AN EXEGETICAL SUMMARY OF
1 TIMOTHY

AN EXEGETICAL SUMMARY OF
1 TIMOTHY

Richard C. Blight

SIL International

Library of Congress Control Number: 2008943578
ISBN: 978-1-55671-230-2

Printed in the United States of America

Copies of this and other publications
of SIL International may be obtained from

International Academic Bookstore
SIL International
7500 West Camp Wisdom Road
Dallas, TX 75236-5699, USA

Voice: 972-708-7404
Fax: 972-708-7363
academic_books@sil.org
www.ethnologue.com

PREFACE

Exegesis is concerned with the interpretation of a text. Exegesis of the New Testament involves determining the meaning of the Greek text. Translators must be especially careful and thorough in their exegesis of the New Testament in order to accurately communicate its message in the vocabulary, grammar, and literary devices of another language. Questions occurring to translators as they study the Greek text are answered by summarizing how scholars have interpreted the text. This is information that should be considered by translators as they make their own exegetical decisions regarding the message they will communicate in their translations.

The Semi-Literal Translation

As a basis for discussion, a semi-literal translation of the Greek text is given so that the reasons for different interpretations can best be seen. When one Greek word is translated into English by several words, these words are joined by hyphens. There are a few times when clarity requires that a string of words joined by hyphens have a separate word, such as "not" (μή), inserted in their midst. In this case, the separate word is surrounded by spaces between the hyphens. When alternate translations of a Greek word are given, these are separated by slashes.

The Text

Variations in the Greek text are noted under the heading TEXT. The base text for the summary is the text of the fourth revised edition of *The Greek New Testament*, published by the United Bible Societies, which has the same text as the twenty-sixth edition of the *Novum Testamentum Graece* (Nestle-Aland). Dr. J. Harold Greenlee researched the variants and has written the notes for this part of the summary. The versions that follow different variations are listed without evaluating their choices.

The Lexicon

The meaning of a key word in context is the first question to be answered. Words marked with a raised letter in the semi-literal translation are treated separately under the heading LEXICON. First, the lexicon form of the Greek word is given. Within the parentheses following the Greek word is the location number where, in the author's judgment, this word is defined in the *Greek-English Lexicon of the New Testament Based on Semantic Domains* (Louw and Nida 1988). When a semantic domain includes a translation of the particular verse being treated, **LN** in bold type indicates that specific translation. If the specific reference for the verse is listed in *A Greek-English Lexicon of the New Testament and Other Early Christian Literature* (Bauer, Arndt, Gingrich, and Danker 1979), the outline location and page number is given. Then English equivalents of the Greek word are given to show how it is translated by commentators who offer their own translations of the whole text and, after a semicolon, all the versions in the list of abbreviations for translations. When reference is made to "all versions," it refers to only the versions in the list of translations. Sometimes further comments are made about the meaning of the word or the significance of a verb's tense, voice, or mood.

The Questions

Under the heading QUESTION, a question is asked that comes from examining the Greek text under consideration. Typical questions concern the identity of an implied actor or object of an event word, the antecedent of a pronominal reference, the connection indicated by a relational word, the meaning of a genitive construction, the meaning of figurative language, the function of a rhetorical question, the identification of an ambiguity, and the presence of implied information that is needed to understand the passage correctly. Background information is also considered for a proper understanding of a passage. Although not all implied information and background information is made explicit in a translation, it is important to consider it so that the translation will not be stated in such a way that prevents a reader from arriving at the proper interpretation. The question is answered with a summary of what commentators have said. If there are contrasting differences of opinion, the different interpretations are numbered and the commentaries that support each are listed. Differences that are not treated by many of the commentaries often are not numbered, but are introduced with a contrastive 'Or' at the beginning of the sentence. No attempt has been made to select which interpretation is best.

In listing support for various statements of interpretation, the author is often faced with the difficult task of matching the different terminologies used in commentaries with the terminology he has adopted. Sometimes he can only infer the position of a commentary from incidental remarks. This book, then, includes the author's interpretation of the views taken in the various commentaries. General statements are followed by specific statements, which indicate the author's understanding of the pertinent relationships, actors, events, and objects implied by that interpretation.

The Use of This Book

This book does not replace the commentaries that it summarizes. Commentaries contain much more information about the meaning of words and passages. They often contain arguments for the interpretations that are taken and they may have important discussions about the discourse features of the text. In addition, they have information about the historical, geographical, and cultural setting. Translators will want to refer to at least four commentaries as they exegete a passage. However, since no one commentary contains all the answers translators need, this book will be a valuable supplement. It makes more sources of exegetical help available than most translators have access to. Even if they had all the books available, few would have the time to search through all of them for the answers.

When many commentaries are studied, it soon becomes apparent that they frequently disagree in their interpretations. That is the reason why so many answers in this book are divided into two or more interpretations. The reader's initial reaction may be that all of these different interpretations complicate exegesis rather than help it. However, before translating a passage, a translator needs to know exactly where there is a problem of interpretation and what the exegetical options are.

Acknowledgments

I am indebted to Jim Cooper and Glenn Graham for the research they did on 1 Timothy. Jim made a first draft of the questions that needed to be answered and then Glenn prepared more detailed drafts of the first two chapters and part of the third before cancer brought his work to an end. Their help speeded my work in writing this volume.

ABBREVIATIONS

COMMENTARIES AND REFERENCE BOOKS

An asterisk (*) indicates a book that translators may find especially helpful as they study the text of 1 Timothy. A dagger (†) indicates that a knowledge of Greek is needed.

AB   Johnson, Luke Timothy. *The First and Second Letters to Timothy.* The Anchor Bible. New York: Doubleday, 2001.

Alf   Alford, Henri. *Alford's Greek Testament,* Vol. 3, Reprinted from 1872 edition. Grand Rapids: Baker, 1980.

BAGD   Bauer, Walter. *A Greek–English Lexicon of the New Testament and Other Early Christian Literature.* Translated and adapted from the 5th edition, 1958 by William F. Arndt and F. Wilbur Gingrich. 2d English edition, revised and augmented by F. Wilbur Gingrich and Frederick W. Danker. Chicago: University of Chicago Press, 1979.

BKC   Litfin, A. Duane. "1 Timothy" in The Bible Knowledge Commentary, New Testament edition. Edited by John F. Walvoord and Roy B. Zuck. Wheaton, Ill.: Victor Books, 1983.

BNTC   Kelly, J. N. D. *A Commentary on the Pastoral Epistles.* Black's New Testament Commentaries. London: A. and C. Black, 1963.

ECC   Quinn, Jerome D., and William C. Wacker. *The First and Second Letters to Timothy.* The Eerdmans Critical Commentary. Grand Rapids: Eerdmans, 1995.

EGT   White, Newport J. D. "The First and Second Epistles to Timothy and the Epistle to Titus" in *The Expositor's Greek Testament,* Vol. 4, Edited by W. Robertson Nicoll. Reprint. Grand Rapids: Eerdmans, 1970.

Herm   Dibelius, Martin, and Hans Conzelmann. *The Pastoral Epistles.* Hermeneia. 4th revised edition 1966, translated by Philip Buttolph and Adela Yarbro. Philadelphia: Fortress Press, 1972.

ICC*†   Marshall, I. Howard. *A Critical and Exegetical Commentary on the Pastoral Epistles.* The International Critical Commentary. Edinburgh, Scotland: T & T Clark, 1999.

LN   Louw, Johannes P., and Eugene A. Nida. *Greek–English Lexicon of the New Testament Based on Semantic Domains.* New York: United Bible Societies, 1988.

Lns   Lenski, R. C. H. *The Interpretation of St. Paul's Epistles to the Colossians, to the Thessalonians, to Timothy, to Titus and to Philemon.* Minneapolis, Minnesota: Augsburg, 1946.

LSA   Blight, Richard C. *A Literary-Semantic Analysis of Paul's First Discourse to Timothy*. Prepublication Draft, 1977.

My   Huther, Joh. Ed. "The Epistles to Timothy and Titus." *Meyer's Critical and Exegetical Hand-book to the New Testament*. Translated from the 4th edition by David Hunter. New York, London: Funk and Wagnalls, 1890.

NAC   Lea, Thomas D., and Hayne P. Griffin, Jr. *1, 2 Timothy, Titus*. The New American Commentary. Nashville, Tenn.: Broadman, 1992.

NCBC   Hanson, A. T. *The Pastoral Epistles*. The New Century Bible Commentary. Grand Rapids: Eerdmans, 1982.

NIBC   Fee, Gordon D. *1 and 2 Timothy, Titus*. Revised edition. New International Biblical Commentary. Peabody, Mass.: Hendrickson, 1988.

NICNT*   Towner, Philip H. *The Letters to Timothy and Titus*. The New International Commentary on the New Testament. Grand Rapids: Eerdmans, 2006.

NIGTC*†   Knight, George W. III. *The Pastoral Epistles*. The New International Greek Testament Commentary. Grand Rapids: Eerdmans, 1992.

NTC   Hendriksen, William. *Exposition of the Pastoral Epistles*. New Testament Commentary. Grand Rapids: Baker, 1957.

NTIC   Johnson, Luke Timothy. *Letters to Paul's Delegates*. The New Testament in Context. Valley Forge, Penn.: Trinity Press International, 1996.

NTL   Collins, Raymond F. *1 & 2 Timothy and Titus*. The New Testament Library. Louisville, Kentucky: Westminster John Knox Press, 2002.

TC   Bernard, J. H. *The Pastoral Epistles*. Thornapple Commentaries. Reprinted from 1899 edition. Grand Rapids: Baker, 1980.

TG   Bratcher, Robert G. *A Translator's Guide to Paul's Letters to Timothy and to Titus*. London, New York: United Bible Societies, 1983.

TH*   Arichea, Daniel C., and Howard A. Hatton. *A Handbook on Paul's Letters to Timothy and to Titus*. New York: United Bible Societies, 1995.

TNTC   Guthrie, Donald. *The Pastoral Epistles*. The Tyndale New Testament Commentaries. Grand Rapids: Eerdmans, 1957.

WBC*   Mounce, William D. *Pastoral Epistles*. Word Biblical Commentary. Nashville, Tenn.: Nelson, 2000.

WP   Robertson, A. T. *The Epistles of Paul*. Word Pictures in the New Testament, Vol. 4. Nashville, Tenn.: Broadman, 1931.

GREEK TEXT AND TRANSLATIONS

GNT	The Greek New Testament. Edited by B. Aland, K. Aland, J. Karavidopoulos, C. Martini, and B. Metzger. Fourth edition. London, New York: United Bible Societies, 1993.
CEV	The Holy Bible, Contemporary English Version. New York: American Bible Society, 1995.
GW	God's Word. Grand Rapids: World Publishing, 1995.
HCSB	Holman Christian Standard Bible. Nashville, Tennessee: Holman Bible Publishers, 2000.
KJV	The Holy Bible. Authorized (or King James) Version. 1611.
NASB	New American Standard Bible. La Habra, Calif.: Lockman Foundation, 1995.
NCV	New Century Version. Dallas: Word Publishing, 1991.
NET	The NET Bible, New English Translation. Version 6r,715, Biblical Studies Press, 2006.
NIV	The Holy Bible, New International Version. Grand Rapids: Zondervan, 1984.
NLT	The Holy Bible, New Living Translation. Second edition. Wheaton, Ill.: Tyndale House, 2004.
NRSV	The Holy Bible: New Revised Standard Version. New York: Oxford University Press, 1989.
REB	The Revised English Bible. Oxford: Oxford University Press and Cambridge University Press, 1989.
TEV	Good News Bible, Today's English Version. Second edition. New York: American Bible Society, 1992.

GRAMMATICAL TERMS

act.	active	mid.	middle
fut.	future	opt.	optative
impera.	imperative	pass.	passive
imperf.	imperfect	perf.	perfect
indic.	indicative	pres.	present
infin.	infinitive	subj.	subjunctive

EXEGETICAL SUMMARY OF 1 TIMOTHY

DISCOURSE UNIT 1:1–20 [ICC, TNTC; NASB]. The topic is the introduction [ICC], the apostle and Timothy [TNTC], misleadings in doctrine and living [NASB].

DISCOURSE UNIT 1:1–2 [AB, ECC, Herm, ICC, NAC, NCBC, NIBC, NICNT, NIGTC, NTL, TH, TNTC, WBC; CEV, GW, HCSB, NCV, NET, NIV, NLT, NRSV, REB, TEV]. The topic is the salutation [ICC, NAC, NIBC, NIGTC, NTL, TH, TNTC, WBC; NET, NRSV], the greeting [AB, ECC, NCBC; GW, HCSB], the initial greeting [Herm, NICNT], greetings from Paul [NLT]. Some versions omit a heading for this greeting section [CEV, NCV, NIV, REB, TEV].

1:1 **Paul an-apostle[a] of-Christ Jesus in-accordance-with[b] a-command[c] of-God our savior[d] and Christ Jesus our hope[e]**

TEXT—Instead of ἐπιταγήν 'command', one important manuscript reads ἐπαγγελία 'promise'. GNT reads ἐπιταγήν 'command' with an A decision, indicating that the text is certain.

TEXT—Instead of Χριστοῦ 'Ιησοῦ 'Christ Jesus' some manuscripts read κυρίου 'Ιησοῦ Χριστοῦ 'Lord Jesus Christ' although GNT does not mention any manuscript support for this variant. 'Lord Jesus Christ' is read by KJV.

LEXICON—a. ἀπόστλος (LN 53.74) (BAGD 3. p. 99): 'apostle' [AB, BAGD, BNTC, ECC, Herm, LN, Lns, LSA, NTC, WBC; all versions], 'special messenger' [BAGD, LN]. An apostle is someone who has been commissioned and sent as a special messenger [LN]. In reference to Paul, 'apostle' refers to the special office that is restricted to the twelve and Paul [Lns, My, NIGTC, NTC, TH, TNTC]. Paul was an apostle in the sense that he had seen the risen Lord who had appointed Paul to preach the gospel. This divine commission had given him the status of being an authoritative leader in the church [NICNT].

b. κατά (LN 89.8) (BAGD II.5.a.δ. p. 407): 'in accordance with' [BAGD, LN], 'according to, in conformity with' [BAGD]. The clause 'in accordance with a command of' is translated 'according to the command of' [HCSB], 'according to the commandment of' [NASB], 'by the commandment of' [KJV], 'by the command of' [AB; GW, NCV, NET, NIV, NRSV, REB], 'by order of' [Lns, NTC; TEV], 'at the order of' [ECC], 'appointed by the command of' [NLT], 'by the commission of' [Herm], 'commissioned by' [BNTC], 'because of the command from' [WBC], '(God our Savior and Christ Jesus) commanded me (to be an apostle)' [CEV], 'because (God and Christ Jesus) commanded it' [LSA]. This preposition indicates a relationship involving a similarity of process [LN]. It introduces the norm which governs something, but often the norm is also the reason, so that the meanings 'in accordance with' and 'because of' merge [BAGD]. It means 'in obedience to the command' [EGT].

c. ἐπιταγή (LN 33.326) (BAGD p. 302): 'command' [AB, BAGD, LN, WBC; GW, HCSB, NCV, NET, NIV, NLT, NRSV, REB], 'commandment' [KJV, NASB], 'order' [BAGD, ECC, LN, Lns, NTC; TEV], 'commission' [Herm]. This noun is also translated as a verb: 'commissioned' [BNTC], 'commanded' [LSA; CEV]. This noun denotes that which has been specifically commanded [LN].

d. σωτήρ (LN 21.31) (BAGD 1. p. 801): 'savior' [AB, BAGD, BNTC, ECC, Herm, LN, Lns, NTC, WBC; all versions], 'deliverer, preserver' [BAGD]. This noun is also translated as a verb phrase: 'who saved us' [LSA]. This noun denotes one who saves [LN]. See this word at 4:10.

e. ἐλπίς (LN 25.61, 25.62) (BAGD 3. p. 253): '(the object of) hope' [BAGD, LN (25.61)], '(the reason or basis for) hope' [LN (25.62)]. The phrase 'our hope' [AB, BNTC, ECC, Herm, Lns, NTC, WBC; HCSB, NCV, NET, NIV, NRSV, REB, TEV] is also translated 'our confidence' [GW], 'who is our hope' [KJV, NASB], 'who gives us hope' [CEV, NLT], 'who will bring about what we await' [LSA]. This noun denotes that which is hoped for [LN (25.61)], or that which constitutes the cause for hoping [LN (25.62)]. It is a firm conviction [TG], a confident expectation [NIGTC], an eager and confident anticipation of what God has in store for believers [WBC]. In the Bible, hope is a desire accompanied by an absolute certainty of its accomplishment [NAC, TNTC].

QUESTION—How is Paul connected with this letter?

Paul is the author of this letter. Some translations show this by beginning the letter 'From Paul' [AB; CEV, GW, NCV, NET, REB, TEV], or 'This letter is from Paul' [NLT]. This letter begins in a form common to letters written at that time: the name of the writer is given first, then comes the name of the recipient, and this is followed by a greeting [AB, BKC, BNTC, NAC, NCBC, NICNT, NTC, NTIC, TC, WBC]. Letters began with the writer identifying himself in the third person form, but as soon as the formal introduction was completed, he referred to himself with first person forms [LSA]. In some languages, it may be necessary to use the first person and second person forms from the start and begin the letter 'I, Paul, write this letter to you, Timothy' [TG].

QUESTION—In the phrase ἀπόστολος Χριστοῦ Ἰησοῦ 'an apostle of Christ Jesus', what relationship is indicated by the genitive form 'of Christ Jesus'?

1. Paul is an apostle who is commissioned and sent by Christ Jesus [BKC, BNTC, EGT, ICC, Lns, My, NAC, NICNT]. The word 'apostle' refers to one who is sent on a mission and the genitive 'of Christ Jesus' indicates that such a one was commissioned by Christ Jesus himself [Lns, NICNT]. Paul was chosen to be Christ's ambassador who was charged to bear witness to the Lord's resurrection and to proclaim his gospel [BNTC, NAC].

2. Paul is an apostle *who represents* Christ Jesus [LSA, NIGTC, NTC, TG, WBC]. This is similar to the preceding meaning, but instead of focusing on the action of being sent on a trip by Christ it focuses on the relationship of representing Christ wherever Paul happened to be [LSA]. The focus is on Paul's authority as an official representative of Christ [WBC]. An apostle is sent as an official representative, carrying with him the authority of the one who sent him [NIGTC, WBC]. Being an apostle is more than a being a messenger; Paul is Christ's representative, an authorized spokesman for Christ [TG]. He was an apostle wherever he might be located and Christ had delegated him with authority in matters of doctrine and life, and the Holy Spirit was with him in a special way, leading him into all truth [NTC].

QUESTION—What is the significance of Paul referring to himself as being an apostle κατά 'in accordance with' the command of both God and Christ?

Paul became an apostle by the direct command of both God and Christ [WBC]. He was appointed by their command [NLT]. This stresses the fact that his appointment was from God and not from people [TG]. His reference to being Christ's personally chosen ambassador adds weight to his letter, not because Timothy needed reassurance, but because the letter would be read to the Ephesian congregation where some resented Paul and questioned his authority [AB, BNTC, NIBC, NICNT, NIGTC, TNTC]. This letter is a written authorization for Timothy to act on Paul's behalf in this apostolic work [Lns].

QUESTION—What was the command of both God and Christ Jesus?

This refers to Paul's commission to be an apostle that came at his conversion (Acts 26:16) [BNTC, Lns, NIGTC, WBC]. God and Christ jointly commanded Paul to be an apostle and the genitive form without a preposition has the double sense of God being the origin of his apostleship and Christ being the mediator [NIGTC]. Both divine names are given to indicate that this came through Christ Jesus whom God had sent [Lns]. In 2 Tim. 1:1 Paul also describes his apostleship as being the result of *the will* of God [BKC, NICNT, WBC]. The descriptions *savior* and *hope* not only designate the relationship of God and Christ Jesus with believers, but these terms imply that the command given to Paul was for the purpose of our salvation and our hope [NTL].

QUESTION—Is there any significance of the word order in the names 'Christ Jesus' and 'Jesus Christ'?

Paul uses the order 'Christ Jesus' at 1:1, 2, 12, 14, 15; 2:5; 3:13; 4:6; 5:21; 6:13. He uses the reverse order 'Jesus Christ' at 1:16; 6:3, 14.

1. The order 'Christ Jesus' may emphasize *Christ* in order to focus on the fact that Jesus is the Messiah [AB, EGT, NIGTC, TNTC]: *Messiah Jesus.* 'Christ' functions as a title for the Messiah, and 'Jesus' is his personal name [AB]. Paul identifies Jesus as being the Messiah promised in the OT in both combinations, 'the Christ, Jesus' or 'Jesus the Christ' [NIGTC].

2. There is no significant difference in the order of the two names [Lns, NTC, NTL, TH]. Probably the name 'Christ' was used as a second proper name for Jesus [NTC, NTL], and in the Greek language it was possible to reverse the order of a person's names with no significance intended in doing so [NTC]. In the NT, when 'Christ' is used as a title for the Messiah, it is usually indicated by the definite article, 'the Christ', but in the Pastoral Letters, Christ is almost always used as a name, not a title [TH].

QUESTION—In what sense is God our 'savior'?

The fact that God is 'savior' fits the theological emphasis of salvation in this letter and Paul also applies the title of *Savior* to God in 2:3 and 4:10 [AB]. Calling God *Savior* is common in the pastoral letters (1 Tim. 2:3; 4:10; Tit. 1:3; 2:10; 3:4). This refers to the saving activity of the Father [NAC]. God is the source of our salvation [Lns, NIBC, NIGTC]. Both God and Christ are referred to as 'Savior' in Paul's letters, God being the initiator of the plan of salvation and Christ being the means by which the plan is carried out [NICNT]. God is called Savior because, through the coming of Jesus, God inaugurated the redemptive process that will be consummated for his people on the last day [BNTC]. The word 'salvation' refers to rescuing someone from danger by placing that one into complete and permanent safety [Lns].

QUESTION—What is meant by Christ Jesus being 'our hope'?

God is the source of our salvation, and our hope is in Christ to complete this salvation at his return [BKC, NIBC]. Christ is the object of our hope [Alf, BAGD (3. p. 253), BNTC, ICC, LSA, NAC, NIBC]. All our hopes are fixed on Christ who is the ground for those hopes [TC]. Christ is 'our hope' because we have placed our hope in him and look forward to his coming again when the salvation we now possess will be bestowed in even fuller measure [BNTC, NTC]. Hope is the confident anticipation of what God has in store for believers and this hope is centered on Christ [WBC]. In Titus this is called the hope of eternal life (Titus 1:2; 3:7), and here the hope that the risen Jesus gives to his disciples is that they too will be resurrected and experience the resultant glory [ECC]. Because Christ died and was resurrected we have a sure hope that he has overcome sin and death to secure eternal life for us, and his return will complete our salvation [NICNT]. Christ is both the source and the object of our hope [My, NTC]. He is the basis of our hope of obtaining salvation in all its fullness because he made this hope possible [NTC]. Christ is the basis of the hope of future salvation [NIGTC]. We look for the unveiling of Christ at the end of time [NAC]. Our hope is to be like Christ (1 John 3:2–3) [EGT].

1:2 to-Timothy a-genuine/faithful[a] child[b] in faith,[c]

LEXICON—a. γνήσιος (LN 73.1) (BAGD 1. p. 163): 'genuine' [AB, LN, Lns, NTC; GW, NET], 'true' [BAGD, ECC, Herm, LSA, WBC; HCSB, NASB, NCV, NIV, NLT, TEV], 'true-born' [REB], 'real' [LN], 'loyal' [NRSV], not explicit [CEV]. The phrase 'a genuine child' is translated 'you are like a son to me' [CEV], 'you are like a true son to me' [LSA], 'a true child to me' [NCV]. Instead of 'a' genuine child, many use the possessive pronoun 'my' [AB, BNTC, NTC, WBC; HCSB, KJV, NASB, NET, NIV, NLT, NRSV, REB, TEV]. Some continue with the third person form: 'his true child' [ECC, Herm]. This adjective means that someone truly has the good character or quality that he is purported to have [LN].

b. τέκνον (LN 9.46, 36.40) (BAGD 2.b. p. 808): 'child' [AB, BAGD, BNTC, ECC, Herm, LN, Lns; GW, HCSB, NASB, NCV, NET, NRSV], 'son' [LSA, WBC; CEV, KJV, NIV, NLT, REB, TEV]. This noun denotes a person of any age for whom one has a special relationship of endearment and association [LN (9.46)], or a person who regards another as being like a father in the faith and thus becomes a disciple of that person [LN (36.40)]. Since Timothy was an adult male, using 'son' instead of 'child' avoids the implication that he was young and immature [LSA, TH].

c. πίστις (LN 31.102) (BAGD 2.d.α. p. 663): 'faith' [BAGD], 'the (Christian) faith' [LN]. The phrase ἐν πίστει 'in faith' [AB, BNTC, ECC, Lns, NTC; GW] is also translated 'in the faith' [HCSB, KJV, NASB, NET, NIV, NLT, NRSV, REB, TEV], 'spiritual (son)' [WBC], 'because you believe' [NCV], 'because you believe in Christ' [LSA], 'because of our faith' [CEV].

QUESTION—What is indicated by the use of the dative case Τιμοθέῳ 'Timothy'?

This indicates that Timothy is the recipient of the letter and it is translated 'to Timothy' [AB, BNTC, Herm, Lns, NICNT, NIGTC, NTC, WBC; all versions except CEV, NLT]. Some make this connection more specific: 'I am writing to Timothy' [NLT] 'writes this to Timothy' [ECC]. Or, Timothy is directly addressed: 'Timothy, (because of our faith, you are like a son to me)' [CEV]. This indicates that Timothy is the immediate recipient of the letter, although it is clear that the letter is to be read aloud to the congregations in Ephesus [BKC].

QUESTION—Why does Paul call Timothy a child?

The kinship term 'child' is used metaphorically since Timothy was not a biological descendant [ICC, LSA, NICNT, TH]. This implies that Paul is the father-authority figure in this relationship [NICNT].

1. Timothy is *like* a child to Paul [all commentaries except Lns]. The connection with Paul is brought out by some who use the possessive 'my child' [AB, BNTC, NTC, TG, WBC; HCSB, KJV, NASB, NET, NIV, REB, TEV]. Some include more than one point of similarity [BNTC, NICNT, NTC].

1.1 The point of similarity is involvement in the beginning of a person's life [BNTC, EGT, LSA, My, NIGTC, NTC, TH]: *like a father is instrumental in the physical birth of his child, so I was instrumental in your spiritual birth*. This assumes that Paul had converted and ordained

Timothy [BNTC]. Paul functioned as God's instrument in imparting spiritual life to Timothy [NTC].

1.2 The point of similarity is the affection one has for a younger person [BKC, BNTC, ICC, NIBC, NICNT, NTC]: *like a father loves his child, so I love you.* They have a relationship of trust and affection [BNTC]. There is a relationship of care and intimacy [NICNT]. Since it is not certain that Paul was directly responsible for Timothy's conversion, it is best to take this as expressing a relationship between people of different ages [ICC]. Probably Paul had not led Timothy to Christ (2 Tim. 1:5 and 3:15), but he likely had ordained him (2 Tim. 1:6) and it is clear that he had great confidence in him [BKC].

1.3 The point of similarity is the role of training a less experienced person [BAGD, ECC, NAC, NICNT, TC, TG, TNTC]: *like a father trains his child in matters of ordinary life, so I am training you in matters of the Christian faith.* 'Child' can be used figuratively for a spiritual child in relation to his master, apostle, or teacher [BAGD (2.b. p. 808)]. Father-son terminology was commonly used for the teacher-student relationship in both Jewish and Hellenistic circles [NICNT, TNTC, WBC]. Paul looked upon Timothy as a son because he had nurtured him in the Christian faith [TG]. Probably Timothy was reared as a Christian by his Jewish-Christian mother and here Paul calls him his child in the sense that Timothy has both received and transmitted Paul's preaching, teaching, and way of life [ECC].

2. Timothy is *like* a child to God [Lns]. The point of similarity is involvement in the beginning of a person's life: like a father gives physical life to his child, so God has given spiritual life to you. In the sphere of faith, Timothy is a real child of God and his only goal is to please his divine Father [Lns].

QUESTION—Does γνησίῳ τέκνῳ mean 'a genuine child' or 'a faithful child'?

1. It refers to the fact that he was a genuine or true child in terms of the metaphor of being Paul's child in the faith [AB, BNTC, ECC, EGT, My, NAC, NIBC, NICNT, NIGTC, NTC, NTL, TG, TH, TNTC, WBC, WP; GW, HCSB, NASB, NCV, NET, NIV, NLT, REB, TEV]. In reference to children, it means 'born in wedlock, legitimate' and when used figuratively of a spiritual relationship, it means 'true' [BAGD (1. p. 163)]. In the metaphor, this adjective establishes the legitimacy of the child, and here the idea of legitimacy guarantees Timothy's true faith and his right to represent Paul in Ephesus [NICNT]. Timothy could be said to be an authentic heir who will carry on the legacy of Paul [NTL]. As a true child of his teacher, he has both received and transmitted Paul's teaching [ECC]. He was a true Christian like Paul himself [TG]. There is nothing false in Timothy's Christianity [BNTC]; it was genuine and sincere [NAC, NTC].

2. It has the meaning of the faithful, loyal, and trustworthy attributes of Timothy's character [EGT; NRSV].

QUESTION—What is meant by the phrase ἐν πίστει 'in faith'?
1. 'Faith' refers to the act of believing [Alf, BNTC, ICC, Lns, LSA, NAC, NIBC, NICNT, NIGTC, NTC, TH, WBC; CEV, GW, NCV].
  1.1 The preposition ἐν indicates the *sphere* of faith in which this relationship exists [ICC, Lns, NAC, NIBC, NICNT, NIGTC, NTC, WBC; probably AB; GW which translate this as 'in faith']: *my genuine child in the sphere of faith*. This phrase describes the Christian life as having a true and ongoing belief in the gospel or in Christ [NICNT]. They shared in their commitment to trust in Christ [ICC]. This shows that Timothy's sonship was spiritual, not physical, and their common faith bound them together [WBC]. With respect to, or in the sphere of, faith Paul had begotten Timothy, and this subjective faith refers to a true knowledge of God and his promises, along with a full confidence in God and his only Son [NTC].
  1.2. The preposition ἐν indicates the *reason* that Timothy is like a son to Paul [BNTC, LSA; CEV, NCV]. He is a true child to Timothy *because* he believes [NCV]. The result of Timothy's faith is that he is a spiritual son to Paul [BNTC].
2. 'Faith' refers to the content of what is believed [ECC, EGT, My, NCBC, TNTC; probably HCSB, KJV, NASB, NET, NIV, NLT, NRSV, REB, TEV which translate this as '*the* faith']. The preposition ἐν indicates their common faith is the sphere in which this relationship exists [ECC, My].

Grace[a] mercy[b] peace[c] from[d] God (the/our) Father and Christ Jesus our Lord.

TEXT—Instead of πατρός 'Father', some manuscripts read πατρὸς ἡμῶν 'our Father'. GNT does not mention this variant. 'Our Father' is read by KJV.

LEXICON—a. χάρις (LN 88.66) (BAGD 2.c. p. 877): 'grace' [AB, BAGD, BNTC, ECC, Herm, LN, Lns, LSA, NTC, WBC; all versions except CEV, GW], 'kindness' [LN], 'favor, gracious help' [BAGD], 'good will' [BAGD; GW]. This noun is also translated as a verb phrase: 'will be kind (to you)' [CEV]. The noun denotes the act of showing kindness to someone in a gracious manner [LN]. See this word at 1:14; 6:21.
  b. ἔλεος (LN 88.76) (BAGD 2.a. p. 250): 'mercy' [AB, BAGD, BNTC, ECC, Herm, LN, Lns, LSA, NTC, WBC; all versions except CEV]. This noun is also translated as a verb phrase: 'will be merciful (to you)' [CEV]. This noun denotes the kindness or concern that is shown to someone who has a serious need [LN].
  c. εἰρήνη (LN 22.42, 25.248) (BAGD 2. p. 227): 'peace' [AB, BAGD, BNTC, ECC, Herm, LN (22.42, 25.248), Lns, LSA, NTC, WBC; all versions], 'tranquility' [LN (22.42)], 'freedom from worry' [LN (25.248)], This noun denotes a set of favorable circumstances involving peace and tranquility [LN (22.42)], or a state of freedom from anxiety and inner turmoil [LN (25.248)]. This corresponds to the Hebrew *shalom*, which refers to one's welfare and health [BAGD].

d. ἀπό (LN 90.15) (BAGD V.4. p. 88): 'from' [AB, BAGD, BNTC, ECC, Herm, LN, Lns, LSA, NTC, WBC; all versions except CEV, NLT, TEV]. 'From God...and Christ...' is translated 'May God...and Christ...give you' [LSA; NLT, TEV], 'I pray that God and Christ will be...May they bless you with...' [CEV]. This preposition indicates the source [LN] or the originator of an action [BAGD].

QUESTION—What is the function of this clause?

Grace and peace are standard words in Paul's greetings when he begins a letter (Rom. 1:7; 1 Cor. 1:3; 2 Cor. 1:2; Gal. 1:3; Eph. 1:2; Phil. 1:2; Col. 1:2; 1 Thess. 1:1; 2 Thess. 1:2; Titus 1:4; Philem. 1:3). The addition of 'mercy' to grace and peace appears only here and in 2 Tim. 1:2. There is no explicit verb in the clause and those who supply a verb differ in its expression.

1. This is a prayer that God and Christ will give these blessings to Timothy [AB, ECC, EGT, LSA; CEV, NLT, TEV]. 'I pray that God our Father and our Lord Jesus Christ will be kind and merciful to you. May they bless you with peace!' [CEV], 'May God our Father and Christ Jesus our Lord give you grace, mercy, and peace' [NLT, TEV]. It is not implied that God has not blessed Timothy in the past, but it means 'may God always, or continuously, bless you' [LSA].

2. This is a statement of what Timothy already enjoys [Lns; GW]. 'Good will, mercy, and peace from God the Father and Christ Jesus our Lord are yours!' [GW].

QUESTION—What is meant by χάρις 'grace' and how does it apply to Timothy?

Grace is goodness offered to undeserving sinners [NAC]. It is God's tender love towards those in need [NTC]. It means to bless someone in undeserved ways [LSA]. Grace is God's undeserved favor [Lns, TH], and for those who are his children, this favor is multiplied in a constant shower of undeserved gifts [Lns]. It refers to the continuing and perfecting aspects of God's grace as he enables Timothy to live that life of good works for which he has been saved [NIGTC]. In all of the discouraging and painful situations Timothy was experiencing, he needed God's grace to sustain him [Lns, NTC, WBC].

QUESTION—What is meant by ἔλεος 'mercy' and how does it apply to Timothy?

'Mercy' describes acts of pity and help [WBC]. It refers to God's kindness, good will, and willingness to forgive [TG, TH]. It stresses the compassionate love that is involved in God's grace [My]. Mercy is God's commiseration with those who are miserable and distressed [Lns, NTC]. It is deliverance out of trouble [NAC]. While *grace* deals with sin and guilt itself and extends pardon, *mercy* deals with the pain and misery that result from sin, and it extends relief [Lns, NIGTC].

QUESTION—What is meant by εἰρήνη 'peace', and how does it apply to Timothy?

1. Peace is that condition when all is well between God and man [Lns, My, NAC, WBC]. This state of peace would assure and give rest to Timothy's soul [Lns]. It is primarily an objective status of one who has been reconciled to God, although from this status comes a subjective feeling of peace [WBC].

2. Peace describes all of God's blessing that enables people to live life in all its fullness so that they will be in a state of physical and mental well-being [TH]. It is a state of spiritual well-being [TG].

3. Peace is a sense of inner peace [NTC]. It is a sense of wholeness, tranquility, and assurance that results from experiencing God's grace and mercy [NTC].

4. This peace is tranquility both within and without, and this was especially needed in the situation Timothy faced at Ephesus [NICNT]. There is an overlap in that the peace with God made possible through Christ enables a believer to meet his problems with tranquility and stability. It also enables believers to continually pursue peace with one another and also to seek to live peacefully with individuals in a hostile world [NIGTC].

QUESTION—Whose father is God in the phrase θεοῦ πατρὸς 'God Father'?

The salutations in Rom., 1 Cor., 2 Cor., Eph., Phil., Col., and Philem. have θεοῦ πατρὸς ἡμῶν 'God our Father', while Gal., 2 Thess., 1 Tim., 2 Tim., and Titus have θεοῦ πατρός 'God Father'. The variations are not significant [WBC]. Here, this is translated 'God Father' [AB], 'God the Father' [BNTC, ECC, Herm, Lns, NTC, WBC; all versions except CEV, KJV, NLT], 'God our Father' [TG, TH; CEV, KJV, NLT]. The word 'our' is to be taken as modifying both names [Lns, TNTC]. God's relationship as Father to humans is brought about by their spiritual birth through Christ [NIGTC].

DISCOURSE UNIT 1:3–3:16 [ICC, NICNT]. The topic is part one of ordering and organizing God's household [NICNT], teachers and church leaders [ICC].

DISCOURSE UNIT 1:3–3:13 [ECC]. The topic is part one of the apostolic commission to Timothy.

DISCOURSE UNIT 1:3–20 [ECC, ICC, NAC, NICNT, NIGTC, WBC; NET, REB]. The topic is the Ephesian problem [WBC], Timothy's task in Ephesus [NET], the explanation of the task to Timothy [NAC], apostolic commands [ECC], Paul's charge to Timothy [REB], regarding false teachers and false doctrine [NICNT], instructions to avoid false doctrine [ICC], Paul's command to Timothy to withstand false doctrine and to further the gospel and its goal, which is love [NIGTC].

DISCOURSE UNIT 1:3–11 [AB, NAC, NIBC, NTL, TH, TNTC; CEV, GW, HCSB, NCV, NIV, NLT, NRSV, TEV]. The topic is the opening commission [AB], the Law [NTL], false doctrine and the misuse of the Law [HCSB], the contrast between the gospel and its counterfeits [TNTC], a warning about false teachers [GW, NIV, NRSV], warnings against false teaching [TH; CEV, NCV, NLT, TEV], the task to prevent the spread of false teaching [NAC], a charge to stop the false teachers [NIBC].

DISCOURSE UNIT 1:3–7 [ECC, Herm, ICC, NCBC, NICNT, NIGTC, WBC]. The topic is the statement of the problem [WBC], a warning against false doctrine [NCBC], Timothy's commission to engage the opponents [NICNT], the charge, the goal, and a description of the false teachers [NIGTC], the command about heterodoxy [ECC], a command to forbid opponents to promulgate false teachings [ICC], a charge to combat the heretics [Herm].

1:3 As[a] I-urged[b] you to-remain in Ephesus (when) I-was-going to **Macedonia,**

LEXICON—a. καθώς (LN 64.14) (BAGD 1. p. 391): 'as' [AB, BNTC, Lns, NTC; HCSB, KJV, NASB, NET, NIV, NRSV], 'just as' [BAGD, LN, LSA, WBC; TEV], not explicit [ECC, Herm; CEV, GW, NCV, NLT, REB]. This conjunction indicates a comparison [BAGD]. It indicates a similarity of events and implies that one thing is in accordance with another [LN].

b. aorist act. indic. of παρακαλέω (LN 33.168): 'to urge' [Lns, LSA, NTC, WBC; HCSB, NASB, NET, NIV, NLT, NRSV, REB, TEV], 'to exhort' [AB], 'to command' [Herm], 'to earnestly ask, to plead, to appeal to' [LN], 'to beseech' [KJV], 'to encourage' [GW], 'to request' [BNTC, LN], 'to ask' [CEV, NCV]. The phrase 'I urged' is translated 'it was at my explicit encouragement that' [ECC]. This verb means asking for something with earnestness and propriety [LN]. It is usually used in speaking to fellow helpers [Alf, NICNT]. Here it is a command in the form of a request [EGT, ICC, NICNT, NTL]. Perhaps Timothy had been reluctant to stay behind [BKC, BNTC, NAC, TNTC]. The verb προσμεῖναι 'to remain' or 'to stay on' gives a hint that Timothy had wanted to make a move [BNTC]. Perhaps Timothy had preferred that Paul stay in order to attend to these matters [Lns]. See this word at 2:1.

QUESTION—What relationship is indicated by καθώς 'as'?
This conjunction indicates a comparison, *'just as…, so…'* [LN], but there is no corresponding 'so' clause in this sentence which continues on through 1:4 [AB, ICC, NAC, NICNT, WBC]. This involves an anacoluthon in which there is an abrupt change within a sentence to a second construction that is inconsistent with the first [Alf, BNTC, ECC, EGT, Herm, ICC, My, NCBC, NIBC, NIGTC, TNTC, WBC]. This anacoluthon indicates an intensity called forth by the urgency of the situation [ECC, WBC]. Paul probably became so caught up in what he was saying that he forgot to complete the thought [NICNT]. This break in the grammatical sequence is treated differently in translations, many restructuring the grammar to eliminate the grammatical break.

1. The grammatical break is left in the translation the same as in the Greek [Alf, ICC, My, NCBC, TC, TNTC]. The sentence 1:3–4 is simply ended

with a dash to indicate that Paul never completed the thought [WBC]: *As I urged you to remain in Ephesus...rather than a plan/stewardship of God the (one) in faith —.*

2. A 'so clause' is supplied, such as 'so I still urge you' or 'so do it' [EGT, Lns, LSA, NIGTC; KJV].

2.1 The supplied clause is inserted at the beginning of the verse [LSA; NRSV]: *I urge you now,* just as I urged you when I was going to Macedonia, remain in Ephesus in order that, etc.

2.2 The supplied clause is inserted before the purpose clause [Lns, NIGTC, WBC]: As I urged you to remain in Ephesus when I was going to Macedonia, *so I still urge you.* The ellipsis 'so I still do' would be understood by the Greek reader at this point [Lns].

2.3 The supplied clause is inserted at the end of verse 4 [EGT, WP; KJV].

3. The infinitive 'to remain' is treated as an imperative so as to make the infinitive clause the apodosis [AB, BNTC, NIBC, NTC; HCSB, NASB, NET, NIV, TEV]: As I urged you when I was going to Macedonia, *remain in Ephesus in order that you command certain ones not to teach differently.*

4. The conjunction 'as' is ignored and the first clause is translated as a statement concerning the original command [ECC, Herm; CEV, GW, NCV, NLT, REB]: *I urged you to remain in Ephesus when I was going to Macedonia.*

QUESTION—What is the background of this verse?

Timothy was in Ephesus when he received instructions from Paul to remain there [BNTC, ECC, ICC, NIGTC], or perhaps he was on this way to Ephesus when he received the instructions [TNTC]. Ephesus was the principal city of Asia Minor (modern Turkey) [BNTC]. Paul went on to Macedonia, which was a Roman province in the northern part of Greece and it included Philippi, Thessalonica, and Berea [BNTC, TH].

1. Paul was with Timothy in Ephesus and was on the point of leaving for Macedonia when he gave instructions to Timothy to remain behind while he went on to Macedonia [AB, Alf, BKC, BNTC, EGT, Herm, Lns, My, NAC, NIBC, NTC]. Paul left Timothy in Ephesus while he traveled on to Macedonia [EGT, Herm, NAC, NIBC].

2. Timothy had been sent to Ephesus and later he traveled to meet Paul, who was on his way to Macedonia. Paul sent him back to Ephesus after giving him these instructions. Later Paul wrote this letter to reinforce Timothy's authority [WBC].

3. Timothy was located in Ephesus, but Paul was somewhere else on his way to Macedonia and had written these instructions to Timothy about remaining there in Ephesus instead of joining him in Macedonia [ECC, ICC].

QUESTION—Why did Paul have to write again what he had previously told Timothy?

Paul sent this letter so that Timothy could present it as evidence to those who objected to Timothy's activities [Lns]. Paul intended that this letter be read out publicly at Ephesus and in other congregations in the surrounding area [BKC, BNTC]. It reinforces Timothy's authority and makes explicit how the church in Ephesus should act [WBC].

in-order-that you-command^a certain (ones) not to-teach-differently^b

LEXICON—a. aorist act. subj. of παραγγέλλω (LN 33.327) (BAGD p. 613): 'to command' [AB, BAGD, LN, LSA, WBC; HCSB, NCV, NIV], 'to order' [BAGD, LN; GW, TEV], 'to charge' [BNTC, ECC, Lns, NTC; KJV], 'to direct' [BAGD], 'to instruct' [BAGD; NASB, NET, NRSV, REB], 'to warn' [CEV]. With the negative μή- 'not', it is translated 'to forbid' [Herm], 'to stop' [NLT]. This verb means to announce what must be done [LN]. It refers to authoritative instructions [NET]. See this word at 4:11; 5:7; 6:13, 17.

b. pres. act. infin. of ἑτεροδιδασκαλέω (LN 33.235) (BAGD p. 314): 'to teach something different' [LN], 'to teach a different doctrine' [BAGD, LN]. The phrase 'not to teach differently' [Lns, NTC] is also translated 'not to teach different doctrine' [AB], 'not to teach any different doctrine' [NRSV], 'not to teach other doctrine' [HCSB], 'not to teach false doctrines' [LSA], 'not to teach false doctrines any longer' [NIV], 'not to teach strange doctrines' [NASB], 'not to continue teaching a different gospel' [WBC], 'not to spread false teachings' [NET], 'not to teach novelties' [BNTC], 'to stop teaching false things' [NCV], 'to stop teaching a different doctrine' [LN], 'to stop teaching false doctrine' [GW], 'to stop spreading their false teachings' [CEV], 'not to propound strange teachings' [ECC], 'to give up teaching erroneous doctrines' [REB] 'that they teach no other doctrine' [KJV], '(forbid) to proclaim other teachings' [Herm]. The phrase 'you command certain ones not to teach differently' is translated 'some people there are teaching false doctrines, and you must order them to stop' [TEV], 'stop those whose teaching is contrary to the truth' [NLT]. This verb means to teach something that is different from what should be taught [LN]. It refers to teaching a heretical doctrine [BAGD]. See this word at 6:3.

QUESTION—What relationship is indicated by the conjunction ἵνα 'in order that'?

It indicates Paul's purpose for urging Timothy to stay in Ephesus [AB, BNTC, ECC, Herm, ICC, Lns, NICNT, NTC, WBC; GW, HCSB, KJV, NASB, NCV, NET, NIV, NRSV]: *remain in Ephesus in order that you command them not to teach differently.*

QUESTION—How is Timothy to command these people?

Paul is telling Timothy to stand before the congregation and command the false teachers to stop [WBC]. However, the verb itself does not imply that this was to be done publicly [My]. Timothy was to act with authority as an apostolic delegate [BNTC, NAC]. In the infinitive form and with the negative particle μή 'not', it means *forbid* them to teach differently [Herm, NIGTC].

QUESTION—Who were the τισίν 'certain ones'?

These men were in some type of leadership positions since they were teaching the Christians in Ephesus [ECC, NAC]. They were men who came from the leadership of the church and were now teaching heresy [ICC, NIBC, NIGTC, WBC]. This is purposely vague, although Paul knew who they were [WP]. They are not named since this is a semi-public letter, but Paul, Timothy, and the congregation knew who they were [BNTC]. Perhaps they are tactfully not named because they had not yet gone to such extremes as did the two men named in 1:20 [WBC], and supplying their names might harden them in their heresy [EGT]. Or, since what he goes on to say about them is not very mild, it includes the two men named in 1:20 [NTC]. Since Paul was now in Macedonia, perhaps Timothy would better know who presently belonged to the group, or the use of 'certain ones' is meant to suggest that those in the group were not as important as they thought they were [NTC]. This indicates that Paul was slightly contemptuous of them [Alf]. Paul would have dealt with such people had they been in Ephesus when he was there, so they must have been men scattered around in the various congregations of the province, and 'certain ones' means whoever and wherever they were [Lns].

QUESTION—What is meant by the verb ἑτεροδιδασκαλέω 'to teach differently'?

In this context it refers to teaching a doctrine that was essentially different from the gospel preached by Paul [BKC, BNTC, NIGTC, WBC] and the other apostles [NET]. The different things they were teaching are explained in the following verse [BNTC, Lns, NIGTC, NTL]. However, myths and genealogies were not all that was involved since 1:6–7 says that they also wanted to be teachers of the Law [NIGTC]. These different teachings were speculative ideas that were contradicted by Paul's explanation of the truth [NAC]. The vagueness of what they taught covers a wide range of teaching [NCBC].

1:4 nor to-devote-their-attention[a] to-myths[b] and genealogies[c] endless,[d]

LEXICON—a. pres. act. infin. of προσέχω (LN 30.35, **31.47**) (BAGD 1.a.β. p. 714): 'to devote their attention to' [Lns], 'to devote themselves to' [AB, NTC, WBC; NIV, REB], 'to occupy themselves with' [GW, NET, NRSV], 'to continually think about' [LSA], 'to give their minds to' [BNTC], 'to spend their time on' [NCV], 'to pay attention to' [BAGD; HCSB, NASB], 'to give heed to' [BAGD; KJV], 'to dote on' [ECC], 'to indulge in' [Herm], 'to waste time on/in' [CEV, NLT], 'to follow' [BAGD], 'to pay close attention to, to consider carefully' [LN (30.35)], 'to hold on to' [**LN** (31.47)], 'to hold firmly to, to continue to believe'

[LN (31.47)]. The phrase 'nor to devote their attention to' is translated 'tell them to give up' [TEV]. This verb means to pay close attention to something, and it may imply being in agreement with it [LN (30.35)], or to hold firmly to a certain belief [LN (31.47)]. They devoted their time, energy, and attention to this, but they should not spend any time at all in it [TH]. Instead of making the gospel central, the myths and genealogies were taught as being the important thing [Lns]. They were preoccupied with those subjects [ICC]. They became absorbed in the extraneous details that made up their doctrines [NICNT]. See this word at 4:1 where it is translated 'giving heed to'.

b. μῦθος (LN 33.13) (BAGD p. 529): 'myth' [AB, BAGD, Herm, LN, Lns, NTC, WBC; GW, HCSB, NASB, NET, NIV, NLT, NRSV, REB], 'legend' [BAGD, LN; TEV], 'tale' [BAGD, ECC, LN], 'story' [BAGD, LN, LSA], 'fable' [BAGD, BNTC, LN; KJV], 'senseless story' [CEV], 'story that is not true' [NCV]. This noun normally denotes a legendary story about supernatural beings, cultural heroes, and events, and it always has an unfavorable connotation in the NT [LN]. A myth is a false and foolish story [Herm] that only the gullible believe [NIGTC]. The word implies that the myths are legendary and untrustworthy [WBC]. See this word at 4:7.

c. γενεαλογία (LN 10.26) (BAGD p. 154): 'genealogy' [AB, BAGD, ECC, Herm, LN, Lns, LSA, NTC, WBC; GW, HCSB, KJV, NASB, NET, NIV, NRSV, REB], 'list of ancestors' [CEV, TEV], 'lists of names in family histories' [NCV], 'spiritual pedigrees' [NLT]. This noun denotes a list of direct descendants or ancestors [LN, Lns, NIGTC, TG, TH, WBC].

d. ἀπέραντος (LN **61.19**) (BAGD p. 84): 'endless' [AB, BAGD, ECC, Herm, **LN**, NTC, WBC; CEV, GW, HCSB, KJV, NASB, NIV, NRSV], 'without limits' [LN], 'interminable' [NET, REB], 'long (lists)' [NCV, TEV]. It refers to a tiresome enumeration of details [BAGD]. The phrase γενεαλογίαις ἀπεράντοιν 'endless genealogies' is translated 'genealogies which seem to be endless' [LSA], 'endless discussion of...spiritual pedigrees' [NLT]. This term refers to a series of things that has no end [LN]. Such teachings went on and on, never coming to a conclusion, always creating more myths and quibbling [WBC]. It is hyperbolic and means that such long lists are tedious [Alf, LSA]. The teaching is wearisome by nature [NIBC]. It led to no conclusions [EGT].

QUESTION—Who are the ones who are not to pay attention to myths and genealogies?

Most commentators think that this command is directed to the false teachers and this tells them not to be involved with myths and genealogies. However, one commentator suggests that this could be directed to the people who are being taught these things by the false teachers [EGT].

QUESTION—What is meant by 'myths' and 'genealogies'?

The two terms are used in a Jewish setting of some sort, but perhaps they also show an incipient Gnostic influence [ICC, NIBC, NIGTC]. The false teachers were not teaching about their own personal genealogies [NIGTC]. Exactly what the terms refer to is uncertain [BKC, NIBC, NIGTC]. These terms describe an untruthful teaching with ethical dimensions that the false teachers tried to authenticate by rooting it in OT history. The term 'genealogies' probably specifies the kind of OT material they exploited for this purpose [ICC].

1. This was a Jewish error concerned with the lists of ancestors in Scripture [ECC, EGT, ICC, Lns, NAC, NIBC, NICNT, NIGTC, NTC, TNTC, WBC]. Titus 1:14 says that these myths were Jewish, so the false teachers were probably Judaizers who did not derive their teachings from mainstream Judaism since they did not really know the law [WBC]. The terms probably refer to the genealogical tables found in those parts of the OT that were often amplified by the Jews with myths woven around them [EGT, NAC, TNTC, WBC]. They were an amplification of OT lists of ancestors, which included inventing the names of wives [Lns].

2. This concerned the Jewish-Christian teachings of incipient Gnosticism of the first century [Alf, BNTC, Herm, My, NCBC, WP]. The heresy was not exclusively Jewish or Gnostic, but was a mixture of both [BNTC, NCBC], and more Jewish than Gnostic [My]. In their system, a series of emanations (aeons) came out of God, each generally thought of as a pair consisting of male and female [NCBC]. This concerns stories about the movements and couplings of the various aeons [NCBC]. The term 'genealogies' refers to Gnostic teachings about groups of aeons [Alf, Herm, My, NCBC]. This teaching concerned theological speculation which arose from the stories and genealogical material in Genesis and the term 'myths' describes such tales from the standpoint of one who disapproved of them. The term 'genealogies' is not restricted to the genealogical lists as such, but is used to describe the narrative parts of the Pentateuch [Herm].

QUESTION—How are 'myths' and 'genealogies' related?

1. They are different things [Alf, ECC, EGT, Lns, LSA, NAC, NIBC, NIGTC, TG, TNTC, WBC]: *nor to pay attention to myths or to genealogies.* This probably is not a hendiadys (mythical genealogies) since these nouns occur separately in Titus 1:14 and 3:9 [ECC, LSA], and 'myths' are referred to alone in 1 Tim. 4.7 [LSA]. Myths were fictional Jewish tales which had developed about the whole body of Mosaic institutions and included additional and allegorical tales of their Jewish ancestors [Lns]. The myths might have been an allegorical treatment of the stories in the OT, while in the genealogies every syllable of the OT lists of ancestors were thought to contain something to edify [EGT].

1.1 The adjective 'endless' modifies the word 'genealogies' [AB, Alf, ECC, LSA, My, NIGTC, TG, TNTC; all versions except NLT, REB]: *myths and endless genealogies.* This refers to very long lists of ancient ancestors [TG].

1.2 The adjective 'endless' modifies the word 'myths' [WBC]: *endless myths and also genealogies*. Since the genealogies were those in the OT, the genealogies wouldn't be called endless [WBC].

1.3 The adjective 'endless' modifies both 'myths' and 'genealogies' [Lns, NIBC; NLT]: *endless myths and endless genealogies*. 'Endless' modifies both, since there was no limit to what they invented about these two subjects [Lns]. This refers to endless discussions of both myths and spiritual pedigrees [NLT].

2. 'Myths' is a general term that is specified as being about 'genealogies' [BNTC, Herm, ICC, My, NIBC, NICNT, NTC]: *nor to pay attention to endless myths about genealogies*. In relation to the standard of truth, they were mere myths, and in regard to their contents, the myths were about genealogical stories that were mainly fictitious [ICC, NTC]. The term 'myths' labels these teachings as being false and harmful, while 'genealogies' indicates that the contents of the myths concerned family trees in which the false teachers sought clues about the deeper sort of piety claimed to have [NICNT]. They would take a name from the genealogies in the OT and expand it into a story [NTC]. These were allegorical or legendary interpretations about the pedigrees of the patriarchs [BNTC].

which cause speculations/disputes[a]

TEXT—Instead of ἐκζητήσεις 'speculation, dispute', some manuscripts read ζητήσεις 'disputes'. GNT reads ἐκζητήσεις 'speculation, dispute' with a B decision, indicating that the text is almost certain.

LEXICON—a. ἐκζήτησις (LN **31.33, 33.442**) (BAGD p. 240): 'speculation, worthless speculation, imaginings' [LN (31.33)], 'meaningless speculation, idle dispute' [LN (33.442)], 'useless speculation' [BAGD]. The phrase 'which cause speculations/disputes' is translated 'since they produce speculations' [WBC], 'that promote speculations' [BNTC; NRSV], 'these promote worthless speculations' [**LN** (31.33)], 'these promote empty speculations' [HCSB], 'such things promote useless speculations' [NET], 'these encourage speculations' [AB], 'which give rise to mere speculation' [NASB, REB], 'these things only lead to meaningless speculations' [NLT], 'whenever people do this, they just speculate' [LSA], 'that can only proffer lucubrations' [ECC], 'which result more in the racking of one's brain' [Herm], 'these raise a lot of questions' [GW], 'which minister questions' [KJV], 'such as furnish questionings' [Lns], 'which foster disputes' [NTC], 'which only produce idle disputes' [**LN** (33.442)], 'these promote controversies' [NIV], 'which only produce arguments' [TEV], 'these things only bring arguments' [NCV], 'such things only cause arguments' [CEV]. This noun denotes ideas that are unrelated to reality [LN (31.33)], or lead to a dispute involving empty speculation [LN (33.442)].

QUESTION—What relationship is indicated by αἵτινες 'which' at the beginning of this clause?

1. This clause gives the reason they are not to pay attention to myths and genealogies [ICC, LSA, My, NAC, NIBC, NICNT, NIGTC, TC, TH, WBC]: do not pay attention to them *because they cause speculations*. The result of this irrelevant teaching contrasts with the true edification which comes from godly instruction [NAC]. The results of false speculation interfere with the responsible fulfillment of the ministry that God has ordained [ICC]. The feminine form αἵτινες 'which' agrees with the preceding feminine noun γενεαλογίαις 'genealogies', but it can also include the masculine noun μύθοις 'myths' [NIGTC].
2. This clause specifies the kinds of myths and genealogies that they are not to pay attention to [ECC, EGT]: do not pay attention to the myths and genealogies *that cause speculations*.
3. This clause states what sort of myths and genealogies these are and gives the reason that such things must not be taught [Lns].

QUESTION—Does the noun ἐκζητήσεις mean 'speculations' or 'disputes' here?

1. This word refers to speculations [AB, BAGD, BKC, BNTC, ECC, EGT, Herm, ICC, **LN** (31.33), Lns, My, NCBC, NIBC, NICNT, NIGTC, TNTC, WBC; HCSB, NASB, NET, NLT, REB], or raising questions [Alf, EGT, Lns, TNTC; GW, KJV]. This describes their searching out more and more of the fancies spun from Scripture names and words [Lns]. They raise questions that cannot be answered or that are not worth answering [EGT]. Paul is not saying that he is opposed to inquiry and controversy as such, but to speculations that are devoid of truth and lead to no good results [NIGTC]. These are controversial or useless speculations [NICNT].
2. This word refers to disputes [Alf, **LN** (33.442), NTC, TG, TH; CEV, NCV, NIV, TEV]. This word is not used anywhere else in the NT and there are no clues from the literature of that time as to its meaning, so many translate it as 'arguments' since this is the likely result of being preoccupied with these things [TH]. They had lengthy debates about dates and definitions [NTC]. The questions led to strife and quarrels [Alf].

rather than a-plan/stewardship[a] of-God the (one) in faith.[b]

TEXT—Instead of οἰκονομίαν 'plan, stewardship', some manuscripts read οἰκοδομήν 'building up'. GNT reads οἰκονομίαν 'plan, stewardship' with an A decision, indicating that the text is certain.

LEXICON—a. οἰκονομία (LN **30.68**, 42.25, 46.1) (BAGD 3. p. 560): 'plan' [**LN** (30.68)], 'purpose, scheme, arrangement' [LN (30.68)], 'task, commission, responsibility' [LN (42.25)], 'management of a household' [LN (46.1)], 'training' [BAGD]. The phrase 'rather than a plan/ stewardship of God' is translated 'rather than God's plan' [HCSB], 'instead of God's own plan' [ECC], 'rather than promoting God's plan'

[GW], 'they do not serve God's plan' [TEV], 'and do not further God's plan for us' [REB], 'rather than God's redemptive plan' [NET], 'rather than God's saving plan' [BNTC], 'rather than God's work' [NIV], 'they do not help God's work' [NCV], 'they don't help anyone to do God's work' [CEV], 'rather than the divine training that is known by faith' [NRSV], 'rather than the stewardship from God' [WBC], 'rather than an administration of God' [Lns], 'rather than furthering the administration of God' [NASB], 'rather than godly edifying' [KJV]. The clause 'rather than a plan/stewardship of God the one in faith' is translated 'rather than faithful attention to God's way of ordering things' [AB], 'which don't help people live a life of faith in God' [NLT], 'than in godly education leading to salvation in faith' [Herm], 'rather than they faithfully manage the household that belongs to God' [LSA], 'rather than faith-centered stewardship required by God' [NTC]. This noun denotes a plan which involves a set of arrangements, and in the NT it is used in reference to God's plan for providing salvation to mankind within the course of history [LN (30.68)], or it is used in reference to a task involving organization and management [LN (42.25)], as in the management of a household [LN (46.1)]. It is God's training in the way of salvation [BAGD].

b. πίστις (LN 31.85) (BAGD 2.d.α. p. 663): 'faith' [BAGD, LN], 'trust' [LN]. The phrase τὴν ἐν πίστει 'the one in faith' [KJV] is also translated 'one in connection with faith' [Lns], 'which centers in faith' [GW], 'which is by faith' [NASB, NIV], 'which is known by faith' [TEV], 'that one receives in faith' [ECC], 'by faith' [WBC], 'which operates by faith' [HCSB, NET], 'which works through faith' [BNTC; REB], 'which is done in faith' [NCV], 'that can only be done by faith' [CEV]. This noun denotes a complete trust and reliance in something [LN]. See the preceding lexical item for AB, Herm, NTC, and NLT. See this word at 1:2, 5, 14, 19; 3:13; 4:12; 6:11.

QUESTION—What is meant by the genitive construction οἰκονομίαν θεοῦ 'a plan/stewardship of God'?

1. This means a plan devised and carried out by God [AB, Alf, BKC, BNTC, ECC, Herm, LN (30.68), Lns, NAC, NIBC, NICNT, NIGTC, NTL, TC, TG, TH; GW, HCSB, NET, NIV, REB, TEV]. It is God's plan of salvation [Herm, NAC, NIGTC, NTL, TH]. It is God's plan or arrangements for redeeming people [NIBC]. It is God's redemptive purpose that is accomplished in history [AB, BNTC]. God administers his plan of salvation through the gospel [NIBC]. It is God's way of ordering reality, specifically God's way of creating and saving the world [AB]. It is God's administration of his grace and the gospel [Lns]. It is God's administration of his plan of salvation through the gospel [NIGTC]. It is the way God shows how he saves people [TH]. It is the ordering of life through the various activities of ministry and service [NICNT].

2. This means the stewardship or responsibility that God entrusts to his stewards, the church leaders [EGT, ICC, LSA, My, NTC, WBC; CEV].

This refers to the stewards of God's household [ICC]. The false teachers were church leaders appointed to be stewards over God's household [WBC]. Stewardship is the care ordained by the Lord with respect to the household of God and concerns the wise administration and distribution of the gospel-mysteries for the edification of the church as they administer spiritual treasures [NTC]. False speculation hinders the performance of the ministry given to the leaders by God [NIGTC].

3. It means the training God has for Christians [Herm, NCBC, TNTC; NRSV]. It is the discipline that belongs to faith [TNTC]. There is a contrast between complicated speculations [LN (33.442)] and simple faith, which is the best training for Christians [NCBC].

QUESTION—What is meant by the plan or stewardship being τὴν ἐν πίστει 'the one in faith'?

1. *When this refers to God's plan.* This means that God's plan of redemption must be received by faith [ECC]. It is received with faithful attention, not with the speculations of the would-be teachers [AB]. God's plan is known and works by means of our faith [BKC]. God's plan works through faith since it is understood and made effective through the faith of those who accept Christ [Alf, BNTC]. God's work is furthered by an attitude of faith or commitment [NAC]. The context emphasizes the gospel as God's work, which is based on or known by faith, and this contrasts with the futility of speculations [NIBC]. God's administration of his plan is brought about by faith, and 'faith' refers to not only initial saving faith but also to a continuing relationship of trust [NIGTC].

2. *When the stewardship refers to what God's stewards do for God.* The stewardship entrusted to God's servants is performed in the sphere of faith [EGT, My]. God requires this stewardship to be faith-centered [NTC]. Their office is accomplished by the faithful ministry of leaders who have genuine faith in Christ [ICC]. The office of stewardship is to be accomplished by faith [WBC].

1:5 Now/but[a] the purpose[b] of-the command[c] is love

LEXICON—a. δέ (LN 89.87, 89.93, 89.124) (BAGD 1, 2, 3. p. 171): This conjunction can mark a sequence of closely related events: 'and, and then' [LN (89.87)], or an additive relation that is not coordinate: 'and, and also, also, in addition, even' [LN (89.93)], or a contrast: 'but, on the other hand' [LN (89.124)]. It can emphasize a contrast: 'but', or mark a simple transition: 'now, then', or mark a resumption of an interrupted discourse: 'and also, but also' [BAGD]. Here it is translated 'now' [Lns; HCSB, KJV], 'but' [AB, Herm, WBC; NASB, NET, NRSV], 'rather' [ECC], 'whereas' [NTC], not explicit [BNTC, LSA; CEV, GW, NCV, NIV, NLT, REB, TEV].

b. τέλος (LN **89.55**) (BAGD 1.c. p. 811): 'purpose' [Herm, **LN**, NTC; NCV, NLT, TEV], 'for the purpose that' [LSA], 'goal' [BAGD, ECC, LN, Lns; WBC; GW, HCSB, NASB, NIV, REB], 'aim' [AB, BAGD; NET,

NRSV], 'intent' [LN], 'object' [BNTC], 'end' [BAGD; KJV], 'outcome' [BAGD]. The phrase 'the purpose of the command' is translated 'my goal in giving you this order is' [GW], 'you must teach people to...' [CEV]. This noun denotes the purpose of a state or event, viewing it in terms of its result [LN, WP]. It indicates the goal of his command [NICNT].

c. παραγγελία (LN 33.328) (BAGD p. 613): 'command' [LN, WBC; NCV, NIV], 'commandment' [AB; KJV], 'order' [BAGD, LN; GW, TEV], 'charge' [BNTC, ECC, Lns, NTC], 'instruction' [BAGD, Herm, LN; HCSB, NASB, NET, NLT, NRSV, REB], 'direction, precept' [BAGD], not explicit [CEV]. This noun is also translated as a verb: 'you should command them' [LSA]. The phrase τῆς παραγγελία 'the command' is translated with possessive pronouns: 'my charge' [BNTC], 'my instruction' [NLT], 'our instruction' [HCSB, NASB]. This noun denotes an announcement that relates to an action that must be done [LN]. See this word at 1:18.

QUESTION—What relationship is indicated by the conjunction δέ 'now/but'?

1. It takes up another point [HCSB, Lns, LSA, TH; probably BNTC; CEV, GW, NCV, NIV, NLT, REB, TEV which do not translate this conjunction]: *now* the purpose of the command is love. This reinforces the command in 1:3 [TH]. It adds an important point concerning the real goal of the charge to Timothy [Lns].

2. It is contrastive [AB, Alf, ECC, Herm, ICC, NCBC, NICNT, NIGTC, NTC, TC, WBC; NASB, NET, NRSV]: *but* the purpose of the command is love. At this point, Paul changes from the sentence structure of 1:3–4 to a new sentence with a new thought beginning with the adversative δέ 'but' [ICC]. This verse contrasts the results of the false teachings with the purposed goals of Paul's command [ICC, NICNT, WBC]. It contrasts the false teachers actions with the apostolic way of love [Alf, NAC]. The purpose of orthodox Christian preaching is contrasted with the speculations resulting from the work of the false teachers [AB, NCBC; NET].

QUESTION—What does τῆς παραγγελία 'the command' refer to?

1. The noun παραγγελίας 'command' refers to its verb form παραγγείλῃς 'you command' in 1:3, so that this refers to what Timothy was to command the false teachers to stop doing [ICC, Lns, LSA, NAC, NIBC, WBC]: *you should command them not to teach differently nor to pay attention to myths and genealogies, and do this for the purpose of bringing about love.*

2. The noun παραγγελίας 'command' refers to the verb παρεκάλεσά σε 'I urged you' in 1:3 so that this refers to Paul's purpose in giving the charge (or command) to Timothy [AB, BKC, BNTC, NICNT, TG, TH; NLT]: *my purpose in commanding you to command them not to teach differently nor to pay attention to myths and genealogies was to bring about love.* This pertains to Timothy's entire commission [AB]. The initial charge was to stop the false teachers, but that charge had a further aim of establishing

love in place of the present arguments [BNTC]. Paul's command to Timothy was designed to promote love by maintaining the purity of the church's teaching [BKC].

3. The noun παραγγελίας 'command' refers to the stewardship concerning the gospel ministry which God gave to pastors and teachers [Herm], or to the purpose of the gospel itself [Alf, Herm, My]. It concerns the preaching of the gospel [NCBC, TC], the true teaching taught by Paul and Timothy [EGT]. The command is God's charge to Christians given in Christian teaching [NIGTC]. The aim of the command of the gospel is love [My]. This was the charge committed to Timothy (1:18) [EGT, TC], and its purpose concerned the comprehensive virtue of love which is the fulfillment of the law (Rom. 13:10) [EGT].

QUESTION—Who are the subjects of the event word ἀγάπη 'love'?

1. The members of the church are to love one another [BNTC, ICC, NIBC, NIGTC, TC, TG, TH; NLT]. Some supply the subject 'people' [NCV], or 'all believers' [NLT]. If the false teachers stop their activities that caused arguments, it will be possible for the church members to again show love for one another [TH].

2. The false teachers are to love others [Lns, LSA, NAC]. The purpose of warning the false teachers was to develop in them a genuine love for God and others [NAC]. The aim was to produce love in the deluded teachers since they could not obtain it through their concentration on the myths [Lns].

QUESTION—Who are the objects of the event word ἀγάπη 'love'?

1. They are primarily to love one another [AB, BNTC, ICC, LSA, NIBC, NICNT, NIGTC, TC, TG, TH]. Here 'love' stands in opposition to the strife and division within the church which the false teaching had brought about [ICC]. If the false teachers stop their activities that have produced quarrels and strife in the congregation, then it is likely that members of the congregation will again begin showing love and concern for one another [TH]. This love is expressed in sacrificial actions done on behalf of others [NICNT]. It refers to a disinterested love that builds the community [AB].

2. They are primarily to love God [ECC]. Since this love comes from the sources of a pure heart, a good conscience, and a sincere *faith*, this is love directed towards God. Also this charge has its basis in Israel's greatest confessional commandment in Deut. 6:4–5, which indicates that nothing is to take precedence over a total and undivided love for God, a love that is to be expressed in the worship prayer of believers [ECC].

3. They are to love both God and people [Lns, NAC, NTC, WBC]. Love is unrestricted and it is to be directed toward God, Christ, church members, and people in general [Lns]. In Scripture, God's love is the basis for a person's own love for both God and others [WBC].

from[a] a-pure[b] heart and a-good[c] conscience[d] and a-sincere[e] faith,

LEXICON—a. ἐκ (LN 90.16) (BAGD 3.g.γ. p. 235): 'from' [BAGD, LN, WBC; GW, HCSB, NASB], 'out of' [Lns; KJV], 'that/which comes from' [AB; NCV, NET, NIV, NLT, NRSV, TEV], 'which springs from' [NTC; REB], 'arising from' [ECC], 'issuing from' [BNTC], 'born of' [Herm], 'by' [LSA]. The phrase ἀγάπη ἐκ καθαρᾶς καρδίας 'love from a pure heart' is translated 'have genuine love' [CEV]. This preposition refers to the source of a state or activity [BAGD, LN].

    b. καθαρός (LN 53.29) (BAGD 3.b. p. 388): 'pure' [BAGD, LN], 'free from sin' [BAGD]. The phrase καθαρᾶς καρδίας 'a pure heart' [AB, BNTC, Herm, NTC; all versions except CEV] is also translated 'a clean heart' [ECC, Lns, WBC], 'genuine (love)' [CEV]. This phrase is also translated as a verb phrase: '(by) having good motives' [LSA]. This adjective means being ritually clean or pure [LN]. It is used here in the moral and religious sense of being free from sin [BAGD].

    c. ἀγαθός (LN 88.1) (BAGD 1.b.β. p. 3): 'good' [LN], 'clear' [BAGD]. The phrase συνειδήσεως ἀγαθῆς 'a good conscience' [AB, BNTC, Herm, NTC; all versions except GW, NLT, TEV] is also translated 'a conscience that is good' [Lns], 'a clear conscience' [ECC, WBC; GW, NLT, TEV]. This phrase is also translated as a verb phrase: '(by) their doing only what they know to be right' [LSA]. This adjective refers to having positive moral qualities in general [LN]. It relates to inner worth, especially moral [BAGD].

    d. συνείδησις (LN 26.13) (BAGD 2. p. 786): 'conscience' [AB, BAGD, BNTC, ECC, Herm, LN, Lns, NTC, WBC; all versions], 'moral sensitivity' [LN]. This noun denotes the faculty that distinguishes between right and wrong [LN]. See this noun at 1:19 and 4:2.

    e. ἀνυπόκριτος (LN 73.8) (BAGD p. 76): 'genuine, sincere' [BAGD, LN], 'true' [CEV]. With its negative prefix, this noun is literally 'without hypocrisy' [AB, BAGD], or 'lacking in pretense or show' [LN]. The phrase πίστεως ἀνυποκρίτου 'a sincere faith' [AB, BNTC, Herm, WBC; GW, HCSB, NASB, NET, NIV, NRSV] is also translated 'a genuine faith' [REB, TEV; similarly NLT], 'a true faith' [NCV; similarly CEV], 'a faith without hypocrisy' [NTC], 'a faith that is unhypocritical' [Lns], 'a faith unfeigned' [ECC; KJV]. This is also translated as a verb phrase: '(by) their sincerely believing (the true doctrine)' [LSA]. This adjective describes the quality of being genuine and sincere [LN].

QUESTION—What relationship is indicated by the preposition ἐκ 'from'?

The following three qualities are the source of this love [AB, Alf, BNTC, ECC, EGT, Herm, ICC, Lns, NAC, NIBC, NICNT, NTC, NTIC, TC, TH, TNTC, WBC]: *a love that arises from a pure heart, a good conscience, and a sincere faith*. Developing these three qualities are the *means* by which people will come to love others [ICC, LSA]: *they will come to love others by having a pure heart, a good conscience, and a sincere faith*. The three qualities are the conditions for the growth of love [WP].

QUESTION—What is a καθαρᾶς καρδίας 'pure heart'?

The heart is the seat of one's personality, the person's very self [ICC, NICNT, NIGTC]. It is the seat of reflection and decisions [AB], the seat of one's mind, emotions, and will [NAC, NICNT]. A heart is pure when the person has no sinful thoughts or hidden motives [TH]. A heart is pure when it is cleansed from sin [ICC, TG, WBC], and directed toward God [ICC]. A pure heart is free from all selfish views and leanings [Alf]. It is free from self-seeking [My]. It is assumed that God has purified the inner person of one who had come to faith in the gospel [NICNT]. There needs to be a continued cleansing as sins are confessed and forgiven [NIGTC].

QUESTION—What is a συνειδήσεως ἀγαθῆς 'good conscience'?

The conscience is an inner awareness of the moral qualities of one's actions [NAC]. It is being conscious of whether one's actions and attitudes are right or wrong before God, and a good conscience results from a positive self-evaluation [NIGTC]. The good conscience is clear of a feeling of guilt [Alf, WBC], and self-reproach [BNTC, TG]. A good conscience is the result of one's heart correctly making decisions about right and wrong [TH]. It approves of only what is good in God's estimation [Lns]. A person with a good conscience makes morally good decisions that lead to godly conduct [ICC]. It is being assured that one is living appropriately to the norms of the gospel, the faith, and sound teaching [NICNT]. This quality and the next are added to the list since the false teachers have both evil consciences and a pretended faith [My].

QUESTION—What is a πίστεως ἀνυποκρίτου 'sincere faith'?

1. This refers to faith in Jesus Christ [BNTC, Lns, TG], or in God [ICC, NAC, NIBC, NIGTC]. Faith includes trusting in God and relying on him [NIGTC]. A person's faith is expressed by accepting Christ's way of life [BNTC]. A sincere faith is an active belief in God and the gospel, and it is accompanied by a lifestyle that evidences the integrity and authenticity of such a commitment [NICNT]. In contrast with a false believer, this describes a true believer who has a single-minded commitment to God [ICC]. This faith is a sincere trust and confidence from the heart [Lns]. Faith would be called insincere if a person was deceived himself or if he deceived others that he had faith [BNTC]. Sincere faith contrasts with the false faith of the false teachers [NIBC].

2. This refers to having such faith in the Christian message that they hold fast to the true Christian teachings and do not accept the false teachings [ECC, LSA, TH]. They will sincerely believe the true doctrine [LSA].

1:6 **(from) which (things) some having-missed-the-mark[a] turned-aside[b] to meaningless-discussion,[c]**

LEXICON—a. aorist act. participle of ἀστοχέω (LN **31.68**) (BAGD p. 118): 'to miss the mark' [BAGD], 'to miss this whole point' [NLT], 'to miss' [BAGD, BNTC, Lns; NCV, NLT], 'to fall short of' [WBC], 'to deviate' [BAGD, ECC; HCSB, NRSV], 'to swerve' [KJV], 'to lose one's way'

[**LN**], 'to abandon the truth' [LN], 'to wander away' [NTC; NIV], 'to stray' [NASB, NET], 'to turn away' [TEV], 'to depart' [BAGD], 'to fail' [BAGD], 'to miss out' [AB], 'to renounce' [Herm], not explicit [REB]. The phrase τινες ἀστοχήσαντες ἐξετράπησαν 'some having missed the mark turned aside' is translated 'some people have left these qualities behind and have turned (to)' [GW], 'who have given up these for nothing but...' [CEV], 'these people have failed to do this' [LSA]. The verb ἀστοχέω is built upon the noun στύχος 'a mark', and with the α-privative prefix (negative in force) it means 'to miss the mark' [ECC, WBC]. This verb means to go astray as a result of departing from the truth [LN]. See this word at 6:21.

b. aorist pass. indic. of ἐκτρέπω (LN 31.65) (BAGD p. 246): 'to turn aside' [AB, NTC, WBC; HCSB, KJV, NASB], 'to swerve aside' [BNTC], 'to turn away' [LN; NET, NLT], 'to turn off' [Lns], 'to turn (to)' [GW, NCV, NIV, NRSV], 'to lose their way' [TEV], 'to slip off' [ECC], 'to go astray' [LN; REB], 'to run after' [Herm]. See LSA and CEV above for translations joining the two verbs. The only other occurrence of this verb in the NT has a medical sense [ECC], where the verb means to wrench or sprain the ligaments of a joint, especially in the legs and feet [LN]. Here the verb is used to indicate a change in direction [ICC]. This verb only occurs in the passive voice in the NT and in all the literature covered by BAGD, but it has the force of the middle voice, 'they have turned themselves away' [BAGD, ECC, NIGTC]. This verb is a figurative expression for turning away from the truth and believing something that is different [LN].

c. ματαιολογία (LN **33.377**) (BAGD p. 495): 'meaningless discussion' [**LN**], 'meaningless talk' [LN; NIV, NRSV], 'useless discussion' [GW], 'useless talk' [NCV], 'empty discussion' [NET], 'empty talk' [BAGD; CEV], 'idle discussion' [LN], 'futile talk' [NTC], 'vain talk' [Lns], 'fruitless discussion' [BAGD; HCSB, NASB], 'foolish discussion' [TEV], 'foolish talk' [Herm], 'foolish chatter' [AB], 'senseless babble' [WBC], 'vain jangling' [KJV], 'mere chattering' [ECC], 'futile verbiage' [BNTC], 'a wilderness of words' [REB]. This noun is also translated as a clause: 'they spend their time in meaningless discussions' [NLT], 'they just discuss what is useless' [LSA]. This noun denotes the kind of talk that has no beneficial purpose and therefore is idle and meaningless [LN].

QUESTION—What is meant by ὧν 'which things'?

This refers back to the three sources of love: 'a pure heart, a good conscience, and a sincere faith' [AB, Alf, ECC, EGT, Lns, My, NAC, NIBC, NICNT, NIGTC, NTC, TC, TG, TNTC, WBC]. The noun ἀγάπη 'love' is not included since it is not coordinate with those three qualities [Lns]. Missing these objectives, they of course missed the final goal of love [Alf, NTC].

QUESTION—Who were the τινες 'some' who missed the mark and turned aside?

They were probably the same people referred to as τισίν 'certain ones' in 1:3 [BNTC, ECC, ICC, LSA, NAC, NIBC, NIGTC, NTC, NTL, TG, TH, WBC]. The use of τινες 'some' has a derogatory sense to it here [Herm, ICC].

QUESTION—What relationship is indicated by the use of the adverbial participle ἀστοχήσαντες 'having missed the mark'?

The participle indicates that this is the reason that they turned aside [NICNT]: *because they missed the mark, they turned aside.*

QUESTION—What is meant by the word ἀστοχήσαντες 'having missed the mark'?

The verb indicates misdirection, missed target, and the like. Here it means that the false teaching resulted in a divergence from the apostolic faith [NICNT].

1. This is a metaphor concerning marksmen [AB, Alf, ECC, EGT, Lns, NAC, NTL, TC, TNTC, WBC; NCV]: *some people have missed their objective, like bad marksmen miss their target.* In 1:5 it speaks of the 'goal' of the command and here 'missing the goal' appropriately follows [AB]. Instead of hitting the target, they deviated from it [ECC]. They had the wrong aim [Lns]. It is doubtful that they really had aimed at a pure heart, a good conscience, and a sincere faith [EGT].

2. This is a metaphor concerning travelers [ICC, LN, NIBC, NICNT, NIGTC, NTC, TNTC; NASB, NET, NIV, TEV]: *some people have missed their objective, like wayward travelers take a wrong turn and miss their destination.* This agrees with the metaphor of the following verb 'turned aside' [LSA]. They have turned away from the right path [ICC]. They were lost and wandering about [NICNT].

3. Some treat this as a dead metaphor and translate without a metaphorical reference [AB, BAGD, Herm, LSA, TH; GW, REB]: 'to deviate, to forsake' [TH], 'to abandon the truth' [LN], 'to fail' [BAGD], 'to miss out' [AB], 'to leave behind' [GW], 'through lack of these' [REB]. One translates this verb 'to renounce' [Herm], implying a more active role than just failing to achieve something.

QUESTION—What is meant by ἐξετράπησαν 'turned aside'?

1. This is a metaphor concerning travelers [AB, Alf, EGT, Herm, Lns, NTC, TC, TG, TNTC, WBC]. They have turned away from the path that leads to the goal of love in 1:5 [Alf]. They had been in the right way, but they did not keep to it when they swerved aside from the straight path [TC]. This implies that some church leaders had started out on the right path of pursing love, but then had turned aside to meaningless discussion [WBC]. The verb ἐκτρέπω is used for any sort of turning and here they turned aside towards foolish speech [AB]. They have unintentionally lost their way and took a wrong path [TG]. Or, they have turned toward a goal of their own choosing [NICNT].

2. Some treat this as a dead metaphor and translate without reference to a
   metaphor [LSA; CEV].

QUESTION—What is meant by ματαιολογίαν 'meaningless discussion'?

Their useless speculation and arguments got nowhere [NTC]. What they
talked about did not get anyone to the goal [Lns]. It does not lead anyone to
holy living [NAC]. In this setting, it refers to the myths and genealogies
which the false teachers regarded as a way of salvation and edification
[ICC]. This refers to the uselessness of the false doctrine [NICNT]. This is
further described in 1:7 [Alf].

1:7 wanting[a] to-be teachers-of-the-law,[b]

LEXICON—a. pres. act. participle of θέλω (LN 25.1, 30.58): 'to want' [AB,
BNTC, ECC, LN (25.1), Lns; all versions except KJV, NRSV, REB], 'to
desire' [LN (25.1), LSA; KJV, NRSV], 'to yearn' [NTC], 'to wish'
[Herm, LN (25.1), WBC], 'to set out (to be)' [REB], 'to purpose' [LN
(30.58)]. This verb means to desire to have or experience something [LN
(25.1)], or to purpose to do something, and generally it is based on one's
preference or desire [LN (30.58)]. They want to be something that they
are not [AB]. They claimed to be teachers of the law but had not really
achieved such a status [NTL].

b. νομοδιδάσκαλος (LN **33.248**) (BAGD p. 541): 'teacher of the Law'
[BAGD, **LN**; NASB], 'teacher of the law' [BNTC, Herm, WBC; HCSB,
KJV, NCV, NET, NIV, NRSV, REB], 'teacher of law' [AB], 'law
teacher' [Lns, NTC], 'teacher of the Law of Moses' [CEV, NLT], 'teacher
of God's law' [TEV], 'expert in the Law' [LN], 'expert in Moses'
Teachings' [GW], 'rabbi' [ECC]. This noun is also translated as a verb
phrase: '(they desire) that they teach the law' [LSA]. The phrase 'to be
teachers of the law' is translated 'to be known as teachers of the law of
Moses' [NLT]. In the NT this noun denotes a person who is skilled in
teaching and interpreting the OT law [LN].

QUESTION—What relationship is indicated by the use of the participle
θέλοντες 'wanting'?

1. This participle indicates a further description of the false teachers [ICC,
   My, NIBC, NICNT, NIGTC, TH; probably AB; CEV, GW, HCSB, NCV,
   NET, NIV, NLT, REB, TEV which begin a new sentence here]. It further
   describes those referred to as 'some' in the preceding verse [NIGTC]. It
   gives the motivations of the false teachers [ICC].

2. This participle indicates a concession to the following participial phrase
   [LSA]: *although they want to be teachers of the Law, they do not
   understand....*

3. This participle indicates the reason they have turned aside to meaningless
   discussion (1:6) [NTC]: *they turned aside to meaningless discussion
   because they want to be teachers of the Law.*

QUESTION—What law did they want to teach?
They wanted to teach the Mosaic Law [AB, Alf, BNTC, EGT, Herm, ICC, My, NAC, NIGTC, TC, TG, WBC; CEV, GW, NASB, NLT]. The absolute phrase ὁ νόμος 'the law' in 1:8 implies that the Law of Moses is meant [AB]. It refers to God's law [TH], recorded by Moses in the Torah, the first five books of the Hebrew Scriptures [TG]. They derived their fantastic myths from the legal portion of the OT [BNTC]. Probably they interwove speculations and ascetic observances with appeals to the OT [Herm]. They probably wanted to have a role in the Christian community equivalent to the role Jewish teachers had in a Jewish community [NICNT].

not understanding[a] neither what (things) they-say[b] nor concerning what (things) they-confidently-speak.[c]
LEXICON—a. pres. act. participle of νοέω (LN **32.2**) (BAGD 1.a. p. 540): 'to understand' [AB, BAGD, **LN**, LSA, NTC, WBC; all versions except CEV, NIV, NLT], 'to comprehend' [LN, Lns], 'to perceive, to gain insight into' [BAGD, LN], 'to know' [Herm; CEV, NIV, NLT]. The phrase 'not understanding' is translated 'having no clear idea of' [BNTC], 'they have no idea of' [ECC]. This verb means to have the ability to comprehend something after having given it careful thought and consideration [LN]. It refers to rational thought or inner contemplation [BAGD]. The verb means more than 'to know' since there is an element of contemplation implied, giving it the meaning of 'understand' or 'comprehend' [WBC].
b. pres. act. indic. of λέγω (LN 33.69) (BAGD I.1.a. p. 468): 'to say' [BAGD, LN], 'to speak' [LN]. The phrase ἃ λέγουσιν 'what they say' [Lns; KJV] is also translated 'what they are saying' [BNTC, ECC, Herm, WBC; HCSB, NASB, NET, NRSV], 'what they are talking about' [CEV, GW, NCV, NIV, NLT], 'the things about which they are speaking' [AB], 'their own words' [LSA; TEV], 'the words they use' [REB], 'the words (or things) which they are speaking' [NTC]. This verb means to speak or talk, and it focuses upon the content of what is communicated by this act [LN]. It refers to an act of communication, whether by speaking or by writing [BAGD].
c. pres. mid./pass. (deponent = act.) indic. of διαβεβαιόομαι (LN 33.322) (BAGD p. 181): 'to speak confidently' [BAGD], 'to state with confidence' [LN], 'to insist' [BAGD, LN]. The phrase μήτε περὶ τίνων διαβεβαιοῦνται 'nor concerning what things they confidently speak' is translated 'or the things about which they speak so confidently' [GW], 'or what they so confidently affirm' [NIV], 'or the things concerning which they insist' [AB], 'or of the things that they insist on' [ECC], 'or the matters about which they make confident assertions' [NASB], 'or the matters about which they speak with so much confidence' [TEV], 'nor the subjects about which they confidently speak' [LSA], 'or the subjects about which they are so dogmatic' [REB], 'nor the themes (or subjects) on

which they are harping with such confidence' [NTC], 'or of the things about which they dogmatize' [BNTC], 'or concerning what things they are so dogmatically asserting' [WBC], 'or concerning what they confidently affirm' [Lns], 'nor whereof they affirm' [KJV], 'or the things about which they make assertions' [NRSV], 'or the things they insist on so confidently' [NET], 'or what they are insisting on' [HCSB], 'nor to what they are bearing witness' [Herm], 'or what they are sure about' [NCV], 'even though they speak so confidently' [NLT], 'even though they think they do' [CEV]. This verb means to state something with confidence and certainty [LN], and with firmness [TH].

QUESTION—What relationship is indicated by the use of the negated participle μὴ νοοῦντες 'not understanding'?

1. This indicates a contrast with the preceding clause [BNTC, ECC, ICC, TH; CEV, GW, NCV, NET, NIV, TEV]: they want to be teachers of the law, *but they do not understand*.... Their purposes and assumptions are contrasted with their total lack of qualifications [ICC]. This refutes their claim of being legitimate teachers of the law [TH].

2. This indicates a concession to the preceding clause [EGT, NTC, WBC, WP; HCSB, NASB, NLT, REB]: they want to be teachers of the law, *although they do not understand*.... The negative participle 'not' expresses Paul's opinion about them [EGT].

3. This indicates the reason they turned aside to meaningless discussion [Lns, LSA, My]: some turned-aside to meaningless discussion *because they don't understand*....

QUESTION—What are the referents of the two clauses 'neither *what things* they say nor concerning *what things* they confidently speak'?

1. The referents of the neuter relative pronoun ἃ 'what (things)' and the interrogative pronoun (used as a relative pronoun) τίνων 'what things' are the same and the focus is placed on the verb διαβεβαιοῦνται 'they confidently speak' [ICC, TG, TH, WBC; CEV, NLT]. 'They don't know what they are talking about, even though they speak so confidently' [NLT]. The things they were saying were the things they were teaching as doctrine [ICC]. These two phrases are practically synonymous [WBC]. The double negative is for rhetorical effect to emphasize their ignorance [ICC, WBC]. Paul is using hyperbole to say that while they attempt to explain different subjects of the Torah, they don't understand the matters they are discussing [TG].

2. The referents of the neuter relative pronoun ἃ 'what (things)' and of the interrogative pronoun τίνων 'what things' (used as a relative pronoun) are different and the pronouns are in focus [AB, Alf, BNTC, ECC, EGT, Lns, LSA, My, NIBC, NIGTC, NTC, TC, TNTC; NASB, REB, TEV].

2.1 The clause 'what *things* they say' refers to the subjective conclusion of these teachers, while the clause 'what *things* they confidently speak' refers to the objective subject matter upon which their opinions were formed [Alf, EGT, Lns, My, NIBC, NIGTC, TC, TNTC]. Being full of speculations and empty talk, they didn't know what they were talking about, nor did they know the meaning of the Scriptures [NIBC]. Often their speech was devoid of meaning and they did not understand the principles of the Law they were expounding [TC]. Perhaps this is talking about the teachers' allegorization of the OT Scriptures [TNTC].

2.2 The clause 'what *things* they say' refers to the ignorance of these teachers as to the meaning of the words they used, while the clause 'concerning what *things* they confidently speak' refers to the nature or realities of the subjects on which they confidently spoke [AB, BKC, ECC, LSA, NTC; NASB, REB, TEV]. They didn't understand their subject, the Law, or what they were saying about it [BKC]. The clause 'what *things* they say' may refer not only to the words they spoke, but also to the written words of OT material they cited [ECC]. They used impressive words and ponderous phrases without really understanding these words that they had added to their vocabulary [NTC]. These teachers did not know the language of the law nor its substance [AB].

DISCOURSE UNIT 1:8–17 [ECC]. The topic is a command about orthodoxy.

DISCOURSE UNIT 1:8–12 [Herm]. The topic is that the gospel was entrusted to Paul.

DISCOURSE UNIT 1:8–11 [ECC, ICC, NCBC, NIGTC, WBC]. The topic is Paul's teachings on law [ECC], the true intention of the Law [WBC], the true purpose of the law [ICC], the use of the law [NCBC], the lawful use of the Law [NIGTC].

1:8 Now/but[a] we-know that the law (is) good,[b] if anyone uses[c] it lawfully,[d]

LEXICON—a. δέ (LN 89.87, 89.93, 89.124) (BAGD 1., 2., 3. p. 171): This conjunction can mark a sequence of closely related events: 'and, and then' [LN (89.87)], or an additive relation that is not coordinate: 'and, and also, also, in addition, even' [LN (89.93)], or a contrast: 'but, on the other hand' [LN (89.124)]. It can emphasize a contrast: 'but', or mark a simple transition: 'now, then', or mark a resumption of an interrupted discourse: 'and also, but also' [BAGD]. Here it is translated 'now' [Lns, NTC; HCSB, NRSV], 'but' [AB, BNTC, Herm, WBC; KJV, NASB, NCV, NET], not explicit [ECC, LSA; CEV, GW, NIV, NLT, REB, TEV].

b. καλός (LN 88.4) (BAGD 2.b. p. 400): 'good' [AB, BAGD, Herm, LN, LSA, WBC; all versions except REB], 'excellent' [BNTC, Lns, NTC], 'fine' [ECC, LN], 'praiseworthy' [LN], 'an admirable thing' [REB], 'useful' [BAGD]. This adjective refers to a positive moral quality [BAGD, LN].

c. pres. mid./pass. (deponent = act.) of χράομαι (LN 42.23) (BAGD 1.a. p. 884): 'to use' [AB, ECC, Herm, LN, Lns, LSA, WBC; GW, HCSB, KJV, NASB, NCV, NET, NIV, NRSV], 'to make use of' [BAGD, LN], 'to make a use of it' [NTC], 'to treat' [BNTC; REB]. This verb is also

translated passively: 'to be used' [CEV, NLT, TEV]. This verb means to
make use of something [LN].

d. νομίμως (LN **72.18**) (BAGD p. 541): 'lawfully' [BAGD], 'according to
the rules' [BAGD, LN], 'correctly' [**LN**]. The clause 'if anyone/someone
uses it lawfully' [WBC; NASB, NCV; similarly Lns; KJV] is also
translated 'if one make a lawful use of it' [NTC], 'provided one treats it as
law' [BNTC; similarly REB], 'if someone uses it legitimately' [NET;
similarly HCSB, NRSV], 'if one knows how to use it according to the
law' [Herm], 'if it is used in the right way' [CEV], 'if anyone uses it
appropriately' [AB], 'if a person uses it correctly' [LSA], 'if one uses it
properly' [NIV], 'if they are used as they were intended to be used' [GW],
'if it is used as it should be' [TEV], 'when used correctly' [NLT], 'there is
still the question of one's using it lawfully' [ECC]. This adverb pertains to
being correct in regard to rules and regulations [LN]. A word play is
involved in the Greek, which says that the νόμος 'law' must be used
νομίμως 'lawfully' [AB, ECC, Herm, Lns, My, NTIC, TC, WBC].

QUESTION—What relationship is indicated by the conjunction δέ 'now/but'?

1. It indicates a transition [BKC, BNTC, Lns, LSA, NTC, NTL, TC, TH,
   TNTC; HCSB, NRSV; probably CEV, GW, NIV, NLT, REB, TEV which
   do not translate this conjunction]: *now we know that....* This introduces a
   digression concerning the place and function of the law [BNTC, LSA,
   NTL, TH, TNTC]. Lest Paul's slighting tone about those 'law-teachers'
   appears to reflect upon the law itself, he now assures Timothy that well-
   informed Christians are well aware of the excellency of the law [BNTC].

2. It indicates a contrast [AB, Alf, ECC, Herm, My, NIBC, NIGTC, WBC;
   KJV, NASB, NCV, NET]: *but we know that....* This is an emphatic
   contrast with the ignorance of the false teachers [AB]. This contrasts the
   false-teachers use of the law with its real value [My]. Their approach to
   the law was wrong, but the law itself is good and it can be used in the
   right way [NIGTC]. What Paul and Timothy know is in contrast with the
   specious knowledge of the false teachers [ECC]. This is a digression in
   response to the false teachers' improper use of the law [NIBC].

QUESTION—What is the referent of 'we' in the verb οἴδαμεν 'we know'?

The pronoun refers to all Christians [NIGTC, TG, TH], or better, it refers to
all *well-informed* Christians [BNTC]. It is a recognized principle that the law
is good [Herm, NTC]. It is an accepted apostolic tradition [NICNT]. 'We'
refers to those who agree with Paul and disagree with the false teachers, so it
would include Paul, Timothy, and other like-minded people [ECC, WBC].
This is knowledge that should be embraced by the readers [ICC].

QUESTION—In what way is the law καλός 'good'?

The law is good because God gave it [NIGTC]. It is in accord with God's
holiness, justice, and truth [Alf]. It refers to the internal excellence of the law
[My]. It is beneficial to people [NIGTC, WBC], and it reveals the will of
God [NIBC, WBC]. It is pleasing, holy, righteous, and attractive [ECC]. It is
noble and honorable [NAC]. It is a true guide for morally and ethically

acceptable conduct [TH]. It is useful and leads to good results [ICC]. The meaning of 'good' is explained in the following qualification, 'if one uses it properly' [NICNT]. Probably the false teachers had accused Paul of teaching that Christians were released from obeying the religious laws, so here Paul points out that they have misunderstood his position, and he agrees with them that the law is good when it is used as it was intended [WBC]. The law would be good even if the condition of using it lawfully was not met, so in this context it means that the law is good *to use* if it is used correctly [LSA, My]. Rather than describing the internal excellence of the law, here the good quality of the law depends on *using* the law according to its nature and meaning [My].

QUESTION—Who is meant by τις 'anyone'?

It refers to anyone in general [Alf, EGT, NIGTC, NTC, WBC]. This statement is an axiomatic truth and so it has an indefinite reference [WBC]. It is indefinite and refers to anyone who uses the law, not just those who teach it [NIGTC]. It may include everyone, but it directly refers to those who teach the law [Alf, My, NAC, TH]. All that is said here refers mainly to a teacher, but it could just as well be applied to any Christian's use of the law [Alf].

QUESTION—What is meant by using the law νομίμως 'lawfully'?

It means that one has to understand that the law has specific functions and limitations [WBC]. The law must be correctly and properly used and applied [TH]. The law must be used in accordance with the spirit in which it was enacted [EGT, NAC], or in accordance with its intended use [NAC, NIGTC]. The law is used properly when it is treated as law that is intended for the lawless, not when it is used as a source for myths and genealogies [NIBC]. Mosaic Law, and any law in general, is to be used as law is intended to be used, that is, to restrain evil-doing [TC]. The lawful use is explained in 1:9–10 [WBC].

1:9 **knowing[a] this, that for-a-righteous[b] (person) law is- not -enacted,[c]**

LEXICON—a. perf. act. participle of οἶδα (LN 28.1) (BAGD 1.e. p. 556): 'to know' [BAGD, LN]. The clause 'knowing this' [Lns, WBC; KJV] is also translated 'bearing this in mind' [NTC], 'realizing' [BNTC; NET], 'recognizing' [REB], 'realizing the fact' [NASB], 'this means understanding' [NRSV], 'we understand this' [AB], 'we know' [HCSB], 'we also know' [NCV, NIV], 'we also understand' [CEV], 'it must be remembered, of course' [TEV], 'that involves knowing' [ECC], 'that is, in the recognition (that)' [Herm], 'for (the law was not intended)' [NLT] 'for example, a person must realize' [GW]. The singular form εἰδώς 'knowing' refers to the preceding singular τις 'anyone' [Alf, EGT, My, NIGTC].

b. δίκαιος (LN 88.12) (BAGD 1.a. or b. p. 195): 'righteous' [BAGD (1.b.), LN, LSA], 'just' [LN], 'law-abiding' [BAGD (1.a.)]. This adjective is translated as a noun phrase: 'the righteous' [Herm; NIV], 'righteous people' [LSA], 'a righteous person' [AB, Lns, WBC; HCSB, NASB, NET], 'the/a righteous man' [BNTC, NTC; KJV], 'good people' [NCV, TEV], 'good citizens' [REB], 'an upright person' [ECC], 'people who do what is right' [NLT], 'the innocent' [NRSV], 'people who please God' [CEV], 'people who have God's approval' [GW]. This attribute can emphasize keeping legal requirements [BAGD (1.a.)], or it can emphasize the religious aspect of not violating God's sovereignty and of keeping God's laws [BAGD (1.b.)]. This adjective means being in accordance with what God requires [LN]. Since it concerns the law, it refers to being righteous before God [AB]. The singular form δικαίῳ 'a righteous (one)' is used generically to refer to all those who are righteous [TH].

c. pres. mid./pass. (deponent = act.) indic. of κεῖμαι (LN **13.73**) (BAGD 2.b. p. 427): 'to be enacted' [LSA, NTC], 'to be established' [Lns], 'to be laid down' [AB, ECC; NRSV], 'to be made' [BNTC; KJV, NASB, NCV, NIV, TEV], 'to be given' [BAGD], 'to be given to control' [CEV], 'to be valid' [BAGD, WBC], 'to exist' [BAGD, **LN**], 'to be (for)' [Herm], 'to be intended (for)' [GW, NET, NLT], 'to be designed (for)' [REB]. This verb means to exist, and it implies that it has been established and thus has continuity and purpose [LN]. The verb refers to enacting the law [Alf, EGT, ICC, TC], and proclaiming it [ICC]. The verb is used figuratively as a legal term meaning 'to be given, to exist, to be valid' [NIGTC]. Here the verb has the sense of 'to be enacted' or 'to be legally valid' [ICC]. The law has not only been given, it is still valid [My].

QUESTION—What relationship is indicated by the use of the participial clause εἰδὼς τοῦτο 'knowing this'?

1. It defines the adverb νομίμως 'lawfully' in the preceding verse [ECC, Herm, ICC, Lns, LSA, My, NIBC, NICNT, NIGTC, TC, TG, TH; NRSV]: if the law is used lawfully, *that is, if it used with the knowledge of the following fact*. It defines what is the appropriate use of the law [ICC]. The issue is in knowing for whom the law was enacted [NICNT]. A teacher uses the law lawfully when he knows and teaches that the law is not established for a righteous person, but for such people as those who are now listed [Lns]. The law is not to be applied to those who live righteously, but to those who live sinfully [WBC].

2. It indicates the grounds for saying that the law is good if it is used lawfully [AB, WBC]: the law is good if it used lawfully, *because of the following fact*. This gives the reason why the statement in 1:8 is true [WBC].

3. It indicates a second thing that is known [BNTC; CEV, NCV, NIV]: we know that the law is good, *and we also know this following fact*.

QUESTION—What is meant by a δίκαιος 'righteous' person?

1. The righteous person is one who keeps the legal requirements and does not break any laws [EGT, ICC, NIGTC, NTC, TC, TNTC; NCV, NRSV, REB, TEV]: *a person who does not break any laws*. This refers to a morally upright person and it is not used here of only those who are

justified by faith [ICC, NIGTC]. 'Righteous' is used in its popular sense [EGT]. A righteous person is contrasted with the following list of wicked people, and if anyone is so good that he naturally keeps the law, then there is no need for a law [NTC]. This is a general principle applicable to any law-abiding person [ICC, TC, TNTC], and it means that they do not need to be told what to do [ICC].

2. The righteous person is a Christian who is justified by faith in Christ and who is living a righteous Christian life [AB, Alf, BKC, BNTC, ECC, Lns, My, NAC, NIBC, NICNT, TH, WBC; CEV, GW]: *a person who is right before God.* The only person who lives righteously is the one who has been made righteous by God [WBC]. Committed believers do not need the law to cause them to live righteously since under the urging of the Holy Spirit they already want to live as God's law says [NAC]. The righteous person is one who has been made upright by God's grace, and no law, whether God's Law in the Torah or Roman law, has the power to make a person upright [ECC]. The law is for those who are unconvinced of their sin and therefore have not turned to Christ [BKC].

QUESTION—Is there significance in the fact that the generic singular 'a righteous person' in the first clause is followed by the list of fourteen plurals that describe all kinds of sinners?

The singular term 'a righteous person' individualizes the person, but all of the wicked people are in the plural form to describe an abominable mass of people [Lns]. Perhaps it suggests that righteous persons are few in relation to those for whom the laws are meant [ECC].

but for-lawless[a] and rebellious[b] (people), for-ungodly[c] and sinful[d] (people), for-unholy[e] and profane[f] (people),

LEXICON—a. ἄνομος (LN 88.140) (BAGD 3. p. 72): 'lawless' [BAGD, LN]. This adjective is translated as a noun or a noun phrase: 'lawbreakers' [CEV, GW, NIV, TEV], 'the lawless' [AB, BNTC, WBC; HCSB, KJV, NRSV, REB], 'lawless people/persons' [ECC, Lns, NTC; NET], 'people/those who are lawless' [NASB, NLT], 'people who break the law' [LSA], 'people who live without the law' [Herm], 'those who are against the law' [NCV], 'people who are disobedient' [NLT]. This adjective pertains to someone who lives without regard to law, and it implies that the person refuses to obey laws [LN]. Having reference to God's laws, it takes on the meaning of being 'godless' or 'wicked' [BAGD].

b. ἀνυπότακτος (LN 36.26) (BAGD 2. p. 76): 'rebellious, disobedient' [BAGD, LN]. This adjective is translated as a noun or noun phrase: 'the rebellious' [WBC; HCSB], 'rebellious people' [NET], 'people/those who are rebellious' [NASB, NLT], 'rebels' [GW, NIV], 'refractory persons' [ECC], 'the insubordinate' [BNTC], 'insubordinate men' [NTC], 'the unruly' [REB], 'those who refuse to follow the law' [NCV], 'the disobedient' [KJV, NRSV], 'disobedient persons' [Lns], 'people who live without obedience' [Herm], 'people who disobey God' [LSA], 'criminals'

[CEV, TEV], 'the reckless' [AB]. This adjective pertains to being rebelliously disobedient [LN].

c. ἀσεβής (LN 53.11) (BAGD 1. p. 114): 'ungodly' [LN, Lns], 'godless, impious' [BAGD]. This adjective is translated as a noun or noun phrase: 'the ungodly' [HCSB, KJV, NASB, NET, NIV], 'ungodly people' [GW], 'people who are ungodly' [NLT], 'the irreligious' [WBC], 'people who do not revere God' [LSA], 'the impious' [BNTC; REB], 'impious people' [Herm, NTC], 'the godless' [AB; NRSV, TEV], 'godless people' [ECC; CEV], 'people who are against God' [NCV]. This adjective pertains to one who lives without regard for any religious belief or practice [LN]. This does not refer to people 'without God', but to people who act impiously toward God [AB].

d. ἁμαρτωλός (LN 88.294) (BAGD 2. p. 44): 'sinful' [LN, Lns], 'sinning' [LN]. This adjective is translated as a noun or noun phrase: 'the sinful' [BNTC; HCSB, NIV, NRSV, REB, TEV], 'sinful men' [NTC], 'people who are sinful' [NCV, NLT], 'people who sin' [LSA], 'sinners' [AB, BAGD, ECC, Herm, WBC; CEV, GW, KJV, NASB, NET]. This adjective refers to sinful behavior [LN]. It refers to people who do wrong in the sight of God [AB].

e. ἀνόσιος (LN **53.47**) (BAGD 1. p. 72): 'unholy' [BAGD, LN, WBC; KJV], 'impious' [LN], 'godless' [**LN**], 'wicked' [BAGD]. This adjective is translated as a noun or noun phrase: 'the unholy' [AB, ECC; HCSB, NASB, NET, NIV, NRSV], 'unholy men' [NTC], 'people who are not holy' [NCV], 'the irreligious' [BNTC; REB], 'impious ones' [Lns], 'wicked people' [CEV], 'people who are wicked' [Herm], 'people who are not pleasing to God' [LSA], 'people who consider nothing sacred' [NLT], 'those who think nothing is holy' [GW], 'those who are not religious' [TEV]. This adjective refers to not being consecrated or devoted to God [LN].

f. βέβηλος (LN **88.115**) (BAGD 2. p. 138): 'profane' [LN, WBC; KJV], 'godless' [BAGD, LN], 'worldly' [**LN**]. This adjective is translated as a noun or noun phrase: 'the profane' [AB, BNTC, ECC; NASB, NET, NRSV], 'the worldly' [REB], 'profane ones/men' [Lns, NTC], 'the irreverent' [HCSB], 'the irreligious' [NIV], 'people who are irreligious' [LSA], 'people who have no religion' [NCV], 'those who are not spiritual' [TEV], 'people who defile what is holy' [NLT], 'those who think nothing is sacred' [GW], 'people who are godless' [Herm], 'evil people' [CEV]. This adjective refers to being profane in the sense of being godless or worldly [LN]. See this word at 4:7; 6:20.

QUESTION—What is meant by *lawless* and *rebellious* people?

These two general terms are in contrast with the righteous person [My, NIGTC, WBC] and they serve as an introduction to the rest of the specific categories in the following list [NICNT, NIGTC]. The two adjectives are virtually synonymous and they refer to people who refuse to be subject to the law [AB, Lns, WBC]. They oppose the law [Alf, Lns, WBC], disobey God

[ICC], are rebellious [NTC], and are not controlled by moral standards [AB]. The lawless are opposed to the law, while the rebellious will not obey proper authority, so that both act as they please [Lns]. Both adjectives refer to people who have a negative attitude toward the law; the lawless disregard and break the law, and the rebellious refuse to submit to it [NAC, NICNT, TH]. They ignore the law and refuse to be disciplined [TNTC]. They act as though there was no law and they refuse to submit to God [ICC]. They oppose the law and refuse to submit to higher authority [My].

1. The phrase refers primarily to God's law [Alf, BNTC, ECC, ICC, My, NICNT, NIGTC, NTC, TNTC, WBC; NET]. The false teachers did follow their mistaken understanding of the Mosaic law, but they were actually opposing the true intentions of that law [WBC]. They know about the law, but they lived as though there was no law [NTC].
2. The phrase refers to any law, whether divine or human [EGT, Lns, TC]. 'Lawless' is used to indicate that they were opposed to law, and 'rebellious' indicates that they were opposed to putting themselves under proper authority [Lns].

QUESTION— What is meant by *ungodly* and *sinful* people?

These two adjectives describe people in relation to their attitude toward God [Alf, My, NAC, TH, TNTC]. These attributes have a more definite reference to God than the preceding pair [My]. They concern moral or spiritual matters [TG]. The two types of people go together in that the ungodly are inwardly irreverent and they outwardly sin by disobeying God [NIBC, TC, WBC]. The ungodly are those who disregard God and his will, and this attitude is accompanied with a life of open sin [Lns]. The ungodly disregard God's authority and even deny his existence and as a result they are sinful [ICC]. The ungodly do not worship God and the sinners commit sinful acts against God [TH]. The ungodly do not revere God and the sinners oppose and defy him [Alf, TNTC].

QUESTION—What is meant by *unholy* and *profane* people?

The two adjectives are virtually synonymous, and they describe unholy conduct that is opposed to God [Lns, NICNT, WBC]. These are practically synonymous with the preceding pair of adjectives [TG]. These adjectives describe attitudes in regard to religious or spiritual matters [TH]. They refer to separation and alienation from God [Alf]. Negatively, they are unholy, and this is expressed positively as being profane [NTC]. They sin by denying God's existence, or by rebelling against his authority [ICC].

QUESTION—Who are the ἀνόσιος 'unholy'?

They are people who regard nothing as being sacred [Lns, TH, TNTC]. They do not customarily worship God [TH]. They disregard their duty to God [NTC], and do not participate in religious rites [ICC].

QUESTION—Who are the βέβηλος 'profane'?

Such people treat nothing as sacred [NAC]. This word is the antonym of the words the NT uses for 'holy' [ICC]. While 'holy' refers to the sphere where God is encountered, the 'profane' refers to everything else that is not in the sphere of the holy [WBC]. The profane are ritually unfit for public worship [ECC]. They treat a holy person, place, or thing as if it were not holy [NAC]. They despise God and blaspheme him [ICC]. They hate God and treat anything spiritual with contempt and ridicule [TH].

for-murderers/strikers-of-fathers[a] and murderers/strikers-of-mothers,[b] for-murderers-of-people[c]

LEXICON—a. πατρολῴας (LN **20.88**) (BAGD p. 637): 'murderers of fathers' [NTC; KJV], 'one who murders his father' [**LN**, LSA], 'one who kills one's father' [AB, BAGD; GW, HCSB, NASB, NCV, NET, NIV, NLT, NRSV, TEV; similarly CEV], 'patricide' [BAGD, ECC, Herm], 'parricide' [BNTC; REB], 'father-smiters' [Lns], 'those who beat their fathers' [WBC]. This noun denotes a person who murders his father [LN].

  b. μητρολῴας (LN **20.87**) (BAGD p. 520): 'murderers of mothers' [NTC; KJV], 'one who murders his mother' [BAGD, **LN**, LSA], 'one who kills one's mother' [AB; GW, HCSB, NASB, NCV, NET, NIV, NLT, NRSV, TEV; similarly CEV], 'matricide' [BAGD, BNTC, ECC, Herm; REB], 'mother-smiters' [Lns], 'those who beat their mothers' [WBC]. This noun denotes a person who murders his mother [LN].

  c. ἀνδροφόνος (LN **20.85**) (BAGD p. 64): 'murderer of people' [**LN**], 'murderer of women and children' [BAGD], 'manslayer' [KJV], 'man-killers' [Lns], 'those who kill their fellows' [NTC], 'those who kill other people' [GW], 'murderer' [AB, BAGD, BNTC, ECC, Herm, WBC; CEV, HCSB, NASB, NET, NIV, NRSV, REB, TEV], 'one who murders other people' [LSA], 'people who murder' [NCV], 'people who commit other murders' [NLT]. This noun denotes a person who murders another person [LN].

QUESTION—Why are πατρολῴαις καὶ μητρολῴαις 'murderers/strikers of fathers and murderers/strikers of mothers' paired by καί 'and' while ἀνδροφόνοις 'murderers' stands alone?

  Grammatically, the pair 'murderers/strikers of fathers and murderers/strikers of mothers' goes with the preceding three pairs of adjectives that are connected with καί 'and'. The noun 'murderers' begins a list that omits the conjunctions that ordinarily join coordinate words. This a figure of speech called *asyndeton*, which is natural in a long listing.

  1. The phrase πατρολῴαις καὶ μητρολῴαις means '*murderers* of fathers and *murderers* of mothers' and are closely related to the following noun ἀνδροφόνοις 'murderers' since all three nouns relate to murder [AB, BAGD, BNTC, ECC, EGT, Herm, LN, LSA, NAC, NIBC, NICNT, NTC, NTL, TG, TH, WP; all versions]. These are separated because the sin of murdering father or mother is a violation of the fifth commandment about honoring one's parents, and the more generic sin of murder is a violation of the sixth commandment about murder [BKC, ECC, NIBC, NTC, NTL, TH]. Murder of parents is the extreme example of not honoring parents, and it includes the lesser acts [BNTC, NTC, TH]. Or, the sin of murdering

parents violates both the fifth and sixth commandments [NAC, NICNT]. Or, each of the three sins represent violations of the sixth commandment against murder [AB, TG, TH]. Since murdering fathers and mothers has just been mentioned, the third sin of murder refers to killing others than parents, so it is accurate to translate this as '*other* murderers' [TG, TH]

2. The phrase πατρολῷαις καὶ μητρολῷαις means '*strikers* of fathers and *strikers* of mothers' and they describe a different kind of act from the following noun ἀνδροφόνοις 'murderers' [Lns, NIGTC, TC, TNTC, WBC]. The compound Greek words πατρολῷαις and μητρολῷαις combine the morphemes for fathers and mothers with ἀλοᾶν 'to hit, to crush, to destroy'. The compounds can mean either 'smiters' or 'murderers' of fathers and mothers, but since the next word in the list is 'murderer', the vice is probably different from murder and means 'strikers'. Also, beating parents would have been more common than killing one's parents [WBC]. The sin of this pair of vices is that of dishonoring parents [TC].

1:10 for-sexually-immoral-persons[a] homosexuals[b] men-stealers[c] liars[d] perjurers,[e]

LEXICON—a. πόρνος (LN 88.274) (BAGD p. 693): 'a sexually immoral person' [BAGD, LN; HCSB, NET], 'the immoral' [TEV], 'immoral man' [NTC; NASB], 'a person who is sexually immoral' [LSA; CEV, NLT], 'one who practices sexual immorality' [BAGD], 'a person involved in sexual sins' [GW], 'a person who takes part in sexual sins' [NCV], 'fornicator' [AB, BAGD, BNTC, Herm, Lns, WBC; NRSV, REB], 'whoremonger' [KJV], 'adulterer' [NIV], 'the incestuous' [ECC]. This noun denotes a man or woman who engages in sexually immoral actions of any kind [LN]. It covers adultery, fornication, and any other sexual activity outside of marriage [NICNT].

b. ἀρσενοκοίτης (LN 88.280) (BAGD p. 109): 'a homosexual' [BAGD, BNTC, ECC, LN, LSA, WBC; CEV, GW, HCSB, NASB], 'a practicing homosexual' [NET], 'a person who practices homosexuality' [NLT], 'a male who practices homosexuality' [BAGD], 'sodomite' [BAGD, NTC; NRSV], 'sexual pervert' [AB; TEV], 'pervert' [CEV, NIV, REB], 'one that defiles himself with mankind' [KJV], 'a person who has sexual relations with people of the same sex' [NCV], 'pederast' [BAGD, Herm, Lns]. This compound noun is literally 'men who lie with males' [ECC]. This noun denotes a male partner in homosexual intercourse [LN]. It denotes the activity of male homosexuality [NICNT].

c. ἀνδραποδιστής (LN 57.187) (BAGD p. 63): 'men-stealer' [KJV], 'slave dealer' [AB, BAGD, LN], 'slave trader' [ECC; NIV, NLT, NRSV], 'a person who sells slaves' [NCV], 'kidnapper' [BAGD, BNTC, Herm, **LN**, Lns, NTC, WBC; CEV, GW, HCSB, NASB, NET, REB, TEV], 'one who kidnaps people' [LSA]. This noun denotes a person who sells another person as a slave, and it includes those who kidnap people and sell them [LN].

d. ψεύστης (LN 33.255) (BAGD p. 892): 'liar' [AB, BAGD, BNTC, ECC, Herm, LN, Lns, NTC, WBC; all versions except NCV, TEV], 'one who lies' [LSA; NCV, TEV]. This noun denotes a person who utters falsehoods and lies [LN].

e. ἐπίορκος (LN **33.466**) (BAGD p. 296): 'perjurer' [AB, BAGD, BNTC, ECC, Herm, **LN**, Lns, WBC; HCSB, NASB, NET, NIV, NRSV, REB], 'one who perjures himself' [LSA], 'a perjured person' [KJV], 'one who gives false testimony' [TEV], 'one who lies when he takes an oath' [GW], 'false swearer' [NTC], 'promise breaker' [NLT], 'a person who will not tell the truth in court' [CEV], 'a person who speaks falsely' [NCV]. This noun denotes a person who swears to something falsely [LN].

QUESTION—Who are πόρνοις 'sexually immoral persons' and ἀρσενο-κοίταις 'homosexuals'?

These two nouns refer to sexual offenses that correspond to the commandment about not committing adultery [AB, Alf, BKC, BNTC, ECC, NAC, NIBC, NIGTC, NTC, TC, TNTC, WBC]. The term πόρνος 'sexually immoral person' is not confined to illicit sexual intercourse between unmarried persons since it includes adultery [ECC, NTC]. The word is usually used of an adulterer or fornicator [ICC, TG], but it covers all forms of sexual vice [BNTC, EGT, NTC]. The first term πόρνος is a generic term to designate persons who engaged in any sexual activity that was prohibited by Jewish tradition [ECC]. The term ἀρσενοκοίταις 'homosexuals' is appropriately paired with the first term [ECC], so as to cover both the heterosexual and the homosexual aspects of immoral sexual activity [NIGTC]. 'Sexually immoral' is generic term while 'homosexual' is a flagrant specific example [NTC]. The Greek word 'homosexual' directly refers to male homosexuals, but this word also refers to all homosexuals whether male or female [NTC, TH].

QUESTION—Who are ἀνδραποδισταῖς 'men stealers'?

This is dramatic example of breaking the commandment against stealing [AB, Alf, BKC, BNTC, ECC, Herm, ICC, Lns, NAC, NIBC, NIGTC, NTC, TC, WBC]. Rabbinic interpretation applied kidnapping to this commandment [Herm, ICC]. It refers to stealing or kidnapping human beings in order to sell them into slavery [ECC, NICNT, TH]. It also refers to selling into slavery men captured in war [AB]. Its primary meaning is 'slave dealer', but here it extends to cover all men-stealers or kidnappers [NTC]. The word means 'men-stealers', whether kidnapers of free men or stealers of other people's slaves [TG, WP]. They enslaved young males and females to exploit them sexually [NTL].

QUESTION—Who are ψεύσταις 'liars' and ἐπιόρκοις 'perjurers'?

These two sins pertain to the commandment about not bearing false witness [AB, Alf, BKC, BNTC, ECC, Lns, NAC, NIBC, NICNT, NIGTC, NTC, TC, WBC]. Paul is extending the meaning of the commandment from courtroom

perjury to include liars who swear to something that is untrue [WBC]. A liar
refers to someone in any circumstance who tells something that is not true
[AB]. The term refers to someone who speaks in a deceptive manner
[NICNT]. 'Perjurer' is a more specific category of liars [ICC, NICNT, NTL,
TH]. A perjurer is someone who takes an oath that he will speak the truth
and then breaks it by lying [NICNT]. He is someone who lies under oath
[AB, ECC], calling upon God as a witness to the truth of what is actually an
untruth [ECC]. A perjurer solemnly asserts something that is false [NTC].
He is someone who does not speak the truth when making an oath or a
promise [TG].

and if any other (thing that) is-contrary[a] to-the sound[b] teaching,

LEXICON—a. pres. mid./pass. (deponent = act.) indic. of ἀντίκειμαι (LN 39.1)
(BAGD p. 74): 'to oppose' [LN], 'to be in opposition' [BAGD]. The
phrase καὶ εἴ τι ἕτερον... ἀντίκειται 'and if any other thing that is
contrary to' [KJV] is also translated 'and whatever else is contrary to'
[NTC; HCSB, NASB, NIV, NRSV], 'and everything else that is contrary
to' [WBC], 'in fact, for any who live contrary to' [NET], 'or who do
anything else contrary to' [TEV], 'or who do anything else that
contradicts' [NLT], 'and if anything else opposes' [Lns], 'and who do
whatever else is opposed to' [AB], 'and for whatever else is against'
[GW], 'and whatever else goes against' [Herm], 'it is for anything else
that opposes' [CEV], 'and anything else that stands opposed to' [ECC],
'and whatever else is antagonistic to' [BNTC], 'and who do anything else
which is forbidden by' [LSA], 'in fact all whose behavior flouts' [REB].
This verb means to oppose something and includes a psychological
attitude in doing so [LN].
   b. pres. act. participle of ὑγιαίνω (LN 72.15) (BAGD 2. p. 832): 'to be
sound, to be correct, to be accurate' [BAGD, LN]. This participle is used
here as an attributive adjective modifying διδασκαλία 'teaching'
[NIGTC]. The phrase τῇ ὑγιαινούσῃ διδασκαλίᾳ 'the sound teaching'
[Herm; HCSB, REB] is also translated 'sound teaching' [NASB, NET,
NRSV], 'sound doctrine' [NTC; KJV, NIV, TEV], 'the healthy teaching'
[AB, Lns, WBC], 'the wholesome teaching' [BNTC; NLT], 'the wholesome instruction' [ECC], 'the correct teaching' [CEV], 'correct doctrine'
[LSA], 'accurate teachings' [GW]. This verb means to be correct in one's
views [LN]. In the Pastoral Epistles the verb 'to be healthy' is used
figuratively with reference to Christian teaching and describes the
teaching as being correct because it is reasonable and appeals to sound
intelligence [BAGD]. See this word at 6:3.
QUESTION—What is the function of this clause?
   This clause sums up all forms of sinful behavior that have not been included
   in the preceding list [ICC, NAC, NIGTC, WBC]. Rounding off the list of
   sinners in this way brings Paul back to his previous warning against false
   teachers [ICC, NIBC]. It seems to imply that there would be no end of a list

that named all the forms of evil committed in human conduct [ECC]. The
conditional particle εἰ 'if' does not indicate a condition of doubt here, but
with the other two members of the expression τι ἕτερον 'any other' it serves
to express a general sense of indefiniteness and implies the existence of other
sins which are also contrary to sound teaching [NIGTC].

QUESTION—What is meant by the phrase τῇ ὑγιαινούσῃ διδασκαλίᾳ 'the
sound teaching'?

'Sound teaching' is a medical metaphor where the physical condition of
well-being was extended to include a teaching that cultivated a condition of
virtue [AB]. It was a current metaphor of the time in philosophical jargon
and meant 'sound' and 'reasonable' [BNTC]. *Sound* doctrine promotes
spiritual *health* [Alf, NTC, WBC]. It implies that the teaching of the false
teachers was unhealthy, diseased, and morbid [ICC, Lns]. Some drop the
metaphor and translate it 'correct' [LSA, NIGTC; CEV], 'accurate' [GW], or
'true' [NIGTC]. The singular form διδασκαλίᾳ 'teaching' refers to the body
of Christian truth [EGT, WBC], the approved apostolic teaching [NICNT],
not a collection of many ideas [WBC]. It refers to the Christian faith
[NIGTC]. The Greek word can apply not only to proper *belief* but to proper
behavior, and here the emphasis is on right behavior that comes from correct
moral teaching [NAC]. It refers to the authentic Christian message pertaining
to conduct [BNTC]. Here it refers to the teaching of the gospel *about* how
Christians should act [TG]. It refers to Paul's interpretation of the Decalogue
[ECC].

1:11 **in-accordance-with**[a] **the good-news**[b] **of-the glory**[c] **of-the blessed**[d] **God,**
LEXICON—a. κατά (LN 89.8): 'in accordance with' [LN], 'in accord with'
   [Lns], 'according to' [Herm; KJV, NASB], 'in agreement with' [GW], 'in
   conformity to' [WBC], 'in harmony with' [NTC], 'based on' [HCSB], 'is
   part of' [NCV], '(the correct teaching) of' [CEV]. This preposition is also
   translated as a verb phrase: '(that/this) accords with' [AB, ECC; NET],
   '(that) conforms to' [NIV, NRSV, REB], '(that) comes from' [NLT],
   '(that teaching) is found in' [TEV], 'because this is what is taught in'
   [LSA], '(such) is' [BNTC]. This preposition indicates a similarity of
   process [LN]. The preposition contains both the meanings 'as deriving
   from' and 'as measured by' [AB]. It is both the source and the standard of
   the good teaching [NICNT]. This preposition also occurs at 1:1.
   b. εὐαγγέλιον (LN 33.217) (BAGD 2.b.α. p. 318): 'good news' [AB,
   BAGD, LN; CEV], 'Good News' [GW, NCV, NLT], 'gospel' [BNTC,
   ECC, Herm, LN, Lns, LSA, NTC, WBC; HCSB, KJV, NASB, NET, NIV,
   NRSV, REB, TEV]. This noun refers to the Christian message about what
   God has done in Christ on behalf of all people [TH]. It is the good news of
   salvation, the Christian message in its broadest sense [ICC]. The good
   news is that the Messiah had come and brought salvation [NICNT].
   c. δόξα (LN 87.23): 'glory' [BNTC, ECC, LN, Lns, WBC; GW, REB],
   'majesty' [Herm], 'greatness' [LN], not explicit [NCV]. This noun is also

translated as an adjective 'glorious' modifying 'good news' [AB, LSA, NTC; HCSB, KJV, NASB, NET, NIV, NLT, NRSV]; or modifying 'God' [CEV, TEV]. This noun denotes the state of being great and wonderful [LN].

d. μακάριος (LN 25.119) (BAGD 2. p. 487): 'blessed' [AB, BAGD, BNTC, ECC, Herm, Lns, LSA, NTC, WBC; all versions except CEV, REB], 'ever-blessed' [REB], 'wonderful' [CEV], 'happy' [BAGD, LN]. This adjective describes the state of being happy because of enjoying favorable circumstances [LN]. See this word at 6:15.

QUESTION—What relationship is indicated by κατά 'in accordance with'?

1. This preposition refers to τῇ ὑγιαινούσῃ διδασκαλίᾳ 'the sound teaching' in 1:10 [AB, ECC, NAC, NIBC, NICNT, NIGTC, NTC, NTL, TC, TH; CEV, HCSB, NCV, NET, NIV, NLT, NRSV, REB, TEV]: *the sound teaching is in accordance with the good news*. The sound doctrine must agree with the gospel itself [TH]. The sound teaching is based on the glorious gospel [HCSB]. The gospel is the source of sound doctrine and also the norm for teaching [AB]. The sound doctrine is contained in the good news [CEV, NCV].

2. This preposition refers to 1:8–10 [BNTC, EGT, ICC, Lns, LSA, My, TNTC; GW]: *everything I said about the law is in accordance with the good news*. This validates Paul's *interpretation* of the use of the law [ICC]. The limited role the law plays is a real part of the gospel that Paul received and it is not just Paul's opinion [BNTC, My, TNTC].

QUESTION—How is the genitive phrase τῆς δόξης 'of the glory' related?

1. The phrase τῆς δόξης 'of the glory' refers to an attribute of 'God', and it describes the content of the good news [BNTC, ECC, Herm, ICC, Lns, My, NAC, NIBC, NICNT, NIGTC, NTIC, TC, TNTC, WBC; GW, REB]: the good news *about the glory possessed by the blessed God*. The gospel makes known God's full glory [NIBC]. Glory is the essence of God, and the gospel reveals God's glory to righteous persons, while the law is for sinners and reveals their sin [WBC]. God's glory refers to all of his attributes as they are seen in his blessedness [Lns]. It is the glory of God's power, majesty, and compassion [BNTC]. This concerns God's personal glory that makes him the transcendent God [ICC]. Here it refers to his glory shown in justifying sinners by providing redemption in Christ without the law [My]. The message of salvation declares that the visible glory of God, with its accompanying qualities of power and majesty, is revealed in the Christ-event [NICNT]. The gospel reveals God's glory as it is made known in the person of Christ [BNTC, My]. Jesus Christ is God's glory [ECC].

2. The phrase τῆς δόξης 'of the glory' functions as the adjective 'glorious', and it modifies the preceding phrase 'the good news' [AB, LSA, NTC, NTL; HCSB, KJV, NASB, NET, NIV, NLT, NRSV]: *the glorious good news*. The good news is glorious in that it displays the glory of God's attributes [NTC]. The genitive construction 'of the blessed God' indicates

the source of the good news [LSA; probably HCSB, NET]: the glorious
good news *from the blessed God*. The genitive construction 'of the
blessed God' indicates both the source of the good news and its content
[AB]: *the glorious good news from God and about God.*

3. The phrase τῆς δόξης 'of the glory' functions as the adjective 'glorious'
and modifies the following phrase 'the blessed God' [EGT, TH; CEV,
TEV]: *the glorious and blessed God*. God's nature is described as glorious
and blessed, and this could be translated 'the wonderful God whom
people praise' [TH]. The genitive construction 'of the blessed God'
indicates the source of the good news [CEV, TEV]: the good news *from
the glorious and blessed God.*

QUESTION—What is meant by God being μακάριος 'blessed'?

This adjective is usually used of people to describe their favorable situation,
as in the beatitudes in Matt. 5:3–12, but here and in 1 Tim. 6:15 it is used as
an attribute of God. It refers to the true happiness of God [Herm, NTL]. God
is happy in being eternally self sufficient and contented [TG]. God
experiences the perfection of bliss [TC, TNTC]. God contains happiness in
himself and he bestows happiness on people [NIGTC]. The adjective relates
to God's happiness and immortality [ICC]. However, 'happy' should not be
used for 'blessed' because happiness implies that unhappiness is also a
possibility [EGT]. Blessedness is an attribute of God that indicates his
absolute perfection [NTC]. God is called blessed because he is the source of
all blessedness [ECC, NAC]. God contains in himself all blessedness and he
bestows this on people [BNTC, NIBC]. Perhaps μακάριος 'blessed' is used
here as a synonym for εὐλογητός 'blessed, praised' so that it would mean
'God who is worthy to be praised' [TH].

with-which I-was-entrusted.[a]

LEXICON—a. aorist pass. indic. of πιστεύω (LN 35.50) (BAGD 3. p. 662): 'to
be entrusted' [AB, BAGD, BNTC, ECC, Herm, LN, Lns, NTC; GW,
HCSB, NET, NLT, REB], 'to be put into the care of' [LN]. The phrase
'with which I was entrusted' is translated actively: 'which he entrusted to
me' [LSA; NIV, NRSV], '(the good news) God has given me' [CEV],
'that he gave me to tell' [NCV], 'which was committed to my trust'
[KJV], 'that was entrusted to me to announce' [TEV]. This verb means to
entrust something to someone's care [LN].

QESTION—Who entrusted the good news to Paul?

God entrusted the gospel into the care of Paul [Lns, NICNT, NTC, TH,
TNTC, WBC; CEV, NCV, NIV, NLT, NRSV]. Paul was entrusted with the
gospel in order that the good news be proclaimed and also to guard against it
being corrupted [TH]. This statement concerns Paul's responsibility to
preserve the message of the gospel in the face of error [ICC]. The
perversions of the gospel (1:9–10) did not proceed from God, so they must
not be allowed to continue [NAC]. This happened when the Lord spoke to

Paul on the Damascus road [BNTC]. It refers to Paul's commission to missionary service (1 Cor. 9:17 and Gal. 2:7) [ICC].

DISCOURSE UNIT 1:12–20 [CEV, NCV, NIV, TEV]. The topic is the Lord's grace to Paul [NIV], being thankful for God's kindness [CEV], gratitude for God's mercy [NCV, TEV].

DISCOURSE UNIT 1:12–17 [AB, ECC, ICC, NAC, NCBC, NIBC, NICNT, NIGTC, NTL, TH, TNTC, WBC; GW, HCSB, NLT, NRSV]. The topic is thanksgiving [NTL], gratitude for mercy [NLT, NRSV], thanks for empowering mercy [AB], Paul's gratitude to Christ Jesus [TH], Paul at prayer [ECC], the apostle's personal experience of the gospel [TNTC], Paul's testimony [HCSB], a testimony about the gospel [NIBC], God's mercy to Paul [GW], God's mercy shown in Paul's life [NCBC], an example of salvation by grace [WBC], the source of Paul's power and commission [ICC], Paul's calling is a pattern of conversion [NICNT], Paul's commission and conversion as an example of the truth of the gospel [NIGTC], the task to preach the gospel [NAC].

1:12 **I-have thanks[a] to-the (one) having-enabled[b] me Christ Jesus our Lord,**

LEXICON—a. χάρις (LN 33.350) (BAGD 5. p. 878): 'thanks' [BAGD, LN], 'gratitude' [BAGD]. The phrase χάριν ἔχω 'I have thanks' is translated 'I give thanks' [AB, ECC; HCSB, REB, TEV], 'I am thankful' [Herm], 'I thank' [WBC; CEV, GW, KJV, NASB, NCV, NIV, NLT], 'I acknowledge my gratitude' [NTC], 'I am grateful' [BNTC, Lns, LSA; NET, NRSV]. This noun denotes the expression of one's thankfulness [LN]. The present tense of the verb ἔχω 'I have' with χάρις 'thanks' indicates that this is Paul's continual practice [Lns, NAC, WBC].

b. aorist act. participle of ἐνδυναμόω (LN 74.6) (BAGD 1. p. 263): 'to enable' [LN, Lns, LSA; KJV], 'to strengthen' [BAGD, LN, WBC; HCSB, NASB, NET, NRSV], 'to give strength' [BNTC, NTC; CEV, NCV, NIV, NLT, TEV], 'to empower' [AB, LN], 'to make strong' [Herm], 'to make equal to the task' [REB]. This verb is also translated as a noun phrase: 'who put his strength in me' [ECC], '(to do his work) with the strength he has given me' [GW]. This verb means to cause a person to have the ability to do something [LN]. The aorist tense of this participle points to some event in Paul's past, probably his conversion and calling on the Damascus Road [NICNT].

QUESTION—Why did Paul thank Christ Jesus instead of God as he usually does?

Here Paul was thinking of his encounter with Christ on the road to Damascus at the time he was called to service [ICC, NICNT]. It was Christ who considered Paul to be trustworthy, who appointed him to his service, and who enabled him to carry it out [NTC].

QUESTION—What relationship is indicated by the participial phrase τῷ ἐνδυναμώσαντί με 'the one enabling me'?

1. This is an adjectival participial phrase that describes Christ Jesus [AB, BNTC, ICC, Lns, NIBC, NICNT, NIGTC, NTC; all versions except CEV]: *I thank Christ Jesus, who enabled me.* Some take this to function as a description of Christ, but also take it to imply that Paul includes this enablement as something to be thankful for, even though his primary reason for thanking Christ is introduced by the following ὅτι 'because' clause [NIBC, NIGTC, NTC].

2. This functions as the reason why Paul thanked Christ Jesus [WBC; CEV]: *I thank Jesus for enabling me.* Then the following ὅτι 'because' clause describes the reason why Christ enabled him [WBC; CEV].

QUESTION—What was it that Christ Jesus enabled Paul to do?

Christ enabled Paul to proclaim the gospel that had been entrusted to him (1:11) [LSA, NAC, NTL, TG]. Christ enabled Paul to serve him [ICC; GW], to do the work Christ gave him to do [EGT, My; TEV]. This enabling refers to religious and moral strengthening [NIGTC]. This refers to the strength he received to perform his work as an apostle [ICC, Lns, NTC, TH, WBC]. Although the immediate reference of the empowering is for serving as an apostle, in the context of heresy it could include God's authentication of Paul's authority in the working of miracles [ICC].

because/that[a] he-considered[b] me trustworthy/faithful[c] appointing[d] (me) to service[e]

LEXICON—a. ὅτι (LN 88.33, 90.21): 'because' [BNTC, ECC, LN (88.33), LSA; CEV, HCSB, NASB, NCV, NET, NRSV], 'for' [AB; REB, TEV], 'since' [LN (88.33), WBC], 'inasmuch as' [LN (88.33)], 'that' [Herm, LN (90.21), Lns, NTC; GW, NIV], 'for that' [KJV], not explicit [NLT].

b. aorist mid./pass. (deponent = act.) indic. of ἡγέομαι (LN 31.1) (BAGD 2. p. 343): 'to consider' [AB, BAGD, BNTC, LN, Lns, LSA, NTC, WBC; HCSB, NASB, NET, NIV, NLT, TEV], 'to hold a view, to have an opinion' [LN], 'to regard' [ECC, LN], 'to judge' [NRSV, REB], 'to think' [BAGD], 'to count' [KJV], 'to know' [CEV], not explicit [Herm; GW, NCV]. This verb means to have an opinion about something [LN].

c. πιστός (LN 31.87) (BAGD 1.a.α. p. 664): 'trustworthy' [BAGD, BNTC, ECC, LN, NTC; NLT], 'worthy of trust' [REB], 'worthy' [TEV], 'dependable' [BAGD, LN], 'reliable' [LN], 'faithful' [AB, BAGD, LN, Lns, WBC; HCSB, KJV, NASB, NET, NIV, NRSV]. The clause 'he considered me trustworthy' is translated 'he considered that I could be trusted' [LSA], 'he knew that he could trust me' [CEV], 'he trusted me' [GW, NCV], 'he has given me his confidence' [Herm]. This adjective refers to the quality of being worthy of trust [LN].

d. aorist mid. participle of τίθημι (LN 37.96) (BAGD II.2.c. p. 816): 'to appoint' [BAGD, BNTC, LN, Lns, LSA, NTC, WBC; GW, HCSB, NIV,

NLT, NRSV, REB, TEV], 'to assign, to give a task to someone' [LN], 'to designate' [Herm, LN], 'to put' [AB; KJV, NASB, NET], 'to place' [ECC], 'to give a work' [NCV], not explicit [CEV]. This verb means to assign someone to a particular role or task [LN].

e. διακονία (LN 35.19, 35.21) (BAGD 3. p. 184): 'service' [AB, BAGD, BNTC, Herm, LN (35.19), Lns, WBC; NASB, NIV, NRSV, REB], 'ministry' [ECC, LN (35.21), NTC; HCSB, KJV, NET], 'task' [LN (35.21)], 'office' [BAGD]. This noun is also translated as a verb: 'to serve (him)' [NCV, NLT, TEV], 'to minister (to people)' [LSA]. The phrase θέμενος εἰς διακονίαν 'appointing me to service' is translated 'has appointed me to do his work' [GW], '(he has given me the strength) for my work' [CEV]. This noun denotes the assistance or help that is rendered by someone who performs certain duties which may be humble or menial in nature [LN (35.19)], or it means the role or position of serving [LN (35.21)].

QUESTION—Does the conjunction ὅτι mean 'because' or 'that' here?

1. This conjunction indicates the reason Paul thanked Christ [AB, BAGD, BNTC, ECC, EGT, ICC, LSA, NAC, NIBC, NICNT, TC, TH, TNTC; CEV, HCSB, NASB, NCV, NET, NRSV]: *I thank Christ Jesus because he considered me faithful and appointed me to service.* The primary reason for thanking Christ is Paul's conversion and call to the ministry [ICC]. Paul was thankful for being considered faithful [TNTC]. There are two reasons for thanking Christ: that Christ judged him to be trustworthy and that Christ appointed him for service [NIBC, TH].

2. This conjunction indicates the contents of what Paul thanked Christ for [Herm, Lns, NIGTC, NTC; GW, KJV, NIV, REB, TEV]: *I thank Christ Jesus that he considered me to be faithful, appointing me to service.* However, there is little difference in taking this to be the reason for thanking Christ or the content of what he thanked Christ for [NTC].

3. This conjunction indicates the reason why Christ enabled Paul [WBC; CEV]: *I thank Christ Jesus that he enabled me because he considered me to be faithful.*

QUESTION—In what way was Paul πιστόν 'trustworthy' or 'faithful'?

1. This describes Paul's quality of being trustworthy and dependable, that is, he was worthy of being trusted by Christ [AB, BNTC, ECC, EGT, Herm, ICC, Lns, LSA, NIBC, NIGTC, NTC, TG, TH, TNTC, WBC; CEV, GW, NASB, NLT, REB]: *Jesus Christ considered that he could trust me.* The word πιστόν 'trustworthy, faithful' is to be connected with ἐπιστεύθην 'I was entrusted' in 1:11, since God entrusted the good news only to someone he considered to be worthy of that trust [BNTC, ECC, Herm, Lns, NICNT, WBC]. This describes Paul as worthy of being appointed [NAC; TEV]. Paul had not yet proven his trustworthiness at the time of his conversion, but the enabling he received changed him from a persecutor of Christians to a trustworthy servant who would be faithful [NIGTC]. It is not that Paul was chosen because he was already a

trustworthy man, but that Christ chose him because he knew that Paul would be trustworthy in the future [EGT, WBC], and that future trustworthiness would be a result of being empowered by God [WBC]. This is not just a general attribute, but it is trustworthiness related to Paul's work in serving Christ [NICNT, TH]. When Christ considered Paul to be trustworthy, he was considering not what Paul was in himself, but what his grace was doing within Paul [NTC]. Christ had shown his confidence in Paul's worth, not that Paul in himself was worthy, but the act of choosing him made him worthy [NAC].

2. This describes Paul's attitude of being faithful to Christ or to the work Christ gave to him [Alf; probably HCSB, KJV, NASB, NET, NIV, NRSV which translate this as 'faithful']: *he considered that I would be faithful to him.* Christ knew that Paul would be faithful to Christ's great trust [Alf].

QUESTION—What relationship is indicated by the use of the participle θέμενος 'appointing'?

1. The participle indicates the result of Christ considering Paul to be trustworthy [LSA, NAC, NIBC, TH]: *he considered me to be trustworthy and so he appointed me to serve.* Christ showed his confidence in Paul's worth by appointing him to the ministry [NAC].

2. The participle indicates Paul's grounds for knowing that Christ considered him to be trustworthy or faithful [AB, Alf, EGT, ICC, Lns, My, WBC]: *I know that he considered me trustworthy, since he appointed me to serve.* This participial clause indicates the grounds for affirming that Christ considered him to be trustworthy [WBC].

3. The participle is practically coordinate with the preceding clause [Herm, NICNT, NIGTC, NTC; GW, NCV, NLT, NRSV, REB, TEV]: *he considered me to be trustworthy/faithful and he appointed me to serve.* Paul was thankful for three benefits: for empowering him, for judging him to be trustworthy, and for appointing him [NTC]. Paul is thankful for being considered trustworthy and then being placed in Christ's service [NIGTC].

QUESTION—What was the διακονίαν 'service' to which Paul was appointed?

1. This is a general term that was used to designate the special office of being a minister to the church [AB, ECC, EGT, Herm, ICC, My, NICNT, NIGTC, NTC, NTL, TC, TH, WBC; HCSB, KJV]: *he appointed me to the ministry.* Service is used of all kinds of commissions to serve in the church, including being an apostle [ICC]. The following verses build on the fact that he is talking about his apostleship [Herm, NIGTC, NTC]. There is no church office, even that of being an apostle, that does not consist in serving rather than being served [WBC]. Christ appointed Paul to represent him [TH]. This ministry of apostolic office was a service he rendered to the Lord [NTC].

2. This is a general term for serving Christ [NIBC, TG; GW, NCV, NIV, NLT, NRSV, REB, TEV]: *he appointed me to serve him.*

3. This is a general term for ministering to people [Lns, LSA]: *he appointed me to minister to people.* It does not mean that his ministry benefited Christ, rather, this is a ministry that benefited people [Lns]. It was a ministry to those who needed help, that is, to people, not the Lord [LSA].

DISCOURSE UNIT 1:13–17 [Herm]. The topic is Paul being an example of God's mercy.

1:13 **formerly**[a] **being a-blasphemer**[b] **and a-persecutor**[c] **and an-insolent-man,**[d]

LEXICON—a. πρότερος (LN 67.18) (BAGD 1.b.α. p. 722): 'formerly' [BAGD, ECC, LN, Lns, LSA, WBC; HCSB, NASB, NET, NRSV], 'previously' [BNTC, NTC], 'before' [LN; KJV], 'earlier' [AB, BAGD], 'once' [Herm; NIV]. The phrase τὸ πρότερον 'formerly' is translated 'in the past' [GW, NCV, REB, TEV], 'I used to' [CEV, NLT]. This adverb pertains to a point of time earlier in a sequence [LN]. It refers to Paul's condition before he was converted [ICC, NIGTC, TG, TH]. These were his actions when he first came in contact with the Christian movement [TH].

b. βλάσφημος (LN **33.403**) (BAGD p. 143): 'blasphemer' [AB, BNTC, ECC, Herm, LN, Lns, NTC, WBC; KJV, NASB, NET, NIV, NRSV], 'defamer' [**LN**], 'slanderer' [BAGD]. The phrase 'being a blasphemer' is translated 'one who was a blasphemer' [HCSB], 'I cursed him' [GW], 'I spoke against Christ' [NCV], 'I used to blaspheme the name of Christ' [NLT], 'I spoke evil of him' [TEV], 'I said evil things about him' [LSA], 'I used to say terrible things about him' [CEV], 'I had met him with abuse' [REB]. This noun denotes a person who defames someone [LN].

c. διώκτης (LN **39.46**) (BAGD p. 201): 'persecutor' [AB, BAGD, BNTC, ECC, Herm, LN, Lns, NTC, WBC; HCSB, KJV, NASB, NET, NIV, NRSV]. The phrase 'being a persecutor' is translated 'I persecuted him' [GW, NCV, TEV], 'I was a person who persecuted him' [**LN**], 'I had met him with persecution' [REB], 'I used to say insulting things about him' [CEV], 'I persecuted his people' [LSA; NLT]. This noun denotes a person who is engaged in persecuting others [LN].

d. ὑβριστής (LN **33.392**) (BAGD p. 832): 'an insolent man/person' [AB, BAGD, Lns, WBC], 'insulter' [**LN**], 'an arrogant man' [HCSB, NET], 'a man who was insanely arrogant' [ECC], 'a violent man' [BAGD; NIV], 'a man of violence' [NRSV], 'a violent aggressor' [NASB], 'a wanton aggressor' [NTC], 'a bully' [BNTC], 'an evil doer' [Herm]. The phrase 'being an insolent man' is translated 'I was insolent to him' [LSA], 'one who insulted him' [**LN**], 'I insulted him' [TEV], 'I was cruel' [CEV], 'I did all kinds of things to hurt him' [NCV], 'who was injurious' [KJV], 'I had met him with outrage' [REB], 'in my insolence' [NLT], 'I acted arrogantly toward him' [GW]. This noun denotes a person who insults another in an arrogant manner [LN].

QUESTION—What relationship is indicated by the use of the present active participle ὄντα 'being'?

1. This participle functions as a concession to the preceding clause [Alf, BNTC, EGT, ICC, LSA, NTC, TC, WBC, WP; NASB, NET, NIV, NLT, NRSV, REB, TEV]: *he considered me faithful and appointed me, even though I was formerly a blasphemer, etc.* This participle relates to both 'considered' and 'appointing' as a concession [NICNT].
2. This functions as a description of 'me' in the preceding clause [ECC, Herm, Lns, NICNT; HCSB, KJV]: *he considered me faithful, a man who was formerly a blasphemer, etc.* This sentence is in apposition to 'me' in the preceding clause and implies that it was an astounding thing for such a man to be considered faithful [Lns].

QUESTION—Is the arrangement of the nouns 'blasphemer, persecutor, insolent man' significant?

Each term is severer than the one before it [ECC, ICC, Lns, NTC, WBC]. These terms are the gospel's judgment of Paul seen through his repentant eyes [WBC]. These terms were accusations made by Paul's own conscience [Alf].

QUESTION—What is meant by Paul being a βλάσφημον 'blasphemer'?

The word refers to being abusive or contemptuous to someone [ECC]. This word means to slander or revile someone, and when directed toward a divine being it is blasphemy [AB].

1. Paul spoke in an offensive way against Christ [EGT, ICC, Lns, My, NAC, NIBC, NICNT, NTC, WBC]. He ridiculed the name of Christ [NTC]. He denied Christ by both what he said and what he did [NAC, NIBC]. He used wicked language full of hate against Christ and tried to force others to do the same [Lns]. From a Christian point of view, this refers to abusing Jesus, the Son of God and God's Messiah, and this was shown by persecuting his followers [ICC]. A blasphemer is one who denies God by carelessly speaking God's name YHWH in a disrespectful way, but in this context, it refers to being scornful about the claim that Jesus was the Messiah and being hostile toward Jesus' followers [NICNT].
2. It was God whom he blasphemed [NICNT, NTL, TH]. Here this probably refers to what he said about God and the things of God [NIGTC]. Paul's persecution of the church amounted to blasphemy against God [NTL].

QUESTION—What is meant by Paul being a διώκτην 'persecutor'?

Paul persecuted the church [AB, BNTC, NAC, TH, WBC]. He tried to force Christians to deny Christ [NIBC]. In persecuting the church, Paul was actually persecuting Christ himself (Acts 9:5; 22:8; 26:15) [EGT, Lns, LSA, NIGTC, NTC, TG, WBC].

QUESTION—What is meant by Paul being a ὑβριστήν 'insolent man'?

This noun means being both insolent and arrogant [AB], or insolent and violent [ICC, NIGTC]. His rude arrogance produced his violence [NICNT]. This refers to an aggressive, rude, and insolent person who treats others with cruelty and violence, and the implied object of this is Christ or his followers

[TH]. He acted like a bully [BNTC, NAC]. This describes adding insult to persecution [Alf]. Paul committed outrages against the followers of Christ [NTC]. Along with verbal attacks he physically mistreated them [TG]. Paul's persecution of the church refers to his acts of violence against God's people [NTL].

yet/but[a] I-received-mercy,[b] because being ignorant[c] I-acted in unbelief.[d]

LEXICON—a. ἀλλά (LN 89.125, 91.2): 'yet' [LN (91.2), LSA; NASB], 'but' [AB, ECC, Herm, LN (89.125), Lns, NTC, WBC; CEV, KJV, NCV, NET, NLT, NRSV, REB, TEV], 'however' [BNTC; GW], not explicit [HCSB, NIV]. This particle is a marker of emphatic contrast [LN].

b. aorist pass. indic. of ἐλεέω (LN 88.76) (BAGD p. 249): 'to receive mercy' [BAGD, LN; HCSB]. The phrase ἠλεήθην 'I received mercy' [HCSB, NRSV] is also translated 'I obtained mercy' [KJV], 'I was shown mercy' [AB, BNTC, WBC; NASB, NIV], 'I was accorded mercy' [NTC], 'I was dealt with mercifully' [REB], 'I was treated with mercy' [Lns; GW, NET], 'mercy found me out' [ECC], 'I received mercy from Christ' [Herm, LSA], 'he had mercy on me' [CEV], 'God showed me mercy' [NCV], 'God had mercy on me' [NLT], 'God was merciful to me' [TEV]. This verb means to show kindness and concern for someone who is in serious need [LN]. Mercy is the expression of God's kindness and compassion [NICNT].

c. pres. act. participle of ἀγνοέω (LN 28.13) (BAGD 1. p. 11): 'to be ignorant, to not know' [BAGD, LN]. The phrase ἀγνοῶν ἐποίησα 'being ignorant I acted' [Lns, WBC] is also translated 'I acted ignorantly' [BNTC, LSA, NTC; GW, NASB, NET, NRSV], 'I acted in ignorance' [NIV, REB; similarly AB], 'I acted from ignorance' [Herm], 'I did it in ignorance' [NLT], 'it was out of ignorance that I had acted' [HCSB], 'I did not know what I was doing' [ECC, **LN** (31.105); CEV, NCV, TEV]. This verb means to lack information about something [LN].

d. ἀπιστία (LN **31.105**) (BAGD 2.b. p. 85): 'unbelief' [BAGD]. The phrase ἐν ἀπιστίᾳ 'in unbelief' [BNTC, Herm, Lns, NTC, WBC; HCSB, KJV, NASB, NET, NRSV], is also translated 'in my unbelief' [ECC; GW]. The phrase 'because being ignorant I acted in unbelief' is translated 'I acted/did it in ignorance and unbelief' [NIV, NLT], 'I acted in the ignorance of unbelief' [REB], 'I acted ignorantly because I did not believe in him' [LSA], 'because as an unbeliever, I did not know what I was doing' [**LN**], 'I did not yet have faith and so did not know what I was doing' [TEV], 'because I didn't know what I was doing, and I had not yet put my faith in him' [CEV], 'because I did not know what I was doing. I did not believe' [NCV], 'in ignorance I acted with faithlessness' [AB]. This noun denotes the state of not believing the gospel about Jesus Christ, and therefore not being a Christian [LN]. It represents an active state of disbelief [AB]. Paul did not believe that Jesus was the Messiah [ICC].

QUESTION—What relationship is indicated by ἀλλὰ 'but'?

1. It indicates contra-expectation [LSA, TH; NASB, NIV]: *formerly I was… yet I received mercy.* Despite his actions, Paul received mercy [TH].

2. It indicates contrast [Alf, ECC, ICC, My, NICNT, NIGTC, WBC]: *formerly I was…, but now I received mercy.* This is a contrast between Paul's sinful condition described in the preceding clause and the mercy shown by God [ECC, WBC], or the Lord [ECC]. This is a contrast that indicates the transition from Paul's former life to his present state [ICC, NICNT]. God's mercy is put in contrast with Paul's lack of it [Alf, My].

QUESTION—What is meant by ἠλεήθην 'I received mercy'?

This refers to divine pity [NTC], or compassion [ICC]. This was a pardon made possible by the fact that Paul had acted from ignorance in unbelief [Herm]. The pardon resulted in Paul's salvation [ICC]. Paul was spared judgment [TH]. This act of mercy was not limited just to the pardon of Paul's persecuting fury, it included all of the aspects of God's grace that was shown to him [EGT, My], such as considering him faithful and appointing him to Christ's service [EGT].

1. Christ was the one who had mercy on him [Herm, LSA, NIGTC, TH; CEV]. Verse 1:12 implies that it was Christ who was merciful to Paul [LSA, TH], and this is supported by 1:16 where he says that Christ showed his patience with him [LSA].

2. God was the one who had mercy on him [BNTC, ICC, NAC, NICNT, TG, TNTC, WBC; NCV, NLT, TEV]. The passive voice of this verb emphasizes that this was totally an act of God [NICNT, WBC], and this shows that salvation is not deserved, but is due to God's mercy and grace [WBC].

QUESTION—What relationship is indicated by the conjunction ὅτι 'because'?

It explains the reason why Paul received mercy [LSA, NAC, NICNT, TNTC]: *I was shown mercy because I acted in unbelief.* Since Paul's misguided past had not been due to a willful ignorance that would increase his guilt, Paul was an object of God's pity rather than judgment [TNTC]. It seems that Paul should have said that he received mercy *in spite of* his ignorance [NCBC]. It does not mean that Paul's ignorance was the *reason* why he received mercy, rather it *explains* why Paul's sins were not regarded as being defiant and unpardonable sins [ICC, NIGTC, WBC]. It explains a consideration that led to his receiving mercy [WBC]. Paul was not claiming that as a result of being ignorant and unbelieving he was without guilt, but that his prior condition became the object of God's mercy [BNTC, NIBC], because his sins had been unwitting and not purposeful as distinguished in Num. 15:22–31 [NIBC].

QUESTION—What is meant by ἐποίησα 'I acted'?

This refers to the actions implied by the three descriptions of Paul in the preceding clause [ICC, NIGTC, WBC]. This summarizes all of Paul's activities in persecuting the church [ECC, NTC].

QUESTION—Why did Paul say that he was 'ignorant'?

Paul was ignorant about Jesus and his church [TH]. This does not mean that Paul knew nothing about Christ, rather his ignorance is explained by 'in unbelief' and his ignorance refers to not recognizing the deity of Christ and the fact that he was the Savior [Lns]. He did not know Jesus' true nature as Lord and Savior [NAC]. Paul did not believe that Jesus was the Messiah, so he thought he was doing right in trying to eliminate the sect that followed Jesus [NIGTC]. Being zealous for the law, Paul did not realize that his actions were sinful [ICC]. Paul was ignorant of the true purpose of the law, and possibly here this means he was ignorant of God's ways in general [WBC]. Since Paul did not believe in Christ he did not realize the true nature of his persecution of Christ's followers [TG]. Paul did not know how grievous his sins were [My].

QUESTION—What relationships are indicated by the use the participle ἀγνοῶν 'being ignorant' and the prepositional phrase ἐν ἀπιστίᾳ 'in unbelief'?

1. The participle ἀγνοῶν 'being ignorant' indicates the manner in which Paul acted [AB, Alf, BNTC, ECC, EGT, Lns, LSA, My, NIGTC, NTC; all versions except HCSB]: *I received mercy because I acted ignorantly.*

   1.1 The prepositional phrase ἐν ἀπιστίᾳ 'in unbelief' indicates the reason why Paul acted ignorantly [Alf, LSA, My, NIGTC; REB]: *I received mercy because I acted ignorantly because I did not believe.* 'In unbelief' describes Paul's condition when he acted, and it provides the basis for his ignorance [Alf, NIGTC]. This corrects a misunderstanding that all acts of ignorance are excusable [Alf].

   1.2 The prepositional phrase ἐν ἀπιστίᾳ 'in unbelief' indicates his state when he acted ignorantly [AB, BNTC, ECC, NICNT, NTC; GW, KJV, NASB, NET, NRSV]: *I received mercy because I acted ignorantly in my state of unbelief.*

   1.3 The prepositional phrase ἐν ἀπιστίᾳ 'in unbelief' indicates the reason Paul received mercy, and his unbelief was the reason he acted ignorantly [TEV]: *I received mercy because I did not believe and so I acted ignorantly.* 'God was merciful to me because I did not yet have faith and so did not know what I was doing' [TEV].

   1.4 The prepositional phrase ἐν ἀπιστίᾳ 'in unbelief' indicates a second manner in which Paul acted [Lns; NIV, NLT]: I received mercy because *I acted in ignorance and in unbelief.*

   1.5 The prepositional phrase ἐν ἀπιστίᾳ 'in unbelief' indicates a second reason he received mercy [TH; CEV]: *I received mercy because I acted ignorantly and because I did not believe.* 'He had mercy on me because I didn't know what I was doing, and I had not yet put my faith in him' [CEV]. 'Christ was merciful to me because I had not yet believed in him and I didn't know what I was doing' [TH].

2. The prepositional phrase ἐν ἀπιστίᾳ 'in unbelief' indicates the manner in which Paul acted and the participle ἀγνοῶν 'being ignorant' indicates the reason Paul acted in unbelief [WBC; HCSB]: *I received mercy because I*

acted in unbelief since I was ignorant. Paul did not commit these sins in defiance to what he knew to be right, his unbelief was caused by his ignorance [WBC].

1:14 And/but[a] the grace[b] of-our Lord super-abounded[c] with[d] faith and love the (one/ones) in[e] Christ Jesus.

LEXICON—a. δέ (LN 89.87, 89.93, 89.124) (BAGD 1., 2., 3. p. 171): This conjunction can mark a sequence of closely related events: 'and, and then' [LN (89.87)], or an additive relation that is not coordinate: 'and, and also, also, in addition, even' [LN (89.93)], or a contrast: 'but, on the other hand' [LN (89.124)]. It can emphasize a contrast: 'but', or mark a simple transition: 'now, then', or mark a resumption of an interrupted discourse: 'and also, but also' [BAGD]. Here it is translated 'and' [AB, LSA, NTC, WBC; HCSB, KJV, NASB, NET, NRSV, TEV], 'indeed' [BNTC, Herm], 'still' [ECC], 'moreover' [Lns], 'but' [NCV], not explicit [CEV, GW, NIV, NLT, REB].

b. χάρις (LN 88.66) (BAGD 2.a. p. 877): 'grace' [BAGD, BNTC, ECC, Herm, LN, Lns, WBC; all versions except CEV, GW, NLT], 'favor, help' [BAGD], 'gift' [AB]. The phrase ἡ χάρις τοῦ κυρίου ἡμῶν 'the grace of our Lord' is translated 'our Lord was very kind to me' [CEV, GW], 'our Lord most graciously favored me' [LSA], '(how) generous and gracious our Lord was!' [NLT]. This noun denotes the kindness shown to someone [LN]. See this word at 1:2; 6:21.

c. aorist act. indic. of ὑπερπλεονάζω (LN **59.49**) (BAGD p. 842): 'to be present in great abundance' [BAGD], 'to be more abundant' [**LN**]. The verb ὑπερεπλεόνασεν 'super-abounded' [ECC; NTC] is also translated 'was more than abundant' [NASB], 'was exceeding abundant' [KJV], 'has been abundantly rich' [Herm], 'was super-abundantly bestowed on me' [BNTC], 'was abundant' [NET], 'overflowed' [WBC; HCSB, NRSV], 'was poured out on me abundantly' [NIV], 'was lavished upon me' [REB], 'exceedingly did abound' [Lns], 'was extravagant' [AB], 'was fully given to me' [NCV], 'was very kind' [GW], 'he has greatly blessed my life' [CEV], 'he filled me completely' [NLT], 'poured out his abundant (grace)' [TEV], 'most graciously (favored me)' [LSA], 'Oh, how (generous and gracious) our Lord was!' [NLT]. This verb indicates that something is present in more abundance than a given quantity [LN].

d. μετά (LN 89.78, 89.123) (BAGD A.II.6. p. 509): 'with' [AB, BAGD, BNTC, Herm, LN (89.78, 89.123), NTC, WBC; CEV, KJV, NASB, NCV, NRSV], 'along with' [ECC; HCSB, NIV, REB], 'accompanied by' [Lns], 'combined with' [LN (89.123)], 'bringing' [NET], 'he brought me to' [GW], 'by means of, through' [LN (89.78)], 'and gave me' [TEV], 'so that I now (believe)' [LSA]. This preposition indicates a relationship in which one thing is combined with another [LN (89.123)], or it indicates means [LN (89.78)]. It indicates a close connection between two nouns, the first noun having the main emphasis [BAGD].

e. The phrase τῆς ἐν Χριστῷ ᾽Ιησοῦ 'the (one/ones) in Christ Jesus' is translated with τῆς 'the' referring *only* to 'love': 'which is in Christ Jesus' [KJV], 'which comes from union with Christ Jesus' [ECC], '(and gave me the love) that Christ Jesus shows people' [GW]; or with τῆς 'the' referring to *both* 'faith' and 'love': 'that are in Christ Jesus' [AB, BNTC, WBC; HCSB, NCV, NIV, NRSV], 'in Christ Jesus' [Herm, NTC; NET], 'which are found in Christ Jesus' [NASB], 'which are ours in Christ Jesus' [REB], 'which are ours in union with Christ Jesus' [TEV], 'we have in Christ Jesus' [BNTC], 'that come from Christ Jesus' [NLT], 'in connection with Christ Jesus' [Lns], 'he has greatly blessed my life with faith and love just like his own' [CEV]. The phrase 'with faith and love the ones in Christ Jesus' is translated 'so that I now believe in Christ Jesus and I love him' [LSA].

QUESTION—What relationship is indicated by δέ 'and/but'?

1. This conjunction is continuative [AB, BNTC, Herm, ICC, Lns, My, NICNT NIGTC, NTC, TH, WBC; HCSB, KJV, NASB, NET, NLT, NRSV, TEV]: *and*. It continues the line of thought begun with 'I received mercy' in 1:13 [NIGTC, TH], and introduces a statement about the super-abundance of grace Paul received when he changed from his state of ignorance and opposition to his new status [NIGTC]. It explains the experience of mercy more fully [ICC, NICNT]. He received mercy from the Lord, and on top of that, the Lord's grace super-abounded towards him [BNTC, Herm, Lns, My; NLT].

2. It is contrastive [Alf, ECC, LSA; NCV]: *being ignorant, I acted in unbelief, but the grace of our Lord super-abounded*. This contrasts Paul's new state with his former state [Alf]. It introduces a second contra-expectation coordinate with the one in the preceding verse: 'yet I received mercy from Christ (1:13)...and our Lord most graciously favored me' [LSA].

QUESTION—Who is 'our Lord'?

1. 'Lord' refers to Christ Jesus [AB, EGT, ICC, Lns, LSA, NIBC, NIGTC, WBC]. Its antecedent is 'Christ Jesus our Lord' in 1:12 [AB, NIGTC].

2. 'Lord' refers to God [BNTC, NAC, NICNT, NTC, TH, TNTC]. Jesus is mentioned later in this verse, so here 'Lord' probably refers to God [TH].

QUESTION—What is meant by the χάρις 'grace' of our Lord?

Grace is God's undeserved love [NAC, TH] and favor towards guilty sinners [BNTC, Lns, NAC, NTC, TH]. It is the Lord's undeserved love and favor [TH]. Grace is God's saving power which produces an entirely new life marked by faith and love in Christ [ICC].

QUESTION—What is meant by the verb ὑπερεπλεόνασεν 'superabounded'?

1. This verb has a superlative force [AB, Alf, BAGD, BNTC, ECC, Herm, LN (59.49), LSA, My, NAC, NIBC, NICNT, NIGTC, NTC, NTL, TH, TNTC, WBC; all versions except NET]. This verb means to be present in great abundance [BAGD, ICC]. The prefix ὑπέρ- before πλεονάζω 'more than enough' adds the idea of 'more than more than enough'

[NTL]. This verb means that the Lord's grace was 'more abundant', but since there is nothing in the context to provide a basis for comparison, the closest equivalent may be 'but the grace of our Lord was very, very much' [LN (59.49)]. We should not take the verb to mean that the Lord's grace surpassed God's mercy or that it surpassed Paul's enmity; the verb means that grace went beyond the measure [My]. His grace surpassed all expectation [AB].

2. This compares the grace shown to Paul in having mercy on him with his former condition [EGT, ICC, Lns, TG]. This expresses a comparison and means grace abounded even more than Paul's former sin did [EGT, Lns]. Although there was an abundance of sin, there was a super-abundance of grace [ICC]. It may imply that this grace was greater than Paul's sin [TG].

3. This verb is translated without an indication of a comparative or a superlative force [NET]: *his grace was abundant.*

QUESTION—What was the Lord's grace that superabounded?

1. In 1:13 it is implied that the Lord acted in *grace* when he was merciful to Paul [Alf, NIGTC, TH, WBC], and here in 1:14 it states that he acted in a *super-abundance of grace* by producing the attributes of faith and love in Paul [Herm, NIGTC, NTL, WBC; CEV, GW, NLT]. Paul received mercy by the Lord's grace, and then the Lord's grace super-abounded towards him by giving him faith and love [BNTC, Herm, My]. Paul received mercy by God's abundant grace, and by that abundant grace Paul gained a new experience of faith and a new attitude of love [NIGTC]. Some translate this to show in what way the Lord's grace superabounded: 'the grace of our Lord completely overflowed with faith and love' [WBC], 'the grace of our Lord has been abundantly rich with faith and love' [Herm].

2. When Paul received mercy (1:13), that act was by the Lord's superabounding grace, and that experience of grace produced a life marked by faith and love so that faith and love were abundant as well as grace [AB, BNTC, ICC, Lns, NTC, TG].

QUESTION—What relationship is indicated by the preposition μετά 'with'?

The preposition μετά 'with' indicates that the Lord's grace was *accompanied with* faith and love [AB, Alf, BNTC, ECC, Lns, NICNT, NTC, NTL, TNTC, WBC; HCSB, NCV, NIV, REB]. Although it doesn't say *how* they happened to accompany grace, we know that grace *kindled* them [Lns]. The preposition μετά 'with' should not be stressed, and the meaning is that the Lord's grace made Paul become a person who had both faith and love [AB]. This is explained in various ways. The Lord's grace *brought with* it faith and love [BNTC; NET]. The Lord acted in his great grace *to produce* faith and love in Paul [Herm, LSA, NAC, NIBC, NTL, TH; NET, NLT]. By the Lord's grace Paul *was given* faith and love [TH, WBC; TEV]. The *effects* of this grace were faith and love [ICC, NIGTC, NTC, TG].

QUESTION—What is the referent of the definite article τῆς 'the' in the phrase μετὰ πίστεως καὶ ἀγάπης τῆς ἐν Χριστῷ Ἰησοῦ 'with faith and love *the (one/ones)* in Christ Jesus' and what relationship is indicated by ἐν in the phrase '*in* Christ Jesus'?

1. The definite article refers to both 'faith' and 'love' [AB, Alf, BNTC, EGT, Herm, ICC, Lns, LSA, NAC, NCBC, NIBC, NIGTC, NTC, TG, TH, WBC; all versions except GW, KJV, NLT]: *with the faith and love that are in Christ Jesus.* The singular article τῆς is used because the two nouns are considered as a unit [NIGTC].

   1.1 It indicates that Paul received the gifts of faith and love because he was in union with Christ Jesus [Alf, ECC, ICC, NICNT, NIGTC, NTC, TG, TNTC, WBC; REB, TEV]. Paul had the graces of faith and love because of his mystic union with Christ [NTC]. These gifts are available only to someone who is in Christ [WBC]. This is translated 'and gave me the faith and love which are ours in union with Christ Jesus' [TEV].

   1.2 It indicates that Paul's 'faith' and 'love' have the quality of Christ's faith and love [AB; CEV, NASB]: *with faith and love just like Christ's own faith and love.* The two qualities that Paul received from the Lord are also the personal qualities of Jesus [AB].

   1.3 It indicates that Paul's faith and love are directed towards Christ Jesus [LSA]: the Lord most graciously favored me *so that I now believe in Christ Jesus and I love him.*

2. The definite article refers to only 'love' [ECC, My, NTL; GW, KJV, NLT]: with faith *and with the love that is in Christ Jesus.* This is translated 'he brought me to faith and gave me the love that Christ Jesus shows people' [GW].

QUESTION—Who are the implied participants of the event nouns 'faith' and 'love'?

This is the faith and love which Paul exercised [BNTC, ICC, Lns, LSA, NAC, NIBC, NICNT, NIGTC, NTC, TC, TH, TNTC, WBC].

1. The object of faith is God or Christ and the object of love is other people [ICC, Lns, NICNT, NIGTC, TC, TG, TH, WBC], especially Christians [NIGTC, TH]. God acted in grace to give Paul the gift of faith in Christ to counter Paul's lack of faith, and he gave Paul the gift of love so he could love those very Christians he had been persecuting. Faith refers to Paul's initial faith that continued throughout his life [WBC]. Both 'faith and love' are brought about by Paul's union with Christ Jesus [AB, BNTC, ECC, ICC, NAC, NIBC, NIGTC, NTC, TG, TH, WBC; NASB, REB, TEV]. Only a person who is in Christ can receive these gifts [WBC]. These are qualities that are expressed by having a living relationship with Christ [BNTC]. These are personal qualities of Jesus and it follows that they are also his to give in grace as a gift [AB]. Faith in Christ and love for believers belong to all those who are in union with Christ Jesus [TG].

2. The object of both faith and love is Christ: Paul now believed in Christ Jesus and loved him [LSA].

1:15 True/trustworthy/faithful[a] (is) the statement[b] and (it is) worthy[c] of-all acceptance,[d]

LEXICON—a. πιστός (LN 31.87) (BAGD 1.b. p. 664): 'true' [LN; CEV, TEV], 'trustworthy' [BAGD, BNTC, LN, WBC; HCSB, NASB, NET, NIV, NLT], 'dependable' [LN], 'reliable' [AB, LN, NTC], 'faithful' [LN, Lns; KJV]. The clause πιστὸς ὁ λόγος 'true/trustworthy/faithful is the statement' is translated 'this is a true saying' [LN (**65.17**); NLT], 'what I say is true' [NCV], 'this is a statement that can be trusted' [GW], 'here is a saying you may trust' [REB], 'a saying which can be believed by people' [LSA], 'the Christian message meant to be believed' [ECC], 'the word stands firm' [Herm]. This adjective pertains to being sure, with the implication of being fully trustworthy [LN (71.17)], or it pertains to being trusted [LN (31.87)]. The phrase πιστὸς ὁ λόγος also occur at 3:1 and the whole clause occurs at 4:8.

   b. λόγος (LN 33.98) (BAGD 1.b.β. p. 478): 'statement' [LN, Lns; GW, NASB], 'saying' [AB, BNTC, LN (65.17), LSA, NTC, WBC; CEV, HCSB, NET, NIV, NLT, REB, TEV], 'the Christian message' [ECC], 'word' [BAGD, Herm, LN], 'what I say' [NCV]. This noun denotes something that has been stated or said, and the focus is on the content of that communication [LN].

   c. ἄξιος (LN 65.17) (BAGD 1.b. p. 78): 'worthy' [BAGD, LN]. See the next lexical item for the translation of the clause. This adjective pertains to having a relatively high degree of comparable merit or worth [LN].

   d. ἀποδοχή (LN **31.52**) (BAGD p. 91): 'acceptance' [BAGD, LN], 'reception' [LN], 'approval' [BAGD]. The clause καὶ πάσης ἀποδοχῆς ἄξιος 'and is worthy of all acceptance' is translated 'and worthy of full acceptance' [NTC], 'is worthy of being fully received' [**LN**], 'and worthy of all acceptance' [AB, Lns; KJV], 'and worthy of complete acceptance' [WBC], 'and which is worthy to be fully accepted by people' [LSA], 'and deserves full acceptance' [NET], 'and deserves complete acceptance' [GW], 'and deserved all recognition' [Herm], 'deserving whole-hearted acceptance' [BNTC; similarly HCSB, NASB, NIV], 'and worth welcoming wholeheartedly' [ECC], 'one that merits a full acceptance' [REB], 'and you should fully accept it' [NCV], 'to be completely accepted and believed' [TEV], 'and everyone should accept it' [NLT], 'and it can be trusted' [CEV]. This noun denotes the appropriate response to the belief that something is true and it lays some emphasis upon the source [LN].

QUESTION—Does the adjective πιστός mean true, trustworthy, or faithful here?

   1. Πιστός focuses on the fact that the statement has the quality of being true in itself [CEV, NCV, TEV]: *the statement is true* (and therefore it is worthy of being fully accepted).

   2. Πιστός focuses on its relationship to people [AB, Alf, BNTC, ECC, EGT, Lns, NAC, NIBC, NTC, NTL, TC, TH; GW, HCSB, NASB, NET, NIV,

NLT, REB]: *the statement can be trusted by people* (and therefore they should fully accept it). Since the words are reliable and trustworthy, they have such importance that they should be accepted by all who hear them [Lns].

3. Πιστός focuses on the fact that the statement in this verse is an accurate presentation of God's message [NIGTC]: *the statement given here is a faithful representation of God's message* (and therefore it is worthy of being fully accepted). Paul is saying that statement is a faithful presentation of God's message [NIGTC].

QUESTION—What does ὁ λόγος 'the statement' refer to?

This refers to the following statement, 'Christ Jesus came into the world to save sinners' [all commentaries and versions]. This statement does not include the following clause 'of whom the foremost am I' [ICC, NIBC, NICNT, NIGTC, NTC, WBC] where Paul sees himself as an example of the sinners Christ came to save [AB, TH, WBC]. It is a statement of the basic truth of the gospel [TH, TNTC]. This is the core of the gospel and it is a saying that had been passed from one to another so that it was embedded in the minds of the Christian community [NTC]. This is a quoted *saying* [NIGTC]. Some translations place quotation marks around the contents of the saying [ECC, Herm, WBC; CEV, HCSB, NET, TEV]. It was a saying known to all Christians [TG, TNTC; probably AB, BNTC, LSA, NTC; CEV, HCSB, NET, NIV, NLT, REB, TEV which translate this word as 'a saying']. There is no verbatim biblical text for this quotation, so Paul has composed a new statement from preexisting materials in agreement with the existing tradition [NICNT]. This saying was current among the disciples [WP]. This was probably an excerpt from some early creed or liturgy [BNTC, NTL]. It was a traditional and authoritative text [ECC, ICC]. It is a brief statement based on what Jesus said about himself [NIGTC]. It is a repetition of Jesus' statement in Matt. 18:11, 'The Son of Man is come to save that which was lost' [Lns, NAC], and Jesus must have restated this many times in his ministry [Lns]. This statement of tradition echoes passages in the Gospels, such as Luke 19:10 'The Son of Man came to seek and save the lost' [AB, BNTC, ICC, NAC, NICNT, NIGTC, NTIC]. It would have been natural for the church to replace the original phrase 'The Son of Man' with 'Christ Jesus' [ICC].

QUESTION—What is meant by πάσης 'all' in the phrase 'all acceptance'?

1. It has an intensive sense [BNTC, ECC, ICC, LN, Lns, LSA, NCBC, NICNT, NIGTC, NTC, NTL, TH, WBC; GW, HCSB, NASB, NCV, NET, NIV, TEV]: it is worthy *to be fully accepted.* It intensifies the event word 'acceptance' [NICNT], This means that it is to be accepted completely, without reservation, hesitation, or doubt [Lns]. We can completely accept the statement without reservation and believe it [TH].

2. It has an extensive sense [Alf, TC, TG; NLT]: it is worthy *to be accepted by all people.* It is worthy of universal acceptance, that is, it is to be

accepted by everyone [TC]. It means that everybody should accept and believe it [TG].

namely-that[a] Christ Jesus came[b] into the world to-save[c] sinners,

LEXICON—a. ὅτι (LN 91.15): 'namely that' [LN], 'namely' [LN], 'that' [AB, LN, Lns, NTC; KJV, NASB], not explicit [CEV]. This word is also translated with a verb: 'it says' [LSA], 'is' [ECC]. Some use a colon to introduce the statement [Herm, WBC; GW, HCSB, NCV, NET, NIV, NLT, REB, TEV]. This is a marker that identifies and explains some statement [LN].

    b. aorist act. indic. of ἔρχομαι (LN 15.81) (BAGD I.1.a.η. p. 311): 'to come' [AB, BAGD, ECC, LN, Lns, LSA, NTC, WBC; all versions], 'to appear, to make an appearance' [BAGD]. This verb means to move toward or up to some reference point as viewed by a character or event [LN].

    c. aorist act. infin. of σῴζω (LN 21.27) (BAGD 2.a.α. p. 798): 'to save' [AB, BAGD, ECC, LN, Lns, LSA, NTC, WBC; all versions], 'to preserve from eternal death' [BAGD]. This verb means to cause someone to experience divine salvation [LN]. This refers to saving sinners from their sins and guilt, and from the punishment of hell [Lns]. Sinners are rescued from spiritual death and destruction [TG]. This refers to delivering sinners from their sin and its consequences to a life of faith and love in Christ [NIGTC]. This refers to rescuing people from sin's guilt, slavery, and punishment and bringing them into a state of being righteous, free, and blessed [NTC]. Sinners are rescued from their sinful condition and given new life [TH]. See this word at 2:4.

QUESTION—What relationship is indicated by the use of the infinitive σῶσαι 'to save'?

    The infinitive indicates Christ's purpose for coming into the world [ECC, Herm, LSA, NICNT, NTC]: Christ Jesus came into the world *in order to save sinners*.

QUESTION—What is meant by saying that Christ Jesus ἦλθεν 'came' into the world?

    This refers to Christ's incarnation [BNTC, ECC, TH, TNTC]. It refers to Christ's descent from heaven to earth and it also includes his incarnation, suffering, and death [NTC]. It refers to Christ's arrival and everything that occurred until he left the world [Lns, NICNT]. It refers to the historical mission of Christ Jesus [ICC, NTL]. In itself, this statement does not imply Christ's preexistence before he came into the world [ECC, Herm, NIGTC], although parallel statements in the writings of John do refer to his preexistence [ECC, NIGTC], with such passages as 'coming from the Father' and 'going to the Father' [NIGTC]. The fact of preexistence can easily be connected with this statement [EGT, Herm, ICC, NIGTC, TNTC]. His preexistence is implicit, but the focus is on his human history and its significance [NICNT].

QUESTION—What is meant by τὸν κόσμον 'the world'?

The world is the earth [My]. It is the location of Jesus' activity [NICNT]. The world is the place where sinful human beings live [ICC, TH], and it is the place where sinners need to be met and redeemed [NIGTC].

of-whom (the) foremost[a] am I.

LEXICON—a. πρῶτος (LN 87.45) (BAGD 1.c.β. p. 726): 'foremost, prominent' [BAGD, LN]. The phase ὧν πρῶτός εἰμι ἐγώ 'of whom the foremost am I' is translated 'foremost of whom am I' [NTC], 'of whom I am the foremost' [WBC], 'among whom I am foremost of all' [NASB], 'to whom I on my part belong as foremost' [Lns], 'and I am the foremost sinner' [GW], 'of whom I am the worst' [NCV, NIV], 'and I am the worst of them' [HCSB, NET, TEV], 'and I am the worst of them all' [NLT], 'of whom I have sinned worst' [LSA], 'of whom I am chief' [KJV], 'I am the first' [BNTC], 'I am the first among them!' [AB], 'and among them I stand first' [REB], 'I am the first one among them' [Herm], 'among them I have first place' [ECC]. One version changes the present tense of εἰμι 'am' to past tense: 'I was the worst sinner of all!' [CEV]. This adjective pertains to being of high rank and implies a special prominence or status [LN]. This adjective refers both to degree and rank [BAGD]. Paul says he was foremost or the greatest sinner [TH]. Paul meant that he was the worst sinner of all [NCBC, NICNT, NTC].

QUESTION—What did the apostle Paul mean by using the present tense when he said πρῶτός εἰμι ἐγώ 'I *am* the foremost sinner'?

In calling himself the foremost sinner, Paul was thinking of his sin in persecuting the church [AB, BNTC, NTC].

1. The present tense indicates that he presently considered himself to still be the foremost sinner [Alf, BNTC, ECC, ICC, Lns, NCBC, NIGTC, NTC, NTL, TC, WP]: *I am the foremost sinner.* This cannot be hyperbolic since Paul's statement of his sin must be real for this to be a valid illustration for all future believers. Since Paul uses the present tense 'I am', this does not mean 'I *was* the foremost sinner', having done the vilest of all things by persecuting the church. This could mean that he was the most *prominent* sinner, since during Paul's lifetime no other person had persecuted the church as Paul had done. However, since this passage stresses God's mercy in salvation, probably Paul expressed his abiding sense of being a forgiven sinner who had previously committed the terrible sin of persecuting Christ's church [WBC]. Paul still considered himself to be a sinner saved by grace and he had a continuing sense of being unworthy to have received that grace [ICC]. Paul deeply regretted his past when he was the most bitter persecutor of all, and even a fully pardoned sinner is still a sinner [NTC]. Although his sins had been forgiven, Paul could say that he was still such a sinner in that he regarded himself as having the status of a redeemed sinner [BNTC]. Paul was still thinking of his condition at that unforgettable moment of his conversion

[ECC]. Although now forgiven and faithful, Paul still regards this classification of himself as being valid [NIGTC]. Paul classifies himself with sinners because of all his sins, both past and present [Lns]. Paul has become the prime example of what it means to be a sinner [NTL]. Or, this does not mean that Paul was worse than every other sinner in existence, but he is speaking from the position of knowing his own sins from personal experience and knowing the sins of others only by observation [Alf, Lns].

2. The present tense indicates that he was in such a state in the past before he was saved [CEV]: *I was the foremost sinner.*

1:16 **Yet/moreover**[a] **because of-this I-received-mercy,**[b]

LEXICON—a. ἀλλά (LN 89.125, 91.2): 'yet' [LN (91.2), LSA; NASB], 'but' [AB, BNTC, ECC, Herm, LN (89.125), Lns, NTC, WBC; all versions except GW, KJV, NASB], 'however' [GW], 'howbeit' [KJV].

b. aorist pass. indic. of ἐλεέω (LN 88.76) (BAGD p. 249): 'to receive mercy' [BAGD, LN]. This repeats the same word that is in 1:13. In doing so, it emphasizes God's mercy, the point of the paragraph [WBC].

QUESTION—What relationship is indicated by ἀλλά 'yet/but'?

1. It indicates contra-expectation [LSA, NTC; NASB; probably some of those which translate this as 'but']: I am the foremost of sinners, *yet I received mercy.*

2. It indicates contrast [Alf, ICC, NICNT, NIGTC, WBC; probably some of those which translate this as 'but']: I am the foremost sinner, *but Christ or God was merciful to me.* This conjunction has its full adversative force in contrasting Paul's sinfulness with God's mercy [Alf, ICC, NIGTC, WBC].

3. It indicates continuity and resumes the thought of 1:13 [EGT, TH]: I received mercy because I ignorantly acted in unbelief; *moreover I received mercy for this reason, that in me, the foremost sinner, Christ Jesus might demonstrate all of his forbearance.* Instead of marking a contrast, it develops the expression of self-depreciation begun in 1:13 [EGT]. This marker of continuity focuses on the reason for mercy being extended to Paul rather than on a contrast between Paul's own opinion of himself and God's graciousness to him [TH].

QUESTION—What is the referent of τοῦτο 'this' in the phrase 'because of this'?

1. It refers to the following ἵνα 'that' clause [AB, EGT, ICC, Lns, LSA, NAC, NICNT, NIGTC, TC, TG, TH, WBC; GW, HCSB, KJV, NASB, NCV, NET]: *I received mercy because of this, namely, that in me Christ Jesus might demonstrate his forbearance for an example.* This points forward to the specific purpose Christ had in showing mercy to Paul [NIGTC].

2. It refers back to the preceding clause where Paul said that he is the foremost sinner [BNTC, ECC, NTC, NTL; CEV, NIV, NRSV; probably

ECC]: *because of the fact that I am the foremost sinner, I received mercy in order that in me Christ Jesus might demonstrate his forbearance for an example.* The greatness of Paul's sin made it necessary that Paul receive mercy [NTC]. From the fact that Paul was the foremost sinner, he now recognizes the reason for God being so gracious in dealing with him [BNTC].

QUESTION—Who had mercy on Paul?

1. Christ was the one who had mercy on him [Lns, LSA, NIGTC]: *Christ had mercy on me.* This verse implies that it was Christ who was merciful to Paul [LSA].

2. God was the one who had mercy on him [NTC, WBC; CEV, NLT, TEV]: *God had mercy on me.*

in-order-that[a] in me, (the) foremost/first,[b] Christ Jesus might-demonstrate[c] all[d] (of-his) forbearance[e]

TEXT—Instead of Χριστὸς Ἰησοῦς 'Christ Jesus', some manuscripts read Ἰησοῦς Χριστός 'Jesus Christ'. GNT does not mention this variant. 'Jesus Christ' is read by BNTC, Herm, Lns, NTC; KJV, NASB, NRSV, REB.

LEXICON—a. ἵνα (LN 89.59) (BAGD I.5. p. 377): 'in order that' [LSA, NTC; TEV], 'so that' [BNTC, ECC, Herm, LN (89.59), WBC; GW, HCSB, NASB, NCV, NET, NIV, NLT], 'for the purpose of' [LN], 'that' [AB, BAGD, Lns; KJV, REB], not explicit [CEV].

b. πρῶτος (LN 60.46, 87.45) (BAGD 1.a. p. 725): 'foremost, prominent' [LN (87.45)], 'first' [BAGD, LN (60.46)], 'earliest' [BAGD]. This repeats the same word that is in 1:15. However in this verse, instead of taking the same meaning of being the foremost sinner as in 1:15, some take the adjective to refer to being a primary example, or being first in time. See the question about the meaning of this term. This term designates the first in a series involving time, space, or set [LN (60.46)], or it pertains to being of a high rank and implies a special prominence [LN (87.45)].

c. aorist mid. subj. of ἐνδείκνυμαι (LN 28.51) (BAGD 1. p. 262): 'to demonstrate' [AB, BAGD, BNTC, LN, LSA; GW, HCSB, NASB, NET], 'to show' [BAGD, Herm, LN; NCV, TEV], 'to display' [Lns, WBC; NIV, NRSV, REB], 'to exhibit' [NTC], 'to make clearly known' [LN], 'to evidence' [ECC]. This verb is also translated 'and let me be (an example)' [CEV], 'could use me (as a prime example)' [NLT]. The verb means to cause something to be known [LN].

d. ἅπας (LN 59.23): 'all, whole' [LN]. The phrase τὴν ἅπασαν μακρο-θυμίαν 'all of his forbearance' is translated 'all his longsuffering' [Lns, NTC], 'all possible forbearance' [AB], 'the endless patience of Christ Jesus' [CEV], 'his utmost patience' [HCSB, NET, NRSV], 'his complete patience' [WBC], 'his full patience' [TEV], 'his unlimited patience' [NIV], 'the full extent of his patience' [BNTC], 'the whole extent of his forbearance' [Herm], 'his inexhaustible patience' [REB], '(evidence) patience to the utmost' [ECC], 'his perfect patience' [NASB], 'his great patience' [NLT], 'his patience' [GW], 'all longsuffering' [KJV], 'he is perfectly patient' [LSA], 'that he has patience without limit' [NCV]. This is an alternative form of πᾶς 'all' and refers to the totality of any object, mass, or collective [LN]. This adjective means 'immense' [ICC], 'utmost' [ECC, NIGTC], or 'perfect' [ECC]. It is intensive to describe his immense patience [NICNT]. It is the utmost patience that Christ is capable of showing [NIGTC].

e. μακροθυμία (LN 25.167) (BAGD 2.b.β. p. 488): 'forbearance' [AB, BAGD, Herm], 'patience' [BAGD, BNTC, ECC, LN, WBC; all versions except KJV], 'longsuffering' [Lns, NTC; KJV]. This noun is also translated as a verb phrase: 'he is patient' [LSA]. This noun denotes a state of emotional calm in the face of provocation [LN]. This refers to putting up with insults and provocation [BNTC]. God shows his patience by being slow to anger and to abound in love [WBC].

QUESTION—What relationship is indicated by ἵνα 'in order that'?

It indicates the purpose Christ had in being merciful to Paul [AB, BNTC, ECC, Herm, Lns, LSA, NAC, NICNT, NIGTC, NTC, TH, WBC; all versions except CEV].

QUESTION—What is meant by ἐν ἐμοὶ 'in me'?

It does not mean 'by means of me', but 'in my case' [Alf, ICC, My, TH, WBC], or 'in dealing with me' [TH; TEV].

QUESTION—What is meant by πρώτῳ 'the foremost/first'?

1. Πρώτῳ means that Paul was the *worst sinner*, the same meaning the word has in 1:15 [AB, BNTC, Lns, LSA, NAC, NIBC, TC, TNTC; CEV, GW, HCSB, NASB, NCV, NET, NIV, TEV]: I received mercy so that Christ Jesus might demonstrate all of his forbearance with me, *the foremost sinner,* as an example to all other sinners. The greatness of God's mercy is best demonstrated when it is shown to the worst of sinners [AB].

2. Πρώτῳ means the *first* in time [My, NCBC; KJV, REB]: 'But I was mercifully dealt with for this very purpose, that Jesus Christ might find in me the first occasion for displaying his inexhaustible patience' [REB]. Christ first showed his entire forbearance in Paul's case [My].

3. This includes both meanings 1 and 2 [Alf, EGT, ICC, NICNT, WP]. The word resumes its meaning in 1:15 and also indicates a temporal sequence necessary for the pattern [ICC, NICNT]. 'First' must be included with 'chief', because of the following phrase 'the ones who are about to believe on him'. He was first in that he was the first example of such full forbearance to be presented to the church [Alf].

4. This means that Paul was the *primary example* of God's mercy [ECC; NLT]: 'But God had mercy on me so that Christ Jesus could use me as a prime example of his great patience with even the worst sinners' [NLT].

5. This includes both meanings 2 and 4 [NTC]. Paul was the foremost example of what Christ's forbearance could accomplish, and he also was the head of a procession of sinners to whom that forbearance is shown [NTC].

QUESTION—How was Christ forbearing towards Paul?

Christ held back his long overdue judgment against Paul [Lns, NAC, NICNT, NIGTC] for persecuting the church [NICNT], in order to give time for repentance and salvation [Alf, NIGTC]. This is the attitude of one who shows mercy [ICC].

for[a] an-example[b] to-the (ones) who are-about[c] to-believe on him for[d] life eternal.

LEXICON—a. πρός (LN 89.60): 'for' [Lns; KJV], 'for the purpose of, in order to' [LN], 'so that' [CEV], 'in order that' [LSA], 'as' [AB, NTC, WBC; HCSB, NASB, NET, NIV, NLT, TEV], not explicit [REB]. This is also translated as a verb phrase: 'that I might become' [Herm], 'making me' [NRSV; similarly NCV], 'using me' [ECC; similarly NLT], '(this patience) serves as' [GW]. This preposition indicates purpose and points to the goal of an event or state [LN].

  b. ὑποτύπωσις (LN **58.59**) (BAGD p. 848): 'example' [AB, BAGD, **LN**, LSA; all versions except KJV, REB], 'illustration' [BNTC, WBC], 'pattern' [KJV], 'model' [ECC, Lns], 'prototype' [Herm], 'sketch' [NTC]. The phrase 'for an example' is translated 'and that I might be typical of all who…' [REB]. This noun denotes a model of behavior that serves as an example to be imitated [LN].

  c. pres. act. participle of μέλλω (LN 67.62) (BAGD 1.c.β. p. 501): 'to be about to' [BAGD, LN]. The phrase τῶν μελλόντων πιστεύειν ἐπ' αὐτῷ 'to the ones who are about to believe on him' is translated 'to/for those who would believe in him' [WBC; GW, HCSB, NASB, NCV, NIV], 'for those who are going to believe in him' [NET], 'of those who are about believe on him' [Lns], 'of those who are going to believe in him' [ECC], 'for/to those who would come to believe in him' [AB; NRSV], 'for those who would come to rest their faith on him' [NTC], 'for the ones who would later believe in him' [TEV; similarly LSA], 'to them which should hereafter believe on him' [KJV], 'all who were in future to have faith in him' [REB], '(an illustration) of the kind of people who were going to believe in him' [BNTC], 'for all those who will in the future attain faith through fellowship with him' [Herm], 'then others will realize that they, too, can believe in him' [NLT], '(so that) others would put their faith in Christ' [CEV]. This verb means to occur at a point in time in the future and it is closely related to another event subsequent to it [LN]. This has a weakened sense here and serves as a periphrasis for the future [BAGD].

  d. εἰς (LN 89.48): 'with the result that, so that as a result, to cause' [LN]. The phrase εἰς ζωὴν αἰώνιον 'for life eternal' [Lns] is also translated 'for eternal life' [ECC, Herm, WBC; HCSB, NASB, NET, NRSV], 'unto eternal life' [AB], 'to life everlasting' [KJV], 'with a view to life everlasting' [NTC], 'and so come to eternal life' [BNTC], 'and receive eternal life' [LSA; NIV, NLT, TEV], 'and gain eternal life' [REB], 'and have eternal life' [CEV], 'and have life forever' [NCV], 'and live forever'

[GW]. This preposition indicates a result and implies a preceding process [LN].

QUESTION—What relationship is indicated by the initial preposition πρός 'for (an example)'?

It indicates the goal of Christ's forbearance [AB, WBC], the purpose of it [Herm, ICC, Lns, LSA, NIBC, NIGTC, NTL; CEV]. However, it is not the only purpose Christ had in showing patience [ICC].

QUESTION—What is the example to the ones who are about to believe on him?

1. Christ's forbearance with Paul is the example [BNTC, NTC, TC, TNTC; GW, NASB, NIV, NLT, TEV]. 'This patience serves as an example for those who would believe in him' [GW], 'in order that Christ Jesus might show his full patience in dealing with me, the worst of sinners, as an example for all those who would later believe in him' [TEV]. What happened to Paul is a sketch of what will happen to others who will similarly receive grace to accept Christ in faith and place their trust in him [BNTC].

2. Paul is the example [AB, ECC, Herm; Lns, NAC, NICNT, NIGTC, NTL, TG, TH, WBC; NCV, NRSV, REB]. 'His patience with me made me an example for those who would believe in him' [NCV], '...making me an example to those who would come to believe' [NRSV], 'that I might be typical of all who were in the future to have faith in him' [REB]. Paul's salvation is an example of Christ's desire and power to save sinners [TG]. Paul's experience as the foremost sinner showed the magnitude of Christ's mercy and patience, and since Christ could reach Paul and enlighten him, then he can reach others who hear the gospel and repent [NICNT]. Paul stands as an example here, and if he is an example *to* them, he would be a model for them to imitate. But probably he is an example *for* them, so that what happened to Paul shows how God's mercy can work in others. This actually comes out to mean that God's power and grace are the example and not any action on Paul's part [AB]. Or, Paul is more than an example, he is a pattern for succeeding events of the same nature. When people come to know how Christ had forbearance with Paul, they will have hope that Christ will also deal with them with forbearance and lead them to believe in him [TH]. Christ used Paul as a model or sketch of the generations of believers who are going to come [ECC]. Paul is a prototype [Herm, NAC], who represents those who will be saved later on [Herm]. Paul's experience shows the sort of pity that God will provide for all sinners [NAC]. Jesus provided a model as a display as to how God would deal in the future with others who will come to believe in him [Lns].

QUESTION—What relationship is indicated by εἰς 'for'?

1. It indicates their goal in believing in Christ [Alf, ICC, My, NICNT; perhaps ECC, HCSB, Herm, Lns, WBC; NASB, NET, NRSV which translate this as 'for']. Eschatological salvation is presented in terms of the Christian hope in eternal life [ICC]. Salvation is viewed from the

standpoint of its goal of eternal life [NICNT]. This is the aim and end of believing [Alf].

2. This indicates the result of believing in Christ [Lns, NIGTC, TC, TG, TH]: to believe in him *and thus have eternal life*. Faith results in eternal life [TH]. They will believe in Christ and be given eternal life [TG].

QUESTION—What is ζωὴν αἰώνιον 'life eternal'?

Eternal life refers to life in the coming kingdom, a life that is also shared by Christians in the present age [BNTC, NAC, NIBC, WBC]. This refers to the spiritual life that begins when we believe in Christ and continues on through all eternity [Lns]. It is a never-ending life in fellowship with God [NIGTC, NTC].

1:17 Now[a] to-the king of-the-ages,[b] immortal[c] invisible[d] only[e] God,

TEXT—Instead of ἀφθάρτῳ ἀοράτῳ 'immortal, invisible', some manuscripts read ἀθάνατῳ ἀοράτῳ 'deathless, invisible' and some manuscripts read ἀφθάρτῳ, ἀοράτῳ, ἀθάνατῳ 'immortal, invisible, deathless'. GNT reads ἀφθάρτῳ ἀοράτῳ 'immortal, invisible' with an A decision, indicating that the text is certain.

TEXT—Instead of μόνῳ θεῷ 'only God', some manuscripts read μόνῳ σοφῷ θεῷ 'only wise God'. GNT does not mention this variant. 'Only wise God' is read by KJV.

LEXICON—a. δέ (LN 89.87, 89.93, 89.124) (BAGD 1., 2., 3. p. 171): This conjunction can mark a sequence of closely related events: 'and, and then' [LN (89.87)], or an additive relation that is not coordinate: 'and, and also, also, in addition, even' [LN (89.93)], or a contrast: 'but, on the other hand' [LN (89.124)]. It can emphasize a contrast: 'but', or mark a simple transition: 'now, then', or mark a resumption of an interrupted discourse: 'and also, but also' [BAGD]. Here it is translated 'now' [Lns, NIGTC, WBC; HCSB, KJV, NASB, NET, NIV], 'so' [ECC, NTC], 'but' [Herm], not explicit [AB, BNTC, LSA; CEV, GW, NCV, NLT, NRSV, REB, TEV].

  b. αἰών (LN 1.2, **67.143**) (BAGD 3. p. 28): 'age, era' [LN (67.143)], 'universe' [LN (1.2)], 'world' [BAGD]. The phrase τῷ βασιλεῖ τῶν αἰώνων 'the king of the ages' [AB, BNTC, NTC; NRSV] is also translated 'the King of the eons' [Lns], 'the king eternal' [WBC; HCSB, KJV, NASB, NIV, REB], 'the eternal King' [LN (67.143); CEV, GW, NET, NLT, TEV], 'the king of eternity' [ECC], 'the King that rules forever' [NCV], 'the King who rules for all time' [LSA], 'the king of the universe' [Herm]. This noun denotes a unit of time that is a particular stage or period of history, but in this passage the genitive plural noun is best understood as an abstract term for an unlimited time [LN (67.143)].

  c. ἄφθαρτος (LN 23.128) (BAGD p. 125): 'immortal' [AB, BAGD, ECC, Herm, LN, LSA; all versions except CEV, NCV, NLT], 'imperishable' [BAGD, LN, Lns, NTC], 'incorruptible' [BNTC, WBC]. This adjective is also translated as a phrase: 'who will never die' [NCV], 'who never dies'

[NLT], 'who lives forever' [CEV]. It pertains to that which is not subject
to decay and death [LN].

d. ἀόρατος (LN 24.4) (BAGD p. 79): 'invisible' [AB, BAGD, BNTC, ECC,
Herm, LN, Lns, LSA, NTC, WBC; all versions except NCV, NLT],
'unseen' [BAGD, LN]. This adjective is also translated as a phrase: 'the
unseen one' [NLT], 'who cannot be seen' [LN; NCV].

e. μόνος (LN 58.50) (BAGD 1.a.δ. p. 527): 'only' [AB, BAGD, BNTC,
ECC, LN, NTC, WBC; all versions except NLT], 'alone' [BAGD, LN],
'sole' [Lns], 'one' [Herm]. This adjective is also translated as a phrase:
'he alone is God' [NLT], 'who is the only true God' [LSA]. This adjective
means the only one in a class [LN].

QUESTION—How is this verse connected with the preceding verses?

Having considered God's grace and mercy shown to such a sinner as
himself, Paul burst into this doxology of praise [BKC, BNTC, Lns, NAC,
NIBC, NICNT, NIGTC, NTC, TG, TNTC, WBC, WP]. This doxology is to
God the Father, not to the trinity [EGT]. Through Christ, God has exhibited
his glorious attributes in all ages [NTC]. God is behind all that has happened
in salvation history [ICC].

QUESTION—What is meant by τῷ βασιλεῖ τῶν αἰώνων 'the King of the
ages'?

The word βασιλεύς 'king' can designate a person who holds the highest
power in any sphere, so it can be properly used to describe God as the
supreme king of all. Also, calling God 'king' is in keeping with the frequent
mention of 'the kingdom of God' in the NT [AB]. Human rulers were called
kings, so by adding 'eternal' he made the appropriate distinction between
human and divine power [NICNT]. The noun αἰώνων 'ages' is a cognate of
the adjective αἰώνιον 'eternal (life)' at the end of the preceding verse so that
there is word play of 'King eternal' with 'life eternal' [BNTC, ECC, NAC,
WBC].

1. Τῶν αἰώνων 'of the ages' is a Hebrew idiom that refers to eternity [Alf,
ECC, LN (67.142), LSA, NIBC, NICNT, NIGTC, TC, TG, TH, WBC; all
versions except NRSV]: *God is the eternal king.* This Hebrew idiom
means that God is an everlasting king [NIGTC, WBC]. God's rule is
unending [NICNT]. It means that God rules in the past, in the present, and
in the future [NICNT, NIGTC]. This speaks of God being eternal since he
rules in and over all of the ages [NIBC, TC].

2. Τῶν αἰώνων 'of the ages' refers to vast periods of time [BKC, BNTC,
ICC, Lns, My, NAC, NTC, TNTC; NRSV]: *God is the king of the ages.*
God is the supreme king who governs all the ages of the world from its
beginning to the end of time [BKC, BNTC, NAC]. God is superior to all
other rulers who can rule in just one age [NTL]. God is king of the present
age and also the age to come [TNTC].

3. Τῶν αἰώνων 'of the worlds' refers to the worlds in existence during the
various ages [BAGD, Herm]: *God is king of the world* [BAGD], or *of the
universe* [Herm].

QUESTION—What is meant by God being ἀφθάρτῳ 'immortal'?

This word is often translated 'imperishable' [BNTC, NIGTC, NTC], and indicates that God will never experience death and decay [BNTC, NTC, TH], or destruction [NIGTC], and therefore he is undying [TH], and immortal [BNTC, ICC, NIGTC]. In Rom. 1:23 God's immortality distinguishes him from mortal creatures that will die [WBC]. This adjective is a synonym of having ἀθανασία 'immortality' in 1 Tim. 6:16 [NTC, WBC].

QUESTION—What is meant by God being ἀοράτῳ 'invisible'?

This is similar in thought to 1 Tim. 6:16 which says that no human has seen or is able to see God [WBC]. Being the supreme *spiritual* being, he is invisible to people [Lns, TG], and he is superior to all that is visible [Lns]. This praise is directed to the unseeable God [ECC, NIGTC], and not to a man-made image [ECC, ICC]. This contrasts with the materialistic idolatry of pagan religions [NICNT]. In the OT, God is hidden from human sight because he is so holy that no human can see him and live [TH].

QUESTION—What is meant by God being the μόνῳ θεῷ 'only God'?

No other God exists [Lns]. God is unique [NAC, NTC] and supreme [NICNT]. This is an affirmation of the first commandment (Exodus 20:3), the central confession of Israel [ECC]. It is a statement of the monotheism of both Testaments [NIGTC, TNTC]. At first, the Israelites were distinguished from all other nations in that they worshipped only one God while others worshipped many gods. But in time, this one God was proclaimed as the only true God of the whole universe [TH]. God has no competitors [NAC].

(be)[a] honor[b] and praise[c] to the ages of-the ages,[d] amen.[e]

LEXICON—a. The implied verbal expression is translated 'be' [AB, BNTC, Herm, NTC, WBC; all versions except CEV, GW, NLT], 'are' [ECC], 'belong to' [GW], 'I pray that...will be given to' [CEV], 'may he be' [LSA], not explicit [Lns; NLT].

b. τιμή (LN 87.4) (BAGD 2.b. p. 818): 'honor' [AB, BAGD, BNTC, ECC, Herm, LN, Lns, NTC, WBC; all versions except GW], 'worship' [GW]. This noun is also translated as a verb: 'be honored' [LSA]. The noun 'honor' denotes an element involved in the assignment of status to someone [LN]. This noun is here understood passively of the respect that one enjoys, or the honor that on possesses [BAGD].

c. δόξα (LN 33.357): 'praise' [LN], 'glory' [AB, BNTC, ECC, Herm, LN, Lns, NTC, WBC; all versions]. This noun is also translated as a verb: 'be praised' [LSA]. This noun denotes the act of speaking about someone in a way that honors that person [LN].

d. αἰών (LN 67.143) (BAGD 1.b. p. 27): 'age' [BAGD, LN]. The phrase εἰς τοὺς αἰῶνας τῶν αἰώνων 'to the ages of the ages' is an idiom meaning an unlimited duration of time [LN]. The phrase is translated 'for the eons of the eons' [Lns], 'forever and ever' [AB, BNTC, LN, NTC; all versions except CEV, GW], 'forever' [LN, LSA, WBC; GW], 'always' [LN;

CEV], 'eternally' [BAGD, LN], 'for all eternity' [ECC, Herm]. The phrase is an emphatic way of saying 'eternally' [TH; NET].

e. ἀμήν (LN 72.6) (BAGD 1. p. 45): 'amen' [AB, BAGD, BNTC, ECC, Herm, Lns, LSA, NTC, WBC; all versions], 'even so' [BAGD], 'truly, indeed, it is true' [LN]. This word denotes a strong affirmation of something that is declared [LN].

QUESTION—Should the implied verb have a imperative sense or an indicative sense?

1. It has an imperative sense [BKC, BNTC, Herm, LN, LSA, NICNT, NTC, WBC; all versions except CEV, GW, NLT]: *let there be given honor and praise to the King.* 'May he be (honored and praised)' is implied to show that Paul desired that everyone would join him in praising God [LSA]. This is an implicit request that this be acknowledged [NICNT].

2. It has an indicative sense [ECC, NIGTC, TC; GW]: *honor and praise belong to the King.* In doxologies the verb is usually omitted and here this doxology is pronounced with certainty and conviction, 'to the king of eternity...*is* honor and glory for all eternity' since God will have his glory and no human can foil him. Human worship and praise only reflect the splendor of the king they honor [ECC]. This doxology is a reverent statement of God's glory, not a prayer [TC].

QUESTION—What is meant by giving the King τιμή 'honor'?

This statement refers to the honor that belongs to God, and those who offer this doxology should recognize this and ascribe this honor to him [NIGTC]. Honor is the esteem and reverence that should be accorded to God [Lns, NAC, TH]. It is the public acknowledgment of God's worth [NICNT].

QUESTION—What is meant by giving the King δόξα 'praise' or 'glory', and how does it differ from τιμή 'honor'?

Δόξα 'glory' describes the shining manifestation of God, and here it either indicates that this radiance continues to be seen in all of its splendor or that praise should be given in response to such glory [NIGTC]. This word is often translated 'glory', but here it does not describe the nature of God, rather it refers to the response of people towards God. It describes the praise of those who see and adore all the greatness of God [Lns]. It refers to acknowledging the majesty and power of God [NAC]. Honor and glory are frequently joined in both the NT and the OT, and the two words are closely related in meaning [NICNT, TG, TH, WBC]. They are basically synonyms [ICC]. Both words have the meaning 'to praise' [TG]. These terms are an acknowledgement of God's honor and together they form a superlative indicating 'all honor' [ICC]. Here the two words are used for their total effect rather than focusing on individual meanings so that the combination means something like 'may people praise you and say that that you are great' [TH]. In speaking the doxology, a worshiper is giving honor and glory to God [NTL].

QUESTION—What is meant by ἀμήν 'amen'?

'Amen' is a transliteration of a Hebrew word that means 'truth' and it is Paul's affirmation of what he has said in the doxology [Lns, NIGTC]. This concludes the doxology by inviting assent by the congregation with 'Amen!' or 'So be it!' [ECC, NICNT, NIGTC, WBC]. The word is an emphatic confirmation [NTC]. The one who reads the letter in front of the congregation is supposed to pause so that the congregation could respond with 'Amen' [BNTC, ICC, NAC, NIBC].

DISCOURSE UNIT 1:18–2:15 [GW]. The topic is guidelines for the church.

DISCOURSE UNIT 1:18–20 [AB, ECC, Herm, ICC, NAC, NCBC, NIBC, NICNT, NTL, TH, TNTC, WBC; HCSB, NLT]. The topic is encouragement and warning for Timothy [WBC], prior examples [NTL], the apostle's charge to Timothy [TNTC], Timothy's task [ECC], the task to prevent a decline of commitment [NAC], Timothy's responsibility [NLT], Paul encourages Timothy to be faithful [TH], the charge renewed [AB, NIBC], the theme of false doctrine resumed [NCBC], an exhortation regarding heretics [Herm], the resumption of the charge to Timothy [NICNT], a renewal of the commission to Timothy [ICC], a command to engage in battle [HCSB], the charge to Timothy reiterated with the negative example of Hymenaeus and Alexander [NIGTC].

1:18 **This command[a] I-entrust[b] to-you, (my) child Timothy, in-accordance-with the prophecies[c] previously-made/leading[d] concerning/to you,**

LEXICON—a. παραγγελία (LN 33.328) (BAGD 2.b.α. p. 613): 'command' [BAGD, LN, WBC; NASB, NCV, TEV], 'commandment' [AB], 'order' [BAGD, LN; GW], 'charge' [BNTC, ECC, Lns, NTC; KJV, NET, REB], 'instruction' [BAGD, Herm, LN; CEV, HCSB, NIV, NLT, NRSV]. This word is also translated as a verb: 'to command' [LSA]. See this word at 1:5.

  b. pres. mid. indic. of παρατίθεμαι, παρατίθημι (LN 35.47) (BAGD 2.b.α. p. 623): 'to entrust' [AB, BAGD, BNTC, LN, WBC; NASB, TEV], 'to commit' [LN, Lns, NTC; KJV], 'to give' [CEV, GW, HCSB, NCV, NIV, NRSV], 'to transmit' [Herm], 'to lay upon' [REB], 'to put before someone' [NET], 'to set out before someone' [ECC], 'to make someone responsible' [LSA]. The phrase ταύτην τὴν παρατίθεμαί σοι 'this command I entrust to you' is translated 'here are my instructions for you' [NLT]. It means to entrust something to someone for safekeeping or for transmitting to others [BAGD, NIGTC].

  c. κατά (LN 89.4, 89.8): 'in accordance with' [LN (89.8), LSA, WBC; NASB, NRSV, TEV], 'in accord with' [Lns], 'in agreement with' [NTC], 'according to' [AB; KJV], 'in keeping with' [HCSB, NET, NIV], 'in remembrance of' [Herm], 'in regard to' [LN (89.4)], 'in relation to' [LN (89.4, 89.8)], 'about' [GW], 'based on' [CEV, NLT]. This preposition is also translated as a verb phrase: 'that accords with' [ECC], 'that agrees with' [NCV], 'I am guided by' [REB], 'relying on' [BNTC]. This preposition indicates a similarity of process [LN (89.8)], or it indicates the relationship of a specific element to something else [LN (89.4)].

d. pres. act. participle of προάγω (LN **13.114**, 15.171) (BAGD 2.b. p. 702): 'to be made long ago, to go or come before' [BAGD], 'to happen previously, to occur formerly, to happen before' [LN (13.114)], 'to lead forth' [LN (15.17)]. The phrase τὰς προαγούσας ἐπὶ σὲ προφητείας 'the prophecies previously-made/leading concerning/to you' is translated 'the prophecies previously made concerning/about you' [WBC; HCSB, NASB], 'the prophecies that were given about you in the past' [NCV], 'the prophecies once made about you' [BNTC; NIV], 'the prophecies once spoken about you' [NET], 'the earlier prophecies made concerning you' [AB], 'the words of prophecy spoken before about you' [L N (13.114)], 'the words of prophecy spoken in the past about you' [TEV], 'the prophecies made earlier about you' [NRSV], 'the prophetic words spoken about you earlier' [NLT], 'the previous prophetic utterances concerning you' [NTC], 'what some prophets once said about you' [CEV], 'what was previously prophesied about you' [LSA], 'the words of the prophets which were once given to you' [Herm], 'the prophecies which went before on thee' [KJV], 'the prophecies proceeding in advance to thee' [Lns]. 'the prophecies that conducted us to you in the first place' [ECC], 'those prophetic utterances which first directed me to you' [REB], 'the prophecies that are still coming to you' [GW]. This verb means to occur previous to some point of time [LN (13.114)], or to lead forth [LN (15.143)].

e. προφητεία (LN 33.460) (BAGD 3.b. p. 722): 'prophecy' [BAGD, LN], 'inspired utterance' [LN], 'the utterance of the prophet' [BAGD]. See the preceding lexical item for translations of this plural noun. See this word at 4:14.

QUESTION—What does ταύτην τὴν παραγγελίαν 'this command' refer to?

1. This command refers backward [AB, BKC, BNTC, ECC, ICC, LSA, My, NAC, NICNT, NIGTC, NTC, TNTC, WBC]. Then the following ἵνα 'in order that' clause indicates Paul's purpose in entrusting this command to Timothy [BNTC, NICNT, NIGTC, NTC, WBC].

1.1 This παραγγελίαν 'command' refers back to the previous use of the same noun παραγγελίας 'command' in 1:5, which refers to the content of its cognate verb form in 1:3 παραγγείλῃς 'you might command' [AB, BKC, BNTC, LSA, My, NAC, TC, WBC; NET]: *I entrust you with the command that you are to give to the false teachers about stopping their wrong teaching in order that you might war the good warfare, holding faith and good conscience.*

1.2 This command refers back to the charge Paul had given Timothy in 1:3–11, the command that Timothy stay on in Ephesus so that he could command the false teachers not to misuse the law [ICC, NIGTC, NTC]: *I commanded you to stay there to do what I instructed you in order that you might war the good warfare, holding faith and good conscience.*

The command concerns Timothy's task instead of the actual teaching he was to give [ICC]. This is a general charge to Timothy (1:5), and probably the appeal to the prophecies about Timothy refers to his ministry as a whole [NIGTC].

2. This command refers forward to the following part of this verse with ἵνα 'that' introducing the *content* of the command [Alf, EGT, Lns, NIBC]: *I entrust this following command to you, namely that you war the good warfare, holding faith and good conscience.* The command in 1:3 was to be given *by* Timothy, not to him, so here Paul's command to Timothy refers to the following clause, which gives both the purport of the command and its purpose [Alf]. It refers directly to the next clause, but it also includes the general contents of the letter [EGT]. The following ἵνα 'that' clause is in apposition to 'this command' and what was explained in the whole of 1:3–17 about the command to silence the false teachers is now pictured as being a military campaign [Lns].

3. This command refers to Paul's instructions that are given throughout the letter [Herm, NCBC, TG; NRSV]: *I entrust this charge that I am giving you in the instructions of this letter so that you might war the good warfare.* It refers to the letter as a whole since the immediately preceding verses do not contain any charge [NCBC]. The charge itself commences at 2:1 [TG].

QUESTION—What is the function of the prepositional phrase '*in accordance with* the prophecies previously made concerning you'?

Paul stresses the fact that when he urged Timothy to command them to stop teaching wrong doctrine, giving such a command is in accordance with the prophecies already made about Timothy and not just Paul's own idea [BNTC, WBC]. This mention of the prophecies is to strengthen Timothy's motivation and indicates that Paul gave these instructions to Timothy so that those prophecies might be fulfilled [ICC].

QUESTION—What is meant by the phrase τὰς προαγούσας ἐπὶ σὲ προφητείας which is literally 'the previously-made/leading prophecies concerning/to you prophecies'?

1. The phrase ἐπὶ σέ means 'concerning you' and modifies the *following* noun προφητείας 'prophecies', thus making the preceding participle προαγούσας mean 'going before in time', that is, 'made before', or 'earlier' [AB, Alf, BAGD, BNTC, Herm, ICC, LN (13.114), Lns, LSA, NAC, NIBC, NICNT, NTC, TG, TH, TNTC, WBC; all versions except GW, REB]: *the prophecies concerning you that were made in the past.* The verb προάγω can mean 'to precede' or 'to lead or bring out or forth' and here it seems to be intransitive and refers to the 'previous prophetic utterances' concerning Timothy [NTC]. Prophets in the church had spoken about Timothy's fitness to serve God, perhaps at his ordination, or at his appointment in Ephesus, or at some other time in his career [BNTC]. Prophecies made at Timothy's ordination probably spoke of what God would do through Timothy [NET]. The prophecies were the

inspired words spoken at Timothy's ordination (4:14) [ICC, NTC], and concerned the content of his commission [ICC]. Probably the prophecies appointed Timothy for special service, summarized his duties, predicted his sufferings, and promised God's help [NTC]. The prophecies made earlier in Timothy's ministry probably concerned his spiritual usefulness [NAC]. The prophecies were spoken over Timothy as he set out on his mission [AB]. The prophecies were words that empowered Timothy with authority, and by means of these words he was able to do battle against the false teachers [AB].

2. The phrase ἐπὶ σέ means 'to you' and modifies the *preceding* participle προαγούσας 'leading', so that it means that the prophecies were leading or pointing *to* Timothy [ECC, EGT, NIGTC, TC; REB]. It means 'those prophetic utterances which first directed me to you' [REB], 'the prophecies that conducted us to you in the first place' [ECC]. The prophecies at Timothy's ordination pointed him out as being suitable for the ministry, thus leading the way to him [EGT]. This is a similar event to that in Acts 13:1–4 where the Holy Spirit spoke through the Christian prophets with the instructions to set apart Barnabas and Saul for the work to which he had called them. Here in 1 Timothy this was probably not a call to accompany Paul and serve him, but a call to ministry in general in view of the statements in 1 Tim. 4:14 and 2 Tim. 1:6, and also the fact that Timothy was no longer with Paul [NIGTC]. In this view, some Christian prophets had prophesied about Timothy and their statements had led Paul to choose Timothy as his co-worker [TH].

in-order-that/that by[a] them you-might-war[b] the good warfare.

LEXICON—a. ἐν (LN 90.11): 'by, with' [LN]. The phrase ἵνα...ἐν αὐταῖς 'in order that/that by them' is translated 'in order that by them' [WBC], 'that in connection with them' [Lns], 'in order that with their aid' [NTC], 'so that by them' [HCSB], 'so that by means of them' [AB], 'so that by following them' [NIV, NRSV], 'that thou by them' [KJV], 'I tell you this so you can follow them and' [NCV], 'If you follow these instructions' [CEV], 'use these prophecies to' [GW], 'use these words as weapons in order to' [TEV], 'that by these (weapons)' [LN (55.4)], 'in order that with such encouragement' [NET], 'encouraged by them' [REB], 'that by being inspired by these prophesies' [LSA], 'so that braced by them' [BNTC], 'that by them' [NASB], 'they were given to help you' [ECC], not explicit [NLT]. This preposition indicates the instrument that serves as a source of information or reason [LN].

b. pres. mid. subj. of στρατεύομαι (LN 55.4) (BAGD 2. p. 770): 'to battle, to fight, to engage in war' [LN], 'to do military service, to serve in the army' [BAGD]. This refers to engaging in a war as a soldier [LN]. The clause στρατεύῃ... τὴν καλὴν στρατείαν 'you might war the good warfare' [NTC] is also translated 'thou mightest war a good warfare' [KJV], 'thou war the noble warfare' [Lns], 'you may fight the good fight'

[BNTC; NET, NIV, NRSV; similarly WBC; NASB, NCV, REB], 'you may wage the good battle' [LN], 'you may strongly engage in battle' [HCSB], 'campaign the fine campaign' [ECC], 'you will fight like a good soldier' [CEV], 'to fight this noble war' [GW], 'you might continue fighting the noble battle' [AB], 'to fight well in the Lord's battles' [NLT], 'you participate in the good warfare' [LSA], 'to fight well' [TEV]. The present tense of the verb has the sense of continuing on in the battle [AB].

QUESTION—What is meant by the metaphor στρατεύῃ τὴν καλὴν στρατείαν 'war the good warfare'?

This is a live metaphor describing a soldier at war [BKC, BNTC, EGT, Herm, ICC, Lns, LSA, NIBC, NICNT, NIGTC, NTC, NTL, TH]. Paul often used military figures of speech and the picture of warfare is appropriate here because Timothy will be in conflict with the false teachers when he follows Paul's instructions to promote the true doctrine and oppose those who are teaching a false doctrine [ICC, LSA, NIBC, TH]. The battle was against perversions of the message of the gospel described in 1:3–12 [AB, BNTC, NAC, NTC]. This would be a spiritual battle [NAC] against the forces of evil [TG]. It is called a *good* warfare because ordinary warfare is usually evil [LSA]. It is good because it is noble by nature [AB, BNTC, NIGTC], and it is in accord with the gospel [NIGTC]. It is an authentic war of faith [NICNT]. It is called good because it is well conducted [Lns, TH]. A good battle is one fought bravely [TG].

QUESTION—What is meant ἐν αὐταῖς 'by them' in relation to fighting the good war?

'Them' refers to the prophecies [BKC, Lns, NIGTC, NTC, WBC].

1. The preposition ἐν indicates the means or instrument with which the fight is waged [AB, BNTC, ECC, Lns, LSA, NAC, NICNT, NTC, NTL, TNTC, WBC; all versions]: *that by means of the prophecies you might fight.* His army is comprised of those prophecies since his whole campaign is a spiritual one [Lns]. The message of the prophecies will serve as a weapon in Timothy's spiritual warfare [NTL, TH, WBC]. Reflection on these prophecies will encourage him that the battle is not just his own but the Lord's and that faithfulness will be rewarded [NTC]. By remembering those prophecies, Timothy will be aided in his fight [NICNT, NIGTC]. He will be aided by recalling his commitment and also the promise of God's help involved in the commission [NICNT].

2. The preposition ἐν 'in' pictures the warrior being encased with his armor for protection [Alf, EGT, LN (55.4), WP]: *that being surrounded and protected by the prophecies you might fight.* The picture is of defensive armor in this metaphor [EGT].

1:19 having[a] **faith/faithfulness and a-good conscience,**[b]

LEXICON—a. pres. act. participle of ἔχω (LN 90.65) (BAGD I.2.e.β. p. 332): 'to have' [AB, BAGD, LN, Lns; HCSB, NCV, NRSV], 'to possess' [BAGD], 'to hold' [KJV], 'to hold on to' [NTC, WBC; NIV], 'to hold firmly to' [NET], 'to keep' [NASB, TEV], 'to be armed with' [BNTC], 'to experience' [LN]. The verb changes according to its collocation with faith and conscience: 'you will be faithful and have a clear conscience' [CEV], 'cling to your faith in Christ, and keep your conscience clear' [NLT], 'continue to have faith and do what you know is right' [NCV], 'as you continue to believe the true doctrine and you do only what you know to be right' [LSA], '(use these prophecies) in faith and with good conscience' [GW; similarly Herm]. This verb is also translated 'with' [ECC]. This verb means 'having', and since Timothy is already a committed believer, it appears that he is being told to maintain or keep that which he already has [TH]. Many commentaries and translations have the idea of holding on to or continuing in his faith and good conscience [Alf, LSA, NIBC, NTC, WBC; NASB, NCV, NET, NIV, NLT, TEV].

b. συνείδησις (LN 26.13) (BAGD 2. p. 786): 'conscience' [BAGD, LN; GW, REB]. The phrase ἀγαθὴν συνείδησιν 'a good conscience' [AB, BNTC, Herm, Lns, NTC, WBC; HCSB, KJV, NASB, NET, NIV, NRSV] is also translated 'a clear conscience' [ECC; CEV, TEV], 'keep your conscience clear' [NLT], 'do what you know is right' [NCV], 'do only what you know to be right' [LSA]. See this noun at 1:5 and 4:2.

QUESTION—What is meant by the use of the participle ἔχων 'having'?

Some think that the metaphor of war is not continued in this verse, so this is not holding faith as a shield, but simply possessing faith [Alf, ECC, EGT, Lns, LSA, My, NIGTC, NTC]. Others think that the metaphor is continued, with faith and a good conscience being pictured as two items of armor to be used in this war [BKC, BNTC, TNTC].

1. This is an attendant circumstance that must take place in addition to the main verb and indicates the manner in which Timothy is to engage in this war [ECC, EGT, Lns, LSA, NIGTC, NTC; CEV, TEV]: *that you might war, while having faith and a good conscience*. This participle indicates how the fight is to be carried out [NIGTC]. As he battles, he is to have these two qualities [Lns, NTC]. This functions as a command [NCV, TEV]: *continue to have faith and a good conscience*.

2. This indicates the means by which the main verb is to be carried out [BNTC, NICNT, TNTC; GW, NET]: *that you might war by having faith and a good conscience*. 'To do this, you must hold firmly to faith' [NET]. This functions as an instruction for Timothy to be armed with these qualities since they are especially relevant to the coming battle [BNTC].

QUESTION—What is meant by having πίστιν 'faith/faithfulness'?

1. Having πίστιν refers to faith as the act of believing [Alf, BNTC, Herm, Lns, LSA, NAC, NCBC, NIBC, NICNT, NIGTC, TH, TNTC, WBC; GW, HCSB, NCV]. It is a relationship term, meaning that he is to trust in Jesus Christ and be committed to him [TH]. It is a personal faith in Christ involving a commitment to him [NAC]. This concerns trusting in God [NIBC, NICNT, NIGTC], and in his revelation [NIGTC]. This is unfeigned trust in God or in the Christian teachings [ICC, NAC, TNTC].

Although most relate this to a general Christian belief, some refer to certain specific objects of this faith: Timothy is to have faith in the truth of the gospel [NTC], or he is to have faith in the prophecies that were made about him [Lns].

2. Having πίστιν refers to the Christian faith which is to be believed [NTC]. This refers to the truth of the gospel [NTC].

3. Having πίστιν refers to being faithful to God [ECC; CEV]: *being faithful.*

QUESTION—What is meant by having a good conscience?

It is doing what one knows to be right [LSA; NCV]. It refers to a conscience that is guided by one's faith [GW]. Only an obedient Christian can have a good conscience [NAC]. It is when a person's moral self-evaluation affirms that he has been obedient to God [NIGTC].

which some having-rejected[a] have-been-shipwrecked[b] concerning the faith,

LEXICON—a. aorist mid. participle of ἀπωθέομαι, ἀπωθέω (LN 31.63) (BAGD 2. p. 103): 'to reject' [BAGD, BNTC, LN, WBC; HCSB, NASB, NCV, NET, NIV], 'to repudiate' [BAGD], 'to refuse to do this' [LSA], 'to refuse to listen to' [LN], 'to spurn' [AB, ECC; REB], 'to despise' [Herm], 'to discard' [NTC], 'to thrust away' [Lns], 'to put away' [KJV]. The phrase 'which having rejected' is translated 'they didn't listen to their consciences' [CEV, TEV], 'have deliberately violated their consciences' [NLT], 'some have refused to let their faith guide their conscience' [GW]. This is a figurative extension of the verb 'to push away' and means that one no longer pays attention to what he previously believed [LN].

b. aorist act. indic. of ναυαγέω (LN 54.26) (BAGD 2. p. 534): 'to be shipwrecked' [LN], 'to suffer shipwreck' [BAGD, LN]. The clause περὶ τὴν πίστιν ἐναυάγησαν 'have been shipwrecked concerning the faith' is translated 'concerning faith have made shipwreck' [KJV], 'have made shipwreck as regards the faith' [Lns], 'have suffered shipwreck concerning the faith' [AB], 'have suffered shipwreck in regard to their/the faith' [NASB, NET], 'have suffered shipwreck with reference to their faith' [NTC], 'have suffered shipwreck in the faith' [Herm], 'have made shipwreck of their faith' [BNTC; REB], 'have shipwrecked the faith' [WBC], 'have suffered the shipwreck of their faith' [HCSB], 'have suffered shipwreck in the faith' [NRSV], 'have shipwrecked their faith' [NIV], 'their faith has been shipwrecked' [NCV, NLT], 'their faith has been destroyed like a wrecked ship' [GW], 'went on to shipwreck in their faith' [ECC], 'have made a mess of their faith' [CEV], 'have made a ruin of their faith' [TEV]. 'they no longer believe what is true, they believe false doctrines' [LSA]. The aorist tense indicates that this event has already occurred [NICNT].

QUESTION—Who are the people designated by τινες 'some'?

These people were the false teachers mentioned in 1:3 as 'certain ones' [NIGTC, NTC, TH].

QUESTION—What have they rejected?

1. The have rejected both faith and a good conscience [AB, LSA, NAC, NIBC, WBC; GW, HCSB, NIV]. These two qualities are said to be the basis of the love that is the purpose for commanding the false teachers to stop teaching false doctrines [AB]. They have rejected their commitment to Christ along with the obedient life that would result from such a commitment [NAC].

2. They have rejected a good conscience [Alf, BNTC, ECC, ICC, Lns, My, NICNT, NIGTC, NTC, TC, TH, TNTC; CEV, NLT, NRSV, REB, TEV]. This speaks of a shipwreck in regard to faith that is brought about by the rejection of a good conscience, not by a rejection of faith [NIGTC]. A person rejects his conscience by disregarding what it said [TG], by refusing to listen to it [ICC].

QUESTION—What relationship is indicated by the use of the participle ἀπωσάμενοι 'having rejected'?

The participle indicates the reason they have been shipwrecked concerning their faith [LSA, TH; CEV, NET, NIV, NLT, REB]: *because they rejected this, they have been shipwrecked.*

QUESTION—What is meant by the metaphor περὶ τὴν πίστιν ἐναυάγησαν 'have been shipwrecked concerning the faith'?

The preceding military metaphor is now followed by a nautical metaphor and the destruction of a ship is compared with the destruction of the faith [TH]. Their faith has been destroyed like a wrecked ship is destroyed [GW]. They suffered moral shipwreck so far as the faith is concerned [EGT]. The metaphor is dropped by some: 'they have made a mess of their faith' [CEV], 'they have made a ruin of their faith' [TEV]. Since the metaphor in the previous verse is about warfare and there is nothing in the context that builds on the figure of a shipwreck, the reference to a shipwreck is to be taken as an idiom for not believing what is true but believing false doctrines [LSA].

1. The phrase τὴν πίστιν 'the faith' refers to their act of believing [BNTC, ICC, Lns, NIGTC, NTC, TH, WP; CEV, GW, HCSB, NASB, NCV, NIV, NLT, REB, TEV]: *their faith.* The verb is intransitive and describes the state of the subject [NICNT], the personal disaster of the false teachers [ICC, NICNT, NIGTC, WP]. This refers to their personal faith, and the definite article in τὴν πίστιν '*the* faith' is used as the equivalent of a possessive pronoun, meaning '*their* faith' [NIGTC, WP]. This agrees with the previous clause and with the stress put on the act of faith throughout the chapter [BNTC]. Their faith was the truth that they had confessed and the name of Christ whom they had named [NTC]. The metaphor means that they no longer believe in Christ [TH].

2. The phrase τὴν πίστιν 'the faith' refers to what Christians believe, the Christian faith [AB, Alf, Herm, LSA, NCBC, NIBC, TC, WBC; NET, NRSV]: *the faith that we believe.* By rejecting complete trust in God's grace, they are in the process of bringing the gospel itself to ruin [NIBC]. Instead of believing the true doctrine, they believe false doctrines [LSA].

This is an objective use of the noun and refers to correct belief [NCBC]. The false teachers have abandoned their personal faith and consciences and as a result have shipwrecked the Christian faith by bringing it into reproach [WBC].

1:20 **among-whom are Hymenaeus and Alexander, whom I-delivered[a] to-Satan, in-order-that they-might-be-taught[b] not to-blaspheme.[c]**

LEXICON—a. aorist act. indic. of παραδίδωμι (LN 57.77) (BAGD 1.b. p. 615): 'to deliver' [BAGD, LSA; HCSB, KJV], 'to deliver over to' [BNTC, Lns, WBC], 'to consign' [REB], 'to give' [NCV], 'to give over to' [BAGD, LN], 'to hand over' [AB, BAGD, ECC, Herm, LN, NTC; GW, NASB, NET, NIV, NLT], 'to turn over to' [BAGD; NRSV], 'to give over to the power of' [CEV], 'to punish by handing (them) over' [TEV]. This verb means to deliver a person into the control of someone else, either to the authorities for punishment or to an enemy who will take undue advantage of the victim [LN]. The verb is in the aorist tense, not the perfect, although the English perfect tense best expresses the force here since these men still remained under the apostle's sentence [Alf, EGT]. The aorist tense followed by a subjunctive indicates that the two were still under this punishment [EGT].

   b. aorist pass. subj. of παιδεύω (LN 36.10, 38.4) (BAGD 2.b.α. p. 604): 'to be taught' [AB; GW, HCSB, NASB, NET, NIV], 'to be trained' [LN], 'to be disciplined' [BAGD, LN, Lns, NTC], 'to be punished' [LN (38.4)]. This passive verb is also translated actively: 'to learn' [LSA; CEV, KJV, NCV, NLT, NRSV, REB]. The clause 'in order that they might be taught not to blaspheme' is translated 'this will teach them to stop their blasphemy' [TEV], 'to teach them a lesson for insulting God' [ECC], 'in order that they might be taught through punishment not to blaspheme' [WBC], 'so that they may be delivered from their blasphemy through punishment' [Herm], 'so that as a result of chastisement they might cease being blasphemous' [BNTC]. The verb means to punish someone for the purpose of improving behavior [LN (38.4)], to discipline with punishment [BAGD], or to train someone in accordance with the proper rules of conduct and behavior [LN (36.10)].

   c. pres. act. infin. of βλασφημέω (LN 33.400) (BAGD 2.b.a. p. 142): 'to blaspheme' [AB, BAGD, LN, NTC, WBC; HCSB, KJV, NASB, NET, NIV, NRSV], 'to be blasphemous' [BNTC; REB], 'to blaspheme God' [NLT], 'to revile, to defame' [LN], 'to dishonor God' [GW], 'to speak against God' [NCV], 'to insult God' [ECC], 'to speak evil about God' [LSA], 'to oppose God' [CEV]. This verb is also translated as a noun phrase: 'their blasphemy' [Herm; TEV]. This verb means to speak against God (or people) in such a way as to harm his reputation [LN]. The verb in the present tense indicates that this was a continuing practice [WBC].

QUESTION—What relationship is indicated by ὧν 'of whom'?

This relative pronoun indicates that the two who are named belong to the class of people Paul has just referred to in the previous clause, people who have rejected a good conscience, so that they have been shipwrecked concerning the faith [Alf, BNTC, ECC, ICC, NIBC, NIGTC, NTC]. They are examples of such people who do this [BNTC, TH, TNTC; NLT]. This pronoun is plural, while the verb ἐστιν 'is' is singular, yet when followed by the two names this is a normal grammatical construction [ICC].

QUESTION—Who were Hymenaeus and Alexander?

These two men were leaders among the false teachers at Ephesus [EGT, NIBC, NIGTC, NTC, WBC]. They were fellow workers at Ephesus [BNTC]. They were probably leaders in the church [NIBC, NICNT, NIGTC, TH]. In 2 Tim. 2:17 Hymenaeus is also mentioned with another man, Philetus, as being among those who were upsetting the faith of some by claiming that the resurrection had already taken place. [AB, Alf, BKC, BNTC, ECC, Herm, ICC, Lns, My, NICNT, NIGTC, NTC, NTL, TC, TG, TNTC, WP]. Alexander was a very common name [ECC, ICC, Lns, NTC], and he is not to be identified with Alexander the metal worker in 2 Tim. 4:14 [BKC, BNTC, Lns, NTC, TNTC]. Alexander cannot be identified [My, TC].

QUESTION—In what way did Paul deliver these two men to Satan?

This language is quite similar to 1 Cor. 5:5 where Paul says about the man who had committed incest, 'you are to deliver this man to Satan for the destruction of the flesh' [AB, BNTC, Herm, Lns], and also to Job 2:6 where God says to the devil, 'I am delivering him over to you; only preserve his life' [AB, BNTC, NICNT]. The text does not say when Paul did this but it could have been at the time of a previous visit to Ephesus [Alf, WBC], or through a letter, or perhaps by means of this very letter [WBC].

1. This refers to a disciplinary pronouncement that Paul was handing the men over to Satan's power [Alf, ECC, Herm, NTL; NET]. This was an act of discipline to restore them [NET]. The next clause shows that this act was not for the purpose of separating them from the congregation but to correct them through exposure to Satan, the destroyer of body and life [Herm]. The purpose of this act was not to cause their deaths but to teach them a lesson [ECC]. Not necessarily accompanied by excommunication, this was an act to correct the two men by putting them under the power of Satan who was ever ready to afflict God's people whenever he was permitted to do so [Alf].

2. This describes what is involved in excommunicating these men from church fellowship [AB, BKC, BNTC, EGT, Herm, ICC, Lns, My, NAC, NCBC, NIBC, NICNT, NIGTC, NTC, NTIC, TC, TG, TNTC, WBC, WP]. This expression was a semi-technical expression to indicate excommunication from the church, the realm of God's care and protection, so that the excommunicated person was now back in the sphere where Satan was at work [BKC, BNTC, NIBC, NICNT]. This involves a formal excommunication initiated by Paul and adopted by the

congregation for the purpose of giving the men over to Satan [Lns]. It was a formal handing over to Satan's malice and power, and here there is the expectation that later they might be restored to the congregation [BNTC]. The purpose clause 'in order that they might be taught not to blaspheme' implies that the purpose of this is the reclamation of the two men [NICNT]. Under the direction of the elders the sentence of excommunication would be carried out by the congregation [NTC]. The world outside the church is Satan's realm, and there they will be exposed to his power and malice [NAC, NIGTC, TG, WBC] when they are separated from the spiritual protection of the church [WBC]. It is not necessary to understand the phrase to mean that they were delivered to Satan's sphere in order that they suffer some physical harm [Lns, NIBC, NICNT, NIGTC]. Or, this expression implies that a person turned over to Satan's power will suffer some kind of physical affliction [BNTC, My, NTC, TC, TNTC, WBC]. The kingdom of Christ and the kingdom of Satan are mutually exclusive, and in Satan's kingdom it was expected the men would suffer a supernatural infliction of bodily sickness [TC]. Satan would be able to punish their bodies, but not their spirits since the purpose of this act is their eventual redemption [WBC].

QUESTION—What is meant by βλασφημέω 'to blaspheme'?

Instead of malicious talk or talk directed against Paul, this is blasphemy in a religious sense, that is, a misrepresentation of the true faith [ICC]. By rejecting a good conscience and making shipwreck of their faith they deserved to be called blasphemers [NIGTC]. They insulted the Lord in their words and deeds [NAC]. By teaching their own doctrines as God's truth, they falsely claimed to have power and authority from God and thus misrepresented God and opposed him [TH]. Blasphemy may refer to their false teaching or their opposition to God [Herm]. Those men blasphemed the true law of the gospel teachings and tried to replace them with their myths [Lns]. These men associated God or Christ with their unholy doctrines, thus bringing shame to God's holy name [Alf]. Paul had been a blasphemer when he preferred Law over grace (1:13), and these men were in that same position [AB, NICNT]. Like Paul, they were persecuting the church and therefore were persecuting Christ by distorting his message for their own purposes and personal gain [WBC].

QUESTION—How would delivering the men to Satan teach them not to blaspheme?

The act of discipline by the church was meant to make the blasphemers realize the seriousness of their sin so that they would repent [Lns, NICNT]. Or, the passive voice in the phrase ἵνα παιδευθῶσιν 'in order that they might be taught' is the divine passive and means that God, not humans, would do the disciplining or educating [AB, WBC]. God can use Satan and his deeds to serve his own purposes in bringing about the good of God's people [NIGTC]. The hope was that these men would realize that they were true sinners and repent of their opposition to the truth and its Author [NTC].

When they are exposed to the malice of others who are opposed to the truth, they will learn their lesson [WBC]. When false teachers are separated from God's people and delivered over to Satan, they will realize that what they have done so displeases God that they have been separated from him [NIGTC]. Or, Satan is pictured here as a teacher who teaches them through physical afflictions to stop their opposition to God [ECC]. The idea is of stern punishment rather than instruction [BNTC, Herm], and this chastisement infers illness or physical disability that would restore them to a better frame of mind [BNTC].

DISCOURSE UNIT 2:1–6:12 [NAC]. The topic is the emphasis that will accomplish the task.

DISCOURSE UNIT 2:1–4:16 [TNTC]. The topic is worship and order in the church.

DISCOURSE UNIT 2:1–4:5 [WBC]. The topic is the correction of improper conduct in the Ephesian church.

DISCOURSE UNIT 2:1–3:16 [REB]. The topic is Christian conduct.

DISCOURSE UNIT 2:1–3:13 [ECC, TH]. The topic is apostolic exhortations [ECC], instruction regarding Christian worship and organization [TH].

DISCOURSE UNIT 2:1–3:1a [ECC]. The topic is prayer and worship.

DISCOURSE UNIT 2:1–15 [ICC, NIGTC; CEV, NCV, NIV, NLT, NRSV, TEV]. The topic is church worship [TEV], how to pray [CEV], instructions concerning prayer [ICC; NRSV], instructions about worship [NIV, NLT], prayer for all and the conduct of women [NIGTC], some rules for men and women [NCV].

DISCOURSE UNIT 2:1–8 [NIGTC, TNTC; NASB, NET]. The topic is a call to prayer [NASB], the importance and scope of public prayer [TNTC], prayer for all [NET], prayer for all is urged and grounded in the existence of one God and one Mediator [NIGTC].

DISCOURSE UNIT 2:1–7 [AB, ECC, Herm, ICC, NAC, NIBC, NICNT, NTL, TH, WBC; HCSB]. The topic is instructions for church worship [TH], instructions on prayer [AB, NTL; HCSB], appropriate prayer in the church [NICNT], the proper objects of prayer [NIBC], prayer and worship: for whom and why [ECC], prayer for all people [Herm, ICC, NAC], salvation is for all people [WBC].

DISCOURSE UNIT 2:1–3 [NCBC]. The topic is how to conduct public prayer.

2:1 Therefore I-urge[a] first[b] of-all (that there) be-made[c] requests,[d] prayers,[e] intercessions,[f] (and) thanksgivings[g] for[h] all people,

LEXICON—a. pres. act. indic. of παρακαλέω (LN 33.168) (BAGD 2. p. 617): 'to urge'. See translations of this word at 1:3. This verb means 'I urge', and it has the same force of the verb in 1:3, not just 'I ask' [WBC].

b. πρῶτος (LN 60.46, 65.52) (BAGD 2.c. p. 726): 'first' [LN (60.46)], 'most important' [LN (65.52)], 'in the first place, above all, especially' [BAGD]. The phrase πρῶτον πάντων 'first of all' [AB, BNTC, ECC, Herm, Lns, LSA, NTC; all versions except NCV] is also translated 'first' [NCV], 'above everything else' [WBC]. This word denotes something that is first in a series [LN (60.46)], or something that exceeds everything else in importance [LN (65.52)].

c. pres. pass./mid. infin. of ποιέω (LN 90.45) (BAGD II.1 p. 683): 'to make' [BAGD, LN], 'to perform, to practice' [LN]. This verb is translated passively: 'to be made' [AB, ECC, Lns, NTC; HCSB, KJV, NASB, NIV, NRSV], 'to be offered' [BNTC; NET, REB], 'to be offered to God' [TEV]. This is also translated in the middle voice: 'to make' [Herm, WBC; GW]. This verb is also translated actively by treating nouns in the list as active verb phrases: 'ask...pray...intercede...thank God' [LSA] 'pray...ask God...intercede...give thanks' [NLT], 'pray...ask God to help and bless...tell God how thankful' [CEV], 'pray...asking God...being thankful' [NCV].

d. δέησις (LN 33.171) (BAGD p. 172): 'request' [LN, WBC; NET, NIV, NLT], 'petition' [Herm, Lns; GW, HCSB, REB, TEV], 'entreaty' [AB, BAGD, ECC; NASB], 'supplication' [BNTC, NTC; KJV, NRSV], 'plea, prayer' [LN]. This noun is also translated as a verb phrase: 'ask God to help them' [NLT]. The phrase 'there be made requests...and intercessions' is translated 'ask God to help and bless them all' [CEV], 'asking God for what they need' [LSA; NCV]. The plural forms of the four nouns imply that there be more than one such prayers, and they also suggest that this involves a number of people in the congregation [ECC, NIGTC]. This noun denotes that which is requested with urgency and implies that there is a need [LN].

e. προσευχή (LN 33.178) (BAGD 1. p. 713): 'prayer' [AB, BAGD, BNTC, ECC, Herm, LN, Lns, NTC, WBC; all versions except CEV, NCV, NLT]. The phrase 'there be made prayers' is translated 'pray (for everyone)' [LSA; CEV, NCV], 'to pray (for all people)' [NLT]. This noun denotes what is said to God or what is requested of him [LN]. It is used in reference to every kind of prayer [My].

f. ἔντευξις (LN 33.347) (BAGD 2.a. p. 268): 'intercession' [BAGD, BNTC, ECC, Herm, LN, NTC; GW, HCSB, KJV, NET, NIV, NRSV, REB], 'request' [TEV], 'petition' [AB, WBC; NASB], 'intercessory prayer' [BAGD], 'approaches' [Lns]. This noun is also translated as a verb phrase: 'intercede on their behalf' [NLT], 'that they intercede for people' [LSA]. See lexical item d. for CEV, NCV. This noun denotes what is said to someone on behalf of someone else [LN]. See this word at 4:5.

   g. εὐχαριστία (LN 33.349) (BAGD 2. p. 328): 'thanksgiving' [AB, BAGD, BNTC, ECC, Herm, LN, Lns, NTC; HCSB, NASB, NIV, NRSV, REB, TEV], 'expressions of thanksgiving' [WBC], 'thanks' [NET], 'prayers of thanks' [GW], 'giving of thanks' [KJV]. The phrase 'there be made thanksgivings' is translated 'that they thank God' [LSA], 'tell God how thankful you are (for each of them)' [CEV], 'give thanks (for them)' [NLT], 'being thankful (to him)' [NCV]. This noun denotes an expression of gratitude for certain benefits or blessings [LN].

   h. ὑπέρ (LN 90.24, **90.36**) (BAGD 1.a.α. p. 838): 'for' [BAGD, BNTC, ECC, Herm, LN (90.36); all versions except NASB, NET], 'for the sake of' [BAGD, LN (90.36)]. 'in behalf of' [AB, BAGD, **LN** (90.36), Lns, NTC], 'on behalf of' [WBC; NASB, NET], 'for the benefit of' [LSA], 'concerning, about' [LN (90.24)]. This preposition indicates the general content, whether in relation to a discourse or to mental activity [LN (90.24)], or it marks a person who is benefited by an event or for whose behalf an event takes place [LN (90.36)].

QUESTION—What relationship is indicated by the conjunction οὖν 'therefore'?

   1. It indicates an exhortation based on what precedes this in chapter 1 [AB, Alf, EGT, ICC, NAC, NIBC, NICNT, TH, TNTC, WBC; KJV]: *therefore*. It refers to the exhortation given in 1:3 [NAC, NIBC, TH, TNTC]. The purpose of the book is stated in 1:3, and here Paul is giving instructions for Timothy to use in combating the errors of the false teachers [NAC]. Or, it is based on the whole of chapter 1 [EGT, TH, WBC]. After a digression in 1:19b–20, it picks up on the general exhortation made in 1:18 [Alf, EGT, ICC, NIBC, NICNT]. Because the false teachers were promoting an exclusivist outlook, it was necessary to emphasize that the gospel is for everyone [NIBC].

   2. It serves as a transition to the next section [BKC, ECC, Lns, LSA, My, NIGTC, NTC; probably Herm; CEV, GW, NCV, NLT which do not translate this conjunction and also probably BNTC; HCSB, NASB, NET, NIV, NRSV, REB, TEV which translate with 'then']: *now, then*. The subject of foolish teachers has been concluded in the previous chapter, and 'then' indicates the next subject [Lns]. Now the body of the letter is to begin [ECC]. Paul begins to treat in detail the things Timothy must do in his ministry [My].

QUESTION—To whom is this exhortation directed?

Some translate with a direct reference to Timothy [TC; CEV, GW, NCV, NLT]: *I urge you to make these prayers.* But this exhortation indicates that Paul was directing Timothy to lead the congregation in praying according to these instructions [NAC]. The unnamed actor of the passive ποιεῖσθαι 'to be made' is the church [ICC, TG]. This is directed to the church through Timothy [BNTC, ECC, EGT, Herm, ICC, Lns, LSA, NAC, NIGTC, WBC;

probably HCSB, KJV, NASB, NET, NIV, NRSV, REB, TEV which translate in the passive voice]: *I urge that these prayers be made by the church.* This section deals with public worship and the conduct that is appropriate for it [BNTC, Herm]. The unnamed persons implied by the passive are Timothy and the congregations he will give these directions to [ICC, Lns, WBC].

QUESTION—What is meant by πρῶτον πάντων 'first of all'?

1. It means the first in a list of things that Paul is going to urge [AB, BNTC, Lns, LSA, NIGTC; NCV]. It means first in a series, not that which is the most important point in the letter [AB]. It is his first requirement in the letter [BNTC]. It indicates that there are more things that he is going to urge [Lns, LSA]. Listing this as the first item to discuss may have happened because it is also of primary importance [NIGTC].

2. It means the first in importance [Alf, BKC, ECC, EGT, ICC, NAC, NTC, TC, TG, TH, TNTC, WBC, WP]. This is the most important instruction needed by the church, and therefore it is the first thing that is mentioned [ICC].

2.1 It refers to the most important point in Paul's exhortations [Alf, EGT, NAC, TG, TH, WBC]. The first matter he takes up is the most important thing of all [TH]. The most significant change that Timothy can bring about is prayer for the salvation of all people and not for just the select few who follow the false teachers [NAC, WBC].

2.2 It refers to the most important thing to do in worship [ECC, ICC, NTC, TNTC]. This concerns the relation of the church to the government since worship cannot be conducted calmly and without disturbance unless it performs this duty [NTC].

QUESTION—What is meant by δεήσεις 'requests' for all people?

This noun describes actual instances of prayer, not just prayer in general [WBC]. It is asking God to act on behalf of others [ICC, NICNT]. This refers to urgently asking for something based on a presumed need [LN (33.171), TH]. It refers to petitions to fill specific needs [ECC, Lns, NIGTC, NTC, TC, WBC]. It concerns deep spiritual needs [NAC]. These needs might refer to illnesses or disturbing events [NTC]. The centrality of prayer is being stressed in this list, and the precise distinctions between the terms should not be pressed [BNTC, Herm]. These are elements to be found in every prayer [TG]. Although some think it concerns a request for oneself, the point here is that all types of prayers should be made for all people [Herm, NIGTC, WBC].

QUESTION—What is meant by προσευχάς 'prayers' for all people?

'Prayers' is the most inclusive category for prayer in this list [AB, Alf, ECC, ICC, Lns, NAC, NICNT, NIGTC, NTC, TC, TH, TNTC, WBC]. Some versions put 'prayers' first in the list and indicate that it includes the other different categories [CEV, NCV, NLT]. The word 'prayers' broadens the scope of 'requests' [ECC]. It can be used of all types of prayer for all people, whether the prayers be general requests or specific petitions [NAC]. In this

context, it may emphasize praying for God's general blessings and care for
all people [NIGTC]. Or, although the noun 'prayers' covers all forms of
reverent address to God [NTC], its position in the middle of a list of near
synonyms suggests that here the meaning is restricted to general requests
about needs that are always present in contrast with the first noun 'requests'
which refers to requests concerning specific situations [NIGTC, NTC].
These general prayers might concern a need for more wisdom or greater
consecration [NTC].

QUESTION—What is meant by ἐντεύξεις 'intercessions' for all people?

This pertains to speaking to God on behalf of someone else [LN (33.347),
TH]. In this context, the noun denotes a pleading in the interest of others
[NTC]. It describes prayers that make requests on behalf of others and it
implies that it is addressed to one who is superior to the intercessor [ICC,
TC, TNTC, WBC]. It is given in an attitude of concern for others,
particularly about their plight or difficulty [NIGTC]. It includes both sinners
and saints [WP].

QUESTION—What is meant by εὐχαριστίας 'thanksgivings' for all people?

This refers to expressions of gratitude for some benefits or blessings [LN
(33.349)]. It is the natural response to the making of requests in prayer
[Herm]. All requests are to be made with conscious expressions of gratitude
to God on behalf of all [NIGTC, TC]. This refers to thanking God for past
mercies [Lns]. This expresses gratitude for the answers of previous prayers
[ICC, NAC, NICNT], and in anticipation for God's future response
[NICNT]. This is the expression of gratitude for God's blessings [NTC]. The
mention of thanksgiving is provides a motivation for making requests to God
[NAC]. Every kind of prayer is also to be accompanied with thanksgiving
[EGT].

QUESTION—What is meant by ὑπὲρ πάντων ἀνθρώπων 'for all people'?

This phrase is to be connected with each of the preceding nouns [Herm, TH].
The church should offer prayers of various kinds for all people [NIBC]. This
phrase gives an intercessory character to all the synonyms that precede it
[Alf]. Probably this indicates that there was a growing exclusiveness of the
surrounding heretical sects [BNTC, ICC, NCBC, TC].

1. This means every person [AB, Alf, BNTC, ECC, ICC, Lns, My, NIBC,
NTIC, TG, TH, WBC]. This reference to 'all people' is the first of the
universal statements in the letter, the others being at 2:4, 5, 6, and 7 [AB,
BNTC, ECC]. This paragraph stresses a concern for universal salvation
[ICC, WBC].

2. This means all groups or classes of people [NAC, NIGTC, NTC]. It would
be impossible to remember in prayer every single person on earth
[NIGTC, NTC], and in this context Paul is thinking of classes of people:
rulers (also implying their subjects), and Gentiles (also implying the
Jews), so that in public worship not a single class is omitted [NTC]. The
repetition in 2:2 of ὑπέρ 'for' in the subgroup 'for all civil rulers'
supports the interpretation that this means all *kinds* of people [NIGTC].

The primary reason for this instruction is inherent in the theology of there being only one God and one mediator, but perhaps he added 'all' to counteract the narrowness of the false teachers [NIGTC]. The false teachers probably were concerned with only a certain elite group [NAC].

2:2 for[a] kings and all (those who) are in a-high-position,[b]

LEXICON—a. ὑπέρ (LN 90.24, 90.36) (BAGD 1.a.α. p. 838): 'for' [BAGD, LN (90.36)], 'for the sake of' [BAGD, LN (90.36)]. 'in behalf of' [BAGD, **LN** (90.36)]. Following ὑπὲρ πάντων ἀνθρώπω 'for all men', the phrase ὑπὲρ βασιλέων 'for kings' [AB, ECC; HCSB, KJV, NASB, NIV, NRSV, TEV] is also translated 'even for kings' [NET], 'on/in behalf of kings' [Lns, NTC, WBC], 'for rulers' [GW], 'for emperors' [Herm], 'for sovereigns' [BNTC; REB], 'Pray for kings' [CEV], 'Pray for rulers' [NCV], 'Pray this way for kings' [NLT], 'they should do this for kings' [LSA]. See this preposition at 2:1.

b. ὑπεροχή (LN **87.26**) (BAGD 2. p. 841): 'high position, high status' [LN], 'authority, prominence' [BAGD]. The clause καὶ πάντων τῶν ἐν ὑπεροχῇ ὄντων 'and all those who are in a high position' is translated 'and all who are in high positions' [NTC; NRSV], 'and all those who are in positions of authority' [AB], 'and all who are in authority' [KJV, NASB, NET, NLT; similarly WBC; HCSB, NIV], 'and all in high station' [ECC], 'and all who occupy high office' [BNTC], 'and all other people who are in high positions' [LSA], 'and all others who are in authority' [NLT, TEV], 'and for all in high office' [REB], 'and for all who have authority' [NCV], 'and for everyone who has authority over us' [GW], 'and all authorities' [Herm], 'and all who are in eminence' [Lns], 'and others in power' [CEV]. This noun denotes a state of high rank or position [LN].

QUESTION—What relationship does this group of people introduced by the preposition ὑπέρ 'for' have with the first group that was similarly introduced by ὑπέρ 'for' in 5:1?

It indicates a specific class of people for whom the church should especially pray [Alf, BKC, BNTC, ECC, ICC, Lns, NAC, NIGTC, TH, TNTC, WBC]. This verse gives an example of how prayer for all men should begin [EGT]. This example is given because Christians tended to leave this class of people out of their prayers [TNTC]. The church should pray for all people as a mass (2:1), and also for all people as nations under the control of their leaders [Lns]. This class of people is singled out because the lives of everyone are affected by their civil authorities [ICC]. It was especially important to pray for the authorities in those days because Christians were suspected of being disloyal to the government [TC].

QUESTION—What should they pray about concerning this class of people?

Besides praying for their conversion, they should pray that the leaders will have wisdom in carrying out their duties and that they will create the conditions for the goals that follow in this verse [NAC]. They should pray that the authorities will cause righteousness and peace to prevail in the land and that the Christians will be protected from calamities [Lns]. They should pray for their prosperity as was done in Jewish models of prayer [ECC]. There will be thanksgiving when decisions of the authorities result in the spread of Christianity [NAC].

QUESTION—What is meant by the plural noun βασιλέων 'kings'?

1. The reference is to the Roman emperor Caesar and all the petty kings of political states under him [AB, BNTC, ECC, ICC, My, NIGTC, NTC]. The plural form covers the Roman emperor and the local rulers as well [BNTC]. This title was applied to the Roman emperors and to regional leaders such as Herod Antipas, Herod Agrippa I, Herod Agrippa II, and Aretas (2 Cor. 11:32) [AB]. It refers to the highest authorities in the government [My].

2. This title refers to the Roman emperors [Alf, Herm, NCBC, NICNT, TC, TNTC]. Although there was only one emperor at a time, the plural form, 'kings' occurs so as to be parallel with the following plural form, 'all those', and especially because this is given as a general rule [Herm]. The plural form is used to make this a general principle applicable at all times [Alf, NCBC, TC, TNTC].

3. The reference is to the emperor of the Roman Empire and to the kings of all other royal forms of governments throughout the world [EGT, Lns, NTC, TH; probably WBC]. Paul knew of kingdoms outside of the Roman Empire where the gospel would be spreading [EGT].

QUESTION—What is meant by πάντων τῶν ἐν ὑπεροχῇ ὄντων 'all who are in authority'?

This is a general description of prominent officials of almost any kind [BNTC, ICC]. They would be the proconsuls, political and religious officials of a province, and even town clerks [NTC]. Or, since it is paired with *kings*, this refers only to civil and government authorities [TH]. These are the government officials who can provide a tranquil and quiet life for those under their charge [ECC]. Praying for *all* of them serves to generalize this prayer instead of universalizing it. Christians were to pray for whatever authorities were over them, rather than for every single authority there was in the whole world [ICC]. They are all the local and regional representatives of the emperor [NICNT].

that[a] we-may-live[b] a-tranquil[c] and quiet[d] life

LEXICON—a. ἵνα (LN 89.26, 90.22): 'that' [LN (90.22), NTC; KJV, NET, NIV, TEV], 'so that' [AB, BNTC, Herm, LN (89.26), Lns; CEV, HCSB, NASB, NCV, NLT, REB], 'in order that' [LN (89.26), LSA], 'for the purpose of' [LN (89.26)]. Some begin a new sentence here: 'Pray for these people so that' [GW], 'Our purpose is' [ECC].

b. pres. act. subj. of διάγω (LN 41.3) (BAGD p. 182): 'to live' [BAGD, LN, LSA], 'to conduct oneself, to behave' [LN], 'to spend one's life' [BAGD]. The verb διάγωμεν 'we may live' [CEV, NIV, TEV] is also translated 'we can live' [LSA; NLT], 'we may/might lead a...life' [AB, BNTC, Lns, NTC; HCSB, KJV, NASB, NET, REB], 'we may be able to lead a...life' [Herm], 'we can have a...life' [GW, NCV], 'we might live our lives in' [WBC], 'to spend a...existence' [ECC]. This verb means to conduct oneself in regard to everyday overt behavior [LN]. The verb refers to the observable life of a person [ICC, NICNT].

c. ἤρεμος (LN **88.104**) (BAGD p. 348): 'tranquil' [BAGD, ECC, NTC; HCSB, NASB, REB, TEV], 'in tranquility' [WBC], '(live) tranquilly' [LSA], 'quiet' [BAGD, BNTC, Herm, **LN**; CEV, GW, KJV, NCV, NRSV], 'peaceful' [AB, LN; NET, NIV, NLT], 'still' [Lns]. This adjective describes an existence or attitude that is quiet and peaceful [LN]. This is a rare word that means to be still and at rest [AB]. It refers to freedom from riots and persecution that would hinder their witness to all people [ICC].

d. ἡσύχιος (LN **88.104**) (BAGD p. 349): 'quiet' [AB, BAGD, ECC, LN; HCSB, NASB, NET, NIV, NLT, REB], 'peaceful' [Herm, **LN**; CEV, GW, NCV, TEV], 'peaceable' [BNTC; KJV, NRSV], '(live) peaceably' [LSA], 'calm' [NTC], 'in calmness' [WBC], 'restful' [Lns]. This adjective describes an existence or attitude that is quiet and peaceful [LN]. This refers to a quiet life away from public turmoil [AB].

QUESTION—What relationship is indicated by ἵνα 'that'?

1. It indicates the purpose or intended result of praying specifically for kings and those in positions of high authority [AB, BNTC, ECC, Herm, ICC, NICNT, NTC, NTL, TH, TNTC, WP; CEV, GW, HCSB, NASB, NCV, NLT, REB]: *pray so that this will be the result.* With such prayers they will not be accused of disloyalty and will be allowed to practice their religion without fear of disturbance [BNTC]. This is not the only purpose for such prayer, but this prayer will maintain an environment favorable to the witness of the church as it seeks the salvation of all people [ICC].

2. The beginning clause of 2:2 is to be taken as parenthetical, so this conjunction indicates the purpose of praying for all people (2:1). If they pray for all people, including authorities, then they won't alienate those outside the church and will not bring reproach upon the church [WBC].

3. It indicates the content or gist of what they are to pray for [EGT, NAC, TC]: *pray that this will happen.* This was the leading thought in their prayers for the authorities [TC].

QUESTION—Is there a significant difference between ἤρεμον 'tranquil' and ἡσύχιον 'quiet'?

Both adjectives are in the same semantic domain in LN, and there is a marked overlap in BAGD and in the translations. These two adjectives refer to an ideal set of circumstances in which the church might live [NICNT]. There is no significant difference between the two words [ICC, LSA, My, TH, TNTC, WBC]. Both words mean 'quiet and tranquil' [TNTC], and they are linked together in order to emphasize the importance of this serenity [My, TNTC]. In languages without such synonyms, a translation could use one word in an emphatic way, such as 'very peaceful' [TH]. Together they refer to a life that is orderly and peaceful, free from danger or trouble [TH]. They refer to living in a dignified way without undue stress [ICC]. They describe a tranquil life free from the hassles that come with a turbulent society [NICNT]. Some explain that there is a difference in that the first term refers to outward circumstances and the second refers to one's inner state [Alf, NTC]. But some reverse these explanations so that the first word refers to the inner state and the second to outward circumstances [EGT, Lns, My].

in^a all godliness^b and dignity.^c

LEXICON—a. ἐν (LN 13.8, 89.84) (BAGD I.4.d. p. 259): 'in' [AB, BAGD, BNTC, ECC, Herm, Lns, NTC; HCSB, KJV, NASB, NET, NIV], 'with' [WBC; TEV], 'marked by' [NLT]. This preposition is also translated as a phrase: 'free to practice (our religion in dignity)' [REB], 'as we conduct ourselves (doing all that is right and proper)' [LSA], 'always lived in (a godly and reverent way)' [GW], 'lives full of (worship and respect for God)' [NCV], 'as (we worship and honor God)' [CEV]. It indicates a state or condition: 'in, with' [LN (13.8)], or the manner in which an event occurs: 'with' [LN (89.84)].

b. εὐσέβεια (LN **53.5**) (BAGD p. 326): 'godliness' [BAGD, BNTC, **LN**, Lns, NTC; HCSB, KJV, NASB, NET, NIV, NLT, NRSV], 'piety' [AB, BAGD, Herm, LN], 'reverence' [WBC], 'reverence toward God' [TEV]. This noun is also translated as a phrase: 'a godly way' [ECC; GW], 'full of worship' [NCV] '(free to practice) our religion' [REB], '(as) we worship God' [CEV], 'doing all that is right' [LSA]. This noun denotes behavior that reflects correct religious beliefs and attitudes [LN]. See this noun at 4:7; 6:3, 5, 11.

c. σεμνότης (LN **88.46**) (BAGD 1. p. 747): 'dignity' [AB, BAGD, Herm; HCSB, NASB, NET, NLT, NRSV, REB], 'godly dignity' [WBC], 'seriousness, respectfulness, probity' [BAGD], 'gravity' [BNTC, Lns, NTC], 'propriety' [**LN**], 'honesty' [KJV], 'proper conduct' [TEV], 'holiness' [BAGD; NIV], 'reverence' [BAGD], 'a reverent way' [ECC; GW], '(full of) respect for God' [NCV]. This noun is also translated 'doing all that is proper' [LSA], '(as) we honor God' [CEV]. This noun denotes befitting behavior, and it implies having such dignity that it attracts respect [LN].

QUESTION—What relationship is indicated by ἐν 'in'?

1. It indicates the manner in which we live a tranquil and quiet life [ICC; GW]. It refers to the state of our beings as we live a tranquil and quiet life [BAGD (I.4.d. p. 259), EGT, LSA, NICNT, TH, TNTC; CEV]: *pray for authorities so that we may live tranquil and quiet lives as we conduct ourselves with all godliness and dignity.* Godliness is expected of Christians in all situations, whether tranquil or turbulent [NICNT].

2. The tranquil life is prayed for so that it will be the setting for reaching the ultimate goal expressed in this clause [NIGTC]: *pray for authorities so*

that we may live tranquil and quiet lives that will allow us to conduct ourselves with all godliness and dignity.

QUESTION—What is meant by πάσῃ 'all'?

This adjective modifies both 'godliness' and 'dignity' [ECC, Lns, NIGTC, TG, TH, WBC]. Both qualities are to be complete [Lns, WBC]. Paul wants godliness and dignity to come their full expression [NIGTC].

QUESTION—What is meant by εὐσέβεια 'godliness'?

1. This word focuses on a person's relationship to God as he lives to please him [BNTC, ICC, Lns, My, NAC, NICNT, NTC, NTL, TG, TH, TNTC, WBC]. This is reverence for God [BNTC], a religious devotion [TNTC]. This word describes the whole of the Christian life as the interplay between the knowledge of God and the observable conduct that emerges from that knowledge [NICNT]. It describes someone who is devoted to God and who has a moral and ethical life that is in keeping with such devotion [TH].

2. This word focuses on the appropriate conduct for a Christian [EGT, Herm, LSA, NIBC, NIGTC]. This word and the next have to do with behavior that can be seen [NIBC]. It refers to one's Christian religion being expressed in daily life [EGT].

QUESTION—What is meant by σεμνότης 'dignity'?

This word refers to dignified conduct toward one's fellow men [ICC, Lns, NIGTC, NTC, NTL, TG, TH]. A settled piety results in moral earnestness, which affects both outward actions and inward intentions [BNTC, NIGTC]. As well as living devoutly (in godliness), taking life seriously is behavior that wins respect from outsiders [ICC, NICNT]. It is a dignified demeanor with a seriousness of purpose [TC, TNTC]. It means respectability [NICNT]. It is gravity that gains respect [EGT]. It refers to proper conduct [NIBC].

2:3 This (is) good[a] and pleasing[b] in-the-opinion-of[c] our savior[d] God,

TEXT—Following τοῦτο 'this', some manuscripts add γάρ 'for'. GNT does not mention this variant. 'For' is read by KJV.

LEXICON—a. καλός (LN 88.4) (BAGD 2.b. p. 400): 'good' [BAGD, LN, WBC; all versions except NRSV, REB], 'excellent' [BNTC, Lns, NTC], 'an excellent thing' [ECC], 'fine' [LN], 'good (to do)' [LSA], 'a noble thing (to do)' [AB], 'right' [NRSV, REB], 'the way it should be' [Herm], 'praiseworthy' [BAGD, LN]. This adjective indicates that which has a positive moral quality [BAGD, LN, WBC], a quality that is favorably valued [LN]. It is rightness of behavior [NICNT]. Here the ideas of 'fitting' and 'right' are probably intended [TH].

b. ἀπόδεκτος (LN **25.85**) (BAGD p. 90): 'pleasing' [AB, BAGD, **LN**, WBC], 'well-pleasing' [Herm], 'acceptable' [BNTC, LN, Lns, NTC; KJV, NASB, NRSV], 'approved' [REB], 'welcome' [ECC], 'welcomed' [NET]. The phrase ἀπόδεκτον ἐνώπιον τοῦ σωτῆρος ἡμῶν θεοῦ 'pleasing in the opinion of our savior, God' is translated 'it pleases God our Savior' [LN (25.85); CEV, GW, HCSB, NCV, NIV, NLT, TEV;

similarly LSA], 'is approved by God our Savior' [REB]. This adjective
refers to that which is pleasing because of its being acceptable [LN].

c. ἐνώπιον (LN 90.20) (BAGD 3. p. 270): 'in the opinion of, in the
judgment of' [BAGD, LN], 'in the sight of' [AB, LN, NTC; KJV, NASB,
NRSV], 'in the eyes of' [ECC], 'before' [Lns, WBC; NET], not explicit
[Herm, LSA; CEV, GW, HCSB, NCV, NIV, NLT, REB, TEV]. This
adjective marks a person whose viewpoint is relevant to an event [LN].

d. σωτήρ (LN 21.31) (BAGD 1. p. 801): 'savior' [AB, BAGD, BNTC, ECC,
Herm, LN, Lns, NTC, WBC; all versions], 'deliverer, preserver' [BAGD].
This noun is also translated as a verb phrase: 'who saved us' [LSA]. The
phrase τοῦ σωτῆρος ἡμῶν θεοῦ 'our savior God' here is similar to the
phrase in 1:1 θεοῦ σωτῆρος ἡμῶν 'God our savior'. The meanings of
both word orders are the same [AB]. Both phrases are translated the same
by many: 'God our savior' [BNTC, Herm, NTC, WBC; all versions].
Savior is not a mere title here but it focuses on the act of saving because
of the following clause 'who want all people to be saved' [Herm].

QUESTION—How is this verse related to what precedes it?

1. Verses 3 gives the grounds for saying that the church should pray for all
people [Alf, BKC, ECC, ICC, Lns, LSA, NIBC, NICNT, NIGTC, NTIC,
TH, WBC; NET]: *pray for all people because this is good and pleasing to
God our savior who wants all people to be saved.* Prayer for the salvation
of all is in accord with God's will [NICNT]. This verse is the first of three
reasons why the church should pray for *all* people [WBC]. The relative
clause of 2:4 explains that praying for all people is good and pleasing to
God because the God who saved us wants to save all people [NIBC].

2. Verse 3 gives the grounds for saying that Christians are to pray for the
authorities [BNTC, NTL]. Following the clause 'that we may live a
tranquil and quiet life', this is the reason for general intercession and
intercession for rulers in particular [BNTC]. Then 2:4 explains why it is
that God is called the Savior [NTL].

QUESTION—What does τοῦτο 'this' refer to?

Some translations include a referent: 'this kind of prayer' [CEV], 'such
prayer' [REB], and 'such prayer for all' [NET].

1. It focuses on praying for all people (2:1) [EGT, Herm, Lns, LSA, NAC,
NIBC, NIGTC, NTIC, TC, TG, TH, TNTC, WBC; NET]. Since 2:2 is
parenthetical, it is unlikely that this statement is building upon that verse
[TC, WBC].

2. It refers to praying for all people, including the authorities (2:1–2) [Alf,
BNTC, ECC, ICC, My, NICNT, NTC; NET]. Prayer for kings and
authorities will include prayer for their salvation [Alf, ECC, NTC]. This
refers to prayer for all people (2:1), and verse 2:2 is merely a continuation
of that thought [Alf]. It refers primarily to 2:1, not that 2:2 is a
parenthesis, but that the points mentioned in 2:2 are included in the
thought of 2:1 [My]. Praying for the salvation of all people and praying

specifically for the effectiveness of the civic powers conforms to God's will [NICNT].

3. It refers to praying for the authorities (2:2) [NTL]. Paul has to argue for his statement about praying for authorities and he says that such prayer for them is good in itself and it is pleasing in God's sight [NTL].

QUESTION—Does the phrase ἐνώπιον 'in the opinion of (God)' modify only 'pleasing' or does it modify both 'good' and 'pleasing'?

1. It modifies only ἀπόδεκτον 'pleasing' [AB, BNTC, ECC, EGT, LN (25.85), LSA, NAC, NTL, TC, TNTC, WBC; CEV, GW, HCSB, NCV, NIV, NLT, REB, TEV]: *this is good and it also pleases God.* In this case, 'good' means that it is intrinsically good [AB, BNTC, EGT, NTL, TC, TNTC, WBC]. A person's own conscience knows that it is good [EGT]. Or, it is good in the opinion of their contemporaries [ECC].

2. It modifies both καλὸν 'good' and ἀπόδεκτον 'pleasing' in God's opinion [Alf, ICC, Lns, My, NTC]: *this is good in God's opinion, and it is also pleasing to him.* To God's eye it is good and to his heart it is pleasing [NTC]. God's judgment pronounces such prayers to be excellent, and therefore he receives them as being acceptable [Lns]. Separating the two adjectives makes an ill-balanced sentence [Alf].

QUESTION—Who is referred to by the possessive pronoun ἡμῶν 'our' savior?

It refers to the Christians who are already saved [BNTC, LSA, NAC, NIBC, NIGTC]: *God who saved us.* God is the actual savior of Christians and furthermore he desires that all people be saved (2:4) [BNTC]. God is mentioned as savior here because the thought in 2:4 is already in mind [My]. It emphasizes the fact that there is a believing community, and the next verse emphatically states that he also wants to be the savior of all people [ECC]. Reminding the church members of their own salvation is a way of urging them to pray for others [NIGTC]. God is the source of salvation [EGT, ICC, NIBC], and since he is the Savior, his people should be involved through their prayers for all [ICC]. God is not satisfied with only our salvation since he wants his salvation to reach all people [NIBC]. The word order 'our Savior, God' hints for a comparison with another 'savior', Caesar, who was called Savior because he provided the Roman empire with peace, order, prosperity, and protection [NICNT, NTL].

DISCOURSE UNIT 2:4–7 [NCBC]. The topic is a credo and a commission.

2:4 who wants[a] all people to-be-saved[b]

LEXICON—a. pres. act. indic. of θέλω (LN 25.1): 'to want' [AB, ECC, Herm, LN, Lns; CEV, GW, HCSB, NCV, NET, NIV, NLT, TEV], 'to desire' [BNTC, LN, LSA, NTC; NASB, NRSV], 'to wish' [WBC], 'will have' [KJV]. The phrase 'who wants' is translated 'whose will it is that' [REB]. This verb means to desire to have something happen [LN].

b. aorist pass. infin. of σῴζω (LN 21.27) (BAGD 2.b. p. 798): 'to be saved' [AB, BAGD, BNTC, ECC, Herm, LN, Lns, NTC, WBC; all versions except REB], 'to be saved (by him)' [LSA], 'to find salvation' [REB].

This verb means to cause someone to experience divine salvation [LN]. It pertains to salvation from sin [ICC, NICNT]. This pertains to escaping God's wrath at the last day [BNTC]. See this word at 1:15.

QUESTION—What is the function of this relative clause?

1. It gives the grounds for the preceding statement in 2:3 that says praying for *all* people is good and pleasing in the opinion of God [BKC, ECC, ICC, LSA, My, NAC, NIGTC, NTC, TNTC; NET]. This also gives a motive for public prayer for all people [ECC]. What is good and pleasing to God is not just the contents of verse 2, because the fact that God wants *all* people to be saved connects directly to verse 1 with its statement that prayer should be made for *all* people [NIBC, TNTC]. There is an intermediate thought in 2:2 that prayer for kings serves to maintain a peace that facilitates the spread of Christianity, but this should not obscure the fact that the focus is on prayer for all in 2:1 [My].

2. This explains why God is called *Savior* [Alf, NTL].

3. It adds to the fact that God, *our* Savior, is the Savior of all Christians [BNTC, Lns]: *God is our Savior and he also desires that all people be saved.* This removes any limitation that might be felt with the phrase '*our* Savior' and the Greek order 'who *all people* he wants to be saved' emphasizes that it is *all people* he wants to experience salvation [Lns].

QUESTION—What is meant by the statement that God 'wants' (θέλει) all people to be saved?

The verb can mean 'want, desire, wish' as most take it, or it can mean 'to have as one's purpose' [TH]. This statement has caused much controversy concerning how God's desire or will that 'all' be saved is to be reconciled with the fact that all people are not in fact saved. Also involved are the doctrines of election and predestination and the interpretations of the Arminians and Calvinists [NTC]. There are arguments that 'all' refers to all whom God predestined, or that the salvation of 'all' refers to God's general (or antecedent) will, but there is also his subsequent will that all who refuse his grace will be punished [BNTC]. However, here the statement about 'all people' is taking issue with the false teachers who had the Jewish belief that God willed the salvation of only the Jewish who were 'righteous', or the Gnostic teaching that salvation belongs only to the spiritually elite followers [BNTC, NTL]. The presence of the false teachers in Ephesus is the background for this statement, not the issues of election, so this is saying that the church must not exclude anyone from the proclamation of the gospel and that is because God desires that all people from all classes of humanity be saved [NCBC, NIBC, WBC]. In contrast to some form of exclusiveness, the stronger sense 'wills' is best in this statement of God's universal intention for mankind, but the element of human response to the gospel should not be downplayed [NICNT].

1. 'All people' means every single individual and although God wants everyone to be saved, his desire that this should happen does not come to pass for each individual [AB, Alf, BKC, ECC, EGT, ICC, Lns, My, NAC,

NIBC, NICNT, NTIC, NTL, TH, WP]. The extent of God's real will (not just the weaker sense of wish or desire) is to save all humankind whether or not they respond to his gracious offer and this does not refer to just the elect whom he has predestined to save [ICC, NICNT]. It refers to all persons individually without distinctions of race or social standing [NAC]. The fact that all are not saved is because God will not override the stubbornness of the human will [Alf, NAC, NTC]. As far as God's will is concerned, he is the savior of *all men*, but actually only 'them that believe' (4:10) are saved because, by his own limitation of his powers, salvation does not depend on God alone, but also on the exercise of the free will of each individual in accepting or rejecting salvation. Those who pray for all men generate a spiritual atmosphere in which God's designs may grow [EGT]. God wills that salvation be open to all people on the basis of faith, and he wills that the gospel be preached to them all [ICC]. Those who do not accept God's universal will for them to be saved will be sent to judgment and perdition by his subsequent will [Lns]. This is what God wills in so far as he can influence people [WP]. This refers to God's resolve that all people be saved, and it is not due to the weakness of God's intent that they are not all saved, but to the stubbornness of the will of those who defy God and go their own way [NAC]. This passive form says that God wants all people *to be saved*, leaving it up to their acceptance of salvation, but it would be wrong to say that God wants *to save* all people, because if that were so, he would save them [Alf]. Or, the passive is used to imply that God is the means for our being saved [Lns]. Or, the passive 'to be saved' is used to indicate that the saving act comes from the person of God, but leaves open the further fact that God saves through the mediator who came to the world to save sinners [ECC].

2. 'All people' means all kinds or classes of people but not every individual, so that those whom God wills to be saved in each class of people will certainly be saved [NIGTC, NTC]. This has the same meaning as 'all people' in 2:1, and these are people from out of every rank and station (such as kings and those in high authority), and tribe and nation (such as Gentiles and Jews) [NIGTC, NTC]. Those who are saved are the ones who are called according to God's will and grace [NIGTC].

and to-come into knowledge[a] of-(the)-truth.[b]

LEXICON—a. ἐπίγνωσις (LN **27.4**, 28.2) (BAGD p. 291): 'knowledge' [BAGD, LN], 'recognition' [BAGD]. The idiom εἰς ἐπίγνωσιν ἔρχομαι 'to come into knowledge' means acquiring knowledge or information about something and emphasizes the process involved in doing so [LN (27.4)]. This idiom is translated 'to come into/to the/a knowledge of' [WBC; HCSB, KJV, NASB, NET, NIV, NRSV], 'to come to know' [REB, TEV], 'to come to full knowledge of' [ECC], 'to come to a realization of' [Lns], 'to know (the) whole (truth)' [CEV], 'to attain knowledge' [BNTC], 'to know' [LSA; NCV], 'to learn' [**LN** (27.4); GW],

'to understand' [NLT], 'to come to the recognition of' [AB, Herm], 'to
come to the acknowledgment of' [NTC]. This verb means to acquire
knowledge or information about something and the process involved in
doing so is emphasized [LN (28.2)].

b. ἀλήθεια (LN 72.2) (BAGD 2.b. p. 36): 'truth' [AB, BAGD, LN], 'the
truth' [BNTC, ECC, Herm, Lns, NTC, WBC; all versions], 'the true
doctrine' [LSA]. This noun denotes the content of what is true or that
which is in accordance with what actually happened [LN]. It especially
refers to the content of Christianity as the absolute truth [BAGD]. See this
word at 3:15; 4:3.

QUESTION—What relationship is indicated by the conjunction καί 'and'?

1. It indicates another thing that God wants to happen [LSA, My, NTL]: *God
wants all people to be saved and also to come to a knowledge of the truth.*
This is one of the benefits of being saved, and 'know' means to learn
about the true Christian doctrine, in contrast with being deceived by the
false doctrine that was being taught by some [LSA]. This knowledge is
one of the ultimate aims of salvation [TNTC]. This is a goal to which
salvation leads [My].

2. It indicates the means by which people are saved [BNTC, EGT, Lns,
NIBC, NIGTC, NTC, TC, TG, TH, WBC]: *God wants all people to be
saved by coming to a knowledge of the truth.* Knowing the truth is the way
by which people experience salvation [NTC, TH]. To be saved, it is
necessary that a person has the knowledge of the truth of the gospel, that
is, the person and work of Christ [NIGTC]. Salvation is God's ultimate
goal, while coming to the knowledge of the truth is God's immediate goal
that leads to salvation [WBC]. 'Salvation' is the state of being saved, so
although grammatically this knowledge appears to be a consequence, it is
actually a precedent condition [EGT]. It is an absolute preliminary to
salvation [BNTC].

3. It explains the preceding clause by restating it [Alf, ECC, Herm, ICC,
NICNT]: God wants all people to be saved, *that is, he wants them to come
to a knowledge of the truth.* In this case 'know' would mean not only to
understand the gospel, but to act on that knowledge and accept it [ECC,
Herm, LSA]. It is a technical term for conversion [Herm]. This clause
describes salvation as a rational decision about the truth of the gospel
[ICC]. This is the human side of the process of salvation and describes the
conversion of someone who comes to faith by the knowledge and
recognition of the truth [NICNT].

QUESTION—What is meant by εἰς ἐπίγνωσιν ἔρχομαι 'to come into
knowledge'?

There are two nouns with the meaning 'knowledge', the simple form γνῶσις
'knowledge' and the compound word ἐπί-γνωσις 'knowledge', which
occurs in this verse. Some commentators take this compound word to be
different from the simple form γνῶσις 'knowledge', while other
commentators think that both forms can be used interchangeably with no

significant difference between them [TH]. Many translate ἐπίγνωσις simply
as 'knowledge' [BAGD, BNTC, LN, WBC; HCSB, KJV, NASB, NRSV].
Some see a difference between the two forms in that the compound form is
more intense than just knowledge [Lns], something like '*full* knowledge'
[Alf, ECC, EGT, NTC, NTL, WP], '*certain* knowledge' [Alf], or '*revealed*
knowledge' [NCBC], instead of ordinary knowledge. Knowledge is more
than just knowing something since it includes both comprehension and
acknowledgement of the truth [Herm, NIGTC]. It is both recognizing and
appropriating the truth by becoming a Christian [NTC, WBC]. It is
recognition of who Jesus is, followed with a total commitment to him [ECC].
The phrase 'to come to a knowledge of the truth' is a synonym for
conversion [BNTC, ICC, NAC, NCBC, NTC]. '*To come* to a knowledge'
indicates a personal and experiential response to such knowledge [NIGTC].
QUESTION—What is meant by ἀληθείας 'truth'?
1. Truth refers to the saving message of the gospel [AB, BNTC, ECC, Herm,
   ICC, Lns, NAC, NIBC, NICNT, NIGTC, NTC, NTL, TG, TH, WBC;
   CEV]. The content of this knowledge is given in 2:5–6 [CEV]. The
   expression 'the truth' refers to the gospel message [NAC]. 'Truth' and
   'the truth' are often used as terms for the gospel about Jesus and his work
   [Herm, Lns]. The truth is the way of salvation that is revealed in the Word
   [NTC]. The gospel enables one to know the truth about God and what he
   wills for humanity [TG]. The good news was being attacked in Ephesus,
   and Paul wants the church to know the true version of the gospel and the
   truth of the good news that God has given them mercy in contrast with the
   requirements of the law [AB]. This refers to obtaining a knowledge of the
   Messiah that culminates in a commitment to him [ECC]. Knowledge is a
   discernment of the truth and appropriating it by faith, so that 'knowing the
   truth' means accepting the gospel message [NIGTC, WBC]. The phrase is
   equivalent to being converted to Christianity [BNTC, Herm]. It includes
   the true version of the gospel preached by Paul and the truth of the gospel
   expressed in 1:12–17 [AB].
2. Truth refers to the whole body of doctrine that Christians believe [BAGD
   (2.b p. 34), BNTC, LSA, NCBC, TNTC]. This knowledge is gained after
   the believer has been saved at conversion [LSA]. Knowledge of the whole
   revelation of God in Christ is the ultimate goal of salvation [TNTC].

2:5 Because (there is) one[a] God, also (there is) one mediator[b] of-God and
of-men, a-human,[c] Christ Jesus,
LEXICON—a. εἷς (LN 60.10, 63.4): 'one' [LN]. The phrase εἷς θεός 'one God'
is translated 'there is one God' [BNTC, WBC; all versions except CEV,
NLT], 'there is only one God' [CEV, NLT], 'there is but *one* God' [NTC],
'there is only one God for all people' [LSA], 'one is God' [Lns], 'God is
one' [AB, ECC, Herm]. The numeral indicates one, as contrasted with
more than one [LN (60.10)], or it indicates something that is united as
one, as contrasted with something that is divided or consisting of parts. In

contexts where God is referred to, this term defines him as a unit rather than characterizing his existence in the form of numerous manifestations or realizations [LN (63.4)].

b. μεσίτης (LN 31.22, **40.6**) (BAGD p. 507): 'mediator' [AB, BAGD, BNTC, ECC, Herm, LN (31.22, **40.6**), Lns, NTC, WBC; GW, HCSB, KJV, NASB, NIV, NRSV, REB], 'go-between' [LN (31.22)], 'intermediary' [NET], 'one who reconciles' [LN (40.6)], 'arbitrator' [BAGD]. The phrase εἷς μεσίτης θεοῦ καὶ ἀνθρώπων 'one mediator of God and of men' is translated 'there is one Mediator who can reconcile God and humanity' [NLT], 'there is only one person who mediates between God and all people' [LSA], 'there is one who brings God and human beings together' [TEV], 'Christ Jesus is the only one who can bring us to God' [CEV], 'there is one way human beings can reach God' [NCV]. This noun denotes someone who helps or causes parties to come together in agreement [LN (31.22)], or it denotes a person who acts as a mediator in bringing about reconciliation between estranged parties [LN (40.6)].

c. ἄνθρωπος (LN 9.1, 9.24): 'human being' [BAGD, LN (9.1)], 'person, individual' [LN (9.1)], 'man' [BAGD, LN (9.24)]. The phrase ἄνθρωπος Χριστὸς Ἰησοῦς 'a human, Christ Jesus' [GW] is also translated 'a person, Christ Jesus' [WBC], 'a man, Christ Jesus' [Lns; HCSB], 'the man Christ Jesus' [ECC, Herm, NTC; KJV, NASB, NET, NLT, TEV], 'Christ Jesus, himself human' [NET, NRSV], 'Christ Jesus, himself a man' [BNTC; REB], 'who is Christ Jesus who himself is a man' [LSA], 'that way is through Christ Jesus who is himself human' [NCV], 'Jesus was truly human' [CEV]. This noun denotes a human being [LN (9.1)], or an adult male person [LN (9.24)].

QUESTION—What relationship is indicated by the conjunction γάρ 'because'?

1. It indicates the grounds for saying that God wants *all* people to be saved (2:4) [AB, Alf, BNTC, ECC, EGT, ICC, Lns, LSA, My, NAC, NIBC, NICNT, NIGTC, NTC, TC, TH, TNTC]. Since God is one, it follows that all people have access to his salvation [NICNT]. This is directly connected with the fact that God wants all people to be saved in 2:4 and only indirectly with the command to pray for all people in 2:1 [Alf, TC]. Verses 5–6 contain two statements that support the claim that God wants all people to be saved: God is *one*, and there is *one* mediator [LSA, NIGTC]. Or, besides taking it as two reasons, the second can be separated so as to make a third reason that Christ gave himself as a ransom for all [TH]. This confirms the fact that the salvation God wants for all people is for *all* mankind [My]. The one God created all people, and therefore he wants to save them all [ECC].

2. It indicates another grounds for saying that prayer should be made for the salvation of all people and that this is pleasing to God [WBC]. Verses 5–6 are probably part of an early creed and are used to support the statement in 2:1 that prayer should be made for the salvation of all people since Christ gave himself as a ransom for all people (2:6). It adds another argument

that all people are united by the oneness of God and the mediator, and therefore all people should be offered the benefit of Christ's ransom [WBC].

3. It explains what the truth is that God wants people to know [CEV]: *God wants everyone to know the whole truth, which is 'There is only one God....'* Verses 2:5–6 apparently are quoted from a creed [CEV].

QUESTION—What is the point of saying that there is *one* God?

This statement rephrases the *Shema* (Deut. 6:4), the central affirmation of Judaism that there is only one God as opposed to many gods [BNTC, ECC, ICC, NIBC, NTL, WBC].

1. This stresses the singularity of God, not the unity of God: there is one God, not two or more Gods [AB, ICC, Lns, NICNT, NIGTC, NTC, NTL, TH, WBC, WP]: *there is one God.* As a number, this word is contrasted with more than one [LN (60.10)]. This statement shows that he who is the only God must then be the God of all people [TH, WBC, WP], and he is not the God of only the false teachers [WBC]. Since there is only one God, there are not many ways of salvation [AB, ICC]. There is not one God for rulers and another God for his subjects (in reference to the preceding context), or one God for the Jews and another God for the Gentiles (in reference to the following context) [NICNT, NIGTC, NTC]. The thrust of the verse focuses on Christ's role: *just as* there is only one God, so also there is only one mediator between God and people, and therefore Christ's work is valid for all mankind. It is also implied that the one gospel that proclaims Christ is that which Paul preaches [ICC].

2. This stresses the unity of God [Alf, EGT, My, TC]: *God is one.* It can indicate something that is united as one, as contrasted to something that is divided or consists in parts, and in Scripture this term defines God as a unit rather than presenting him in the form of numerous manifestations or realizations [LN (63.4)]. God is one in essence and one in purpose [Alf]. The unity of God means that God stands in the same ultimate relationship with all of his creatures, and his mercy reaches everyone [TC]. He has only one purpose for all people, because if he did have different purposes for different individuals, then the Godhead would be divided in its nature [My]. This statement of the unity of God is suggested by the singular σωτῆρος 'Savior' in 2:3, and it has nothing to do with the doctrine of the trinity [EGT].

QUESTION—What is meant by μεσίτης 'mediator'?

The word *mediator* is found elsewhere in the NT. In Galatians 3:19–20 the term refers to Moses where the law needed him to be a mediator to convey the law to Israel. The term refers to Christ in Hebrews 8:6; 9:15; 12:24 where Christ is described as the mediator of the new covenant, but here in 1 Timothy the term is used of Christ without qualifications [NCBC]. Christ is the mediator *between* God and human beings [AB, Alf, Lns, NCBC, NIBC, NTC, WBC; GW, HCSB, KJV, NASB, NET, NLT, NRSV, REB, TEV]. The two parties are *God*, who has been offended, and *mankind*, whose sins offend God [NTC]. A mediator may represent one of the parties to the other, or he may bring together opposing parties while belonging to one of the parties or to both of them [ICC]. That there is only one God implies that there can be only one mediator between God and mankind [ICC, My]. The result of mediation may be described in terms of reconciliation or a new covenant, but in any case the mediator has brought God and people into a new relationship that can be described by metaphors such as a new covenant, adoption, redemption, and salvation [NICNT].

1. The mediator acts as an intermediary to reconcile God and people [Alf, BNTC, ECC, ICC, Lns, My, NIBC, NTC, TH]. A mediator is someone who mediates between two parties to remove a disagreement [BAGD (p. 507)], and to bring about reconciliation [LN (40.6)]. Here the mediator is related to both parties, and he has the task of bringing about reconciliation between the parties [ICC]. In today's usage, the word 'mediator' makes us think of the role of a labor mediator who draws up an agreement acceptable to both labor and management in a dispute, so 'intermediary' better describes Christ's role [TG; NET]. God does not need to change his will or purpose that all people be saved and that Christ Jesus is the one through whom people can be saved by God and united to him [TG]. Christ is mediator in that through him God accomplishes his purpose of saving people and only through him people can reach the goal God appointed for them [My]. Through Christ and his work of redemption human beings are restored to fellowship with God [BNTC]. Christ removed the separation caused by sin between God and mankind and he reconciled mankind with God [NAC]. God was offended by the sins of mankind, so Christ stood between as a mediator in order to take upon himself the wrath mankind deserved and thus provided a way of peace with God, and he reveals this to men as he persuades them to accept the good news [NTC].

2. The mediator helps to bring agreement between God and mankind and also guarantees this agreement [Herm, NAC, TNTC]. He helps parties to come to an agreement, with the implication of guaranteeing the certainty of the arrangement [LN (31.22)]. Christ was the mediator of a covenant such as is described in Hebrews 8:6 [Herm]. Besides the first meaning of 'mediator', it also presents Christ as a negotiator who establishes a new arrangement between God and mankind and only through him can sinful humans come to God [NAC].

QUESTION—What is the significance of specifying that Christ Jesus is a human?

The word ἄνθρωπος 'man' does not have an article, so it emphasizes the humanity of Jesus rather than the fact that he is a male [Alf, ICC, NIBC, NICNT, NTIC, NTL, TG, TH, WBC; NET]. This does not deny Christ's divinity [NTC, WBC]. It is understood that Christ Jesus is God, but here it is stressed that at the same time he is also man and this implies that being a human is pertinent to his mediating between God and mankind [LSA]. The word 'human' explains how Christ could be an adequate mediator between God and mankind since he was a mediator who was both God and man. Therefore Christ understood both parties and his sympathy was with both [EGT]. That Christ was a human is specified in order to identify him with those whom he represents as a mediator [NIGTC]. It was as a human being that Christ mediates between God and humanity and as a man he offered himself to die to redeem humanity [ICC, NICNT, My, WBC]. This emphasizes the fact that the Messiah whom God anointed was able to mediate between God and human beings because he was also a human being [WBC]. This emphasizes Christ's identity with those he represents as mediator [Lns, NIGTC]. Jesus' mediation is accomplished on the basis of his common humanity and in his giving himself as a ransom in behalf of all humanity [NTIC]. Or, this presents Christ as the second Adam who redeems humanity [Alf, NAC, NIBC].

2:6 the (one who) gave[a] himself (as) a-ransom[b] for[c] all,

LEXICON—a. aorist act. participle of δίδωμι (LN 13.142) (BAGD 6. p. 193): 'to give, to grant, to allow' [LN], 'to give up, to sacrifice' [BAGD]. The phrase ὁ δοὺς ἑαυτὸν 'who gave himself' [AB, ECC, Herm, **LN** (37.130), Lns, NTC, WBC; all versions except GW, NLT, REB] is also translated 'who/he gave his life' [LSA; NLT], 'who sacrificed himself' [GW, REB]. This verb means to grant someone the opportunity or occasion to do something [LN]. This verb emphasizes the fact that this was a voluntary self-offering [NICNT], At Gethsemane Christ actually gave himself into the power of his enemies to voluntarily die as a ransom for all [Lns].

b. ἀντίλυτρον (LN **37.130**) (BAGD p. 75): 'ransom' [AB, BAGD, ECC, Herm, **LN**, Lns, NTC, WBC; HCSB, KJV, NASB, NET, NIV, NRSV], 'a means of release' [LN], 'a payment to free (all people)' [NCV]. This noun is also translated as a verb: 'to ransom' [LSA], 'to rescue' [CEV], 'to redeem' [TEV], 'to purchase freedom for someone' [NLT], 'to win freedom for someone' [REB], 'to free from sin' [GW]. This noun denotes the means or the instrument by which a release or deliverance is made [LN].

c. ὑπέρ (LN 90.36) (BAGD 1.a.ε. p. 838): 'for' [BAGD, ECC, Herm, LN, Lns, NTC, WBC; all versions except CEV, NCV, TEV], 'on behalf of' [BAGD, LN], 'in behalf of' [AB], 'for the sake of' [LN]. Some which translate the noun 'ransom' as a verb make 'all' the object of the verb, thus leaving out the preposition: 'to ransom all people' [LSA], 'to rescue all of us' [CEV], 'to free all people' [NCV], 'to redeem the whole human race' [TEV]. This preposition indicates the person who is benefited by an action, or in whose behalf an event occurs [LN].

QUESTION—How is this clause related to what precedes?

This goes on to define Christ's work with a free version of Christ's statement in Mark 10:45 that 'the Son of Man came to give his life as a ransom for many' [BNTC, ECC, ICC, LSA, NCBC, NICNT]. The emphasis in Paul's argument is on the phrase *for all* [BNTC].

1. It describes how Christ fulfilled his office of mediator (2:5) [BNTC, Herm, Lns, LSA, My, NICNT, NIGTC, NTC].
2. It indicates the grounds for the universality of the redemptive plan in 2:4 [NIBC, TC, TH]. After the two statements that there is one God and that there is one mediator between God and people, this statement follows as a third proof for the claim that God wants to save all people [NIBC, TC, TH].
3. It indicates the grounds for praying for all people [WBC]. This is the point of the creed and a second grounds for the command to pray for all people in 2:1 [WBC].

QUESTION—What is meant by Christ being an ἀντίλυτρον 'ransom'?

The universality of the effect of Jesus' death is described with the metaphor of a ransom that is paid to free all people [ECC]. A ransom is a sum of money that is paid to a slave owner in order to release a slave from slavery [Herm, NAC, TG, TH, WBC]. 'Ransom' denotes the means or instrument by which a release or deliverance is made possible [LN (37.130)]. The word 'ransom' means the price that is paid to gain the freedom of someone, and since the word is accompanied with the idea of a payment (having *given himself*) on behalf of all people, this appears to be a live metaphor [LSA]. Mankind is in captivity to sin [NAC]. Mankind is pictured as a huge society that is enslaved morally and ethically by human sin and evil [ECC]. Jesus paid the ransom, and that ransom was his own life [Lns, WBC]. Jesus gave himself as a ransom by giving himself up to death [My]. Jesus was both the ransom and the one who paid the ransom [ECC, Lns, My, WBC]. Jesus himself was the ransom that was paid by dying on the cross [ECC, NAC]. The result of paying the price of the ransom was freedom [WBC]. Theological problems arise if the figure is filled out so as to include the one to whom the ransom is paid [LSA], since mankind is enslaved not by some person, but by sin and evil [ECC]. The phrase is a formula, so it is pointless to ask who received the ransom payment [Herm]. What is in focus is that Christ gave up his life in order to save people [LSA]. The NT never suggests that Christ's death was the ransom price God paid to Satan in order to set people free [TG]. To avoid the problem of who paid what in order to free people, it could be translated, 'He offered himself as the means by which God will free all people from the power of sin and death' [TH]. Christ died on behalf of all people, but the saving effects of his death are limited to those who respond in faith [NAC, TNTC]. Or, although this noun can mean 'ransom' with the idea of payment, here it has the meaning of 'redemption', as used in Exodus where instead of a payment being involved, it has the sense of deliverance from bondage [NIBC].

QUESTION—Does the phrase ἀντίλυτρον ὑπὲρ πάντων 'a ransom for all' include the idea that Christ died *in the place of* all?

1. The verb means that Christ gave up himself to die *in the place of* those he ransomed and the preposition ὑπέρ 'for' means he did this for the benefit of all [ECC, ICC, Lns, NAC, NICNT, NIGTC, NTC, NTL, TC, TNTC, WBC, WP]. Jesus not only represented humankind, but he stood in its place as a substitute for its benefit [NICNT]. This is the only occurrence of the noun ἀντίλυτρον 'ransom' in the NT, and the noun has the prefix ἀντί- 'in exchange for, in place of' with the stem λύτρον 'ransom', so this compound noun gives the meaning 'a substitute ransom', and by adding the preposition ὑπέρ 'for' to the noun gives the meaning that Christ's death was substitutionary and for the advantage of all [NTC]. This was a substitutionary act and with the preposition ὑπέρ 'in behalf of' the context gives the meaning that he died *instead of* us [Lns]. In Mark 10:45 the phrase is λύτρον ἀντὶ πολλῶν 'a ransom *in the place of* all', so the idea of substitution was already associated with the ransom. It may be incidental that there is a change from ἀντί to ὑπέρ, but probably ὑπέρ means 'for', perhaps expressing the idea of representation [ICC]. The preposition ὑπέρ 'for' can mean either 'on behalf of' or 'in the place of', and since 'on behalf of' or 'for the sake of' fits in all three occurrences of the preposition at 2:2, 2:2, and 2:6, it is best to take that meaning here [NIGTC]. Or, the noun ἀντίλυτρον 'ransom' includes the idea of substitution, and historically the preposition ὑπέρ had started sharing the meaning of ἀντί so that the phrase could be emphasizing the idea of substitution [WBC].

2. The verb means only that Christ died to set free those whom he ransomed and the preposition ὑπέρ 'for' means that he did this for the benefit of all [AB, Alf, BNTC, EGT, My, NIBC, TG, TH]. It is useless to speculate about the complex meanings involved. The important fact is that Christ died for *all* people, therefore making it obligatory to pray for all without distinction [BNTC].

the testimony[a] (in) its/his-own times.[b]

LEXICON—a. μαρτύριον (LN 33.262, 33.264) (BAGD 1.a. p. 494): 'testimony' [BAGD, LN (33.264)], 'witness' [LN (33.262, 33.264)]. The phrase τὸ μαρτύριον 'the testimony' [AB, Herm, NTC; NASB, NIV] is also translated 'a testimony' [HCSB], 'this testimony' [Lns], 'the testimony to this' [ECC], 'to be testified' [KJV], 'the witness' [WBC], 'this was attested' [NRSV], 'this message is valid' [GW], 'revealing God's purpose' [NET, REB], 'God showed us this' [CEV], 'This is the message that God gave to the world' [NLT], 'This was the proof that God wants everyone to be saved' [TEV], 'He is proof that came' [NCV]. This noun denotes information about a person or an event of which the speaker has direct knowledge [LN (33.62)], or the content of what is witnessed or said [LN (33.264)]. This noun denotes that which serves as testimony or

proof and may consist of an action, circumstance, or anything else. Here
the redeeming death of Jesus is referred to as God's testimony [BAGD].

b. καιρός (LN 67.1) (BAGD 2.b. p. 395): 'time' [BAGD, LN], 'occasion'
[LN]. The phrase καιροῖς ἰδίοις 'in its own times' is translated 'in its
proper time' [NIV], 'in its determined time' [Herm], 'at the right time'
[CEV, NCV, NRSV, TEV], 'at just at the right time' [NLT], 'at the proper
time' [WBC; HCSB], 'in due time' [KJV], 'at his appointed time' [NET],
'at God's good time' [REB], 'was given at the right time' [AB], 'given at
the proper time' [NASB], 'to be borne in due season' [NTC], 'has
occurred in due time' [ECC], 'for their own seasons' [Lns], '(is valid) for
every era' [GW]. This noun denotes a point of time as an occasion for a
particular event [LN]. It may be used with qualifying phrases to define the
specific character of the time, such as the 'definite', 'fixed', or 'right' time
[BAGD].

QUESTION—How is this clause related to what precedes?

The clause is problematic with respect to its meaning and also to its
connection to the phrases before and after it [AB]. The clause is appended
without conjunctions that would indicate its relationship to what has
preceded it [NICNT]. This statement is enigmatic [BNTC], very elliptical
[ECC], obscure [NCBC, TG, TNTC], vague [NICNT], and difficult to
understand [ICC, NAC, WBC; NET].

1. This is part of a creed that Paul quoted in 2:5–6 [NCBC; CEV, HCSB].
2. This is a comment Paul added about the creed or statement of faith that is
   quoted in 2:5–6a [BNTC, ECC, NAC, NIBC, WBC; NRSV]. The
   quotation is neater without this final addition [BNTC], which disrupts the
   structure of the creed [WBC]. This phrase is properly introduced with a
   dash to indicate the lack of a grammatical connection with the preceding
   clause [NIBC; NRSV].
3. No creed was being quoted and this is an additional statement [AB, Lns,
   NICNT, NTC; probably GW, NASB, NCV, NET, NIV, NLT, REB, TEV
   which do not indicate that a creed is being quoted]. The basic element in
   Christ being mediator is that he gave himself as a ransom for all, and now
   this clause indicates the second element, that Christ's death as a ransom
   must be proclaimed [NTC].

QUESTION—What is meant by μαρτύριον 'testimony'?

The noun 'testimony' can refer to spoken reports or to an event that serves as
a testimony [AB]. It refers to either to the act of giving a testimony or to the
content of the testimony [NICNT].

1. The testimony is the information contained in the preceding clauses, and
   that is the message to be passed on to others [ECC, ICC, Lns, NIBC,
   NTC]: *who gave himself as a ransom for all, and the testimony to this
   information was given at the right time.* The testimony was to be given by
   Paul [ICC], or by the apostles [ECC, Lns]. It pertains to 2:5–6a [ECC,
   Lns]. The apostles testified to the message contained in 2:5–6a [Lns]. The

apostles witnessed to all people by telling about the crucified mediator between God and human beings [ECC].

2. The testimony is the event of Christ giving himself as a ransom for all, and this event serves as a testimony to be understood by those who hear about it [BNTC, Herm, ICC, Lns, LSA, NAC, NCBC, NIGTC, NTC, NTL, TG, TH, WBC; NET]: *who gave himself as a ransom for all, and this act of giving himself was itself a testimony that was given at the right time.* Here 'testimony' has the idea of being the proof or evidence of the fact that God really wants all people to be saved [NAC, NTL, TH; NET]. Christ's sacrifice of his life was a witness to God's desire to save all people [BNTC]. Christ's ransom for 'all people' was a witness to the Ephesian church that all people are to be offered the gospel [WBC], and prayer should be offered for all [ICC].

3. The testimony is the fact that God sent his Son at the appointed time [TNTC].

QUESTION—What is referred to by the plural reflexive pronoun ἰδίοις 'its/their own'?

'In its own times' is in the plural, but it can be taken as an idiom referring to only one event since the same plural occurs in 6:15 where it clearly refers to just one event [ICC, LSA, NIGTC, WBC]. Or, the plural could refer to the continuing apostolic testimony that was given many times [ECC, EGT, Lns], so that this means the apostles testified in or for *their* own times, and their testimony stands until the last day [Lns].

1. The reflexive pronoun is treated as singular, and it refers to τὸ μαρτύριον 'the testimony' [Herm, NAC, NICNT, NIGTC, NTC; GW, NIV]: *the testimony in its own time.* 'In its determined time' implies that God determined the time [Herm]. The development of God's plan of salvation by Christ paying the ransom had now come, and it is implied that believers should proclaim this testimony [NAC].

2. The reflexive pronoun is treated as singular, and it refers to God [BNTC, NICNT, TC, TH, WBC; NET, REB]: *the testimony in his/God's own time.* This refers to God's present witness at his own appointed time [WBC]. The phrase 'in his own times' means that at the proper or right time chosen by God [NICNT, TH]. God made known the evidence that he wants all people to be saved [TH].

3. The reflexive pronoun is treated as plural, and it refers to the apostles and others [ECC, Lns, TG]: *the testimony for the apostles' own times.* The testimony to the things in 2:5–6a refers to the apostolic proclamation of this in various times and places [ECC]. The testimony about Christ's self-sacrifice was afterwards testified to by the apostles and others at the right time [TG]. This refers to the witness of the apostles to the gospel, and their testimony stands for all times [Lns].

4. The reflexive pronoun refers both to the act of Christ giving himself being a witness to God's desire to save all people, and to Paul being appointed to continue to bear testimony to this act [NIGTC].

QUESTION—What time is meant by καιροῖς ἰδίοις 'its/his *own times*'?

This was the time God appointed for the testimony to be given [Alf, BNTC, ECC, Herm, ICC, NAC, NCBC, NIBC, NICNT, NIGTC, NTC, NTL, TH, WBC; CEV, NET, REB, TEV]. Here, ἰδίοις 'own' may be better translated as 'appointed' [NET], 'determined' [Herm], 'proper' [NIGTC, TH, WBC; HCSB, NASB, NIV], 'right' [AB, TG; CEV, NCV, NLT, NRSV, TEV], 'good' [REB], or 'appropriate' [AB, NICNT, NTC, TH].

1. This refers to the event of Christ's atonement for sin [BNTC, Herm, NCBC, WBC; NET]. God is the savior, so salvation happened according to God's schedule [WBC]. God had planned Christ's atoning work from all eternity, but it came to light at the time God intended [NET]. Christ's death was the fulfillment of what God had promised, and it happened in God's good time [NCBC]. Christ's dying for mankind happened at the very time in history that God had fixed for accomplishing his purpose for the salvation of all people [BNTC]. This was the time determined by God in his promises [Herm].

2. This refers to the time when news of Christ's atonement was proclaimed [ECC, Lns, NICNT, NTC]. The next verse suggests that at the right eschatological time God called Paul to be an apostle to bear witness of the event described in 2:5–6a [NICNT]. The due time was the time God had set for the apostolic testimony to the one God and his one mediator. It was a time when people were suitably disposed toward the faith, and since the apostolic testimony continues, it shows God's continuous desire for all human beings to be saved and come to the knowledge of the truth [ECC]. It refers to the time of the NT, since in the OT there could only be promises and prophesies about God's will and the coming mediator, but now all those promises are fulfilled and can be testified to [Lns]. The testimony was to be borne in the due season when it was appropriate and favorable, and this season extends through the entire new dispensation [NTC].

2:7 For[a] which I-was-appointed[b] a-herald[c] and an-apostle,

LEXICON—a. εἰς (LN 89.48, 89.57, 90.23): This preposition is a marker of result, and probably there is the implication of a preceding process: 'with the result that, so that as a result, to cause' [LN (89.48)], or it indicates purpose or intent (intended result): 'for the purpose of, in order to' [LN (89.57)]. The prepositional phrase εἰς ὅ 'for which' is translated: 'for this' [BNTC; HCSB, NASB, NET, NRSV], 'of this' [REB], 'whereunto' [KJV], 'for which purpose' [NTC], 'and for this purpose' [NIV], 'this/that is why' [CEV, NCV, TEV], 'and' [NLT], 'for which testimony' [Lns], 'for that testimony' [ECC], 'it is with reference to this witness that' [WBC], not explicit [AB, Herm, LSA; GW].

b. aorist pass. indic. of τίθημι (LN 37.96) (BAGD I.2.a.α. p. 816): 'to be appointed' [AB, BNTC, ECC, Herm, LN, Lns, LSA, NTC, WBC; GW, HCSB, NASB, NET, NIV, NRSV, REB], 'to be chosen' [NCV, NLT], 'to be designated, to be assigned, to be given a task' [LN], 'to be ordained' [KJV], 'to be made' [BAGD], 'to be sent' [TEV]. This passive verb is also translated actively with God as the subject: 'God chose me to be' [CEV]. This verb means to assign someone to a particular function, task, or role [LN, TH]. The aorist tense indicates that this appointment took place at a specific point of time in the past [NIGTC]. The passive voice implies that the author of this appointment was either God or Christ [NIGTC]. It was God [My, NICNT, NTL, WBC], it was Christ [TH].

c. κῆρυξ (LN 33.259) (BAGD 2. p. 431): 'herald' [AB, BNTC, ECC, Lns, NTC, WBC; HCSB, NIV, NRSV, REB], 'preacher' [BAGD, Herm, LN; CEV, KJV, NASB, NET, NLT]. The noun is also translated as a verb: 'to proclaim' [TEV], 'to tell (the Good News)' [NCV], 'to spread (this Good News)' [GW], 'to preach (this message)' [LSA]. This noun denotes a person who preaches [LN].

QUESTION—What relationship is indicated by the prepositional phrase εἰς ὃ 'for which'?

The pronoun ὃ 'which' may refer to the phrase τὸ μαρτύριον 'the testimony' in the last clause of 2:6 or to the gospel message described in 2:5–6a, but there is no significant difference in meaning between them [WBC].

1. The preposition indicates that the *purpose* for his appointment to be a herald and an apostle was to proclaim τὸ μαρτύριον 'the testimony' (2:6) about the message of 2:5–6a [Alf, BNTC, My, NAC, NIBC, NICNT, NIGTC, NTC, TH, TNTC; CEV, GW, HCSB, NASB, NET, NIV, TEV]: *for which purpose I was appointed a herald and an apostle.* God appointed Paul to be a teacher to the Gentiles for the purpose of bearing testimony to all people [NIBC, NTC]. The proclamation of this universality of the gospel was the one object to which Paul's appointment as a herald and an apostle was directed [Alf]. As a final argument for God's universal purpose to save mankind, the apostle appeals to his own special role in the proclamation of the gospel. It was in order to spread abroad precisely this μαρτύριον 'testimony' about God's universal will to save people [BNTC, NIBC]. God appointed Paul to the office of apostleship for the purpose of carrying out his plan for the salvation of all men [NTC].

2. The preposition indicates that Paul's appointment to be a herald and an apostle was *with reference to* τὸ μαρτύριον 'the testimony' (2:6) [Lns, LSA, WBC]: *with reference to which testimony I was appointed a herald and an apostle.* God's universal purpose is to save all people and the truths of God's oneness, the oneness of the mediator, and the presentation of the mediator as the one who gave himself a ransom for all are the primary arguments in this section. Paul's relationship to the proclamation of this testimony is stated in a relative clause, and as a secondary argument it adds the final argument to all that Paul has said about God's universal desire to save all people and to have the churches pray for them

accordingly. [Lns]. This is a relative clause depending on τὸ μαρτύριον 'the testimony' n 2:6. But it also probably functions as the outcome or result of the declaration in 2:4 that God desires that all people be saved and come to the knowledge of the truth [Lns, LSA].

QUESTION—What is meant by the noun κῆρυξ 'herald'?

A herald is one who is sent to make a loud public announcement, and here his appointment was to be a herald and an apostle, sent forth to be a teacher of the Gentiles [Lns]. 'Herald' refers to a messenger who is given the task of proclaiming a message [NICNT]. This noun's basic meaning emphasizes the work of a herald as one who makes his message public, and although it is the gospel that is proclaimed here, 'to preach the gospel' lacks that emphasis [WBC]. The supreme King is sending out his herald to proclaim that there is peace through a ransom [NTC]. The noun κῆρυξ 'herald' seems to empha-size evangelism and exhortation, while the noun διδάσκαλος 'teacher' in the last part of the verse emphasizes instruction [NIGTC]. The word 'herald' pictures him as being an announcer of good news [NIBC]. This noun had acquired a distinctively Christian connotation, 'a preacher' [BAGD (2. p. 431), EGT, Herm, My, TH; CEV, KJV, NASB, NET, NLT]. The words κῆρυξ καὶ ἀπόστολος 'a herald and apostle' states that that Paul is a 'herald-apostle' or an 'apostolic herald' since each noun complements and illuminates the other [ECC] 'Apostle' distinguishes his status as a herald to be that of divine origin [NICNT].

(I-speak truth, I do- not -lie[a])

TEXT—Following λέγω 'I speak', some manuscripts add ἐν Χριστῷ 'in Christ'. GNT rejects this addition with an A decision, indicating that the text is certain. 'In Christ' is read by KJV.

LEXICON—a. pres. mid. (deponent = act.) indic. of ψεύδομαι (LN 33.253) (BAGD 1. p. 891): 'to lie, to tell a falsehood' [BAGD, LN]. The clause ἀλήθειαν λέγω οὐ ψεύδομαι 'I speak the truth, I do not lie' is translated 'I am speaking the truth; I am not lying' [WBC; similarly AB, Herm, Lns; KJV], 'I am telling the truth, I am not lying' [LSA, NTC; CEV, GW, HCSB, NASB, NCV, NET, NIV, NRSV], 'I am telling the truth and not telling lies' [BNTC], 'I am not lying; I am telling the truth' [TEV], 'this is no lie, it is the truth' [REB], 'it is a fact, though it sounds incredible' [ECC], 'I'm not exaggerating—just telling the truth' [NLT]. The verb ψεύδομαι 'to lie' denotes the communication of something that is false for the purpose of misleading someone [LN]. Here it is used in a formula of affirmation [BAGD].

QUESTION—How is this clause related to the context?

This clause is an emphatic parenthesis expressing corroboration [AB, BNTC, ECC, Herm, Lns, NAC, NIBC, NICNT, NTC, TC, TH, WBC; HCSB, KJV, NASB, NCV, NET, NIV, NLT, NRSV, REB]. This is done with great precision by the use of an antithetic parallelism in which one part expresses the thought positively, and the other negatively [TH]. Some say that this parenthesis must be regarded as being directed to the church and other readers, not for Timothy himself who already knew that Paul would not lie [NAC, NIBC, TNTC, WBC]. Since this letter was semi-public, it was added so that Timothy would have the strongest possible assertion of Paul's apostleship in order to combat those at Ephesus who denied this, and Timothy's own commission to work there depended upon the authenticity of Paul's office [TNTC]. Paul could bring no witnesses for the type of appointment he had received from God, so here he was certifying these instructions for all the churches so that no one would question them or Timothy's authority [Lns].

1. It is connected with the preceding clause 'for which I was appointed a herald and an apostle', so emphasizing Paul's authority [Alf, LSA, My, NIGTC; HCSB, KJV, NRSV, REB]. There were those in Ephesus who denied Paul's apostleship, and it is in reference to them that he makes this solemn affirmation [My, NIGTC]. The interpretation that this is to be taken with the following clause is not probable since Paul elsewhere, in nearly all of his epistles, begins them with an insistence upon the genuineness of his apostolic office [NIGTC]. This may be intended to highlight a contrast with the false teachers who had no such authority as Paul had [LSA]. Moreover, if Paul had meant this clause to be taken with the following clause, διδάσκαλος ἐθνῶν 'a teacher of the Gentiles', he would have preceded this clause with a καί 'and' [My].

2. It is connected with the following phrase διδάσκαλος ἐθνῶν 'a teacher of the Gentiles', thus emphasizing the Apostle's mission to the Gentiles [BNTC, EGT, Herm, ICC, Lns, NAC, NIBC, NICNT, TC, WBC]. It is better to take this clause as introducing the Apostle's claim to be a teacher of the Gentiles since he is writing about the universality of the gospel message [Lns, NIBC, NICNT, TC]. This affirmation is aimed at the apostle's claim to being a teacher of the Gentiles, unlike other contexts in which his apostolic office was questioned. This suggests that the false teachers were excluding the Gentiles from their offer of salvation [WBC]. It rounds out the argument began in 2:1 concerning the universality of the gospel for the Gentiles and so points forward to the phrase 'a teacher of the Gentiles'. It was Paul's conviction that apostleship and the gospel for the Gentiles were indissolubly bound together. This vehement parenthesis accentuates the writer's claim to have been assigned the mission to the Gentiles in contrast to the false teachers' exclusivist teachings [BNTC, NIBC]. The force of this comment indicates that this concept must have been contested [ICC]. This interpretation has the advantage of giving full value to the phrase 'a teacher of the Gentiles, etc.', and of making this whole verse the logical development of 2:5–6 [BNTC].

3. It is connected with the whole verse [ECC, NTC, TG, TH, TNTC; GW, NLT, TEV]. Some translations put this affirmation at the end of the verse [TG, TH; GW, NLT, TEV]. Grammatically, this exclamatory interjection could be taken with the preceding phrase or with the following, or with

both, but here it functions to separate the title κῆρυξ καὶ ἀπόστολος 'a herald and apostle' from the title διδάσκαλος ἐθνῶν 'a teacher of (the) Gentiles' [ECC]. It is only natural to assume that those who taught false doctrine in Ephesus would also begin to question Paul's apostolic authority, *especially* with reference to his appointment to proclaim to *Gentiles* the gospel of God's grace. This is the reason for the injection of this parenthesis into the text [NTC].

a-teacher[a] of-Gentiles[b] in[c] faith and truth.

LEXICON—a. διδάσκαλος (LN 33.243): 'a teacher' [AB, LN, Lns, WBC; KJV, NRSV], '(as) a teacher' [Herm; NASB], '(and) a teacher' [HCSB, NET, NIV], '(the Gentiles') teacher' [ECC], 'instructor' [LN]. This noun is also translated as a verb: '(I was appointed) to teach' [BNTC, LSA; CEV, GW, NCV, NLT, TNTC], 'to instruct' [REB]. This noun denotes a person who provides instruction [LN]. 'Teacher' is in apposition to both 'herald' and 'apostle', so 'a teacher' is correct [Lns].

  b. ἔθνος (LN 11.37): The plural form of this noun is translated 'Gentiles' [AB, ECC, Herm, Lns, LSA, WBC; CEV, HCSB, KJV, NASB, NET, NIV, NLT, NRSV, REB], 'those who are not Jews' [NCV], 'people who are not Jewish' [GW], 'the nations' [BNTC], 'heathens, pagans' [LN]. Used in the plural form, this noun designates those who do not belong either to the Jewish or the Christian faith [LN, NIGTC].

  c. ἐν (LN 89.84, 90.23): This preposition indicates content as a means of specifying a particular referent: 'concerning, with respect to, with reference to, about, in' [LN (90.23)], or it indicates the manner in which an event occurs: 'with' [LN (89.84)]. The prepositional phrase ἐν πίστει καὶ ἀληθείᾳ 'in faith and truth' [AB, BNTC, ECC, Herm, Lns, WBC; HCSB, NASB, NET, NRSV] is also translated 'in faith and verity' [KJV], 'about faith and truth' [CEV, GW, NLT], 'what they should believe and what is true' [LSA], 'to believe and to know the truth' [NCV], 'in the true faith' [REB], '(a teacher) of the true faith' [NIV].

QUESTION—How is this phrase related to what precedes?

This phrase carries the chief emphasis in the sentence [BNTC, My, NIBC, NICNT, NTC]. It was specifically for the purpose of giving testimony to *all* men, that Paul was appointed to be a teacher of the Gentiles [My, NIBC, WBC]. The fact that God has chosen him to teach the gospel to Gentiles and not just Jews, is clinching proof that God wishes to save all men [BNTC], and therefore the church has the obligation to pray for *all* men [BNTC].

QUESTION—How is διδάσκαλος 'teacher' related to the preceding designations κῆρυξ καὶ ἀπόστολος 'herald and apostle'?

  1. The three terms belong in a series that describes three offices: herald, apostle, and teacher [NAC, NTIC; HCSB, NET, NIV]: *I was appointed to be a herald, an apostle, and a teacher.* As a *herald*, Paul proclaimed the truth, as an *apostle* he had a divine commission, but he also had an office

that the other apostles did not have, that of being a *teacher of the Gentiles* [NAC].

2. The terms *herald* and *teacher* describe functions of the office of *apostle* [ICC, NICNT, NIGTC, NTL, TG]: *I was appointed to be an apostle who heralds the gospel and teaches the Gentiles.* Paul is not enumerating three different offices, since elsewhere Paul considers his office of apostle to include both proclamation and teaching [NIGTC]. 'Herald' and 'teacher' sum up the task of an 'apostle', and perhaps these two categories are to be distinguished by their purposes and audiences [ICC, NICNT]. God appointed Paul to the office of apostle, while the activities of *herald* and *teacher* embrace and interpret that office [NTL]. The idea is that God made Paul an apostle to proclaim the Good News to the Gentiles and to teach them the true faith [TG].

3. The terms *herald* and *apostle* are two offices, while *teacher* is a function of both of the first two [BNTC, Herm, Lns, My, NTC, TH; CEV, GW, NASB, NLT, REB, TEV]: *I was appointed to be a herald and an apostle to teach the Gentiles.* This interpretation is supported by the fact that *herald* and *apostle* are coordinate nouns with the conjunction καί 'and' connecting them, while there is no conjunction before the noun *teacher* [TH]. The conjunction καί 'and' does not join 'teacher' to the phrase 'herald and apostle' since 'teacher' is in apposition to that preceding phrase. So Paul is saying that he was the Lord's herald and apostle *as* a teacher of the Gentiles [Lns]. The term *teacher* is in apposition to 'a herald and an apostle', thus giving a further definition of his commission [My].

QUESTION—What relationship is indicated by ἐν 'in'?

1. The preposition ἐν 'in' specifies what Paul was to teach [EGT, Lns, LSA, NIBC, NIGTC, TC, TG, TH, WBC; CEV, GW, NCV, NIV, NLT, REB; probably Alf, My, NAC, NTC, TNTC which describe the preposition as the *realm* or *sphere* of the teaching]: *I was appointed to teach the Gentiles about faith and truth.* The awkwardness of adding two additional objective genitives to διδάσκαλος 'teacher' after having named personal objects with it by the objective genitive ἐθνῶν 'Gentiles' led Paul to use the preposition ἐν 'in' with the meaning 'in connection with' [Lns].

2. The preposition ἐν 'in' indicates the manner in which Paul was to teach [ECC, NCBC, NICNT]: *I was appointed to teach the Gentiles with sincerity and truth.* He taught them in a faithful and true manner [NCBC].

QUESTION—What is meant by πίστει 'faith' and ἀληθείᾳ 'truth'?

1. Both 'faith' and 'truth' are objective, denoting the content of Paul's teaching [Alf, EGT, Lns, LSA, NIBC, TC, TG, TH, WBC; CEV, GW, NIV, NLT, REB]: *to teach the Gentiles about faith and about truth.* Since both of these nouns are often used objectively throughout the Pastoral Epistles to describe the gospel, it is preferable to take this interpretation [WBC]. The fact that these nouns occur without an article is no objection

to this interpretation because common Christian terms are used without the definite article in these epistles [EGT].

1.1 They are understood as separate terms [Alf, EGT, Lns, LSA, TC, WBC; CEV, GW]: *a teacher of Gentiles about the faith and the truth.* These nouns denote the content of Paul's teaching—what they should believe and what is true [LSA]. According to this interpretation, ἀληθείᾳ 'truth' must be explained in light of the phrase 'to come to the knowledge of the truth' in 2:4 [Alf, Lns, TC], 'the truth'; being the truth of the gospel [Alf, Lns], and then it is only natural to understand πίστει 'faith' to be 'the faith' [Alf, TC].

1.2 Although 'and' makes them grammatically coordinate, they form a hendiadys in which one of the nouns is subordinate, not coordinate, to the other [NIBC, TG, TH; NIV, REB]: *a teacher of the Gentiles in respect to the true faith.* The two nouns form one idea with ἀληθείᾳ 'true' modifying πίστει 'faith': 'the true faith', or 'the true teachings about Jesus' [TH].

2. Πίστει 'faith' is subjective, while ἀληθείᾳ 'truth' is objective [My, NAC, NIGTC, NTC; NCV]: *to teach the Gentiles to believe and to teach them about truth.* Πίστει 'faith' has a subjective relationship and ἀληθείᾳ is 'truth', the objective benefit received in faith [My]. 'Faith' refers to the Gentiles' faith [LSA, NAC, NIGTC, NTC; NCV], their subjective response to the truth of the gospel [NAC, NTC]. What Paul means is that he and his message were used by God as the means to bring to the hearts and minds of the Gentiles a living faith in the truth of the gospel [NTC].

3. Both πίστει and ἀληθείᾳ are subjective with the meanings 'faithfulness' and 'truthfulness', and they denote the *manner* in which Paul imparted his teaching [ECC, NCBC, NICNT]: *a teacher of the Gentiles, teaching them sincerely and truthfully.* It is best to take the phrase with an adjectival sense, meaning that Paul was a teacher who was *trustworthy* and *sincere* [ECC].

DISCOURSE UNIT 2:8–3:1a [ECC, Herm, NTL]. The topic is by whom and how prayer and worship is to be offered [ECC], men and women at prayer [NTL], prayer by men and women [Herm].

DISCOURSE UNIT 2:8–15 [AB, ICC, NAC, NIBC, NICNT, TH, WBC; HCSB]. The topic is the proper demeanor in prayer [NIBC], gender roles in worship [AB], instructions to men and women [HCSB], the behavior of men and women in the public worship assembly [NICNT], men and women at prayer and in the church meeting [ICC], holy living by men and women [NAC], the place of women in worship [TH], questions about disruption and leadership [WBC].

DISCOURSE UNIT 2:8 [ECC, NAC, NCBC]. The topic is the resumption of the theme of prayer [NCBC], prayer and worship by men [ECC], an appeal to men [NAC].

2:8 **Therefore**[a] **I-want**[b] **the men in every place**[c] **to pray**[d]

LEXICON—a. οὖν (LN 89.50): 'therefore' [AB, LN, LSA, WBC; HCSB, KJV, NASB, REB], 'consequently, accordingly, so then' [LN], 'so' [BNTC, LN; NCV, NET], 'then' [LN, Lns, NTC; NRSV], 'now' [ECC], 'as far as (prayer is concerned)' [Herm], not explicit [CEV, GW, NIV, NLT, TEV]. This conjunction indicates result, often implying the conclusion of a process of reasoning [LN (89.50)].

  b. pres. mid./pass. (deponent = act.) indic. of βούλομαι (LN 25.3): 'to want' [AB; all versions except KJV, NRSV, REB], 'to desire' [LN, LSA, WBC; NRSV], 'to wish' [Herm], 'to will' [NTC; KJV], 'to intend that' [Lns]. The verb is translated 'it is my desire' [REB], 'it is my wish that' [BNTC], 'my wish is that' [ECC].

  c. τόπος (LN 80.1): 'place' [LN]. The phrase ἐν παντὶ τόπῳ 'in every place' [AB, BNTC, Lns, NTC, WBC; HCSB, NASB, NET, NRSV] is also translated 'everywhere' [Herm; CEV, GW, KJV, NCV, NIV, REB], 'in every church service' [TEV], 'in every place of worship' [ECC; NLT], 'in every place the men pray' [LSA].

  d. aorist mid./pass. (deponent = act) infin. of προσεύχομαι (LN 33.178): 'to pray' [AB, BNTC, LN, LSA, WBC; all versions except GW, NIV, NRSV], 'to offer prayer' [NTC], 'to offer prayers' [GW], 'to speak to God' [LN]. This verb is also translated as a phrase: 'to lift up in prayer' [NIV], 'that prayers be said (by men)' [NRSV], 'to do the praying' [Lns], 'as far as prayer is concerned' [Herm], to take part in the prayer [ECC]. This verb means to speak to God or make requests of him [LN]. This verb includes all of the forms of prayer mentioned in 2:1: requests, prayers, intercessions, and thanksgivings [NICNT, NIGTC, WBC].

QUESTION—What relationship is indicated by οὖν 'therefore'?

  1. This indicates the beginning of a new discussion [Alf, BNTC, EGT, Herm, ICC, Lns, My, NAC, NIBC, NTC, NTL, TC, TH, WBC]. Παρακαλῶ οὖν 'I urge therefore' is the initial phrase of section 2:1–7 (which has the theme of the universality of the offer of salvation), and that phrase is paralleled here with Βούλομαι οὖν 'I want therefore', the initial phrase for section 2:8–15 (which has the theme of preventing disruptions in the church), so that both sections mention prayer as a beginning point [WBC]. The subject of prayer in 2:1–2 is now resumed with further instructions about it [Alf, BNTC, EGT, Herm, ICC, LSA, My, NAC, NTC, NTL, TH]. The previous section had dealt with the proper scope of prayer, especially that it is to be offered universally for all people, and now Paul goes on to the attitudes appropriate to prayer [BNTC, NAC]. The sense of the verse is this: 'therefore, while we are on the subject, as the people gather to pray, be sure that it is for prayer [NIBC]. However, the instructions concerning women in 2:9–15 go beyond the women being silent in worship and deals with their behavior in regard to the congregation, their husbands, and society in general [TH].

2. This indicates a conclusion to the previous discussion [NIGTC; NET]: *since God wants the church to pray for all people, therefore it should pray in the proper manner.* It is a summary exhortation and closes the preceding paragraph so that 2:9 begins a new paragraph [NIGTC].

QUESTION—What is meant by the verb βούλομαι 'I want'?

This verb expresses not only Paul's desire but, coming from an apostle, it has the force of a command [AB, BNTC, ECC, EGT, Herm, ICC, Lns, My, NAC, NCBC, NICNT, NIGTC, NTC, TC, TG, TH, TNTC, WBC]. The verb is imperatival in force [ICC, WBC]. This is a courteous and polite, yet firm, expression of an authoritative command [BNTC, TH].

QUESTION—What is meant by saying that τοὺς ἄνδρας 'the men' should pray in the manner he describes?

The definite article τούς 'the' indicates that ἄνδρας 'men' denotes the male sex [AB, Alf, Lns, NAC, NTL, TG, WP], especially since the noun ἄνδρας 'men' denotes men as distinct from women [Lns, NCBC, NIGTC, TH]. It stands in contrast to γυναῖκας 'women' in the following verse [ECC, Lns, My, NIGTC, TNTC]. Paul is speaking of public congregational prayers here [Lns, My, NAC, NIGTC, NTC, TH, WBC].

1. Paul's directive meant that *only* the men are to pray [AB, BNTC, ECC, EGT, Lns, NCBC, NIGTC, NTC, NTIC, TNTC, WP]. The men only, and no women at all, were to do the praying in the public worship services [Lns]. The men are specified because it was the men who led the worship service [NCBC, NIGTC, NTIC, TC]. This followed the practice of the Jewish synagogues [ECC, Lns, NTC]. Men went to the synagogue to learn, but the women were there only to listen [NTC, TC]. Although women would be present in public worship, they should pray silently [NTC]. The fact that the sex of the persons who pray is stressed suggests that the conventions of the Jewish synagogue had been breaking down in the congregations at Ephesus [BNTC].

2. Paul's directive that the men are to do the praying must be understood in a nonrestrictive sense [NAC, NIBC, TH, WBC]. Paul is not saying that only men should pray, but it is possible that the analogy of the Jewish synagogues would suggest that only the men could offer public prayer and this may have carried over into the worship services of the church. Or anger and quarreling were reflected more prominently in the prayers of the men than in those of the women [WBC]. The false teachings were engendering controversies attended by anger and strife (1:4). The men are mentioned because they were especially affected in this particular way. With the women, on the other hand, the effect of the false teachings can be found in 5:3–16 and 2 Tim. 3:5–9, and the instructions that follow in 2:9–15 seem to address their problems [NIBC]. So in this verse Paul is not saying that the men must pray, nor that only the men should pray, but that when the men do pray, it should be without getting into arguments [NAC, NIBC].

3. Paul's directive is addressed to every believer, not just the men: 'I want everyone everywhere to lift innocent hands toward heaven and pray...' [CEV].

QUESTION—What is meant by ἐν παντὶ τόπῳ 'in every place'?

1. It refers to every house-church in and around the city of Ephesus [AB, Alf, NIBC, NTC, TH]: *in every place where you Ephesians pray*. This is a *local* command respecting prayer [Alf]. This phrase is best explained by the fact that the Ephesian church, like many others, consisted of different assemblies meeting in several house-churches [AB, NIBC, NTC, TH]. It means 'wherever *you* meet for worship' [TH].

2. It refers to wherever Christian worship services were held at any location [BNTC, ECC, EGT, ICC, Lns, My, NAC, NICNT, NIGTC, TC, WBC; REB, TEV]: *wherever Christians meet to worship*. This concerns prayer in every *meeting place of worship* [ECC]. Or, the place is *every city or town* where public worship is held [Lns]. While 2:8–15 is directed to a specific historical situation that existed in Ephesus, Paul gives no explicit indication that his solutions to the problems involving anger mixed with prayer, immodest and extravagant dress, and the problem of church leadership would be limited to just the worship services in Ephesus [NAC, WBC]. The directions apply to every church without exception, and Paul makes no allowance for conditions that may be peculiar to any particular locality [EGT]. This passage speaks only of the prayer of the assembled congregation, therefore 'in every place' cannot refer to all the various places an individual Christian might pray, and Paul's intention is to have these instructions carried out in all congregations everywhere [Lns, My].

raising-up[a] holy[c] hands without anger[c] and disputing/doubt.[d]

LEXICON—a. pres. act. participle of ἐπαίρω (LN **15.105**) (BAGD 1. p. 281): 'to raise up' [BAGD, LN], 'to raise' [BNTC, Herm], 'to lift up' [BAGD, ECC, Lns, NTC; HCSB, KJV, NASB, NET, NIV, NRSV, REB], 'to hold up' [BAGD]. The phrase ἐπαίροντας ὁσίους χεῖρας 'raising up holy hands' [**LN**] is also translated 'by lifting up holy hands' [WBC], 'lifting up their hands in a holy manner' [NCV], 'with their hands lifted up with piety' [AB], 'they should raise their hands in prayer' [GW], 'with holy hands lifted up to God' [NLT], 'to lift innocent hands toward heaven' [CEV], 'men who are dedicated to God and can lift their hands in prayer' [TEV], 'whose hands they raise while they pray are not used to sin' [LSA]. This verb means to cause something to move up [LN].

b. ὅσιος (LN53.46, 88.24) (BAGD 1.a. p. 585): 'holy' [BAGD, BNTC, ECC, Herm, Lns, NTC, WBC; HCSB, KJV, NASB, NET, NIV, NLT, NRSV], 'consecrated, devout' [BAGD, LN], 'godly, dedicated' [LN], 'pious' [BAGD], 'innocent' [CEV], 'not used to sin' [LSA], not explicit [GW]. Instead of modifying 'hands', this is translated as an adverb modifying the verb 'raising up': 'in a holy manner' [NCV], 'with piety' [AB], 'with a pure intention' [REB]; or modifying 'men': 'men who are dedicated to God' [TEV]. This adjective pertains to something being dedicated or consecrated to the service of God [LN].

c. ὀργή (LN **88.173**) (BAGD 1. p. 578): 'anger' [AB, BAGD, BNTC, Herm, **LN**, WBC; HCSB, NCV, NET, NIV, NRSV, REB, TEV], 'wrath' [BAGD, ECC, Lns, NTC; KJV, NASB]. The phrase χωρὶς ὀργῆς 'without anger' is translated 'free from anger' [NLT], 'without being angry' [CEV], 'who are not angry with anyone' [LSA], 'after putting aside their anger' [GW].

d. διαλογισμός (LN 31.37) (BAGD 2. p. 186): 'dispute' [BAGD; NET, NIV], 'dissension' [NASB], 'argument' [AB, BAGD, LN (33.446); HCSB, NCV, NRSV, REB, TEV], 'controversy' [NLT], 'quarrelsomeness' [BNTC], 'strife' [Herm], 'evil deliberation' [NTC], 'resentment' [ECC], 'wrong consideration' [Lns], 'doubt' [BAGD, LN (31.37); KJV]. This noun is also translated as a verb phrase: 'disputing' [NIV], 'arguing' [WBC], 'arguing with each other' [CEV], '(after putting aside) any quarrels they have with anyone' [GW], 'who do not doubt that God will answer' [LSA]. This noun denotes doubt about the truth or certainty of something [LN (31.37)], or it denotes an argument over a difference of opinion [LN (33.446)].

QUESTION—What relationship is indicated by the use of the participial phrase ἐπαίροντας ὁσίους χεῖρας *raising up* holy hands'?

The use of the participle ἐπαίροντας 'raising up' indicates the manner in which they are to pray [My, NIGTC, WBC]. The apostle is laying stress, not on the fact that men are to pray, but on *how* they are to pray [My, WBC]. It introduces the ethical conditions to be met by the one who prays [ICC]. The gesture of raising the hands here is incidental to the qualifying adjective ὁσίους 'holy' [TNTC]. The emphasis is placed upon the adjective ὁσίους 'holy', with the following phrase 'without anger and disputing' giving a further explanation [WBC]. The focus is on the proper inner attitude of the man who raises his hands in prayer [BNTC, EGT, ICC, Lns, NAC, NIGTC, NTC, TH, TNTC, WBC]. The position in prayer is mentioned as a matter of fact, and it is not a part of the command about how to pray [TH]. This phrase 'lifting up holy hands' is not meant to require a particular gesture that is appropriate to prayer, rather the phrase merely avoids a repetition of the verb προσέρχεσθαι 'to pray', and the point is that the men who are to conduct the public worship of the church must be upright men who have hands that are holy [EGT].

QUESTION—What is the significance of praying with upraised hands?

The normal position in prayer was to stand with arms outstretched [BNTC, NAC, NTC, TG, TH, WBC], with the palms being turned upwards [BNTC, NTC, TG, WBC]. Raising our hands signifies the offering of the instruments we use in our daily lives [NIGTC], or it pictures us as expectantly waiting for a gift from above [NTC]. It indicates that one is pleading to God who is located above us [Lns]. Lifting the hands in prayer indicates the person's full commitment to God [ECC]. This was the customary way in which prayers were offered at worship services [BNTC, ICC, My, TNTC]. It is not a command to conform to a certain posture when praying, it merely mentions the mode of prayer practiced in the early church [NAC].

QUESTION—What is meant by ὁσίους χεῖρας 'holy hands'?

The phrase 'holy hands' contains a *metonymy* in which 'hands' stand for the person, and since raised hands suggest a person in prayer, this can be translated 'pray with their hands lifted up with piety' [AB]. Or, this is a *synecdoche* in which a pertinent part of a person stands for the whole person in prayer since it is the person, not his hands, who is to be holy [ICC, TH], and this can be translated 'These must be men who are pure in that they live lives acceptable to God, and when they lift up their hands to pray, they must do so without having anger in their hearts or quarreling with others' [TH]. They are hands that have not been used to sin [Alf, Lns, LSA, My], and are unpolluted from previous crimes [Lns]. This is the spiritual and moral sense of 'holy', not a sense of something forbidden, or taboo. Here 'holy' refers to people who are set apart to serve God, who do not do any kind of evil, and who lead a life that is acceptable to God [TH]. In the NT, human holiness refers to being dedicated to God, and spiritual purity may also be meant [TG]. The adjective ὁσίους 'holy' means that a person's conduct is appropriate and acceptable to God [WBC], and is above reproach [TC]. The way they lived would show their passion to please God [NAC]. The physical lifting of the hands was important in the Jewish act of prayer, and the physical purity of the hands was originally a prerequisite for the one who approached God (Ex. 30:19-21). The 'holy hands' in Judaism, would include at least the implication of 'hands ceremonially washed', alluding to the practice of washing the hands before entering the sanctuary (Ex. 30:19-21), and this act came to symbolize the inner purity expressed by that external act of cultic purity [ICC, NICNT, WBC].

QUESTION—What is meant by χωρίς 'without' anger and disputing/doubt?

The preposition χωρίς 'without' means 'without *expressing* or *practicing* anger and disputing/doubt' [ICC]. Paul defines what he means by 'holy hands' with the following phrase 'without anger and strife' [AB, Herm], so the stress really falls upon this following phrase rather than upon the formulaic phrase 'raising holy hands' [Herm]. This clause is at least *one aspect* of what is meant by holiness [ICC], but it does not include all of its other aspects, such as those mentioned in the following chapters [NIGTC]. This is the attitude they must have in order to pray with their hands lifted up with piety [AB]. This is a necessary preparation of their hearts that they must make before coming to church [NTC]. This means that the men who pray must be those who show by their lives that they are not characterized by an angry disposition, nor do they quarrel with others. But it could imply that before taking part in the prayers, they should be made pure by being forgiven and cleansed by confessing their sins related to anger and quarreling [TH].

Raising their hands in public prayer is futile if their hearts are not free of ill-will [BNTC]. All wrong thoughts of any kind must be removed from the heart when they pray [Lns]. This instruction to the men is also relevant to the women [ICC].

QUESTION—What is meant by ὀργή 'anger' here?

Anger is the presence of indignation against someone else [NAC, NTC]. Their thoughts must not be filled with anger as they pray [Herm, TG]. They must not have an angry or wrathful attitude towards another person [NIGTC], and if it should arise, it must be removed by forgiving that person who provoked the anger [ICC, NIGTC]. When one is angry, he cannot have the patience, kindness, and forgiveness that are necessary in maintaining and fostering relationships [NICNT]. Anger in one's heart make him unfit for all aspects of worship, as do wrong thoughts of any kind [Lns].

QUESTION—Does the noun διαλογισμός mean 'disputing' or 'doubt' or something else?

This noun can mean either 'doubt' or 'dispute' [NIGTC]. In the NT διαλογισμός denotes thoughts or intentions, even evil intentions (Matt. 15:19), or it denotes doubts (Luke 24:38), or a dispute (Luke 9:46) [AB].

1. It means 'disputing' [AB, BNTC, Herm, ICC, NAC, NCBC, NIBC, NICNT, NIGTC, TC, TG, TH, TNTC, WBC; all translations except KJV]. They should have no desire to argue [TG]. The reference to disputes has to do with the quarrels and controversy that the teaching of the false teachers aroused (1:6–7) [NAC, NIBC, TH, WBC]. This phrase is both an appeal to the men not to imitate the false teachers (1:3) and a subtle denunciation of them [TH]. Because it is linked here with 'anger', it has the sense of 'dispute' or 'argument' rather than 'doubt' [Herm, ICC, NIGTC]. The hostile attitude of anger develops into hostile actions [NICNT]. The fact that the whole context, including the following section relating to women, is related to one's attitude towards others and one's impact upon them, makes it very likely that this refers to disputes rather than to doubt [NIGTC].

2. It means 'doubting' [EGT, LSA; KJV]. 'Anger' is directed against other people, while doubt is directed against God [EGT, LSA]. This refers to doubting that God will answer their prayers [LSA]. The phrase 'without anger and doubt' indicates two conditions that are necessary for effectual prayer: freedom from irritation toward one's fellow-men and confidence toward God [EGT].

3. It denotes any kind of 'evil thought' [ECC, Lns, My, NTC] directed against one's fellow man [Lns, My, NTC], and also against God [Lns]: *without anger or any evil thoughts against anyone*. Διαλογισμοῦ should not be translated by either 'doubt' or 'disputing' [Lns, My]. Here it indicates an evil deliberation against another, such as a deliberation going on within the mind concerning what kind of evil deed one will commit against his neighbor [NTC]. The close connection of 'wrong thoughts' with 'anger' indicates that the word not only has a bad sense here, but that

it is directed against one's neighbor [My]. It involves the resentment that arose from being criticized by other members of the congregation [ECC].

DISCOURSE UNIT 2:9–3:1a [ECC]. The topic is prayer and worship by women.

DISCOURSE UNIT 2:9–15 [NAC, NCBC, NIGTC, TNTC; NASB, NET]. The topic is an appeal to women [NAC], the status and demeanor of Christian women [TNTC], instructions for women [NIGTC; NASB], the conduct of women [NET], how women should behave and the scriptural authority for this advice [NCBC].

2:9 Similarly[a] also (I want)[b] women to-adorn/dress[c] themselves in proper[d] clothes/behavior[e] with decency[f] and sensibility,[g]

TEXT: Some manuscripts omit καί 'also' following ὡσαύτως 'similarly'. GNT places it in brackets in its text, indicating that the word may be regarded as part of the text, but it is not completely certain. 'Also' is omitted by BNTC, EGT, Lns, My, NIGTC, NTC; CEV, GW, NASB, NET, NLT, REB.

LEXICON—a. ὡσαύτως (LN 64.16) (BAGD p. 899): 'similarly, likewise' [BAGD], 'in the same way' [BAGD, LN], 'just as, in like manner' [LN]. The phrase ὡσαύτως καί 'similarly also' is translated 'similarly' [BNTC, NTC], 'similarly, I also (wish)' [ECC], 'in like manner also' [KJV], 'likewise also' [AB, WBC], 'and likewise' [Herm], 'likewise' [Lns; NASB, NET], 'also' [HCSB, NCV, NIV, NRSV, TEV], 'and (I want)' [LSA; NLT], not explicit [CEV, GW, REB]. This adverb indicates a similarity [LN].

b. (I want): The supplied verb is 'I want' [GW, NASB, NIV, NLT, TEV], 'I wish' [ECC], 'I desire' [LSA, WBC; NRSV], 'I intend' [Lns], 'I will that' [KJV], 'I would like' [CEV], '(the women) are to' [HCSB, NET], '(women) should' [AB, Herm; NCV], '(women) must' [REB].

c. pres. act. infin. of κοσμέω (LN 79.12) (BAGD 2.a.α. p. 445): 'to adorn, to decorate' [BAGD, LN], 'to beautify' [LN]. The phrase ἐν καταστολῇ κοσμίῳ...κοσμεῖν ἑαυτάς 'to adorn/dress themselves in proper clothes/ behavior' is translated 'to adorn themselves with proper clothing' [NASB], 'should adorn themselves in respectable attire' [WBC], 'adorn themselves in adorning dress/attire' [Lns, NTC], 'adorn themselves in modest apparel' [KJV], 'adorn themselves in appropriate dress' [AB], 'to show their beauty by dressing in appropriate clothes' [GW], 'to make themselves attractive in a becoming costume' [ECC], 'must dress in becoming manner' [REB], 'to dress themselves in modest clothing' [HCSB], 'to dress modestly' [NIV], 'to dress in suitable apparel' [NET], 'wear suitable clothing' [LSA], 'should wear proper clothes' [NCV], 'to be modest in their appearance' [NLT], '(do likewise,) in modest deportment' [Herm]. The longer phrase 'to adorn themselves in proper/modest deportment/clothes with decency and propriety' is translated 'in becoming costume, should adorn themselves modestly and chastely' [BNTC], 'should dress themselves in a proper manner with modesty and good sense' or 'women should be modest and sensible about the clothes they wear and dress properly' [LN (49.12)], 'to be modest and sensible about their clothes and to dress properly' [TEV], 'should dress themselves modestly and decently in suitable clothing' [NRSV], 'to wear modest and sensible clothes' [CEV]. This verb means to cause something to be beautiful by decorating it [LN].

d. κόσμιος (LN **66.10**, 88.48) (BAGD 2. p. 445): 'proper' [LN (66.10); NASB, NCV], 'appropriate' [AB; GW, NLT], 'respectable' [WBC], 'suitable' [LN (66.10), LSA; NET, NRSV], 'modest' [BAGD, Herm, LN (88.48); CEV, HCSB, KJV, NLT], 'well-ordered, moderate, becoming' [LN (88.48)], 'in adorning (dress/attire)' [Lns, NTC], 'in a becoming (costume)' [BNTC, ECC], 'in becoming manner' [REB]. This adjective is also translated as an adverb modifying 'to dress': 'properly' [TEV], 'modestly' [NIV]. This adjective refers to being attractive in respect to what is proper and suitable [LN (66.10)], or being modest in the sense of being moderate and well-ordered [LN (88.48)].

e. καταστολή (LN **49.12**) (BAGD p. 419): 'clothes' [CEV, GW, NCV, NRSV], 'clothing' [LN (66.10), LSA; HCSB, NASB, NRSV], 'apparel' [LN (88.48); KJV, NET], 'attire' [NTC, WBC], 'costume' [BNTC, ECC], 'dress' [AB, Lns], 'manner of dress' [LN], 'deportment' [BAGD, Herm], 'appearance' [NLT]. This noun is also translated as a verb: 'to dress' [NIV, TEV], 'to dress in (becoming manner)' [REB]. This noun denotes clothing as a symbol of behavior [LN]. It refers to outward deportment expressed by one's clothing [BAGD].

f. αἰδώς (LN 88.49) (BAGD 1. p. 22): 'modesty' [BAGD, LN]. The phrase μετὰ αἰδοῦς 'with decency' [HCSB, NIV] is also translated 'with modesty' [AB, Lns, NTC, WBC; NET], 'with shamefacedness' [KJV], 'with chastity' [Herm], 'with (sensible) discretion' [ECC], 'that are modest' [GW] 'that show respect' [NCV], '(they should wear) decent (clothing)' [NLT], 'to be modest (about their clothes)' [LSA; TEV], '(adorn/dress themselves) modestly' [BNTC; NASB, NRSV, REB]. This noun is conflated with the preceding adjective κοσμίῳ 'modest': '(wear) modest clothes' [CEV]. This noun denotes the quality of modesty and it implies that because of that modesty the person is respected [LN].

g. σωφροσύνη (LN 88.93) (BAGD 2. p. 802): 'sensibility' [LN], 'good judgment' [BAGD], 'good sense' [NTC; HCSB], 'discretion' [AB], 'prudence' [Herm], 'sobriety' [Lns; KJV], 'self control' [NCV, NET], 'moderation' [BAGD, LN, WBC], 'propriety' [NIV]. This noun is also translated as an adjective: '(that are) respectable' [GW], '(be) sensible (about their clothes)' [LSA; TEV], 'with sensible (discretion)' [ECC], '(wear) sensible (clothes)' [CEV], '(wear) appropriate (clothing)' [NLT]; or as an adverb modifying the verb 'dress': 'soberly' [REB] 'decently' [NRSV], 'chastely' [BNTC], 'discreetly' [NASB]. This noun denotes behaving oneself in a sensible manner, and it implies that the person doing so possesses a thoughtful awareness of what is in her best interest [LN (88.93)]. See this word at 2:13.

QUESTION—What verb is modified by the adverb ὡσαύτως 'similarly'?

Grammatically, 2:9 is dependent upon 2:8 since 2:9 does not contain a finite verbal form [WBC]. The adverb ὡσαύτως 'similarly' is used to introduce another of the apostle's regulations [EGT]. If just βούλομαι 'I want' is carried over from 2:8, 'similarly I want' would mean that Paul had instructions for the women just as he had instructions for the men. However, if both the verbs βούλομαι 'I want' and προσεύχεσθαι 'to pray' are carried over from 2:8, it would mean that the women should engage in prayer the same way as the men were to engage in prayer [NIGTC].

1. The subject of public worship and prayer is continued, but now with reference to the conduct of women, and the verb βούλομαι 'I want' is carried over from 2:8 [BNTC, ECC, Herm, My, NAC, NTC, NTIC, TH, WP]: *similarly I also have directions for the women attending public worship meetings: I want them to do the following.* The loosely attached adverb ὡσαύτως 'similarly' and the phrase 'to learn in silence' (2:11) both indicate that Paul is still on the subject of public prayers and that he is laying down rules for women's dress and deportment at these meetings [BNTC]. Of course, the guidelines for their behavior in worship services would also apply to their behavior elsewhere [NAC, TH, WP].

2. The subject of public prayer is continued, but now with reference to the conduct of women and *both* the verb βούλομαι 'I want' and the verb προσεύχεσθαι 'to pray' are carried over from 2:8 so that everything that was said in 2:8 concerning the men is also here applied to the women, i.e., that women in the Christian assemblies, in contrast to Jewish and pagan practices, should participate in vocal public prayer in precisely the same manner as the men [ECC, Herm, ICC]: *similarly, I want the women to pray like I told the men to pray, and I also want them to adorn themselves, etc.* The construction is peculiar in that the instructions about the behavior of the women are not limited only to when they are at prayer [ICC].

3. The subject now encompasses the general deportment and dress of women, and the verb βούλομαι 'I want' is to be carried over from 2:8 [Alf, EGT, Lns, LSA, NICNT, NIGTC, TC, TNTC, WBC]: *similarly I have directions for the women: I want them to do the following.* The immediate context continues to be the disruptive effects of women's dress in church meetings, yet with 2:10 there is a shift to the topic of good deeds, which Paul sees as having ramifications for other social contexts [WBC]. That the apostle has widened his discussion here from public prayer is seen in the fact that he would hardly be concerned for the modesty and discretion of women *only* in the public worship services, and the 'good works' he mentions in 2:10 could hardly refer only to those done in the public worship services. Then, too, the conclusion of this section in 2:15, 'in faith and love and sanctification with prudence', certainly has in view the Christian life in its widest extent [NIGTC]. The

apostle is calling attention to the general duties of women, rather than just the single point of their conduct in public worship, though the subject of public worship did lead to this topic and has not entirely disappeared from his thoughts. [Alf].

QUESTION—What is meant by the phrase κοσμεῖν ἑαυτάς 'to adorn themselves'?

1. The phrase means 'to adorn, to beautify' themselves [AB, Alf, BAGD (2.a.α. p. 445), BNTC, ECC, EGT, Herm, ICC, LN, Lns, My, NICNT, NIGTC, NTC, TH, WBC; GW, KJV, NASB]: *I want women to adorn themselves with proper clothing.* The scope of κοσμεῖν 'to adorn' is larger than just 'to dress'. The verb was used metaphorically, for instance, to speak of slaves adorning the doctrine of God by their submission to their masters (Titus 2:10). This metaphorical extension is significant in the present text where its force is to show that Paul's primary focus is not so much on what women wear, though this is included, but on what their spiritual priorities are. Paul wants them to be adorned with good deeds rather than being adorned with expensive clothes. Thus this flexible usage of κοσμεῖν 'to adorn' prepares for the shift of emphasis that becomes explicit in 2:10 [WBC]. Their beauty should be shown by what they do, not by wearing expensive clothes or jewelry or having fancy hairstyles [GW]. Adornment to make themselves beautiful can be connected to the following verse with the idea that their adornment is doing good works. Or, it can be connected to the following part of this verse with the idea that their adornment is not to include elaborate hairstyles, etc. [ICC].

2. It means 'to dress themselves' or 'to wear' [LSA, NTL; CEV, HCSB, NCV, NET, NIV, NLT, NRSV, REB, TEV]: *I want women to dress themselves in proper clothing.* Used of women, the verb usually means to dress or attire oneself [NTL].

QUESTION—What is meant by adorning or dressing themselves ἐν καταστολῇ κοσμίῳ 'in proper/modest/adorning clothes/behavior'?

1. The phrase describes the type of clothes women should wear:

1.1 They should wear 'proper, suitable' clothes [Alf, EGT, ICC, LN (66.10), LSA, TH, WBC; GW, NASB, NCV, NIV, NRSV, TEV]: *I want the women to adorn or dress themselves in proper clothes.* This adjective means 'orderly', as opposed to a disorderly appearance [EGT]. It means that their apparel is not to be excessive, but to be proper and suitable [ICC]. This word means well-ordered and moderate (not excessive) or proper and suitable, or simple and unassuming [TH]. They are to dress themselves in clothes that are proper [NASB, NCV, TEV], suitable [NIV, NRSV], respectable [WBC], and appropriate [AB; GW].

1.2 They should wear clothes that reflect the moral qualities of the women who wear them [CEV, HCSB, KJV, NIV]: *I want the women to adorn or dress themselves in modest clothes.*

1.3 They should wear clothes that give them a pleasing appearance [AB, BNTC, ECC, Lns, NTC, WP; REB]: *I want the women to adorn or dress themselves in clothes that enhance their beauty.* There is a play on words here: κόσμιος –κοσμέω 'in adorning attire–adorn themselves' [Lns, NTC]. Those who argue that here this adjective must mean 'virtuous' or 'honorable' ignore the fact that this is the meaning of the term when it describes a person's character. This is of little value when it modifies a noun that indicates dress rather than character. As such, the more literal meaning 'adorning or becoming attire' suggests itself as the proper meaning [NTC]. Paul wanted the women to wear clothes that were attractive [BNTC], becoming [ECC, WP], adorning [NTC], and well-arranged [WP].

2. The phrase describes the deportment or demeanor women themselves [ECC, EGT, Herm, My, NAC, NICNT, NIGTC, NTL, TNTC, WBC; NLT, REB]: *I want women to adorn themselves in a proper manner.* This adjective reflects the correct attitude of mind in regard to dress [TNTC]. 'Women should dress themselves in a proper manner with modesty and good sense' or 'women should be modest and sensible about the clothes they wear and dress properly' [LN (49.12)]. They are to dress in a becoming manner [REB]. They are to be modest in their appearance [Herm; NLT]. While the focus of the noun in this verse is upon the women's attire, it also overlaps into the meaning 'deportment' since Paul is speaking of the character of a woman's inner person, and like κοσμεῖν 'to adorn', its wider meaning continues to prepare the way for the true emphasis of 2:10 [WBC]. A woman who is κοσμίῳ 'modest' in her dress dresses tastefully, not provocatively [NAC]. In her outer dress, a woman would either signal modesty and dignity or promiscuous availability [NICNT]. It must be understood in terms of internal disposition and conduct which is observable. As such, it embraces a person's whole deportment, habits, clothing, life-style; in fact, all of the outward signs of the interior disposition that a person employs. [ECC]. The idea here is something that can outwardly be recognized, 'deportment' as it is exhibited externally in look, manner, or dress [EGT, NIGTC], but principally exhibited in dress [EGT].

QUESTION—What relationship is indicated by the prepositional phrase μετὰ αἰδοῦς καὶ σωφροσύνης '*with* decency and sensibility'?

1. These are two qualities that the women should have as they wear appropriate clothes [AB, ECC, EGT, Herm, ICC, Lns, My, NAC, NIBC, NICNT, NIGTC, NTC, NTL, TC, TNTC, WBC; NET]: *they are to do so with decency and sensibility.* The preposition μετὰ 'with' indicates attendant circumstances, and this clause carries the discussion from mere appearance to the attitudes of discretion and decorum that befit a Christian woman. It stands in direct contrast to the following negative clause which portrays the seductiveness and wealthy display of a worldly woman [ICC]. The outward clothing must be accompanied by the inward qualities of modesty and sobriety [Lns]. Their clothes will show the qualities that the women possess [NCV]. The two nouns indicate the state of mind or

attitude that is necessary for a person who is concerned about modesty [NIGTC].

1.1 The noun αἰδοῦς 'decency' means that in wearing their clothes, women are to do so with decency [ICC; HCSB, NIV], modesty [AB, BNTC, ICC, Lns, NICNT, NIGTC, NTC, TNTC, WBC; NASB, NET, NRSV, REB, TEV], self-respect [NTL], shamefacedness [EGT, TC; KJV], respectfulness [NCV], sensibleness [ECC], chastity [Herm], discretion and propriety [ICC, NICNT]. This implies that they would not wear clothes that were showy and sexually enticing [ICC]. It describes modesty that will not overstep womanly reserve [TC].

1.2 The noun σωφροσύνης means that in wearing their clothes, women are to do so with good sense [NTC; HCSB, NET, TEV], discretion [AB, ECC; NASB], sound judgment [NIGTC; NET], prudence [Herm], propriety [NIBC; NIV], sobriety [Lns; KJV, NET, REB], moderation [NIGTC; WBC; NET], self control [Alf, EGT, NIGTC, NTL, TC, TNTC; NCV, NET], discreetness [EGT], decency [NIGTC; NRSV], good judgment in the matter of dress [NIBC].

2. These are two descriptions of the clothes they are to wear, and they define what kind of clothing is meant under the description of κοσμίῳ 'proper or modest' clothing mentioned in the preceding clause [TH; CEV, GW, NLT].

2.1 The noun αἰδοῦς 'decency' means clothes that are decent [NLT], modest [CEV, GW], chaste [BNTC],

2.2 The noun σωφροσύνης 'sensibility' means clothes that are sensible [TH; CEV], appropriate [NLT], respectable [GW], moderate [TH].

QUESTION—What is meant by αἰδοῦς 'decency'?

Αἰδοῦς is here defined as 'shamefastness' (denoting a woman who is held *fast* by an honorable sense of shame) [Alf, EGT, Lns]. It is a reluctance to overstep the limits of womanly reserve and modesty [Alf, Lns, NIGTC, NTC]. It is the innate shrinking from anything immodest [My]. It denotes feminine reserve in matters of sex [BNTC, NAC], which includes avoiding clothing and adornment which would be either showy and extravagant or sexually enticing [ICC].

QUESTION—What is meant by σωφροσύνης 'propriety'?

Literally, σωφροσρνης means 'soundness of mind', and here it refers to 'sensible' attire [NTC]. The word here has a reference to 'good judgment' in matters of dress [NIBC]. Basically it means 'restraint' or 'self-control' [Alf, Lns, NICNT, WBC]. The shortcoming of 'self-restraint' is that it is a word too indicative of *effort*, as if the unchaste desires were continually breaking their bounds, and must be continually held in check. Rather the idea is that in the person who is σώφρων 'self-controlled, prudent', the better nature is established in its rule and no such continual struggle has any place [Alf]. It expresses the mean between two extremes and means 'moderation' [WBC], or 'proper reserve', so that when they *adorn* themselves, it is not in queer old-fashioned attire nor in immoral or indecent attire [NTC]. Or, some find a sexual connotation here [BAGD (2. p. 802), BNTC, Herm, My, NAC, NIGTC]. Applied specifically to women, as it is here, it may suggest chastity and sexual purity as a form of self-control [ICC]. It had a definite sexual nuance [BAGD, BNTC, Herm] and was almost the equivalent of 'chastity' [BNTC, Herm, My, NIGTC]. It expresses control of the desires [BNTC, My, NAC], particularly in matters of sex [NAC].

not with braided-hair[a] and gold[b] or pearls[c] or expensive[d] clothing,

TEXT—Instead of καί 'and' preceding χρυσίῳ 'of-gold', some manuscripts read ἤ 'or'. GNT does not mention this variant. 'Or' is read by KJV.

LEXICON—a. πλέγμα (LN **49.28**) (BAGD p. 667): 'braided hair' [LN, WBC; KJV, NASB, NCV, NET, NIV; similarly NRSV], 'braids' [AB, Herm, LN, Lns, LSA; NTC], 'fancy hairdos' [CEV], 'fancy hair styles' [TEV], 'elaborate hairstyles' [BNTC; HCSB, REB], '(their) hairstyles' [GW], '(not draw attention to themselves by) the way they fix their hair' [NLT], '(their beauty is not in their) coiffure' [ECC].

    b. χρυσίον (LN 6.189) (BAGD p. 888): 'gold' [AB, BNTC, Herm, Lns, LSA, NTC, WBC; HCSB, KJV, NASB, NCV, NET, NIV, NLT, NRSV], 'adorned with gold' [REB], 'gold jewelry' [LN; GW], 'gold ornaments' [BAGD, ECC, LN; TEV], 'jewelry' [BAGD], 'jewelry made of gold' [CEV]. This noun denotes something made of gold [LN].

    c. μαργαρίτης (LN 2.43) (BAGD 1. p. 491): 'pearls' [AB, BNTC, ECC, Herm, LN, Lns, LSA, NTC, WBC; all versions except CEV, REB], 'adorned with pearls' [REB], 'jewelry made of pearls' [CEV]. This noun denotes a smooth rounded gem formed by concretion within the shells of certain mollusks, and it was valued because of its lustrous color [LN].

    d. πολυτελής (LN 65.3) (BAGD p. 690): 'expensive' [BAGD, BNTC, Herm, LN, Lns, NTC; all versions except KJV, NASB], 'costly' [AB, BAGD, LSA, WBC; KJV, NASB], 'valuable' [LN], 'extravagant' [ECC]. This adjective describes something as being of great value or worth [LN].

QUESTION—How is this clause related to the previous one?

In a contrasting negative form ('not with'), this clause gives a further delineation of the proper attire that is described in the first part of the verse [LSA, NIBC, NIGTC]. It is possible that the specific items to avoid are named because they are intrinsically wrong for Christian women, or it could be hyperbole to be taken relatively in connection with the idea of adorning their inner persons (2:10) and not the outer, or it could be general principles related to practices of that time which were contrary to Christian lifestyle [NIGTC]. This describes the kind of adornment to avoid [ICC]. Some supply an additional connection: 'they should not have' [CEV], 'their adornment must not be with' [NET], 'not decorate themselves with' [Herm], 'not using' [NCV], 'not adorn herself' [NTC], 'their beauty is not in' [ECC], 'and not draw attention to themselves by they way they fix...or by wearing...' [NLT].

QUESTION—What is meant by πλέγμασιν 'braided hair'?

This noun describes anything that may be twisted [ICC], entwined, woven, or braided [BAGD (p. 667), LN (49.28), NIGTC], and here the reference is to women's hair [BAGD, ICC, Lns]. The reference is not to today's common braids, but to putting up the hair in a showy and unusual fashion [Lns, NTC]. Paul may be referring to a style in which women wore their hair in an enormously elaborate arrangement with braids and curls interwoven or piled high like towers [NAC], rising to some inches above the head [TH], with gems, gold, or pearls decorating it [ICC, NAC, TH]. This was obviously done with the object of being conspicuous so as to outshine rivals and to make other women envious [Lns]. Such a practice demonstrates pride and self-centeredness [NAC]. Some commentators mention that we must not suppose that the mere braiding of the hair is here forbidden [NTC, WBC], but rather ostentatious arrangement and ornamentation [TH].

QUESTION—What is meant by χρυσίῳ ἤ μαργαρίταις 'gold or pearls'?

Χρυσίῳ 'gold' refers to gold ornaments and jewelry [BAGD (p. 888), ICC, TH, WP]. Both gold and pearls decorated women's elaborate hairstyles [NAC]. If 'gold' referred to hair decorations, then 'pearls' might refer to earrings [ECC]. Pearls are decorations used by women [ICC]. In Roman times, pearls were highly valued [ECC] and fabulously priced [NTC].

QUESTION—What is meant by ἱματισμῷ πολυτελεῖ 'expensive clothing'?

The noun ἱματισμῷ 'clothing' is a general term for clothing of any kind, and here it is women's clothing. The adjective πολυτελεῖ 'expensive' has a negative, derogatory connotation of being 'exorbitant, excessively priced' [TH, WBC]. The phrase contrasts with the phrase καταστολῇ κοσμίῳ 'modest apparel' used previously in this verse [My].

2:10 but what is-proper[a] for-women claiming[b] reverence-for-God/ religion,[c] with/by-means-of[d] good deeds.[e]

LEXICON—a. pres. act. indic. of πρέπω (LN 66.1) (BAGD p. 699): 'to be proper' [**LN** (33.219)], 'to be fitting' [BAGD, LN], 'to be right' [LN], 'to be seemly or suitable' [BAGD]. The phrase ὃ πρέπει 'what is proper' is translated 'what is fitting' [Herm], 'in a way fitting to' [AB], 'which is right' [NCV], 'this is what is proper' [GW], 'as is proper' [NTC; HCSB, NASB, NET, NRSV, TEV], 'what is appropriate' [WBC], 'appropriate for' [NIV], 'what befits' [Lns], 'as befits' [BNTC; REB], 'which becomes' [KJV], 'that suits' [ECC], 'should do' [CEV], 'doing what women should do' [LSA], 'should (make themselves attractive by)' [NLT]. This verb implies that a moral judgment may be involved [LN]. It is implied that the proper standard was known and generally accepted [NICNT].

b. pres. mid./pass. (deponent = act.) participle of ἐπαγγέλλομαι (LN **33.219**) (BAGD 2. p. 281): 'to claim' [BNTC, LSA; CEV, GW, NLT, REB, TEV], 'to make a claim' [NASB], 'to profess' [BAGD, ECC, Herm, **LN**, Lns, NTC; KJV, NET, NIV, NRSV], 'to assert' [LN], 'to affirm'

[HCSB], 'to say' [NCV], 'to be committed to' [WBC], 'to be dedicated to' [AB]. This verb means to announce something in an open and emphatic way [LN]. It means to profess and lay claim to something [NIGTC], to claim that a person is in a certain state or condition [TH].

c. θεοσέβεια (LN **53.1**) (BAGD p. 358): 'reverence for God' [BAGD; NET, NRSV], 'piety' [BAGD, LN], 'godly piety' [Lns], 'godliness' [WBC; KJV, NASB], 'real godliness' [ECC], 'the service of God' [AB], 'the worship of God' [Herm], 'religion' [BAGD, **LN**]. This noun is also translated as a verbal phrase: 'to have reverence for God' [GW], 'to be devoted to God' [NLT], 'to worship God' [LSA; NCV, NIV], 'to love God' [CEV], 'to be God-fearing' [NTC], 'to be religious' [BNTC; REB, TEV]. This noun denotes the appropriate beliefs and devout practice of the obligations one has in relating to supernatural persons and powers [LN].

d. διά (LN 89.76, 90.8): See translations of this word in the following lexical item. This preposition indicates the means by which one event makes another event possible: 'by means of, through, by' [LN (89.76)] (so Alf, ECC, Lns, NIGTC, NTC, WBC), or it indicates the instrument by which something is accomplished: 'by means of, through, with' [LN (90.8)] (so BNTC, EGT, Herm, ICC; KJV, NET, NIV, REB, TEV). The verb κοσμέω 'to adorn' is reflexive, not transitive, so 'adorn themselves' can be construed with either ἐν 'with' (2:9) or διά 'by means of/with' (2:10) [Lns].

e. ἔργον (LN 42.11) (BAGD 1.c.β. p. 308): 'deed' [BAGD, LN], 'act' [LN], 'accomplishment' [BAGD]. The phrase δι' ἔργων ἀγαθῶν 'with/by means of good deeds' is translated 'with good deeds' [BNTC; NET, NIV, REB, TEV], 'with good works' [Herm; KJV, NRSV], 'by means of good works' [Lns, NTC; NASB], 'by their doing good deeds' [LSA], 'by the good things they do' [NLT], '(their beauty will be shown) by what they do' [GW], 'through good works' [AB], 'it comes through their excellent deeds' [ECC], 'namely, in good deeds' [WBC], 'they should do good deeds' [NCV], 'should do helpful things for others' [CEV]. This noun denotes that which is done and may possibly focus on the effort involved [LN].

QUESTION—What relationship is indicated by the initial conjunction ἀλλά 'but'?

This conjunction indicates a positive contrast with the preceding negative clause [BNTC, ECC, ICC, Lns, LSA, NIGTC, NTC, TH, WBC]: *women should not adorn themselves with braided hair and gold or pearls or expensive clothing, but with/by means of the following*. The verb construction intended to be understood is κοσμεῖν ἑαυτάς 'to adorn themselves', which governs 2:9 and carries over to this verse [ICC, NICNT, NIGTC]. Paul does not mean that all adornment is to be avoided, but that the greatest asset they have is a devout and godly life [NTC].

QUESTION—Following the initial conjunction ἀλλά 'but', how are the
following two phrases related in this verse?

1. The final phrase δι' ἔργων ἀγαθῶν 'with/by means of good deeds' is in
   contrast with the preceding negative clause in 2:9, while the first phrase
   modifies 'good deeds' [Alf, BNTC, ECC, EGT, Lns, NIBC, NIGTC,
   NTC, TC, TG, TH; all versions]: women should adorn themselves (2:9),
   not with braided hair and gold or pearls or expensive clothing (2:10b), *but
   with/by means of* good deeds. The clause 'what is proper for women
   professing reverence for God/religion' is a parenthetical remark about
   'good deeds' [ECC, EGT, Lns, TC]. The final phrase 'with/by means of
   good deeds' is kept last for emphasis, so that the whole argument is: 'Let
   women dress with decency and sensibility, not with…, but with/by means
   of good works' [NIGTC]. Women should be admired for their good
   deeds, not for their expensive clothing and jewelry [TG]. The verb
   κοσμέω 'to adorn' is reflexive, not transitive, so 'adorn themselves' can
   be construed with either (ἐν) 'with' (2:9) or διά 'by means of/with' (2:10)
   [Lns]. It says that they adorn themselves *by means of* good deeds since the
   adorning that results from their good deeds is brought about *by means of*
   what they do, not with what they wear [Alf].
2. The first clause after ἀλλά 'but' is in contrast with the preceding negative
   clause in 2:9, while the final phrase δι' ἔργων ἀγαθῶν 'with/by means of
   good deeds' defines it [AB, Herm, ICC, LSA, My, WBC]: women should
   adorn themselves *not* with braided hair and gold or pearls or expensive
   clothing, (2:10b), *but with* what is proper for women professing reverence
   for God/religion, *namely,* with good deeds.

QUESTION—Does the noun θεοσέβειαν refer to 'reverence for God' or
'religion' in this verse?

1. It refers to the act of revering and worshiping God [Alf, ECC, Herm,
   NIGTC, NTC, NTL, WBC; HCSB, KJV, NASB, NCV, NET, NIV, NLT,
   NRSV]: *women who claim to revere God.* This word has a strong ethical
   connotation and emphasizes a woman's personal relationship to God
   [NIGTC].
2. It refers to adhering to a system of beliefs and its demands for appropriate
   behavior [BNTC, ICC, LN (53.1), NCBC, NIBC; CEV, GW, REB, TEV]:
   women who claim to be religious. Women are to demonstrate their claim
   to faith by showing the appropriate adornment, which is nothing more
   than the Christian character and conduct that is expected of all believers
   [ICC].

QUESTION—What is meant by ἔργων 'good deeds'?

The adjective ἀγαθῶν 'good' is used in the moral sense [AB, BAGD,
NIGTC], and it emphasizes the internal and ethical quality of the deeds, and
this is in contrast with the visible beauty of decorative jewelry and clothing
[ECC]. The phrase 'good deeds' combines the internal ('good') with the
external ('deeds') to indicate the kind of adornment that befits godliness
[ICC]. Practicing good deeds reveals the moral disposition of the women

who live a life of productive virtue [AB]. Good deeds are the response of a believer to God's grace and mercy and they do not earn salvation [BNTC]. Good deeds include general benevolence [BNTC, NAC], and reverent godliness [NAC]. Good deeds are the actions performed to benefit others [ICC, Lns, NICNT, TH], as a result of the outworking of one's faith [NICNT]. There is no need to restrict the scope of 'good deeds' [Lns]. Some of the good deeds are mentioned in 5:10 [WBC].

2:11 Let- a-woman -learn[a] in silence/quietness[b] in all subjection.[c]

LEXICON—a. pres. act. impera. of μανθάνω (LN 27.12) (BAGD 1. p. 490): 'to learn' [BAGD, LN; TEV], 'to be instructed, to be taught' [LN]. The phrase γυνὴ μανθανέτω 'let a woman learn' [AB, NTC; NCV, NRSV; similarly Lns; KJV] is also translated 'a woman must learn' [LSA; GW, NET], 'a woman should learn' [Herm, WBC; HCSB, NIV], 'a woman ought to learn' [BNTC], 'women should learn' [CEV, NLT, TEV], 'a woman must (quietly) receive instruction' [NASB], 'their role is to learn' [REB], 'let a married woman learn' [ECC]. This verb means to acquire information as the result of either formal or informal instruction [LN].

b. ἡσυχία (LN 33.119, 88.103) (BAGD 2. p. 349): 'silence' [BAGD, LN (33.119)], 'quiet life, peaceful life' [LN (88.103)]. The phrase ἐν ἡσυχίᾳ 'in silence' [NTC; GW, HCSB, KJV, NRSV, TEV] is also translated 'being silent' [LSA], 'by being silent' [Herm], 'by being quiet' [CEV], 'in quietness' [Lns, WBC; NIV], 'quietly' [AB, BNTC, ECC; NASB, NCV, NET, NLT], 'listening quietly' [REB]. This noun denotes a state of silence and may focus on the person's attitude [LN (33.119)], or it denotes a manner of life that is quiet and peaceful [LN (88.103)].

c. ὑποταγή (LN 36.18) (BAGD p. 847): 'subjection, subordination' [BAGD], 'obedience' [BAGD, LN], 'submission' [LN]. The phrase ἐν πάσῃ ὑποταγῇ 'in all subjection' [Lns] is also translated 'with all subjection' [KJV], 'in/with full submission' [HCSB, NIV, NRSV], 'in/with all submissiveness' [WBC; NET], 'with entire submissiveness' [NASB], 'with complete submissiveness' [BNTC, NTC], 'with due submission' [REB], 'in complete subordination' [AB], 'subordinating herself' [Herm], 'fully subjecting herself to those with authority' [LSA], 'in all humility' [TEV], 'being ready to cooperate in everything' [NCV], 'in keeping with her position' [GW], '(learn) by paying attention' [CEV]. This noun is also translated as an adverb: 'submissively' [NLT], 'quite obediently' [ECC] This noun denotes submitting to the orders or directives of someone [LN].

QUESTION—What is the significance of the lack of a connective particle to introduce this verse?

This asyndeton, together with a shift to the third person imperative [ICC], introduces a new topic [ICC, Lns, NICNT, NIGTC, WBC]. The reader's attention is arrested by the lack of a connective particle and this feature

introduces Paul's second point in regard to women [Lns]. Some begin a new
paragraph here [ECC, NIGTC, WBC; GW, NCV, NIV, NLT].

QUESTION—What is indicated by the use of the singular noun γυναικί 'a
woman'?

1. This is a reference to women in general in regard to their relationship to
   the congregation [Alf, BAGD (1. p. 168), BNTC, Herm, ICC, Lns, LSA,
   My, NAC, NIBC, NIGTC, NTC, TH, TNTC, WBC]. As in 2:9 and 2:12,
   the singular γυναικί 'woman' functions as a generic noun, which is
   appropriate for the statement of a general truth [WBC]. It is characteristic
   of Paul to use *woman* as an individualizing singular. Just as the plural
   γυναῖκας 'women' in 2:9 refers to all *women* as a class [Lns], so the
   singular here refers to a 'woman' as such, each and every one of them. It
   certainly does not single out 'a wife' [Lns, NAC], just as τοὺς ἄνδρας
   'the men' in 2:8 does not mean 'the husbands' [Lns].

2. This refers to married women [ECC, EGT, NICNT]. The previous two
   verses use the plural when referring to women in general so that the
   directive of 2:8 applies to all women. But 2:11–15 turns upon the singular
   use of the term. In the Pastoral Epistles, the singular occurs in the set
   phrase 'a man of one woman' or 'a woman of one man' (1 Tim. 3:2, 12;
   5:9 and Titus 1:6). These phrases always refer to a married woman, a
   wife. Therefore, here the singular γυναικί 'a woman' is intended to
   narrow the reference in 2:11–15 to a married woman [ECC]. The generic
   singular form 'wife' is used to state a general principle [NICNT].

QUESTION—What environment is assumed in this verse?

The environment is the church's worship service [Alf, BKC, BNTC, ICC,
My, NAC, NCBC, NIBC, NICNT, NIGTC, NTC, TC, TG, TH, TNTC,
WBC]. This verse is paralleled very closely in thought by 1 Cor. 14:33b–35
'as in all the congregations of the saints, women should remain silent in the
churches' [BNTC, ECC, EGT, ICC, Lns, My, NIGTC, NTC, NTIC, TC,
TNTC]. Or, this primarily refers to church meetings, but 2:12 indicates that
there may also be a reference to the relationship of men and women in
general, and in particular, the relationship between a woman and her
husband [TH]. The subject of public meetings brought on this directive, but
the following instructions show that this applies to their behavior wherever
they might be [Alf].

QUESTION—What is meant by γυνὴ ἐν ἡσυχία μανθανέτω 'let a woman
learn in silence'?

The verb implies learning through instruction [BAGD (1. p. 490), ICC,
NAC, NICNT, NIGTC, TG, TH], which, of course, implies paying attention
[NAC], and listening [Herm, TH, TNTC; NLT]. The reference is to listening
to public exhortation and the application of the OT Scriptures [WBC]. They
learned from the formal instruction given by gifted teachers in the church
concerning the gospel, the OT, and all aspects of living [NICNT]. The
question of the part women were to play in the worship service was a
burning one since silence was expected of women in the Jewish synagogue

services [BNTC, NAC], and yet there is evidence of a spirit of emancipation that was spreading among women in the young Christian congregations [BNTC, TNTC].

1. Ἐν ἡσυχίᾳ 'in silence' means women were not to speak during the worship service [Lns, My, NIGTC, NTC, TH, TNTC]. The women were not to teach or speak to a public assembly [Lns, My, NTC, TH], or even ask questions [TH]. Women must not place themselves on an equality with men by assisting in the worship service by teaching (2:12) [Lns].

2. Ἐν ἡσυχίᾳ 'in quietness' means a woman must have a quiet demeanor [BKC, ECC, ICC, NAC, NIBC, NICNT, WBC]. Paul's purpose in using this phrase is not that a woman must remain absolutely silent so much as it is that she must have a quiet, orderly, teachable spirit [BKC, NAC]. Four times in the NT this noun and its cognate adjective and verb are used in reference to complete silence, and four other times these words denote a quiet demeanor. Several considerations favor the meaning 'quiet demeanor' here: (1) 1 Cor. 11:5 allows a vocal role for women in the worship services, (2) the cognate adjective ἤρεμος denotes a quiet demeanor in 1 Tim. 2:2, (3) neither the present context nor the word ὑποταγῇ 'submissiveness' in the next phrase, or forbidding them to teach in 2:12 demand total silence, since 'quiet demeanor' provides sufficient contrast to διδάσκειν 'to teach' [WBC]. The ἡσυχία 'quietness' enjoined here is the same as the ἡσύχιον βίον 'quiet life' enjoined in 2:2 where it is not limited to women [NIBC]. In Acts 22:2 and 2 Thess. 3:12, the noun does not denote complete silence [BKC, ECC]. It means that she should have a quiet demeanor, not necessarily remaining in complete silence [ICC, NIBC]. Quietness is the appropriate posture and attitude appropriate of deference to the teacher, and it would keep her out of any argumentation during the lesson [NICNT]. She was to listen attentively and show deference to the person teaching, since all believers in attendance, both women and men, were in the position of learners. Other forms of utterance such as praying, singing, prophesying, or encouraging are not ruled out. The reference here is a limited one and probably refers to speaking out of turn and thereby interrupting the service [ICC].

QUESTION—What is meant by ἐν πάσῃ ὑποταγῇ 'in all subjection', and to whom is a woman to be in subjection?

The noun ὑποταγή 'subjection' contains the three elements of recognition, subordination, and obedience [TH]. The adjective πάσῃ 'all' indicates the highest degree [NIGTC], or *complete* subjection [ICC]. This describes what Paul means by ἐν ἡσυχίᾳ 'in silence' [Lns, NIBC, WBC].

1. A woman should be in subjection to the church leaders [ECC, Lns, NAC, NIBC, NIGTC, TNTC, WBC], or to any of the men who were teaching during the service [Herm, ICC, NICNT, NTC, TG, TH]. Since the context has to do with learning, the object of her submission is likely to be the teaching elders, who were responsible for teaching the true gospel and for refuting error. Nowhere does Paul ever teach that all women must be

submissive to all men. So this interpretation places this verse in line with
other scriptural calls, to men and women alike, for obedience to ruling
authorities, whether they be secular or spiritual [WBC]. The role and
attitude of the woman in being submissive as a learner do not necessarily
apply to all that submission might imply in other relationships such as
master-slave and husband-wife relationships [NICNT]. Here ὑποταγῇ
'submission' describes the attitude or posture appropriate to a learner, and
it implies acceptance of the teaching and of the authority of the teacher. It
was an attitude which was doubtlessly also expected of the men in
attendance who were not teaching (just as women who prayed must also
do like the men in 2:8, and lift holy hands without anger and dispute as
they pray) [ICC]. 'In all subjection' means that the women's submission
to men is to be the norm for the relationship of women to men within the
authority functions of the church [NIGTC]. It means that women must
subordinate themselves to *what* the men in the congregation teach [Herm],
without contradicting them [My]. Learning in silence should not be
accompanied by a rebellious attitude, but with submissiveness to God's
law for her life. While the NT gives her full spiritual equality with men as
a sharer in salvation and all its blessings, it does not imply any basic
change in her nature as a woman who is not to exercise authority over a
man by teaching or preaching in an official manner at church [NTC]. This
passage does not refer to a woman's subjection to her husband [Lns]. The
use of πάσῃ 'all' in the sense of 'full' subjection probably implies a
broader category than just husbands in that it probably also covers the
young widows treated in 5:13 [NIBC].

2. A woman (wife) should be in subjection to her husband [EGT].

2:12 **And/but I-do- not -permit[a] a-woman to-teach nor to-have-authority-over/to-domineer-over[b] a-man, instead[c] (I want her) to-be in silence/quietness.[d]**

LEXICON—a. pres. act. indic. of ἐπιτρέπω (LN 13.138) (BAGD 1. p. 303): 'to
permit' [BAGD, LN, Lns; LSA, NTC, WBC; NIV, NRSV, REB], 'to
allow' [BAGD, BNTC, ECC, Herm, LN; GW, HCSB, NASB, NCV,
NET, TEV], 'to let' [LN; NLT], 'to suffer' [KJV], 'to entrust (teaching to
a woman)' [AB]. This active form is also translated passively: '(they
should not) be allowed' [CEV]. This verb means to allow someone to do
something [LN].

b. pres. act. infin. of αὐθεντέω (LN **37.21**) (BAGD p. 121): 'to have
authority over' [BAGD, Herm, LSA; GW, HCSB, NCV, NIV, NLT,
NRSV, TEV], 'to exercise authority over' [Lns, NTC, WBC; NASB,
NET], 'to wield authority over' [BNTC], 'to entrust authority over' [AB],
'to control' [LN], 'to dominate' [**LN**], 'to domineer over' [BAGD], 'to
dictate to' [REB], 'to boss' [ECC], 'to usurp authority over' [KJV]. The
phrase 'to have authority over a man' is translated 'to tell men what to do'

[CEV]. This verb means to control someone in a domineering manner [LN].

   c. ἀλλά (LN 89.125): 'instead' [LN; GW, HCSB], 'rather' [LSA], 'on the contrary' [LN], 'but' [LN, Lns, NTC, WBC; KJV, NASB, NCV], 'but rather' [Herm], not explicit [AB, BNTC, ECC; CEV, NET, NIV, NLT, NRSV, REB, TEV]. This conjunction indicates a contrast [LN].

   d. ἡσυχία (LN 33.119, 88.103) (BAGD 2. p. 349): 'silence' [BAGD (33.119), LN], 'quiet life, peaceful life' [LN (88.103)]. See translations of this word in 2:11.

QUESTION—What relationship is indicated by the initial conjunction δέ 'and/but'?

   1. Δέ 'and, now, moreover' is continuative [ECC, Lns, LSA, WBC; perhaps CEV, GW, NIV, NLT, NRSV, REB, TEV which do not translate this conjunction]: *and I do not allow a woman to teach*. It specifies more closely what the apostle has stated in 2:11 [Lns, WBC]. It serves to qualify one part of what has been said rather than to rework the whole in a negative statement [ECC]. It introduces the second qualifying clause explaining what Paul means by ἐν ἡσυχίᾳ 'in quietness' and defines in practical, contrasting terms what learning in quietness involves [WBC]. The fact that a woman is not to lead in public prayer was indicated in 2:8 and now the fact that she is not to teach in the worship service is added [Lns].

   2. Δέ 'but' is adversative [Alf, Herm, ICC, My, NIBC, NICNT, NIGTC, NTC; KJV, NASB, NCV, NET]: *but I do not permit a woman to teach*. The positive imperative μανθανέτω 'let (a woman) learn' is now followed by the prohibition οὐκ ἐπιτρέπω 'I do not permit (a woman to teach)' [ICC, My, NICNT, NIGTC; NET].

QUESTION—What is meant by οὐκ ἐπιτρέπω 'I do not permit'?

It has the connotation of one who properly speaks from the authority inherent in or delegated to him [ECC, ICC, NAC, NIGTC, WBC, WP]. It carries the same authority that βούλομαι 'I want' carries in 2:8 [ICC, NICNT]. The other uses of ἐπιτρέπω 'I permit' by Paul indicate that he used this verb authoritatively, and this has no implication that it is just a personal opinion or that its present tense indicates a temporal limitation to the situation in Ephesus. Paul regularly uses first person singular present tenses for universal and authoritative instructions [NIGTC, WBC]. Paul does not permit a woman to teach nor to have authority over a man because the *Torah*, the law, does not permit it (1 Cor. 14:34), as the following references to Genesis 2:13–24 indicate [Lns, NIGTC, NTC]. Or, the present tense οὐκ ἐπιτρέπω 'I am not permitting' implies that these are specific instructions to this situation in Ephesus and must not be interpreted as a universal imperative for all situations [NIBC]. Culturally, the role of teacher was assigned to males in public settings [AB].

QUESTION—What is meant by διδάσκειν 'to teach', what are the implied limits of this prohibition, and who is the implied object of this teaching?

This prohibition is made more emphatic by positioning the infinitive διδάσκειν 'to teach' at the beginning of the clause [ICC, Lns, LSA, My, NTC]. It is in emphatic opposition to μανθανέτω 'let (a woman) learn' [My, WBC]. Paul is not referring to the imparting of secular knowledge [Lns, NAC]. This does not prohibit a woman from teaching children or other women [Lns, NIGTC, WBC].

1. The implied object of διδάσκειν 'to teach' is the congregation as a whole, and this indicates that women were not to have positions as teachers in church meetings [Alf, BNTC, EGT, ICC, Lns, My, NAC, NIBC, NICNT, TC, TG, TH, TNTC, WBC, WP]: *I do not permit a woman to teach the congregation, nor to have authority over a man.* Διδάσκειν 'to teach' pertains to teaching in a church meeting, and Paul is concerned about giving authoritative instruction in a congregational setting [ICC, NAC, WBC]. That the women not teach and not speak relate to a church setting, while not having authority over a man relates to all settings [My]. Women must not have a position of authority over men, and since teaching is one way in which authority is exercised in the church, women should not teach in the church [Lns, WBC]. This does not prohibit teaching in an informal setting [NAC]. The time when Aquila and his wife taught Apollos in their home does not provide an exception to this command [Lns]. Culturally, only men taught in church [TH, TNTC]. Or, the prohibition to teach was brought about by a specific group of Ephesian women whose teaching was influenced by the heretical teaching of the false teachers [ICC]. This prohibition applies to the house churches in Ephesus, although in churches in other locations women could prophesy and probably teach from time to time (1 Cor. 14:26) [NIBC].

2. The implied object of διδάσκειν 'to teach' is ἀνδρός 'a man', and this indicates that women are not to have the role of teaching men in a church meeting [Herm, NIGTC, NTC, WBC]: *I do not permit a woman to teach a man, nor to have authority over a man.* The object of διδάσκειν 'to teach' is ἀνδρός 'man' (in the next clause), so the persons not to be taught were men and, since men were part of the congregation, women were not to teach in public meetings of the church [NIGTC]. A woman must subordinate herself to what the men teach [Herm]. For a woman to teach in an official manner in church is the same as exercising authority over a man [NTC, WBC], and this is against God's law concerning the role of women [NTC].

3. Διδάσκειν 'to teach' has no limits; since it refers to wives teaching not only (although primarily) within the church, but also at home and anywhere else where they would be in the position of teaching their husbands [ECC, NCBC]. Teaching under the auspices of the church was done with apostolic authentication, and here this is explicitly denied to Christian wives since they were not to teach their husbands who

presumably would be present in the public service [ECC]. The noun ἀνδρός 'a man' refers, not to men in general, but to a woman's husband, and her teaching would amount to be lording it over her husband [NCBC].

QUESTION—What connotation does the infinitive αὐθεντεῖν 'to have authority' or 'to domineer' have?

This rare verb is parallel to ὑποταγῇ 'subjection' in the preceding verse, and it has two basic meanings. If it means 'to exercise authority', then Paul is prohibiting all types of authoritative teaching. If it means 'to domineer', in the sense of exercising authority in a coercive manner, then Paul is prohibiting the type of authoritative teaching that is done in a domineering way, and leaves the way open for women to teach men in a proper way [WBC].

1. The verb αὐθεντεῖν has a neutral connotation, meaning 'to have authority, to exercise authority' [NAC, NIGTC, WBC; all versions except KJV, REB]: *I do not permit a woman to have authority over a man.* Women are not to be in positions of authority in the church [WBC]. It refers to having a leadership function in the church, and it carries no negative connotation that 'to usurp authority' or 'to domineer' would suggest [NIGTC].

2. The verb αὐθεντεῖν has a negative connotation, meaning 'to domineer, to dominate' [Alf, BNTC, ECC, EGT, Herm, ICC, Lns, My, NIBC, NTC, TC, TG, TH, TNTC; REB]: *nor to domineer over a man.* The verb has the connotation of being domineering and laying down the law to a man [BNTC], and of being overbearing and heavy-handed [ICC]. A woman is not to assume the role of ruling or domineering over men [NTC, TH, TNTC]. Here, the verb may indicate that women were being forward and challenging [Herm, TH], or contradicting [NIBC], what the men were teaching in public worship [Herm]. Perhaps the women argued from what they were learning from the Gnostic teachers in Ephesus [NIBC].

QUESTION—What is meant by οὐδὲ αὐθεντεῖν ἀνδρός 'nor to have authority over a man'?

1. This prohibits a woman to have authority over a man in any situation [AB, BNTC, Herm, Lns, My, NAC, NIGTC, TH, TNTC, WBC]. This statement is based on the section in Genesis about creation and the fall which indicates that it is the man's role to be in authority and it is the woman's role to be in subjection [Lns, NTC]. The activity of teaching in a church meeting is a specific example of having authority over men [BNTC, Lns, NAC, NIGTC, NTC, WBC]: *a woman must not teach nor is she to have any other kind of authority over a man.* This clause forbids women to teach in church meetings. A teacher who instructs God's people publicly not only tells them what they need to know, but in his capacity of a teacher he stands before his audience to rule and govern it with God's Word, and this is a position God has given to men and has withheld from women [Lns]. Teaching is one of the ways authority in the church is

exercised, and since women should not have authority in the church, they
are not teach in the church [WBC].

2. This prohibits a woman to have authority over a man in regard to her
teaching in Ephesus [ICC, NIBC, NICNT]. There was something wrong
with the content of the teaching by a specific group of women in Ephesus,
and their teaching was being done in a heavy-handed manner that abused
the authority of the men, probably due to a trend of emancipation [ICC].

3. This prohibits a wife to have authority over her husband [ECC, NCBC].
Although the sexes are equal before God, the subordination of a wife to
her husband comes by entering into the marriage relationship [ECC].

QUESTION—What relationship is indicated by the conjunction ἀλλά 'but' in
the clause '*but* to be in silence'?

'Αλλά 'but' introduces a contrast between the infinitives 'to teach' and 'to
have authority over' [EGT, Lns, LSA, NIGTC]. This clause does not say that
a woman is to be silent in the whole gathered assembly in regard to every
aspect such as praying, prophesying, and singing, but only in regard to the
conduct to which it is contrasted, that of teaching and exercising authority
over men, just as the ἐν ἡσυχίᾳ 'in silence' of 2:11 is applied specifically to
the learning situation [NIGTC]. The concluding injunction to silence here
could hardly apply to the Christian home, therefore it must relate to the
assembled community [TNTC].

QUESTION—To what verb is the infinitive εἶναι 'to be' connected?

The verb βούλομαι 'I want' (which occurs in 2:8) is implied by the use of
οὐκ ἐπιτρέπω 'I do not permit' in the first part of the verse [Alf, ECC,
EGT, Herm, LSA, My]. The contrast with οὐκ ἐπιτρέπω 'I do not permit' is
'I enjoin' [ECC].

2:13 Because Adam first[a] was-formed,[b] then[c] Eve.

LEXICON—a. πρῶτος (LN 60.46) (BAGD 1.a. p. 725): 'first' [AB, BAGD,
BNTC, ECC, Herm, LN, LSA, NTC, WBC; all versions except CEV].
The clause 'Adam first was formed, then Eve' is translated 'Adam was
created before Eve' [CEV]. This particle denotes the first in time of a
series of events [BAGD, LN].

b. aorist pass. indic. of πλάσσω (LN **42.31**) (BAGD 1.b.α. p. 666): 'to be
formed' [BAGD, **LN**, NTC; GW, KJV, NCV, NIV, NRSV], 'to be
molded' [BAGD, LN], 'to be made' [AB, LN, LSA], 'to be created'
[BNTC, Herm, WBC; CEV, HCSB, NASB, REB, TEV]. This passive
verb is also translated actively: 'God made Adam' [NLT], 'God fashioned
Adam' [ECC]. This verb means to form an object [LN]. It refers to God's
creating activity in forming Adam [BAGD]. The passive form implies that
God was the actor [ECC, ICC].

c. εἶτα (LN **67.44**) (BAGD 1. p. 234): 'then' [AB, BNTC, ECC, **LN**, NTC,
WBC; all versions except CEV, NLT, REB], 'only then' [Herm],
'afterwards' [LSA; NLT, REB], 'later' [LN]. See lexical item a. for the

translation in CEV. This adverb indicates a point of time that follows
another point of time [LN].

QUESTION—What relationship is indicated by the initial conjunction γάρ
'because', and what is the role of this verse in the argument?

The conjunction γάρ indicates the first *grounds* for Paul's statement in
2:11–12 [AB, Alf, BNTC, EGT, ICC, Lns, LSA, My, NAC, NCBC, NICNT,
NIGTC, NTC, NTIC, NTL, TC, TG, TH, WBC]. God intended that men
have authority over women since he made Adam first and then afterwards he
made Eve. The order of creation indicates that God intended male authority
and female submission [AB, BKC, ICC, Lns, NTL, WBC]. The argument is
that something chronologically first is in some sense superior, an argument
Paul also used in 1 Cor. 11:7–9 [AB, BKC, BNTC, NCBC, TC, TNTC]. This
brief statement about the order of creation found in Genesis 2 is meant to
appeal to the whole account about what God did and said about Adam in Eve
in that account [NIGTC]. The argument is based on the fact that Adam was
created *before* Eve, and also that Adam became the *source* of the creation of
Eve [TH]. Not only is the order of creation involved, but also the fact that
God created Eve (1) for the sake of Adam, in that she was to be his helper
(Gen. 2:18–25) and also his glory (1 Cor. 11:7–9), and (2) God created them
so that it was Adam's nature to lead and Eve's nature was to follow [NTC].
In Jewish practice, the first-born male child inherited the responsibility of
leadership in the home and in worship. Since Adam was both male and the
oldest, he received the leadership role of the first-born son, and this also
applied to the church congregation in having the leadership role being the
responsibility of the male, not the female [NAC]. Or, this first reason does
not appear to be a perfectly logical reason [EGT, NTIC], and the argument
really rests in the next verse where Adam's superiority in intellect is shown
by the Fall [EGT].

2:14 And Adam was- not -deceived,[a] but the woman (who) having-been-
deceived[b] came-to-be in transgression.[c]

LEXICON—a. aorist pass. indic. of ἀπατάω (LN 31.12) (BAGD 1. p. 82): 'to
be deceived' [AB, BAGD, BNTC, LN, LSA, NTC; all versions except
CEV, NCV], 'to be mislead' [BAGD, LN], 'to be fooled' [ECC; CEV],
'to be tricked' [NCV], 'to be beguiled' [Lns], 'to be seduced' [Herm].
This verb and its intensive form ἐξαπατάω (b. below), denote causing
someone to have misleading or erroneous views about the truth [LN].

b. aorist pass. participle of ἐξαπατάω (LN 31.12) (BAGD p. 273): 'to be
deceived' [AB, BAGD, BNTC, LN, LSA; GW, HCSB, KJV, NASB,
NIV, NLT, NRSV, TEV], 'to be mislead' [LN], 'to be led astray'
[BAGD], 'to be tricked' [NCV], 'to be made a fool of' [ECC]. This
passive verb is also translated actively: 'to yield to temptation' [REB], 'to
succumb to the seduction' [Herm]. Some indicate that this is an intensive
form of the verb: 'to indeed be deceived' [NTC], 'to be fully deceived'
[NET], 'to be completely fooled' [CEV], 'to be completely beguiled'

[Lns]. This verb is in the same semantic domain as ἀπατάω in a. above, but with the prefix ἐκ- it has an intensive meaning [LN].

c. παράβασις (LN 36.28) (BAGD p. 612): 'transgression' [BAGD, LN], 'disobedience' [LN]. The phrase ἐν παραβάσει γέγονεν 'came to be in transgression' [Lns] is also translated 'fell into transgression' [AB, BNTC, NTC; NASB, NET], 'and transgressed' [HCSB], 'she transgressed what God had commanded' [LSA], 'fell into sin' [Herm; REB], 'and sinned' [CEV], 'and became a sinner' [NCV, NIV], 'and became a transgressor' [NRSV], 'was in the transgression' [KJV], 'and sin was the result' [NLT], 'and she turned to sin' [ECC], 'and brought sin into the world' [GW], 'and broke God's law' [TEV]. This noun denotes an act that is contrary to law or an established custom, and it implies that the violation is intentional [LN]. Eve's transgression was not obeying God's plain command even though she knew and spoke about both the command and the threat of what would happen if she disobeyed [Lns].

QUESTION—What relationship is indicated by the conjunction καί 'and'?

1. It connects this statement to the γάρ 'because' in 2:13 as a second supporting grounds for Paul's prohibition in 2:12 [AB, Alf, BNTC, ECC, Herm, ICC, Lns, LSA, NAC, NIBC, NTC, NTIC, TG, TH, TNTC]: *and also because*.

2. The grounds for following the respective roles of men and women is given in 2:13 by referring to the creation of Eve from Adam, so this verse serves as an example of the dire consequences of reversing the leadership roles established by God [NICNT, NIGTC].

QUESTION—What is meant by the statement 'Adam was not deceived'?

It means that Adam was not deceived by the serpent, in contrast to Eve who was deceived by the serpent [ECC, NTIC]. Adam was without fault in the matter of deception [Alf, TG]. Instead of being deceived, Adam sinned willfully [My, NIGTC, TC, TH]. This does not dissolve Adam of his guilt (Rom. 5:12), which was greater than Eve's because he sinned with his eyes open when he tasted the fruit [BKC, BNTC, TNTC]. Although Eve might seem to be the first to sin, Adam was probably present and failed to say anything to stop Eve, and his sin of omission occurred at the same time of Eve's sin of commission [WBC]. Adam's guilt was greater because he sinned fully knowing what he was doing [Alf, BNTC, NTC]. Some think that it is implied that Adam was not deceived by the serpent but by Eve [ICC, NIBC].

QUESTION—What is meant by the verb ἐξαπατηθεῖσα 'having been deceived'?

The shift from ἠπατήθη '(not) deceived' in regard to Adam to the compound verb ἐξαπατηθεῖσα 'having been deceived' in regard to Eve could merely be a stylistic variation, or the compound verb could signify an intensification of the meaning [ICC, WBC]. since the emphatic use of the compound verb fits the context. Then it would mean that Adam was *not at all* deceived, but Eve was *completely* deceived by the serpent's deception [WBC].

1. This verb concerning the woman being deceived has the same sense as the verb ἠπατήθη that is used in reference to Adam not being deceived [EGT, LSA, NICNT, TH, TNTC; all versions except CEV, NET]. The change of verb was only stylistic, since this very verb is used in 2 Corinthians 11:3 without any added nuance of being intensive [NICNT]. Paul has used the compound verb in five places in his writings and the simple verb only once, so probably the compound verb came naturally to his mind [EGT].
2. This verb has an ἐκ- prefix which intensifies the verb and means that she was *completely* deceived [Alf, ECC, Lns, NAC, NTC, NTL, TC; CEV, NET].
3. This refers to the woman being sexually seduced by the Serpent [Herm, NCBC]. There is Jewish tradition that the serpent indulged in unchaste practices with Eve [Herm, NCBC], a situation that is emphatically denied with respect to Adam [Herm].

QUESTION—What relationship is indicated by the use of the participle ἐξαπατηθεῖσα 'having been deceived'?

The participle indicates the reason why the woman transgressed [EGT, ICC, LSA, NCBC, NIBC, NIGTC, TH, WBC; NLT]: *because the woman was deceived, she transgressed.* Eve was tricked, yet she was still responsible for her actions and God punished her with increased pain in childbirth [WBC].

QUESTION—What is the significance of referring to Eve as ἡ γυνή 'the woman'?

In the Septuagint account of Genesis 3, Eve is referred to as ἡ γυνή 'the woman' [NIGTC]. The woman whom the Serpent deceived was certainly Eve, but by calling her 'the woman', her sex is emphasized so that in the next verse Paul can continue with the generalization '*she* (any woman) shall be saved' and with the plural form 'if *they* remain in faith' [Lns]. This signifies that the traits of the first woman Eve, are also transmitted to all of her female descendents [BNTC]. The characters and propensities of Adam and Eve are transmitted to their descendants, and since God ruled that Eve's desire would be to her husband and Adam was to rule over her, this applied to the entire female sex [BNTC]. This may signal a connection to the women of 2:9–12 [ICC], and this also prepares for the reference to women in general with the third person plural verb μείνωσιν '*they* remain' in 2:15 [Alf, ICC, NIGTC]. Paul has emphasized the sex instead of the individual since he wants to give the incident a general application [EGT]. Eve is the representative woman [NAC, NIBC], and in the same way Eve was deceived by Satan, some women in Ephesus have turned away to follow Satan (5:15) by being deceived by the false teachers who were involved in things taught by demons (4:1) [NIBC].

QUESTION—What is the significance of the woman being the one who was deceived and transgressed God's command?

God appointed Eve to have a subordinate position to Adam, but she deserted her position when she sinned by taking the leadership into her own hands [Lns, NIGTC]. A lower rank in the order of creation is accompanied by a

greater moral weakness that is more susceptible to suggestions [AB]. Eve
was the gullible one, so she, and all women, cannot be trusted to teach
[BNTC]. Since Adam sinned without being deceived, he would appear to be
even more guilty than Eve, but here Paul is making the point that women in
general are more easily led astray and therefore should not be placed in the
position of teachers [TNTC].

QUESTION—What is meant by the phrase ἐν παραβάσει γέγονεν 'came to be
in transgression'

The perfect tense of the verb γέγονεν 'having come to be' indicates a
permanent, abiding state [NTL, TNTC]. The past event is viewed as having a
continuing present influence upon the subject so that the woman passed into
a new state of being in sin and remained there [Alf, ECC, ICC, NAC,
NIGTC, TC]. The preposition ἐν 'in (transgression)' has the idea of coming
into a state or condition of sin [ECC, EGT, ICC] at a definite point in time
[EGT]. The perfect tense of the verb 'having come to be' makes a
connection between the historic person of Eve and the consequent effect on
all women in 2:15 [WBC]. The word παραβάσει 'transgression' denotes the
willful breach of God's definite command [Alf, ECC, ICC], or law [ICC,
My, NIGTC, TC, TH]. The man also is in the state of transgression, but that
is not treated here [Alf].

2:15 But she-will-be-saved[a] in/through[b] the childbearing,[c]

LEXICON—a. fut. pass. indic. of σῴζω (LN 21.27) (BAGD 2.b. p. 798): 'to be
saved' [BAGD, LN]. The singular verb σωθήσεται 'she will be saved'
[AB, Herm; HCSB, Lns, NTC, WBC; KJV, NCV, NRSV] is also
translated 'a woman will be saved' [TEV], 'she will be delivered' [NET],
'she and all women will be saved' [GW], 'women will be saved' [LSA;
CEV, NIV, NLT], 'women will be preserved' [NASB], 'salvation for the
women will be' [REB], 'a person will be saved (rearing children)' [ECC].
This verb means to cause someone to experience divine salvation [LN].

b. διά (LN 13.8, 89.76, 89.80) (BAGD A.III.1.c. p. 180): 'in' [LN (13.8);
KJV, REB], 'through' [AB, BAGD, BNTC, Herm, LN (89.76), WBC; all
versions except CEV, KJV, REB], 'by means of' [BAGD, LN (89.76)],
'by' [LN (89.76); CEV], 'by way of' [Lns, NTC], 'with, while at the same
time' [LN (89.80)], 'as (they bear children)' [LSA], not explicit [ECC].
This preposition indicates a state or condition of the person [LN (13.8)],
or the means by which one event causes another event to happen [BAGD,
LN (89.76)], or it indicates attendant circumstances, often implying means
[LN (89.80)].

c. τεκνογονία (LN **23.52**) (BAGD p. 808): 'the bearing of children'
[BAGD]. The prepositional phrase διὰ τῆς τεκνογονίας 'in/through the
childbearing' is translated 'through childbearing' [AB, BNTC, WBC;
HCSB, NET, NIV, NLT, NRSV], 'by way of childbearing' [Lns], 'by way
of her childbearing' [NTC], 'through the bearing of children' [NASB],
'through bearing children' [Herm], 'in the bearing of children' [REB], 'as

they bear children' [LSA], 'in childbearing' [KJV], 'through having children' [**LN**; NCV, TEV], 'by having children' [CEV], 'rearing children' [ECC], 'through the birth of the child' [GW]. This noun denotes the birth of a child [LN].

QUESTION—What relationship is indicated by the conjunction δέ 'but'?

1. Δέ 'but' indicates a contrast with the preceding statement that the woman is a transgressor (2:14) [AB, Alf, BNTC, ECC, EGT, Herm, LSA, My, NIBC, NIGTC, WBC]: *the woman came to be in transgression, but/yet she will be saved.* Despite all its enduring effects, the woman's original transgression is not irreversible [ECC]. Δέ 'yet' indicates a contra-expectation [AB, LSA; NRSV]: *yet, in spite of that, she will be saved.*

2. Δέ 'but' indicates a contrast between the men's position of teaching in and conduct of worship services with the women's position of domesticity in the home [BNTC, Lns, NTC]. The δέ 'but' merely adds a further comment about the status of women in the church in contrast with that of the men [Lns]. The writer states that women are to find their salvation, not in teaching or conducting worship services in the church, to which the men are appointed (2:8, 12), but in the sphere of the home and child rearing [BNTC, Lns, NTC].

QUESTION—To whom does the third person singular subject of the passive verb σωθήσεται 'she will be saved' refer?

1. 'She' refers to all women collectively [AB, Alf, BNTC, Herm, ICC, Lns, LSA, NAC, NIBC, NIGTC, NTL, TH, TNTC; CEV, GW, NASB, NIV, NLT, REB]: *women will be saved in/through childbirth.*

1.1 The subject 'she' in the verb σωθήσεται '*she shall be saved*' refers to women in general and this implied plural is made explicit by the subject 'they' in the verb μείνωσιν '*they* remain' in the next clause [AB, Alf, BNTC, Herm, ICC, Lns, LSA, NAC, NIBC, NICNT, NTL, TC, TNTC]. 'She' is identified by specifying 'women' [LSA; CEV, NASB, NIV, NLT, REB]. This is not talking about Eve's salvation, but the salvation of the women in Ephesus [NIBC]. In 2:14 the singular noun ἡ γυνὴ 'the woman' who was deceived (aorist tense) refers to Eve, but now the tense is changed to 'she will be saved' (future tense) so as to refer to women in general [BNTC, Lns, LSA]. The singular pronoun indicates a generic use of the word [TH]. Or, verses 2:13–14 are parenthetic so that the implied subject of 'she' is the generic use of γυναικί 'a woman' in 2:11–12 [ICC, NTL].

1.2 The formal reference here is first of all to Eve, as in 2:14, but it is applied to include all women generally [My, NIBC, NIGTC, NTC, WBC; GW]. 'She' refers to 'the woman' in 2:14 [NTC]. 'She' is identified by specifying the implied extension: 'she and all women' [GW]. Paul is talking about Eve, as reflected in the facts that the passive verb σωθήσεται 'she shall be saved' is singular and the future tense is in reference to Eve's perspective. Yet Paul is not talking about Eve in isolation, but she is used as *a typological parallel* representing the

Ephesian women. He demonstrates this by switching to a plural verb ἐὰν μείνωσιν 'if *they* remain' in the final clause of this verse [NTC, WBC], and the shifts in number and tense in this paragraph make good sense in the logic of Paul's argument when the use of a typological parallel is kept in mind [WBC].

2. This refers to any Christian parent, male or female [ECC]: *a person will be saved through rearing children*. As with the impersonal plural μείνωσιν 'they continue' later in this verse, the antecedent of the impersonal singular σωθήσεται 'she shall be saved' is the mention of Adam and his wife, Eve in 2:14, so that this refers to any Christian parent, man or woman, and was so understood by some of the early church fathers [ECC].

QUESTION—What is meant by σωθήσεται 'she will be saved'?

1. The word σωθήσεται 'she shall be saved' refers to spiritual salvation in the comprehensive sense, from the forgiveness of sins to the eternal, eschatological redemption [AB, BAGD, BNTC, ECC, Herm, ICC, Lns, LSA, My, NAC, NIBC, NICNT, NIGTC, NTC, TH, TNTC, WBC; all versions]. The term παραβάσει 'transgression' in the preceding clause defines from what she shall be saved [WBC]. They will be saved *from* their sins [ICC, NIBC, TH], or their sinful condition [TH], and they will be saved *for* eternal life [NIBC]. Being saved is receiving forgiveness of sins [NAC]. The passive voice indicates that this deliverance from eternal death is wrought for her by God [ECC, TH]. Or, she will be saved by Christ since the future tense shifts the attention here from Eve to the promised future deliverance through the seed of the woman (Gen. 3:15), which is Christ [NIGTC].

2. The reference of σωθήσεται 'she will be saved' is to physical safety throughout the process of childbirth [TC; this is also given as an alternative translation in CEV, NLT, TEV]: *women will be brought safely through childbirth* if they continue in faith, etc.

3. The word σωθήσεται 'she shall be saved' refers to being preserved from insignificance [BKC].

QUESTION—What is meant by the woman being saved διὰ τῆς τεκνογονίας 'in/through the child-bearing'?

1. Τῆς τεκνογονίας 'the childbearing' refers to the birth process and the reference is general, i.e., to the birth of any child [AB, BAGD (p. 808), BKC, BNTC, EGT, Herm, LSA, NIBC, NTC, TC, TG, TH, WBC; all versions except GW]. The article τῆς in the phrase '*the* childbirth' refers to the well-known childbearing that is common in motherhood [Lns]. Or, the article in 'the childbearing' is simply inelegant Greek [ECC]. The term τεκνογονίας 'childbearing' refers to a life of bearing *children*, not to just a single event of bearing one child [ECC, ICC, NAC, NIBC]. Some think that the physical act of childbirth is meant to encompass the whole process of not only bearing children, but also of rearing them [ICC, Lns, NAC]: *but women will be saved through the rearing of children*. Paul

employs a synecdoche (a part for the whole), so that 'childbearing' is used to describe a woman's work of motherhood as a whole [NAC]. Paul uses the word 'childbearing' as a synecdoche to stand for all of a woman's God-assigned roles, with the birth process being put as a specific example because the false teachers were specifically downplaying the importance of marriage, and probably also of childbirth [WBC]. The natural function of woman in general is childbearing and all that this implies in a Christian family. The subject 'the woman' also includes young girls and women who never marry, or women who have married and remain childless, but God's providence in individual lives does not destroy his general purpose for women [Lns]. Paul is saying that a woman's salvation and the practical working out of that salvation does not consist in her role in the church. Rather, she is to accept the role God assigned to her, one specific function being childbearing, and work out her salvation (Phil. 2:12) by performing the good works, which give evidence of salvation, in this area of life [WBC].

1.1 The preposition διά 'in' indicates attendant circumstances [BAGD (A.III.1.c. p. 180), EGT, ICC, Lns, LSA, NAC, NICNT, NTC, TC]: *as they bear children, women will be saved if they remain in faith, etc.* Childbearing is not a means of being saved, rather it is the natural function of a woman in a Christian family and it is implied that women are not in the least curtailed in the matter of salvation when they follow their God-given role and let men attend to the public work of teaching [Lns]. Women prove that they are saved when they become the kind of wives and mothers whose good deeds include marriage and assuming the God-appointed role of raising children [NAC]. In the context of transgression (2:14) and the following conditions for salvation which follow, taking διά to indicate an attendant circumstance is the simplest interpretation, and this is pertinent here after the women had been told what they should not be doing in 2:11–12 [LSA].

1.2 The preposition διά 'through' indicates means [BKC, BNTC, Herm, TH, WBC; CEV]: *but the women will be saved by means of bearing children, if they also remain in faith, etc.* Accepting her God-given role of bearing children (Gen. 3:16) is her path to salvation, not by usurping the role of men, such as teaching in church [BNTC]. The context indicates that διά 'through' indicates the efficient, not the ultimate, means of a woman's salvation [WBC]. Or, women will be saved from insignificance by means of their role in the family. They will not find meaning in life in seeking the male role, but by fulfilling God's design for her to be both wife and mother [BKC].

2. Τῆς τεκνογονίας 'the child-bearing' refers to the birth of 'the Child', that is, to the birth of Christ [NIGTC; GW; this is given as an alternative translation in the footnotes of CEV, NLT]: *she shall be saved by means of the birth of the Child (Christ).* This is consistent with the normal meaning of διά 'through' being the means by which she is saved, with the force of

the definite article with τεκνογονίας '*the* child-bearing', and with the
high probability that in speaking of her transgression the apostle would
not fail to mention the sustaining prophecy of the woman's Offspring
(Gen. 3:15) [NIGTC].

3. When the verb σωθήσεται 'she will be saved' is taken to refer to physical
deliverance throughout the process of childbirth [TC; this is also given as
an alternative translation in CEV, NLT, TEV] and the preposition διά
means 'during, in the course of' [LN (67.136)]: *she will be brought safely
through childbirth*. When a woman fulfills a woman's duty of bearing a
child, it shall be accompanied with pain, but nevertheless she will be
safely brought through giving birth if she continues in faith, etc. [TC]

**if they-continue[a] in faith/faithfulness and love and holiness[b] with sensi-
bility.[c]**

LEXICON—a. aorist pass. indic. of μένω (LN 68.11) (BAGD 1.a.β. p. 504): 'to
continue' [BAGD, BNTC, LN, LSA, NTC; HCSB, KJV, NASB, NCV,
NET, NIV, NRSV, REB], 'to remain' [AB, BAGD, Herm, LN, Lns,
WBC], 'to keep on' [LN], 'to stay' [CEV], 'to persevere' [ECC; TEV], 'to
continue to live (in)' [NLT], 'to lead lives' [GW]. This verb refers to
remaining in a given activity or state [LN]. Figuratively, it refers to
someone who does not leave the realm or sphere in which he finds himself
[BAGD]. The aorist tense has the force of 'to definitely remain' [Lns].

b. ἁγιασμός (LN 53.44) (BAGD p. 9): 'holiness' [AB, BAGD, ECC, WBC;
all versions except CEV, NASB], 'consecration' [BAGD, LN], 'dedication' [LN], 'sanctification' [BAGD, BNTC, Herm, Lns, NTC], 'sanctity'
[NASB]. This noun is also translated as an adjective: 'holy' [CEV]; or as
a clause: 'to live acceptably to God' [LSA]. This noun is used in the moral
sense of the process, or more often, the result, of the state of being made
holy [BAGD]. It denotes dedication to the service of God and loyalty to
him, although in some contexts it suggests a resulting moral behavior with
the emphasis upon the religious activity and observances which reflect
one's dedication or consecration to God rather than upon a manner of life
[LN].

c. σωφροσύνη (LN 32.34, **88.93**): 'sensibility' [**LN** (32.34)], 'good sense'
[NTC; HCSB], 'sound judgment' [LN], 'propriety' [NIV], 'moderation,
sensibility' [LN (88.93)], 'moral discretion' [AB], 'self-control' [NCV,
NET], 'self-restraint' [NASB], 'dignity' [Herm], 'modesty' [WBC; NLT,
NRSV, REB, TEV], 'chastity' [BNTC], 'sobriety' [Lns; KJV]. This noun
is also translated as an adjective: 'sensible' [ECC], 'modest' [LSA; CEV],
'respectable' [GW]. This noun denotes behaving oneself in a sensible
manner, and it implies that the person doing so possesses a thoughtful
awareness of what is in one's best interest [LN (88.93)], or it denotes
understanding practical matters so as to act sensibly [LN (32.34)]. See this
word at 2:9.

QUESTION—What is meant by ἐάν 'if'?

The conjunction ἐάν 'if' indicates the condition that must be met to receive salvation and remain in it [NIGTC]. This conjunction introduces the condition which joins the successful outworking of this salvation to the continued practice of behavior which is specifically Christian in nature [ICC]. Their salvation is made sure by their resolve to observe these qualities [TH]. Since salvation is not acquired by mere good works [BNTC, My, NIBC, NIGTC], and since motherhood is the common lot of women [BNTC, My], the apostle adds a vital condition [BNTC, My, NIBC]. It means that even though a woman's salvation has already been objectively provided and accomplished, she does not just automatically experience it. To be experienced, it requires an abiding and living faith which is manifested and expressed in a holiness of life that is appropriate for women [NIGTC].

QUESTION—Who is the referent of the third person plural subject of the verb μείνωσιν 'they remain', and what is the significance of the aorist tense of this verb?

1. It refers to women in general [AB, Alf, BKC, BNTC, Lns, LSA, My, NAC, NCBC, NIBC, NICNT, NIGTC, NTC, TG, TH, WBC], or, more specifically, to Christian women as a class since the following condition must be met [Herm, ICC, Lns, NTC, TNTC]. The referent of the generic plural here is the same as in the generic singular in the previous clause [Alf, NTC, TG, TH; NET]. It is not unusual to find the singular changing to the plural if the subject in question has the characteristic of a noun of multitude [TH]. This transition to the plural verb is awkward, and this has led some commentators to the view that it refers to the husband and wife or to the conduct of the woman's children. But this would constitute an abrupt change of subject that is difficult to accept. The awkwardness disappears if one remembers that throughout this paragraph, Paul has been writing about women in the plural or referring to them as a class in the singular [BNTC]. This cannot refer to the children of the women, since that would make the women's salvation dependent upon the conduct of her offspring [TH, WBC]. Likewise, it probably doesn't refer to a woman and her husband because it is the women who are the focus of the verse [TH] and, in the final analysis, neither a husband nor her children are necessary to a woman's salvation [WBC].

2. It refers to a husband and wife [ECC, EGT]. With this interpretation the plural μείνωσιν 'they continue' has as its antecedent the mention of Adam and his wife, Eve, in 2:14 so that the virtues which are mentioned in this clause are explicitly urged upon husbands as well as wives [ECC]. After speaking of a women in her marriage relationship, 'they' refers to the woman and her husband [EGT].

QUESTION—What is the relationship between the nouns πίστει 'faith', ἀγάπῃ 'love', and ἁγιασμῷ 'holiness'?

A woman's faith will activate the qualities of love and holiness [NAC, NIBC]. Πίστει 'faith' is the quality that apprehends salvation, ἀγάπῃ 'love' (both to God and to men) is the invariable fruit of faith, and ἁγιασμῷ 'holiness' of the life is the end result [Lns]. 'Faith' and 'love' are the aim of the commandment given in 1:5, while 'holiness' is the character of the Christian community that is committed to the holy God [AB]. Faith and love bring about holiness [TC].

QUESTION—What is meant by πίστει 'faith/faithfulness'?

1. It refers to having faith, that is, the act of believing [AB, Alf, BNTC, EGT, Herm, ICC, Lns, LSA, NAC, NCBC, NIGTC, NTC, TH, TNTC, WBC; all versions except CEV]. Πίστει 'faith' is used in the active sense of 'believing' [NIGTC]. This refers to faith in Christ [BNTC, ICC, TG, TH, WBC] and his work on the cross [WBC], or to faith in God [EGT].

2. It refers to the attribute of 'faithfulness' [ECC; CEV]: *if they remain faithful.* None specify as to what they are to remain faithful.

QUESTION—What is the implied object of the event noun ἀγάπη 'love'?

1. The object of ἀγάπη 'love' is fellow Christians [BNTC, EGT].

2. The object of ἀγάπη 'love' is other people [LSA, TG, TH, WBC]. This word represents the horizontal relationship of the Christian life [TH].

3. The object of ἀγάπη 'love' is both God and people [Lns].

QUESTION—What is meant by ἁγιασμῷ 'holiness'?

It means 'holiness' [AB, NICNT, NIGTC, TG, TH, TNTC, WBC; all versions except NASB], or 'sanctification' [BAGD, BNTC, Herm, Lns, NTC; NASB]: *if they remain in faith and love and live a consecrated Christian life.* The word is used in a moral and ethical sense [BAGD, TH]. Holiness describes the state of belonging to the Lord [NTL]. This refers to a life dedicated to God and because of that, it is characterized by blameless conduct [TH]. It refers to the daily dying to sin and renewal unto holiness, and perhaps has a special emphasis here on active opposition to all immorality and uncleanness in thought and act [NTC]. Though translating ἁγιασμῷ as 'sanctification', one commentator states that it applies to the degree in which women keep their married life consecrated and not merely carnal [BNTC]. The meaning is parallel to that in 1 Thess. 4:3, 4, 7 where the term demands sexual purity in Christian marriage [ECC].

QUESTION—What relationship is indicated by μετά 'with' in the prepositional phrase μετὰ σωφροσύνης 'with sensibility'?

The preposition μετά 'with' is used to show a close connection between nouns, with the focus being upon the first mentioned noun(s) [BAGD (A.II.6 p. 509)]. With the word 'sensibility' occurring at both 2:9 and here, Paul ends on the same note with which he began. He wants women to dress modestly (2:9) since this is appropriate to their salvation (2:15) [WBC].

1. The phrase μετὰ σωφροσύνης 'with sensibility' is connected with the preceding three qualities 'faith and love and holiness' [AB, BAGD (A.II.6 p. 509), BNTC, Herm, ICC, LN (89.123), Lns, My, NTC, NTL, TH, WBC; GW, HCSB, NCV, NRSV, REB, TEV]: *if they remain in faith and love and holiness, doing all of this with sensibility.* Σωφροσύνης 'prudence/modesty' is mentioned with the preceding cardinal virtues of

the Christian life because it is particularly becoming as it resides in the mind of a woman [My]. It is listed separately as a key virtue which must accompany the others [ICC]. It indicates the way in which a woman expresses her faith, love, and holiness [TH].

2. The phrase is connected only with ἁγιασμῷ 'holiness' [ECC, TG]: *if they remain in faith and love, and in holiness with sensibility.* The phrase refers to a sensible holiness of sexual self-control and responsibility [ECC]. She will be pure and sensible in her conduct [TG].

3. It is treated as a fourth virtue: 'if they stay faithful, loving, holy, and modest' [LSA, TNTC; CEV, NLT]. The four nouns in this clause are the four conditions for a woman's salvation [LSA].

QUESTION—What is meant by σωφροσύνης 'sensibility/modesty'

It refers to the attribute of being sensible in what they do [ECC, LN (32.34), NTC, TG; HCSB], especially in regard to having self-control [ICC, NIGTC, NTC; NASB, NCV, NET], being chaste [BNTC, ICC], discrete and prudent [AB], dignified [Herm], respectable [GW], modest [LSA, NTL, TH, WBC; CEV, NLT, NRSV, REB, TEV], and unassuming [TG]. This results in keeping their proper place in church services [Lns]. The use of the term in this concluding statement probably refers not only to restraint and discretion in clothing and adornment (2:9), but also, to the woman's role versus the man's in the church, reflecting a woman's lifestyle and attitude which restrain her from being immodest or ostentatious, as well as from violating the order which the Creator-Savior has instituted [NIGTC]. Here, as in 2:9, the emphasis is on self control, which, in the case of women, must be expressed in behavior that is chaste [ICC]. Modesty was the virtue most admired by the society in which they lived [NTL].

DISCOURSE UNIT: 3:1–16 [NIGTC; GW, NASB, NIV]. The topic is the overseers and deacons [NASB, NIV], qualifications for bishops and deacons [NIGTC], guidelines for leaders in the church [GW].

DISCOURSE UNIT: 3:1–13 [ICC, NAC, NICNT, TH, TNTC; HCSB, NET, NLT]. The topic is the leaders in the church [NLT], church leadership by committed servants [NAC], the qualifications of church leaders [TH, TNTC; HCSB], qualifications for overseers and deacons [ICC, NICNT; NET].

DISCOURSE UNIT: 3:1–7 [AB, ICC, NAC, NCBC, NIBC, NICNT, NIGTC, TH, TNTC, WBC; CEV, NCV, NRSV, TEV]. The topic is overseers [WBC], bishops [NIGTC, TH, TNTC], church officials [CEV], elders in the church [NCV], leaders in the church [TEV], qualifications for bishops [NCBC; NRSV], qualifications for overseers [ICC, NAC, NIBC, NICNT], qualifications for the supervisor [AB].

3:1a Trustworthy/true[a] (is) the saying/statement.[b]

TEXT—Instead of πιστὸς ὁ λόγος 'trustworthy (is) the saying', some manu-scripts read ἀνθρώπινος ὁ λόγος 'human (is) the saying' and one manuscript omits this phrase. GNT reads πιστὸς ὁ λόγος 'trustworthy (is) the saying' with an A decision, indicating that the text is certain.

LEXICON—a. πιστός (LN 31.87, 71.17) (BAGD 1.b. p. 664): 'trustworthy' [BAGD, BNTC, LN (31.87), WBC; HCSB, NASB, NET, NIV, NLT], 'dependable' [BAGD, LN (31.87)], 'reliable' [AB, LN (31.87), NTC], 'sure' [LN (71.17); NRSV], 'true' [CEV, KJV, NCV, TEV], 'faithful' [BAGD, LN (31.87), Lns]. This adjective is also translated as a verb phrase: '(a statement) that can be trusted' [GW], '(a saying) you may trust' [REB], 'which can be believed by people' [LSA], 'meant to be believed' [ECC], 'stands firm' [Herm]. This adjective indicates that something can be trusted [LN (31.78)], or, that something is sure, with the implication that it is worthy of being fully trusted [LN (71.17)]. See this word at 1:15.

    b. λόγος (LN 33.98) (BAGD 1.b.β. p. 478): 'saying' [BNTC, LN, LSA, NTC, WBC; HCSB, KJV, NET, NIV, NLT, NRSV, REB, TEV], 'word' [Herm, LN], 'message' [ECC], 'statement' [LN, Lns; NASB], 'opinion' [AB]. The clause πιστὸς ὁ λόγος 'trustworthy/true (is) the saying' is translated 'this is a statement that can be trusted:' [GW], 'this is a true saying' [TEV], 'what I say is true' [NCV], 'it is true that' [CEV], 'that is the Christian message, meant to be believed' [ECC]. This noun denotes that which has been stated and its primary focus is on the contents of the communication [LN]. This refers to divine revelation through Christ and his messengers [BAGD]. See this word at 1:15; 4:9.

QUESTION—How is this short sentence connected to its context?

    1. It is connected forward to 3:1b [Alf, BKC, BNTC, ICC, Lns, LSA, My, NAC, NCBC, NIBC, NICNT, NIGTC, NTC, TH, TC, TNTC, WBC; all versions]: *this saying/statement is trustworthy, namely that if anyone desires the office of bishop, etc.* Many end this clause with a colon to connect it with the clause that follows [Lns; GW, HCSB, NASB, NCV, NET, NIV, NRSV, REB, TEV]. Without this introductory formula, the connection with the verses that follow would be much too abrupt [NIGTC]. Neither 2:15 nor any of the verses preceding it seem to be a maxim or saying that would have been current in the church [BNTC, ICC, NAC, NTC]. Here, as in 1:15, the saying introduces a new train of thought that emphasizes the dignity of the office before taking up the qualifications that the office requires [TNTC]. In view of the deep interest there was in church order at that time, the saying could easily have arisen and Paul used this saying to commend the importance of the office of bishop and introduce the qualifications for the office [NIGTC]. Perhaps this saying had arisen to develop an esteem for the office of bishop and thus encourage candidates to offer themselves for that position [BNTC].

    2. It is connected backward to 2:15 [AB, ECC, EGT, Herm, NTIC, NTL, WP]. This sentence closes the preceding paragraph and a new paragraph begins with 3:1b [ECC, Herm, WP]. If this connection is taken, then all of the faithful sayings would be dealing with the issue of salvation, and here

this formula would highlight the significance of 2:15 [ICC, NIGTC, WBC]. It is connected with 2:15, by saying that it is a reliable *opinion* instead of a saying [AB, NTIC].

QUESTION—Does the noun λόγος mean a commonly known 'saying' or an original 'statement'?

1. It means a 'saying' that was commonly held and well known [BKC, BNTC, ECC, LN, LSA, NAC, NCBC, NIGTC, NTC, TNTC; HCSB, KJV, NET, NIV, NLT, NRSV, REB, TEV]. The five 'trustworthy sayings' (1 Tim. 1:15, 3:1, 4:9; 2 Tim. 2:11; Titus 3:8) were trustworthy proverbs or maxims that were then current, and the present one harmonizes beautifully with the entire paragraph that follows [NTC]. This formula introduces a saying concerning the office of bishop [NIGTC]. Paul is probably referring to the common knowledge that the office of an overseer was a noble task despite the fact that some of the leaders in Ephesus had performed poorly [NAC].

2. It means a 'statement' that Paul writes here in his letter [AB, ICC, Lns, NIBC, NICNT, NTIC, WBC; CEV, GW, NASB, NCV]. Instead of a current *saying*, this is probably simply Paul's affirmation of the truth of the following statement [ICC]. Probably these words had become a kind of reinforcement formula for Paul, meaning 'what I am about to say is of special import' [NIBC], or what he just wrote was reliable [AB]. It is a trustworthy statement because it is true [Lns]. The formula is used, not to indicate that the citation is from traditional material, but to give solemnity to it [WBC].

DISCOURSE UNIT: 3:1b–7 [ECC, Herm, NTL]. The topic is overseers [NTL], the bishop [ECC], the conduct of bishops [Herm].

3:1b **If anyone aspires-to[a] (the) office-of-overseer[b] he-desires[c] a-good work.[d]**

LEXICON—a. pres. mid. indic. of ὀρέγομαι (LN **25.15**) (BAGD p. 579): 'to aspire to' [BAGD, BNTC, ECC, **LN**, Lns, LSA, NTC, WBC; HCSB, NASB, NET, NLT, NRSV, REB], 'to strive for' [Herm], 'to strive to attain, to eagerly long for' [LN], 'to be eager (to be)' [TEV], 'to set one's heart on (being)' [GW, NIV], 'to strive for' [BAGD], 'to desire' [BAGD; CEV, KJV], 'to seek' [AB], 'to want to become' [NCV]. This verb means to eagerly desire to accomplish a goal [LN, TH].

b. ἐπισκοπή (LN **53.69**), (BAGD 3. p. 299): 'the office of overseer' [BAGD, NTC, WBC; NASB, NET], 'the office of a bishop' [Herm; KJV, NRSV], 'the position as an overseer' [BAGD], 'the office, or position as church leader' [LN], 'a ministry as a church leader' [**LN**], 'leadership' [REB], 'oversight' [BNTC], 'overseership' [Lns], 'the episcopate' [ECC]. Instead of indicating an office or position, some translate the noun as pertaining to the individual who fills the office: 'an overseer' [LSA; HCSB, NIV], 'a supervisor' [AB], 'an elder' [NCV, NLT], 'a church leader' [CEV, TEV], 'a bishop' [GW]. This noun denotes a religious position that involves both service and leadership [LN]. It is especially used of the office of a bishop [BAGD].

c. pres. act. indic. of ἐπιθυμέω (LN 25.12) (BAGD p. 293): 'to desire' [BAGD, Herm, Lns, LSA, NTC, WBC; all versions except CEV, REB], 'to desire very much' [LN], 'to long for' [BAGD, LN], 'to set one's heart on' [BNTC, ECC], 'to want (to be)' [CEV], not explicit [REB]. This verb means to greatly desire to do something or have something [ECC, LN, TNTC, WBC]. It means to set one's heart upon something and here it may be used simply as a stylistic variation of the preceding verb ὀρέγομαι 'to aspire to' [NIGTC]. The two verbs in this sentence are virtually synonymous [ICC, NICNT].

d. ἔργον (LN 42.42) (BAGD 2. or 4. p. 308): 'work' [BAGD (2.), LN, LSA], 'task' [BAGD (2.), LN], 'occupation' [BAGD (2.)], 'thing' [BAGD (4.)]. The phrase καλοῦ ἔργου 'a good work' [Herm, WBC; KJV, NCV, NET] is also translated 'an excellent work' [TEV], 'an excellent task' [Lns], 'a fine work' [ECC], 'a noble work' [NTC; HCSB], 'a noble task' [NIV, NRSV], 'an honorable position' [NLT], 'an honorable ambition' [REB], 'something excellent' [GW], 'a worthwhile job' [BNTC], 'something worthwhile' [CEV]. This noun denotes the activity that a person normally does [LN], such as in the execution of an office [BAGD (2.)]. This could have a weakened form here of 'thing' [BAGD (4.)]. It refers to an excellent occupation or work of ministry [ICC].

QUESTION—What is meant by the noun ἐπισκοπῆς 'the office of overseer'?

This refers to any office of supervisory capacity within the local church [BNTC, EGT, ICC, Lns, My, NAC, NIGTC, NTC, NTIC, TH, WBC; NIV, TEV]. The noun ἐπισκοπή is used here to mean the *position* or *office* held by an ἐπίσκοπος 'overseer' (3:2) [ICC, NIGTC]. This is an alternative term to designate the office of elder [BNTC, ICC, Lns, My, NIGTC, NTC, NTIC, WBC, WP; NCV, NLT]. This noun is derived from the verb ἐπισκοπέω 'to have responsibility for the care of someone' and means 'overseership' [WBC]. An overseer is someone who has general oversight over others, and the use of the singular form refers to the office of overseer, an office that could be held by many people [BNTC, ICC, WBC]. This is the office of a church leader, and ἐπίσκοπος 'overseer' is just one of several terms in the NT to describe such leaders. The most common term is πρεσβύτερος 'elder', but also ὑποιμήν 'pastor' is used in Eph. 4:11. Although the terms describe different aspects of leadership, they all designate the same office [BKC]. The words ἐπίσκοπος 'overseer' and πρεσβύτερος 'elder' are titles for the same office, the designation 'overseer' pertaining to the nature of the work and the designation 'elder' pertaining to a person's age and dignity [EGT, Lns, NTC]. This pertains to being a church leader, one who leads the believers [TH]. An overseer directs the affairs of the church and this includes pastoring and teaching [NAC]. The title 'bishop' in the sense of being a superintendent over a diocese did not appear until the second century [BNTC, Lns, NAC], and translating this as 'bishop' is anachronistic [ICC].

However, some have translated ἐπίσκοπος as 'bishop' [ECC, Herm; GW, KJV, NRSV, REB]. The use of the singular indefinite pronoun τις 'anyone' indicates that this is to be taken as a statement of a general truth [WBC], or as referring generically to the *class* of overseers [BNTC, NET], and it does not indicate a single leader at the top of a hierarchical structure of church leaders [NET].

3:2 **Therefore it-is-necessary[a] (that) the overseer[b] be above-reproach,[c]**

LEXICON—a. pres. act. indic. of δεῖ (LN 71.34): 'to be necessary' [LN, Lns, WBC], 'must' [AB, LN, LSA, NTC; all versions], 'should' [BNTC, Herm], 'has to' [ECC]. This verb means that something must take place as a matter of necessity [LN]. The necessity is inherent in the office of overseer [Lns].

b. ἐπίσκοπος (LN 53.71) (BAGD 2. p. 299): 'overseer' [BNTC, Lns, LSA, NTC, WBC; HCSB, NASB, NET, NIV], 'church leader' [LN; TEV], 'elder' [NCV, NLT], 'supervisor' [AB], 'superintendent, guardian' [BAGD], 'official' [CEV], 'bishop' [BAGD, ECC, Herm; GW, KJV, NRSV, REB]. This noun denotes the one who serves as a leader in a church, and it combines the ideas of both leadership and service since this person had the responsibility of caring for the needs of the congregation as well as directing the activities of the members [LN]. It refers to a person who has a definite function or a fixed office within the church [BAGD, NIGTC].

c. ἀνεπίλημπτος (LN 33.415) (BAGD p. 65): 'above reproach' [BNTC, NTC, WBC; HCSB, NASB, NET, NIV, NRSV, REB], 'without reproach' [Herm], 'beyond reproach, above criticism' [LN], 'irreproachable' [BAGD, ECC, Lns], 'without fault' [TEV], 'blameless' [AB; KJV]. The phrase ἀνεπίλημπτον εἶναι 'be above reproach' is translated 'have a good reputation' [CEV, GW], 'be a man whose life is above reproach' [NLT], 'not give people a reason to criticize him' [NCV], 'he must conduct himself in such a way that on one can justifiably reproach him' [LSA]. This adjective describes a person who cannot be criticized [LN].

QUESTION—What relationship is indicated by the conjunction οὖν 'therefore'?

1. The conjunction indicates a conclusion drawn from the preceding clause [AB, BNTC, Lns, LSA, NIBC, NICNT, NIGTC, NTC, TC, WBC; CEV, HCSB, KJV, NASB, NET, REB]: *the office of overseer is a good work, therefore an overseer must be above reproach.* The importance of the office requires the qualifications that follow [NICNT].

2. The conjunction continues the discussion about the office of an overseer [NIV, NRSV; probably GW, NCV, TEV which omit the conjunction]: *now the overseer must be above reproach.*

QUESTION—What is the significance of the singular noun ἐπισκοπῆς 'an overseer' here and the indefinite plural noun διακόνους 'deacons' in 3:8?

It probably does not imply that in any one congregation there were many deacons but only one overseer. The singular ἐπισκοπῆς 'an overseer' is to be taken as a general reference referring to the class of overseers [BNTC, EGT, LSA, My, NAC, WBC; NET], or the singular form refers to the category of the men who had been given oversight in the church and to teach [NIGTC]. Perhaps the singular form was influenced by the singular τις 'anyone' in 3:1, and there is no significant contrast intended with the plural 'deacons' in 3:8 [BNTC, LSA, NIGTC]. Presuming that the πρεσβύτεροι 'elders' in 5:17 are the same people as the overseers, there would be more than one overseer in a congregation [BNTC, LSA]. This word does not have the monarchial sense of a bishop over the elders [WP]. Or, it could be that only one overseer served in a single house-group so that there was a group of overseers in Ephesus because there were various house-groups in that city [NAC]. Or, in Ephesus there was one leadership position occupied by a supervisor, then a board of elders, and also subordinate officials called deacons or servers [NTIC].

QUESTION—What is meant by ἀνεπίλημπτον εἶναι 'to be above reproach'?

The overseer must not be vulnerable to attack or criticism in regard to his Christian life in general, and especially concerning the list of characteristics that follow [NIGTC]. He must be irreproachable [WP]. Since this requirement is the responsibility of the overseer and not of those who would reproach him if he did wrong, it is implied that an overseer must conduct himself in such a way that no one can *justifiably* reproach him [LSA]. He is to be above reproach in the estimation of fellow church members, and if enemies bring accusations against him those charges will be proved to be empty whenever fair methods of investigation are applied [NTC]. His character and actions must give no basis for an accusation or reproach against him [BKC, BNTC, ECC, NICNT]. This person must be of such a character that no one can *justly* charge him of unfitness [Lns, NAC]. This denotes a person against whom it is impossible to bring a charge of wrongdoing such as could stand in an impartial examination [EGT]. It implies not only that the candidate has a good report, but that he deserves it [NTC, TC, TNTC, WBC]. This is equivalent to the concluding requirement of the list in 2:7, that he must have a good testimony from the ones outside [NICNT].

of-one wife[a] a-husband, sober,[b] sensible,[c] dignified,[d] hospitable,[e] able-to-teach,[f]

LEXICON—a. γυνή (LN 10.54): 'wife' [LN]. The phrase μιᾶς γυναικὸς ἄνδρα 'of one wife a husband' is translated 'a "one-woman" man' [WBC], 'one wife's husband' [Lns, NTC], 'the husband of one wife' [AB, BNTC, Herm; HCSB, KJV, NASB, NET, REB], 'the husband of only/but one wife' [LSA; NIV], 'a husband to one wife' [ECC], 'have only one wife' [GW, NCV, TEV], 'be faithful to his wife' [NLT], 'be faithful in

marriage' [CEV], 'married only once' [NRSV]. The noun γυνή denotes a
woman, and in Greek a wife is simply called 'his woman', 'my woman',
with the context normally indicating whether 'woman' or 'wife' is meant
[LN].
  b. νηφάλιος (LN **88.87**) (BAGD p. 538): 'sober' [AB, BAGD, Herm, **LN**;
     GW, REB, TEV], 'clear-minded' [WBC], 'clear-headed' [BAGD,
     BNTC], 'self-controlled' [BAGD; CEV, HCSB, NCV], 'temperate'
     [ECC, Lns, NTC; NASB, NET, NIV, NRSV], 'restrained' [LN], 'vigilant'
     [KJV]. This adjective is also translated as a verb phrase: 'think clearly'
     [LSA], 'exercise self-control' [NLT]. This adjective describes a manner of
     behavior that is sober or restrained [LN]. Included in this word's range of
     meanings is being temperate in the use of alcoholic beverages [BAGD].
     The adjective means temperate or sober, and can be used figuratively as
     being self-controlled and sober-minded [NICNT]. See this word at 3:11.
  c. σώφρων (LN 88.94) (BAGD p. 802): 'sensible' [ECC, LN, LSA; CEV,
     HCSB, NRSV], 'wise' [NCV], 'temperate' [REB], 'moderate' [LN],
     'prudent' [AB, BAGD, Herm; NASB], 'thoughtful' [BAGD], 'self-
     controlled' [BAGD, BNTC, NTC, WBC; NET, NIV, TEV], 'sober'
     [KJV], 'sober-minded' [Lns]. This adjective is also translated as a verb
     phrase: 'use good judgment' [GW], 'live wisely' [NLT]. This adjective
     describes a person as being sensible or moderate in behavior [LN].
  d. κόσμιος (LN **88.48**) (BAGD 1. p. 445): 'dignified' [BNTC, LSA, WBC],
     'respectable' [AB, BAGD; GW, HCSB, NASB, NET, NIV, NRSV],
     'respected by others' [NCV], 'well-behaved' [CEV], 'courteous' [REB],
     'of good behavior' [KJV], 'urbane' [ECC], 'moderate' [Herm, **LN**],
     'modest, well-ordered, becoming' [LN], 'orderly' [Lns; TEV], 'virtuous'
     [NTC], 'honorable' [BAGD]. This adjective is also translated as a verb
     phrase: 'have a good reputation' [NLT]. This adjective describes a person
     who is modest in the sense of being moderate and well-ordered [LN].
  e. φιλόξενος (LN 34.58) (BAGD p. 860): 'hospitable' [AB, BAGD, BNTC,
     Herm, LN, Lns, LSA, NTC, WBC; GW, HCSB, NASB, NET, NIV,
     NRSV, REB], 'given to hospitality' [KJV], 'friendly to strangers' [CEV],
     'one who likes guests' [ECC]. This adjective is also translated as a verb
     phrase: 'welcome strangers in his home' [TEV], 'ready to welcome
     guests' [NCV], 'enjoy having guests in his home' [NLT]. This adjective
     describes a person who shows hospitality to strangers [LN].
  f. διδακτικός (LN **33.233**) (BAGD p. 191): 'able to teach' [**LN**; CEV, GW,
     NASB, NCV, NIV, NLT, TEV], 'able to teach well' [LSA], 'an able
     teacher' [HCSB, NET], 'apt to teach' [Lns], 'an apt teacher' [AB; NRSV],
     'a good teacher' [REB], 'a skilled teacher' [BNTC, ECC], 'skilled in
     teaching' [WBC], 'skillful in teaching' [BAGD, Herm], 'qualified to
     teach' [NTC]. This adjective describes someone who is able to teach
     [LN].

QUESTION—How is the preceding qualification of 'being above reproach' related to this list of qualifications?

The list of qualifications in 3:2b–6 are specifics of the general requirement that an overseer must be above reproach [AB, ICC, Lns, LSA, NIBC, NICNT, NIGTC, NTC, TH].

QUESTION—What is meant by being μιᾶς γυναικὸς ἄνδρα 'of one wife a husband'?

The phrase μιᾶς γυναικὸς ἄνδρα is literally 'of one woman a man' and when used in a marriage situation, it means 'of one wife a husband', putting the focus on 'one wife' [AB, BAGD (2.b. p. 231), BNTC, ICC, Lns, LSA, NIBC, WBC]. Some show this focus by translating this as 'only one wife' [BAGD, LSA; GW, NCV], 'but one wife' [NIV], and 'a "one-wife" man' [WBC]. Probably this assumes that most overseers will be married and this requirement pertains to those who are married, leaving it possible that there could also be unmarried overseers [ICC, Lns, LSA, NTC]. The history of interpretation of this requirement has had those who think it excludes candidates who were unmarried, or who were polygamous, or who were divorced, or who remarried after the first wife had died [NET].

1. This means that an overseer is to have only one wife in his lifetime, and this prohibits remarriage after his first wife has died [Alf, BNTC, ECC, EGT, TC]. What is expressly forbidden by this phrase is contracting a second marriage under any circumstances, whether after the death or divorce of the first spouse [BNTC, EGT]. The meaning of this phrase must take into consideration the parallel phrase in 5:9: ἑνὸς ἀνδρὸς γυνή 'wife of one husband' [Alf, EGT, TC]. For ordinary Christians, remarriage after the death of a mate was not forbidden, but it was forbidden to the bishop and the deacon, and even the widows who were put on the church's list, since they were to uphold the highest ideals [EGT, TC]. Evidence from literature and funerary inscriptions, both pagan and Jewish, indicate that remaining unmarried after the death a spouse or divorce was considered exemplary, while remarriage was taken as a sign of moral weakness and self-indulgence [BNTC]. The Church's ministers were expected to be exemplary in their conduct and to content themselves with a single marriage in their lifetime [BNTC, ECC].

2. This means that a married overseer must not remarry after a divorce [NCBC]. Divorce was allowed by both Greek and Roman law and it was common for men and women to divorce and to marry another mate during the former mate's lifetime, but this passage specifically excludes overseers from remarrying after divorce [NCBC].

3. 'Wife' is used in an extended sense and means that an overseer must not have any other sexual partners besides his legal wife, thus prohibiting adultery [ICC, Lns, My, NAC, NIBC, NICNT, NIGTC, NTC, TH, WBC, WP; NLT]. Instead of prohibiting some unsanctioned form of marriage, this is a positive requirement of being faithful in marriage [ICC, NICNT]. This means that his marriage must be monogamous and acceptable in the

opinion of the community [NICNT]. An overseer must be entirely faithful to his wife, and he does not act as pagans often did by having immoral relationships with another woman [NTC]. The Greek phrase refers to a 'one-woman kind of man' [ICC, NAC, WBC]. He can have only one wife at a time [WP].

QUESTION—What is meant by νηφάλιος 'sober'?

1. It is understood in its literal sense, having reference to being temperate in the consumption of wine [ECC, EGT, Herm]. Since this quality is also required of women officials (3:11) and aged men (Tit. 2:2), the probable reference here is to the moderate use of wine and so equivalent to μὴ οἴνῳ πολλῷ προσέχοντας 'not addicted to much wine' in 3:8 [ECC, EGT, Herm].

2. It is understood in its extended figurative sense of a life characterized by a sober outlook and self-control [AB, Alf, BKC, BNTC, Lns, LSA, My, NAC, NIBC, NICNT, NIGTC, NTC, NTL, TC, TH, TNTC]. Drunkenness is specifically stigmatized in the next verse, so this should be taken in its extended sense [AB, BNTC, LSA, My, NAC, NIBC, NICNT, NIGTC, NTL]. Since the following characteristic of σώφρων also has the meaning of 'self-controlled', the two words must refer to different aspects of self-control, and here it refers to the sober, clear-headed aspect [NIGTC]. Its focus is on clarity of mind [BNTC, LSA], being self-controlled [BAGD, NIGTC; CEV, HCSB, NCV, NLT], well-balanced [BKC, NICNT], well possessed and reasonable [AB]. He is not given to excess [NAC, NTC, TH], but is moderate, well-balanced, calm, steady, careful, and sane [NTC], and temperate [Lns, TC]. He is to be temperate in all things, not only in regard to intoxicants, but also in regard to his mind. He is to be spiritually temperate, not being carried away with such false teachings as those mentioned in 1:4, etc. [Lns].

QUESTION—What is meant by σώφρων 'sensible'?

This is a person who follows sound reason, and is not under the control of any passion [NTC]. He is sound and balanced in judgment, not flighty and unstable [Lns, NAC]. He is not ready to accept nonsense such as was being spread by the false teachers at Ephesus, but is always ready and willing to learn [NTC]. It means to be in control over his behavior along with the impulses and emotions behind it [NICNT]. Some of the terms commentators use to translate this adjective are self-controlled [AB, BAGD, BNTC, ICC, NAC, NIGTC, NTC, TH, TNTC, WBC], prudent [AB, BAGD (p. 802), ICC, NIGTC, NTIC], thoughtful [BAGD, ICC, NIGTC], sensible [NTC], of sound mind [NTC, TH], discreet [NTC], balanced [NAC], sober minded [WP], serious and earnest [EGT].

QUESTION—What is meant by κόσμιος 'dignified'?

While the preceding term σώφρων 'sensible' deals with the overseer's *inward* character [BNTC, TC, WBC], this term deals with his *external* deportment [BNTC, TC, WBC], deportment that causes others to regard him as being 'respectable' [NIGTC]. This is a quality of a character that is orderly in mind and habits, and its outward marks of being tidy and courteous are not in focus [Lns]. Commentators translate σώφρων with the terms respectable [AB, BAGD (1. p. 445), NAC, NICNT, NIGTC, TG], dignified [EGT], orderly [EGT, Lns, NAC, NIGTC, NTC, NTL, TC, TH, WP], disciplined [ICC], virtuous [NIGTC, NTC], honorable [AB], well behaved/well-mannered [ICC, NIGTC, NTL, TG, TH, TNTC], well balanced [NTIC].

QUESTION—What is meant by φιλόξενος 'hospitable'?

Christian hospitality here does not have the modern connotation of one who entertains friends, or even the poor [Lns]. Rather, it refers to taking in Christian strangers or acquaintances when they are traveling [Lns, NAC, TH], or fleeing from persecution and are without means of any kind [Lns]. A hospitable person is literally a φιλόξενος, 'friend of strangers', i.e., he supplies their necessities [NTC, TH]. Widows and orphans were dependent upon the kindness of relatives and friends, and also poverty and hunger were far more prevalent than they are today in the Western world. Messages between churches from one section of the Christian world to another were carried and delivered by personal messengers [NTC]. Hospitality was a requirement for every Christian to show [ICC, NIBC, NICNT, NIGTC, NTC, TC, WBC] according to his opportunity and ability to furnish it, but hospitality was an even more important requirement for one who held the office of an overseer [BNTC, NIGTC, NTC, NTL, WBC], who normally was expected to take on this duty and be a model for others [ICC]. The overseer had the duty of keeping an open house for traveling Christian delegates, and also of showing hospitality to such needy members of the local congregation as might occur [BNTC].

QUESTION—What is meant by διδακτικός 'able to teach'?

An apt teacher is a person who possesses everything that would fit him for teaching including the willingness to teach [EGT, My]. The presupposition here is that the candidate for bishop has already been engaged in teaching prior to his becoming a candidate so that this quality has been demonstrated [ICC]. The man who occupied the office of bishop was not only to be a man involved with teaching, but was skilled in it [Alf, ICC, My, NIGTC, WP]. This skill was especially needed by a minister because it would ordinarily be his responsibility to instruct the believers and to refute false teachers [Alf, My, NAC, NCBC, NIBC, TH, WBC]. When we consider how much Paul's mind was occupied with the false teachers in Ephesus and the dangers they caused, this requirement for the overseer's office would lay upon these men the responsibility of correcting false teaching by teaching the truth [Alf, BNTC, NIGTC, NTL, TC]. This skill enables him to both understand and communicate the truth of the Scriptures to others and also to refute those who mishandle that truth. This skill would be used publicly or in informal private settings [BKC].

3:3 **not drunken,**[a] **not a-violent-man,**[b] **but forbearing,**[c] **not-quarrelsome,**[d] **not-loving-money,**[e]

TEXT—Following μὴ πλήκτην 'not a violent man' some manuscripts add μὴ αἰσχροκερδῆ 'not shamefully greedy'. GNT does not mention this variant. 'Not shamefully greedy' or 'not greedy of filthy lucre' is read by KJV.

LEXICON—a. πάροινος (LN 88.288) (BAGD p. 629): 'drunken' [BAGD]. This adjective is also translated as a noun: 'drunkard' [LN, WBC; NET, NRSV, TEV], 'drinker' [ECC], 'heavy drinker' [LN; CEV, NLT], 'a slave of drink' [BNTC]; as a verb phrase: 'given to drunkenness' [NIV], 'given to drink' [REB], 'given to wine' [Herm; KJV], 'addicted to wine' [AB, NTIC; HCSB, NASB], 'one sitting long beside wine' [Lns], 'one who lingers beside his wine' [NTC], 'he must not drink much wine' [LSA], 'he must not drink too much wine' [NCV], 'he must not drink excessively' [GW]. This adjective describes a person who habitually drinks too much and thus becomes a drunkard [LN].

b. πλήκτης (LN **88.137**) (BAGD p. 669): 'violent person/man' [LN; GW, TEV], 'pugnacious man' [BAGD], 'striker' [Lns; KJV], 'bully' (BAGD, ECC, **LN**; HCSB), 'troublemaker' [CEV]. This noun is also translated as an adjective: 'belligerent' [LSA], 'violent' [WBC; NET, NIV, NLT, NRSV], 'pugnacious' [NASB]; as a verb phrase: 'he must not like to fight' [NCV], 'not given to brawling' [Herm; REB], 'not be violent' [AB], 'not given to violence' [BNTC], 'not given to blows' [NTC]. This noun denotes a pugnacious and demanding person [LN].

c. ἐπιεικής (LN 88.63) (BAGD p. 292): 'forbearing' [BAGD, LN], 'patient' [KJV], 'yielding' [BAGD, Lns], 'kind' [BAGD, Herm; CEV], 'gentle' [AB, BAGD, ECC, LN, LSA; all versions except CEV, KJV, REB], 'gracious' [LN, WBC], 'genial' [NTC], 'of a forbearing disposition' [REB], 'reasonable' [NTIC], 'yielding' [Lns], 'magnanimous' [BNTC]. This adjective describes someone as being gracious and forbearing [LN].

d. ἄμαχος (LN **39.24**) (BAGD p. 44): 'not quarrelsome' [LSA, WBC; GW, HCSB, NIV, NLT, NRSV], 'not argumentative' [ECC], 'not contentious' [LN, NTC; NET], 'not fighting' [Lns], 'not a brawler' [KJV], 'peaceful' [**LN**; TEV], 'peaceable' [BAGD, Herm; NASB, NCV], 'gentle' [CEV]. This adjective is also translated as a verb phrase: 'not given to battle' [AB], 'not a lover of battle' [NTIC], 'avoiding quarrels' [REB], 'free from quarrelsomeness' [BNTC]. This adjective describes someone who has a lack of conflict and contention [LN].

e. ἀφιλάργυρος (LN **25.109**) (BAGD p. 126): 'not loving money' [BAGD; NCV, NLT], 'not fond of money' [NTC], 'not silver loving' [Lns], 'not greedy' [BAGD, LSA; HCSB], 'not avaricious' [REB], 'not covetous' [Herm; KJV], 'not loving wealth, one who does not love money' [LN], 'not one who likes money' [ECC], 'free from the love of money' [NASB, NET], 'free from attachment to money' [BNTC]. This adjective is also translated as a noun phrase: 'not a lover of money' [AB, **LN**, NTIC, WBC; NIV, NRSV]; as verb phrase: 'he must not love money' [GW,

TEV], 'they must not love money' [CEV]. This adjective describes a person as not being desirous or greedy for money [LN].

QUESTION—What is meant by πάροινον 'drunken'?

The word is a compound word that is literally παρά- 'alongside of' and οἶνος 'wine' and this gives the picture of someone who spends too much time with wine [WBC], one who lingers beside his wine [NTC], a man given over to wine [TC], one who is given to drunkenness [NICNT]. This adjective means the same as the phrase οἴνῳ πολλῷ προσέχοντας 'being much addicted to wine' in 3:8 [LSA, NIGTC, WBC], and wine is probably in focus here as well in 3:8 [Herm, Lns, LSA, NTC; KJV, NCV]. The Christians probably knew that other intoxicants were undesirable, so Paul focused on the commonly used wine, which could also be intoxicating when used excessively [LSA].

1. The phrase is to be taken in its literal meaning of intemperance in drinking wine [ECC, Herm, ICC, Lns, LSA, NAC, NIGTC, NTC; CEV, KJV, NCV, NLT], of being drunk [BAGD, ICC, Lns, NAC, NCBC, NIBC, NICNT, NTC, TC, TG, TH, TNTC, WBC; NIV], or of being addicted to wine [AB, BNTC, Herm, NTIC; HCSB, KJV, NASB, REB]: *he must not drink too much wine and become drunk.* It corresponds to and overlaps conceptually with νηφάλιος in the sense of 'temperate' in 3:2 [ECC]. Here it denotes one who is in the habit of drinking wine [WBC]. But it cannot be inferred from the use of the word here that Paul is absolutely and entirely prohibiting the drinking of wine [BNTC, NIBC, NTC, TG, TH, WBC]. What is being prohibited here is drunkenness [BNTC, NIBC, NTC]. In places where good drinking water was scarce, wine became the common, ordinary drink and drinking a moderate amount of wine is not the issue, rather it is the drunkenness that would result from drinking too much wine [TH].

2. The phrase is used in an extended sense denoting the behavior which manifests itself as a result of being drunk [Alf, EGT, My, WP]: *he must not be quarrelsome from his wine.* It is not simply synonymous with 'wine-lover' or with 'addicted to much wine' since the focus is on the man's behavior, not just the fact that he was drunk, and it refers to a man made insolent and rude by much wine [Alf, EGT]. It is not simply referring to drunkenness, but to the impudence and arrogance brought on by intoxication [My]. He is not to be a brawler [WP].

QUESTION—What is meant by πλήκτης 'a violent man'?

The word πλήκτης is literally 'a giver of blows' [WBC].

1. This noun has the literal meaning of being a violent person who physically strikes others [AB, Alf, BNTC, ECC, Herm, ICC, Lns, My, NAC, NICNT, NTC, TC, TH, TNTC, WBC; GW, KJV, NCV, NET, NIV, NRSV, REB, TEV]: *he must not be a violent man.* This term suggests a violent person, a brawler, or a bully [WBC]. It is probably better to adopt the literal meaning here as setting forth the opposite of an overseer's character [Alf]. Paul was thinking of a quick-tempered man [Lns], who, in

his anger [TH], was ever ready to strike someone with his fists [Lns, My, NAC, NTC, TH]. This describes an overseer who tries to intimidate others and will even strike them to keep them from wrongdoing [BNTC, ECC].

2. It has the extended meaning of the word and refers to the *attitude* of a belligerent person [LSA, NIGTC; CEV, NLT]: *he must not be belligerent.* Probably the extended sense is intended in which the attitude of a quick-tempered man or even a bully is meant, without implying that physical blows must be involved [LSA]. Various terms are used to suggest this figurative sense: 'troublemaker' [CEV], 'quarrelsome' [NLT], and 'pugnacious' [BAGD, NIGTC].

QUESTION—What relationship is indicated by the conjunction ἀλλά 'but'?

1. This conjunction indicates that the following description ἐπιεικής 'forbearing' is in contrast with the preceding description πλήκτην 'violent man' [ECC, Lns, LSA, NAC, NTC, WBC; NIV, NRSV]: *not a violent man, but forbearing.* The adjective ἐπιεικής 'forbearing' is followed by the adjective ἄμαχος 'not quarrelsome' which is another antonym of πλήκτης 'violent man'. Instead of being coordinate with 'forbearing' so as to function as another contrast with 'a violent man', it is coordinate with πλήκτης 'a belligerent man' as another example in the list for two reasons, (1) it is not joined to the positive virtue of 'forbearing' by a conjunction καί 'and' [LSA], and (2) the negative prefix α- in ἄμαχος 'not quarrelsome' makes it fit in well in the list of the other four negative traits in this verse [ECC, LSA, WBC]. The person indicated by 'forbearing' is the very opposite of a violent man given to blows [NTC].

2. This indicates that the following two descriptions ἐπιεικής 'forbearing' and ἄμαχος 'not quarrelsome' are in contrast with the preceding description of πλήκτην 'a violent man' [NIGTC]: *not a violent man, but forbearing and peaceable.*

3. This indicates that the following description ἐπιεικής 'forbearing' is in contrast with the *two* preceding descriptions πάροινος 'drunken' and πλήκτην 'belligerent' [AB, Alf; GW]: *not drunken or a violent man, but forbearing.*

4. This indicates that the following *two* descriptions ἐπιεικής 'forbearing' and ἄμαχος 'not quarrelsome' are in contrast with the *two* preceding descriptions πάροινος 'drunken' and πλήκτην 'belligerent' [ICC, NICNT; NCV, TEV]: *not drunken or a violent man, but forbearing and not quarrelsome.* The hostile attitudes just prohibited by the two negative phrases are replaced by the positive attitudes of gentleness and peaceableness [ICC].

5. This indicates that the three following descriptions are in contrast with the *two* preceding descriptions πάροινος 'drunken' and πλήκτην 'belligerent' [BNTC, Herm, NTL; CEV, NASB, NLT, REB]: *not drunken or a violent man, but gentle, not quarrelsome, and not loving money.*

QUESTION—What is meant by ἐπιεικής 'forbearing'?

This adjective is contrasted with being a πλήκτης 'violent man' [LSA]. There is no single word or expression in the English language that is the full equivalent of what is meant by ἐπιεικής 'forbearing' [Lns, NICNT, NTC]. Words and expressions which commentators and translators have used to express this word are forbearing [BNTC, NAC, TC, TNTC], patient and tolerant [NICNT, TH], yielding [BAGD, ICC, Lns, NAC, NTC], conciliatory [ICC, NTC], gentle [AB, Alf, BAGD, ECC, ICC, LN, Lns, LSA, My, NAC, NIBC, NICNT, NIGTC, NTC, WP], kind [AB, BAGD, Herm, ICC, NAC, NIGTC, TNTC], reasonable [Alf, NTC], fair [NTC], considerate [NAC, NTC], tolerant [NICNT], moderate [My], gracious [BNTC, NIGTC, WBC], magnanimous [BNTC, TNTC], genial [NTC]. Such an overseer is gracious, and instead of insisting on his full rights, he will submit to injury and injustice [WBC]. No matter how exasperating church members might be, the overseer will be forbearing and gracious [BNTC].

QUESTION—What is meant by ἄμαχος 'not quarrelsome'?

Some indicate that this term means 'peaceable, peaceful' [AB, BAGD, Herm, LN, My, NAC, NICNT; NASB, NCV, TEV], and 'gentle' [CEV], but one commentator objects to these renderings because they sacrifice the negative character inherent in the term [Alf]. Some prefer to retain the force of the negative α- prefix of the term and translate: not quarrelsome [Alf, BNTC, LSA, NAC, WBC; HCSB, NIV, NLT, NRSV], not argumenative [ECC], not contentious [LN, NAC, NIGTC, NTC, TC, TH, WP; NET], not fighting [Lns], 'not a lover of battle' [NTIC], 'not a brawler' [KJV]. Others accept either 'not quarrelsome' or 'peaceable' [ICC, NICNT, NIGTC, TH, WBC]. This adjective is a strong term that describes active and serious bickering, which could even lead to physical combat [WBC]. A quarrelsome man is a verbal, and possibly a physical, fighter. He is pugnacious, contentious, and grasping [NAC]. While a person might not be eager to come to blows, he might still be disputatious [NTC]. What Paul wants is a leader with a peaceable attitude who rejects all forms of threatening and fighting [NAC]. He would heal rifts caused by bitter arguments and help unite the congregation [NICNT].

QUESTION—What is meant by ἀφιλάργυρος 'not loving money'?

The adjective ἀφιλάργυρος literally means 'not loving silver' [Lns, LSA]. It means not a lover of money [AB, Alf, LN, Lns, LSA, My, NAC, NICNT, NIGTC, NTC, NTIC, TH, WBC; all translations except KJV], not greedy [ICC, NICNT, NIGTC, TG], not stingy [Lns], not covetous [Herm; KJV]. Such a man does not use his ministry for personal gain [BKC]. Although 'not a lover of money' may lead to liberality in people who have plenty of money, still it is a totally distinct concept from liberality and refers to the quality of abstinence from the love of money [Alf]. This has the same meaning as the requirement for deacons in 3:8, μὴ αἰσχροκερδεῖς 'not greedy for gain' [WBC].

3:4 managing[a] (his) own household[b] well,[c] having children in obedience,[d] with all respect/dignity[e]

LEXICON—a. pres. mid. participle of προΐσταμαι, προΐστημι (LN 36.1) (BAGD 1. p. 707): 'to manage' [BAGD, BNTC, LSA, NTC, WBC; all versions except CEV, KJV, NCV], 'to direct' [BAGD, LN], 'to guide, to lead' [LN], 'to superintend' [Lns], 'to govern' [Herm], 'to rule' [AB, BAGD; KJV]. The clause τοῦ ἰδίου οἴκου καλῶς προϊστάμενον 'managing his own household well' is translated 'he must be a good family leader' [NCV], 'he must be outstanding in his direction of his own home' [ECC], 'church officials must be in control of their own families' [CEV]. This verb means to influence others so as to cause them to follow a recommended course of action [LN]. See this verb at 3:12.

    b. οἶκος (LN 10.8) (BAGD 2. p. 560): 'household' [AB, BAGD, BNTC, LN, LSA, NTC, WBC; HCSB, NASB, NET, NLT, NRSV, REB], 'family' [BAGD, LN; CEV, GW, NCV, NIV, TEV], 'home' [ECC], 'house' [Herm, Lns; KJV]. This noun denotes a family consisting of all those related by blood and marriage who live in the same house or homestead, and it includes the servants and slaves as well [LN]. See this word at 3:12, 15; 5:4.

    c. καλῶς (LN 65.23) (BAGD 1. p. 401): 'well' [AB, BAGD, BNTC, Herm, LN, Lns, LSA, NTC, WBC; all versions except CEV, HCSB, NCV], 'competently' [HCSB], 'appropriately, in the right way' [BAGD], 'good' [LN; NCV], 'outstanding' [ECC], not explicit [CEV]. This adverb describes the state of having events measure up to their intended purpose [LN].

    d. ὑποταγή (LN 36.18) (BAGD p. 847): 'obedience, submission' [BAGD, LN]. The clause τέκνα ἔχοντα ἐν ὑποταγῇ 'having children in obedience' is translated 'having children who obey him' [NLT], 'with children who are obedient' [ECC], 'and keeps his children in obedience' [Herm], 'they must see that their children are obedient' [CEV], 'and must see that his children obey him' [NIV], 'and make his children obey him' [TEV], 'he must cause that his children obey him' [LSA], 'his children should obey him' [GW], 'having children in subjection' [Lns; KJV], 'and controls his children' [REB], 'having his children under control' [HCSB], 'keeping his children under control' [BAGD; NASB], 'and keep his children in control' [NET], 'keeping his children submissive' [NRSV], 'keeping his children in submission' [BNTC, NTC], 'having submissive children' [WBC], 'with his children in subordination' [AB], 'having children who cooperate' [NCV]. This noun denotes submission to the orders or directives of someone [LN]. It means that the children must be characterized by submissiveness to their father [WBC].

    e. σεμνότης (LN 88.46) (BAGD 1. p. 747): 'respectfulness, reverence, dignity, seriousness, probity' [BAGD], 'propriety, befitting behavior' [LN]. The phrase μετὰ πάσης σεμνότητος 'with all respect/dignity' is translated 'with complete reverence' [AB]. It is translated with *the children* having this quality: 'with all respect' [TEV], 'with full respect' [NCV], 'with proper respect' [NIV], 'and always respectful' [CEV], 'and respectful in every way' [NRSV], '(who) respect him' [NLT], 'and that they completely respect him' [LSA], '(his children should) respectfully (obey him)' [GW], '(keeps his children in) respectful (obedience)' [Herm], 'and quite reverent' [ECC]; or it is translated with *the overseer* having this quality: 'with all dignity' [Lns, WBC; HCSB, NASB], 'with true dignity' [NTC], 'without losing his dignity' [NET, REB], 'with unruffled dignity' [BNTC], 'with all gravity' [KJV]. This noun denotes behavior that is befitting, and implies a measure of dignity that leads to respect [LN].

QUESTION—What is the significance of the requirement that the overseer must manage his own household well?

This relates to the administrative capabilities of a potential overseer [AB]. Before managing the household of God, he must show that he can manage his own household [WBC]. His leadership and caring abilities are shown by his management of his own household in the aspects of his ruling, directing, and leading it [NIGTC]. The verb προϊστάμενον 'managing' denotes ruling over, governing, caring for, and being concerned about the household [TH]. Direction and management of the household also has the idea of caring for it [ICC]. It is an effective exercise of authority accompanied by sensitive compassion, and in 3:5 the role of 'managing' is accompanied by ἐπιμελέομαι 'caring for', suggesting that this leadership is accomplished more by showing mercy than by delivering ultimatums [NAC]. It also includes managing the affairs of the household [LSA].

QUESTION—What is meant by οἴκου 'household'?

The noun οἴκου 'house' is used here as a metonymy, the object 'house' being used for what is in it or associated with it [WBC], that is, the people constituting the 'home' [ECC]. It means 'family' [ECC, LSA, NAC, NIGTC, TG, TH; CEV, NIV, TEV], or 'household' [Alf, BNTC, ICC, Lns, LSA, My, NCBC, NIGTC, NTC, WBC; NLT]. A similar requirement for deacons is in 3:12 where it says 'let them manage their children and their households well', and this implies that 'household' includes any people living in the same house [LSA]. This would include any slaves living there [ICC, LN, My, TG], in short, all the dependents who live in the house [LSA].

QUESTION—How is the clause τέκνα ἔχοντα ἐν ὑποταγῇ 'having children in obedience' related to the preceding clause?

This clause gives a specific example of what is meant by 'managing his own household well' [BKC, ICC, Lns, LSA, NICNT, NIGTC, NTC, TH, WBC]. This clause narrows the scope of the preceding broad qualification and focuses upon the candidate's oversight of his children as he fills his role as father and householder [ICC]. The way in which a man rules his house indicates his capacity for leadership and government and this is most obvious when there are children in the home [NTC]. One important aspect of

managing one's family well is ensuring that the children behave properly
[TH, WBC]. The lack of such success in ruling his own house well would
disqualify the candidate from ruling the church [Alf]. This requirement does
not mean that an overseer *must* have children, but when he does have a
family, as most men did, the children must be obedient [EGT, Lns, NAC,
NIBC, NIGTC].

QUESTION—What is the phrase μετὰ πάσης σεμνότητος 'with all respect/
dignity' connected with, and who shows this respect or dignity?

The clause is placed so that the children seem to be the intended reference,
and it would then mean that the children should have respect or reverence for
their father. However, the noun σεμνότητος 'respect' does not usually have
a transitive quality, and if it is not transitive here, this would refer to the
father's own dignity. This interpretation is supported by 3:2 where the
dignified appearance of the overseer is an important qualification [AB].
Either interpretation makes good sense. If it refers to the respectful attitude
of the children as they obey their father, it would be proof that he knows how
to discipline in a good way. If it refers to the attitude of the father, the
meaning 'dignity' would apply, and this would indicate his ability to
maintain discipline without violence or loss of dignity [LSA].

1. This phrase is connected to the noun τέκνα 'children', and it refers to the
children's attitude of respect for their father as they obey him [Alf, ECC,
Herm, LSA, My, NIBC, TH; CEV, GW, NCV, NIV, NLT, NRSV, TEV]:
with all respect for him (or, for everyone). The children respond with an
affection for their father that is mingled with respect and some awe
[ECC]. 'Respectful' probably refers to the children's conduct in general
so that they are 'respectful to everyone', showing respect to their parents
and to others as well [TH]. This probably means that people will
recognize both his children's obedience and their generally good behavior
[NIBC].

2. This phrase is connected to the participle ἔχοντα 'having', and it refers to
the action of the father that is to be done with dignity [BNTC, ICC, Lns,
NAC, NTC, NTL, TC, TNTC, WBC; HCSB, KJV, NASB, NET, REB]:
with all dignity having children in obedience. A father must act in a
dignified way as he secures obedience from his children [Lns]. He does so
with a dignified bearing [NTL]. The father must use strict discipline, but
he must do so without fuss or resorting to violence [BNTC]. The
overseer's manner in training his children can be described as being 'in all
seriousness' as he uses a blend of authority and compassion [NAC].

3:5 for/but[a] if anyone does- not -know (how) to-manage (his) own household, how[b] can-he-care-for[c] a-church[d] of-God?

LEXICON—a. δέ (LN 89.87, 89.93, 89.124) (BAGD 1., 2., 3. p. 171): This
conjunction can mark a sequence of closely related events: 'and, and then'
[LN (89.87)], or an additive relation that is not coordinate: 'and, and also,
also, in addition, even' [LN (89.93)], or a contrast: 'but, on the other

hand' [LN (89.124)]. It can emphasize a contrast: 'but', or mark a simple transition: 'now, then', or mark a resumption of an interrupted discourse: 'and also, but also' [BAGD]. Here it is translated 'for' [AB, ECC, Herm, NTC, WBC; KJV, NLT, NRSV, REB, TEV], 'because' [LSA], 'now' [Lns], 'but' [NASB, NET], not explicit [BNTC; CEV, GW, HCSB, NCV, NIV].

b. πῶς (LN 92.16) (BAGD 1.d. p. 732): 'how?' [AB, BAGD, BNTC, ECC, Herm, LN, Lns, NTC, WBC; all versions], 'by what means?' [LN]. The particle is omitted by making this a statement instead of a question: 'he certainly cannot care for God's church' [LSA]. This is an interrogative particle that has reference to means [LN]. When used in a rhetorical question where an assumption is called into question or rejected altogether, πῶς 'how?' is equivalent to a strong assertion meaning 'by no means' or 'it is impossible that' [BAGD].

c. fut. pass. (deponent = act.) indic. of ἐπιμελέομαι (LN **30.40**, 35.44) (BAGD p. 296): 'to take care of' [BAGD, ECC, Herm, LN (35.44), Lns, NTC; all versions except CEV, NET, REB], 'to care for' [BAGD, LSA, WBC; NET], 'to look after' [BNTC; CEV], 'to provide whatever is needed' [LN (35.44)], 'to think about, to be concerned about, to give attention so as to respond' [LN (30.40)], 'to take charge of' [AB; REB]. This clause is translated by keeping the question form: 'how can he give proper consideration to (the needs of) God's church?' [**LN** (30.40)]. This is also translated as a statement: 'he certainly cannot care for God's church' [LSA]. This verb means to give proper consideration to some matter, 'to think about, to be concerned about, to give attention so as to respond' [LN (30.40)], or to care for something with diligent concern [LN (35.44)].

d. ἐκκλησία (LN 11.32) (BAGD 4.e.α. p. 241): 'church' [BAGD, LN], 'congregation' [BAGD, LN]. The phrase ἐκκλησίας θεοῦ 'a church of God' is translated 'the church of God' [Herm, WBC; KJV, NASB, NET, TEV], 'God's church' [BNTC, ECC, Lns, LSA, NTC; GW, NCV, NIV, NLT, NRSV], 'God's people' [CEV], 'God's assembly' [AB], 'a congregation of God's people' [REB]. This noun denotes a congregation of Christians [LN].

QUESTION—What relationship is indicated by the conjunction δέ 'for/but'?

1. The conjunction δέ functions as a transitional particle [Lns, WBC]. It introduces an explanation [WBC]. The conjunction dé 'now' indicates that this rhetorical question is the point of the requirement presented in 3:4 [Lns]. This verse provides the underlying reason or grounds for the stipulation the writer has made in 3:4 [AB, BKC, BNTC, ECC, Herm, ICC, LSA, NIGTC, NTC, TH, TNTC, WBC; KJV, NLT, NRSV, REB, TEV; probably CEV, GW, HCSB, NCV, NIV which omit the conjunction], more particularly 3:4a [LSA]: *(it is necessary that) he manage his own household well, for if anyone does not know how to manage his own*

household, he certainly won't be able to take charge of God's church!
This is parenthetical in nature [BKC, My, TNTC].
2. The conjunction δέ indicates a contrast [Alf, My; NASB, NET]. 'But'
   indicates a contrast is being made by presenting an imagined situation that
   is the opposite case of the preceding clause of 3:4 [Alf]: *(it is necessary
   that) he manage his own household well, but if anyone does not know how
   to manage his own household then, etc.*

QUESTION—What is the function of the question *'how* can he take care of a
congregation of God, etc.'?

This is a rhetorical question which expects a negative answer [AB, BAGD
(1.d. p. 732), BNTC, ECC, ICC, Lns, LSA, NIGTC, TH, TNTC, WBC,
WP]: *he cannot take care of a congregation!* It makes a forceful assertion
[BAGD, LSA, TH] that the one who cannot manage his own household
certainly cannot be trusted with caring for God's church [TH]. The argument
is from the lesser to the greater [ECC, EGT, ICC, Lns, LSA, My, NIGTC,
TC, TNTC], and means that if a man cannot fulfill the lesser responsibility
of managing his own household, he will not be able to take on the greater
responsibility of caring for God's household [LSA].

QUESTION—What is meant by ἐπιμελήσεται 'take care of' and how does it
relate to the infinitive προστῆναι 'to manage' in the preceding conditional
clause?

The verb ἐπιμελήσεται 'take care of' means 'to care for, look after' [BAGD
(p. 296), BNTC, ECC, EGT, ICC, Lns, NAC, NIBC, NIGTC, NTC, TH,
WBC]: *how can he take care of God's church?* The use of the two verbs
'manage' and 'care for' brings together the ideas of authority and sensitive
concern in the overseer's role [ICC, TH, WBC]. 'Take care of' indicates a
more solicitous and incessant watchful regard than 'manage' does [NTC].
'Manage' has do with church government, while 'to care for' pictures the
personal care and attention that a father would give to his family [EGT].
However, the verb refers to guidance and leadership as well as to a caring
concern [NIBC]. Some focus on this leadership aspect [AB, Alf, My]: *how
can he take charge of God's church?* The verb not only expresses the more
general meaning 'to take care of something' but it also has the more definite
idea of 'to fill an office' or 'to be an overseer over something', which is the
sense in which it is used here [My].

QUESTION—What is meant by ἐκκλησίας θεοῦ 'a church of God'?

This phrase should be translated in an indefinite manner [BNTC, ECC, Lns]
since any local church is indicated [BNTC, ICC, Lns, LSA, NICNT, NIGTC,
NTC, TNTC, WBC]: *a congregation of God.* Paul is speaking in general
terms and not of any specific local assembly [WBC]. This is a general
principle that is about the overseer's role in any church [NIGTC, WBC]. The
anarthrous reference here is a general way of referring to a community of
believers, but it could also refer to a specific congregation [TH]. A 'church
of God' is a church that belongs to God [NIGTC, WP]. 'God's church'
means a congregation of God's people or a Christian church, and a

translation should not imply that there are other churches that do not belong
to God [TG].

3:6 **not recently-converted,**[a]

LEXICON—a. νεόφυτος (LN **11.21**) (BAGD p. 536): 'newly converted'
[BAGD]. The clause μὴ νεόφυτον 'not recently converted' is translated
'he must not be recently converted' [LSA], 'not a recent convert' [**LN**,
NTC, WBC], 'he must/should not be a recent convert' [AB, BNTC; NET,
NIV, NRSV, REB], 'he must not be a new convert' [HCSB; similarly
NASB], 'not a novice' [Lns; KJV], 'he must not be a neophyte' [ECC],
'he must not be a new Christian' [GW], 'but an elder must not be a new
believer' [NCV], 'they must not be new followers of the Lord' [CEV],
'nor should he be newly baptized' [Herm], 'he must be mature in the
faith' [TEV]. This adjective literally describes something that is newly
planted [AB, BAGD, LN, NICNT, NIGTC] and here it is used
figuratively to describe someone who is newly 'planted' in the Christian
church, that is, 'newly converted' [BAGD, NIGTC]. It is applied to
someone who has recently become a member of a religious group [LN].

QUESTION—How is this requirement for an overseer connected to the
preceding requirements?

It is connected to the previous accusatives (3:2–3), all of which are
dependent upon the words in 3:2 δεῖ τὸν ἐπίσκοπον εἶναι 'it is necessary
that the overseer be' [ECC, LSA, My], and the preceding verse 3:5 functions
as a parenthesis inserted in the list [ECC, My; GW, HCSB, KJV, NASB,
NCV, NIV, NRSV]. It consists of a final negative qualification of the
candidate for the office of a bishop [Alf]. This requirement marks a shift
from the candidate's family status to his own experience in faith [TH]. It
leaves the subjects of virtues and conduct to add a qualification that is
simply based upon a time lapse between the candidate's baptism and his
consideration for the post of an overseer [ECC].

QUESTION—What is meant by νεόφυτον 'newly converted'?

This term refers to someone who was only recently converted to the
Christian faith [AB, BAGD, BNTC, EGT, LN, Lns, LSA, NAC, NCBC,
NIBC, NTC, TH, WBC; HCSB, NASB, NET, NIV, NRSV, REB], or who
had been only recently baptized [ECC, Herm, TC, TNTC]. He is a novice in
experiencing the Christian life [LSA]. This requirement is directed not so
much against a youthful candidate as against one who is young in the faith,
whether young or old in years [Lns, NAC, NTC, WBC]. In the letter to Titus
this requirement was not included because Crete was a new territory, and
only recent converts were available for leadership roles in the newly formed
congregations, and in such a situation there was no danger of falling into
conceit. However in Ephesus, where the church was fully established and
there were already prominent elders, the elevation of a novice might fill such
a man with conceit [Lns]. In Paul's first missionary journey, he did not

appoint elders in every church until he revisited those churches later (Acts 14:23) [NTC].

in-order-that not[a] having-become-conceited[b] he-might-fall[c] into (the) judgment[d] of-the devil.[e]

LEXICON—a. ἵνα μή (LN 89.62): 'in order that…not' [AB, LN, NTC], 'so that…not' [BNTC, LN; NASB, TEV], 'lest' [ECC, Herm, LN, Lns, WBC; KJV], 'or (he might)' [GW, HCSB, NCV, NET, NIV, NRSV], 'if they are, (they might)' [CEV], 'because (he might)' [LSA; NLT], not explicit [REB].

b. aorist pass. participle of τυφόομαι, τυφόω (LN **88.218**) (BAGD 1. p. 831): 'to be conceited' [BAGD, Lns, LSA, WBC; HCSB, NASB, NIV], 'to be arrogant' [GW, NET], 'to be puffed up' [BAGD, Herm], 'to be puffed up with conceit' [NRSV], 'to be inflated with vanity' [ECC], 'to be beclouded by conceit' [NTC], 'to swell up with pride' [TEV], 'to get swollen-headed' [BNTC], 'to get a false sense of his own importance' [AB], 'to become proud' [CEV, NLT], 'to be extremely proud' [**LN**], 'to become too proud of himself' [NCV], 'to be lifted up with pride' [KJV], 'conceit (might bring on him)' [REB]. This verb is a figurative extension of τυφόομαι 'to be crazy, to be demented', a meaning that does not occur in the NT where it means 'to be insanely arrogant, to be extremely proud, to be very arrogant' [LN]. See this word at 6:4.

c. aorist act. subj. of ἐμπίπτω (LN **90.71**) (BAGD 2. p. 256): 'to fall' [AB, BAGD, ECC, Herm, Lns, NTC, WBC; HCSB, KJV, NASB, NET, NIV, NLT, NRSV], 'to experience' [**LN**], 'to incur' [BNTC], not explicit [LSA; CEV, GW, NCV, REB, TEV]. This verb means to suddenly experience something that is difficult or bad [LN].

d. κρίμα (LN 56.24, 56.30) (BAGD 4.b. p. 450): 'judgment' [AB, LN (56.24), Lns, WBC; NIV], 'condemnation' [BAGD, ECC, Herm, LN (56.30), NTC; HCSB, KJV, NASB, NRSV], 'punishment' [NET, REB], 'sentence, verdict' [LN (56.24)]. The clause εἰς κρίμα ἐμπέσῃ τοῦ διαβόλου 'fall into the judgment of the devil' [WBC] is also translated 'fall into the devil's judgment' [Lns], 'incur the judgment of the devil' [BNTC], 'fall under the devil's condemnation' [ECC], 'fall into the condemnation of the devil' [Herm, NTC; HCSB, NRSV; similarly KJV], '(conceit) might bring on him the devil's punishment' [REB]. Some translate the genitive phrase τοῦ διαβόλου 'of the devil' as being *objective*, indicating that the devil was condemned: 'and fall under the same judgment as the devil' [NIV], 'and fall into the condemnation incurred by the devil' [NASB], 'and fall into the judgment reserved for the devil' [AB], 'and thus experience the condemnation meted out to the Devil' [**LN**], 'and be judged guilty just as the devil was' [NCV], 'and be doomed along with the devil' [CEV], 'and be condemned, as the Devil was' [TEV], 'as a result he will be condemned by God like the devil was condemned by God' [LSA], '(he might become arrogant) like the devil and be condemned' [GW]. Some translate the genitive phrase τοῦ διαβόλου 'of the devil' as being *subjective,* indicating that the devil does the punishing: 'and fall into the punishment that the devil will exact' [NET], 'and the Devil would cause him to fall' [NLT]. This noun denotes the judge's legal decision concerning the accused as to whether or not he is guilty [LN (56.24)], or it denotes the guilty verdict of a judgment, making the guilty person liable to punishment [BAGD, LN (56.30), NICNT].

e. διάβολος (LN 12.34): 'devil' [AB, BNTC, ECC, Herm, Lns, NTC, WBC; all versions except HCSB, NLT, TEV]. Some translate this noun as a proper noun: 'Devil' [LN; HCSB, NLT, TEV], 'Satan' [LN]. This noun has been borrowed from Aramaic and it is a title for the 'adversary', the Devil, a name given to the principal supernatural evil being [LN].

QUESTION—What relationship is indicated by ἵνα μή 'in order that not'?

This phrase indicates the purpose or reason for the prohibition 'not a recent convert' in the preceding phrase, [AB, BNTC, ECC, Herm, ICC, Lns, LSA, My, NIBC, NIGTC, NTL]. It introduces a purpose with a negative intent [ICC, NIGTC, WP] and serves to indicate what is likely to happen if a newly converted Christian were to be made an overseer [NIGTC].

1. There are two related reasons, the first being stated as an aorist passive participle τυφωθείς 'having become conceited' and the second is the following clause 'he might fall into the condemnation of the devil' [BNTC, Herm, ICC, NIBC, NICNT, NIGTC, NTC; possibly AB, BNTC, Herm; CEV, GW, HCSB, NASB, NCV, NET, NIV, NLT, NRSV, TEV which use *'and'* to connect the participle with the clause following it). The second clause is also the result of the first [BNTC, LSA, NICNT, NIGTC, NTC]: *so that he will not become conceited and then fall into judgment.*

2. The reason is stated in the final clause 'he might fall into the condemnation of the devil', with the participle τυφωθείς 'having become conceited' giving the situation that would make it possible for him to fall into condemnation [ECC, Lns, WBC; probably KJV, REB which translate the participle *'having* become conceited' as subordinate to the last clause]: *so that, becoming conceited, he will not fall into judgment.*

QUESTION—What is meant by the participle τυφωθείς 'having become conceited'?

The word τυφωθείς literally means 'to be filled or enveloped by smoke', and it became an idiom for either being conceited or being blinded and foolish [ICC, LSA, WBC].

1. It simply means to be conceited, proud, or arrogant [AB, BAGD, LN, Lns, LSA, NIBC, NIGTC, NTC, NTL, TH, TNTC, WBC, WP; all versions]. He raises a smokescreen of pride [WP]. His conceit enfolds him as though it were a smoky fog [Lns, TNTC]. This means that he is arrogantly proud [TH]. It is an arrogance that comes from having a sense of one's superior position [AB]. The translation should be 'conceited' if the following

phrase 'into judgment of the devil' means the judgment incurred by Satan, since it would then be making a comparison between the recent convert and Satan, both being condemned for their conceited pride [WBC].

2. The metaphor refers to the clouding of the mind and judgment of a person as *the result of* becoming conceited because of such a rapid advancement [Alf, BNTC, ECC, EGT, ICC, My, NAC, NCBC, TC]. When a recent convert is promoted to a prominent position in the church his pride may cause his spiritual alertness to be blunted, and he will become morally blind [NAC]. He may become infatuated and dazzled by the authority and power that comes with the office [ICC]. The person who is inflated with vanity will have a delirious delusion that he sees something that is not really true [ECC]. He is blinded or bewildered from pride so that he cannot see himself or others as they really are [Alf, My], nor can he understand the matters with which he is concerned [EGT]. His mind and judgment are beclouded as a result of the conceit brought about by his rapid advancement [BNTC]. Self-conceit has a bewildering and confusing effect on such a person [TC].

QUESTION—What is meant by εἰς κρίμα ἐμπέσῃ 'he might fall into condemnation'?

This describes the result of becoming conceited, and the phrase 'falling into condemnation' is an idiom for incurring judgment [LSA]. While the term 'judgment' itself is neutral, the dread expressed in this clause by 'falling into' such a judgment definitely gives an adverse sense to the meaning of 'judgment' [Alf]. The word 'judgment' here indicates the result of the action of a judicial pronouncement of a verdict [Lns]. Here judgment is a judicial verdict that results in condemnation [ICC, My]. Judgment in this context focuses on the sentence or condemnation that is passed [LSA, NICNT, NTC], since a sin has been the occasion for bringing about the judgment [LSA].

QUESTION—What is meant by the genitive phrase κρίμα τοῦ διαβόλου 'the judgment of the devil'

1. This refers to the judgment that the devil *received* from God [AB, Alf, BKC, EGT, **LN**, Lns, LSA, NIBC, NIGTC, NTC, TG, TH, TNTC, WBC, WP; CEV, GW, NASB, NIV, TEV]: *the conceited overseer will be judged by God just like the devil was judged by God.* This interpretation carries an implied comparison between the judgment upon the conceit of the overseer and the judgment upon the conceit of the devil [BKC, LSA, TG, TH, WBC]. The overseer is in danger of receiving the same judgment pronounced and executed upon the devil [NTC]. This fits the tradition that the devil was punished because of the proud arrogance he showed toward God [AB]. God's judgment was on the devil's pride, and here the conceited novice might also be judged for his pride since his conceit could smother his new faith and carry him into that fatal sin committed by the devil [Lns]. Joining 'judgment', where it clearly indicates a condemnatory judgment, with the genitive 'of the devil' with a subjective sense so that

the devil is the one who makes the judgment is theologically objectionable [Alf, Lns, NTC], since the NT never presents the devil as ever passing a sentence of condemnation upon anyone [Lns, LSA, NTC].

2. This refers to the punishment carried out or caused by the devil [BNTC, ECC, ICC, My, NAC, NCBC, NICNT, NTL; NET, NLT].

2.1 This refers to a judgment that the devil will carry out upon the conceited overseer [BNTC, ECC, NICNT, NTL; NET, NLT]: *the conceited overseer will be punished by the devil.* This is related to the function of the devil in 1:20 where Hymenaeus and Alexander were delivered to Satan so that they might be taught not to blaspheme [ECC; NET]. The condemnation is not the final eschatological judgment, but the chastisement that the devil carries out with the power he has to administer all the evils that afflict mankind, including death [ECC]. The devil's active role in the next verse favors an active role for the devil here in pronouncing the condemnation he has designed for God's people [NICNT]. If instead of a subjective genitive, this was to be taken as an objective genitive where a judgment is passed *upon* the devil, then this does nothing to prepare the way for the following statement about the trap set by the devil in 3:7 [BNTC].

2.2 This refers to a condemnation brought about by the devil [ICC, My, NAC, NCBC]: *the conceited overseer will be accused by the devil when God judges that man.* The parallelism here with 'the snare of the devil' in 3:7 supports this interpretation [ICC, My, NAC, NCBC]. That parallelism shows that this refers to the condemnation of the man that is brought about by the devil tempting an overseer to be proud [ICC, NCBC]. In this case, the 'judgment' or 'condemnation' may be a temporal, not eschatological, judicial punishment that is decreed by God upon the vain neophyte, with the physical chastisements being inflicted by the devil, as in 1:20 and 1 Cor. 5:5 [ECC].

3. This refers to the judgment made by a slanderous person. Here διάβολος means 'slanderer' instead of 'devil' and it refers to a person who delights in finding fault with anyone who professes to follow a strict rule of life [TC].

3:7 And/but[a] it-is-necessary also to-have a-good-testimony[b] from[c] the (ones) outside,[d]

LEXICON—a. δέ (LN 89.87, 89.93, 89.124) (BAGD 1., 2., 3. p. 171): This conjunction can mark a sequence of closely related events: 'and, and then' [LN (89.87)], or an additive relation that is not coordinate: 'and, and also, also, in addition, even' [LN (89.93)], or a contrast: 'but, on the other hand' [LN (89.124)]. It can emphasize a contrast: 'but', or mark a simple transition: 'now, then', or mark a resumption of an interrupted discourse: 'and also, but also' [BAGD]. Here it is translated 'and' [AB, BNTC, WBC; NASB, NET], 'furthermore' [HCSB], 'moreover' [Lns, LSA; KJV,

NRSV, REB], 'also' [NLT], 'finally' [CEV], 'but' [ECC], not explicit [Herm, NTC; GW, NCV, NIV].

b. μαρτυρία (LN 33.262, 33.264, **33.265**) (BAGD 2.c. p. 493): 'testimony' [BAGD, LN (33.264)], 'reputation' [LN (33.265)], 'witness' [LN (33.262, 33.264)]. The phrase μαρτυρίαν καλὴν ἔχειν ἀπό 'to have a good testimony from' is translated 'have excellent testimony from' [Lns], 'have a favorable testimony from' [NTC], 'have a good report of' [KJV], 'have the commendation of' [AB], 'enjoy a fine recommendation from' [ECC], 'have a good reputation with' [BNTC, WBC; NASB, NIV, REB], 'who has a good reputation among' [**LN** (33.265); similarly Herm; HCSB], 'who is respected by' [TEV], 'be well respected by' [CEV], 'have the respect of' [NCV], 'be well thought of by' [NET, NRSV]. This is also translated with the outsiders being the subject of the verb: 'speak well of (him)' [LSA; GW, NLT]. This noun denotes the giving of information about a person or an event arising out of the speaker's direct knowledge [LN (33.262)], or it denotes the content of what one has said or to which he has borne witness [LN (33. 264)], or it denotes what is said about a person based upon an evaluation of that person's conduct [LN (33.265)].

c. ἀπό (LN 90.7, 90.15) (BAGD V.4. p. 88): 'from' [BAGD, LN], 'by, with' [LN]. See the preceding lexical item b. for translations of this preposition with the different ways of translating μαρτυρία 'testimony'. This usage of the preposition may indicate cause, means, or outcome [BAGD (V. p. 87)]. More specifically, it may indicate the source of the action denoted in the verb [BAGD, LN (90.15), My, NIGTC]. This preposition is a marker of both agent and source. This arises from the fact that ἀπό 'from, by' as a marker of agent involves communication which may very well give rise to a double sense of both the agent and the source of the communication [LN (90.7, footnote 1)].

d. ἔξωθεν (LN **11.10**) (BAGD 1.b.β. p. 279): 'from outside' [BAGD, LN]. The phrase τῶν ἔξωθεν 'the (ones) outside' is translated 'those outside' [WBC], 'those on the outside' [BAGD], 'those without' [Lns], 'them which are without' [KJV], 'outsiders' [AB, BNTC, ECC, **LN,** NTC; HCSB, NIV, NRSV], 'the outside world' [REB], 'those/people outside the church' [NASB, NLT, TEV], 'those outside of the congregation' [Herm], 'people who are not in the church' [NCV], 'those outside the faith' [NET], 'people who are not Christians' [GW], 'non-Christians' [LSA], 'people who are not followers' [CEV]. When used as a substantive with the definite article as here, this adverb becomes a figurative extension of the meaning of ἔξωθεν 'from outside' (under LN 84.15) and denotes all persons who are not members of a particular in-group [LN (11.10)]. This means people who were not members of the Church, i.e., non-Christians [BAGD, BNTC, ECC, My, NIGTC, NTC, TG, WBC, WP], both pagan and Jewish [BNTC]. They are those who have not believed the gospel [NAC].

QUESTION—What relationship is indicated by δέ 'and, but'?

1. The conjunction δέ 'and, moreover' is additive and developmental [AB, Alf, BNTC, Lns, LSA, My, NICNT, NIGTC, NTC; CEV, HCSB, KJV, NET, NLT, NRSV, REB; probably GW, NCV, NIV, TEV which omit the conjunction]: *moreover it is also necessary*. With 3:6 the apostle has finished the list of requirements that pertain to the estimation in which the candidate for overseer is held by the members of his congregation, and now he proceeds to treat the opinions of outsiders concerning him. An overseer with a bad reputation among the outsiders would nullify any powerful influence for good that the church could have among them to lead them to Christ [NTC]. The conjunction δέ 'moreover' does not introduce something opposed to 3:6, but rather adds a new requirement to those listed in 3:2–6 [My], and this requirement is accompanied by an emphatic καί 'also, moreover' to indicate that it is equally as important as the preceding ones [ICC, NIGTC]. The words 'it is necessary' connect this back with the identical term in 3:2 [Lns, My], verses 2–6 having formed a single sentence. This reverts back to the very first requirement that an overseer must be ἀνεπίλημπτον 'above reproach', and adds that this applies not only to the opinion of the congregation, but also to the opinion of those outside the church [ECC, Lns].

2. The conjunction δέ 'but' is adversative [ECC, TC, WBC]: *but it is also necessary*. This is in contrast with an overseer who is a new convert that has become conceited [ECC]. This conjunction has a weak adversative force which contrasts those who fall prey to the judgment of the devil (2:6) with the overseers who are to be above reproach [WBC].

QUESTION—What is meant by having μαρτυρίαν καλὴν 'a good testimony' from others?

In matters of religion and morals, this testimony is a judgment that is passed upon one person by another [BAGD], usually referring to a positive judgment, and here it refers to a good reputation or recommendation [ICC]. A 'good testimony from outsiders' means 'a good reputation with outsiders' [Herm, NICNT, NIGTC, NTL], and it concerns a good verdict on the overseer's commitment to his religious faith [NIGTC]. In the matter of his wider reputation, he must be well regarded in society [NICNT]. This is a testimony given by outsiders concerning the moral worth of the overseers [AB]. This testimony is about the overseer's life since his conversion [Lns].

in-order-that he-might- not -fall[a] into reproach[b] and a-trap[c] of-the devil.

LEXICON—a. aorist act. subj. of ἐμπίπτω (LN 90.71) (BAGD 2. p. 256): 'to fall' [BAGD], 'to experience, to encounter' [LN]. This verb means to suddenly experience something that is difficult or bad [LN]. See translations of this verb in the following lexical item. See this verb at 3:6.

b. ὀνειδισμός (LN 33.389) (BAGD p. 570): 'reproach, disgrace, reviling' [BAGD], 'insult' [BAGD, LN]. The phrase εἰς ὀνειδισμὸν ἐμπέσῃ 'fall into reproach' [WBC; KJV, NASB] is also translated 'be reproached by people' [LSA], 'fall into disgrace' [AB, ECC; HCSB, NET, NIV, NRSV], 'be disgraced' [CEV, NLT, TEV], 'be criticized by others' [NCV], 'be exposed to scandal' [REB], 'incur slander' [BNTC], 'become the victim of disgraceful insults' [GW]. This noun denotes the act of speaking in a disparagingly manner about someone who does not deserve it [LN].

c. παγίς (LN 6.23) (BAGD 2. p. 602): 'trap' [BAGD, LN], 'snare' [BAGD, LN]. The phrase εἰς...ἐμπέσῃ...παγίδα τοῦ διαβόλου 'fall into a trap of the devil' is translated 'fall into...the trap of the devil' [AB], 'fall into...the devil's trap' [HCSB, NIV, NLT, TEV], 'fall into the devil's snare' [Herm], 'fall into...a/the snare of the devil' [ECC; KJV, NASB, NRSV], 'caught in the devil's trap' [BNTC; NCV], 'be caught by the devil's trap' [NET], 'be caught in the devil's snare' [REB], 'be caught in the trap which the devil has set for him' [LSA], 'be trapped by the devil' [CEV], '(disgraceful insults) that the devil sets as traps for him' [GW], '(lest he fall into reproach,) which is the snare of the devil' [WBC]. This noun denotes an object that is used to trap or snare animals, principally birds [LN]. This is used figuratively of something that suddenly and unexpectedly brings danger or death [BAGD].

QUESTION—What is the function of the negative clause ἵνα μὴ ἐμπέσῃ... 'in order that he might not fall...'?

It indicates the purpose or reason for the preceding requirement of having a good testimony from the outsiders [ECC, ICC, LSA, My, NICNT, NIGTC]: *it is necessary also to have a good testimony from the outsiders in order that he might not fall into their reproaches.* He must guard against behavior that is against the standard of morality held by society [NICNT]. A man who does not have this good testimony and is nevertheless chosen to be an overseer may easily fall into reproach [NTC, TH]. If an overseer does not do what he publicly proclaims and teaches he will receive well-deserved derision from the outsiders [BNTC, ECC].

QUESTION—Who would reproach an overseer who did not have a good testimony from outsiders?

An overseer who did not have a good testimony with the outsiders would be reproached by those outsiders [BNTC, ECC, ICC, NICNT, NIGTC, NTC, TH]. The outsiders would be ready to put an unfavorable interpretation on his slightest word or deed [BNTC, NIGTC]. The outsiders would perhaps accuse him of hypocrisy [TH]. Not only would the outsiders reproach him, but also the Christians would reproach such a man who was a disgrace to them in his sacred office of overseer [Lns].

QUESTION—How are the phrases 'fall into reproach' and '(fall into) a trap of the devil' connected?

1. Falling into reproach is one situation to be avoided, and falling into a trap set by the devil is a subsequent situation that would probably result from the first [AB, BNTC, Herm, ICC, Lns, My, NICNT, NIGTC, NTC, NTL; probably HCSB, KJV, NASB, NCV, NET, NIV, NRSV, REB, TEV which translate these as two separate events]: *fall into the reproach of*

outsiders and then fall into a trap of the devil. He must beware of falling into these two things [AB]. If the overseer incurs slander, he may well get caught in a snare set by the devil to discredit the leader, and this would in turn discredit the church [BNTC]. He may fall into the devil's snare when people reproach him [Herm]. If this man sees that he can get away with reproachable conduct and still be overseer, he may become so bold as to think he could get away with anything, and then he would fall into the devil's trap, that is, fall into the devil's power [NTC]. Reproach from others, especially from Christians, would separate the overseer from them, and then the devil would lay his snare to catch him into his deadly power like an animal is caught and then killed [Lns].

2. Falling into reproach is described as falling into a trap that the devil has set for him [LSA, NIBC, WBC; CEV, GW, NLT]: *he will fall into the reproach of outsiders, that is, he would fall into the trap of the devil.* The devil's plan is to discredit the overseer, so when outsiders reproach the overseer, the devil's plan has been accomplished, and therefore falling into the reproach of the outsiders is described as falling into the trap that devil has set for him [LSA]. The preceding καί 'even' explains the preceding statement about falling into reproach [WBC]. This is translated 'or he might become the victim of disgraceful insults that the devil sets as traps for him' [GW], 'so that he will not be disgraced and fall into the devil's trap' [NLT], 'then they won't be trapped and disgraced by the devil' [CEV].

3. Here διάβολος means 'slanderer' instead of 'devil' and the phrase 'of the slanderer' goes with both situations [TC]: *he will fall into the reproaches and traps prepared by slanderers.*

QUESTION—What is meant by the metaphor 'fall into a trap of the devil'?

This pictures the devil as setting a trap [NICNT, WP; NET]. It refers to falling into the power of the devil [Lns, NTC, TG]. This depicts the devil's role in tempting and leading the overseer into the kinds of sins that Paul has just written about and thus be brought into disrepute [NICNT]. Satan has set out many traps for preachers, such as pride, money, women, and ambition [WBC, WP]. There is a somewhat parallel reference in 2 Tim. 2: 26 about the opponents escaping from the trap of the devil where they were held captive to do his will [NET]. It describes a relapse into sin [Herm]. The man could lose his senses when he fell into reproach and be ensnared to obey the devil instead of God [NIGTC].

DISCOURSE UNIT: 3:8–16 [AB]. The topic is behavior in the household of God.

DISCOURSE UNIT: 3:8–13 [ECC, Herm, ICC, NAC, NCBC, NIBC, NICNT, NIGTC, NTL, TH, TNTC, WBC; CEV, NCV, NRSV, TEV]. The topic is church officers [CEV], deacons [NIGTC, TH, TNTC, WBC], deacons in the church [NCV], servers [NTL], helpers in the church [TEV], the conduct of deacons, [Herm], qualifications for deacons [ICC, NCBC, NIBC, NICNT;

NRSV], the deacons and women ministers [ECC], qualifications of deacons and women helpers [NAC].

3:8 Deacons[a] similarly[b] (must be)[c] respectable,[d]

LEXICON—a. διάκονος (LN **53.67**) (BAGD 1.c. p. 184): 'deacon' [BAGD, BNTC, ECC, Herm, **LN**, Lns, LSA, NTC, WBC; all versions except CEV, TEV], 'church officer' [CEV], 'church helper' [TEV], 'one who helps the believers' [LN], 'helper' [AB]. This noun denotes an official of the church [BAGD], who serves as a deacon, with the responsibility of caring for the needs of the believers [LN].

　　b. ὡσαύτως (LN 64.16) (BAGD p. 899): 'similarly' [BAGD, BNTC, ECC, NTC], 'likewise' [AB, BAGD, Herm, LSA, WBC; HCSB, KJV, NASB, NET, NIV, NRSV, REB], 'in the same way' [BAGD, LN; NCV, NLT], 'in like manner' [LN, Lns], 'also' [GW], not explicit [CEV]. This adverb indicates a similarity [LN]. See this word at 2:9.

　　c. (must be): The supplied verb is 'must be' [LSA, NTC; GW, KJV, NASB, NCV, NET, NLT, NRSV, REB], 'must' [TEV], 'have to be' [ECC], 'should be' [AB, BNTC, Herm, LN (88.47); CEV, HCSB], 'are to be' [NIV], 'it is necessary to be' [WBC], not explicit [Lns]. The words δεῖ εἶναι 'it is necessary to be' in 3:2 are meant to be supplied here [Alf, EGT, ICC, Lns, NAC, NIGTC, TC, WBC, WP].

　　d. σεμνός (LN 88.47) (BAGD 1.a. p. 747): 'worthy of respect' [BAGD, LN; HCSB, NIV], 'well respected' [NLT], 'worthy of honor' [BAGD], 'honorable' [Herm, LN], 'of good character' [**LN**; GW], 'dignified' [AB, BAGD, Lns, NTC, WBC; NET, REB], 'serious' [BAGD, BNTC, ECC, LSA; CEV, NRSV], 'grave' [KJV]. This adjective is also translated as a noun phrase: 'men of dignity' [NASB]; or as a verb phrase: 'respected by others' [NCV], 'have a good character' [TEV]. This adjective describes appropriate behavior that is dignified and worthy of respect [LN]. See this word at 3:11.

QUESTION—What relationship is indicated by the conjunction ὡσαύτως 'similarly'?

　　There are qualifications for overseers as listed above and likewise there are qualifications for deacons [My, NIGTC]. Like the office of overseer, the office of the deacon was also important [TH], and it likewise required an exemplary moral character and qualifications [Lns, TH]. It also indicates that this new list of qualifications is similar to the preceding list of qualifications for the overseers [Alf, BNTC, Lns, My, NAC, TH, WBC].

QUESTION—Who was a διάκονος 'deacon'?

　　The word διάκονος means 'helper' [AB, TH], or 'servant' [TH]. By the time this letter was written it had become a technical term to designate an office or position in the church, evidently a position of leadership ranking below that of the office of 'overseer' (or 'elder') [ICC, NAC, NIBC, NIGTC, TH]. Deacons were official church workers [WBC]. The word διάκονος 'deacon' refers to the office of 'deacon' and also describes the function of the office as serving in the church [NIGTC]. They served in carrying out the menial tasks of the church and thus enabled the elders to give their attention to more important matters [BKC]. They were assistants to the overseers and there is no suggestion that they had the responsibilities of teaching or hospitality [BNTC, Lns]. Official teaching duties were assigned to overseers, but this does not mean that deacons could not teach, since the requirements listed here concern the type of persons deacons were to be and not their duties [WBC]. These people had a fixed role in the community with specific duties, but the nature of this service is not specified in this letter [NTL]. Another view is that church offices such as bishop and deacon were a later development when the position of deacon was a stepping stone to a higher rank. At this stage of church organization, it is better to use the term 'helper' to indicate one who helped in practical tasks [NTIC].

QUESTION—What is meant by σεμνός 'respectable'?

The cognate noun σεμνότητος 'respect/dignity' has already been used in 2:2 to refer to an essential quality of Christians in general, and in 3:4 it refers to overseers in particular [BNTC, TH]. This adjectival form σεμνούς 'respectable' has the same range of meanings as its cognate noun in 3:4 [AB]. When referring to a person, it means that the person is worthy of respect [NIGTC]. It refers to having a dignity of bearing [AB, NIBC, NTIC]. Their behavior must be dignified and serious so as to receive the respect of others [EGT, ICC, NIBC]. The word expresses the ideas of dignity, restraint, virtue, temperance, honor, and modesty [ECC]. It combines such ideas as dignity, earnestness of purpose, and winsome attractiveness [NAC], or the ideas of being noble, worthy, and esteemed [WBC]. The work of a deacon required that he be sensible and steady [Lns].

not double-worded,[a]

LEXICON—a. δίλογος (LN **88.235**) (BAGD p. 198): 'double-tongued' [BAGD, Herm, LN, Lns, NTC; KJV, NASB, NRSV], 'two-faced' [**LN**; GW, NET], 'hypocritical' [LN; HCSB], 'insincere' [BAGD, LSA], 'duplicitous' [AB]. This adjective is also translated as a noun: 'liar' [CEV], 'gossip' [WBC]; or as a verb phrase: 'indulging in double talk' [REB], 'saying things they do not mean' [NCV], 'retailing gossip' [ECC]. The litotes 'not double-word' is also translated as a positive statement: 'be sincere' [NIV, TEV], 'have integrity' [NLT], 'consistent in what they say' [BNTC]. This adjective describes contradictory behavior that is based upon pretense or hypocrisy [LN].

QUESTION—What is meant by being δίλογος 'double-worded'?

The word is composed of two morphemes δι- 'two' and λογος 'word', that is, 'double-worded', and this refers to giving a false impression of one's true intentions by using deceptive words [AB, NTIC]. It refers to saying one thing to one person and saying something different to another person [BNTC, EGT, ICC, Lns, My, NCBC, NICNT, NTC, TH, TNTC, WP]. It means to say one thing while knowing that something different is really true

[NTC,]. This phrase has reference to insincerity [EGT, ICC, LSA, NIGTC, TH; NIV, TEV], hypocrisy [HCSB], or lying [CEV]. Some convert this negative phrase into a positive quality involving sincerity [NIV, TEV], or integrity [NLT]. They must be fully trustworthy in what they say [NIBC]. They are to be honest and not hypocritical [BKC]. This has special reference to gossiping [ECC, NAC, WBC]. This describes a person who reveals secrets instead of keeping them [WBC]. Since his duties would make him a frequent visitor in homes, he needed to be consistent in what he reported to those to whom he was responsible. He was not to spread rumors to different groups of listeners [NAC].

not indulging[a] in-much wine,[b]

LEXICON—a. pres. act. participle of προσέχω (LN 68.19) (BAGD 1.c. p. 714): 'to continue to give oneself to, to continue to apply oneself to' [LN], 'to occupy oneself with, to devote oneself to' [BAGD]. The clause οἴνῳ πολλῷ προσέχοντας 'indulging in much wine' [NIV, NRSV] is also translated 'given to much wine' [KJV], 'devoting themselves to much wine' [Lns], 'given to excessive drinking' [NET], 'drinking a lot of wine' [HCSB], 'drink too much wine' [NCV, TEV], 'like to drink much wine' [LSA], 'be heavy drinkers' [CEV, NLT], 'over-fond of wine' [AB], 'given to excessive drinking' [REB], 'given to heavy drinking' [BNTC], 'given to immoderate enjoyment of wine' [Herm], 'addicted to wine' [WBC], 'addicted to much wine' [NTC; NASB], 'addicted to heavy drinking' [ECC], 'be addicted to alcohol' [GW]. This verb means to be devoted to something [LN].

   b. οἶνος (LN 6.197) (BAGD 1. p. 562): 'wine' [AB, BAGD, Herm, LN, Lns, LSA, NTC, WBC; HCSB, KJV, NASB, NCV, NRSV, TEV], 'alcohol' [GW], not explicit [BNTC, ECC; CEV, NLT, REB]. This noun denotes a fermented beverage that is made from the juice of grapes [LN].

QUESTION—What is meant by this requirement?

This requirement does not imply that total abstinence was required on the part of a deacon [Lns, NTC, TH]. It does not forbid the use of wine, the common drink of the time, but rather it forbids the love of too much of it [Lns]. This forbids excessive use of wine [ICC, NICNT]. He must not be enslaved to much wine [NIGTC]. The qualified deacon must be moderate in his consumption of wine, if he does drinks some [NTC]. The verb προσέχοντας 'indulging' refers to being *addicted* to wine [ECC, ICC, My, NTC, TC, WBC; GW, NASB].

not greedy-for-dishonest-gain,[a]

LEXICON—a. αἰσχροκερδής (LN **25.26**) (BAGD p. 25): 'greedy for dishonest gain' [BNTC], 'greedy of shameful gain' [NTC], 'greedy for money' [CEV, HCSB, NRSV, TEV], 'shamefully greedy for material gain' [**LN**], 'shamefully greedy' [LN], 'greedy of filthy lucre' [KJV], 'out for shameful gain' [Lns], 'pursuing dishonest gain' [NIV], 'dishonest with money' [NLT], 'fond of sordid gain' [NASB], 'greedy for gain' [WBC;

NET], 'greedy' [Herm, LSA], 'money-minded' [ECC], 'given to money-grubbing' [REB]. This clause is translated 'they must not use shameful ways to make money' [GW], 'they must not try to get rich by cheating others' [NCV], 'not willing to do anything for a profit' [AB]. This adjective describes someone as being shamefully greedy for material gain or profit [LN].

QUESTION—What is meant by the adjective αἰσχροκερδής 'greedy for dishonest gain'?

Αἰσχροκερδής is a compound word from αἰσχρός 'shameful, disgraceful' and κέρδος 'gain' [WBC]. This suggests that the office of deacon carried some sort of financial responsibility, perhaps administrating food and money to widows [TH], and to other needy people [BNTC, NCBC, TH, WBC]. This forbids seeking the office of deacon for the purpose of material profit [Alf, ICC, My, NAC, NIGTC, WBC]. Titus 1:11 and 1 Pet. 5:2 indicate that what is referred to is not dishonest dealing but using a Church office for the purpose of material benefit [My, NAC]. What the Apostle is talking about is undertaking a ministry when the motivation is financial gain rather than simply the desire to serve God and his people [NIGTC]. This term is synonymous with its counterpart ἀφιλάργυρος 'not loving money' in 3:3 [NIGTC]. Or, this term is much stronger than ἀφιλάργυρος 'not loving money' [BNTC, WBC], and indicates the seriousness of the problem of teaching for the sake of becoming rich, as Paul's opponents were doing in Ephesus (1 Tim. 6:5) [WBC].

1. This focuses on the attitude of being greedy [Alf, ECC, EGT, Herm, LN, LSA, NAC, TG, WBC; CEV, HCSB, NET, NRSV, REB, TEV]. It probably means that greed itself is shameful and not that a person is trying to make money by using dishonest means [Alf, EGT, LN, TG]: *not have shameful greed for money*. If he were to seek to gain money in a dishonest way, it would obviously be wrong, so here Paul is saying that a deacon is not to be greedy and not use his office for material benefit [NAC].

2. This adds to the attitude of being greedy by describing it as an illicit means of obtaining money [AB, BNTC, Lns, NIBC, NTC, NTIC, TC, TH, TNTC; GW, KJV, NASB, NCV, NIV, NLT]. This word has some form of dishonesty included in its meaning [TH; NLT]. It describes the way of gaining money as being shameful [Lns, NTC; GW, NCV], dishonest [BNTC; NIV], sordid [NASB], cheating [NCV]. It refers to the illicit disposal of the church funds that they are in charge of distributing [TC]. It speaks of shamelessly doing anything for a profit [NTIC]. It forbids disgraceful means of gain, whether by embezzling the alms entrusted to them or by currying favors to obtain money [Lns].

3:9 holding[a] the mystery[b] of-the-faith with a-clear[c] conscience.

LEXICON—a. pres. act. participle of ἔχω (LN 18.6) (BAGD I.1.c.β. p. 332): 'to hold' [AB, ECC; HCSB, KJV], 'to hold to' [NASB, NET, TEV], 'to hold on to' [LN, WBC; NASB], 'to hold fast to' [BNTC; NRSV], 'to hold firmly to' [CEV], 'to keep hold of' [NTC; NIV], 'to keep' [BAGD], 'to possess' [Lns; GW], 'to follow' [NCV], 'to be committed to' [NLT], 'to cherish' [Herm], 'with a firm hold on' [REB], 'to believe' [LSA]. This verb literally means to hold on to an object [LN]. This is a figurative use of 'to keep' or 'to preserve' [BAGD].

b. μυστήριον (LN 28.77) (BAGD 2. p. 530): 'mystery, secret' [BAGD, LN]. The phrase τὸ μυστήριον τῆς πίστεως 'the mystery of the faith' [BNTC, ECC, Lns, WBC; HCSB, KJV, NASB, NET, NRSV, REB] is also translated 'the mystery of our faith' [NTC], 'the mystery of faith' [AB, Herm], 'the mystery of the Christian faith' [GW], 'the mystery of the faith now revealed' [NLT], 'the secret of the faith that God made known to us' [NCV], 'the deep truths of the faith' [NIV], 'the revealed truth of the faith' [TEV], 'what God has shown us about our faith' [CEV], 'the doctrine which was not known until God revealed it' [LSA]. This noun denotes the content of something that had not been known before, and it is implied that it has now been revealed to at least some people [LN]. In this verse, the expression 'the mystery of the faith' is a formula meaning 'the faith' or the Christian religion [BAGD]. See this word at 3:16.

c. καθαρός (LN 53.29, 79.48) (BAGD 3.b. p. 388): 'clean' [LN (79.48)], 'pure' [BAGD, LN (53.29)], 'free from sin' [BAGD]. The phrase ἐν καθαρᾷ συνειδήσει 'with a clear conscience' [BNTC; HCSB, NASB, NET, NIV, NLT, NRSV, TEV] is also translated 'with a clean conscience' [ECC, WBC], 'in a clean conscience' [Lns], 'with a pure conscience' [AB, Herm, NTC], 'in a pure conscience' [KJV]. Some put this phrase first in the verse: 'And they must have a clear conscience (and hold firmly to…)' [CEV], 'They must have clear consciences about (possessing the mystery…)' [GW], 'With a clear conscience (they must follow the secret…)' [NCV], 'They must be men who combine a clear conscience (with a firm hold on…)' [REB], 'and they must sincerely (believe the doctrine)' [LSA]. This adjective describes the state of being ritually clean or pure [LN (53.29)], or the state of not being dirty [LN (79.48)]. It is used here in the moral and religious sense of being free from sin [BAGD]. See this word at 1:5 where it is translated 'pure' when applied to the heart.

QUESTION—What relationship is indicated by the use of the participle ἔχοντας 'holding' and what is meant by this verb?

This verse states positively what the three preceding qualifications have stated negatively [ICC, Lns, NAC, NTC]. This requirement is most important of all [BKC, BNTC, NTL]. This concludes the initial instructions about deacons by adding the important need for a deacon's faith in his life [NIGTC], and the force of δεῖ εἶναι 'it is necessary to be' in 3:2 is to be added here, 'they *must* hold to the faith' [AB, NIGTC; CEV, GW, NIV, NLT, NRSV, TEV]. The participial phrase 'holding to the mystery of the faith' indicates that the deacons have already accepted the faith [NIGTC].

They are to *maintain* the mystery of the faith with a clean conscience [ECC]. The extended sense of the verb ἔχοντας 'having' is 'being faithful to' the faith [TH]. The adherence of the candidate must be unquestioned [NICNT]. One holds to the 'body of revealed doctrine' when he maintains his faith in its teachings, continues to believe in them, and remains loyal to them [TG].

QUESTION—What is meant by τὸ μυστήριον τῆς πίστεως 'the mystery of the faith'?

1. 'The faith' is to be taken objectively as *the Christian doctrine* that is the content of the mystery [BAGD, BNTC, ECC, EGT, Herm, ICC, Lns, NAC, NCBC, NIBC, NICNT, NIGTC, TH, TNTC, WBC, WP; GW; probably HCSB, KJV, NASB, NCV, NET, NIV, NLT, NRSV, REB, TEV which translate it 'the faith']: *the mystery about the faith.* The participle 'holding to' refers to a solid commitment to the gospel [WBC], and since the subjective side of faith is already expressed in the participle ἔχοντας 'holding to', the objective concept of 'the faith' must be in view here [NIGTC]. 'The faith' is the objective body of Christian teaching [BNTC], the revealed truth of the Christian faith [NIGTC, TNTC; NET], the teachings that are accepted as being true and definitive [TH], the key articles of the Christian creed [BNTC, EGT], the gospel [Lns, NTL, WBC]. The 'mystery' is all of the hidden truths that are not accessible to reason, but which are made known by divine revelation [BNTC]. The mystery refers to a knowledge of God's plan that is beyond the understanding of sinners but which has been revealed through the gospel [WBC]. The mystery is God's plan of redemption which had been hidden from the beginning, but by the coming of Christ it has at last been revealed to those who have eyes to see [BNTC]. Some treat 'the faith' as being in apposition to the mystery (the mystery *is* the gospel) [AB, EGT, NTL]. The phrase means 'the faith as revealed' [EGT]

2. 'Faith' is to be taken subjectively as *the act of believing* the mystery [Alf, My, NTC, TC]: *the mystery that they believe.* The mystery refers to the secret of salvation in Christ, the mystery which faith has embraced and then rests upon [TC]. The mystery is the subject matter of faith, and the mystery refers to the divine truth that remains hidden until the knowledge of it is revealed by God's Spirit [My]. It is God's revelation about the person of Christ [Alf]. Or, Christ himself is called *the mystery* because he is God revealed in the flesh for the salvation of Jews and Gentiles on equal terms, and the participle 'holding to' refers to a person keeping in the closest possible union with Christ [NTC].

QUESTION—What is meant by holding the mystery ἐν καθαρᾷ συνειδήσε 'with a clear conscience'?

The preposition ἐν 'with' indicates that a clear conscience is to accompany the act of holding to the mystery of the faith [ECC, ICC, Lns, WBC]. The emphasis of this verse is on the requirement of having a good conscience [BNTC, Herm, My, NAC, NIGTC]. Or, the words 'holding to the faith' and 'having a clean conscience' form a loosely connected whole so that the condition of the conscience is determined by one's commitment to the faith [ICC].

1. The clear conscience refers to the deacon's life in general [AB, Alf, BKC, BNTC, Lns, NCBC, NICNT, NIGTC, NTC, NTL, TC, TH, WBC]. These words are not to be applied just to the official life of deacons, rather it concerns the earnestness of their Christian character [Alf]. The knowledge of the faith must be accompanied with appropriate behavior [NICNT, WBC], that of living so as to have a conscience clear from any stain of sin [WBC]. Any man who is double-worded, or indulges in much wine, or is greedy cannot hold to the Christian faith with a clean conscience [Lns, NTC]. Without a conscience that is free from stain and self-reproach, the attempt to hold the mystery of the faith is unproductive [BNTC]. A conscience is clear when the person has the conviction that he has done nothing wrong and is not motivated by selfish desires in what he does [TH]. This is the good conscience of 1:5 and adds the idea of a deacon serving the common good, especially in matters of finances [AB].

2. The clear conscience refers specifically to their act of *holding to* the mystery of the faith [My, NAC, NIBC, NIGTC, TG; GW]. The clear conscience does not refer to a virtuous life in general, but to the purity and uprightness of the conscience in regard to holding the mystery of faith, in contrast with the heretics' consciences which were stained by mingling truth with errors (4:2) [My]. The conscience is clear when a deacon continually obeys God's truth as it is revealed in Scripture, something that the false teachers did not do [NAC]. He keeps the revealed doctrines of the church with a clear conscience when he does so without doubts as to their truth and validity and thus unquestioning accepts them [TG]. The moral self-consciousness of a deacon is καθαρά 'clean' or 'clear' when he seeks to live according to the ethical demands of the revealed faith [NIGTC].

3:10 And also[a] let- these (men) -be-tested[b] first,[c]

LEXICON—a. καὶ δέ: 'and also'. This phrase is translated 'and also' [NTC, WBC; HCSB, KJV, NET], 'and too' [REB], 'also' [NASB], 'too' [BNTC, LSA], 'and' [NRSV], 'too, moreover' [Lns], not explicit [AB, ECC, Herm; CEV, GW, NCV, NIV, NLT, TEV].

b. pres. pass. impera. of δοκιμάζω (LN 27.44) (BAGD 1. p. 202): 'to be put to the test' [BAGD], 'to be examined' [BAGD], 'to be examined carefully, to be investigated' [LN]. The phrase οὗτοι δοκιμαζέσθωσαν 'let these men be tested' is translated 'let them be tested' [Lns, NTC; NRSV], 'they should be tested' [AB, Herm, WBC; TEV], 'they must be tested' [HCSB, NIV; similarly NASB, NET], 'these should have a testing' [BNTC], 'let them be put to the test' [ECC], 'they must be examined' [LSA\, 'they must undergo scrutiny' [REB], 'a person must be evaluated' [GW], 'let them be closely examined' [NLT], 'let these be proved' [KJV], 'they must prove themselves' [CEV]. This passive verb is also translated actively: 'test them' [NCV]. This verb means to try to learn the nature or truth about someone by the process of careful study, evaluation, and judgment [LN]. Here the verb means to examine the candidates for the office of deacon [BAGD]. The imperative tense of this verb indicates that this is a required step in selecting deacons, they *must* be tested [TH].

c. πρῶτος (LN 60.46) (BAGD 2.a. p. 726): 'first' [AB, BAGD, ECC, Herm, LN, Lns, LSA, NTC, WBC; all versions except NLT], 'before (they are appointed as deacons)' [NLT], 'preliminary' [BNTC]. This adverb means the first in a series involving time [LN]. Here it means that before a potential deacon is installed, he must be tested [TG]. The sequence *first* and *then* are important, and it indicates that first the candidates are to be judged, and only then may they serve [NTL].

QUESTION—What relationship is indicated by the conjunction δέ 'and'?

The conjunction δέ 'and' relates this verse to the previous one [Lns, LSA, WBC], and adds a somewhat different type of qualification from the preceding ones [Lns, LSA, My]. This has no adversative force here [WBC]. It introduces a caution and implies a slight contrast of a necessary addition to their present character [Alf].

QUESTION—What relationship is indicated by καί 'also'?

1. Καί 'also' indicates that the deacons are being compared with the overseer [BKC, ICC, Lns, LSA, NAC, NIGTC, NTC]: *the overseer must be tested, and also deacons must be tested.* This verse states explicitly a requirement for appointing deacons that is only implied in appointing an overseer [Lns, LSA, NAC, NIGTC, NTC, TH]. The requirements for an overseer that are listed in 3:2–7 imply that such a testing was also required for an overseer [Lns, LSA, NIGTC].

2. Καί 'also' means that in addition to the requirements for a deacon given in 3:8–9, there is also the requirement that they be tested [Alf, NICNT, TH, WBC; probably AB, ECC, Herm; CEV, GW, NCV, NIV, NLT, NRSV, TEV which do not translate this word]. There is no connection with the requirements listed for overseers [Alf]. Here the phrase καὶ δέ 'and also' means 'and also in the second place' [WBC]. This is not an additional, unspecified test, but rather it is an assessment of the candidates in regard to the qualifications already set out [NICNT]. It is likely that 'also' refers to 3:9 and indicates that potential deacons should be tested to find out if they really do hold fast to revealed truth of the faith [TH].

QUESTION—What is meant by δοκιμαζέσθωσαν 'let them be tested'?

1. They must be evaluated as to their fitness for serving in the church [BKC, Herm, ICC, Lns, LSA, My, NAC, NICNT, NIGTC, NTC, NTL, TC, TNTC]. The members of the congregation are the ones who would test the candidates [ICC, NAC, NIGTC, NTC, NTL, TC, TH, TNTC]. The deacons' character and past conduct must be reviewed in order to see if they meet the qualifications that have been listed [LSA]. The congregation would carefully evaluate the candidate's life in light of the list of requirements for the position [NIGTC], the five qualities in 3:8–9 being

the minimal qualities required [NTL]. This doesn't mean that the candidate must serve a trial period, but that he must sustain the test of having the attention of the whole church plus outsiders focused on his character and life to ascertain if he has been blameless [NTC]. The present tense of δοκιμαζέσθωσαν 'let them continue to be tested' suggests a continual testing of potential candidates while they are members of the congregation so that when deacons are needed, they may be chosen from the available group of such tested men [Lns, NAC]. They must prove their qualities in regard to life and ministry over time by their ordinary activities [BKC].

2. They must have a probationary period in which the candidate would prove to be capable of the duties of a deacon [CEV, KJV]: *they must prove themselves* [CEV].

then[a] **let-them-serve-as-deacons,**[b] **being above-reproach.**[c]

LEXICON—a. εἶτα (LN 67.44) (BAGD 1. p. 234): 'then' [AB, BAGD, BNTC, ECC, Herm, LN, Lns, LSA, WBC; all versions except REB], 'afterwards, later' [LN], 'next' [BAGD], 'and only (if)' [REB]. This adverb refers to a point of time that follows another point [LN].

b. pres. act. impera. of διακονέω (LN **53.66**) (BAGD 5. p. 184): 'to serve as a deacon' [BAGD, **LN**, LSA], 'to be a deacon' [LN]. The imperative form διακονείτωσαν 'let them serve as deacons' [ECC; NASB, NCV, NET, NIV, NLT, NRSV] is also translated 'they can serve as deacons' [HCSB], 'should serve as deacons' [BNTC], 'he may become a deacon' [GW], '(only if...) may they serve as deacons' [REB], 'they can serve as officers' [CEV], 'let them use the office of a deacon' [KJV], 'let them serve' [WBC], 'they are able to serve' [TEV], 'let them minister' [Lns], 'they can carry out their service' [AB], 'they should execute their duty' [Herm]. This verb means to serve God in some special way, and here it means to serve as a deacon [LN]. The verb itself means 'to serve', but since this passage is not talking about serving in general, it means to serve as deacons [NICNT, WBC]. The imperative tense here means that after passing the test they *are allowed* to serve as deacons [TH].

c. ἀνέγκλητος (LN 33.433) (BAGD p. 64): 'irreproachable, blameless' [BAGD], 'without accusation' [LN]. The phrase ἀνέγκλητοι ὄντες 'being above reproach' is translated 'if they are beyond reproach' [NASB], 'if they are found above reproach' [WBC], 'if they are irreproachable' [Herm], 'being blameless' [AB], 'being found blameless' [KJV], 'if they are found blameless' [NET], 'if they prove blameless' [HCSB], 'if they prove themselves blameless' [NRSV], 'if they are without fault' [LSA], 'if no fault has been found in them' [BNTC], 'if no one has anything against them' [CEV], 'if there is nothing against them' [NIV], 'if you find nothing wrong in them' [NCV], 'if they are of unimpeachable character' [REB], 'if he has a good reputation' [GW], 'if they pass the test' [NLT, TEV], 'as being men unaccused' [Lns], 'those who are unimpeachable' [ECC]. This adjective describes someone who cannot be accused of anything wrong [LN].

QUESTION—What is meant by the use of the participle ὄντες 'being'?

1. This indicates a condition [Alf, BNTC, Herm, ICC, LSA, NIGTC, TC, WBC, WP; all versions]: *if they are found to be above reproach, then let them serve as deacons.*

2. This indicates the kind of men they are [ECC, Lns]: *let the ones who are unreprovable serve as deacons.*

QUESTION—What is meant by the adjective ἀνέγκλητοι 'above reproach'?

This word 'above reproach' is a synonym of ἀνεπίλημπτον 'above reproach' in 3:2 [BKC, NAC, NIBC, NICNT, NIGTC, NTC, TH, WBC]. A fair appraisal will judge them as being blameless if they have all of the positive qualifications of the list and none of the negative traits listed [NIGTC]. It means to be free of accusation in public and civil matters [NICNT]. No specific charge of wrongdoing can be made against them [NAC]. Also see the answer in 3:2.

3:11 Women[a] similarly[b] (must be)[c] respectable,[d]

LEXICON—a. γυνή (LN 9.34, 10.54): 'woman' [LN (9.34)], 'wife' [LN (10.54)]. The plural form is translated 'women' [Herm, Lns, NTC; CEV, NASB, NCV, NRSV], 'women deacons' [BNTC], 'women helpers' [AB], 'women in this office' [REB], 'women who are ministers' [ECC], 'wives' [WBC; HCSB, KJV], 'their wives' [LSA; GW, NET, NIV, NLT, TEV]. This noun denotes an adult female person of marriageable age [LN (9.34)], or a woman who is married to a man [LN (10.54)].

b. ὡσαύτως (LN 64.16) (BAGD p. 899): 'similarly' [BAGD, BNTC, ECC, NTC], 'likewise' [AB, BAGD, Herm, LSA, WBC; NASB, NRSV, REB], 'likewise also' [NET], 'in the same way' [BAGD, LN; NCV, NIV, NLT], 'just as, in like manner' [LN, Lns], 'even so' [KJV], 'also' [CEV, GW, TEV], 'too' [HCSB]. This adverb indicates a similarity [LN]. See this word at 2:9; 3:8.

c. (must be): The supplied verb is 'must be' [NTC, WBC; all versions except NIV], 'must' [LSA], 'should be' [AB, BNTC, Herm], 'have to be' [ECC], 'are to be' [NIV], not explicit [Lns]. The words δεῖ εἶναι 'it is necessary to be' in 3:2 are meant to be supplied here [WBC, WP].

d. σεμνός (LN 88.47) (BAGD 1.a. p. 747): 'worthy of respect' [BAGD, LN; HCSB, NIV], 'worthy of honor' [BAGD], 'honorable' [Herm, LN], 'of good character' [LN; GW, TEV], 'noble' [BAGD], 'dignified' [AB, Lns, NTC, WBC; NASB, NET, REB], 'serious' [BAGD, ECC; CEV, NRSV], 'serious minded' [BNTC], 'grave' [KJV]. This adjective is also translated as a verb phrase: 'be respected' [NLT], 'be respected by others' [NCV], 'conduct themselves suitably' [LSA]. This adjective describes appropriate behavior that is dignified and worthy of respect [LN]. See this word at 3:8.

QUESTION—What relationship is indicated by ὡσαύτως 'similarly'?

This word connects these qualifications with the qualifications of the deacons and indicates that all three sets of positions have requirements that must be met [EGT, Lns, NIGTC]. This verse is awkwardly placed since it is inserted in the midst of the qualifications of men who are candidates for being deacons [TG].

QUESTION—Who are the γυναῖκας 'women'?

1. They are female deacons [AB, Alf, BNTC, ECC, EGT, ICC, Lns, NICNT, NTIC, NTL, TC, TG, TH, WP; REB]. The connective ὡσαύτως 'like-wise' appears to signal a difference between men and women having the same function and the requirements are similar to those for the men deacons [AB, BNTC, ECC, Lns, NICNT, NTL]. It would be strange to have the wives of the deacons singled out when the wife of an overseer is not mentioned although she had an even more influential position, so here this refers to deacons who are women [BNTC, ECC, NICNT]. They are referred to in this way because there was no separate technical term for a woman deacon [BNTC, NICNT, WBC], and the Greek at that time used the masculine form for either men or women [ECC, NICNT, NTL, WBC]. Probably these were unmarried women who devoted themselves to public ministry [ECC, Lns].

2. They are woman helpers who served the church in some way [NAC, NTC]. These women helpers would have a special ministry within the congregation [NAC]. These women were the deacons' assistants who would perform ministries more suited to women, the widows in 5:9 being examples of some who assisted in counseling and comforting younger women [NTC].

3. They are the wives of the deacons [LSA, My, NCBC, NIGTC, WBC; GW, NET, NIV, NLT, TEV]. After discussing personal qualities required of the candidates in 3:8–10, Paul now turns to the candidates' home life in 3:11–12, with the requirements that his wife must be dignified, he must be faithful to that wife, and he must govern his children well [NIGTC, WBC]. Referring to the wife of a deacon, it simply means that like deacons must be respectable, so also must their wives be respectable [WBC].

QUESTION—What is meant by σεμνάς 'respectable'?

This is the feminine form of the same adjective σεμνούς used in 3:8 for deacons.

not slanderers,[a] sober,[b] faithful/believing[c] in all.

LEXICON—a. διάβολος (LN 33.397) (BAGD 1. p. 182): 'slanderer' [LN, Lns, NTC, WBC; HCSB, KJV, NRSV], 'gossiper' [AB; LN], 'a gossip' [GW], 'scandalmonger' [REB], 'malicious gossip' [NASB], 'malicious talker' [NIV], 'devils at gossip' [ECC]. This substantive is also translated as an adjective: 'slanderous' [BAGD, Herm; NET]; or as a verb phrase: 'must not slander others' [NLT], 'must not gossip' [CEV, TEV], 'be given to gossip' [BNTC], 'speak evil about people' [LSA], 'speak evil of others' [NCV]. This word denotes someone who engages in slander or gossip [LN].

b. νηφάλιος (LN 88.87) (BAGD p. 538): 'sober' [AB, Herm, LN; KJV, REB, TEV], 'clear-minded' [WBC], 'self-controlled' [BAGD; HCSB, NCV], 'restrained' [LN], 'temperate' [BNTC, ECC, Lns, NTC; NASB, NET, NIV, NRSV]. This adjective is also translated as a verb phrase: 'exercise self-control' [NLT], 'must not be heavy drinkers' [CEV], 'must not drink too much wine' [LSA], 'must control their tempers' [GW]. This adjective describes a sober or restrained manner [LN]. See this word at 3:2.

c. πιστός (LN 31.86, 31.87) (BAGD 1.a.α. p. 664): 'faithful, trustworthy, dependable' [BAGD, LN (31.87)], 'reliable' [LN (31.87)], 'trusting' [LN (31.86)]. The phrase πιστὰς ἐν πᾶσιν 'faithful in all' is translated 'faithful in all things' [Lns, LSA, WBC; KJV, NASB, NRSV], 'faithful in every respect' [AB; NET], 'faithful in everything' [HCSB], 'faithful in everything they do' [CEV, NLT], 'trustworthy in everything' [NCV, NIV], 'trustworthy in every way' [GW, REB], 'honest in everything' [TEV], 'reliable in everything' [BNTC, Herm], 'reliable in all matters' [NTC], 'believers in every sense' [ECC]. This adjective pertains to being trusted [LN (31.87)], or to trusting in (God) [LN (31.86)].

QUESTION—What is meant by διαβόλους 'slanderers'?

This refers to the gossiping that their position of serving members of the congregation would easily lead to [BNTC]. A deaconess would visit widely among the congregation and might be tempted to tell others anything bad she had found out [Lns]. Slanderers are those who say harmful things about others [TH]. This is the same word translated 'devil' in 3:6–7, but here it means spreading lies, and positively it means that she should be known for speaking the truth [NICNT].

QUESTION—What is meant by νηφαλίους 'sober'?

This is the same word used in 3:2 as a requirement for an overseer.

1. It is understood in its literal sense, having reference to being temperate in the consumption of wine [AB, Alf, BNTC, EGT, ICC, LSA, NICNT, NTL; CEV]. It is equivalent to the phrase μὴ οἴνῳ πολλῷ προσέχοντας 'not indulging in much wine' used in 3:8 as a requirement for the deacons [AB, Alf, ICC].

2. It is understood in its extended sense of a life characterized by a sober outlook with self-control [BKC, Lns, My, NAC, NIGTC, NTC, TC, TG, TH, WBC; GW, HCSB, NCV, NLT]. They were to be moderate, well-balanced, and steady people [NTC]. This refers to moderation in all their behavior [NAC]. This means to be free from any type of excess [TH]. This woman must not only be temperate in her use of alcohol, but clear-minded in everything else that she does [NIGTC, WBC].

QUESTION—What is meant by the phrase πιστὰς ἐν πᾶσιν 'faithful in all'?

1. Here πιστάς has the passive sense of being faithful, trustworthy, and dependable [AB, BAGD, BKC, BNTC, Herm, Lns, LSA, My, NIBC, NICNT, NIGTC, NTC, TC, TNTC, WBC, WP; all versions]. The words ἐν πᾶσιν 'in all matters' mean all matter in reference to her duties, not her character [AB]. Being deaconesses who distribute help, they would have special temptations [WP]. The requirement of being fully trustworthy is added to cover all the other descriptions that might be listed [WBC].

2. Here πιστάς has the active sense of trusting or believing [ECC, NTL]. The words ἐν πᾶσιν 'in all matters' mean that they are to be Christian women in the widest possible sense of that term [ECC].

3:12 Let- deacons -be husbands of-one wife,[a] managing[b] children well and their own households.[c]

LEXICON—a. γυνή (LN 10.54): 'wife' [LN]. The phrase ἔστωσαν μιᾶς γυναικὸς ἄνδρες 'be husbands of one wife' [BNTC, ECC, Lns] is also translated 'be "one-woman" men' [WBC], 'be men who have one wife' [AB], 'be husbands of one wife' [ECC; HCSB, KJV, NET], 'be husbands to/of only one wife' [LSA; NASB], 'must have only one wife' [NCV], 'be married only once' [NRSV], 'should be the husband of one wife' [Herm], 'must be faithful in marriage' [CEV]. Some translate the plural subject διάκονοι 'deacons' with the singular form 'deacon' to better relate an individual deacon to his own wife and his own children and household, 'let *a deacon*': 'be the husband of one wife' [REB], 'be the husband of but one wife' [NIV], 'be one wife's husband' [NTC], 'must have only one wife' [GW, TEV], 'be faithful to his wife' [NLT]. The noun γυνή denotes a woman, and in Greek a wife is simply called 'his woman', 'my woman', etc, with the context normally indicating whether 'woman' or 'wife' is meant [LN]. See 3:2 for the same requirement for an overseer.

b. pres. mid. participle of προΐσταμαι, προΐστημι (LN 36.1) (BAGD 1. p. 707): 'to manage' [AB, BAGD, LSA, NTC, WBC; GW, NIV, NLT, NRSV], 'to be able to manage' [TEV], 'to rule' [BAGD; KJV], 'to direct' [BAGD, LN], 'to govern' [Herm], 'to guide, to lead' [LN]. The phrase καλῶς προϊστάμενοι 'managing well' is translated 'managing competently' [HCSB], 'managing properly' [BNTC], 'excellently superintending' [Lns], 'outstanding in the direction of' [ECC], 'be good at managing' [REB], 'be good managers' [NASB, NET], 'be good leaders' [NCV], 'they must be in full control of' [CEV]. See this verb at 3:4.

c. οἶκος (LN 10.8) (BAGD 2. p. 560): 'household' [BAGD, LN], 'family' [BAGD, LN]. The phrase τῶν ἰδίων οἴκων 'their own households' [BNTC, WBC; HCSB, NASB, NET; similarly NTC; REB] is also translated 'their households' [NRSV; similarly NIV, NLT], 'their own houses' [KJV], 'their own homes' [ECC, Lns], 'their homes' [Herm], 'their own families' [NCV], 'their families' [GW; similarly TEV], 'the rest of their households' [LSA], 'everyone else in their home' [CEV], 'their own household affairs' [AB]. This noun denotes a family consisting of all those related by blood and marriage who live in the same house or homestead, and includes the servants and slaves as well [LN]. Since a deacon's children are part of his household, it is implied that he must manage his children and *the rest of* his household well [LSA, NICNT; CEV]. See this noun at 3:4, 15; 5:4.

QUESTION—Following the requirements for 'women' in 3:11, how is this verse related to the requirements of the deacons in 3:8–10?

If Paul was referring to what was required of the *deacon's wives* in 3:11, then this verse is simply a return to more requirements for the deacons and perhaps the mention of the wives had naturally led to the deacons' relations with their wives and families. However, if Paul was referring to a separate office of *deaconess* in 3:11, then this verse appears to be an afterthought that required something more to be said about the deacons [NIBC].

QUESTION—How do these requirements for deacons differ from the requirements for an overseer that are given in 3:2 and 3:4?

The requirements for an overseer concerning a wife (3:2) and managing his household well (3:4) are the same as those given here for deacons. There is a slight difference concerning children. The overseer must have his children in subjection (3:4), and here the deacon must manage his children well. However, the difference is slight since when a father manages his children well, the children will be obedient [WBC]. The separate references to the household and the children in 3:4 have been conflated here [ECC].

QUESTION—How can many deacons be the husbands of one wife?

In the command 'let deacons be husbands of *one wife*', the singular 'one wife' is the individualizing singular that is common with plurals ('deacons') [Lns]. To avoid the idea of one wife having many husbands, some translations have changed the plural nouns 'deacons' and 'husbands' to the generic singular forms 'a deacon' and 'a husband' [NTC; GW, NIV, NLT, REB, TEV], or the plural form 'deacons' is kept but the singular form 'husband' is used [Herm]. One of these versions reverts back to the plural form 'deacons' for the second requirement about deacons managing *their* children and households well [GW].

3:13 Because[a] the (ones) having-served[b] well acquire[c] a-good standing[d] for-themselves

LEXICON—a. γάρ (LN 89.23): 'because' [LN, LSA], 'for' [BNTC, ECC, Herm, LN, Lns, NTC, WBC; HCSB, KJV, NASB, NET, NRSV, REB], not explicit [AB; CEV, GW, NCV, NIV, NLT, TEV]. This conjunction indicates the cause or reason between events [LN].

   b. aorist act. participle of διακονέω (LN 35.19) (BAGD 5. p. 184): 'to serve' [AB, LN, NTC, WBC; GW, NET, NIV], 'to render service, to help' [LN], 'to serve as deacons' [BAGD, BNTC; HCSB, NASB, NCV, NRSV]. The phrase οἱ καλῶς διακονήσαντες 'the ones having served well' is translated 'those who perform their service well' [Herm], 'those who do well as deacons' [NLT], 'those who do a good work' [LN (57.61)], 'they who ministered excellently' [Lns], 'those helpers who do their work well' [TEV], 'those who serve well as officers' [CEV], 'they who have used the office of a deacon well' [KJV], 'deacons with a good record of service' [REB], 'if deacons served well' [LSA], 'men who give outstanding diaconal service' [ECC]. This verb means to give assistance by performing certain duties, which may often be of a humble or menial nature [LN].

c. pres. mid. indic. of περιποιέομαι (LN **57.61**) (BAGD 2. p. 650): 'to acquire' [LN, Lns, NTC, WBC; HCSB], 'to achieve' [LN], 'to gain' [AB, ECC; GW, NET, NIV, NRSV], 'to win' [**LN**; TEV], 'to obtain' [Herm; NASB], 'to secure' [BNTC], 'to purchase' [KJV], 'to make' [NCV], 'to be rewarded' [NLT], 'to earn' [CEV], 'to be entitled to' [REB], not explicit [LSA]. This verb means to acquire possession of something and implies that it takes effort to do so [LN]. The present tense indicates that this is an ongoing process [Lns, WBC].

d. βαθμός (LN **87.3**) (BAGD p. 130): 'standing' [BAGD, **LN**], 'rank' [BAGD, LN], 'status' [LN]. The clause βαθμὸν ἑαυτοῖς καλὸν περιποι-οῦνται 'acquire a good standing for themselves' [WBC; HCSB] is also translated 'gain a good standing for themselves' [NET, NRSV], 'win for themselves a good standing' [TEV], 'secure a good standing for themselves' [BNTC], 'obtain for themselves a high standing' [NASB], 'are acquiring for themselves excellent standing' [Lns], 'will acquire for themselves a noble standing' [NTC], 'gain an excellent standing' [NIV], 'gain a fine standing for themselves' [ECC], 'purchase to themselves a good degree' [KJV], 'will earn a good reputation' [CEV], 'will gain an excellent reputation' [GW], 'will be rewarded with respect from others' [NLT], 'are making an honorable place for themselves' [NCV], 'have thereby gained a good position for themselves' [AB], 'obtain for themselves a good position' [Herm], 'are entitled to high standing' [REB], 'people will respect them' [LSA]. This noun denotes a standing in society in regard to one's rank or status [LN].

QUESTION—What relationship is indicated by the conjunction γάρ 'because'?

1. This indicates the reason why deacons should serve well by meeting the requirements listed in 3:8–12 [Alf, BNTC, Herm, ICC, Lns, My, NIBC, NICNT, NIGTC, NTC, TC, TG, TH, WBC]. This verse serves as an incentive for living up to those requirements by pointing out the two resulting rewards [Lns, WBC]. Although the conjunction indicates the grounds for listing the requirements, it also serves as an incentive for faithfully fulfilling them [NTC].

2. This indicates the grounds for setting forth the requirements for deacons in 3:8–12 [LSA, NTC]. This shows how Paul knows that deacons must fulfill all of the requirements he listed, and the conjunction means 'I know this is true, for…' [NTC].

QUESTION—Who are the 'ones' who serve well?

1. They are the deacons mentioned in 3:8–12 [Alf, BKC, BNTC, ECC, Herm, ICC, LSA, NIBC, NIGTC, NTC, NTL, TC, TH, WBC; CEV]. There is nothing in 3:12 itself that directly relates to this verse, so this verse is related to the whole paragraph of 3:8–12 [WBC]. This concerns the male deacons [BNTC]. Or, this includes the women discussed in 3:11 [ECC, NICNT, NTC, WBC].

2. They are all who have been mentioned in this chapter: the overseers, the men deacons, and the women deacons [Lns]. The verb διακονήσαντες 'having served' is not a technical term relating to 'serving as deacons' but is a general term of any type of service and here it pertains to all who serve in their various offices [Lns].

QUESTION—What is the significance of the verb tenses in the statement 'the ones having served (aorist tense) well are acquiring (present continuative) a good standing'?

The deacons should have the qualities listed in 3:8–12 upon entering their office, and these qualities must be maintained as they serve and acquire a good reputation within the community [WBC]. The aorist tense 'having served' considers the deacons' service as a whole [ECC]. The aorist 'having served' does not mean that they are no longer in office. Those who have served are still in office and so they still 'are acquiring' (present tense) a good standing [Lns].

QUESTION—What is meant by acquiring a good βαθμός 'standing' for themselves?

The word βαθμός 'standing' literally means a step [Alf, BNTC, ICC, LSA, NIBC, NIGTC, NTC, TC, TH, WBC, WP], or a base or foundation [BNTC, LSA], or threshold [NIGTC]. The word 'step' is used figuratively for either an advancement of grade or rank [BAGD, ICC, NIGTC, WBC]. In this context it could refer to the attainment of a good standing or reputation or to an advancement from the office of deacon to the office of overseer [LSA, WBC]. It can mean a promotion to a higher rank, or influence and esteem within the church, or a standing before God [TH].

1. This means they will acquire a good standing in the estimation of others [BKC, BNTC, Herm, ICC, LSA, My, NCBC, NIBC, NICNT, NTC, NTL, TC, TG, TH, TNTC, WBC]. People will respect such a deacon [LSA, TC], and have a greater trust in him [TC]. This does not refer to advancement in rank since it says that a deacon will acquire a *good* standing, not a *better* standing [ICC, WBC].

1.1 This refers to gaining a good standing in the esteem of the congregation [BKC, BNTC, My, NIBC, NICNT, NTC, TC, TG, TH, TNTC]. The congregation will think highly of them because they have served in a worthy manner [NTC]. Their fellow Christians are the ones who will understand and appreciate their humble service even though such service is unattractive according to worldly standards [BKC].

1.2 This refers to gaining a good standing in the esteem of the whole community [NCBC, WBC]. Their good service will cause their office as deacon to be influential and respected in the community [WBC].

1.3 This refers to gaining a good standing in the esteem of both the community and God [ICC, NTL, TNTC].

2. This means they will acquire a good spiritual standing in God's estimation [Alf, NIGTC]. Both βαθμόν 'standing' and παρρησίαν 'confidence' are modified by the final phrase 'in faith in Christ Jesus' so that the encouragement for faithful service is their *progress* in their standing (βαθμόν) and confidence or boldness in reference to the sphere of their faith in Christ, in which they already stand [NIGTC]. This refers to their standing on the Day of Judgment when they have finished the course [Alf].

3. This means they will acquire the good position of being deacons [ECC, Lns]. In 3:1 it says that the office of overseer is καλοῦ ἔργου 'a good work', and here acquiring βαθμὸν καλὸν 'a good standing' means that the ones who meet the requirements and serve well acquire a good position [ECC]. This is not a comparison between a prior standing and a standing which they will attain later on, rather it is the excellent standing in their office that they acquire by serving excellently in that office [Lns].

4. This means that they will acquire a higher position in the church, a 'step' up in regard to promotion [ECC, EGT; REB]. Those who serve καλῶς 'well, good' will be appreciated by the believers who will then promote those deacons to the καλοῦ 'good' work (3:1) of an overseer [ECC].

and much confidence[a] in faith[b] that (is) in Christ Jesus.

LEXICON—a. παρρησία (LN 25.158) (BAGD 3.b. p. 630): 'confidence, joyousness' [BAGD], 'boldness, courage' [BAGD, LN]. The phrase καὶ πολλὴν παρρησίαν 'and much confidence' [AB] is also translated 'and great confidence' [WBC; NASB], 'and great assurance' [NIV], 'and will have confidence' [NTC; GW], 'and will have increased confidence' [NLT], 'as well as great assurance' [BNTC], 'and great boldness' [HCSB, KJV, NET, NRSV], 'a great boldness' [Lns], 'and they will be very bold' [NCV], 'and are able to speak boldly' [TEV], 'and a right to speak out' [ECC], 'and they will be able to speak very boldly' [LSA], 'and will be highly respected' [CEV], 'and the right to be heard' [REB], 'and real cheerfulness' [Herm]. This noun denotes the state of being bold and confident [LN]. It means courage, confidence, boldness, or fearlessness especially before people of high rank, and in relation to God this can refer to the joy or confidence that is either the result or the accompaniment of faith [BAGD].

b. πίστις (LN 31.85) (BAGD 2.b.β. p. 663): 'faith, trust' [BAGD, LN]. The phrase ἐν πίστει τῇ ἐν Χριστῷ 'Ιησοῦ 'in faith that is in Christ Jesus' [AB; HCSB, KJV, NASB, NET, NRSV] is also translated 'in faith, which is in Christ Jesus' [WBC], 'in faith in Christ Jesus' [Lns], 'in their faith in

Christ Jesus' [BNTC; NCV, NIV, NLT], 'as a result of their faith in
Christ Jesus' [GW], '(be respected) for their faith in Christ Jesus' [CEV],
'(speak out) for the faith that is theirs in Christ Jesus' [ECC], 'in the faith
which centers in Christ Jesus' [NTC], '(speak boldly) about their faith in
Christ Jesus' [TEV], '(speak very boldly) about what they believe
concerning Christ Jesus' [LSA], '(be heard) on matters of the Christian
faith' [REB]. This noun denotes the presence of complete trust and
reliance [LN]. This refers to the state of having faith in Christ [BAGD].
See this word at 1:2, 4, 5, 14, 19; 4:12; 6:11.

QUESTION—What is meant by acquiring much confidence ἐν πίστει τῇ ἐν
Χριστῷ Ἰησοῦ 'in faith that is in Christ Jesus'?

1. They will have confidence and boldness in speaking to people [ECC,
   NCBC, NTC, NTL, TC, TG, TH, WBC].
   1.1 'Faith' is the act of believing in Christ Jesus [ECC, TC, TH, WBC; GW,
       NCV, NIV, NLT, TEV]. They will have confidence to speak out boldly
       to people because of their personal faith in Christ Jesus [ECC, NIGTC,
       TC, WBC]. They will speak confidently and frankly about the faith that
       is theirs to both believers and unbelievers, and this confidence is based
       on their faith in Christ [ECC]. The will acquire boldness to speak about
       their faith and commitment to Christ Jesus [TH]. As a deacon serves
       well, his personal faith in Christ is strengthened and as a result the
       proclamation of his faith becomes bolder [WBC]. Their progress and
       confidence is experienced in the sphere or framework of trust in Christ
       [NIGTC, TC].
   1.2 'Faith' is the content of 'the faith', the facts about Jesus Christ [LSA,
       NTC, NTL; NET]. This is the faith that is centered in Christ Jesus, and
       knowing that they have done their best as deacons, they will confidently
       speak freely and gladly about Christ [NTC]. They will speak boldly
       about what they believe concerning Christ [LSA]. 'Faith' refers to *what*
       Christians believe, so this concerns the deacons' boldness to act on the
       truth they believe in [NET]. In this setting, 'faith' refers to what people
       believe, and the words 'in Christ Jesus' may be a formula used
       adjectivally so that this means 'confidence in regard to the Christian
       faith' [NTL].
2. They will have an increasing boldness before people as they proclaim the
   gospel and they also will have an increasing confidence in drawing close
   to God, an assurance motivated by their faith in Christ [BNTC].
3. They will have confidence and assurance about their own personal faith in
   Christ [Alf, BKC, ICC, NICNT]. They will develop confidence in the
   sincerity of their own faith in Christ after their true motives for service
   have been tested by their humble service [BKC]. The deacons will have a
   greater sense of confidence in God and in their assurance of salvation
   [ICC]. This is the confidence they have towards God upon making an
   advance in their faith in Christ [Alf]. Their faithful service as deacons will

deepen their faith and further strengthen their relationship with God and Christ [NICNT].

4. They will have confidence and boldness in carrying out their duties as deacons [Lns, My]. After serving excellently for some time, a person will be able, to carry out his office with the boldness and assurance that comes from his faith in Christ Jesus [Lns].

5. Deacons will be highly respected by others for their faith in Christ Jesus [CEV].

DISCOURSE UNIT: 3:14–16 [Herm, ICC, NAC, NCBC, NIBC, NICNT, NTL, TNTC, WBC; CEV, HCSB, NCV, NET, NLT, NRSV, TEV]. The topic is the purpose of the letter [NIBC], the heart of the corpus [WBC], a word concerning the church [Herm], the truths of our faith [NLT], the mystery of our religion [CEV, NRSV], the mystery of godliness [HCSB], the great secret [TEV], the secret of our life [NCV], the church and the faith [NICNT], the church and the mystery of the faith [ICC], the character of the church [TNTC], conduct in God's church [NET], the church's great confession [NTL], the correct application of Christian truth [NAC], a *midrash* and a hymn [NCBC].

DISCOURSE UNIT: 3:14–15 [ECC, TH]. The topic is the Pauline introduction [ECC], a summary statement of purpose [TH].

3:14 I-write these (things) to-you hoping[a] to-come[b] to you soon;[c] **3:15** but if I-delay,[d] so-that you-may know

LEXICON—a. pres. act. participle of ἐλπίζω (LN 30.45) (BAGD 2. p. 252): 'to hope' [AB, ECC, LN, Lns, LSA, NTC, WBC; all versions], 'to expect' [LN]. This verb is also translated as a noun: '(writing) in the hope of' [BNTC, Herm]. This verb means to expect to do something, and it usually implies that there is some benefit involved [LN].

b. aorist act. infin. of ἔρχομαι (LN 5.7): 'to come' [AB, BNTC, ECC, Herm, LN, Lns, LSA, NTC, WBC; HCSB, KJV, NASB, NCV, NET, NIV, NRSV, REB], 'to go' [LN], 'to visit' [CEV, GW], 'to be with you' [NLT], 'to come and see you' [TEV]. This verb means to move from one place to another, and it can be viewed either as a coming or a going [LN].

c. The phrase ἐν τάχει 'in haste' is translated 'soon' [Herm, LN (67.56), LSA; all versions except KJV, NASB], 'very soon' [LN (67.56)], 'quickly' [WBC], 'shortly' [AB, BNTC, Lns, NTC; KJV], 'before long' [ECC; NASB]. The phrase ἐν τάχει pertains to a point of time subsequent to another point of time with emphasis upon the brief interval between the two points of time [LN]. 'Soon' usually indicates a short period of time, maybe just a matter of weeks [TG].

d. pres. act. subj. of βραδύνω (LN **67.124**) (BAGD p. 147): 'to delay' [BAGD, LN]; The phrase ἐὰν δὲ βραδύνω 'but if I delay' [**LN**; TEV] is also translated 'but if I wait' [WBC], 'but if I tarry long' [KJV], 'yet in case I am slow' [Lns], 'still, if I do delay' [ECC]. This active voice is also translated passively: 'but if I am delayed' [AB], 'if I am delayed' [CEV], 'but if I should be delayed' [NTC; HCSB], 'but in case I am delayed' [Herm; NASB], 'but in case I should be held up' [BNTC], 'in case I am delayed' [GW, NET, REB], '(so that,) if I am delayed' [NIV, NLT, NRSV], '(so that,) even if I am delayed' [LSA], '(then) even if I am delayed' [NCV]. This verb means to extend a period of time because of delay or slowness [LN]. The verb βραδύνω is active intransitive 'I wait' or 'I delay', and not the passive 'I am delayed' as in most translations. So Paul was thinking of the possibility that something would come up, such as the need for his ministry elsewhere, that would cause him to make a decision to put off his coming to Ephesus for a while [WBC]. He would be delayed if he was not able to go when he planned [TG].

QUESTION—What is meant by ταῦτά 'these' that he writing?

Paul is writing these things [AB, Lns, LSA, NIGTC, NTIC, WBC; HCSB, KJV, NASB, NCV, NLT], these instructions [BKC, BNTC, My, NICNT, TC; CEV, NET, NIV, NRSV], these matters [ECC], this [GW, REB], all this [Herm], or this letter [TEV]. This refers to the specific instructions on appropriate conduct in church [WBC]. It refers to the contents of chapters 1–3 [NIBC, WBC], or chapters 2–3 [EGT, ICC, Lns, LSA, My, NAC, NICNT, NIGTC, NTC, TC; NET]. However, if referring to chapters 2 and 3 at this point in the letter, any additional teaching later in the letter would share the same purpose [EGT, ICC, NAC, NICNT]. This refers to the entire letter [BNTC, TH; TEV].

QUESTION—Who is the referent of σοί 'you'?

This returns to the direct address to Timothy that was last used at 1:18 [ICC]. This letter would confirm the advice Paul already had given Timothy when they were together in Ephesus, and it would strengthen Timothy's authority before the congregation, which contained false teachers who oppose him [NAC, TNTC].

QUESTION—What relationship is indicated by the use of the participle ἐλπίζων 'hoping'?

It indicates a concession [AB, Alf, ECC, ICC, Lns, LSA, NIBC, NIGTC, NTC, NTIC, WBC; NCV, NET, NIV, NLT]: I write these things to you, *although I hope to come to you soon.* The word ἐάν 'if' at the beginning of 3:15 seems to indicate that Paul rather expected to be delayed [Lns, NIBC, NIGTC]. Also the conjunction δέ 'but' (3:15) indicates a contrast between the two verses and indicates that the 'if' clause is more likely to happen than the concession clause in 3:14 [NIGTC]. Or, the Greek seems to suggest that that it is not likely that there will be a delay [TH]. Paul did not know it, but his hope was not to be realized [WP].

QUESTION—What relationship is indicated by ἵνα 'so that'?

This indicates the *purpose* for writing these things [BKC, BNTC, ICC, LSA, NAC, NICNT, NTC, NTL, WBC; CEV, HCSB, NASB, NIV, NLT, NRSV], or the *reason* for writing them [NIGTC]. This purpose is valid whether or not Paul is delayed, although when he does arrive there will presumably be more to be said [ICC].

QUESTION—How are these clauses connected?

The syntax of 3:14–15 is awkward [WBC], clumsy [BNTC, ICC], rough [ICC, NIBC], and unusual [ECC]. Yet the meaning is clear [NIBC]. Verse 15 is an incomplete sentence in Greek, and implies a main clause, 'I am writing to you these things' [NAC, TH]. Translations adjust the syntax in various ways, such as repeating the verb 'I write', moving the conjunction 'so that', or moving the clause with 'I hope' to the beginning: I write these things to you, although I hope to come to you soon; but if I am delayed, *I write* so that you may know [AB, ECC, NTC; HCSB, NASB], I write these things to you, although I hope to come to you soon, *so that* if I am delayed, you may know [LSA; NLT], I hope to come to you soon, but I write these things to you *so that*, if I am delayed, you may know [CEV, NRSV], I hope to come to you soon, but I write these things to you in case I am delayed so that you may know [GW, NET, REB], Although I hope to come to you soon, I write these things to you now *so that* if I am delayed, you may know [NIV], Although I hope to come to you soon, I write these things to you now. Then, even if I am delayed, you may know [NCV], I write these things to you in the hope of coming to you soon, but in case I am delayed you should at least know [Herm].

how it is necessary to-conduct-oneself/yourself[a] in (the) household/house[b] of-God, which is (the) church[c] of-a-living[d] God

LEXICON—a. pres. pass. infin. of ἀναστρέφομαι, ἀναστρέφω (LN 41.3) (BAGD 1.b.β. p. 61): 'to conduct oneself' [BAGD, LN, LSA, NTC, WBC; NASB, NET, NIV, NLT, TEV], 'to conduct one's life' [Herm], 'to behave oneself' [Lns], 'to behave' [AB, BAGD, ECC, LN; CEV, GW, KJV, NRSV], 'to act' [HCSB], 'to live' [LN; NCV]. The phrase 'how it is necessary to conduct oneself' is translated 'what is proper conduct' [REB], 'the behavior suitable (in God's household)' [BNTC]. This verb means to conduct oneself, usually focusing upon one's overt daily behavior [LN]. This passive verb has a reflexive sense, 'to conduct *oneself*' [TH, WBC].

b. οἶκος (LN 7.2, 10.8) (BAGD 1.b.α. or 2. p. 560): 'household' [AB, BNTC, Herm, LN (10.8); HCSB, NASB, NET, NIV, NLT, NRSV, REB, TEV], 'family' [LN (10.8); CEV, GW, NCV], 'members of God's family' [LSA; GW], 'everyone who belongs to God's family' [CEV], 'house' [BAGD, ECC, LN (7.2), Lns, NTC, WBC; KJV], 'temple, sanctuary' [LN (7.2)]. This noun denotes a building normally serving as a dwelling place, although it can also refer to certain public buildings such as a temple [LN (7.2)], or it denotes a family living in the same house [LN (10.8)]. This is a figurative use of 'house' to refer to Christendom as God's spiritual temple (1.b.α), or it refers to Christians as God's family (2.) [BAGD]. See this word at 3:4, 12; 5:4.

c. ἐκκλησία (LN 11.33) (BAGD 4.e.α. p. 241): 'church' [AB, BAGD, BNTC, ECC, Herm, LN, Lns, LSA, NTC, WBC; all versions]. This noun denotes the totality of Christian congregations [LN]. The local congregation as well as the universal church is called the church of God [BAGD]. Church is used here in a universal sense, although in 3:5 and 5:16, the household refers to a local manifestation of the church [ICC].

d. pres. act. participle of ζάω (LN 23.88) (BAGD 1.a.ε. p. 336): 'to live' [AB, BAGD, BNTC, ECC, Herm, LN, Lns, LSA, NTC, WBC; all versions], 'to be alive' [LN]. This verb means to live and is used to refer to God as a being who is not subject to death [BAGD].

QUESTION—Whose conduct is referred to?

1. It refers to the conduct of those who are in the household of God [Alf, BKC, BNTC, ECC, Herm, My, NAC, NIBC, NICNT, NIGTC, NTIC, TG, TH, WBC; all versions except KJV]: *how it is necessary to conduct oneself.* The Greek should be translated 'how it is necessary to behave' [NTIC, WBC; NET]. It is assumed that the text means 'how *one* ought to behave', not 'how *you* ought to behave', and this agrees better with the semi-public character of this letter and also with the idea of the church being God's household [BNTC]. Since Timothy's opponents are the ones causing trouble, they are the subject of this verb, not Timothy, although of course this includes Timothy who is to be an example to the church [WBC]. No definite subject should be supplied since 'these things' that he was writing are not about what Timothy should do but what was to prevail in the church [My]. Instead of '*how* one ought to behave', it is better expressed 'what kind of conduct befits a member of God's household' [NIBC].

2. It refers to the conduct of Timothy who is addressed as 'you' in 3:14 [ICC, Lns, NTC, NTL, TNTC, WP; KJV]: *how it is necessary to conduct yourself.* It is more natural to supply 'you' than 'any one' here [WP]. These instructions are directed to Timothy to make sure that suitable appointments are made [TNTC]. This instructs Timothy how to conduct himself as Paul's representative when he arranges the worship and the offices in God's house [Lns, NTC]. The instructions in the preceding chapters informed Timothy about the fitting behavior expected in God's church [ICC]. It is not so much Timothy's personal behavior that is in view, but it is his role as a leader who exhorts the congregation about how they should act as members of God's household [NTC].

QUESTION—What is meant by the οἴκῳ θεοῦ 'household/house of God'?

1. It means the household or family of God [AB, BNTC, ECC, EGT, Herm, ICC, NIBC, NICNT, NIGTC, NTIC, NTL, TG, TH, TNTC, WP; all versions except KJV]. This picks up the thought of 3:4, 5, and 12 where 'household' is in focus [BNTC]. The church is compared to a human family with its close relationships between its members, and here they are members of God's family [TH]. God is the father, and the believers are brothers and sisters in his family [NAC, NIBC]. Although the terminology of calling the household a house is developed in the next clause, the conduct being discussed concerns the interaction of the members of God's

family [NIGTC]. The noun refers to the Christian community as it is gathered together, and there is no development of this figure in the following clause which talks about a pillar and foundation [Herm]. The metaphor will shift from a household to a building [NIBC, WP].

2. It means the house of God [Alf, Lns, My, NTC, WBC; KJV]. The following references to a house's pillar and foundation suggest that here οἴκῳ should also refer to a house and give a picture of God's temple, which of course would house God's family. Since there is no definite article, this is picturing each local congregation in a general truth that applies to all churches [WBC]. Believers are God's house, or temple (1 Cor. 3:16; 6:19; 2 Cor. 6:16) [NTC], because God dwells in them [Alf, Lns, My, NTC]. The church is God's house where he dwells and where everything must be as God wants since it belongs to him [Lns].

QUESTION—What is the function of the relative clause ἥτις ἐστὶν ἐκκλησία θεοῦ ζῶντος 'which is the church of a living God', and what is implied by describing God as 'living'?

The feminine gender pronoun ἥτις 'which' modifies the masculine noun οἴκῳ 'house', but it has been attracted to the feminine gender of ἐκκλησία 'church' [EGT, ICC, Lns, NICNT, NIGTC, NTC, WBC, WP]. It indicates the reason for being concerned about one's conduct in the household of God [Lns, NTC; CEV, NET]: how one ought to conduct oneself in the household of God, *because it is the church of a living God.* This moves out of the metaphorical use of 'household' to the designation the 'assembly of God's people', probably referring to the church in universal terms [NICNT]. This clause highlights the awesome responsibility one has in following such conduct [NIGTC]. The adjective 'living' brings out a contrast with dead idols [BNTC, NAC, NIGTC, TG, TH], but also describes God as one who is actively working in the world among people [TH]. Or, the context does not focus on a contrast with idols, so 'the living God' emphasizes God's presence with his people [ICC, NICNT]. It brings out God's personal presence among them [Alf], or his continual providence in guiding his church [TC]. As a *living* God, he gives life and salvation to those who believe in him, and he gives them the vitality to serve and obey him [NIGTC]. The living God is not merely the God of Israel's past history, but the God who has chosen the people among whom he now dwells [NTL]. God is described as living forever [TG]. The emphasis of this clause is that the church belongs to a living God, not a dead deity who can do nothing, and since he is living he will discipline those who damage his house [WBC].

a-pillar[a] and a-foundation/bulwark[b] of-the truth.[c]

LEXICON—a. στῦλος (LN 7.45) (BAGD p. 772): 'pillar' [AB, BAGD, BNTC, ECC, LN, Lns, NTC, WBC; all versions except CEV, NCV, NET], 'column' [BAGD, LN], 'support' [Herm; NCV, NET]. The phrase στῦλος καὶ ἑδραίωμα τῆς ἀληθείας 'a pillar and foundation of the truth' is translated 'the strong foundation of truth' [CEV], 'which upholds the true doctrine' [LSA]. This noun denotes an upright shaft that is used as a building support [LN].

b. ἑδραίωμα (LN **31.93**) (BAGD p. 218): 'foundation' [BAGD, LN, Lns, NTC; CEV, GW, HCSB, NCV, NIV, NLT], 'support' [AB, **LN**; NASB, TEV], 'mainstay' [BAGD], 'ground' [KJV], 'pedestal' [ECC], 'buttress' [BNTC], 'bulwark' [NET, NRSV, REB], 'protector' [WBC], 'fortress' [Herm], 'basis' [LN]. This noun denotes that which provides the basis or foundation for belief or practice [LN].

c. ἀλήθεια (LN 72.2): 'truth' [AB, BNTC, ECC, Herm, LN, Lns, NTC, WBC; all versions], 'the true doctrine' [LSA]. This noun denotes the content of that which is true and thus in accordance with what actually happened [LN]. See this word at 2:4; 4:3.

QUESTION—What is the function of this added description?

1. It is an added description of the household of God [all commentaries except ECC; all versions]. It is in apposition to ἐκκλησία 'church' and describes the church's responsibility and function [ICC, NICNT]. It emphasizes the importance of being the church of the living God [ECC].

2. It is a description of Timothy [ECC]: 'There you, Timothy, are a pillar and pedestal for the truth'. In Rev. 3:12 this figure is used of individuals when it says 'The one who overcomes I will make a pillar in the temple of my God' [ECC].

QUESTION—What is meant by τῆς ἀληθείας 'the truth'?

'The truth' is a synonym of 'the gospel', which is referred to in 2:4 where it says that God wants all people to come to knowledge of the truth [LSA, WBC]. The truth is the gospel [Lns, NICNT], the true gospel [ICC], the truth of the gospel [NIBC], the orthodox faith [BNTC]. It means the true teaching, the accepted Christian doctrine [NAC, NIGTC, TG, TH]. The 'truth' is further described in the following verse as the mystery of godliness [LSA].

QUESTION—What is meant by the church being a στῦλος 'pillar' of the truth?

A pillar supports the roof structure [Lns]. A common metaphor is used here to mean 'a support' [BNTC, Herm, My, NAC, NTIC, WP; NASB, NLT, TEV]. 'Pillar' is used in a figurative sense to picture one of the functions of the church as being to *support* the proclamation of the true gospel [LN, TG, TH, WBC]. The church supports the truth of the gospel [NTC]. Since the function of the pillar is to 'support' or 'uphold' the truth, it could be stated that the church 'causes people to know the true doctrine' [LSA].

QUESTION—What is meant by the church being a ἑδραίωμα 'foundation' of the truth?

1. This metaphor has the much the same meaning as the preceding metaphor of the pillar and both refer to being *supports* of the truth [AB, ICC, Lns, LSA, My, NAC, NCBC, NICNT, NIGTC, NTCNTIC, NTL, TH, WP; CEV, NASB, NLT, TEV]. The foundation metaphor intensifies the metaphor of the pillar [Lns]. Together they are used to refer to a firm foundation [NICNT, NTL]. Like a pillar *supports* the roof and as the foundation *supports* the entire superstructure, so the church *supports* the

truth of the gospel [Lns, NTC]. In the midst of false teachings, the church supports the truth like the foundation and pillar of a house support and stabilize a house [TH]. The church exists to provide a powerful and steadfast support for the truth [NICNT]. The picture is of a building having many pillars that support the roof, with the pillars themselves resting on the foundation, so that the church is the foundation that supports the truth of the Christian faith by the commitment of its members to present the gospel to the world [NAC]. By their actions and words they are to uphold the truth of Christianity [NIGTC]. The truth is supported and borne by the church as it preserves the truth [My].

2. This metaphor has the meaning of bulwark, the strong wall-like structure that is raised for defense, and as the pillars *support* the gospel, the bulwarks surround the gospel to *protect* it [BKC, BNTC, NIBC, TC, TG, WBC]. Those who use the metaphor of a 'foundation' are not clear as to whether they are thinking of the function of support or protection, but it should not be taken to mean that that the gospel is subordinate to the church and nowhere in Scripture is there a suggestion that the church is the foundation of the gospel since 1 Cor. 3:10–11 says that no other foundation can anyone lay that that which is laid, which is Christ [WBC]. The church will both support the truth and be a bulwark against the assaults of the false teachers as it safeguards the true teaching by its continual witness [BNTC]. They are to keep the truth safe [TG]. The church has been entrusted to uphold the truth of the gospel and proclaim it [NIBC]. Without the church's permanent witness the truth might be endangered [TC].

QUESTION—Is there a significance in the lack of the article 'the' with the nouns στῦλος καὶ ἑδραίωμα 'a pillar and a foundation'?

1. Some use the indefinite article '*a* pillar and support' [AB, BNTC, ECC, NTIC, TC, WBC]. The church is not *the* pillar and *the* foundation because the church is only a part of God's defense of the truth, and God is not dependent on the church in Ephesus or anywhere else to protect the proclamation of Christ. Besides the church, one could add the Scriptures as having this function [WBC].

2. Many supply the article so as to read '*the* pillar and foundation' [Herm, ICC, Lns, NAC, NICNT, NIGTC, NTL, TC, WP; all versions]. It should not read 'a pillar' and 'a foundation' as though there were other supports of the truth, since the absence of the articles stresses the qualitative force of the two nouns [Lns, NTC].

DISCOURSE UNIT: 3:16 [ECC, TH]. The topic is a hymn [ECC], a hymn to Christ [TH].

3:16 And admittedly[a] great[b] is the mystery[c] of religion:[d]
LEXICON—a. ὁμολογουμένως (LN **33.276**) (BAGD p. 569): 'admittedly' [LN], 'confessedly' [BAGD, Lns, NTC], 'by common confession' [NASB], 'undeniably' [BAGD, WBC], 'most certainly' [BAGD, Herm;

HCSB], 'without doubt' [NCV], 'without any doubt' [NRSV], 'without controversy' [KJV], 'without question' [NLT], 'beyond all question' [BNTC; NIV, REB], 'there is no denying it' [ECC], not explicit [CEV]. This adverb is also translated as a verb phrase: 'one must admit' [**LN**], 'we all agree' [NET], 'we confess' [AB], 'no one can deny' [TEV], 'is acknowledged to be (great)' [GW]. This adverb is derived from the verb ὁμολογέω 'to admit' and it pertains to what should be admitted or acknowledged publicly [LN]. The word means 'by common consent', referring to the unanimous belief of Christians [BNTC, NAC]. All must confess the undeniable fact that the gospel is great [WBC]. Only the church will admit this because only the church knows the mystery [Lns].

b. μέγας (LN 87.22) (BAGD 2.b.β. p. 498): 'great' [AB, BAGD, BNTC, ECC, LN, Lns, NTC, WBC; all versions except NET], 'amazing' [NET], 'important' [BAGD, LN], 'sublime' [BAGD]. This adjective pertains to being great in terms of status [LN], in terms of rank and dignity [BAGD]. This word means extraordinary or astounding [TG], or important [BKC].

c. μυστήριον (LN 28.77) (BAGD 2. p. 530): 'mystery, secret' [BAGD, LN]. The phrase τῆς εὐσεβείας μυστήριον 'the mystery of religion' is translated 'the mystery of our religion' [BNTC, Herm; CEV, NRSV, REB], 'the secret of our religion' [TEV], 'the mystery of our faith' [NLT], 'the mystery of godliness' [AB, ECC, WBC; HCSB, KJV, NASB, NIV], 'the mystery of the godliness' [Lns], 'the mystery that gives us our reverence for God' [GW], 'the mystery of our devotion' [NTC], 'the secret of our life of worship' [NCV]. This noun phrase is also translated as a verb phrase: 'our religion contains amazing revelation' [NET]. This mystery has been kept secret in the past ages but now it has been revealed [BNTC]. The mystery is about our faith (3:9) and devotion [NTC]. The mystery is explained in the rest of the verse, so a translation might say 'the revealed truth of our religion' [TG]. See this word at 3:9.

d. εὐσέβεια (LN 53.1) (BAGD p. 326): 'religion' [BAGD, BNTC, Herm, LN; CEV, NET, NRSV, REB, TEV], 'our faith' [NLT], 'reverence for God' [GW], 'piety' [LN], 'godliness' [AB, ECC, Lns, WBC; HCSB, KJV, NASB, NIV], 'devotion' [NTC]. This noun denotes the appropriate beliefs about supernatural persons and the obligations that relate to them [LN]. This refers to the duty a person owes to God in terms of piety, godliness, and religion [BAGD]. The word εὐσέβεια has a range of meanings and here it refers to the whole system of belief and approach to God in religion, and as such it is the basis for our devotion and reverence toward God and our conduct in living in godliness and piety [NET]. It refers to the teachings of God [TH]. 'Godliness' describes the whole Christian life into which one puts his faith into practice [ECC].

QUESTION—What is the function of this statement?

Paul now develops the thought of τῆς ἀληθείας 'the truth' in 3:15 [EGT, ICC]. The mention of 'the truth' in 3:15 has brought about this almost ecstatic outburst about the Christian religion [BNTC, NIBC]. To justify his use of 'great', Paul describes the essence of the Christian religion [BNTC] by quoting an excerpt from a hymn about Christ [BNTC, ICC, NAC, NCBC, NIBC, NICNT, NTIC, NTL, TG, TH, WP]. It is a liturgical statement of the apostolic church, perhaps a creed or a hymn [ECC, NIGTC]. It is evident that the following is an excerpt since it lacks any principal clause and simply begins with the pronoun ὅς 'who' [Alf, BNTC, ECC, NAC, NIGTC]. The pronoun's antecedent is in a section of the liturgical text that is not included here and it evidently refers to Christ [NIGTC]. This introduces a summary of the Christian confession [AB]. The content of the mystery is set forth in the following citation [NIBC, NIGTC, NTL], although it is only a part of it [NIBC]. A colon is used to signify that this statement refers to the following clauses [AB, Herm, Lns; all versions].

who was-manifested[a] in flesh,[b]

TEXT—Instead of ὅς 'who', some manuscripts read ὅ '(that) which' and some manuscripts read θεός 'God'. GNT reads ὅς 'who' with an A decision, indicating that the text is certain. 'God' is read by KJV.

LEXICON—a. aorist pass. indic. of φανερόω (LN 24.19) (BAGD 2.b.β. p. 853): 'to be manifested' [AB, BNTC, Lns, NTC; HCSB, KJV, REB], 'to be shown' [NCV], 'to be revealed' [BAGD, ECC, Herm, WBC; NASB, NET, NLT, NRSV], 'to be made to appear, to be made visible, to be caused to be seen' [LN], 'to appear' [BAGD, LN; GW, NIV, TEV], 'to come' [CEV]. This verb means to become visible [LN]. It speaks of Christ's appearance into the world [BAGD].

b. σάρξ (LN **8.4**) (BAGD 2. p. 743): 'body' [BAGD, LN], 'physical body' [LN]. The clause ὃ ἐφανερώθη ἐν σαρκί 'who/he was manifested in flesh' [AB, BNTC, Lns; REB] is also translated 'who/he was manifested in the flesh' [NTC; HCSB], '(God) was manifest in the flesh' [KJV], 'who/he was revealed in flesh' [WBC; NRSV], 'who/he was revealed in the flesh' [Herm; NASB, NET], 'he who was revealed in human flesh' [ECC], 'who was revealed in a human body' [NLT], 'he appeared in a body' [NIV], 'who appeared in a physical body' [**LN**], 'he appeared in human form' [TEV], 'Christ came as a human' [CEV], 'Christ appeared as a human being', or 'Christ became a person' [**LN**], 'he appeared in his human nature' [GW], 'he was shown to us in a human body' [NCV]. This noun denotes a living body, but in order to avoid a mistaken interpretation that Christ took on the body of someone else or merely indwelt some miraculous human form rather than he actually become a human being, it may be necessary in some instances to translate this as 'a human being' or 'a person' [LN].

QUESTION—What is meant by the clause ὃ ἐφανερώθη ἐν σαρκί 'who was manifested in flesh'?

This quote refers to the incarnation [BKC, BNTC, EGT, ICC, My, NAC, NCBC, NIBC, NICNT, NIGTC, TC, TG, TNTC, WP]. The verb φανερόω 'to manifest' is a common term in the NT, and it is sometimes used of the coming of Christ into the world [WBC]. This states that Christ appeared on earth as a real man [BNTC]. The focus is not on his birth, but on the fact of his humanity, the state in which he did his work [NICNT]. This passive verb implies that God the Father made Christ known [ICC, NICNT, NIGTC]. Or, an actor is not implied, and it simply means that Jesus 'appeared' or 'became visible' in the world as a human being [TG, TH; CEV, GW, NIV, TEV]. If the definite article had accompanied the word 'flesh', the phrase ἐν τῇ σαρκί 'in *the* flesh' would undoubtedly refer to Christ's earthy nature, but the absence of the article is not significant since definite articles are often omitted from prepositional phrases like this [WBC]. 'Flesh' refers to ordinary human existence [AB], the God-man's humanity [BNTC, WBC]. 'Flesh' is not only the physical body, but it is all that belongs to a human body and nature in regard to body, soul, and spirit [Lns, NAC], of course with the exception of sin [NAC]. Christ was manifested in the flesh during his entire earthly life [Lns], from the time of his birth until his burial [NTC]. Christ's pre-existence is probably implied [BNTC, My, NCBC, NIBC, NIGTC, TC, TNTC], or it is at least compatible with the use of this passive form [WBC]. In Christ, God has appeared in a human body [NAC]. Or, another interpretation refers this manifestation to Christ's appearances after his resurrection and those appearances proclaimed his bodily resurrection [NTL].

was-vindicated[a] by/in Spirit/spirit,

> LEXICON—a. aorist pass. indic. of δικαιόω (LN 88.16) (BAGD 3.d. p. 198): 'to be vindicated, to be justified' [BAGD], 'to be proved to be right' [BAGD, LN], 'to be shown to be right' [LN]. The clause ἐδικαιώθη ἐν πνεύματι 'was vindicated by/in Spirit/spirit' is translated 'was vindicated by the Spirit' [NTC; NET, NIV, NLT], 'was vindicated in the Spirit' [NASB], 'justified by the Spirit' [HCSB], 'justified in the Spirit' [KJV], 'was approved by the Spirit' [GW], 'was shown to be right by the Spirit' [TEV], 'was made victorious in the Spirit' [ECC], 'the Spirit proved that he pleased God' [CEV], 'was vindicated in spirit' [BNTC, WBC; NRSV, REB], 'vindicated in the spirit' [Herm], 'proved right in spirit' [NCV], 'was justified in spirit' [Lns], 'he was made righteous by spirit' [AB]. This verb means to demonstrate that something is morally right [LN].

QUESTION—What is meant by the phrase ἐδικαιώθη ἐν πνεύματι 'was vindicated by/in Spirit/spirit'?

Most translate ἐδικαιώθη as 'was vindicated' [BNTC, Herm, LN, NICNT, NTC, WBC; all versions except GW, KJV]. Some translate it as 'was justified' [AB, Lns; KJV], but the only explanation given has the same sense as 'vindicated'. The verb ἐδικαιώθη 'was justified' is to be taken in the forensic sense of being declared righteous, and this happened when God *declared* Jesus to be righteous by raising him from the dead. However, unlike other men who must have another's righteousness imputed to them,

Jesus was sinless [Lns]. God demonstrated Jesus' innocence [NICNT]. Two other interpretations that are not explained are: Christ was 'made victorious in the Spirit' [ECC], and he was 'approved by the Spirit' [GW].

1. The preposition ἐν has the instrumental sense 'by' and the noun πνεύματι refers to the Holy Spirit [BKC, ECC, NIGTC, NTC, TH; all versions except NCV, NRSV, REB]: *was vindicated by the (Holy) Spirit.* The vindication concerned the righteousness of Christ [Alf; CEV]. At Christ's baptism and temptation the Spirit showed that he both approved and proved Christ's righteousness [Alf]. The Spirit vindicated the Son of God in human history by powerfully acting throughout Jesus' ministry up to the resurrection [ECC, NTC], and it was especially by means of his resurrection that the Holy Spirit vindicated Jesus' claim that he was the Son of God [NTC]. By means of the resurrection the Holy Spirit vindicated Christ's claim to be the promised Messiah and the Son of God [NIGTC]. The Holy Spirit confirmed that the things Jesus did were correct [TH].

2. The preposition ἐν indicates the relationship of 'by means of' and the noun πνεύματι refers to the Holy Spirit [BNTC]. This says that God vindicated Christ by showing that Christ was righteous when the Holy Spirit raised him from the dead [BNTC].

3. The preposition ἐν has the specifying sense 'in regard to', and the noun πνεύματι refers to Christ's spiritual nature [BNTC, Herm, Lns, My, NIBC, TC, TG, TNTC, WBC, WP; NCV, NRSV, REB]: *was vindicated in respect to his spirit.* It is best to take ἐν to mean 'in' since it does not have an instrumental sense in the other five lines of this hymn and there is no article modifying 'spirit', so this refers to Jesus' spirit, not 'the Holy Spirit' [WBC]. Here it is Christ's spirit in contrast with Christ's flesh in the preceding line [NIBC, WBC]. Although Christ always knew who he was, the world needed a revelation to vindicate his real identity [WBC]. This refers to Christ's spiritual existence or spiritual form, and here it means that in regard to his spiritual existence he was shown to be Lord [TG]. In Christ's spiritual activities, his words and deeds proved him to be the Son of God just as he claimed to be [TC]. This would mean that in respect to Christ's spiritual nature, in spite of being executed as a malefactor, he was vindicated when God raised him for the dead and thus declared him to be righteous and in fact the Son of God [BNTC]. This refers to Christ's human spirit, and God vindicated him in the spiritual realm by declaring Christ to be his Son [TNTC].

4. The preposition ἐν has the specifying sense 'in regard to' and the noun πνεύματι refers to the spiritual realm. In the spiritual realm, at his resurrection Christ was publicly proved to be the Son of God as he had claimed to be [NAC].

was-seen[a] **by-angels/messengers,**

LEXICON—a. aorist pass. indic. of ὁράω (LN 24.1) (BAGD 1.a.δ. p. 578): 'to be seen' [LN], 'to appear, to become visible' [BAGD]. The clause ὤφθη ἀγγέλοις 'was seen by angels' [Lns, NTC; all versions except KJV] is also translated 'seen of angels' [KJV], 'gazed on by angels' [BNTC], 'made manifest to the angelic powers' [Herm], 'he who was seen by God's messengers' [ECC]. Instead of the passive voice, this is translated as the middle voice: 'appeared to angels' [WBC], 'he appeared to messengers' [AB]. The passive verb frequently is used to refer to an active exhibition of the person described and means that he 'appeared' to angels [NICNT].

QUESTION—Does ἀγγέλοις mean 'angels' or 'messengers'?

1. Jesus was seen by angels [Alf, BKC, BNTC, EGT, ICC, Lns, My, NAC, NIBC, NICNT, NIGTC, NTC, NTIC, NTL, TC, TG, TH, WBC, WP; all versions]. The angels observed Christ's incarnate life [Alf, EGT, TC] and gained a fuller knowledge of his person [TC]. Angels showed their interest in Jesus' birth and in his triumph over Satan, they addressed Jesus' disciples after his ascension, and they welcomed Jesus back to heaven, but Jesus' glorious resurrection is the main point [NTC]. Angels saw the victory of Christ's resurrection and his following resurrection appearances [NIGTC, WP], so that the cosmic nature of Christ's work and its significance was known from the time of his resurrection [NIGTC]. The first ones who saw Jesus after his resurrection in his glorified human nature were some angels [Lns]. The angels throughout the universe witnessed Christ's victorious ascent [WBC]. Or, this refers to the angels' worship of Christ when he ascended to heaven and was glorified [BKC, BNTC, NIBC]. Jesus appeared to the angles in heaven after his exaltation [ICC, NAC, NICNT]. Christ assumed authority over all the angels, and they saw his glory [TG].

2. Jesus was seen by messengers [AB, ECC]. The basic meaning of ἄγγελος is 'messenger', and this easily applies to those disciples who were witnesses of his resurrection and then went out to proclaim the message [AB]. The messengers who had seen the risen Jesus were the ones who heralded the news to the nations [ECC].

was-proclaimed[a] **among nations/Gentiles,**[b]

LEXICON—a. aorist pass. indic. of κηρύσσω (LN 33.206) (BAGD 2.b.β. p. 431): 'to be proclaimed' [LN], 'to be announced' [BAGD, LN], 'to be made know' [BAGD]. The clause ἐκηρύχθη ἐν ἔθνεσι 'was proclaimed among the nations/Gentiles' is translated 'was proclaimed among the nations' [BNTC; NASB, REB], 'was preached in nations' [Lns], 'was preached among the nations' [Herm, WBC; NIV, TEV; similarly AB], 'was announced to the nations' [NLT], 'was announced throughout the nations' [GW], 'Christ was preached to the nations' [CEV], 'was heralded among the nations' [NTC], 'proclaimed among Gentiles' [NET, NRSV], 'preached among the Gentiles' [HCSB], 'preached unto the Gentiles' [KJV], 'was preached to those who are not Jews' [NCV], 'was heralded to the pagans' [ECC]. This verb means to announce in a formal or official manner by a herald [LN]. The heralds were preachers [BAGD].

b. ἔθνος (LN 11.55): 'nation, people' [LN]. The plural form ἔθνεσιν is translated 'nations' [AB, BNTC, Herm, Lns, NTC, WBC; CEV, GW, NASB, NIV, NLT, REB, TEV], 'Gentiles' [HCSB, KJV, NET, NRSV], 'those who are not Jews' [NCV], 'pagans' [ECC]. The word ἔθνος denotes the largest unit of a socio-political community and means 'nation' or 'people' [LN (11.55)]. However, the plural form τὰ ἔθνη 'the nations' can have an extended meaning that refers to those who do not belong to the Jewish or Christian faith, with the meaning 'heathen', 'pagans', or 'Gentiles' [LN (11.37, 11.38)]

QUESTION—What is meant by ἐκηρύχθη ἐν ἔθνεσιν 'was proclaimed among nations/Gentiles'

1. This refers to being proclaimed among the nations [AB, BNTC, Herm, ICC, Lns, My, NIBC, NIGTC, NTC, NTL, TG, TH, WBC; CEV, GW, NASB, NIV, NLT, REB, TEV]. Christ was made known to not only the angels in heaven, but also to all rational beings on earth [BNTC]. These are the nations of the *known* world [NIBC]. Jesus was heralded in their midst, and there is no intent to distinguish between Jews and Gentiles [Lns]. Jesus was universally proclaimed as the Savior of the world [NTC]. The focus is on all people, not just the Gentiles [NIGTC], and this does not exclude the Jews [ICC].

2. This refers to being proclaimed among the Gentiles [ECC, NICNT; HCSB, KJV, NCV, NET, NRSV]. This refers to all those who were not Jews [ECC]. The phrase ἐν ἔθνεσιν 'among the nations/Gentiles' itself does not exclude the Jews, but 'among the Gentiles' marks a salvation-historical benchmark as another eschatological point [NICNT].

was-believed-in[a] in[b] (the) world,

LEXICON—a. aorist passive indic. of πιστεύω (LN 31.85) (BAGD 2.a.α. p. 661): 'to be believed in' [BAGD, BNTC, LN, NTC; GW, NCV, NLT, NRSV, REB, TEV], 'to be believed on' [HCSB, KJV, NASB, NET, NIV], 'to be believed' [AB, Herm, Lns, WBC], 'to be trusted' [BAGD, LN], 'to be received in faith' [ECC]. This passive form is also translated in the active voice with people as the subject 'people...put their faith in him' [CEV]. This verb means to believe so as to have complete trust and reliance in someone [LN].

b. ἐν (LN 83.13): 'in, within' [LN]. The phrase ἐν κόσμῳ 'in the world' [ECC, Herm, Lns, WBC; GW, HCSB, KJV, NASB, NCV, NET, NIV] is also translated '(people) in this world' [CEV], 'by the world' [AB, NTC], 'throughout the world' [BNTC; NLT, NRSV, REB, TEV]. This preposition refers to a position defined as being within certain limits [LN].

QUESTION—Who believed in him?

This is the response to the announcement that was proclaimed among the nations [NIBC, NICNT]. The translation 'was believed *by* the world' is to be joined with 'preached among nations', but the locative sense is not meant to be lost since this is to be understood 'throughout the world' without implying that all of the people in the whole world believed the proclamation about Jesus [AB]. On earth people believed the gospel, but this does not say that everyone believed [WBC]. People all over the world believed in Jesus [TH]. Jesus was received by faith in the world [ECC]. People from every tribe and nation began to worship Jesus as their Lord and Savior [NTC].

was-taken-up[a] in/to glory.[b]

LEXICON—a. aorist pass. indic. of ἀναλαμβάνω (LN 15.203) (BAGD 1. p. 56): 'to be taken up' [BAGD, BNTC, ECC, LN, NTC, WBC; CEV, HCSB, NASB, NCV, NET, NIV, NRSV, TEV], 'to be lifted up' [Herm], 'to be taken to' [GW, NLT], 'to be raised to' [REB], 'to be received up' [Lns; KJV], 'to be carried away, to be taken away' [LN]. This verb means to carry something away from some point [LN]. This verb is used in reference to Christ's ascension in Mk 16:19 and Acts 1:2, 11, 22.

b. δόξα (LN 1.15): 'glory, heaven' [LN]. The clause ἀνελήμφθη ἐν δόξῃ 'was taken up in glory' [AB, BNTC, ECC, NTC, WBC; HCSB, NASB, NCV, NET, NIV, NRSV], is also translated 'was taken to heaven in glory' [GW, NLT], 'lifted up in glory' [Herm], 'was received up in glory' [Lns]. Some translate 'glory' as being his destination: 'he was taken up to glory' [CEV], 'raised to heavenly glory' [REB], 'received up into glory' [KJV], 'he was taken up to heaven' [LN; TEV]. As a noun this denotes a place that is glorious and is used as a reference to heaven. Some scholars, however, interpret δόξα in 1 Timothy 3:16 as an abstract and thus translate ἐν δόξῃ as 'in a glorious way' or 'in a wonderful way' or 'in a way that revealed his glory' [LN].

QUESTION—Does the phrase ἐν δόξῃ refer to the manner in which Christ was taken up or to the location to which he was taken?

1. It refers to the glorious manner in which Jesus was taken up to heaven [Lns, NAC, NIBC, NICNT, NTC, TC]. Christ's exaltation was glorious [NIBC]. The glorified Jesus was gloriously received into heaven [Lns]. This glory was Christ's permanent condition manifested in his ascension and which now continues in heaven [TC]. Glory was the brightness and majesty of God's presence in Jesus [NAC]. Christ was taken up in glory when he was received in heaven as its victorious king and the innumerable multitude sang 'Worthy is the Lamb' [NTC].

2. It refers to the presence of glory in heaven to where Jesus was taken [AB, Alf, BNTC, LN, NIGTC, TG, TH; CEV, TEV; probably KJV, REB]. 'Glory' describes the presence and radiance of God [AB, NIGTC]. To enter into glory is to enter into God's presence [NIGTC]. Christ was taken up into glory at his ascension and there reigns in glory [Alf]. 'Glory' is the

dazzling brightness of God's presence, so this indicates that Jesus was taken up into the realm of God's glory where he would reign along with his Father [BNTC].

DISCOURSE UNIT: 4:1–6:21a [ICC, NICNT]. The topic is the attitude of the church leader to the church and the groups in it [ICC], ordering and organizing God's household [NICNT].

DISCOURSE UNIT: 4:1–16 [ICC, NICNT, NIGTC, TH, TNTC; NASB, NET, NIV, REB]. The topic is instructions to Timothy [NIV], instructions on Timothy's proper conduct as a church leader [TH], Timothy's duties as a teacher in the face of heresy [ICC], Timothy's ministry in the later times [NET], threats to the safety of the church [TNTC], false teaching [REB], apostasy [NASB], apostasy: a good minister's discipline [NIGTC], regarding godliness, and Timothy's responsibility [NICNT].

DISCOURSE UNIT: 4:1–7a [AB]. The topic is opposition to healthy teaching.

DISCOURSE UNIT: 4:1–5 [ECC, Herm, ICC, NAC, NCBC, NIBC, NICNT, NIGTC, NTL, TH, TNTC, WBC; CEV, GW, HCSB, NCV, NLT, NRSV, TEV]. The topic is false teachers [TEV], a word concerning false teaching [Herm], warnings against false teachers [TH; NCV, NLT], renewed warning against false teachers [NCBC], the false teaching censured [NIBC], the source of the heresy [WBC], demonic influence [HCSB], the emergence of heresy [NICNT], the rise of heresy and the need for sound doctrine [ICC], understanding false practice [NAC], latter times [NTL], a prophecy [ECC], a prophecy about the last times [GW], people will turn from their faith [CEV], the approaching apostasy [TNTC], apostasy and its false asceticism [NIGTC], false asceticism [NRSV].

4:1 **Now/but the Spirit explicitly[a] says that in later/(the)-last[b] times some will-depart-from[c] the faith,**

LEXICON—a. ῥητῶς (LN **33.94**) (BAGD p. 736): 'explicitly, expressly' [BAGD], 'thusly, just as said, in so many words' [LN]. The phrase τὸ πνεῦμα ῥητῶς λέγει 'the Spirit explicitly says' [HCSB, NASB, NET, NRSV; similarly AB] is also translated 'the spirit expressly declares' [AB], 'the Spirit expressly states' [BNTC; similarly Lns, NTC; KJV], 'God's Spirit explicitly says' [CEV], 'the Holy Spirit has explicitly said' [LSA], 'the Spirit clearly says' [WBC; NCV, NIV; similarly GW, TEV], 'the Holy Spirit tells us clearly' [NLT], 'here is the Spirit expressly declaring' [ECC], 'this is exactly what the Spirit says' [**LN**], 'the Spirit speaks thusly' [**LN**], 'the Spirit explicitly warns us' [REB]. This adverb pertains to what is spoken or has been spoken [LN]. It emphasizes the clarity of the prophecy [TH, WBC], and its explicitness [TH]. This means 'in express words', a phrase that is especially used with quotations [My].

b. ὕστερος (LN **61.16**, 67.50) (BAGD 1.b. p. 849): 'later, afterward' [LN (67.50)], 'last' [BAGD, LN (61.16)], 'final' [LN (61.16)]. The phrase ἐν ὑστέροις καιροῖς 'in later times/the last times' is translated 'in later

times' [AB, LSA; GW, NASB, NIV, NRSV, TEV], 'in the later times'
[NCV, NET], 'in future times' [Herm], 'in later seasons' [Lns, NTC], 'in
time to come' [REB], 'these latter times' [ECC], 'in the latter times'
[HCSB, KJV], 'in the last times' [BNTC, **LN** (61.16), WBC; NLT], 'in
the last days' [CEV]. This adjective refers to a subsequent event [LN
(67.50)], or to something being final in a series [LN (61.16)].

    c. fut. mid. indic. of ἀφίστημι (LN 39.41) (BAGD 2.a. p. 127): 'to fall
away, to become apostate' [BAGD], 'to revolt, to rebel' [LN]. The phrase
ἀποστήσονταί τινες τῆς πίστεως 'some will depart from the faith'
[NTC; HCSB, KJV] is also translated 'some will fall away from the faith'
[NASB; similarly Herm], 'some will turn away from the true faith'
[NLT], 'some people will stop believing the faith' [NCV], 'some will
abandon the faith' [BNTC; NIV; similarly TEV], 'some will renounce the
faith' [NRSV], 'some will forsake the faith' [REB], 'some will desert the
faith' [NET], 'some believers will desert the Christian faith' [GW], 'some
people will distance themselves from the faith' [AB], 'some people will
apostatize from the faith' [ECC, Lns], 'many people will turn from their
faith' [CEV], 'some people will stop believing the doctrine' [LSA]. One
translation takes τῆς πίστεως 'the faith' to modify τίνος 'some': 'some
(people) of the faith will apostatize' [WBC]. The intransitive use of the
verb ἀφίστημι means 'to go away, to withdraw', and in this context it
means 'to desert, to fall away', or 'to become apostate' in the sense of
giving up the faith or denying it [ICC].

QUESTION—What relationship is indicated by δέ 'now/but'?

    1. This indicates transition or a resumption of an interrupted discourse [AB,
EGT, ICC, Lns, LSA, NICNT, WBC; HCSB, KJV, NCV, NET, NLT,
NRSV; probably ECC, Herm; CEV, GW, NIV, REB, TEV which do not
translate this conjunction]. After a digression about the Christian mystery,
Paul returns to the topic of the false teachers that was hinted at in 3:15
[BNTC]. Paul now points out the types of problems that the church will
have [WBC]. There may be an implicit contrast between the preceding
verse and the apostasy which will now be discussed, but the conjunction is
to be taken as making a fresh start with a new topic [EGT, ICC].

    2. This indicates a contrast [Alf, My, NIBC, NIGTC, NTC, TC, TH; NASB]:
but, however. The church is glorious, but apostasy is threatening and those
who are members of church outwardly are not all members inwardly [Alf,
NTC]. It is true that the church is the bulwark of the truth, but there are
those who will undermine the truth [TH], and abandon it [NIBC]. The
church is the bulwark of the truth, yet error will arise even in the church
[TC]. The mystery of our religion is great (3:16), but some will depart
from the faith [My].

QUESTION—How did the Spirit explicitly say this?

It is not possible to identify the prophecy [BNTC, LSA, NIBC, TH, WBC,
WP]. It could be that the Spirit revealed this to Paul at this time or in the
past, or that the Spirit revealed this to Christian prophets, and the message

had been circulating in the church [NICNT]. The Spirit probably spoke through some anonymous prophet [ECC]. Probably this refers to Christian prophets who were inspired by the Holy Spirit [EGT, ICC, TC, TG], and Paul was one of them [EGT]. This could refer to Paul's prophecy in Acts 20:29–30 where he told the church in Ephesus about men arising who would speak perverse thing that would draw the disciples after them [WBC]. Or, the Spirit was presently saying this to Paul [Alf, NTC] and probably to others as well [Alf]. This prophecy was a warning by direct revelation from the Spirit to Paul, to other apostles, and perhaps to a few others such as Agabus [Lns]. Or, this was not a specific prophecy, but the gist of repeated teaching by Jesus, other apostles, and even Paul [BKC, TNTC]. The present tense of λέγει 'says' indicates the abiding validity of a previous prophecy [ICC, NIGTC, WBC]. The 'later times' is future to the giving of the prophecy, and since this prophecy is presented as a present danger that has already begun to take place at the time of writing this letter, the present tense is to be taken as a vivid description of a past event [LSA].

QUESTION—Does the ὑστέροις καιροῖς mean 'later times' or 'the last times'?

1. This means it will happen in times later than the time of the prophecy [Alf, Herm, Lns, LSA, NTC, TC, WP]. These later times are short periods of time that follow earlier ones and the later times were future to the speaker of the prophecy [Alf, TC, WP], and now the prophecies were coming true [WP]. The earlier times had already passed when the letter was written and later times would appear in which there would be apostasy in one or more of them [Lns]. These later seasons were eras included in the new dispensation, and the error that was already present would grow and develop in the manner described in 4:3 [NTC]. This is translated 'future times' because of the artificial futuristic expression 'will depart from' which shows that the author applied this to a present danger [Herm].

2. This means 'the latter times' or 'the last days', referring to the days before the return of Christ [AB, BNTC, ECC, EGT, ICC, NAC, NIBC, NICNT, NIGTC, TG, WBC]. Although this expression ὑστέροις καιροῖς 'later times' is different from the expression ἐσχάταις ἡμέραις 'last days', both refer to the last days [EGT, NAC]. The word ὑστέροις 'later' is a comparative adjective, but here it can have the superlative force of 'last' [ICC]. The 'latter days' are the last days in apocalyptic literature [AB]. This is referred to as 'the last times', and since this is applied to the time of writing the letter, it shows that the Second Coming was thought to be imminent [BNTC]. This is a warning concerning the future Last Days, but Paul believed that this condition was already in operation [EGT, NICNT]. The future tense of 'will depart from the faith' comes from the time that the prophecy had been originally given, and that future time had now become the present time of the writing of the letter [WBC]. It is the eschatological period of the Spirit and salvation [NICNT]. Paul is using

the emphatic future language of prophecy to speak of a present situation
[NIGTC].

QUESTION—What is meant by some people departing from the faith?

The 'faith' is used in the objective sense [Alf, BNTC, Lns, NTC, TC], the
body of redemptive truth [NTC, TG], the body of doctrine that Christians
believe [LSA]. It concerns the content of what is believed as does 'the
mystery of the faith' in 3:9 [BNTC], and 'the truth' in 3:15 [NIBC]. The
phrase τῆς πίστεως 'the faith' can refer to either the Christian doctrine or
the Christian religion, but here probably doctrine is in view [TH]. In contrast
with those who hold on to the mystery of our religion (3:16), are those who
depart from the faith, that is, from the entire Christian view of reality and the
way of life, not just their religious profession [AB]. This is apostasy from
Christian faith [NICNT]. They fall away from their own personal belief in
'the faith' [NIGTC]. This refers to a gradual decline of their views [Alf]. The
word 'some' refers to professing Christians in Ephesus [Alf, NAC], who are
led away from the faith by the false teachers [Alf, My]. Or, rather than belief
in a creed, it refers to their faith in God through Christ [WP].

giving-heed-to[a] deceitful[b] spirits[c] and teachings of-demons,[d]

LEXICON—a. pres. act. participle of προσέχω (LN 30.35, 31.47) (BAGD
1.a.α. p. 714): 'to give heed to' [BAGD, Lns, LSA, NTC; KJV], 'to pay
attention to' [BAGD, BNTC; HCSB, NASB, NRSV], 'to pay close
attention to, to consider carefully' [LN (30.35)], 'to occupy oneself with'
[NET], 'to dote on' [ECC], 'to be devoted to' [WBC], 'to devote oneself
to' [AB], 'to surrender one's mind to' [REB], 'to believe' [LN (31.9)], 'to
hold firmly to, to continue to believe' [LN (31.47)], 'to adhere to' [Herm],
'to follow' [BAGD; GW, NCV, NIV, NLT], 'to obey' [TEV], 'to be
fooled by' [CEV]. This verb means to pay close attention to something,
possibly implying being in agreement with it [LN (30.35)], or to hold
firmly to a certain belief [LN (31.47)]. This is more than just 'paying
attention to' the spirits, but includes following, obeying, and giving
allegiance to them [TG]. See this word at 1:4 where it is translated 'to
devote their attention to'.

b. πλάνος (LN **31.9**) (BAGD 1. p. 666): 'deceitful' [BAGD, LN], 'leading
astray' [BAGD], 'causing someone to be mistaken, that which deceives'
[LN]. The phrase πνεύμασιν πλάνοις 'deceitful spirits' [Lns, WBC;
HCSB, NASB, NRSV] is also translated 'deceiving spirits' [AB; NET,
NIV], 'deceptive spirits' [BNTC; NLT], 'spirits which deceive' [**LN**
(31.9); GW], 'spirits who deceive people' [LSA], 'lying spirits' [TEV],
'spirits that lie' [NCV], 'spirits of error' [Herm], 'subversive spirits'
[REB], 'seducing spirits' [NTC; KJV], 'seductive spirits' [ECC], 'fooled
by evil spirits' [CEV]. This adjective pertains to causing someone to be
mistaken [LN].

c. πνεῦμα (LN 12.37) (BAGD 4.c. p. 676): 'spirit' [AB, BNTC, ECC,
Herm, Lns, LSA, NTC, WBC; all versions except CEV], 'evil spirit'

[BAGD, LN; CEV], 'demon' [LN]. This noun denotes an evil supernatural being or spirit [LN].

    d. δαιμόνιον (LN 12.37) (BAGD 2. p. 169): 'demon, evil spirit' [BAGD,
LN]. The phrase καὶ διδασκαλίαις δαιμονίων 'and teachings of
demons' [WBC; NCV] is also translated 'and the teachings of demons'
[AB; HCSB; similarly NRSV], 'and the teachings of devils' [BNTC],
'and teachings that come from demons' [NLT], 'and things taught by
demons' [NIV], 'and doctrines of demons' [Lns, NTC; NASB], 'and
doctrines of devils' [KJV], 'and by teachings that come from demons'
[CEV], 'and demonic teachings' [Herm; NET], 'and demonic doctrines'
[ECC], 'and demon-inspired doctrines' [REB], 'and follow the teachings
of demons' [TEV], 'they will believe the teachings of demons' [GW],
'specifically, they will give heed to false doctrines that these evil spirits
teach' [LSA]. This noun denotes an evil supernatural being or spirit [LN].

QUESTION—What relationship is indicated by the use of participle προσέχοντες 'paying attention to'?

    1. It indicates the means by which they depart from the faith [My, NICNT,
NTC, WBC; NRSV]: some will depart from the faith *by paying attention
to deceitful spirits.* This indicates how the apostasy is brought about [My].

    2. It indicates the reason for their departure from the faith [BNTC, NIGTC]:
some will depart from the faith *because they will pay attention to deceitful
spirits.* This is the ultimate cause of some falling away [NIGTC].

    3. It indicates an attendant circumstance that takes place in addition to the
preceding main verb [NET, NIV, REB]: some will depart from the faith
while paying attention to deceitful spirits.

    4. It describes and defines the people who will depart from the faith [ECC]:
some people, *those who pay attention to deceitful spirits,* will depart from
the faith.

    5. It functions as a second part of the content of what the Spirit says [LSA];
the Spirit has said that in later times some will stop believing the doctrine
and that they will give heed to spirits that deceive people [LSA].

QUESTION—What is meant by προσέχοντες πνεύμασιν πλάνοις 'paying
attention to deceitful spirits'?

    1. The πνεύμασιν 'spirits' are evil spirits [Alf, EGT, ICC, LSA, My,
NICNT, NIGTC, NTC, NTL, TC, TG, TH, TNTC]. They are supernatural
spirits [TNTC]. These spirits are not men, but demons who seduce and
lead humans astray [EGT, LSA, My, NTC]. The spirits seduce people
away from the truth to believe in what is false [My]. The deceit of the evil
spirits influenced the apostasy [ICC]. These spirits are the ultimate cause
of the human introduction of errors that will appear in the church [TC].
The false teachers transmitted the lies of these spirits [TG]. The verb
προσέχοντες 'paying attention to' is the same verb used in 1:4 where
Timothy was to command certain ones not to *pay attention to* myths and
endless genealogies, and this makes it clear that the same people are again

in view [AB]. Satan and his allies were influencing the actions of Paul's opponents and their resistance to the truth [BNTC].

2. The πνεύμασιν 'spirits' are the false teachers [Lns, NAC]. Since the false teachers in Ephesus are described as 'deceiving and being deceived' in 2 Tim. 3:13, this is a reference to the false teachers themselves [NAC]. They are the false teachers who are called spirits because they represent the deceitful spirits who speak through them, and this is similar to 1 John 4:1–3 which speaks about testing the spirits [Lns].

QUESTION—What is the difference between πνεύμασιν 'spirits' and δαιμονίων 'demons'?

The demons are evil spirits [Alf, EGT, ICC, LSA, My, NICNT, NIGTC, NTC, NTL, TC, TG, TH, TNTC]. The terms 'demons' and 'spirits' probably refer to the same beings [Alf, EGT, LSA, My, NTC]. Here, the word 'demon' is the specific meaning of the generic term 'spirit' [LSA].

QUESTION—What is meant by the genitive construction διδασκαλίαις δαιμονίων 'teachings of demons'?

The teachings are those taught by demons [Alf, BNTC, EGT, ICC, Lns, TC, TNTC; NIV, WP]. The demons are the source of these teachings [Lns, NAC, NICNT; CEV, NET, NLT], and probably those which translate this phrase as 'teachings *of* demons' consider the demons to be in some way the source of the teachings [AB, My, NIGTC, NTC, WBC; GW, HCSB, KJV, NASB, NCV, NIV, NRSV, TEV]. They inspired the doctrines [REB]. This statement about demons is explained by the preceding clause about evil spirits [WP]. Probably those which translate this phrase 'demonic teaching' consider the teachings to be demonic in nature [ECC, Herm, NIBC]. It is not that the men who opposed Paul were demon-possessed; rather, they were the agents of the demons [WBC]. These were human teachings that are inspired by demons [TH]. False teachers taught the false teachings of the demons [TG]. The false doctrines taught by the false teachers were given to them by demons [BKC].

4:2 in[a] hypocrisy[b] of-liars,[c] having-been-seared/branded[d] (in their) own conscience,[e]

LEXICON—a. ἐν (LN 89.26, 89.76): 'by means of, through, by' [LN (89.76)], 'because of, on account of, by reason of' [LN (89.26)]. The phrase ἐν ὑποκρίσει ψευδολόγων 'in hypocrisy of liars' is translated 'in hypocrisy of lie-speakers' [Lns], 'in hypocrisy they speak falsely' [AB], '(teachings of demons) coming from the deceit of men who are liars' [LN (33.255)], '(demonic teachings) based on deceitful preaching by liars' [Herm], 'such teachings come through hypocritical liars' [NIV], 'such teachings come from the false words of liars' [NCV], 'such teachings are spread by deceitful liars' [TEV], 'by the hypocrisy of liars' [WBC], 'they will also be fooled by the false claims of liars' [CEV], 'through the hypocrisy of liars' [HCSB, NRSV], 'through the plausible falsehoods of those' [REB], 'influenced by the hypocrisy of liars' [NET], 'by means of the hypocrisy of liars' [NASB], 'by causing men who lie to insincerely teach these false doctrines' [LSA], '(the apostasy comes about) as a result of the hypocrisy of liars' [BNTC], 'speaking lies in hypocrisy' [KJV], 'these people will speak lies disguised as truth' [GW], 'these people are hypocrites and liars' [NLT], 'these lying frauds' [ECC], '(these doctrines are) embodied in the insincere utterance of those who speak lies' [NTC]. This preposition indicates the means by which one event makes another event possible [LN (89.76)], or the cause or reason, with the instrument in focus [LN (89.26)].

    b. ὑπόκρισις (LN 88.227) (BAGD p. 845): 'hypocrisy, pretense' [BAGD, LN], 'deceit' [LN (33.255)]. See translations of this word above in lexical item a. This noun denotes the feigning of certain purposes or motivations that are quite different from the real ones [LN]. It means to pretend to be someone that one really isn't [WBC].

    c. ψευδολόγος (LN 33.255) (BAGD p. 891): 'liar' [BAGD, LN]. See translations of this word above in lexical item a. This noun denotes someone who tells falsehoods and lies [LN].

    d. perf. pass. participle of καυστηριάζομαι (LN **27.54**) (BAGD p. 425): 'to be seared' [BAGD, LN], 'to be branded with a red-hot iron' [BAGD]. The clause κεκαυστηριασμένων τὴν ἰδίαν συνείδησιν 'having been seared/ branded in their own conscience' is translated with the metaphor of searing the conscience: 'whose consciences have been seared as with a hot iron' [NIV], 'their consciences have been scarred as if branded by a red-hot iron' [GW], 'whose consciences are seared with a hot iron' [NRSV; similarly KJV], 'whose consciences are seared' [HCSB, NET; similarly NTC], 'seared in their own consciences' [BAGD], 'such as have been seared as to their own conscience' [Lns], 'their own consciences are seared' [**LN**], 'whose consciences are dead, as if burnt with a hot iron' [TEV], 'whose consciences are destroyed as if by a hot iron' [NCV], 'seared in their own conscience as with a branding iron' [NASB], 'with their cauterized consciences' [ECC], 'since their own consciences have been cauterized' [AB]. Some translate with the metaphor of branding: 'whose consciences have been branded' [BNTC; similarly WBC], 'whose consciences have been permanently branded' [REB], 'who carry a brand on their consciences' [Herm]. Some treat this phrase as an idiom without a metaphor: 'they refuse to listen to their consciences' [**LN**], '(who lie) and do not feel guilty' [LSA], 'whose consciences have lost all feeling' [CEV], 'and their consciences are dead' [NLT]. The idiom 'to be seared in/as-to the conscience' means to be unwilling to learn from one's conscience [LN].

    e. συνείδησις (LN 26.13) (BAGD 2. p. 786): 'conscience' [BAGD, LN]. See this word at 1:5, 19.

QUESTION—What relationship is indicated by the preposition ἐν 'in' in the phrase 'in hypocrisy of liars'?

    1. The preposition ἐν is connected with what precedes in 4:1 [Alf, BKC, BNTC, ECC, EGT, ICC, Lns, My, NICNT, NIGTC, NTC, TG, TH,

TNTC, WBC; CEV, HCSB, NASB, NCV, NET, NIV, NRSV, REB, TEV].

1.1 The preposition indicates the cause of people departing from the faith to devote their attention to deceitful spirits and teachings of demons [BNTC, Lns, NAC, WBC, WP; CEV, HCSB, NASB, NET, NRSV, REB]: some will depart from the faith…*because of the hypocrisy of liars*. The hypocritical liars will lead them into apostasy [WBC].

1.2 The preposition indicates the means or instrument by which the teachings of demons were taught [BKC, ECC, EGT, Herm, ICC, NAC, NIGTC, NTC, TG, TH, TNTC; NCV, NIV, TEV]: some will depart from the faith *through the teaching of hypocritical liars*. The preposition ἐν indicates that the teachings were mediated 'by means of' or 'through' human beings who were liars [NIGTC, TH]. The demons used the liars to mislead the Ephesians [NAC]. The hypocritical liars are the human agents for the teachings of devils [EGT, TH]. 'Such teachings come through hypocritical liars' [NIV]. 'Such teachings are spread by deceitful liars' [TEV]. The teaching coming from the demonic powers was mediated through the deceitful teaching of liars, and the prepositional phrase indicates the instrument that led people into apostasy [ICC]. The doctrines of demons were embodied in the insincere utterance of liars [NTC]. The teachings of demons were taught by hypocritical liars, or the demons spoke through such people [TG]. 'Liars' is in apposition to the preceding word 'demons' and describes the spokesmen for the spirits and demons as 'these lying frauds' [ECC]. The demonic teachings were 'based on deceitful preaching by liars' [Herm].

2. The preposition adds a further description of the 'some' in 4:1 [AB, NICNT; GW]. In English, this description begins a new sentence as it shifts the focus from the demonic source of the false teaching to the participation of the humans who will teach those demonic doctrines [NICNT]. 'In hypocrisy' indicates the manner in which the liars speak [AB]. 'These people will speak lies disguised as truth' [GW].

QUESTION—Who were the people described in this verse?

1. This refers to the false teachers who were used by the deceitful spirits to get people to depart from the faith [BKC, BNTC, EGT, Herm, ICC, Lns, My, NAC, NICNT, NTC, TC, TG, TH, WBC; CEV, HCSB, NASB, NCV, NET, NIV, NRSV, REB, TEV]. The spirits (demons) used men who spoke lies [NTC]. The demons used these men as their agents [BNTC]. Although the liars are included among those who departed from the faith, there were some in that group who were not actively deceiving others, so this should be connected with the phrase 'giving heed to deceitful spirits and teachings of demons' rather than the phrase 'will depart from the faith' [EGT, My].

2. This refers to the people who will depart from the faith [AB, Alf, ECC, NTIC, NTL; GW]. The members of the congregation who have gone

astray have a scarred conscience instead of a pure and clean conscience that they should have (1:5, 19; 3:9) [NLT].

QUESTION—In what way were they hypocrites?

They were doing and teaching things that they knew to be wrong [WBC]. They spoke as though they were pious and learned men in order to cover up the fact that they were really arrogant and immoral [NTC]. After turning from the truth, the false teachers pretended to be Christian teachers who taught the truth, but they did so in order to deceive people [ICC]. They claimed to be Christian teachers who were godly and had a better revelation, but they were not who they claimed to be and their teaching was not what they claimed it to be [NICNT].

QUESTION—What is meant by the verb κεκαυστηριασμένων 'having been seared/branded'?

1. This refers to being seared or cauterized by a hot iron [BAGD, BKC, ECC, ICC, LN, Lns, NCBC, NICNT, NIGTC, NTC, NTIC, NTL, TH; all versions except CEV, NLT, REB]. This means that their consciences have been cauterized so that they were no longer bothered by their consciences [ECC, Lns, NTC]. Their consciences did not forbid them to act deceitfully or else they did not pay attention to their consciences [ICC]. In this case, the metaphor is: like skin has lost all of its feeling after being badly burned, so their consciences are dead and no longer warn them of doing wrong [TG]. They have lost the use of their consciences and were no longer aware that they acted wrongly [TH].

2. This refers to being marked with a branding iron [Alf, BNTC, Herm, My, NAC, NIBC, TC, WBC, WP; REB].

2.1 The brand identifies their owner [BNTC, NAC, NIBC, WBC]. Their consciences have brand marks burned in them to show that Satan owns them much like the foreheads of slaves had brand marks to show who their owners were, and here this indicates that they were instruments of demonic powers [BNTC]. The false teachers bore the brand on their consciences and the passive voice points to Satan being the one who branded them in order to mark them as his property and his agents [WBC]. They have been branded by Satan to signify that they belong to him and do his will [NIBC]. Branded by Satan to do his will, they did his will when they misled the Ephesians [NAC]. In this case, the metaphor is: like animals and runaway slaves are branded with the mark of their owners, so these people have the Devil's mark of ownership on them and they are completely ruled by him [TG].

2.2 The brand identifies them as those who are guilty of sin [Alf, My, TC]. This probably refers to a penal branding of criminals who have the brand of sin in their consciences [TC]. As criminals bore a brand on their foreheads to mark them as criminals, so the heretics bore a brand on their consciences of the knowledge that they are guilty [My]. Their consciences were seared by crime [Alf].

3. No comparison is intended since this is an idiomatic expression for not being sensitive to distinctions of right and wrong [LSA; CEV, NLT].

4:3 forbidding[a] to-marry, (commanding)[b] to-abstain-from[c] foods,[d]

LEXICON—a. pres. act. participle of κωλύω (LN 13.146) (BAGD 2. p. 461): 'to forbid' [BAGD], 'to prevent, to hinder' [BAGD, LN]. The clause κωλυόντων γαμεῖν 'forbidding to marry' [WBC; KJV; similarly Lns] is also translated 'they forbid people to marry' [NCV, NIV; similarly LSA, NTC], 'they forbid marriage' [AB, Herm; HCSB, NRSV; similarly BNTC; NASB, REB], 'these liars will forbid people to marry' [CEV], 'they will prohibit marriage' [NET], 'interdict marriage' [ECC], 'they will try to stop others from getting married' [GW], 'they will say it is wrong to be married' [NLT], 'such people teach that it is wrong to marry' [TEV]. This verb means to prevent something from happening [LN].

b. (commanding). The verb κωλυόντων 'forbidding' governs the two infinitives 'to marry' and 'to abstain' that follow it. This is a case of zeugma [Alf, BNTC, ECC, EGT, ICC, Lns, NAC, NIGTC], in that the verb 'forbidding' collocates only with the first infinitive and, having a negative meaning, it does not give the proper sense if translated 'forbidding to abstain from foods'. Therefore some supply a verb that is opposite in meaning from 'forbidding' to go with the second infinitive: 'and commanding' [KJV], 'and order them' [NIV; similarly LSA], 'and demand' [ECC, Herm; HCSB, NRSV], 'demanding' [WBC], 'and require' [NET], 'and insist on' [NASB], 'and bid' [BNTC], 'and enjoining them' [NTC], 'and tell them' [NCV]. Another solution is to use a verb that collocates with both situations and still gives the proper meaning: 'will forbid people to marry or to eat certain foods' [CEV], 'will try to stop others from getting married and from eating certain foods' [GW], 'teach that it is wrong to marry and to eat certain foods' [TEV], 'they will say it is wrong to be married and wrong to eat certain foods' [NLT], 'they forbid marriage, forbid eating foods' [AB].

c. pres. mid. infin. of ἀπέχομαι, ἀπέχω (LN 13.158) (BAGD 3. p. 85): 'to abstain from' [BAGD, BNTC, Lns, LSA, NTC; KJV, NASB, NIV], 'to keep away from' [BAGD], 'to avoid doing, to keep from doing' [LN], 'to try to stop' [GW], 'not to eat' [NCV]. This verb is also translated as a noun: 'abstinence' [Herm, WBC; HCSB, NRSV, REB]. Some use the same verb that they use in the first clause [AB; CEV, GW, NLT, TEV]. This verb means to continue to avoid doing something [LN]. It means to keep away from, or to abstain from something [ICC].

d. βρῶμα (LN 5.1, **5.7**) (BAGD 1. p. 148): 'food' [BAGD, LN (5.1)], 'meat' [**LN** (5.7)], 'solid food, flesh' [LN (5.7)]. The plural form βρωμάτων 'foods' [AB, BNTC, ECC, Herm, Lns, NTC, WBC; HCSB, NASB, NET, NRSV, REB] is also translated 'meats' [KJV]. It is also translated so as not to appear to forbid all kinds of food: 'certain foods' [LSA; CEV, GW, NCV, NIV, NLT, TEV]. This noun denotes any kind of food or nourishment [LN (5.1), TH], or any type of solid food, particularly meat [AB, ICC, LN (5.7)].

QUESTION—Who are the people who are the actors of the participle κωλυόντων 'forbidding'?

This participle modifies the lying hypocrites (4:2) and specifies some of the things they taught [BNTC, ECC, ICC, My, NICNT, TG; CEV]. This gives two examples of the false teachings [ICC, NAC, NIBC, TH].

QUESTION—Why would these people forbid marriage?

Marital restrictions were found in both Judaism and Gnosticism, and the false teachers in Ephesus wanted to enforce rules of asceticism [WBC]. The heretics probably thought that people would gain a higher degree of holiness by abstaining from marriage [NAC]. They thought that marriage was inherently wrong [NIGTC]. The Gnostics taught that the human body and its functions, and even all matter, were evil, so religious people should be emancipated from marriage and sex [BNTC]. Since these incipient Gnostics thought that matter was evil, they believed that all bodily appetites were evil, including the normal desires for sex and food [BKC]. This probably refers to abstinence from sexual activity both within and outside of marriage [ICC, NICNT]. Probably they believed that the resurrection to a spiritual life had already occurred and in this new order there would be no marriage, and they would be like the angels who do not marry [NIBC].

QUESTION—Why would these people forbid people to eat food?

Of course this does not mean that people should not eat any food at all and starve to death, so some translations indicate that the restrictions were for *certain* foods [ICC, LSA, TG, TH; CEV, GW, NCV, NIV, NLT, TEV]. The false teachers praised the practice of fasting [NTC], and they insisted that the church must follow their dietary restrictions [WBC]. It could mean abstinence from meat, or from alcohol, or food that was considered unclean by the Jews [ICC]. This probably had some connection with the OT laws on ritual cleanliness and diet [BNTC, ECC, TG]. It is possible that this means people should not eat certain kinds of food, but probably it means that they taught that people should eat as little food as possible [TH]. The word βρωμάτων 'foods' probably is used in a specialized sense of 'meat' [Alf, My, NIGTC], and the false teachers were forbidding the eating of meat because they considered it wrong to do so [NIGTC]. Probably this was concerned with the Jewish distinctions between clean and unclean meat, and so it does not mean *all* meat [My].

which God created[a] for receiving/sharing[b] with thanksgiving[c] by-the believers/faithful[d] and the (ones) having-known[e] the truth.[f]

LEXICON—a. aorist act. indic. of κτίζω (LN 42.35) (BAGD p. 455): 'to create' [AB, BAGD, ECC, Herm, LN; all versions]. The phrase ἃ ὁ θεὸς ἔκτισεν '(to marry, to abstain from foods,) which God created' [Herm; KJV, NIV, NRSV] is also translated '(foods) which God created' [BNTC, NTC; NASB, NCV, REB], '(foods) that God created' [WBC; HCSB, NET], 'these foods were created by God' [LSA], 'But God created these/those foods' [CEV, NLT, TEV], 'God created food' [GW], 'things that God created' [ECC], 'which things God created' [Lns], 'these are things God created' [AB]. This verb means to create something that has not existed before [LN].

b. μετάλημψις (LN **57.129**) (BAGD p. 511): 'receiving, taking' [BAGD], 'eating' [LN], 'sharing' [BAGD, LN]. The clause εἰς μετάλημψιν 'for receiving/sharing' is translated 'for reception' [Lns], 'to be received' [Herm, WBC; GW, HCSB, KJV, NET, NIV, NRSV], 'in order that people receive them' [LSA], 'to be enjoyed' [REB], 'to be eaten' [CEV, NCV, NLT, TEV], 'to share in' [ECC], 'to be shared in' [NASB], 'to be shared' [AB], 'to be partaken of' [BNTC], 'may partake of them' [NTC]. This noun denotes the activity of receiving something from what one is to have a share in, but in 1 Tim. 4:3 it refers to the activity of eating and therefore one may translate it 'which God created for people to eat' [**LN**].

c. εὐχαριστία (LN 33.349) (BAGD 2. p. 328): 'thanksgiving' [BAGD, LN], 'thankfulness' [LN]. The phrase μετὰ εὐχαριστίας 'with thanksgiving' [AB, BNTC, Herm, Lns, NTC, WBC; KJV, NET, NIV, NRSV, REB] is also translated 'with thanks' [NCV, NLT], 'with thankful hearts' [CEV], 'with prayers of thanks' [GW], 'after a prayer of thanks' [TEV], 'with gratitude' [HCSB], 'thankfully' [ECC], 'gratefully' [NASB], 'and that they thank God for the food' [LSA]. This noun denotes an expression of gratitude for benefits or blessings [LN].

d. πιστός (LN 31.86, 31.87), (BAGD 2. p. 665): 'believing, faithful' [BAGD], 'trusting' [LN (31.86)], 'faithful, trustworthy, dependable, reliable' [LN (31.87)]. The phrase τοῖς πιστοῖς 'the believers/faithful' is translated 'the believers' [BAGD, Lns], 'believers' [ECC; REB], 'those who are believers' [TEV], 'those who believe' [BNTC, NTC; GW, HCSB, KJV, NASB, NET, NIV, NRSV], 'people who believe' [NCV], 'people who believe in Christ' [LSA], 'his followers' [CEV], 'those who have come to the faith' [Herm], 'those who are faithful' [AB, WBC], 'faithful people' [NLT]. This adjective pertains to trusting [LN (31.86)], or to being trusted [LN (31.87)].

e. perf. act. participle of ἐπιγινώσκω (LN 28.2) (BAGD 2.a. p. 291): 'to know' [BAGD], 'to know about, to know definitely about' [LN]. The phrase τοῖς πιστοῖς καὶ ἐπεγνωκόσι τὴν ἀλήθεια 'by believers and the ones having known the truth' is also translated '(created) for the believers and those who have realized the truth' [Lns], '(created) for believers and persons who have recognized the truth' [ECC]. The conjunction καί 'and' is epexegetical and further defines the believers [Lns], so most translate so as to make it clear that the believers and the ones having known the truth are the same people: 'by those who believe and who know the truth' [NIV, NRSV], 'by people who believe and have come to know the truth' [BNTC], 'by those who believe and know the truth' [GW, HCSB, NASB, NET; similarly NCV], 'of them which believe and know the truth' [KJV], 'by his followers who know the truth' [CEV], 'by those who are believers and have come to know the truth' [TEV], 'by believers who have come to knowledge of the truth' [REB], 'those who believe and acknowledge the truth' [NTC], 'by all those who have come to the faith and to the recognition of the truth' [Herm], 'people who believe in Christ and who know the true doctrine' [LSA], 'by those who are faithful and know the truth' [WBC], 'by those who are faithful and have come to a recognition of the truth' [AB]. Instead of taking τοῖς πιστοῖς to refer to 'the believers', this is taken to refer to the attribute of being faithful: 'by faithful people who know the truth' [NLT]. This verb means to have definite information about something [LN].

f. ἀλήθεια (LN 72.2) (BAGD 2.b. p. 36): 'truth' [BNTC, LN]. The phrase τὴν ἀλήθεια 'the truth' [AB, BNTC, ECC, Herm, NTC, WBC; all versions] is also translated 'the true doctrine' [LSA]. This noun denotes the content of that which is true and thus in accordance with what actually happened [LN]. It is used especially of the Christian doctrine as the absolute truth [BAGD]. See this word at 2:4; 3:15.

QUESTION—What is the referent of ἃ 'which' in the phrase 'which God created for receiving with thanksgiving'?

1. It refers to the forbidden foods that God created for eating with thanksgiving [BNTC, EGT, Herm, ICC, LN, LSA, NAC, NIBC, NICNT, NIGTC, NTC, TG, TH, WBC; CEV, GW, HCSB, NASB, NCV, NET, NLT, REB, TEV]. The neuter pronoun ἃ 'which' refers at least to the plural noun 'foods' and some interpret it to also refer to the verb 'to marry'. However because marriage and food are in two different categories, an event and an object, it is simpler to take the pronoun to refer only to the foods that have been created by God [LSA]. Although Paul's argument could also apply to marriage, the emphasis is on the question of food because it is the nearer antecedent and the falseness of their view of marriage is self-evident [NIGTC]. Grammatically the relative pronoun 'which' refers to 'foods', and Paul's previous positive statements about marriage (2:15; 3:2, 12) and his encouragement to young widows to get married (5:14) are a sufficient correction to the prohibition of marriage [NICNT]. They were to thank God for the food they ate and when they did this, it was an acknowledgement that the food came from God [TG]. The food was to be received with a prayer of thanksgiving according to the custom of the Jews [BNTC, ICC, NIBC], and Jesus had continued this custom [BNTC, ICC].

2. It refers to both marriage and foods that God created for partaking in with thanksgiving [AB, ECC, Lns, NTIC, NTL, TNTC]. The neuter pronoun ἃ 'which' includes both marriage and food, and this speaks of sharing a life in marriage and sharing food with others [AB, ECC, Lns]. God created both marriage and foods, so forbidding either of them is to dispute his creative purpose [Lns]. Both marriage and foods are God's gifts to all

human beings and Christians should receive them with thanksgiving even though others do not understand this and shun his gifts [NTL].

QUESTION—What relationship is indicated by the preposition εἰς 'for'?

It indicates God's purpose in creating them [AB, BNTC, ECC, ICC, LSA, NIGTC, NTC, WBC]: *he created them in order to be received/shared with thanksgiving.* God created food to meet human needs [NICNT].

QUESTION—Does the verb μετάλημψιν mean 'receiving' or 'sharing', and how is thanksgiving involved?

1. It means receiving and eating [BKC, Herm, ICC, Lns, LSA, NAC, NIBC, NIGTC, NTIC, NTL, TH, WBC, WP; all versions except NASB]: *which God created to be received with thanksgiving.* This food was created for believers to eat after a prayer of thanks [NAC, TH]. It does not imply that such food was created only for believers [EGT, NAC], yet only those who know the truth can offer the prayer of thanks that sanctifies the food [NAC]. Accepting food with thanksgiving makes it holy [Herm].

2. It means sharing or partaking [AB, BNTC, ECC, NICNT, NTC; NASB]: *which God created to be shared with thanksgiving.* Paul may have had the corporate life of the church in mind [NICNT]. Probably this refers to the act of sharing in a meal, and then the thanksgiving would refer to the prayer of thanksgiving that came before the meal [NICNT, TH]. There is a communal aspect to this sharing of food with others and the thanksgiving would be spoken in prayer [AB]. Since God created these things for them, they should of course thank him for this [ECC].

QUESTION—What is the argument that Paul is presenting here?

Genesis indicates that God created food for human nourishment, therefore Christians should receive and eat that food with thanksgiving [ICC, NICNT]. The false teachers were forbidding people to eat the very food that God had created to be eaten with thanksgiving, so Paul's argument is that God created food for human needs and because of that all food is inherently clean. So when the false teachers said that certain foods were not suitable for eating, they implied that God's purposes had failed [WBC].

QUESTION—What is meant by τοῖς πιστοῖς 'the believers/faithful'?

1. The word πιστοῖς refers to those who believe [BNTC, ECC, EGT, Herm, ICC, Lns, LSA, My, NICNT, NIGTC, NTC, TC; all versions except NLT]: *the believers.* Instead of meaning 'faithful' as in other parts of the letter, the word πιστοῖς refers to people who trust in Christ and are committed to him, or it used as a technical term for 'believers' [TH].

2. The word πιστοῖς refers to those who remain faithful [AB, WBC; NLT]: *the faithful.*

QUESTION—What is meant by τοῖς πιστοῖς καὶ ἐπεγνωκόσι τὴν ἀλήθειαν 'the believers and ones having known the truth'?

The words 'believers' and 'those who know the truth' refer to the same people, the members of the Christian community [AB, BNTC, Herm, Lns, LSA, NCBC, NIBC, NICNT, NTC, TC, TH, WBC; all versions]. This is correct because there is just one definite article used for the two descriptions

[NIGTC, TH]. The conjunction καί 'and' is epexegetical and further defines the believers [Lns, My]. Believers who have come to know the truth describes authentic believers in contrast to the false teachers [NICNT]. Those who are not Christians are not able to thank God from the heart [NTC].

QUESTION—What is meant by τὴν ἀλήθειαν 'the truth'?

1. The truth is the true message believed by Christians [BNTC, TG, TH], the Christian gospel [BNTC, ECC, EGT, ICC, NAC, TG]. 'The truth' can describe the message of the gospel or the body of Christian teaching [TH]. It is the Christian faith [ECC]. The perfect tense indicates that they have 'come to know' the truth contained in the gospel [ICC].

2. 'The truth' refers to the true facts that Paul brings out in his argument [AB, NIGTC, NTC; probably Lns]. The perfect active participle in the phrase 'having known the truth' emphasizes an abiding awareness of the truth that Paul is treating here, that God has created all things and that they are good, and therefore should be received with thanksgiving [NIGTC]. The believers have been brought to the realization of this blessed truth [Lns]. They have come to recognize the truth that these things are God's creation, and so they must give thanks to their creator [AB].

4:4 Because[a] every created-thing[b] of-God (is) good[c]

LEXICON—a. ὅτι (LN 89.33): 'because' [AB, LN, LSA], 'for' [BNTC, ECC, Herm, LN, NTC; HCSB, KJV, NASB, NET, NIV, NRSV], 'since' [WBC; NLT], 'seeing that' [Lns], not explicit [CEV, GW, NCV, REB, TEV]. This conjunction indicates the cause or reason for something [LN].

b. κτίσμα (LN 42.38) (BAGD p. 456): 'what has been created, creature' [BAGD, LN], 'creation' [LN]. The phrase πᾶν κτίσμα θεοῦ 'every created thing of God' is translated 'every creation of God' [NET], 'every creature of God' [AB, Lns, NTC; KJV], 'everything created by God' [BAGD, BNTC; HCSB, NASB, NRSV], 'everything God created' [CEV, GW, NIV, NLT], 'everything God has created' [REB, TEV; similarly Herm, LSA], 'everything in God's creation' [ECC], 'all of God's creation' [WBC], 'everything God made' [NCV]. This noun denotes something that has been created [LN]. It denotes the result of creating [WP], that which is created by God [ICC, TH], everything existing [NIGTC]. Here it refers to *things* that have been created as opposed to human beings who have been created [ICC].

c. καλός (LN 88.4) (BAGD 2.c.β. p. 400): 'good' [AB, BAGD, BNTC, Herm, LN, LSA, WBC; all versions], 'excellent' [Lns, NTC], 'fine' [ECC]. This adjective describes a positive moral quality [LN].

QUESTION—What relationship is indicated by the conjunction ὅτι 'because'?

This indicates the grounds for the preceding statement in 4:3 that God created food to be received with thanksgiving [AB, Alf, BNTC, EGT, LSA, My, NAC, NICNT, NIGTC, NTC, TC, TH, TNTC, WBC; HCSB, KJV,

NASB, NET, NIV, NRSV]: *(food) which God created for receiving with thanksgiving, because every created thing of God is good if it is received with thanksgiving.* This is the principle that abolishes all food laws [BNTC].

QUESTION—What is meant by καλός 'good'?

1. It is morally and intrinsically good [BKC, BNTC, ICC, NAC, NIBC, NIGTC, NTIC, TC, TH; probably all which translate this as 'good']. The OT in Gen. 1:31 states that all God created was good [Alf, BKC, ICC, NAC, NIGTC, TC, TH]. This adjective means having absolute worth [TC], being inherently good [NIBC]

2. It is ritually pure [WBC]. Since the next verse speaks of it being ἁγιάζεται 'sanctified', this must mean that all food is made ritually pure. The food is not unclean in itself, but in relation to the eater who might have scruples about eating it, it becomes clean to him when he receives it with thanksgiving [WBC].

and nothing (is to be) rejected[a] being-received[b] with thanksgiving.[c]

LEXICON—a. ἀπόβλητος (LN 57.141) (BAGD p. 89): 'rejected' [BAGD, LN]. The phrase οὐδὲν ἀπόβλητον 'nothing is to be rejected' [AB, BNTC; NASB, NIV, NRSV, REB, TEV] is also translated 'nothing should be rejected' [LSA; GW, HCSB], 'none of it is to be rejected' [Herm], 'nothing should be refused' [NCV; similarly KJV], 'nothing is fit to be thrown away' [NTC], 'nothing to be thrown away' [Lns], 'no food is to be rejected' [NET], 'we should not reject any of it' [NLT], 'none is despicable' [ECC], 'nothing is unclean' [WBC]. This phrase is also translated 'you may eat anything' [CEV]. This adjective describes something as being rejected [LN]. The word 'rejected' is literally 'to be thrown away', and some think that it can have the sense of being taboo [TH]. Here it has the sense of 'tabooed' [TNTC]. In this context, it would be rejected as being considered ritually or otherwise unclean [NICNT].

b. pres. pass. participle of λαμβάνω (LN 57.125) (BAGD 2. p. 465): 'to be received' [BAGD, LN], 'to be accepted' [LN], not explicit [CEV]. The participle λαμβανόμενον 'being received' [Lns] is also translated 'if it is received' [AB, NTC, WBC; GW, HCSB, NASB, NET, NIV; similarly KJV], 'if it is accepted' [NCV], 'provided it is received' [BNTC; NRSV], 'provided it is accepted' [REB], 'when received' [ECC], 'which is received' [Herm], 'but receive it' [NLT], 'but everything is to be received (with…)' [TEV]. The clause μετὰ εὐχαριστίας λαμβανόμενον 'being received with thanksgiving' is translated 'if they thank God for it when they receive it' [LSA], 'if you give thanks' [CEV]. This verb means to receive or accept an object from the one who gives it [LN]. Although this verb is not the same word as the noun μετάλημψις 'receiving' in 4:3, both the root and the meaning are the same [TH].

c. εὐχαριστία (LN 33.349) (BAGD 2. p. 328): 'thanksgiving' [BAGD, LN], 'thankfulness' [LN]. For the phrase μετὰ εὐχαριστίας 'with thanksgiving' see the identical phrase in 4:3.

QUESTION—What relationship is indicated by the conjunction καί 'and'?
This introduces the corollary developing from the preceding clause [BNTC]. Everything God created is good, therefore nothing should be rejected [NTIC, TH; NLT]. The conjunction introduces a fresh subject [ICC].

QUESTION—What relationship is indicated by the use of the participle λαμ-βανόμενον 'being received'?
This clause can be taken in three ways: (1) nothing is to be rejected *if* it can be received with thanksgiving, (2) nothing that is received with thanksgiving is to be rejected, or (3) nothing is to be rejected, *but* it is to be received with thanksgiving [ICC]. It implies that 'nothing *that God has made* is to be rejected' [Alf]. This refers to ἅ 'which' in the phrase '*which* God created for receiving with thanksgiving' at 4:3 where it lists those who think that it refers to food and those who think it refers to both marriage and food.

1. The participle indicates the condition for the preceding clause [Alf, BNTC, EGT, ICC, LSA, NAC, NICNT, NTC, TC, WBC, WP; CEV, GW, HCSB, NASB, NCV, NET, NIV, NRSV, REB]: *nothing is to be rejected if it is received with thanksgiving*. The repeated emphasis in 4:3–5 is on thanksgiving, so rejection is contrasted with reception with thanksgiving, an act that recognizes that God is the giver of these good gifts [NIGTC]. Thanksgiving here means more than a spirit of gratitude, it refers to voicing that gratitude in table prayers [ICC, NAC, NICNT, TC, WBC]. This seems to imply that without a thankful heart, even good food can become unacceptable food [NAC]. Perhaps an objection might be made that certain kinds of good food were to be rejected because of God's commands in the Mosaic Law, but here it means that thanksgiving annuls the Law in each particular case because anything over which thanksgiving can be said is no longer to be included in the category of tabooed things [EGT].

2. The participle indicates the conclusion of the previous clause [Lns, NAC, NTIC; NLT, TEV]: *nothing is to be rejected, therefore it should be received with thanksgiving*. Since all God has created is good, we can eat all that God has made [NAC].

4:5 Because[a] it-is-sanctified[b] by[c] (the) word[d] of God and prayer/inter-cession.[e]

LEXICON—a. γάρ (LN 89.23): 'because' [LN, LSA; NCV, NIV, TEV], 'for' [AB, Herm, LN, Lns, NTC, WBC; KJV, NASB, NET, NRSV], 'for then' [BNTC; REB], 'for we know' [NLT], 'since' [HCSB], not explicit [ECC; CEV, GW]. This conjunction indicates the cause or reason between events [LN].

b. pres. pass. indic. of ἁγιάζω (LN 53.44) (BAGD 1. p. 8): 'to be sanctified' [BNTC, Lns, WBC; HCSB, KJV, NASB, NET, NRSV], 'to be consecrated' [BAGD, LN, NTC; NIV], 'to be dedicated to God' [LN], 'to be made holy' [AB, BAGD, Herm; NCV, REB], 'to be hallowed' [ECC], 'to be made acceptable' [NLT]. This passive voice is also translated actively with the subject being the 'word of God and intercession': 'make it acceptable to God' [TEV], 'set it apart as holy' [GW], 'will make it fit to eat' [CEV]. This verb means to dedicate something to the service of God [LN]. It means to set something aside or to make it suitable for ritual purposes [BAGD].

c. διά (LN 89.76): 'by' [AB, BNTC, ECC, LN, NTC; HCSB, KJV, NCV, NET, NIV, NLT, NRSV, REB], 'by means of' [LN, Lns; NASB], 'through' [Herm, LN, WBC], 'because' [LSA], not explicit [CEV, GW, TEV]. The clause is translated 'because the word of God and the prayer make it acceptable to God' [TEV], 'the word of God and prayer set it apart as holy' [GW], 'what God has said and your prayer will make it fit to eat' [CEV]. This preposition indicates the means by which one event makes another event possible [ECC, LN, NIGTC].

d. λόγος (LN 33.98) (BAGD 1.b.α. p. 478): 'word' [BAGD, LN], 'message, statement' [LN]. The phrase λόγου θεοῦ 'word of God' is translated 'the word of God' [BNTC, NTC, WBC; GW, HCSB, KJV, NASB, NIV, NLT, TEV], 'God's word' [AB, Herm, Lns; NET, NRSV, REB], 'what God said' [CEV], 'what God has said' [NCV], 'God's word in Scripture' [ECC], '(because) God says so' [LSA]. This noun denotes that which has been stated or said, and the primary focus is upon the content of the communication [LN].

e. ἔντευξις (LN **33.347**) (BAGD 2.c. p. 268): 'prayer' [AB, BNTC, Herm, Lns, NTC, WBC; all versions except TEV], 'the prayer' [TEV], 'request' [LN], 'intercession' [**LN**], 'intercessory prayer' [BAGD, ECC]. The noun is also translated as a clause '(because) they pray concerning it' [LSA]. This noun denotes intercession on behalf of someone else [LN]. See this word at 2:1.

QUESTION—What relationship is indicated by the conjunction γάρ 'because'?

This explains the reason for the preceding clause 'being received with thanksgiving' [BNTC, ECC, ICC, Lns, NAC, NCBC, NICNT, NIGTC, TNTC]: *nothing that is received with thanksgiving is to be rejected, because it is sanctified, etc.* It explains what Christian thanksgiving does [Lns, My]. It gives the reason for not rejecting any food [LSA, NIBC, TH].

QUESTION—What is meant by ἁγιάζεται 'it is sanctified'?

1. *When it refers to foods.* It is made acceptable to God [Alf, ICC, LSA, NAC, NIBC, NIGTC, NTC, TH, TNTC, WBC; TEV]. This refers to consecrating food to God [TH]. By means of God's blessing on the food when we pray, the food has been set apart for holy use [NTC]. It is made holy [Alf, WP] in the sense of being fit for godly use by Christians [Alf]. The verb has the general sense of food being declared acceptable and therefore good for eating [NIGTC]. Or, it means to make something suitable for ritual purposes, and here this probably concerns foods offered to idols and then put on sale in food markets [ICC]. The food is holy as contrasted with heathen taboos [TNTC]. Such food is not unclean in itself, but one's scruples about it or a failure to be thankful might make it

ritually unclean to that person [WBC]. This does not mean that besides having the intrinsic goodness of being God's creation, an additional sanctification is imparted to the food. [BNTC, NAC, NIBC]. Rather, it means that by the prayer of thanksgiving the person acknowledges that the food is a good gift from God, and thus he will regard it as being sacred [BNTC, NAC].

2. *When it refers to both marriage and foods.* Public prayer is the means by which God consecrates both Christian marriage and nourishment [ECC]. Married people are joined together by God so that it is a pure and holy work of God, and Christians are to eat or drink, and whatever they do to the glory of God (1 Cor. 10:31) [Lns].

QUESTION—What is meant by λόγου θεοῦ 'the word of God'?

The word of God (1) may refer to what God has said in the Scriptures concerning food, (2) or it may mean that when prayer is made to God, asking him to bless the food, he, in effect, does utter a blessing, (3) or it may mean that when thanksgiving is given, Scripture is read or quoted as part of the ceremony [LSA]. It could refer to the Christian message that includes the words of Jesus in declaring the goodness of all food (Mark 7:1–23), and the sanctity of marriage (Mark 10:2–9) [AB].

1. The word of God refers to the teaching of Scripture [ECC, ICC, NAC, NIBC, NIGTC, WBC]. It is a statement from God [NIGTC]. In Genesis God says that his creation was good, and since that includes food, all foods are clean [NIBC, NIGTC, WBC]. In the gospel message, the believers learn that there are no food laws [NAC].

2. The 'word of God' refers to excerpts from Scripture that were quoted in the prayer of thanksgiving [Alf, BNTC, EGT, Herm, Lns, TC, TH, TNTC, WP]. This refers to God's Word quoted in the prayer of thanksgiving [TH]. The 'word of God' is in some sense coordinate with prayer and refers to a scriptural prayer or a prayer that is in harmony with God's revealed truth [EGT]. Prayers in the marriage ceremony and prayer said at meals contain words and references from the Scriptures [AB].

QUESTION—What is meant by ἐντεύξεως 'prayer/intercession'?

1. This means their prayers [AB, BNTC, ECC, EGT, Herm, Lns, NAC, NICNT, NTIC, TC, TNTC, WBC; CEV, GW, HCSB, KJV, NASB, NCV, NET, NIV, NLT, NRSV, REB, TEV]. This is a general word for prayer [NIGTC]. It is speaking freely to God [Lns], and here it refers to the table prayer of thanking God for food [AB, BNTC, NAC, NICNT, NIGTC, TNTC, WBC]. This concerns public prayers at both meals and weddings, and these might take the forms of blessings or thanksgiving [ECC].

2. This means intersession or request on behalf of the food [Alf, ICC, LN]. This refers to prayer at mealtime, but it differs from the prayer of thanksgiving mentioned in 4:4 since this prayer concerns a request that God will cleanse or consecrate food that has been bought in the market after it had been offered to idols [ICC]. Intercession is made on behalf of

the κτίσμα 'created thing', asking that it may be sanctified to one's use [Alf].

DISCOURSE UNIT: 4:6–6:19 [ECC]. The topic is the second part of the apostolic commission to Timothy.

DISCOURSE UNIT: 4:6–5:2 [NLT]. The topic is being a good servant of Christ Jesus.

DISCOURSE UNIT: 4:6–16 [ECC, NAC, NCBC, NIGTC, NTL, TH, TNTC, WBC; CEV, GW, NCV, NRSV, TEV]. The topic is Paul's advice to Timothy [CEV], a charge to Timothy [NTL], personal notes to Timothy [WBC], Timothy's personal responsibilities [NIBC], Timothy's performance of his task [NAC], a good servant of Christ Jesus [NCV, TEV], an apostolic teacher [ECC], appropriate conduct for a church leader [TH], guidelines for serving Christ [GW], how a church leader should behave [NCBC], a good minister of Jesus Christ [NRSV], a good minister's discipline [NIGTC], methods of dealing with false teaching [TNTC].

DISCOURSE UNIT: 4:6–10 [Herm, ICC, NAC, NICNT; HCSB]. The topic is a good servant of Jesus Christ [HCSB], instructions for Timothy [Herm], the need for instruction that leads to godliness [ICC], facing falsehood [NAC], sound teaching and godliness [NICNT].

4:6 These (things) teaching[a] the brothers[b] you-will-be a-good servant[c] of-Christ Jesus,

TEXT—Instead of Χριστοῦ Ἰησοῦ 'Christ Jesus', some manuscripts evidently read Ἰησοῦ Χριστοῦ 'Jesus Christ', although GNT does not mention this variant. 'Jesus Christ' is read by KJV.

LEXICON—a. pres. mid. participle of ὑποτίθεμαι, ὑποτίθημι (LN 33.230) (BAGD 2. p. 848): 'to teach, to suggest, to make known' [BAGD], 'to instruct, to give instructions' [LN]. The phrase ταῦτα ὑποτιθέμενος 'these things teaching' is translated 'if you teach these things' [CEV], 'if you put these instructions before (the brothers)' [BNTC; NRSV], 'if you give these instructions' [LN; TEV], 'if you explain these things' [NLT], 'if you propose these things' [AB], 'if thou put (the brethren) in remembrance of these things' [KJV], 'if you instruct (the brothers) in this way' [Herm], 'if you point these things out' [HCSB, NIV], 'when you point these things out' [GW], 'when you suggest matters such as the preceding' [ECC], 'by placing these things before (the brethren)' [WBC], 'by telling these things' [NCV], 'by pointing out such things' [NET], 'by offering such advice as this' [REB], 'in pointing out these things' [NASB], 'by submitting these things/matters' [Lns, NTC], 'these things are to be taught by you' [LSA]. This verb means to provide instruction about what should be done [LN]. The meaning of this verb ranges from 'suggest' all the way to 'order' [BAGD]. Here it means to teach [NIGTC], expound [TC], advise, command [My], remind [EGT, TH], propose [NTIC], suggest

[Alf, EGT, NAC, TNTC, WP], or give [TG]. This present participle gives the idea of *continuing* to put these instructions before the church [WBC]. He will submit these things to the brethren by bringing them to their attention [Lns].

b. ἀδελφός (LN 11.23): 'fellow believer, (Christian) brother' [LN]. The phrase τοῖς ἀδελφοῖς 'the brothers' [BNTC, Herm, LSA, NTC; HCSB, NIV] is also translated 'our brothers' [GW], 'your brothers' [ECC], 'the brothers and sisters' [NCV, NET, NLT, NRSV], 'the brethren' [AB, Lns, WBC; KJV, NASB], 'the brotherhood' [REB], 'other followers' [CEV], 'the believers' [TEV]. This noun denotes a close association of a group of persons having a well-defined membership, and here it refers specifically to fellow believers in Christ [LN]. The word 'brothers' was commonly used in the early church to match the imagery of the church being a family (as also in 5:1) [NIGTC, WBC]. Although Timothy held a prominent position in the church, he was still a brother to the members of the congregation [ICC].

c. διάκονος (LN 35.20) (BAGD 1.a. p. 184): 'servant' [BAGD, LN]. The phrase καλὸς ἔσῃ διάκονος 'you will be a good servant' [WBC; CEV, HCSB, NASB, NCV, NET, NRSV, TEV] is also translated 'you will be a worthy servant' [NLT], 'you will be a true servant' [Herm], 'you are a good servant' [GW], 'you will prove to be a good servant' [REB], 'you will be a good helper' [AB], 'you will be a good minister' [KJV, NIV], 'you will be an excellent minister' [Lns, NTC], 'you will be a fine minister' [ECC], 'you will be an admirable minister' [BNTC], 'in order that you serve them well' [LSA]. This noun denotes a person who renders service [LN]. This is the same word used to describe the office of the deacon in 3:8, but it is used here with the generic meaning of one who serves [BNTC, ICC, NCBC, TC, WBC]. Paul could not mean that Timothy was a deacon instead of an overseer [NIBC].

QUESTION—What is the referent of ταῦτα 'these things'?

This refers to 4:1–5 [Alf, BNTC, Lns, NAC, NTC]. This probably refers specifically to the refutation of the false teachers' command to abstain from foods since Paul has just gone into such detail about this in 4:3b–5 [ICC, LSA, NICNT, TC]. Or, this refers to 3:14–4:5 [ECC]. Or, this refers to the whole letter up to this point as it concerns law, grace, salvation, and conduct in the church [WBC].

QUESTION—What relationship is indicated by the use of the present participle ὑποτιθέμενος 'teaching'?

1. It indicates the means by which Timothy will become a good servant [Lns, LSA, My, NIBC, NICNT, NTC, TG, WBC; NCV, NET, REB]: *by teaching these things, you will be a good servant.* We can assume that Paul knew that Timothy wanted to be a good servant, so Paul used that desire to motivate him to teach these things: 'these things are to be taught by you to the brothers in order that you serve them well' [LSA].

2. It indicates the condition to be met in order to be a good servant [AB, BNTC, ECC, Herm, ICC, TH; CEV, GW, HCSB, KJV, NIV, NLT, NRSV, TEV]: *if you teach these things, then you will be a good servant*. This is the first condition for him to be a good servant, the second being that of nurturing himself [TH]. The verb ἔσῃ 'will be' is a logical future, so if he gives them this teaching, it will show that he is a good servant [ICC].

QUESTION—Whom will Timothy serve?

1. He will be serving Christ Jesus well [EGT, NICNT, TG, TH; probably all versions except KJV, NIV, which simply translate this as 'servant of Christ Jesus']. The noun is used in a general sense of serving Christ in any capacity [TG].

2. He will be serving the brothers well [Lns, LSA, NTC, WP; probably KJV, NIV which translate this as 'ministers of Christ Jesus']. 'A minister of Christ Jesus' does not mean that he will be ministering to Christ. Rather, the ones who will benefit from his service will be the brothers, so the genitive construction 'of Christ Jesus' means that Christ has appointed him to this ministry, or perhaps that Timothy belongs to Christ [Lns, LSA]. This speaks of his service *for* Christ [WP]. A good minister will warn people against departing from the truth and will show how to deal with error as he represents Christ Jesus [NTC].

being-nourished/being-trained[a] by-the words[b] of-the faith and-of-the good teaching[c] that you-have-followed.[d]

LEXICON—a. pres. mid./pass. participle of ἐντρέφω (LN 33.242) (BAGD p. 269): 'to be trained' [BAGD, LN], 'to be taught' [LN], 'to be brought up, to be reared' [BAGD]. The participial phrase ἐντρεφόμενος 'being nourished/being trained by' is translated 'nourished by' [AB; HCSB], 'being nourished on' [NTC], 'yourself nourished on' [ECC], 'constantly nourished on' [NASB, NRSV], 'as being nourished by' [Lns], 'nourished up in' [KJV], 'having nourished yourself on' [NET], 'then you will be nourished by' [GW], 'sustained by' [BNTC], 'as you feed yourself spiritually on' [TEV], 'you will be made strong by' [NCV], 'nurtured in' [REB], 'one who is nourished by' [NLT], 'and in order that you may become strong (spiritually) by means of' [LSA], 'being trained daily by' [WBC], 'you will show that you have grown up on' [CEV], 'brought up in' [NIV], 'one who is being reared by' [Herm]. This verb means to provide instruction and training, and it implies that the one who teaches is skilled in some area of practical knowledge [LN].

b. λόγος (LN 33.98) (BAGD 1.b.β. p. 478): 'word' [BAGD, LN], 'message, statement' [LN]. The phrase τοῖς λόγοις τῆς πίστεως 'the words of the faith' [BNTC, ECC, Lns, NTC, WBC; HCSB, NASB, NCV, NET, NRSV] is also translated 'the words of the Christian faith' [GW], 'the teachings about our faith' [CEV], 'the precepts of our faith' [REB], 'the truths of the faith' [NIV] 'the words of faith' [AB, Herm; KJV, TEV], 'the message of faith' [NLT], 'the message which we all believe' [LSA]. This noun denotes that which has been stated or said, and the primary focus is upon the content of the communication [LN]. See this word at 4:5.

c. διδασκαλία (LN 33.224) (BAGD 2. p. 191): 'teaching' [BAGD, LN]. The phrase καὶ τῆς καλῆς διδασκαλίας 'and the good teaching' [NCV, NLT; similarly Herm, WBC; HCSB, NET, NIV] is also translated 'and of good doctrine' [KJV], 'and of the excellent doctrine' [Lns, NTC], 'and of the true teaching' [TEV], 'and of the admirable doctrine' [BNTC], 'and of the sound doctrine' [NASB], 'and of the sound instruction' [REB], 'and of that fine instruction' [ECC], 'and of the sound teaching' [NRSV], 'and by the noble teaching' [AB], 'and the excellent teachings' [GW], 'and (have grown up) on the good instructions' [CEV], 'which is the good doctrine' [LSA]. This noun denotes the instruction provided in either a formal or informal setting [LN].

d. perf. act. indic. of παρακολουθέω (LN 36.32) (BAGD 2. p. 619): 'to follow' [BAGD, LN], 'to be a follower of, to conform to' [LN]. The phrase ᾗ παρηκολούθηκας 'that/which you have followed' [BNTC, WBC; HCSB, NET, NIV, NRSV, REB, TEV; similarly NLT] is also translated 'which you have been following' [Lns, NTC; NASB, NCV], 'which you have followed closely' [GW], 'in which you have followed' [AB], 'of which you have become a follower' [Herm], 'which you obeyed' [LSA], '(the good instructions) you have obeyed' [CEV], 'whereunto thou hast attained' [KJV], 'with which you are quite familiar' [ECC]. This verb means to conform to a particular system of instruction or teaching [LN]. It means to follow with one's mind, to understand [BAGD].

QUESTION—Does ἐντρεφόμενος mean 'being nourished' or 'being trained' here?

The participle ἐντρεφόμενος may be either middle or passive. If it is middle, it means 'nourishing yourself', but if passive, it means 'educated in' [ICC, NICNT].

1. This verb means to be nourished [AB, BKC, BNTC, ECC, ICC, Lns, LSA, My, NAC, NIBC, NICNT, NIGTC, NTC, NTL, TG, TH, TNTC, WP; all versions except CEV, NIV]. This is used figuratively to refer to being spiritually fed with spiritual food consisting of the words of the faith and of the good doctrine [TG]. This refers to constant spiritual nourishment by (or on) the food of the words of the faith and of the good doctrine [Lns, NAC, NTC]. This nourishment is necessary in order to be a good minister who instructs others [NIGTC]. Various terms are used to express this idea: nourished [ECC, Lns, NTC, TH; GW, HCSB, KJV, NASB, NET, NLT, NRSV], sustained [BNTC], fed on [TEV], and made strong by [LSA; NCV]. The connotation of the metaphor is that of having strength and health [Lns]. The metaphor of being nourished has the idea of becoming spiritually strong [LSA]. He is to feed his heart on the words

of the faith and the good teaching he has followed [TH]. Being a present participle, it refers to being *continually* nourished [ICC, NIBC, NICNT, NIGTC, TH, TNTC].

2. This verb means to be trained [Alf, BAGD, EGT, Herm, LN, NTIC, WBC; probably CEV, NIV]. Since this passage concerns correct doctrine, the metaphor of training is to be preferred over the metaphor of being nourished [WBC]. This means to be continuously training himself in the words, not nourishing himself with them [Alf]. The present tense refers to Timothy's daily training, not just to his past upbringing [EGT, WBC].

QUESTION—What relationship is indicated by the use of the participle ἐντρεφόμενος 'being nourished/trained'?

1. It is adjectival and describes 'a good servant' [ECC, Herm, Lns, NICNT, NTC; NLT, REB]: *you will be a good servant, one who is nourished by the words of the faith.* By doing his duty, he will fit this description [NTC]. This states in what respect Timothy will be a good minister of Christ [Lns].

2. It is the second purpose of teaching the brothers [LSA]: *teach the brothers these things in order that that you serve them well, and in order that you may be nourished by means of the words of the faith.*

3. It indicates the result of teaching these things [ICC; GW]: *when you teach these things, then you will be nourished by the words of the faith.* If you give them this teaching, it will show that you are a good servant and that you are nourished by these words [ICC].

4. This is the second condition to be met in order to be a good servant [TH]: *if you teach these things and are nourished by the words of the faith, then you will be a good servant.*

5. This indicates the manner in which he will become a good minister [BKC, NAC]: *by being nourished by the words of the faith, you will become a good minister.*

QUESTION—What is meant by τοῖς λόγοις τῆς πίστεως 'the words of the faith'?

The *words of the faith* refer to the statements of what is to be believed [Lns], the Christian doctrine [EGT, NICNT, NTC, TG, TNTC], the Christian creed [TC], the apostolic teaching [NICNT], the contents of the gospel [Alf, ECC, ICC, NIBC, NICNT]. These are words that come from the Scriptures and the gospel [AB]. 'Faith' is used in an objective sense here [BKC, NIGTC], and faith is an appropriate description of the words since they demand a response of faith on the part of those who hear [NIGTC].

QUESTION—What is meant by καὶ τῆς καλῆς διδασκαλίας 'and the good teaching' ?

The phrase τοῖς λόγοις 'the words' is qualified by the two genitive constructions τῆς πίστεως 'of the faith' and τῆς καλῆς διδασκαλίας 'of the good teaching' [NIGTC]. While 'the words of *the faith*' refer to the basic gospel message, 'the words of *the good teaching*' refer to the doctrinal teaching contained in the gospel, so this is saying that the reading of the gospel is to be accompanied by the correct doctrinal understanding of the gospel [WBC]. Both pertain to the Christian message, but 'the words of the faith' focus on the total content of message, while 'the words of the good teaching' focus on the actual proclamation of the content in a form of an authoritative statement of what the church should believe. Together they mean 'the words of the Christian message and the true teachings that you have followed or obeyed' [TH]. The words of the faith refer to the total body of the Christ doctrine, while the second phrase refers to the same as it is being imparted little by little to the congregation [EGT]. The 'words of the good teaching' are the good instructions Timothy had always followed [Alf, TG] in his spiritual journey [TH]. It refers to formal doctrinal statements [TC]. The good teaching refers to Paul's interpretation of the OT Scriptures [ECC]. It refers to what Paul taught Timothy [BKC, NIBC, TNTC], either about the contents of the gospel or the correct use of Scripture as in 2 Tim. 3:14–16 [NIBC]. This phrase is almost synonymous with 'the words of the faith' [ICC, NICNT]. The good teaching is the same as the sound teaching in 1:10 [Herm]. 'Teaching' is an appropriate description since this is the purpose of the words, and 'good' distinguishes these words from the erroneous teachings of demons (4:1) [NICNT, NIGTC]. The good teaching is sound teaching, and this describes the gospel as measurably superior to false teaching [NICNT].

QUESTION—What is meant by the final phrase ᾗ παρηκολούθηκας 'that you have followed'?

The words 'that you have followed' refer to Timothy's long association with the gospel [WBC]. The perfect tense indicates that throughout the past Timothy had followed the doctrine of the faith and was continuing to do so [Lns, NICNT, NIGTC]. He had always followed them [TG]. He followed those words by diligently studying and practicing them [BNTC]. He followed the words by using his mind to understand and appropriate them [NIGTC]. Or, he had faithfully learned Paul's instructions to him and carried them out [BKC, NIBC].

4:7 **But the profane[a] and old-womanish[b] myths[c] avoid.[d]**

LEXICON—a. βέβηλος (LN **88.115**) (BAGD 1. p. 138): 'profane, godless' [LN], 'worldly' [BAGD, **LN**]. See the following lexical item for translations of this word. This adjective describes something as profane in the sense of being worldly or godless [LN]. It means that something is profane, accessible to everyone, or unhallowed [BAGD]. See this word at 1:9; 6:20.

   b. γραώδης (LN 9.38) (BAGD p. 167): 'like old women say, like old women do' [LN], 'characteristic of old women' [BAGD]. The phrase τοὺς βεβήλους καὶ γραώδεις μύθους 'the profane and old-womanish myths' [Lns, NTC] is also translated, 'profane and old-women myths' [AB], 'profane and old wives' fables' [KJV], 'profane old wives' tales' [ECC], 'those profane old wives' fables' [BNTC], 'godless old wives' tales' [Herm], 'profane myths and old wives' tales' [NRSV], 'godless myths that old women like to tell' [GW], 'godless myths and old wives' tales' [NIV], 'godless ideas and old wives' tales' [NLT], 'worldly fables fit only for old women' [NASB], 'godless myths such as old women are likely to tell' or 'godless and useless legends' [**LN** (9.38)], 'the profane and silly myths' [WBC], 'foolish stories that disagree with God's truth' [NCV], 'worldly and foolish legends' [LN (88.115)], 'irreverent and silly myths' [HCSB], 'godless, silly stories' [LSA], 'superstitious myths, mere old wives' tales' [REB], 'worthless, senseless stories' [CEV], 'those myths fit only for the godless and gullible' [NET], 'those godless legends, which are not worth telling' [TEV]. This adjective is derived from γραῦς 'old woman' and refers to something characteristic of old women [BAGD, LN].

c. μῦθος (LN 33.13) (BAGD p. 529): 'myth, tale, story, legend, fable' [BAGD, LN]. See the preceding lexical item for translations of this noun. This noun denotes a legendary story or account, and in the NT it always has an unfavorable connotation [LN]. See this word at 1:4.

d. pres. mid./pass. (deponent = act.) impera. of παραιτέομαι (LN **27.60**) (BAGD 2.b. p. 616): 'to avoid' [BAGD, LN], 'to reject' [BAGD], 'to refuse to pay attention to, to pay no attention to' [LN]. The imperative παραιτοῦ 'avoid' is translated 'stay away from' [AB], 'keep away from' [TEV], 'don't have anything to do with' [CEV, GW], 'have nothing to do with' [BNTC, ECC, LSA; HCSB, NASB, NIV, NRSV, REB], 'reject' [Herm, WBC; NET], 'refuse' [KJV], 'shun' [NTC], 'pay no attention to' [LN], 'do not waste time arguing over' [NLT], 'disdain to be bothered with' [Lns]. This verb means to not pay attention to something [LN]. The present tenses indicate a continual action [WBC].

QUESTION—What relationship is indicated by δέ 'but, now'?

1. It indicates a contrast with the preceding verse [AB, BNTC, Herm, ICC, LSA, NIBC, NICNT, NTC, TC, TNTC, WBC; KJV, NASB, NCV, NET, TEV]: *but*. The negative prohibition in this verse contrasts with the positive exhortation in 4:6 [ICC]. The phrases 'the words of the faith' and 'those profane old wives' fables' are in direct antithesis [BNTC, ECC, NTC, TNTC, WBC].

2. The words of faith and good doctrine are opposites of the myths, but there is not a contrast between the two main sentences about 'you will be a good servant' and 'avoid myths', so here δέ 'and' merely continues the admonition [Lns].

QUESTION—What is meant by the adjective βέβηλος 'profane'?

Profane describes something that is separate from and in opposition to what is holy, and this aptly describes the false teaching that had no religious basis or content [BNTC]. It is the opposite of holy, that is, it is secular without anything sacred [NIBC, TH]. There is nothing sacred about the myths [ICC, Lns], they are unworthy of a religious person's attention [Lns]. The heresy is pagan in its thrust [NICNT].

QUESTION—What is meant by γραώδης 'old-womanish' myths?

It means that the myths were fit for only superstitious old women with limitless credulity [BNTC]. They were fit only for senile and silly old crones to chatter about [Lns]. This refers to drivel belonging to the category of silly superstitions [NTC]. The myths are the endless myths and genealogies referred to in 1:4 [ICC, NTC]. Possibly it means superstitious nonsense that is based on OT material [ICC]. It describes something that is frivolous and not worthy of serious attention [NAC]. It is insignificant in its contribution [NICNT]. The expression was often used sarcastically in Greek philosophical writings [NIBC, TH]. The expression had become an idiom for any insignificant chatter, and some translators drop this idiom and merely give the intended meaning [TH]: silly [LSA, WBC; HCSB], foolish [NCV], senseless [CEV], frivolous [TNTC], useless [LN (9.38)]. The article in the phrase 'the profane and old-womanish myths' indicates that Paul is referring to the Ephesian heresy [WBC].

QUESTION—How was Timothy to 'avoid' those myths?

The myths refer back to the wild inventions contained in the myths at 1:4 [Lns, My, NIBC, TC, TH]. When people came to Timothy with these stories, he was not treat them seriously by discussing and arguing about them, rather he was to firmly and politely beg to be spared from discussing such foolishness [Lns]. He was to have nothing to do with them [TC], and steer clear of them [NICNT]. He was not to waste his time with those who teach these myths, but keep himself free for better things [ICC]. This false teaching was best ignored [NAC].

DISCOURSE UNIT: 4:7b–16 [AB]. The topic is modeling healthy teaching.

And/but[a] train[b] yourself for/in godliness.[c]

LEXICON—a. δέ (LN 89.87, 89.93, 89.124) (BAGD 1, 2, 3. p. 171): This conjunction can mark a sequence of closely related events: 'and, and then' [LN (89.87)], or an additive relation that is not coordinate: 'and, and also, also, in addition, even' [LN (89.93)], or a contrast: 'but, on the other hand' [LN (89.124)]. It can emphasize a contrast: 'but', or mark a simple transition: 'now, then', or mark a resumption of an interrupted discourse: 'and also, but also' [BAGD]. Here it is translated 'and' [NET], 'but' [Lns; NCV], 'rather'; [BNTC, WBC; GW, HCSB, KJV, NIV], 'instead' [AB; NLT], 'on the other hand' [NASB], not explicit [ECC, Herm, LSA, NTC; CEV, NRSV, REB, TEV].

b. pres. act. impera. of γυμνάζω (LN **33.88**, 36.11): 'to train, to undergo discipline' [LN (36.11)], 'to discipline oneself, to keep oneself disciplined' [LN (33.88)]. The clause γύμναζε σεαυτὸν πρὸς εὐσέβειαν 'train yourself for godliness' [AB, WBC; NET] is also translated 'train yourself for godly living' [NTC], 'train yourself in order that you live more godly' [LSA], 'train yourself to live a godly life' [GW], 'train yourself to be godly' [NIV, NLT], 'train yourself to serve God' [NCV], 'keep yourself in training for a godly life' [TEV], 'keep yourself in training for the practice of religion' [REB], 'train yourself for sound religion' [BNTC], 'train for action that aims at godliness' [ECC], 'discipline yourself for the purpose of godliness' [NASB], 'keep yourself disciplined for a godly life' [**LN** (33.88)], 'work hard to be truly religious' [CEV], 'exercise thyself unto godliness' [KJV], 'train yourself in godliness' [HCSB, NRSV], 'continue to train yourself in piety' [Herm], 'exercise yourself with respect to godliness' [Lns]. This verb means to undergo vigorous training with the goal of increased physical and/or moral strength [LN (36.11)], or to control oneself by thorough discipline [LN (33.88)].

c. εὐσέβεια (LN 53.5) (BAGD p. 326): 'godliness' [AB, BAGD, ECC, LN, Lns, WBC; HCSB, KJV, NASB, NET, NRSV], 'piety' [Herm, LN], 'godly living' [NTC], 'a godly life' [LN; TEV], 'sound religion' [BNTC], 'the practice of religion' [REB]. The noun is also translated as a verb phrase: 'live more godly' [LSA], 'live a godly life' [GW], 'to be godly' [NIV, NLT], 'be truly religious' [CEV], 'serve God' [NCV]. This noun denotes behavior that reflects correct religious beliefs and attitudes [LN]. See this noun at 2:2; 6: 3, 5, 11.

QUESTION—What relationship is indicated by δέ 'and, but'?

1. It indicates a transition to a new topic [LSA; NET; probably Herm, NTC; CEV, NRSV, REB, TEV which do not translate this conjunction]. In addition to teaching the good doctrine (4:6), he is also to train himself to live more and more godly [LSA].

2. It indicates a contrast [AB, BNTC, ECC, ICC, Lns, My, NICNT, WBC; GW, HCSB, KJV, NASB, NCV, NIV, NLT]. He recommends a different kind of activity [ICC]. This is an alternate route to godliness [NICNT]. The contrast is between myths and true godliness [WBC].

QUESTION—What is meant by the command γύμναζε σεαυτὸν 'train yourself'?

This is an athletic metaphor [AB, BKC, BNTC, NAC, NIGTC, NTC, WBC] that refers to bodily exercise [Alf, ECC, ICC, Lns, TG, TH, TNTC], and this metaphor is carried on in 4:10 with the verbs 'we toil and strain' [Lns]. This exercise is concerned with Christian growth [ICC], and spiritual discipline [BKC, NTC]. It refers to working at progressing toward virtue in the moral and spiritual sphere [NICNT]. It is used to emphasize the effort that is involved to progress toward a greater virtue [AB], that of godliness [ECC]. The metaphor refers to genuine Christian self-discipline [BAGD]. The grounds of comparison may be either sparing no effort to attain the goal, or divesting oneself of anything that could encumber physical and spiritual progress [NTC]. The present imperative indicates that this training for a godly life is to be continuous and persistent [TH].

QUESTION—What relationship is indicated by the preposition in the phrase πρὸς εὐσέβειαν 'for/in godliness'?

1. It indicates the goal of Timothy's training [AB, Alf, BNTC, ECC, ICC, LN, LSA, My, NAC, NICNT, NTC, TC, TG, TH, WBC; all versions

except HCSB, NRSV]: train yourself *in order to become more godly*. It refers to conducting himself more and more in a godly manner [LSA]. The metaphor of exercise is used of spiritual discipline that helps a person become godly [ICC].

2. It indicates that area in which one trains himself [Herm, Lns, NIGTC; HCSB, NRSV]: train yourself *in the matter of godliness*. Timothy is told to exercise the godliness he already has for the purpose of becoming more godly [NIGTC].

QUESTION—What is meant by εὐσέβεια 'godliness' [BNTC].

This describes true Christianity [BNTC], true Christian piety [BNTC], living a good Christian life [TG], a life totally consecrated to God [WBC]. The root of this noun refers to awe and reverence, so the noun indicates a worship arising from awe and worship and also a life of obedience that is fitting to that reverence [NIGTC]. It is the observable outworking of the knowledge of God and truth in appropriate ways [NICNT]. It is a life that shows reverence to God [TH]. It involves both right belief and obedient action [NAC]. Note that here godliness itself is not being discussed, but the training that leads to godliness is the subject [TH].

4:8 **Because**[a] **the bodily**[b] **training is profitable**[c] **for a-little**[d] **but the godliness is profitable for all,**[e]

LEXICON—a. γάρ (LN 89.23): 'because' [LN, LSA], 'for' [BNTC, Herm, LN, Lns, NTC, WBC; HCSB, KJV, NASB, NET, NIV, NRSV, REB], 'whereas' [ECC], not explicit [AB; CEV, GW, NCV, NLT, TEV]. This conjunction indicates the cause or reason between events [LN].

b. σωματικός (LN **8.2**) (BAGD 2. p. 800): 'bodily' [BAGD, LN], 'physical' [LN], 'corporeal' [BAGD]. The phrase ἡ σωματικὴ γυμνασία 'the bodily training' is translated 'bodily training' [BNTC, Herm, **LN**], 'bodily exercise' [Lns, WBC; KJV], 'the training of the body' [HCSB, REB], 'training the body' [AB; GW, NCV], 'physical training' [NTC; NIV, NLT, NRSV], 'physical exercise' [ECC; NET, TEV], 'bodily discipline' [NASB], '(if) he trains his body' [LSA], 'exercise (is good for) your body' [CEV]. This adjective describes something as pertaining to a physical body [BAGD, LN].

c. ὠφέλιμος (LN **65.40**) (BAGD p. 900): 'beneficial' [BAGD, LN], 'useful, advantageous' [BAGD]. See the following lexical item for translations of this word. This adjective pertains to a benefit to be derived from some object, event, or state [LN]. This word means beneficial or advantageous for someone [NIGTC].

d. ὀλίγος (LN 78.8) (BAGD 3.b. p. 564): 'little' [BAGD, LN], 'to a small degree, slight' [LN]. The phrase πρὸς ὀλίγον ἐστὶν ὠφέλιμος 'is profitable for a little' is translated 'is useful for a little' [ECC], 'is only of little profit' [NASB], 'is profitable (only) with respect to little' [Lns], 'is beneficial to a small extent' [**LN**], 'is beneficial up to a point' [BNTC], 'is useful in a limited way' [AB], 'has a limited benefit' [HCSB], 'is of some benefit' [NTC], 'is of some value' [NIV, NRSV], 'has some value' [TEV], 'is of value for a little while' [WBC], 'brings limited benefit' [REB], 'has some value' [NET], 'helps a little' [GW], 'benefits a little' [LSA], 'helps in some ways' [NCV], 'is good' [CEV, NLT], 'is of little benefit' [Herm], 'profits little' [KJV]. This adjective describes something as being on a relatively low point on a scale of extent [LN].

e. πᾶς (LN 58.28): 'all sorts of, every kind of' [LN] The phrase πρὸς πάντα ὠφέλιμός ἐστιν 'is profitable for all' is translated 'is profitable for all things' [KJV, NASB], 'is profitable with respect to everything' [Lns], 'is useful for everything' [ECC], 'has value for all things' [NIV], 'is beneficial all the way' [BNTC], 'is valuable in every way' [NET, NRSV, TEV], 'is of benefit in every way' [NTC], 'is beneficial in every way' [HCSB], 'is useful in every way' [AB], 'helps in every way' [CEV, GW], 'helps you in every way' [NCV], 'brings the greatest possible benefits' [Herm], 'the benefits are without limit' [REB], 'is much better' [NLT], 'a person benefits very much' [LSA]. This pronominal adjective denotes a totality of kinds or sorts [LN]. The spiritual benefits do not cease at the death of the body, they are for both the present life and for the future life [TH].

QUESTION—What relationship is indicated by the conjunction γάρ 'because'?

It indicates the grounds for the command in 4:7 [BNTC, ECC, Herm, ICC, Lns, LSA, My, NAC, NICNT, NIGTC, NTC, WBC; HCSB, KJV, NASB, NET, NIV, NRSV, REB]: *train yourself in godliness because godliness is profitable for all things.* This supports the statement that Timothy should strive for godliness [NICNT, WBC].

QUESTION—What is meant by this clause in which the prepositional phrase πρὸς ὀλίγον 'for a little' is contrasted with πρὸς πάντα 'for all'?

1. The adjectives ὀλίγον 'little' and πάντα 'all' refer to the value of physical training to develop the body and of spiritual training to develop godliness, so that the argument is that physical exercise has some value, but spiritual exercise in godliness has a great deal more value [Alf, BAGD, BKC, ICC, LSA, My, NIBC, NIGTC, NTC, NTIC, NTL, TG, TH; CEV, GW, HCSB, KJV, NASB, NCV, NET, NIV, TEV]: *training to develop the body has some value, but training to develop godliness is valuable in all ways.* While the text says 'godliness is profitable', in the context of training this is talking about *training* in godliness being profitable [ICC, My, NIGTC, NTC, TG, TH]. 'Spiritual exercise is valuable in every way' [TEV]. It is spiritual exercise that needs to be practiced [ICC].

1.1 This acknowledges that there is some value in bodily training [AB, Alf, BKC, BNTC, ECC, ICC, LN, Lns, LSA, My, NIBC, NIGTC, NTC, NTIC, NTL, TG, TH, WBC; all versions except KJV]: *physical training has a little value, that is, it is of some value.* The comparison is between physical training and training for godly living, and although Paul does not belittle the benefits of physical training with its rewards of health, vigor, and beauty of one's physical form, it is very much inferior to the reward of the everlasting life in fellowship with God that is promised to a godly life [NTC]. It means that if you exercise you will get some benefit [TH], it will bring some good results [TG]. 'A little' means 'in a limited way', because physical exercise only affects one's human life [AB, NTIC]. This is not meant to encourage Timothy to take up physical exercise, it merely acknowledges that physical exercise is of some value [NIBC].

1.2 This does not affirm a positive value of physical training and perhaps downgrades it [Herm; probably KJV]: *physical training has little value.*

2. The adjectives ὀλίγον 'little' and πάντα 'all' refer to the value of ascetic training to control body and spiritual training to develop godliness, so that the argument is that disciplining the body to control bodily appetites may have some value, but spiritual exercise in godliness has value in every way [EGT, Lns, NAC, TC]. This is directed against prohibitions to marry and to eat meats (4:3), and although extreme bodily discipline is renounced, Paul admits that there is some profit in seeking to control the body [EGT, NAC]. This refers to training the body to keep its appetites in control by sober temperance in all bodily matters, and although this is a part of true godliness, it is only 'little' part in comparison with all that real godliness includes [Lns].

3. The adjectives ὀλίγον 'little' and πάντα 'all' refer to the temporal nature of physical exercise and godliness so that the argument is that the value of physical exercise lasts only for a little while the value of godliness lasts forever [ECC, WBC]. The main issue is not how much value physical exercise and godliness have, but how long exercise and godliness last [WBC]. The effects of a physical workout are momentary when compared with the effects of godliness which result in *eternal* life [ECC].

having promise[a] of-life[b] of-the now and of-the coming[c] (life).

LEXICON—a. ἐπαγγελία (LN 33.288) (BAGD 2.a. p. 280): 'promise' [BAGD, LN]. The phrase ἐπαγγελίαν ἔχουσα ζωῆς 'having promise of life' [KJV] is also translated 'having promise for the (present) life' [Lns], 'holding promise for the (present) life' [NIV, NRSV], 'promising benefits in (this) life' [NLT], 'it bears a promise of life' [AB], 'has the promise of life' [GW], 'it holds promise for the (present) life' [HCSB, NET], 'it promises life' [CEV], 'because it promises life' [TEV], 'because it holds a promise for the (present) life' [WBC], 'because a person can expect that' [LSA], 'since it holds promise for the (present) life' [NASB], 'since it holds the promise of life' [BNTC], 'since it holds out promise for (this) life' [REB], 'since it contains the promise of a life' [ECC], 'as it holds promise of life' [NTC], 'for it promises life' [Herm], 'by bringing you blessings in (this) life' [NCV]. This noun denotes the content of what is promised [LN].

b. ζωή (LN 23.88) (BAGD 1.a. p. 340): 'life' [BAGD, LN]. See the lexical item above for translations of this word. This noun denotes life in the physical sense [BAGD].

c. pres. act. participle of μέλλω (LN 67.62) (BAGD 2. p. 501): 'to be about to' [LN], 'to come, future' [BAGD]. The phrase ζωῆς τῆς νῦν καὶ τῆς μελλούσης 'life of the now and of the coming one' is translated 'for the present life and for the life to come' [Lns; HCSB, NASB, NET, NIV, NRSV], 'for the present life and for the coming life' [WBC], 'not only for this life but also for the life to come' [REB], 'of life here and now and of life to come' [BNTC], 'in this life and in the life to come' [NLT], 'life that is now and that is going to be' [ECC], 'in this life and in the future life, too' [NCV], 'life now and in eternity' [Herm], 'life now and in the world to come' [GW], 'of the life that now is, and of that which is to come' [KJV], 'while he lives now and when he lives in the future life' [LSA], 'life both now and in the future' [AB], 'life both for the present and for the future' [TEV], 'life now and forever' [CEV]. This verb means to occur at a point of time in the future, and it implies that another related event is subsequent to it [LN].

QUESTION—What relationship is indicated by the use of the participial phrase ἐπαγγελίαν ἔχουσα 'having promise'?

It indicates the grounds for saying that godliness is profitable for all things [BNTC, ECC, Herm, Lns, LSA, NAC, NICNT, NIGTC, NTC, NTL, TC; NASB, REB, TEV]. Godliness has promise in that this promise is inherent in the nature of godliness [NIGTC]. Godliness is the way to receive what God promises [ICC]. The promise is that godliness bears benefits in this age and in the age to come [WBC]. By means of spiritual exercise people can obtain the kind of life that God has promised to give [TH]. The practice of godliness will enable the believer to experience God's promise of eternal life in the present age, and this will carry on into the age to come [NICNT].

QUESTION—What is meant by the genitive construction ἐπαγγελίαν ζωῆς 'promise of life'?

The genitive ζωῆς 'of life' explains that what is promised is life now and to come [AB, Alf, Lns, NTC]. It is the life promised by God [Alf, NICNT, NIGTC, TH]. Or, godliness has inherent in itself a promise of life [NTL]. The life of the now is the present earthly life, and the life to come is the future life that follows the earthly life [My, WP]. This is not talking of two kinds of life as suggested by a translation such as 'for the present life and for the life to come'. Rather, this is the genitive of quality and means the content of the promise is life in its fullness both in the present age and in the age to come [NTC]. The word 'life' includes both the present and future aspects of salvation [ICC]. 'Life' is the eternal life that has already begun [NIBC, NICNT]. This life is the eternal life that God has promised, a life that starts now and instead of ceasing at death, goes on forever [TH]. Godliness 'has the promise of life' in that a person exercises in godliness because his hope is in God who has promised life and gives it in the Savior [NIGTC].

4:9 True/trustworthy/faithful (is) the statement and (it is) worthy of-all acceptance,[a]

LEXICON—a. See the exact wording of this whole verse at 1:15. The first clause, 'True/trustworthy/faithful (is) the statement' also occurs at 3:1.

QUESTION—What is the statement that this refers to?

There is no doubt that this same formula refers to what follows it in 1 Tim. 1:15 and it refers to what precedes it in Titus 3:8. However, in this verse the reference is not certain [TC].

1. The statement is contained in the preceding verse 4:8. However it is not certain whether this refers to all of 4:8 or to only the positive endorsement of godliness in the last part of that verse [NICNT].

1.1 The statement consists of all of verse 4:8 with the exception of its initial conjunction γάρ 'because' [AB, BKC, ECC, EGT, ICC, Lns, LSA, My, NIGTC, NTC, TH, WP; CEV, HCSB, NET, NLT]. Some translations enclose the statement in quotation marks [CEV, NET, NLT] or use a distinctive formatting [HCSB]. Although this same formula in 1:15 refers to what follows it, here the following clause begins with γάρ 'because' and does not seem to have the characteristics of the kind of statement that is described here in 4:9, so evidently this refers back to 4:8 which speaks of the promise of life both now and in the future [AB].

1.2 The statement consists of the last part of 4:8: 'godliness is profitable for all, having promise of life of the now and of the coming one' [BNTC, NAC, NIBC, NTL, TC]. This is the part that Paul elaborates on in 4:10 [BNTC, NAC, NIBC].

2. The statement is contained in the following verse 4:10.

2.1 The statement consists of the second part of 4:10, 'we have put our hope on a living God, who is a savior of all people, especially of believers [Alf, TNTC, WBC; NIV]. The clause 'and for this reason we labor and strive' is an introductory comment to the saying [WBC], and can be treated as a parenthetical comment [NIV].

2.2 The statement consists of all of 4:10 except for Paul's added comment, 'especially of believers' [REB].

4:10 Because[a] to[b] this we-labor[c] and we-struggle,[d]

TEXT—Instead of ἀγωνιζόμεθα 'we struggle', some manuscripts read ὀνειδιζόμεθα 'we suffer reproach'. GNT reads ἀγωνιζόμεθα 'we struggle' with a C decision, indicating that the committee had difficulty in making the decision. 'We suffer reproach' is read by KJV.

LEXICON—a. γάρ (LN 89.23): 'because' [LN], 'for' [BNTC, LN, NTC, WBC; KJV, NASB, NRSV], 'certainly' [GW], 'in fact' [HCSB, NET], 'yes' [Lns], not explicit [ECC, LSA; CEV, NCV, NLT, TEV]. This conjunction indicates the cause or reason between events [LN].

b. εἰς (LN 89.57, 89.48): 'for the purpose of, in order to' [LN (89.57)], 'with the result that, so that as a result' [LN (89.48)]. The phrase εἰς τοῦτο 'to this' is translated 'to this end' [NRSV], 'for this' [HCSB, NASB, NIV], 'this is why' [NCV, NET, NLT, REB], 'that's why' [CEV], 'this is the reason why' [LSA], '(we work hard and struggle) to live a godly life' [GW], 'therefore' [KJV], not explicit [TEV]. This preposition indicates intent and often implies an expected result [LN (89.57)], or it indicates result, usually of a preceding process [LN (89.48)].

   c. pres. act. indic. of κοπιάω (LN 42.47) (BAGD 2. p. 443): 'to labor' [BAGD, LN; HCSB, KJV, NASB], 'to toil' [BAGD, BNTC, LN, Lns, LSA, WBC; NRSV], 'to work hard' [BAGD, LN; CEV, GW, NET, NLT, TEV]. This is also translated as a noun phrase: 'our job' [ECC]. This verb means to engage in hard work, and it is implied that there are difficulties and trouble involved [LN]. This verb pertains to physical, mental, or spiritual exertion [BAGD].

   d. pres. mid./pass. (deponent = act.) indic., of ἀγωνίζομαι (LN 68.74) (BAGD 2.b. p. 15): 'to struggle' [BNTC, LSA, WBC; CEV, GW, NET, NLT, NRSV, TEV], 'to strive' [BAGD; HCSB, NASB], 'to strain' [Lns], 'to make every effort to, to do everything possible to, to strain oneself to' [LN]. This is also translated as a noun phrase: 'our contest' [ECC]. This verb means to strive to do something with great intensity and effort [LN]. It means to fight or struggle, and it can be used figuratively of any type of struggle or striving [BAGD]. See this word at 6:12.

QUESTION—What relationship is indicated by the conjunction γάρ 'because'?

  1. It indicates the grounds for Paul's declaration in 4:9 that the saying is true and should be accepted [EGT, ICC, NIBC, NTC]. If Paul didn't believe it, he wouldn't be toiling and striving so hard, so this affirms his conviction of the truth expressed in the faithful saying [NTC]. That 4:9 is true is confirmed by the fact that Paul's hard toil for the gospel has as its purpose the fulfillment of their hope in God to grant salvation to all believers [ICC].

  2. It confirms or emphasizes the trustworthiness of the statement [Herm, Lns, WBC]. Subjective actions cannot establish objective facts, so instead of giving a reason, it gives a consequence by saying that the statement is so trustworthy that Paul and Timothy labor and strive in the way they do [Lns]. The saying is not only trustworthy and worthy of full acceptance, but it also expresses the very goal of Paul's missionary activities [WBC]. This is a transition that applies the message to be believed to the ministry of Paul and Timothy [ECC].

  3. It gives the reason for Paul's declaration in 4:8 that godliness is profitable in all things [My, NAC, NICNT, NIGTC].

QUESTION—What is meant by the phrase εἰς τοῦτο 'to this' and to what does 'this' refer?

  1. The phrase εἰς τοῦτο means 'for this purpose' [BNTC, EGT, Herm, ICC, My, NTC, TH, WP; GW, NRSV; probably HCSB, NASB, NIV which translate it 'for this']: *this is our purpose in laboring and struggling.*

  1.1 They labor and strive in order to live a godly life [BKC, BNTC, Herm, My, WP; GW]. They labor and strive to reach the goal of the Christian training in 4:8 [Herm], that is, to be spiritually fit [TH]. Their purpose is to develop the godliness mentioned in 4:8 [BKC].

1.2 They labor and struggle with the goal of securing the blessed life mentioned in 4:8 [BNTC, EGT].

1.3 They labor and struggle to the end or purpose that people all over the world shall hear and accept the gospel and obtain eternal life [NTC].

2. The phrase εἰς τοῦτο means 'for this reason' [AB, LSA, NAC, NIBC, NICNT, TG, WBC; CEV, KJV, NCV, NLT, REB]: *this is the reason why we labor and struggle.*

2.1 This refers back to the trustworthy statement (4:9) that training for godliness leads to life (4:8) [AB, LSA, NIBC]: *training for godliness leads to life, and for this reason we labor and struggle.*

2.2 They labor and struggle because of their hope in the living God who wants to save all people (4:10b) [AB, LSA, TG, WBC; CEV, NCV, REB]. Paul labors and strives 'with respect to this reason', that he has set his hope on the living God [WBC].

2.3 They labor and struggle in their missionary labors because of what has been said in 4:8 about godliness and its promise of eternal life [NICNT].

QUESTION—Who is the referent of 'we' in the verbs κοπιῶμεν καὶ ἀγωνιζό-μεθα 'we labor and we struggle'?

The first person plural 'we' refers to Paul and Timothy [Herm, Lns, NICNT, NTC, WBC], or to Paul, Timothy, and perhaps others [TH], or to Paul and his coworkers [BNTC, ECC, ICC, NIGTC], or to Christians in general [Alf, EGT, My, NTL, TG].

QUESTION—In what way did they 'labor and struggle'?

Paul uses the metaphor to describe the laboring and buffeting he and his associates put up with in order to spread the gospel [BNTC] in missionary work [ICC, NICNT]. As in many of his letters, Paul uses these verbs to refer to the energy expended in the work of evangelizing and of encouraging Christian growth [LSA]. It refers to the work of proclaiming the gospel [NIGTC]. It refers to their missionary work and pastoral care, picturing this as hard work and wearisome routine [ECC]. It refers to their exertions to spread godliness among the people and to maintain it against the false teaching [Lns]. Their striving is not for their own fulfillment and perfection, but for the sake of the gospel [ICC]. Or, although these two verbs were usually used to describe the work of evangelism, in this verse they primarily relate to the Christian life [NTL], and the reproach that Christians face in the world [My]. The two verbs are virtually synonyms, the first referring to hard work and the second to intense struggle, and here the focus is on the activities involved in attaining spiritual fitness, not physical fitness [TH].

1. Both of these verbs continue the athletic metaphor where athletes toil and struggle in their training to receive a victor's wreath [AB, Herm, Lns, NIBC, TNTC, WBC]. 'Labor' refers to hard work, and this word was commonly used to refer to the work of Christians, but in company with

the next verb 'struggle', a word used in athletic contests, 'labor' also has athletic overtones [WBC].

2. The verb 'labor' refers to work, while 'struggle' is an athletic metaphor [ECC, NICNT, NTC]. 'Labor' refers to the elders' jobs of preaching and teaching, while 'struggle' refers to the metaphor of exercises in a gymnasium [ECC]. These two terms refer to the effort and risk involved in the work of the gospel [NICNT]. 'Labor' refers to manual labor or toil, while 'struggle' refers to the spiritual arena in which they struggle against the forces of darkness [NTC].

because we-have-put-our-hope^a on (the) living God,

LEXICON—a. perf. act. indic. of ἐλπίζω (LN **25.59**) (BAGD 3. p. 252): 'to put one's hope in someone' [BAGD], 'to hope, to hope for' [LN]. The clause ἠλπίκαμεν ἐπὶ 'we have set our hope on' [BNTC] is also translated 'we have put our hope in' [CEV, HCSB], 'we have placed our hope in' [**LN**, WBC; TEV], 'we have fixed our hope on' [NASB], 'we have set our hope on' [NET; similarly ECC; NRSV], 'we hope in' [NCV], 'our hope is in' [NLT], 'we place our confidence in' [GW], 'we trust in' [KJV], 'we expect that God will do this (because he lives)' [LSA]. This verb means to confidently look forward to something that is good and beneficial [LN]. The perfect tense indicates a settled, continuous state of hope [BKC, BNTC, EGT, NAC, NICNT, NIGTC, TH, TNTC]. This hope refers to an expectation of the future, accompanied by trust, and patience in waiting [NIGTC].

QUESTION—What relationship is indicated by the conjunction ὅτι 'because'?

It indicates the reason why they labored and strived [BKC, BNTC, Herm, ICC, Lns, My, NAC, NIBC, NICNT, NIGTC, NTC, NTL, TH, TNTC, WBC; CEV, HCSB, KJV, NASB, NRSV, TEV]: *we labor and we strive because we have put our hope in the living God.* Their hope is on the living God who promised the gift of godliness [NTC]. Their hope is in God who can give life for the present and the future [NIBC, NTL].

QUESTION—What is the function of the participle ζῶντι 'living'?

It functions as a grounds for having hope in God [BNTC, LSA]. Only a living God is able to keep his promise for the future and he is the basis of their hope [Lns, NAC, NTC]. This hope in God includes the knowledge that he is the savior of all [NIGTC]. Hope in God gives a certainty that he will fulfill his promise [My].

who is savior^a of-all people, especially^b of-believers.

LEXICON—a. σωτήρ (LN 21.31) (BAGD 1. p. 801): 'savior' [AB, BAGD, BNTC, ECC, Herm, LN, NTC, WBC; all versions]. This noun is also translated as a verb phrase: 'who saves' [LSA]. This noun denotes one who saves [LN]. See this word at 1:1.

b. μάλιστα (LN 18.7) (BAGD 1. p. 489): 'especially' [BAGD, BNTC, LN; CEV], 'very much, particularly' [LN], 'most of all, above all, particularly' [BAGD]. The phrase μάλιστα πιστῶν 'especially of believers' [NASB,

NET] is also translated 'especially of those who believe' [GW, HCSB, KJV, NCV, NRSV, TEV], 'but especially of those who have faith' [CEV], 'particularly of believers' [ECC], 'and particularly of all believers' [NLT], 'particularly of those who believe' [WBC], 'specifically, he saves those who believe in Christ' [LSA]. This adverb indicates a very high point on a scale of extent [LN].

QUESTION—What is the function of this clause?

It gives the grounds for having hope in God [LSA].

QUESTION—What is meant by the phrase μάλιστα πιστῶν 'especially of believers'?

1. This does not indicate a special position for the believers [AB], but makes the point that God's desire for all people be saved is particularly realized among the believers [AB, LSA]. God wants all people to be saved and he provided Christ as the ransom to make salvation available for all [BKC], yet God's desire to be savior comes to pass only for those who believe [BKC, Lns]. God wants to save all and all could be saved, but only those who believe are actually saved [Alf, EGT, Herm, TG]. God is the potential savior of all people, but only those who believe are actually saved [EGT, ICC, LSA, NIBC, NICNT, NTL]. That all are not saved is due to their stubborn opposition to God's will [NAC]. Or, 'all' is limited to believers: he is the Savior of all people, that is, of all who believe [NIGTC]. Or, Paul expresses his certainty about the believers, although he does not deny that others may receive salvation [BNTC].

2. The word 'Savior' is used in two senses [NTC, TNTC]. God is the savior of all men in the sense that he showers blessings on all men, but in a special sense he is savior to believers by imparting salvation and everlasting life to them [NTC, TNTC]. In the first sense, God is the Preserver of all people and in the second sense God singles out believers as special recipients of his saving power [TNTC].

DISCOURSE UNIT: 4:11–5:2 [Herm; HCSB]. The topic is Timothy as an example [Herm], instructions for ministry [HCSB].

DISCOURSE UNIT: 4:11–16 [ICC, NAC, NICNT]. The topic is the demonstration of Christian behavior [NAC], Timothy as a teacher [ICC], Timothy, a paradigm of the healthy teacher [NICNT].

4:11 Command[a] these (things) and teach[b] (them).

LEXICON—a. pres. act. impera. of παραγγέλλω (LN 33.327) (BAGD p. 613): 'to command' [AB, BAGD, BNTC, LN, LSA, NTC, WBC; HCSB, KJV, NCV, NET, NIV], 'to order' [LN, Lns], 'to charge' [ECC], 'to insist on' [BAGD; GW, NLT, NRSV, REB], 'to prescribe' [NASB], 'to preach' [Herm], 'to instruct, to urge' [BAGD]. This imperative is translated 'give these instructions' [TEV], 'tell everyone to do what you say' [CEV]. This verb means to announce what must be done [LN]. See this word at 1:3; 5:7; 6:13, 17.

b. pres. act. impera. of διδάσκω (LN 33.224) (BAGD 1. p. 192): 'to teach'
   [AB, BAGD, BNTC, ECC, Herm, LN, Lns, LSA, NTC, WBC; all
   versions]. This verb means to provide instruction in either a formal or
   informal setting [LN].

QUESTION—What are ταῦτα 'these things' that Timothy is to command and
to teach?

It must refer to what precedes this [ICC, NICNT]. Since similar verbs occur
at 4:6, 5:7, 6:2, and 6:17, it is probable that 'these things' relate to the verses
close at hand, likely the preceding section that consists of general truths for
believers, and not the following verses that refer almost exclusively to
Timothy [NCBC, NIGTC]. These things could refer to everything in the
letter up to 4:10, or it could refer to 4:1–10, or 4:6–10, or to 4:8–10, or just
4:10 [TH]. These things refer to 4:3–5 [LSA], or 4:6–10 [NAC]. Perhaps it
includes everything from 2:1 [NIBC]. Or, it refers to all the various portions
of advice Paul has given in the letter [BNTC, WBC]. It refers to all that Paul
has said about godliness [My].

QUESTION—Does this verse end the preceding paragraph or start a new
paragraph?

It begins a new paragraph [ECC, Herm, ICC, NAC, NICNT, NIGTC, NTC,
NTL, WBC; all versions except KJV]. This verse is a transition verse and
could also be taken as the conclusion to the preceding paragraph [NCBC,
NIGTC]. If it ends the preceding paragraph, it limits 'these things' to what
precedes, perhaps to only the immediately preceding verses. However, if it
begins a new paragraph, it has the disadvantage of being wrongly understood
to refer forward to the following verse [TH].

QUESTION—How are the two verbs 'command' and 'teach' related?

The order of the verbs 'command' and 'teach' is surprising, but understand-
able in that the stress on the preceding passage has been on heretical
practices and the need for piety. Timothy already has been instructed to give
commands to certain people in 1:3, and he is also to be a moral instructor to
the whole church [AB]. Timothy is to command false teachers to cease their
teaching, and he himself is to continue teaching the true doctrine [WBC].
These two verbs stress teaching and exhortation, the term 'command'
referring to the implementation of the preceding discussion and 'teach'
referring to doctrinal instruction in a congregational setting [NICNT].
Timothy is to take from the preceding verses what should be expressed as
exhortation and what may be taught as instructions for the church [ICC]. It is
clear from 4:6 that he is to teach the members of the church [ICC, NIGTC,
TG]. Some of the things he is to command are the direct commands in 4:7
and the implied commands in 4:3–4, 6, 8–9 [Alf, NTC], and he is to teach
things such as the coming apostasy (4:3), what God considers good (4:4–5),
and that the benefits from godly living transcend the results of physical
training (4:8–10) [NTC]. 'Command' refers to orders given by someone in
authority, and here Timothy is to command what Paul has communicated.
'Teach' refers to teaching the truths behind those orders [NIGTC, TC].

Timothy is to provide authoritative directions with his instructions for the church [ICC]. These two verbs indicate that Timothy is to teach with a note of authority so that his natural timidity is replaced with firmness [TNTC]. Or, there is no reason to think that Paul would have used a timid man to be his representative in the Asian churches [Lns]. In relation to the outworking of the two verbs, teaching the fundamentals comes before commanding what should be done about them [EGT]. Some translations reverse the order of the verbs: 'teach these things and tell everyone to do what you say' [CEV], 'teach these things and insist that everyone learn them' [NLT], 'insist on these things in your teaching' [REB].

4:12 **Let- no-one -despise[a] your youth,**

LEXICON—a. pres. act. impera. of καταφρονέω (LN 88.192) (BAGD 1. p. 420): 'to despise' [AB, BAGD, LN, Lns, NTC; HCSB, KJV, NRSV], 'to scorn, to look down on' [BAGD, LN], 'to disdain' [ECC], 'to treat with contempt' [BAGD], 'to be contemptuous' [Herm]. The whole clause is translated 'let no one depreciate you because you are young' [LSA], 'let no one look down on you because you are young' [NET; similarly NASB, NIV, TEV], 'don't let anyone look down on you for being young' [GW], 'don't let anyone think less of you because you are young' [NLT], 'let no one underrate you because you are young' [BNTC; REB], 'let no one treat you contemptuously because of your youth' [WBC], 'do not let anyone treat you as if you are unimportant because you are young' [NCV], 'don't let anyone make fun of you, just because you are young' [CEV]. This verb means to feel contempt for someone who is considered to be of no value [LN]. See this word at 6:2.

QUESTION—How young was Timothy?

There is no way to determine Timothy's exact age, but he was younger than Paul [Alf, NTL, TC, TH], and younger than many of the church leaders and members who were under his charge [TH, TNTC]. 'Youth' can refer to people from their early teens to their mid-forties [ECC, Lns]. Timothy was in his late twenties or early thirties [WBC], or in his thirties [NIGTC]. Timothy's age was probably between 22–27 [NTC], 25–30 [TG], 30–35 [NAC, NIBC], 35–40 [Lns]. Timothy was very young for the position he held [NTC]. The elders of congregations were commonly much older than Timothy, and in a case of disagreement some might despise him because he was a 'youth' in comparison with them [Lns, NTC, WBC].

QUESTION—How would Timothy prevent people from despising him?

This command directs Timothy to avoid giving others an opportunity to despise him [TG, WBC]. Timothy would avoid adverse remarks by having the type of character and conduct that Paul describes [Lns]. He must see to it that he was respected by how he conducted himself [NTC]. Criticism of Timothy's youth would be overcome by demonstrating maturity in his life and conduct [NIGTC]. This command would encourage Timothy in his work, and it would also impress the congregation about Timothy's authority when this letter was read to them in church [BNTC, NIBC].

but be an-example[a] (for) the believers in speech,[b] in conduct,[c]

LEXICON—a. τύπος (LN 58.59) (BAGD 5.b. p. 830): 'example' [BAGD, LN], 'model' [LN]. The phrase τύπος γίνου 'be an example for' [Lns, WBC; HCSB, TEV] is also translated 'be/become an example to' [BNTC, Herm; NCV, NLT, REB; similarly KJV], 'keep on being a pattern for' [ECC], 'become a model to' [AB; similarly NTC], 'set an example for' [CEV, NET, NIV, NRSV], 'show the people by example how they should' [LSA], 'make (your speech...) an example for' [GW], 'in (speech...) show yourself an example of' [NASB]. This noun denotes a model of behavior that is an example to be imitated [LN].

b. λόγος (LN 33.99) (BAGD 1.a.α. p. 477): 'speech' [LN; GW], 'speaking' [LN], 'word' [BAGD]. The phrase ἐν λόγῳ 'in speech' [AB, BNTC, NTC, WBC; HCSB, NIV, NRSV, REB] is also translated 'in your speech' [NET, TEV], 'in word' [ECC, Herm, Lns; KJV], 'with your words' [NCV], 'in what you say' [NLT], 'by what you say' [CEV], 'speak good things' [LSA]. This noun denotes the act of speaking [LN].

c. ἀναστροφή (LN 41.3) (BAGD p. 61): 'conduct, behavior' [BAGD, LN]. The phrase ἐν ἀναστροφῇ 'in conduct' [Herm, Lns, NTC, WBC; HCSB, NRSV] is also translated 'in your...conduct' [NET, TEV], 'in behavior' [AB, BNTC, ECC; GW, REB], 'in life' [NIV], 'in the way you live' [NLT], 'in conversation' [KJV], 'with...your actions' [NCV], 'by what you do' [CEV], 'conduct yourself well' [LSA]. This noun denotes one's conduct in regard to daily behavior [LN].

QUESTION—What relationship is indicated by ἀλλά 'but'?

This means 'rather, in order that they may respect you, show them by example how they should conduct themselves' [LSA].

QUESTION—Do the words τύπος γίνου 'be/become an example' indicate that he hadn't been an example up to then?

The present imperative verb γίνου 'become' does not mean that he had not yet become an example, rather, it indicates that he has been such an example and that he should continue to be such an example [Lns, My]. He was to keep on becoming an example to believers [ECC, WP].

QUESTION—In what way was Timothy to be an example?

Timothy was to be an example for them to follow [AB, BKC, BNTC, Herm, LSA, NCBC, NIBC, NIGTC, NTC, NTIC, NTL, TC, TG, TH, WBC, WP; CEV, GW, HCSB, NCV, NET, NLT, NRSV, REB]. The use of the genitive in the phrase τῶν πιστῶν 'the believers' means 'to believers' rather than 'what believers should be' [NIGTC]. The definite article with the word 'believers' specifies the believers to be those among whom Timothy lived [NIGTC]. Timothy was to be an example of what true believers are [NAC, NTC; KJV, NASB]. Timothy would be a spiritual example of what a believer can be, and the believers in Ephesus would be able to develop godliness by following his example [NAC].

QUESTION—What is meant by λόγος 'speech'?

This refers to his day-to-day conversation with others [BNTC, NIGTC, NTC, TH, WBC], since preaching is covered in the next verse [BNTC, NTC]. Or, it includes all forms of speaking including teaching [Lns]. It is everything he says in public and private [Alf, WP]. It means all types of verbal expression [NAC]. It concerns the intent, tone, and manner of his speech [NTL]. He should not get involved in arguments [NIBC].

QUESTION—What is meant by ἀναστροφή 'conduct'?

This refers to his general conduct in life [BNTC, NAC, TH, WBC]. It includes one's habits and ways of dealing with others [NTC].

in love[a], in faith/faithfulness,[b] in purity.[c]

TEXT—After the phrase ἐν ἀγάπῃ 'in love', some manuscripts include the phrase ἐν πνεύματι 'in spirit'. GNT does not mention this alternative. The phrase 'in spirit' is read by KJV.

LEXICON—a. ἀγάπη (LN 25.43) (BAGD I.1.a. p. 5): 'love' [LN; GW]. The phrase ἐν ἀγάπῃ 'in love' [BNTC, Herm, Lns, NTC, WBC; HCSB, NIV, NRSV, REB] is also translated 'in your...love' [NET, NLT, TEV], 'in charity' [ECC; KJV], 'by love' [AB], 'by your love' [CEV], 'with...your love' [NCV], 'love people' [LSA]. This noun denotes love for someone that is based on sincere appreciation and high regard [LN] See this word at 1:5, 14; 2:15; 6:11.

    b. πίστις (LN 31.85) (BAGD 2.d.γ. p. 663): 'faith' [BAGD, LN; GW], 'trust' [LN]. The phrase ἐν πίστει 'in faith' [BNTC, Herm, Lns, NTC, WBC; HCSB, KJV, NIV, NRSV] is also translated 'in your faith' [NLT, TEV], 'by faith' [AB], 'by your faith' [CEV], 'with...your faith' [NCV], 'trust God' [LSA], 'in fidelity' [REB], 'in faithfulness' [ECC], 'in your... faithfulness' [NET]. This noun denotes complete trust and reliance [LN]. It denotes the Christian virtue of true piety [BAGD]. See this word at 1:2, 4, 5, 14, 19; 3:13; 6:11.

    c. ἁγνεία (LN **88.29**) (BAGD p. 10): 'purity' [BAGD, **LN**; GW]. The phrase ἐν ἁγνείᾳ 'in purity' [BNTC, ECC, Herm, NTC, WBC; HCSB, KJV, NIV, NRSV, REB] is also translated 'in your...purity' [NET, NLT, TEV], 'in pureness' [Lns], 'by purity' [AB], 'by your purity' [CEV], 'with...your pure life' [NCV], 'you must be completely chaste' [LSA]. This noun denotes the quality of moral purity [LN].

QUESTION—How are these three descriptions related to the preceding two descriptions?

Some translate these as equal members in a list of five virtues [BNTC, ECC, Herm, Lns, NTC, WBC; GW, HCSB, KJV, NASB, NCV, NET, NIV, NLT, TEV]. Some join the preceding two nouns with the conjunction 'and', 'in speech and conduct', and then add these with connections such as 'as well as' [CEV], 'in' [NRSV, REB], 'by' [AB]. The first two go together, and the general word ἀναστροφή 'behavior' is specified by the three inward qualities that influence the kind of behavior that Paul particularly wished to be exemplified [AB]. It is not useful to classify these as being inward qualities since they all must be expressed outwardly so that the congregation can see them and imitate them [NIGTC]. Speech and conduct refer to outward demeanor; love, faith and purity are qualities that become apparent in word and conduct [Lns].

QUESTION—What is meant by ἀγάπη 'love'?

This is love for others [BNTC, LSA, NTC, TH], especially Christians [TH]. Love for others includes other believers, neighbors, and even enemies [NTC]. Love is for both God and others [NAC].

QUESTION—What is meant by πίστει 'faith'?

1. This is the quality of trusting God or Christ [LSA, NICNT, NIGTC, NTC]. It is belief in God [NICNT]. While love is a horizontal relationship with others, faith is a vertical relationship with God [NTC]. This speaks of growth in basic Christian trust [NIGTC].

2. This is the quality of faithfulness [BAGD, BNTC, NAC, TG]. It is an attitude of faithfulness and trustworthiness [NAC], reliability and dependability [TG].

3. This is the quality of both trusting in Christ and being faithful to him [TH].

QUESTION—What is meant by ἁγνεία 'purity'?

1. Purity pertains to all of his life and motives [Alf, BKC, BNTC, Lns, My, NAC, NIGTC, NTC, NTL, TC, TG, TH, WP]. It is general moral purity [Lns]. Here the word is used of Timothy's character and probably refers to the purity and integrity of his motives [NIGTC]. This means to be in conformity with God's law, both in thought and action [NTC]. It is living an upright moral life, especially being free from immoral acts [TH]. Of course this includes purity in matters of sex [BNTC, Lns, NAC, NIGTC, TG].

2. Here purity refers specifically to chastity in matters of sex [BAGD, LSA, NCBC, NICNT, WBC]. Since Timothy is not to give grounds for his youth to be criticized, this emphasis is appropriate [NICNT].

4:13 Until I-come attend-to[a] the reading,[b] the exhortation,[c] the teaching.[d]

LEXICON—a. pres. act. impera. of προσέχω (LN 68.19) (BAGD 1.c. p. 714): 'to continue to give oneself to, to continue to apply oneself to' [LN], 'to give oneself to, to occupy oneself with, to devote or apply oneself to' [BAGD]. This imperative is translated 'attend to' [NTC], 'give attendance to' [KJV, NET], 'give attention to' [HCSB, NASB, NRSV], 'pay attention to' [AB], 'concentrate on' [ECC; GW], 'be devoted to' [WBC], 'devote yourself to' [BNTC; NIV, REB], 'focus on' [NLT], 'give your time and effort to' [TEV], 'continue to' [NCV], 'continue (the reading)' [Herm], 'be sure to keep on (reading...) and don't stop (preaching, etc.)' [CEV], 'be sure that you (read, etc.)' [LSA]. This verb means to continue to do something with close attention and devotion [LN]. The present imperative means to keep on doing this [WP]. See this word at 1:4 where it is translated 'pay attention to'.

b. ἀνάγνωσις (LN 33.68) (BAGD 1. p. 53): 'reading' [AB, BAGD, LN, WBC; KJV], 'public reading' [BAGD; HCSB], 'Scripture reading' [BNTC], 'the reading aloud of the scriptures' [Herm], 'the public reading of Scripture' [NTC; NASB, NET, NIV, NRSV, REB; similarly TEV]. 'your public reading of the Scriptures' [ECC], This noun is also translated as a verb: 'to read the Scriptures to the people' [NCV], 'read the Scriptures to the congregation' [LSA], 'reading the Scriptures to the church' [NLT], 'reading Scriptures/Scripture in worship' [CEV, GW]. This noun denotes the reading of something written, and the reading is normally done aloud [LN].

c. παράκλησις (LN 25.150) (BAGD 1. p. 618): 'exhortation' [AB, BAGD, BNTC, Herm, WBC; HCSB, KJV, NASB, NET, REB], 'exhorting' [NTC; NRSV], 'preaching' [ECC; CEV, TEV], 'encouragement' [BAGD, LN]. This noun is also translated as a verb phrase: 'exhort them' [LSA], 'strengthen them' [NCV], 'giving encouraging messages' [GW], 'encouraging the believers' [NLT]. This noun denotes encouragement or consolation, either by verbal or non-verbal means [LN].

d. διδασκαλία (LN 33.224) (BAGD 1. p. 191): 'teaching' [AB, BNTC, Herm, LN, NTC, WBC; CEV, HCSB, NASB, NET, NIV, NRSV, REB, TEV], 'instruction' [ECC], 'the act of teaching or instruction' [BAGD], 'doctrine' [KJV]. This noun is also translated as a verb phrase: 'teach them' [LSA; NCV], 'teaching them' [NLT], 'teaching people' [GW]. This noun denotes instruction in either a formal or informal setting [LN].

QUESTION—What is meant by the words ἕως ἔρχομαι 'until I come'?

In 3:14–15 Paul said that he hoped to come to Timothy quickly, but there might be a delay [AB, BNTC, ICC, NTL, WBC]. These are Timothy's duties while Paul was traveling [Lns]. It reminds Timothy to keep on doing these things [TG], and it does not imply that Timothy was to stop doing these things after Paul arrived [ECC, NCBC, TG]. It does not mean that when Paul arrived, he would take over the duties mentioned here. Instead, it appears that when Paul arrived, he would give Timothy new duties [TH].

QUESTION—What is the significance of the definite article τῇ 'the' before each of the three nouns?

The article before each of the three nouns here indicate that they were standard parts of church worship [BNTC, NICNT, TH, WBC]. These three items are picked because they are based on Scripture, but more would be done in a meeting [ICC]. Of course worship would also include prayer, singing, personal testimonies, and the Lord's Supper, but the three items that are mentioned would be a way of combating false teaching that occurred in Ephesus [NAC, NIBC].

QUESTION— How was Timothy to attend (πρόσεχε) to these things?

1. This refers to how Timothy was to personally conduct meetings of the congregation [AB, Alf, BNTC, ECC, NIBC, NICNT, NTL, TH, TNTC, WBC].
2. This refers to Timothy's duty to pay close attention to what was going on in the various congregations in the area [Lns, NTC]. This isn't telling Timothy to read, exhort, and teach when he conducted meetings, but to pay close attention to what was going on in the various congregations he was responsible for. He must pay close attention to what was being read and taught since there were people in the churches who might ask for certain parts of the genealogies or law to be read so they could go on to pin their myths and false teachings on them. Timothy has already been told to stop such things in 1:4 [Lns]. Timothy was to see to it that all the churches of Ephesus and its surroundings had these three elements in their public worship [NTC].
3. This refers to what happened in church, whether it was carried out by Timothy himself or it was the activities organized by him [ICC].

QUESTION—What is meant by τῇ ἀναγνώσει 'the reading'?

This refers to reading the Scriptures to the congregation [EGT, NICNT, NTL, TH, TNTC, WBC], and the words 'the reading' was a technical term for this practice [NTL], This refers to reading the Old Testament to the believers [TG]. It means the reading of the Old Testament Scriptures plus the growing New Testament [BNTC, ICC, NICNT, NIGTC, NTC, TH]. It would include Paul's own letters [AB, NICNT, NIGTC, TC].

QUESTION—What is mean by τῇ παρακλήσει 'the exhortation'?

This noun denotes exhortation, encouragement, or consolation [AB, BAGD, ICC, LN, NTC, TH]. The word refers to warning against error as well as giving advice and encouragement [NTC]. The word refers to either reprimand or encouragement as motivation to change one's behavior [NTL]. After the reading of Scripture, there would be a period of encouraging and exhorting the people to follow the Scripture that had been read [WBC]. Probably in this context the word means exhortation rather than comfort, and 'exhortation' refers to preaching to the congregation [AB]. Exhortation refers to the exposition and application of the Scriptures [BKC, BNTC, TG]. The phrase 'the exhortation' refers to the sermon [ICC, TC], which would explain the Scriptures and lead to commands or encouragement for the congregation depending on the type of Scripture that was read [ICC]. The preaching would include moral instruction with an appeal to the will [NAC]. It refers to explaining the meaning and relevance of the passages that were read [TH]. It probably focuses on explaining the true faith in contrast with the false teachings [ICC]. This verb means to summon the congregation to respond to the scripture that has been read, and the summons would take the form of exhortation or comfort depending on the message of the passage [NIGTC]. Probably this does not mean that exhortation precedes teaching since exhortation is actually based on instruction [WP].

QUESTION—What is meant by τῇ διδασκαλίᾳ 'the teaching'?

This third duty is to bring a fuller understanding of the meaning of the text of the Scriptures that had been read to the congregation [WBC]. This refers to teaching facts about doctrine and morals [NTC], or the duties of the believers [TG]. It would not be limited to the text that was read at that meeting [Lns]. Teaching would be intermingled with the preaching [AB]. The teaching gives information about the Christian faith [NAC, TNTC]. It was catechetical instruction about Christian doctrines [BKC, BNTC, TH].

4:14 Do- not -neglect[a] the gift[b] in you, which was-given to-you

LEXICON—a. pres. act. impera. of ἀμελέω (LN **30.50**) (BAGD p. 44): 'to neglect' [BAGD, ECC, **LN**, LSA, WBC; all versions except CEV, NCV], 'to disregard, to pay no attention to' [LN], 'to be unconcerned about' [BAGD], 'to be careless about' [Lns], 'to be careless with' [AB], 'to grow careless about' [NTC], 'to leave unused' [BNTC]. The negative command 'do not neglect' is also translated positively: 'use (the gift)' [Herm; CEV, NCV]. This verb means to not think about something and as a result not be able to respond appropriately to it [LN]. This command does not imply blame [My]. Or, this suggests that Timothy should stop neglecting this gift [NAC].

b. χάρισμα (LN 57.103) (BAGD 2. p. 879): 'gift' [BAGD, LN, NTC, WBC; HCSB, KJV, NRSV], 'gracious gift' [ECC, LN], 'gift of grace' [Herm], 'spiritual gift' [NASB, TEV], 'special gift' [BNTC], 'the special gift for service' [AB], 'charisma' [Lns]. The phrase τοῦ ἐν σοὶ χαρίσματος, ὃ ἐδόθη σοι 'the gift in you, which was given to you' is translated 'your gift, which was given you' [NIV], 'the gift you were given' [CEV], 'the gift you have, which was given to you' [NCV], 'the spiritual gift you have, given to you' [NET], 'the spiritual gift you received' [NLT], 'the gift which you received' [GW], 'the spiritual endowment given you' [REB], 'what God has graciously enabled you to do' [LSA]. This noun denotes that which is given freely and generously [LN]. This denotes a special non-material gift that God graciously bestows on individual Christians [BAGD].

QUESTION—What was τοῦ χαρίσματος 'the gift'?

It was a spiritual gift to equip Timothy for his ministry [AB, BKC, BNTC, ICC, My, NIBC, NICNT, NIGTC, TG, TH, TNTC, WBC]. The gift was the ability to teach and preach [EGT, NAC], and also the ability to understand the gospel and to be able to recognize error [NAC]. It was the gift of teaching and ruling the church [Alf]. It was the gift of discernment that enabled him to discern whether a teaching was true or false [NTC]. Or, the preceding verse suggest that he had received the non-miraculous gifts of prophecy and discerning the spirits so that he could understand and teach the true message of the gospel and detect deviations from it [Lns]. It is unusual to speak of a spiritual gift being in Timothy instead of being given to him, but since the Spirit indwells him, the Spirit's gifts can also be thought of indwelling Timothy [ICC].

QUESTION—Who is the implied actor in the passive phrase ὃ ἐδόθη σοι 'which was given to you'?

1. The source of the gift was God [Alf, BKC, ECC, EGT, Lns, NICNT, NIGTC, NTC, NTL, TC, TG, WBC, WP]: *the gift in you that God gave you.* In 2 Tim. 1:6 it speaks of τὸ χάρισμα τοῦ θεοῦ 'the gift of God' [NIGTC].

2. The source of the gift was the Holy Spirit [BNTC, My, NIBC, TH]: *the gift in you that the Holy Spirit gave you.* That the Spirit is the source of spiritual gifts is made clear in 2 Tim. 1:7 [NIBC], or in 1 Cor. 12:4 [My].

QUESTION—How could the gift be neglected?

Timothy would neglect the gift he had in him by failing to use the spiritual power and authority he had received, thus failing to meet the obligations that came with the possession of the gift [ICC]. The phrase 'do not be careless of' is a litotes in which a strong positive command is expressed by a negative statement, and the present imperative stresses that this command is of an ongoing character [ECC, ICC, Lns, TG, TH]: *diligently keep on using your gift.*

through/with[a] prophecy[b]

LEXICON—a. διά (LN 89.76) (BAGD III.1.a. or c. p. 180): 'by means of, through' [BAGD (III.1.a.), LN], 'by' [LN], 'with' [BAGD (III.1.c.)]. This preposition can indicate the means by which one event makes another event possible [BAGD (III.1.a.), LN], or it can indicate attendant circumstances [BAGD (III.1.c.)]. See the following lexical item for translations of this preposition.

b. προφητεία (LN 33.460) (BAGD 3.b. p. 722): 'prophecy' [BAGD, LN], 'inspired utterance' [LN]. The phrase διὰ προφητείας is translated 'through prophecy' [AB, WBC; GW, HCSB, NCV, NRSV], 'through prophetic utterance' [NTC; NASB], 'through a prophetic message' [NIV], 'through the word of the prophet' [Herm], 'by means of prophecy' [Lns], 'by prophecy' [KJV], 'by prophetic words' [NET], 'by means of men prophesying about you' [LSA], 'under prophetic direction' [ECC], 'under the guidance of prophecy' [REB], 'through the prophecy spoken over you' [NLT], 'when the prophets spoke' [CEV, TEV], 'to the accompaniment of prophecy' [BNTC]. This noun denotes an utterance that is inspired by God [LN, NIGTC]. See this word at 1:18.

QUESTION—What relationship is indicated by the preposition διά 'through/with'?

1. The preposition διά indicates the means by which the gift was given to Timothy [Alf, BKC, ECC, Lns, LSA, My, NIBC, TC, WBC; all versions except CEV, NET, TEV]: *the gift that was given to you through prophecy.*

1.1 The gift was given through a specific prophecy spoken at the time the gift was given [BKC, ECC, LSA, TC, WBC]. The gift had come to

Timothy through a prophetic message at the time of his ordination [BKC]. Prophecy was the medium through which the gift came [TC]. This refers to the prophetic participation involved in the bestowment of God's gift [ECC].

1.2 The gift was given over a period of time. Timothy received the ability to teach and discern false teachings by means of listening to the teachings of Paul, the most capable prophet of all [Lns].

2. The preposition διά indicates attendant circumstances [AB, BNTC, EGT, ICC, NICNT, NTC, TG, TH, WBC, WP; CEV, NET, TEV]: *the gift that was given to you and this was accompanied by prophecy.* Here the preposition indicates accompanying circumstances, so that this can be stated 'accompanied by prophecy' [BNTC; NET]. This preposition has the same meaning as the following preposition μετά 'with', so instead of saying that the prophecy was the efficient cause of Timothy's gifts, the prophecy was uttered when God gave the gift [EGT, WBC]. Prophecy wasn't the means by which the gift was given since the passive verb 'was given' refers to God or the Holy Spirit as being the giver, so the prophecy was the words spoken by a prophet or prophets who confirmed and identified the gift, thus authorizing his ministry to the church [NICNT]. The Holy Spirit had given Timothy God's gift when people spoke about what would happen to him in the future [TH]. Some appear to say that the gift had been given to Timothy and leave it open as to when it was made known by prophecy [BNTC, TG]. When the prophecy was uttered, God's gift to Timothy was made known [TG]. Paul's choice of Timothy was endorsed by Spirit-inspired utterances of men who were prophets [BNTC].

QUESTION—What was the message of the prophecy?

Perhaps it was God's message of what he would do through Timothy's ministry [TH; NET]. The prophecy probably informed the elders that God had gifted Timothy for his task [NIGTC]. The prophecy affirmed that Timothy had been called by God [ICC, NAC, NCBC]. Or, the Holy Spirit inspired certain men to speak at Timothy's ordination to endorse the choice of Timothy [BNTC]. Or, the prophecy inspired by the Spirit at the time of ordination might have been a word of promise, exhortation, or prayer [My]. The prophecy made Timothy aware of the kind of gift he had received and the character of the work he was to do [NTC]. Or, the prophecy consisted of the teachings of the prophet Paul [Lns].

with (the) laying-on[a] of-the hands of-the council-of-elders.[b]

LEXICON—a. ἐπίθεσις (LN **85.51**) (BAGD p. 293): 'the laying on' [LN]. The phrase μετὰ ἐπιθέσεως τῶν χειρῶν τοῦ πρεσβυτερίου 'with the laying on of the hands of the council of elders' is translated 'with the laying on of hands by the council of elders' [HCSB, NRSV], 'with the laying on of hands by the presbytery' [NASB; similarly NTC; KJV], 'together with laying on of the hands of the presbytery' [Lns], 'after the elders had laid their hands (on you)' [**LN**], 'when the elders laid their hands on you' [REB], 'when the elders laid hands on you' [NET, TEV], 'when the group of elders laid their hands on you' [NCV], 'with the laying on of the hands of the body of elders' [WBC], 'with a laying on of hands by the board of elders' [AB], 'when the body of elders laid their hands on you' [NIV], 'when the elders laid their hands upon you' [Herm], 'when the elders of the church laid their hands on you' [NLT], 'when...the group of church leaders blessed you by placing their hands on you' [CEV], 'with an imposition of the hands of the presbytery' [ECC], 'along with the laying on of hands for ordination as an elder' [BNTC], 'when the spiritual leaders placed their hands on you to ordain you' [GW], 'and by means of the elders laying their hands on you' [LSA]. This noun denotes the event of placing something on something [LN].

b. πρεσβυτέριον (LN **11.84**) (BAGD 2. p. 699): 'the council of elders' [BAGD, LN; HCSB, NRSV], 'group of elders' [LN], 'group of church leaders' [CEV], 'body of elders' [WBC; NIV], 'elders' [Herm, **LN**, LSA; NET, REB, TEV], 'spiritual leaders' [GW], 'presbytery' [Lns, NTC; KJV, NASB]. This noun denotes a council of elders [LN].

QUESTION—What relationship is indicated by the preposition μετά 'with'?

1. It indicates attendant circumstances [AB, BNTC, ECC, EGT, Herm, Lns, NICNT, NIGTC, NTC, TC, TH, WBC, WP; all versions]. Receiving the gift and the prophecy was accompanied by the laying on of hands [NIBC, NTC, TC]. The elders responded to the prophecy by obediently laying their hands of Timothy [NIGTC].

2. It indicates the second means God used in giving the gift [LSA].

QUESTION—What was the significance of laying hands on Timothy?

This action signified ordination to a ministry [BNTC, My, NCBC, NIBC, NIGTC, TC; GW]. It was a commissioning ritual to identify a person's call to some specific task (Acts 6:6; 13:3; 1 Tim. 1:18; 4:14; 5:22) [WBC]. It symbolized a transfer of power from those in whom it resided to the one on whom they placed their hands [NTL]. Or, instead of an ordination ceremony, it was a special church service to recognize and affirm Timothy's gift and thus allow Timothy to freely minister among the Ephesians [NAC]. It consecrated Timothy to his office of authority over several congregations [Herm]. Or, it was an act signifying the giving of blessing [CEV]. This ceremony served to remind Timothy and the congregation that he had spiritual gifts that had been confirmed by prophecy [ICC, NAC]. The verb refers to an act of *pressing* one's hands on a person and is to be distinguished from another act of placing hands on someone for blessings and healing [BNTC].

QUESTION—What was the πρεσβυτέριον 'council of elders'?

The council of elders was the Christian counterpart to the Jewish elders in a synagogue [TG]. This council was a body of elders in the Ephesian church [Alf, BNTC, NAC, NIGTC, WBC], but calling them a presbytery would be anachronistic since such an office was not in existence until the second century [WBC].

4:15 Practice/consider[a] these (things), be in[b] these (things),

LEXICON—a. pres. act. impera. of μελετάω (LN **30.20** or **68.20**) (BAGD 2. p. 500): 'to practice' [BAGD, LN (68.20)], 'to continue to do' [LN (68.20)], 'to ponder, to let one's mind dwell on, to keep thinking about, to fix one's attention on' [LN (30.20)]. The imperative μελέτα is translated 'practice' [Herm, **LN** (68.20); GW, HCSB, TEV] 'continually practice' [WBC], 'continue to do' [NCV], 'put into practice' [NRSV], '(these matters) are what you are to do' [LSA], 'to continue to care for' [Lns], 'let (these things) be your constant care' [NTC], 'make (these matters) your business' [REB], 'take pains with' [NASB, NET], 'be diligent in' [NIV], 'keep thinking carefully about' [**LN** (30.20)], 'meditate upon' [KJV], 'let (these matters) be your study' [ECC], 'remember' [CEV], 'pay attention to' [AB], 'give your mind to' [BNTC], 'give your complete attention to' [NLT]. This verb means to continue to perform certain activities with care and concern [LN (68.20)], or to keep on giving serious consideration to something [LN (30.20)]. The present tense indicates the continuous aspect of the four present imperatives in 4:15–16, showing Paul's concern that this be a day-to-day activity [WBC]. Many point out the importance of this continuative aspect [LN, Lns, NTC, WP; NCV]. Timothy is told to continue in what he already was doing [Lns], he was to keep on doing it [WP].

b. The phrase εἰμὶ ἐν 'be in' is an idiom (LN **68.20**) (BAGD III.4. p. 225) meaning to continue to perform certain activities with care and concern (LN **68.20**). The imperative clause ἐν τούτοις ἴσθι 'be in these things' is translated 'in these things ever be' [Lns], 'be absorbed in them' [ECC; NASB, NET; similarly NTC], 'make them your absorbing interest' [REB], 'occupy yourself with these things' [Herm], 'immerse yourself in them' [WBC], 'be committed to them' [HCSB], 'on them you are to concentrate' [LSA], 'give yourself to these things' [**LN**], 'devote yourself to these things' [BAGD; NRSV, TEV], 'devote your life to them' [GW], 'busy yourself with these things' [BNTC], 'give yourself wholly to them' [KJV, NIV], 'give your life to doing them' [NCV], 'throw yourself into your tasks' [NLT], 'think about them' [CEV], 'live by them' [AB].

QUESTION—What is the referent of ταῦτα 'these things'?

This refers to the various things to be done in 4:1–14 [NTC], 4:6–14 [NCBC], 4:11–14 [Lns], 4:12–13 [ICC, NICNT], 4:12–14 [Alf, NAC, TH], 4:13 [TG, TNTC], 4:13–14 [Herm], or the whole letter [NCBC]. It is a generic reference to Paul's teachings [ECC]. The phrase 'in these things' means 'in this kind of activity' [Herm].

QUESTION—What is meant by the command μελέτα 'practice/consider (these things)'

1. This is a command to keep doing the preceding things [EGT, Herm, ICC, My, LSA, NICNT, TH, WBC, WP; GW, HCSB, NCV, NRSV, TEV]. Since the purpose of this command is that people should *see* Timothy's progress, the focus of the verb is on 'practice', not 'meditate' [WBC]. The command 'put into practice' is the positive equivalent of the preceding verse's command 'do not neglect' [TH].

2. The is a command to be completely involved in the preceding things [ECC, Lns, NAC, NIGTC, NTC, TNTC, WBC; CEV, KJV, NASB, NET, NIV, NLT, REB]. It is more comprehensive than just practicing them [NIGTC]. This thought is repeated in the following command for emphasis [Lns]. He was to ponder over the directions [NAC, TC], and then put them into operation [NAC].

QUESTION—What is meant by the command ἐν τούτοις ἴσθι 'be in these things'?

This refers to intense and total involvement in these things [NIGTC]. It means to be completely committed to them [ICC], to be completely wrapped up in them [Lns, NTC, TH], to be fully devoted to them [NICNT], and to be absorbed in them [TH, TNTC]. Although the verb 'to be' does not mean 'immerse', this phrase indicates Paul's intention that he be immersed in these things [WBC]. Together, the two commands make the point very emphatically [TH].

in-order-that your progress[a] may-be-evident[b] to-all.

LEXICON—a. προκοπή (LN **13.57**) (BAGD p. 707): 'progress' [BAGD, BNTC, ECC; Herm, **LN**, NTC, WBC; all versions except CEV, KJV], 'advancement' [BAGD, LN, Lns], 'profiting' [KJV]. The whole clause is translated 'so everyone can see how well you are doing' [CEV], 'in order that all people may see that you are improving in doing them' [LSA]. This noun denotes the change of one's state for the better by advancing and making progress [LN].

b. φανερός (LN 28.58) (BAGD 1. p. 852): 'evident, clearly known, easily known, plain, clear' [LN]. The phrase φανερὰ ᾖ πᾶσιν 'may/will be evident to all/everyone' [NTC; HCSB, NASB] is also translated 'may be obvious to all' [BNTC], 'may be manifest to all' [Lns], 'may/might be visible to all' [Herm, WBC], 'may be seen by all/everyone' [NCV, TEV], 'may appear to all' [KJV], 'can be perceived by all' [ECC], 'may be plain to all' [REB], 'everyone can/may/will see' [CEV, GW, NET, NIV, NLT; similarly LSA; NRSV]. This adjective describes something that can be clearly and easily known [LN].

QUESTION—What relationship is indicated by the conjunction ἵνα 'in order that'?

The conjunction indicates the immediate purpose of the preceding commands [Lns, LSA, NICNT, NIGTC, TH, WBC, WP], or the contemplated result [Lns, NTC].

QUESTION—What is Timothy to make progress in?

Timothy was to make progress or advancement in the faith [NIGTC], the development of his life as a Christian [TH], his Christian character and effective ministry [ICC, NTC, TC, TG], being a faithful minister of the gospel [NIBC, TNTC], the duties of his office [Alf]. This concerns his work so that as people observed him, they could see that he was the man suited for his position in the church [Lns]. Or, this refers to improving in accomplishing the commands in the preceding orders [LSA].

4:16 **Watch[a] yourself and the teaching,[b] continue[c] in-them;**

LEXICON—a. pres. act. impera. of ἐπέχω (LN 27.59) (BAGD 2.a. p. 285): 'to pay attention to, to keep on the lookout for, to be alert for, to be on one's guard against' [LN], 'to take pains' [BAGD]. The phrase ἔπεχε σεαυτῷ 'watch yourself' [**LN**, WBC; TEV] is translated 'keeping close watch on yourself' [REB], 'look to yourself' [BNTC, NTC], 'take heed unto thyself' [KJV], 'pay attention to yourself' [ECC], 'pay close attention to yourself' [NASB, NRSV], 'be attentive to yourself' [AB], 'continue to heed to thyself' [Lns], 'be conscientious about yourself' [HCSB], 'be conscientious about how you live' [NET], 'watch your life closely' [NIV], 'focus on your life' [GW], 'keep a close watch on how you live' [NLT], 'be careful about the way you live' [CEV], 'be careful in your life' [NCV], 'take heed that you conduct yourself well' [LSA], 'take pains with yourself' [Herm]. This verb means to be in a continuous state of readiness to learn of any future danger, need, or error, and then to respond appropriately [LN]. The present imperatives in this verse mean *keep on* doing it, not *begin doing it* [Lns, WP].

b. διδασκαλία (LN 33.224) (BAGD 1. p. 191): 'teaching' [BAGD, LN], 'instruction' [BAGD]. The phrase καὶ τῇ διδασκαλίᾳ 'and the teaching' [WBC] is also translated 'and with the teaching' [Herm], 'and to the teaching' [Lns, NTC], 'and unto the doctrine' [KJV], 'and doctrine' [NIV], 'and your teaching' [AB, LN; GW, HCSB, TEV], 'and to the teaching' [AB], 'and to your teaching' [NASB, NRSV], 'and in your teaching' [NCV], 'and on your teaching' [NLT, REB], 'and what you teach' [CEV, NET], 'and that you teach the good doctrine' [LSA], 'and to your instructions' [ECC]. This noun denotes instruction that is provided in a formal or informal setting [LN].

c. pres. act. impera. of ἐπιμένω (LN 68.11) (BAGD 2. p. 296): 'to continue' [BAGD, LN], 'to remain in, to keep on' [LN], 'to persist in' [BAGD]. The clause ἐπίμενε αὐτοῖς 'continue in them' [KJV] is also translated 'continue in these things' [NRSV], 'keep on doing these things' [TEV],

'keep on doing this' [CEV], 'continue to do this' [LSA], 'continue to do
what I've told you' [GW], 'persevere in these things' [HCSB, NASB],
'persevere in these activities' [ECC], 'persevere in them' [NTC; NIV,
REB], 'persevere in this' [NET], 'be persistent in them' [WBC], 'stay true
to what is right' [NLT], 'remain steady in both' [AB], 'keep remaining in
them' [Lns], 'hold on to these things' [Herm], 'stick to the directions
given' [BNTC]. This verb means to continue in an activity or state [LN].
It means to persist or continue in something [ICC, NICNT], to persevere
in them [NICNT].

QUESTION—What is meant by the command ἔπεχε σεαυτῷ 'watch yourself'?
This refers back 4:12 and perhaps 4:14 as well [TH]. This means he is to fix
his attention on himself in regard to his spiritual progress [ICC]. It refers to
his conduct [NICNT, WBC], and character [AB, NICNT] both as a Christian
and as a minister [TG]. His moral conduct must conform to the Christian
standard [NCBC]. He must scrutinize his behavior [NAC], since he is an
example for the believers (4:12) [NIBC]. This is described in 4:7 as being
trained in godliness [NIGTC]. He is to focus his mind on his duties and his
gift [NTC]. He must see to it that he carefully follows Paul's instructions in
this letter [BKC]. It means to be all that he should be in his responsible
position [Lns]. Timothy must hold tightly to what he is [WBC].

QUESTION—What is meant by the command ἔπεχε... τῇ διδασκαλίᾳ
'watch...the teaching'?
1. 'The teaching' refers to the content and quality of Timothy's instruction
[AB, ICC, NAC, NCBC, NIGTC, TC, TG, TH, WBC]. Timothy must
heed his own presentation of the truth [TC]. The noun 'teaching'
emphasizes the act of teaching, although the content of the teaching is not
excluded [NIBC]. 'Teaching' refers back to 4:13, and this command
pertains to both the activity of teaching and to the content of what is
taught [TH]. Timothy must pay close attention to what he teaches [TG].
He must scrutinize his theology [NAC]. His teaching must conform to the
norm of Christian orthodoxy [NCBC]. It refers to holding to biblical
doctrine and not be caught up in the teachings of his opponents [WBC].
Timothy is to be loyal to the teaching and constantly urge others to accept
it [NIGTC]. Here it refers to paying attention to doctrine in regards to
teaching others [ICC]. The words τῇ διδασκαλί 'the teaching' refers the
good teaching that Timothy had received and followed (4:6) [LSA,
NIGTC], the apostolic teaching [NICNT]. He will be loyal to the teaching
and constantly urge that teaching on others [NIGTC].
2. 'The teaching' refers to the teaching that is done by whoever teaches
under Timothy's supervision in the Ephesian churches [Lns, NTC]. Paul
is not speaking about Timothy's personal preaching, which was not in
doubt [Lns]. Or, it includes both the teaching of Timothy and of the others
in the district [NTC].

QUESTION—What is the referent of αὐτοῖς 'them'?
1. The pronoun αὐτοῖς 'them' refers to ταῦτα 'these things' in 4:15 [Alf,
   BNTC, ECC, Herm, ICC, Lns, TC, WBC; possibly NICNT]. It is
   impossible to take αὐτοῖς 'them' as referring to 'yourself and your
   teaching' so it has to go back to ταῦτα 'these things' in the preceding
   verse [BNTC].
2. The pronoun αὐτοῖς 'them' refers to the two aspects of his life just
   mentioned in this verse, watching himself and watching the teaching [AB,
   NIBC, NIGTC, NTC, TG, TH; possibly NICNT]. He will discharge his
   duties and obligations as teacher and leader of the congregation [TH].
   These two obligations clarify what is meant by 'these things' in 4:15
   [NIBC].
3. The pronoun αὐτοῖς 'them' refers to all the instruction from 4:12 onward
   [My].

**because doing[a] this you-will-save[b] both yourself and the (ones) hearing[c]
you.**
LEXICON—a. pres. act. participle of ποιέω (LN 90.45): 'to do, to practice'
   [LN]. The phrase τοῦτο ποιῶν 'doing this' is translated 'by doing so'
   [NET, REB], 'by doing this' [Lns, LSA, NTC, WBC; HCSB], 'if you do'
   [NIV, TEV], 'if you do this' [AB, ECC; GW], 'if you do that' [Herm], 'in
   doing this' [KJV, NRSV], 'in acting thus' [BNTC], 'as you do this'
   [NASB]. This is combined with the preceding clause: 'keep on doing this
   and you will...' [CEV], 'if you continue to live and teach rightly, you
   will...' [NCV], 'stay true to what is right for the sake of your own
   salvation' [NLT].
   b. fut. act. indic. of σῴζω (LN 21.27) (BAGD 2.a.β. p. 798): 'to save'
   [BAGD, LN]. The clause σεαυτὸν σώσεις 'you will save yourself' [AB,
   BNTC, ECC, Herm, LSA, NTC, WBC; CEV, GW, KJV, NCV, NET,
   NIV, NRSV, REB, TEV; similarly Lns] is also translated 'you will ensure
   salvation for yourself' [NASB], '(for the sake of) your own salvation'
   [NLT]. This verb means to cause someone to experience divine salvation
   [LN]. See this word at 1:15; 2:4, 15.
   c. pres. act. participle of ἀκούω (LN 24.52): 'to hear' [LN, Lns, LSA, NTC,
   WBC; CEV, GW, KJV, NASB, NLT, TEV], 'to listen to' [AB, BNTC,
   ECC; NCV, NET]. This verb is also translated as a noun phrase: 'your
   hearers' [Herm; HCSB, NIV, NRSV, REB]. 'Hear' is used in reference to
   hearing the gospel and Christian instruction [ICC].
QUESTION—What relationship is indicated by γάρ 'because'?
   This conjunction indicates the grounds for the preceding exhortation [My,
   NIBC, NICNT, NIGTC, NTC]: *continue in them because by doing this you
   will save yourself and others.* This gives an incentive for sticking to the
   directions that had been given [BNTC, Lns]. Or, it gives the purpose and
   goal of the exhortation [ECC].

QUESTION—What relationship is indicated by the participle ποιῶν 'doing'?

1. The participle indicates the means of saving himself and those who hear him [ICC, LSA, NIBC, NTC, TH; HCSB, NET, REB]: *by doing this, you will save*....

2. The participle indicates the condition for saving himself and those who hear him [AB, ECC, Herm, My, NTIC, TG; GW, NIV, TEV]: *if you do this, you will save*....

QUESTION—What is meant by σεαυτὸν σώσεις 'you will save yourself'?

This refers to being saved from eternal damnation [Alf, BNTC, ECC, ICC, Lns, My, NAC, NICNT, NIGTC, NTC, NTL, TC, TG, TH, TNTC, WBC, WP]. This agrees with the other references to salvation in this letter (1:15; 2:4, 15), which refer to Christian salvation [NIGTC]. It is final salvation at the end of this age, and salvation means not being subject to judgment and the power of death [TH]. This has the sense of Phil. 2:12–13 where it speaks of working out your own salvation by God working in you both to will and to work for his own pleasure [TNTC]. Timothy's endurance in these things would not merit his salvation, but it would give evidences that he was heading for salvation since holy living and sound teaching are the fruits of saving faith [NAC]. It means that he would *further* his salvation [My]. The future tense does not mean that salvation is not a present aspect of Christian life. Rather, it refers to the effect that Timothy's life and teaching will have in regard to the greater realization of the fullness of salvation God has for him and the church [NICNT]. Or, Paul himself feared the possibility of not being saved by the gospel he preached to others, so he tells Timothy that he must be fully committed to doing this because in so doing he will bring himself and his congregation to final salvation [ICC]. It is by a life of holy living and diligence in teaching that salvation both in the present and the future is obtained [NTC]. If he fails to follow these instructions he will suffer the loss of eternal life for himself and his listeners [TG].

QUESTION—What is meant by 'you will save the ones hearing you'?

The salvation of the hearers was the goal of his ministry [NIGTC]. This refers to the people listening to Timothy as he exhorts and teaches them [TH]. God is the one who saves any person, but he saves people by the use of means, so the one who uses these means can be said to save someone [Lns, NIGTC, NTL, TH]. Only God can save, but in a secondary sense the NT speaks of a person saving himself (Phil. 2:12) and others (James 5:19–20 and Jude 23) [BKC]. The verb 'hearing' implies that the one hearing accepts the teaching, and this is the equivalent of the verb 'to believe' [ECC]. 'Hearing' in this context includes both response and obedience to that which is heard [WBC]. The preacher's example of perseverance builds the same trait in his congregation [NAC, NIBC].

DISCOURSE UNIT: 5:1–6:19 [TH]. The topic is further instructions regarding Timothy's ministry.

DISCOURSE UNIT: 5:1–6:2 [ECC, NIGTC, TNTC; NCV, NIV]. The topic is discipline and responsibility [TNTC], duties toward others [NIGTC], the apostolic supervisor of the orders in the church [ECC], rules for living with others [NCV], advice about widows, elders, and slaves [NIV].

DISCOURSE UNIT: 5:1–6:2a [ICC, NICNT, TH, WBC; GW, NET, NRSV, REB, TEV]. The topic is how Timothy is to relate to different groups in the church [TH, WBC], regarding other groups in God's household [NICNT], the treatment of various groups in the church [ICC], instructions about specific groups [NET], guidelines for dealing with other Christians [GW], responsibilities toward believers [NRSV, TEV], church discipline [REB].

DISCOURSE UNIT: 5:1–16 [AB, NAC; CEV, NASB]. The topic is responsibilities toward church groups [NAC], how to act towards others [CEV], honor widows [NASB], crisis in the care of widows [AB].

DISCOURSE UNIT: 5:1–2 [ECC, ICC, NAC, NCBC, NIBC, NICNT, NIGTC, NTL, TH, TNTC, WBC]. The topic is people of various ages [TNTC, WBC], responsibilities toward elder and younger believers [TH], responsibilities to men and women [NTL], responsibilities toward believers [NIBC], proper treatment for all ages [NAC], proper treatment of age groups [NICNT], how to behave towards various groups [NCBC], how to deal with the old and the young [ICC], how the minister should exhort others [NIGTC], part one of the domestic code [ECC].

5:1 Do- not -rebuke[a] an-older-man[b] but appeal[c] as[d] (to) a-father,

LEXICON—a. aorist act. subj. of ἐπιπλήσσω (LN **33.420**) (BAGD p. 297): 'to rebuke, to reprove' [BAGD, LN], 'to denounce' [**LN**]. The imperative μὴ ἐπιπλήξῃς 'do not rebuke' [Herm, LSA, WBC; HCSB, KJV, TEV] is also translated 'do not sharply rebuke' [NASB], 'do not rebuke harshly' [BNTC; NIV], 'do not speak harshly to' [NRSV], 'never speak harshly to' [NLT], 'do not address harshly' [NET], 'do not treat harshly' [NTC], 'never use harsh words when you correct' [GW], 'never be harsh with' [REB], 'do not speak angrily to' [NCV], 'never scold' [ECC], 'do not castigate' [AB], 'do not assault' [Lns], 'don't correct' [CEV]. This verb is a figurative extension of ἐπιπλήσσω 'to strike' and it expresses strong disapproval [LN]. This verb means to express strong rebuke, even to the point of striking the person [AB].

b. πρεσβύτερος (LN 67.102) (BAGD 1.a. p. 699): 'an older man' [AB, BAGD, BNTC, Herm, LN, Lns, LSA, NTC, WBC; all versions except KJV], 'an elderly man' [ECC], 'an elder' [KJV]. This masculine pronominal adjective denotes the older of two males [BAGD, LN]. The singular form here is generic, as seen by the plural forms of the following categories [NICNT, NIGTC]. The use of the singular indicates that this appeal is to be done with individuals in private [ECC].

c. pres. act. impera. of παρακαλέω (LN 25.150, 33.168) (BAGD 2. or 5. p. 617): 'to appeal to' [BAGD (2.), LN (33.168)], 'to urge, to exhort'

[BAGD (2.)], 'to encourage' [BAGD (2.), LN (25.150)], 'to console' [BAGD (5.), LN (25.150)], 'to conciliate, to speak to in a friendly manner' [BAGD (5.)]. The imperative παρακάλει 'appeal' is translated 'appeal to him' [BNTC; NASB, NET, NLT, REB, TEV], 'plead with him' [NCV], 'entreat him' [KJV], 'exhort him' [AB, LSA; HCSB, NIV], 'admonish him' [Herm, Lns, NTC], 'talk to him' [GW], 'speak to him' [NRSV], 'encourage him' [WBC; CEV], 'keep encouraging him' [ECC]. This verb means to earnestly ask for something with propriety [LN (33.168)], or to cause someone to be encouraged or consoled [LN (25.150)]. The present imperative form indicates that this is to be an ongoing action [ECC, NIGTC]. This word has a range of meanings such as encouraging, comforting, exhorting, entreating, appealing to, and admonishing, and in this situation admonishing is predominant [Lns, NTC].

d. ὡς (LN 64.12): 'as, like' [LN]. The phrase ὡς πατέρα 'as a father' [BNTC; Lns, WBC; HCSB, KJV, NASB, NET] is also translated 'as if he were your father' [AB; GW, NCV, NIV, REB, TEV], 'as if he were your own father' [ECC], 'as one would a father' [Herm], 'as to a father' [NRSV], 'as you would to your own father' [NLT], 'as you would a father' [NTC], 'as you would your own father' [CEV], 'as you would exhort him if he were your father' [LSA]. This conjunction indicates a relationship between events or states [LN].

QUESTION—Why was this command necessary?

At times in his pastoral duties, Timothy will have to correct the faults of some of members of the congregation [NTC]. Admonition will always be needed in a congregation [Lns]. It is presupposed that people in these various classes were church members who were guilty of some transgression [My]. After telling Timothy to command and teach the true doctrine so as to counter the false teachings (4:6, 11), to let no one despise his youth (4:12), and to attend to exhortation and teaching (4:13), his attitude in doing so is now addressed so that he won't be harsh and overbearing in performing these duties [NIGTC]. He is not to rebuke the members of the church, but this prohibition does not apply to the false teachers [WBC].

QUESTION—What is meant by πρεσβύτερος 'older man'?

Although this noun can be used of the office of 'elder' in the church as in 5:17, here it is clear that it pertains to the age and sex of the men [Alf, BKC, BNTC, ECC, EGT, Herm, ICC, Lns, My, NAC, NCBC, NIBC, NIGTC, NTC, TC, TG, TH, TNTC, WP], since it contrasts with the categories of younger men, older women, and younger women [Alf, ICC, NIGTC, TH]. An older man would be at least forty [NICNT]. Of course, some of these older men could also be elders in the church [ECC]. The comparative idea had all but vanished in the language, and this section is talking about old men, young men, old women, and young women [NTC].

QUESTION—What is meant by the imperative verb παρακάλει 'appeal'?
It means to appeal to someone to do something [LSA, NIGTC, TH; HCSB, KJV, NASB, NCV, NET, NIV, NLT, REB, TEV]. What Timothy taught in his ministry was to be urged upon and applied to the congregation, so the meanings 'appeal' or 'exhort' are intended here [NIGTC]. In this context it means to advise, admonish, exhort, or to appeal to someone [TG, TH], to warn or instruct [TG]. This is especially pertinent when the older men have done something wrong [TG]. Instead of rebuking someone, he is to encourage that person [ICC, WBC; CEV] to follow the correct teachings [WBC]. Probably this means to console, conciliate, and speak in a friendly manner [ICC].

QUESTION—How would Timothy appeal to an older man 'as a father'?
Timothy is to appeal to him in the same way he would appeal to his own father [AB, ECC, Herm, LSA, NTC; CEV, GW, NCV, NIV, NLT, REB, TEV]. When Timothy needs to instruct or exhort an older man, he should show respect [ICC, NIGTC, NTC], speak with deference and politeness [NICNT], and use consideration, tact, gentleness, and moderation [NTC].

younger-men[a] as brothers
LEXICON—a. νέος (LN 67.116) (BAGD 2.b.β. p. 536): 'young, younger' [BAGD, LN]. The phrase νεωτέρους ὡς ἀδελφούς 'younger men as brothers' [Herm, Lns, NTC, WBC; HCSB, KJV] is also translated 'to the younger men as brothers' [NASB], 'encourage young men as if they were your own brothers' [ECC], 'exhort younger men as you would exhort them if they were your brothers' [LSA], 'treat younger men as/like brothers' [BNTC; NCV, NIV, REB], 'treat the younger men as your brothers' [TEV], 'treat younger men as you would your own brother' [CEV], 'act toward younger men as towards brothers' [AB], 'talk to younger men as if they were your brothers' [GW], 'talk to younger men as you would to your own brothers' [NLT], 'speak to younger men as brothers' [NET, NRSV]. This masculine pronominal adjective denotes a living male who is relatively young, often the younger of two persons [LN].

QUESTION—Who are they younger than?
In the context of older women and younger women (5:2), it means that they are younger than the older men, not necessarily younger than Timothy [NICNT, TH, WBC]. They would be men who were Timothy's own age or younger [WBC]. He should treat them in the spirit of equality [NAC, NTC].

QUESTION—What verb should be supplied with the three categories of younger men, older women, and younger women?
1. The verb παρακάλει 'appeal' that was applied to the older men is also the implied command for treating each of the following categories of people [Alf, BNTC, ECC, Lns, LSA, NIBC, NIGTC, NTC, TH]: (don't rebuke younger men, but) *appeal to them as you would to your brothers.* The

contrast 'do not rebuke but appeal' extends to Timothy's dealing with all the categories in 5:1–2 [ICC, NIGTC].

2. For the three last categories of the church members, Paul passes beyond finding fault with them and refers to more general relations with them [BNTC, EGT]: *treat younger men as you would your brothers.* It means to treat, behave towards, or deal with them [EGT]. Some translations supply the verb 'treat' with the young men, older women, and young women [BNTC; CEV, NCV, NIV, REB, TEV], or the verbs 'talk/speak to' [GW, NET, NLT, NRSV].

5:2 **older-women[a] as mothers,**

LEXICON—a. πρεσβύτερος (LN 67.102) (BAGD 1.a. p. 699): 'older one' [BAGD, LN]. The phrase πρεσβυτέρας ὡς μητέρας 'older women as/like mothers' [BNTC, ECC, Herm, Lns, NTC, WBC; HCSB, NASB, NCV, NET, NIV, REB, TEV] is also translated 'the elder women as mothers' [KJV], 'older women as if they were your mothers' [GW], '(treat) older women as you would your own mother' [CEV, NLT], '(toward) older women as towards mothers' [AB], '(speak to) older women as mothers' [NRSV, REB]. This feminine pronominal adjective denotes the older of two females [BAGD, LN].

younger-women[a] as sisters in all purity.[c]

LEXICON—a. (LN 67.116) (BAGD 2.b.β. p. 536): 'young, younger' [BAGD, LN]. The phrase νεωτέρους ὡς ἀδελφούς 'younger women as sisters' [Herm, Lns, NTC; HCSB, NASB, NET, TEV] is also translated 'the younger as sisters' [WBC; KJV, NRSV], 'the younger as your sisters' [REB], 'younger women like/as sisters' [NCV, NIV], 'young women as if they were your own sisters' [ECC], 'young women as sisters' [BNTC], 'younger women as if they were your sisters' [GW], '(treat) younger women as you would your own sisters' [NLT], 'toward younger women as toward sisters' [AB], 'exhort younger women as you would exhort them if they were your sisters' [LSA]. The whole clause is translated 'show the same respect to younger women that you would to your sister' [CEV]. This feminine pronominal adjective denotes a living female who is relatively young, often the younger of two persons [LN].

b. ἁγνεία (LN 88.30) (BAGD p. 10): 'purity' [LN], 'propriety' [BAGD]. The phrase ἐν πάσῃ ἁγνείᾳ 'in all purity' [Lns, NTC; NASB, REB] is also translated 'with all purity' [WBC; KJV, NLT, TEV], 'in complete purity' [ECC], 'with complete purity' [NET], 'with absolute purity' [NIV, NRSV], 'in all propriety' [Herm], 'with all propriety' [HCSB], 'in complete propriety' [BNTC], 'while keeping yourself morally pure' [GW], 'always treat them in a pure way' [NCV], 'that is, in all purity' [AB], 'you must be completely chaste' [LSA]. See the preceding lexical item for the translation of this phrase [CEV]. This noun denotes the quality of moral purity [LN].

QUESTION—What does ἐν πάσῃ ἁγνείᾳ 'in all purity' modify and what is meant by 'purity'?

1. The concerns Timothy's relationship with the younger women while dealing with them [BKC, BNTC, ECC, My, NAC, NIBC, NIGTC, NTC, TC, TG, TNTC, WBC, WP]. Or, it is how he is to deal with all women, but particularly with the younger ones [TH]. Here the general term 'purity' means with chastity [NIGTC], with a heart free from immoral thoughts [TH], with propriety so that there is no reason to accuse him of sexual misconduct [TG]. He is to have a purity that avoids evil thoughts and deeds [NAC]. This is necessary in the cases where a male minister must deal personally and privately with younger women [NIGTC]. This would help prevent Timothy from getting into situations in which his propriety could be called into question [NICNT].

2. This concerns Timothy's relationship will all four categories of people [Lns, NTL]. The phrase modifies the verb παρακάλει 'appeal' in 4:1, which is also implied for the other three categories of people, so it means to admonish each category without flaw or fault [Lns]. All people of every age group are to be encouraged with the kind of holiness and dedication to God for which Timothy was noted [NTL].

DISCOURSE UNIT: 5:3–6:2a [NLT]. The topic is advice about widows, elders, and slaves.

DISCOURSE UNIT: 5:3–16 [ECC, Herm, ICC, NCBC, NIBC, NICNT, NIGTC, NTL, TH, TNTC, WBC; HCSB]. The topic is widows [Herm, TNTC, WBC], the order of widows [ECC], "real widows" and other widows [NTL], how to deal with the problem of widows [NCBC], proper treatment of widows [NIGTC], care of widows [NIGTC], the support of widows [HCSB], instructions about widows [ICC, NIBC], responsibilities toward widows [TH].

DISCOURSE UNIT: 5:3–8 [NAC, NIGTC, TNTC]. The topic is widows in need [TNTC], the care of true widows [NAC], the obligations of descendants [NIGTC].

5:3 Honor[a] widows the (ones) (who are) really[b] widows.

LEXICON—a. pres. act. impera. of τιμάω (LN **57.117**) (BAGD 2. p. 817): 'to honor' [BAGD], 'to give assistance to, to provide for the needs of, to support and honor' [LN]. The command χήρας τίμα 'honor widows' [Herm, WBC; GW, KJV, NASB, NET, NRSV] is also translated 'show respect for widows' [TEV], 'as widows honor (those who)' [Lns, NTC], 'give proper recognition to those widows (who)' [NIV], 'enroll as widows' [REB], 'officially recognize widows' [BNTC], 'support and honor those widows' [LN], 'honor widows by taking care of them' [LSA], 'take care of widows' [NCV], 'support widows' [HCSB], 'take care of any widow' [CEV, NLT], 'provide financial support for widows' [AB], 'honor the claims of widows' [ECC]. This verb means to provide financial assistance and other kinds of aid as an appropriate means of showing respect [LN].

b. ὄντως (LN **70.2**) (BAGD 2. p. 574): 'really' [BAGD, LN], 'certainly, truly' [LN] The phrase τὰς ὄντως χήρας 'the ones who are really widows' is translated 'those who are really widows' [**LN** (70.2); similarly BNTC; NRSV], 'who are truly widows' [AB, WBC; NCV], 'who are genuinely widows' [HCSB], 'who are widows indeed' [KJV, NASB], 'those genuinely widows' [Lns], 'if they are true widows' [Herm], 'who deserve that title' [ECC], 'only those who are widows in the fullest sense' [REB], 'who are really what is implied in the name widows' [NTC], 'who are really desolate widows' [LSA], 'who really are all alone' [TEV], 'who really are left alone' [**LN** (57.117)], 'who have no families' [GW], 'who are really in need' [NIV], 'who are truly in need' [NET], '(any widow) who is really in need' [CEV], '(any widow) who has no one else to care for her' [NLT]. This adverb pertains to actual existence [LN]. This word is also used attributively: 'the real widow', making a contrast with a so-called widow who has relatives, or is still of a marriageable age [BAGD]. See this word at 5:5, 16.

QUESTION—Who is to honor widows?

The second person singular imperative verb τίμα 'honor' seems to direct this command to Timothy alone, but Paul is actually using this command to instruct the church [NIGTC, WBC]. This is shown by the plural verbs in 5:4 ('let them learn') and 5:7 ('they be irreproachable') [NIGTC, WBC]. Also the indefinite adjective τίς 'any' in 5:4, 8, and 16 indicate that these instructions are general rules [WBC]. Paul is telling Timothy, as the leader of the church, to ensure that 'real' widows be cared for [NTL].

QUESTION—What is meant by the command χήρας τίμα 'honor widows'?

The word τίμα 'honor' is also used in the commandment to honor one's father and mother (Matt. 15:4), and it means to show respect [EGT, NAC, TG, TH, WBC, WP], and high regard [NTC]. This includes having consideration for them [NTC], and sympathy [TH]. All widows should be respected, so the verb here must include the sense of honoring this class of widows by giving them material support [ICC, My]. It pertains to both honor and financial support, and both meanings are intended here [TNTC; NET]. In this context, showing respect to widows in a practical way would be to pay attention to their needs [AB, LN, LSA, NAC, NTC, TG, TH; CEV, HCSB, NCV, NET, NLT]. It should be understood here as 'provide the support that honor demands' [NICNT]. Here it should be translated 'provide financial support' [AB, NTIC].

QUESTION—What is meant by the phrase τὰς ὄντως χήρας 'the ones who are really widows'?

This does not deny that there were other women who were widows in the normal sense of those whose husbands have died, but here it is referring to widows who qualify for being widows who are to be cared for by the church [NIGTC, WBC]. The theme of this discussion concerns widows that the church should support financially, and the translation 'provide financial support' is demanded here [AB]. They are genuine widows in relation to the category of those widows whom the church should support [ICC]. They were really in need [BKC], truly destitute [Alf, NCBC, TNTC]. They are widows who have no other means of material support except the church [NTC, TH], and the next verse explains that they are widows who have no children or relatives to take care of them [TC, TG].

5:4 **But if any widow has children or grandchildren, they-should-learn**[a] **first to-show-piety-toward**[b] **their own household**[c]

LEXICON—a. pres. act. impera. of μανθάνω (LN 27.12) (BAGD 4. p. 490): 'to learn' [AB, BAGD, BNTC, ECC, Herm, LN, Lns, LSA, NTC, WBC; all versions except NLT], 'to be instructed, to be taught' [LN]. The phrase 'they should learn first' is translated 'their first responsibility is' [NLT]. This verb means to acquire information as the result of instruction, whether in an informal or formal context [LN]. This means to appropriate to oneself through experience and practice [BAGD].

b. pres. act. infin. of εὐσεβέω (LN **71.29**) (BAGD 2. p. 326): 'to show piety toward' [BAGD], 'to fulfill one's duties, to complete one's religious duty' [LN]. The phrase τὸν ἴδιον οἶκον εὐσεβεῖν 'to show piety to their own household' is translated 'to show piety toward their own family' [Herm], 'show piety at home' [KJV], 'to practice piety in regard to their own family' [NASB], 'to carry out their religious duties toward their own family' [**LN**], 'to put their religion into practice by caring for their own family' [NIV], 'to practice their religion toward their own family first' [HCSB; similarly BNTC], 'to carry out their religious duties toward their own family' [TEV], 'their religious duty to their own family' [NTC; NRSV], 'to show godliness to their own household' [WBC; similarly AB], 'their first responsibility is to show godliness at home' [NLT], 'to do their duty to their own family' [NCV], 'to fulfill their duty toward their own household' [NET], 'to respect their own family' [LSA; GW], 'to be dutiful to their own family' [Lns], 'to show loyalty to the family' [REB], 'to learn the meaning of reverence for one's own home' [ECC], 'to serve God by taking care of her' [CEV]. This verb means to fulfill one's socio-religious obligations [LN].

c. οἶκος (LN 10.8) (BAGD 2. p. 561): 'household, family' [LN]. This noun denotes a family consisting of all those related by blood and marriage who live in the same house or homestead, and includes the servants and slaves as well [LN]. See this word at 3:4, 12, 15.

QUESTION—What relationship is indicated by δέ 'but'?

This conjunction indicates a contrast between the help given to two kinds of widows [AB, BNTC, ICC, Lns, NIGTC, NTC, WBC; all versions except GW, NRSV, REB which do not translate this conjunction]. Here an exception is given of the kind of widow who is not a 'real' widow [ICC, NTC]. In contrast with the 'real' widows who are to be supported by the church, the widows who have families should be supported by their families [WBC]. The church should care for true widows, but families should care for the widows in their own families [WBC]. The church is to honor widows by caring for their needs, but if a widow has a family that should take care of her, then this is not the church's obligation [NIGTC].

QUESTION—Who are the referents of the pronoun 'they' in the verb μανθανέτωσαν 'they should learn'?

1. This refers to the widow's children and grandchildren [AB, Alf, BNTC, ECC, EGT, ICC, Lns, NAC, NCBC, NICNT, NIGTC, NTC, TC, TH, TNTC, WBC, WP], her living descendants [NIGTC]. Since 'they' is third person plural, it is best to take it as referring to the children and grandchildren rather than the singular noun 'widow [NIGTC, WBC]. The issue in this passage is not the widows' duties, but which widows should be cared for by the church [WBC]. In this case, it is presumed that the children or grandchildren are adults who are able to take on the duty of helping the widow [ECC, ICC].

2. This refers to the subject of the preceding conditional clause τις χήρα 'any widow' [My]. The singular phrase 'any widow' is to be taken as a collective idea and so it is correct to use the plural verb 'they should learn' as Luther has understood this [My]. If this view is taken, the point is that if widows have children or grandchildren, then they should not seek to be enrolled to work in the church, but should show their piety by staying at home to care for their own families, thus showing respect to their own forbearers by caring for their own children just as their parents and grandparents had done for them [ICC].

QUESTION—What is meant by μανθάνω 'learn'?

They are to learn to do something rather than to know something [ECC]. This verb means to get into the practice of doing something [TG, TH], to become proficient in a duty [TH], to appropriate to oneself [NIGTC].

QUESTION—What is to be done πρῶτον 'first'?

This is what they are to learn before anything else [TG]. The first duty of children is to show filial piety [EGT]. This is their first duty in showing loyalty to their family [REB], their first religious duty towards those who raised them [NTC]. Before doing other works of love, the members of the family must first show piety toward their own family [Herm]. The first responsibility for caring for needy members of the family falls on that family [BKC]. It means that this is a religious duty that should be given first priority [ICC, NICNT, NIGTC, TH], before other forms of Christian service [ICC]. This is of primary importance [WBC].

What is meant by εὐσεβεῖν 'show piety'?

This refers to their religious duty [NIGTC, TG]. Usually translated 'godliness' in the sense of worshipping God, the word is used here in an ethical sense of fulfilling one's religious obligations, doing the things that they should do because they are Christians [TH]. This is the conduct coming from a godly person [WBC]. It is putting their religion into practice [BKC,

NICNT]. In this case, they show the godliness Paul referred to in 4:7 by caring for their aged parents or other relatives [NAC].

QUESTION—What is meant by τὸν ἴδιον οἶκον 'their own household'?

This means their own household [WBC, WP; NET], family [AB, Lns, LSA, NICNT, NIGTC, NTC, TG; GW, HCSB, NASB, NIV, NRSV, REB, TEV], relatives [NAC], at home [KJV, NLT]. One translation applies this specifically to the widow: 'by taking care of her' [CEV]. This general term covers the whole household, so this general category is used as a basis for requiring care for an elderly mother or grandmother [ICC]. The adjective ἴδιον 'their own' is singular in agreement with the singular noun 'household', but it refers back to the plural subject of the sentence [NIGTC]. They are to show piety/godliness at home [KJV, NLT].

and to recompense[a] the recompense[b] to-the progenitors.[c]

LEXICON—a. pres. act. infin. of ἀποδίδωμι (LN 57.155) (BAGD 3. p. 90): 'to recompense, to reward, to return' [BAGD], 'to pay' [LN], 'to render' [BAGD, LN]. See translations of this verb in the following lexical item. This verb means to make a payment, and it implies that the payment is in response to an obligation that has been incurred [LN]. It means to render what is due [NIGTC]. The present tense indicates that they are to keep on giving it back [NIGTC, WP].

  b. ἀμοιβή (LN **57.168**) (BAGD p. 46) 'a recompense' [BAGD, LN], 'repayment' [LN], 'a return' [BAGD]. The phrase καὶ ἀμοιβὰς ἀποδιδόναι τοῖς προγόνοις 'and to recompense the recompense to the progenitors' is translated 'and so repay what they owe to their parents and grandparents' [REB], 'specifically, they are to repay what they owe their progenitors' [LSA], 'and give back some repayment to those who gave them birth' [AB], 'and to repay their parents or grandparents' [NCV], 'and to repay their parents' [HCSB; similarly NLT], 'and so repay their parents' [NET], 'and so repaying their parents and grandparents' [NIV], 'to make repayment to their parents and grandparents' [**LN**], 'to pay back to their parents and grandparents for what these have done for them' or 'to help their parents and grandparents because of what these have done to help them' [**LN**], 'and to requite their parents' [KJV], 'and in this way repay their parents and grandparents' [TEV], 'and make some repayment to their parents' [NRSV], 'and to make some return to their parents' [WBC; NASB], 'and of giving recompense to their forebears' [ECC], 'and to make a proper return to their forbears' [BNTC], 'and duly render requital to their parents' [Lns], 'and make a real return to their parents' [NTC], 'by repaying their parents' [GW], 'and to show gratitude to their forebears' [Herm], '(by taking care of her,) as she once took care of them' [CEV]. This noun denotes that which is given as a means of recompense or repayment [LN]. The phrase is tautologous since both the verb and noun mean to give back or return [AB]. This noun means 'requital', and the verb and the noun are usually translated together as 'to requite' in the sense of returning the good they have received from their parents [Lns].

c. πρόγονος (LN 10.20) (BAGD p. 704): 'ancestor, forefather' [LN]. This noun denotes a person who is several preceding generations removed from the reference person [TH]. The translation 'parents' must be understood to include more than one generation [NIGTC]. Here it means living relatives born earlier, specifically parents and grandparents, the counterpart to children and grandchildren [NICNT].

QUESTION—What relationship is indicated by καί 'and'?

It indicates the specific action of respect they are to render their family [Lns, LSA, NIGTC, WBC]. This is an explanatory clause to tell what is meant by 'to show godliness' [NICNT, WBC]. Rather than a separate action, it indicates the outcome of showing piety to one's family [ICC].

QUESTION—What is meant by τοῖς προγόνοις 'the progenitors'?

1. It refers to the parents and the grandparents of the people who are to recompense them [LN (57.168), Lns, LSA, NIGTC, NTC, TG, TH; NCV, NIV, REB, TEV], forebears [BNTC, ECC, Herm]. Since both children and grandchildren are included in the preceding sentence ('nephews' in the KJV meant grandchildren in 1611), this refers to both parents and grandparents here [NICNT, TG]. This generic term for persons several generations removed from the person referred to is used here in a narrow sense to refer to both grandparents and parents [TH]. It includes a father or grandfather as well as a mother or grandmother [Lns]. It includes caring for the whole household, but especially the widows [NIGTC, TH]. In this context, it primarily refers to a widowed mother or grandmother [NIBC, NIGTC]. This presumes that the children and grandchildren referred to here are grown up and capable of helping support the widows in their family [TH].

2. It means the parents of the people who are to recompense them [AB, Lns, NTC, WBC; GW, HCSB, KJV, NASB, NET, NLT, NRSV], 'those who gave them birth' [AB].

3. It means the widow who has children or grandchildren [CEV].

QUESTION—What is the recompense they are to pay back?

The children are to repay their parents and grandparents by returning the care that they had received from them [NIGTC]. They have received life and sustenance from their forefathers, and they are now to repay their forefathers in their need [ECC].

Because this is pleasing[a] in-the-opinion of-God.

TEXT—Instead of ἀπόδεκτον 'pleasing', some manuscripts read καλὸν καὶ ἀπόδεκτον 'good and pleasing'. GNT does not mention this variant. 'Good and pleasing' is read by KJV.

LEXICON—a. ἀπόδεκτος (LN 25.85) (BAGD p. 90): 'pleasing' [BAGD, LN], 'acceptable' [LN]. The phrase 'this is pleasing in the opinion of God' is translated 'this is pleasing in God's sight' [GW, NRSV], 'this is pleasing before God' [WBC], 'this is well pleasing before God' [Herm], 'this is pleasing to God' [NIV], 'this pleases God' [LSA; HCSB], 'this is what pleases God' [NET, TEV], 'that has God's approval' [REB], 'this is what God wants them to do' [CEV], 'this is commendable in God's sight' [BNTC], 'this is acceptable in the sight of God' [Lns, NTC; NASB], 'this is an acceptable thing before God' [AB], 'this is a welcome thing in the eyes of God the Father' [ECC], 'that is (good and) acceptable before God' [KJV]. This adjective refers to something that is pleasing because of its acceptability [LN]. This clause is included in 2:3.

QUESTION—What relationship is indicated by γάρ 'because'?

This conjunction indicates the grounds for giving the preceding command [ECC, LSA]. It is the ultimate reason why the preceding command should be obeyed [NIGTC, WBC].

QUESTION—What is the referent of τοῦτο 'this'?

It refers to the children's act of showing honor to their parents and grandparents [ECC, NTC], and caring for them [NIGTC, TH].

QUESTION—Why does Paul know that this is pleasing to God?

Probably it is pleasing to God because it fulfills the fifth commandment about honoring one's father and mother [BNTC, ICC, NIBC, NICNT, TNTC].

5:5 Now/but the (one) (who is) really[a] a-widow and having-been-left-alone[b] has-put-her-hope[c] on God

LEXICON—a. ὄντως (LN 70.2) (BAGD 2. p. 574): 'really' [BAGD, LN], 'certainly, truly' [LN]. This word is also used attributively: 'the real widow', making a contrast with a so-called widow who has relatives, or is still of a marriageable age [BAGD]. This adverb pertains to actual existence [LN]. See this word and a discussion of the phrase 'one who is really a widow' at 5:3.

b. perf. pass. participle of μονόομαι, μονόω (LN **10.13**) (BAGD p. 528): 'to be left alone' [BAGD; NASB, NIV], 'to be absolutely alone in the world' [BNTC], 'to be solitary' [Herm], 'to be desolate' [KJV], 'to be without a family' [LN], 'to be without relatives' [LN], 'to be completely on her own' [NET]. The phrase ἡ ὄντως χήρα καὶ μεμονωμένη 'the one who is really a widow and having been left alone' is also translated without joining the two descriptions with the conjunction 'and': 'the true widow, who is all alone' [NCV], 'the real widow, left all alone' [HCSB; similarly NRSV], 'the genuine widow, namely the one having been left alone' [Lns], 'the real widow, the one who was left all alone' [NTC], 'the widow proper, one who is a completely destitute woman' [ECC], 'a true widow, a woman who is truly alone in this world' [NLT], 'a widow in the full sense, one who is alone in the world' [REB], 'the real widow is one who, having been left alone' [AB], 'a widow who is all alone, with no one to take care of her' [TEV], 'the true widow, who has been left totally alone' [WBC], 'a widow who has no family' [GW], 'the really desolate widow' [LSA], 'a widow who is really in need is one who doesn't have any relatives' [CEV]. This verb means to be left without a family, and in this verse it implies that she has no relatives who would be in a position to help her [LN].

    c. perf. act. indic. of ἐλπίζω (LN 25.59) (BAGD 3. p. 252): 'to put one's hope in something' [BAGD], 'to hope' [LN]. The phrase ἤλπικεν ἐπὶ θεόν 'has put her hope on God' [AB] is also translated 'has put her hope in God' [HCSB; similarly NCV, NIV], 'has set her hope on God' [Lns, NTC, WBC; NET, NRSV; similarly BNTC], 'has fixed her hope in/on God' [ECC; NASB], 'has placed her hope in God' [Herm; NLT, TEV], 'has placed her confidence in God' [GW], 'puts all her trust in God' [REB], 'she has faith in God' [CEV], 'trusts in God' [KJV], 'expects that God will help her' [LSA]. This verb means to look forward with confidence to that which is good and beneficial [LN]. It indicates a settled attitude of depending on God to supply her needs [AB, Alf, BNTC, ICC, NAC]. The perfect tense indicates that in the past she had turned to God in the expectation of having her needs met by him, and this resulted in an attitude that characterizes her at the present time [LSA].

QUESTION—What relationship is indicated by δέ 'now, but'?

    1. This conjunction indicates a resumption of the discourse [AB, My, NIBC, NTC, TH; KJV, NASB; probably CEV, GW, HCSB, NCV, NIV, NRSV, TEV which do not translate the conjunction]: *now*. This returns to the discussion of a 'real widow' in 1:3 and defines what such a widow is [AB, My, NIGTC, TH].

    2. This conjunction indicates a contrast [Alf, ECC, ICC, Lns, NIGTC, WBC; NET]: *but*. This indicates a contrast with the widow who is provided for by her family (5:4) [ICC, NIGTC, WBC].

QUESTION—How is the phrase καὶ μεμονωμένη *'and* having been left alone' related to the preceding phrase?

    It functions as an added description to clarify the preceding phrase, and this can be translated 'namely, the one who is on her own' [ICC]. It is appositional [Lns, NIGTC], and gives the basic description of a real widow as being without a family to care for her [NICNT, NIGTC, WBC]. It explains what a true widow is [My, NTL, TC]. This emphasizes the widow's helplessness [TH].

QUESTION—What does the widow hope for?

    The widow hopes that God will help her [LSA, TH; CEV] and supply what she needs [ICC]. God has made many promises about widows and his protection of them in his word [Lns]. She confidently anticipates that God will intervene and provide for her [NICNT, WBC]. The widow's hope includes her expectations for the future, her trust in God's care, and her patience in waiting [NIGTC]. Her life is filled with the hope of eternal life [ECC]. That she depends only on God and trusts completely in him is the fitting attitude of a widow who has no one on earth to help her [TH].

and continues[a] in the requests[b] and the prayers[c] night and day.

LEXICON—a. pres. act. indic. of προσμένω (LN **68.11**) (BAGD 1.b. p. 717): 'to continue' [AB, BAGD, **LN**, LSA, NTC, WBC; HCSB, KJV, NASB, NCV, NET, NIV, NRSV, TEV], 'to keep on' [LN; similarly CEV], 'to stay on' [ECC], 'to remain in/on' [Herm, Lns], not explicit [AB; NLT]. This verb is also translated as an adverb: 'regularly' [REB]. This verb means to continue in an activity [LN].

   b. δέησις (LN 33.171) (BAGD p. 172): 'request, prayer' [LN], 'plea' [LN; NET], 'entreaty' [BAGD, ECC, WBC; NASB], 'petition' [AB, Lns; HCSB], 'supplication' [BNTC, Herm, NTC; KJV, NRSV]. The noun is also translated as a verb phrase: '(continues to pray) for God's help' [NCV; similarly CEV, GW], 'asking God for his help' [NLT; similarly NIV, TEV], '(continues) to ask God that he will help her' [LSA], 'attends the meetings for prayer (and worship)' [REB]. This noun denotes that which is asked for with urgency based on a need [LN]. See this word at 2:1.

   c. προσευχή (LN 33.178) (BAGD 1. p. 713): 'prayer' [AB, BAGD, BNTC, ECC, Herm, LN, Lns, NTC, WBC; HCSB, KJV, NASB, NET, NRSV]. This noun is also translated as a verb: 'she (continues) to pray' [LSA; NCV, NIV, TEV], 'she (keeps) praying to him' [CEV], 'she prays' [NLT], 'by praying' [GW], 'attends the meetings for (prayer and) worship' [REB]. This noun denotes what is said to God or what is requested of him [LN]. See this word at 2:1.

QUESTION—What relationship is indicated by καί 'and'?

The conjunction καί 'and' indicates the practical expression of the widow's hope in God [ICC, NICNT]. This adds a further description of such a widow to emphasize her true godliness [WBC].

QUESTION—What is the significance of the articles with the nouns ταῖς δεήσεσιν καὶ ταῖς προσευχαῖς 'the requests and the prayers'?

The significance of the articles is uncertain [NICNT]. The articles could mean the appointed times of requests and prayers in church or at private devotions, but the articles do not necessarily mean this [ICC]. The articles could refer to the public prayers at the church, or they may indicate possession, meaning her requests and her prayers, or they may merely designate the two great divisions of prayer [Alf].

1. It means the widow's requests and prayers that she continually makes [Lns, NTC, WBC; probably all versions except REB]. The articles indicate that they are the widow's very own prayers coming from her soul [Lns].

2. It means at the appointed time for requests and prayer to be made [BNTC, ECC, TG; REB]. She attends the prayers and supplication [BNTC], 'and regularly, night and day, attends the meetings for prayer and worship' [REB]. Probably this refers to her prayers in church, not her private prayers [TG].

QUESTION—How are the two activities connected in the description 'continues in requests and prayers'?

The word προσευχή is the generic word for prayer, and δέησις is a more specific word to describe entreaties made in prayer [NIGTC, TH]. The requests are made in her prayers: she keeps praying to God, asking for his help [CEV]. Some show this by reversing the order of the nouns: she continues to pray, asking God for his help [GW, NCV, NIV, NLT, TEV]. Some translate the clause as though they were two different activities: she continues in her requests and prayers [LSA; HCSB, KJV, NASB, NET, NRSV, REB].

QUESTION—Is there any significance in the order 'night and day' and what does it mean to pray night and day?

Paul uses this same order in 1 Thess. 2:19; 3:10; 2 Thess. 3:8; 2 Tim 1:3, and it may simply be his favored idiom, perhaps because he personally started work before dawn [NIGTC]. This reflects the Jewish way of regarding a day to begin at sunset [ECC, NCBC, NIBC, NTL, TH, WBC]. This phrase reinforces the statement that she continually prays [NIBC]. The phrase uses hyperbole to indicate persistent dedication to a life of prayer [ECC]. The widow doesn't pray all night and all day without ever stopping, but prayer is such a regular habit for her that no matter whether it is night or day, she still comes to God in prayer [TH]. The genitive forms of νυκτὸς 'night' and of ἡμέρας 'day' mean that she prays by night and by day, and not *all* night and *all* day [WP]. Part of every night and part of every day she prays [NTC].

5:6 But the (one) living-indulgently[a] has-died[b] (while) living.

LEXICON—a. pres. act. participle of σπαταλάω (LN 88.252) (BAGD p. 761): 'to live indulgently' [BAGD, LN], 'to live luxuriously or voluptuously' [BAGD]. The phrase ἡ σπαταλῶσα 'the one living indulgently' is translated 'a widow given to self-indulgence' [REB; similarly AB], 'the widow who lives in order that she may indulge herself' [LSA], 'she who is self-indulgent' [HCSB], 'the widow who uses her life to please herself' [NCV], 'the widow who lives for pleasure' [GW, NIV, NRSV; similarly WBC; KJC, NET, NLT], 'a widow who gives herself to pleasure' [TEV], 'she who gives herself to wanton pleasure' [NASB], 'the one who is giving herself up to luxury' [NTC], 'the one luxuriating' [Lns], 'the one who lives voluptuously' [Herm; similarly ECC], 'a widow who thinks only about having a good time' [CEV]. This verb means to indulge oneself excessively and to satisfy one's own appetites and desires [LN].

b. perf. act. indic. of θνήσκω (LN 23.99) (BAGD 2. p. 362): 'to die' [BAGD, LN]. The phrase ζῶσα τέθνηκεν 'has died while living' is translated 'has died while still living' [ECC], 'is dead even while she lives' [HCSB, NASB, NET, NIV, NRSV; similarly BNTC, Herm; KJV], 'she is dead though she is still alive' [BAGD] 'has already died, even though she lives' [TEV; similarly AB], 'is already dead, even though she is still alive' [CEV; similarly GW], 'is really dead while she is alive'

[NCV], 'even though living, has died' [WBC; similarly Lns, NTC], 'is as good as dead' [REB], 'is spiritually dead even while she lives' [NLT], 'the widow is spiritually dead who lives (in order that she may indulge herself)' [LSA]. This verb refers to the process of dying [LN]. The verb is used figuratively of spiritual death [BAGD].

QUESTION—What relationship is indicated by δέ 'but'?

This conjunction indicates a contrast with the 'the one who is really a widow' in 5:5 [AB, Alf, BNTC, ECC, ICC, Lns, NAC, NICNT, NIGTC, TH, WBC]. The contrast is between a 'real' widow who is destitute and this widow who has the means to live a luxurious self-indulgent life [AB, ICC, NIGTC]. It is implied that she is not eligible to be cared for by the church and has no claims on the church because she was not destitute [AB, ICC, NCBC, NIGTC]. Some also point out the contrast between the godly widow who trusts in God and lives for him and this spiritually dead widow who lives only to please herself [NIGTC, WBC]. This implies that she has no claims on the church because she had not set her hope on God and did not live a godly life [Alf, BKC, BNTC, Lns, NAC, WBC]. The context seems to indicate that such widows were seeking church support, but if they were supported, they would just live self-centered lives given over to their selfish pleasure [WBC].

QUESTION—What is meant by the verb σπαταλάω 'to live in pleasure'?

This describes a sinful hedonistic life-style, but the specifics are not named [NIGTC]. Her life is described as being self indulgent [AB, BAGD, LN, NIBC, NIGTC, WBC], hedonistic [ICC], given to pleasure [WBC], voluptuous [BAGD, ECC, Herm, ICC, NAC, NIGTC], sensual [BNTC], luxurious [BAGD, NAC, NICNT, NTC], extravagant [TH]. Her sin is that she is misusing her wealth to live for pleasure instead of helping others [ICC]. She is a merry widow who enjoys the money that was spent on her [Lns]. It could be that she was involved in sexual sin since this would be a temptation for a widow and would provide for financial needs [NIGTC]. Some think that she probably was guilty of immoral behavior [NCBC, NTC, TG]. However, there is nothing in the text to suggest that she was guilty of sexual immorality [ICC, TH, WBC].

QUESTION—What relationship is indicated by the use of the present participle ζῶσα 'living' to describe this widow?

The participle indicates a concession [WBC]: *although she is living, she has died.* Translations use 'although' [BAGD, Lns, NTC; GW], 'even though' [AB, WBC; CEV, TEV], 'while' [BNTC, ECC, Herm; HCSB, KJV, NASB, NCV, NET, NIV, NRSV], 'even while' [NLT].

QUESTION—What is meant by the paradox that she was dead while she was still living?

1. This means that such a widow is spiritually dead while she is physically alive [Alf, BAGD, BKC, ECC, ICC, Lns, LSA, NAC, NCBC, NIBC, NICNT, NTL, TC, TH, WBC; NLT]. Only having eternal life constitutes real life [NTL].

2. This means that the widow is as good as dead while she is physically alive [AB, NTC; REB]. Even though she attended church, she was dead to all higher interests in religious matters [NTC].

5:7 **And/also these (things) command,[a] in-order-that they-will-be irreproachable[b]**

LEXICON—a. pres. act. impera. of παραγγέλλω (LN 33.327) (BAGD p. 613): 'to command' [AB, BAGD, LN, WBC; HCSB], 'to order' [BAGD, LN, Lns], 'to charge' [ECC; similarly KJV], 'to prescribe' [NASB], 'to insist on' [GW], 'to instruct' [BAGD], 'to give (these commands/instructions)' [Herm; NRSV, TEV], 'to issue (these instructions)' [BNTC], 'to reinforce (these commands)' [NET], 'to add (these instructions to the rest)' [REB]. Some make explicit the ones who are to be commanded: 'command the church' [LSA], 'give these instructions to the church' [NLT], 'tell the believers to do these things' [NCV], 'tell all of this to everyone' [CEV], 'give the people these instructions' [NIV]. This verb means to announce what must be done [LN]. See this word at 1:3; 4:11; 6:13, 17.

b. ἀνεπίλημπτος (LN 33.415) (BAGD p. 65): 'irreproachable' [BAGD, ECC, Lns], 'above reproach' [BNTC, WBC; NASB, NRSV, REB], 'beyond reproach' [Herm, LN; NET], 'without reproach' [AB], 'above criticism' [LN], 'no one will be open to criticism' [NLT], 'no one may be open to blame' [NIV], 'blameless' [KJV]. The adjective is also translated as a verb: 'so they won't be blamed' [HCSB], 'in order that no one can reproach them' [LSA], 'so that no one can criticize them' [NCV], 'so that no one can find fault with them' [TEV], 'so that widows will have good reputations' [GW], 'so they will do the right thing' [CEV]. This adjective describes someone who cannot be criticized [LN]. It means that they cannot be *rightly* criticized [TG].

QUESTION—What relationship is indicated by καί 'and/also'?

1. This means 'and' [ECC, Lns, LSA, NCBC; KJV; probably CEV, GW, HCSB, NCV, NET, NLT, TEV which do not translate the conjunction]. It indicates a transition from a moral principle to a command [ECC].

2. This means 'also' and adds this command to a preceding command [BKC, BNTC, ICC, NICNT, NIGTC, NTC, TC, WBC; NASB, NIV, NRSV, REB]. Paul is reminding Timothy of the previous requirement to command 'the things' referred to in 4:11 [NIGTC, NTC, TC]. These instructions about the rules for genuine widowhood are to be added to the instructions given in the first part of chapter four [BNTC]. They are to add this instruction to the rest of the instructions [REB].

QUESTION—Who are the ones Timothy is to command, and what should he command them?

1. Timothy is to command the church [AB, BKC, LSA, NTC, TC; CEV, NCV, NIV, NLT]. Some say that Timothy is to give this command to the church [LSA; NLT], the believers [NCV], the people [NIV], the householders [AB], everyone [CEV]. Timothy is to command the church

that the children or grandchildren of 'real' widows are to take care of those widows [LSA]. Timothy is to give orders to the church about the criteria for enrolling widows [BKC, BNTC, ECC, TC]. Timothy is to command the things contained in 5:3–6, 8 [Lns, NTC], and in 4:11 [NTC]. 'These things' refer to the responsibilities of the children in 5:4 and the responsibilities of the widows in 5:5 [TNTC].

2. Timothy is to command the children and grandchildren of needy widows to practice piety by caring for their parents [EGT, ICC, NICNT, NIGTC, WBC]. The content of this command refers to what Paul has written in 5:4 about the duties of the children of the widows [ICC, LSA, NICNT, NIGTC]. This refers to children of the widows and not the widows [NIGTC].

3. Timothy is to command the widows to live according to the description given in 5:5 and not be like those widows described in 5:6 [Alf, My, NAC, NIBC, NTL]. In 5:11–15 the younger widows were the source of the problem [NAC]. By announcing these things to the congregation, he will be exhorting the widows in it [My].

QUESTION—What relationship is indicated by ἵνα 'in order that'?

This conjunction indicates the purpose for commanding these things [AB, BNTC, ECC, Herm, ICC, Lns, My, NIBC, NICNT, NIGTC, NTC, NTL, WBC; all versions]. Obedience to this command will ensure that they will be blameless [ICC].

QUESTION—Who is in danger of being reproached?

1. The whole church will be reproached by outsiders [EGT, Lns, NTC]. This concerns all those involved in 5:3–8 [EGT, Lns, NTC]. It concerns the widows who are like those in 5:6, the children who fail in their duties written in 5:4, and the whole church if it does not honor the widows and know how to distinguish between the widows that should be honored and those that should not be honored [Lns, NTC]. Reproach would come from outsiders and also from members of the church [NTC].

2. The children and grandchildren of widows will be reproached by others if they don't take care of their widowed mothers or grandmothers [AB, ICC, LSA, NICNT, WBC].

2. The widows will be reproached if the wrong widows are enrolled [Alf, BKC, BNTC, ECC, My, NIBC, NTL, TC; GW, REB]. The instructions are about 'real' widows because if the official list of widows included some who are described in 4:6, the reputation of the order of widows would be harmed [BNTC]. Timothy must exhort the widows so that they will be blameless [NTL].

5:8 And/but if anyone does- not -provide-for[a] (one's) own[b] and especially/ namely[c] (one's) household,[d]

LEXICON—a. pres. act. indic. of προνοέω (LN 35.39): 'to provide for' [AB, ECC, Herm, Lns, NTC; HCSB, NASB, NET, NIV, NRSV], 'to make provision for' [REB], 'to look after' [BNTC, LN], 'to take care of' [**LN**,

LSA; CEV, GW, TEV], 'to care for' [WBC; NCV, NLT]. This verb means to care for or look after someone and implies that this is a continuing responsibility [LN]. This probably refers to the long-term responsibility one has for another, not just providing for material needs [TH].

b. ἴδιος (LN 57.4): 'one's own' [LN]. This pronominal adjective is translated 'his own' [Lns, NTC, WBC; KJV, NASB, NET], 'his own relatives' [AB, BNTC, LN (10.11), LSA; GW, HCSB, NCV; similarly NIV], 'their relatives' [CEV, NLT, TEV], 'relatives' [NRSV], 'his relations' [REB], 'his own people' [ECC, Herm]. This word indicates something that is the exclusive property of someone [LN].

c. μάλιστα (LN 78.7) (BAGD 1. p. 489): 'especially' [AB, BAGD, BNTC, LN, Lns, LSA, NTC, WBC; all versions], 'particularly' [ECC, LN], 'not even for' [Herm]. This adverb denotes a very high point on a scale of extent [LN].

d. οἰκεῖος (LN **10.11**) (BAGD 1. p. 556): 'family' [LN, LSA], 'his own family' [Herm; NET], 'his family members' [Lns; NRSV; similarly BNTC, NTC; NCV, TEV], 'members of his own family' [**LN**], 'his immediate family' [ECC; GW, NIV], 'those of his household' [NAS; similarly NLT], 'his household members' [WBC; similarly AB; HCSB, REB], 'relatives' [LN; CEV]. This noun denotes a person who belongs to a particular household or extended family [LN].

QUESTION—What relationship is indicated by δέ 'and/but'?

1. This conjunction is a continuative [Alf, BNTC, ECC, Lns, LSA, NTC; HCSB, NRSV, REB; probably CEV, GW, NCV, NIV which do not translate this conjunction]: *and, now*. It adds something that is different from the preceding text by offering a principle [Lns]. It states the principle behind the command in 5:4 [BNTC].

2. This conjunction indicates a contrast [AB, Herm, WBC; KJV, NASB, NET, NLT, TEV]: *but*. If it is a contrast, being irreproachable by obeying the command to care for one's own family is contrasted with denying the faith by not caring for one's family [NIGTC, WBC]. Those who start this verse with 'but' indicate that this verse is not part of the instructions referred to in 5:7 [TH].

QUESTION—Who is τίς 'anyone'?

The use of 'anyone' is used to state a general principle that is applicable to the entire church [Alf, ICC, Lns, NIGTC, WBC]. However, in this context it refers especially to the householder who is responsible for the members of his household [ICC, Lns]. Or, it refers back to the children and grandchildren in 5:4 and is still speaking about widows in need [NIBC, TC, TH, WBC].

QUESTION—Who are ἰδίων '(his) own', and how is this to be connected with following phrase 'especially/namely (μάλιστα) his household'?

1. 'His own' refers to the person's whole family wherever they live, while μάλιστα 'especially' makes his responsibility even stronger for those living under his roof [EGT, Herm, ICC, LSA, NAC, NIBC, NIGTC, NTC,

TC, TG, TH, TNTC, WBC; all versions]. The word ἰδίων refers to his relatives [LSA, NIGTC; CEV, GW, HCSB, NCV, NET, NIV, NLT, NRSV, TEV], his relations [REB], his extended family [WBC]. These relatives are related to the person, but they are not members of the immediate family [TG]. The word ἰδίων '(his) own' refers to the members of his family in a broad sense so that children of grandparents are involved, while the immediate family in one's household is shown to be a special responsibility [NIGTC]. The word ἰδίων '(his) own' refers to the members of his family in a broad sense, and his immediate family is highlighted as being a special responsibility [ICC, NIGTC, TNTC]. Those living under his roof may also include relatives [NAC]. Taking care of one's relatives in general begins with those in one's own family [TH].

2. 'His own' refers to all those living in the household, both servants and members of the family and 'especially' makes his responsibility even stronger for family members. All dependents are included, covering parents if they are dependent, wife, children, and other relatives such as orphaned nephews and nieces [Lns].

3. 'His own' refers to the general obligation to care for widows in one's own family, while there is a special obligation to care for widows who are fellow Christians in the 'household of faith' [NTL].

he-has-denied[a] the faith and is worse[b] (than) an-unbeliever.

LEXICON—a. perf. mid./pass. (deponent = act.) indic. of ἀρνέομαι (LN 34.48) (BAGD 3.d. p. 108): 'to deny' [LN], 'to repudiate, to reject' [BAGD]. The clause τὴν πίστιν ἤρνηται 'he has denied the faith' [BNTC, Herm, NTC; HCSB, NASB, NET, NIV, NRSV, REB; similarly AB, Lns; TEV] is also translated 'those...have denied the true faith' [NLT], 'he has denied the Christian faith' [GW], 'he has denied what we believe' [LSA], 'he has disowned the faith' [ECC, WBC], 'has turned against the faith' [NCV], 'have given up their faith' [CEV]. This verb means to deny any relationship of association with someone or something [LN].

b. χείρων' (LN 65.29) (BAGD p. 881): 'worse' [AB, BAGD, BNTC, ECC, Herm, LN, Lns, LSA, NTC, WBC; all versions]. This comparative adjective indicates that something is less satisfactory than something else [LN].

QUESTION—What is τὴν πίστιν 'the faith'?

This means the Christian faith [BNTC, ECC, ICC, NCBC, NIGTC, NTC, TG, TNTC, WBC; GW], the doctrine that is held by the church [Lns], the teachings that Christians believe [LSA, TH]. This refers to the revelation of the will of God concerning the believer's conduct [ECC]. It refers to one's entire way of life [AB]. Actually, the objective aspects of the faith can hardly be separated from the subjective aspects [ICC, WBC], but the article places the emphasis on the corporate sense [WBC]. Behavior resulting from one's faith is authentic Christianity [NICNT]. He is denying his profession of faith [NTC].

QUESTION—What is meant by denying the faith?

Denying the faith means to deny or disavow any relationship with it, and such a denial could be shown by words or actions [TH]. This does not refer to a formal repudiation of the Christian faith, but to a practical denial of the Christian teachings by failing to do what is taught in them [ICC]. His denial is not by words, but by committing the sin of neglecting to support the members of his family [NTC]. By his act he is denying the teaching that he ought to believe and obey [Lns]. This describes a person who claims to be a believer while virtually denying the Christian faith by not even living up to pagan standards of decency, let alone Christian standards [WBC].

QUESTION—In what way is such a Christian worse that someone who is not Christian?

Non-Christians generally keep their family obligations, so they are morally better than a Christian who does not keep family obligations [ICC]. Both the attitude and actions of such a Christian are worse that those who are not Christians [NIGTC]. The person who is a Christian has God's law which says 'honor your father and your mother', so when that person fails to obey this law, he is worse than the many unbelievers who do instinctively what that law commands [NIGTC]. Among non-Christians, it was normal to take care of widows in their families, so a Christian family that failed to do this was behaving worse than the non-Christians [TG]. Not all unbelievers provide for members of their families, but when an unbeliever does not do so, it is not as bad as the believer who has the true teaching and yet denies it [Lns].

DISCOURSE UNIT: 5:9–16 [NIGTC, TNTC]. The topic is the enrollment of widows who are to be cared for by the church and also younger widows [NIGTC], a warning to younger widows [NAC].

DISCOURSE UNIT: 5:9–10 [TNTC]. The topic concerns widows as Christian workers.

5:9 (Let) a-widow be-put-on-the-list[a] being[b] **not less (than) sixty years, of-one husband a-wife,**[c]

LEXICON—a. pres. pass. impera. of καταλέγω (LN **33.34**) (BAGD p. 413): 'to have one's name on a list, to be entered on a list' [LN], 'to be put on the list' [NASB, NET, NRSV], 'to be on the list of widows' [NCV], 'to be placed/put on the list of widows' [NTC; CEV, GW, NIV], 'to be on the official list' [BNTC], 'to be put on the list for support' [NLT], 'to be placed on the official support list' [HCSB], 'to be put on the roll' [REB], 'to be enrolled' [AB, BAGD, LN, Lns, LSA, WBC], 'to be enrolled as a widow' [Herm], 'to be taken into the number' [KJV]. This passive verb is also translated actively with the widow as the object: 'do not put any widow on the list unless...' [**LN**], 'do not add any widow to the list of widows unless...' [TEV], '(follow these rules) for enrolling a widow' [ECC]. This verb means to be enrolled in the sense that a person's name is put on a list in order for that person to be identified as a member of a particular group [TH].

b. perf. act. participle of γίνομαι (LN 13.3) (BAGD II.2.b. p. 160): 'to be' [BAGD, LN]. The clause μὴ ἔλαττον ἐτῶν ἑξήκοντα γεγονυῖα 'being not less than sixty years' is translated 'not be less than sixty years old' [AB, Lns, LSA, WBC], 'not be less than sixty years of age' [NTC], 'if she is not less than sixty years old' [NRSV], 'only if she is not less than sixty years old' [NASB], 'unless she is at least 60 years old' [HCSB, NET], 'who is at least sixty years old' [GW, NLT], 'she must be at least sixty years old' [CEV, NCV], '(a widow) under sixty years of age (should not)' [REB], 'who is not younger than sixty' [Herm], 'she must have lived no less than sixty years' [ECC], '(not be taken) under threescore years old' [KJV], 'unless she is over sixty' [BNTC; NIV], 'unless she is over sixty years of age' [TEV]. The verb means to possess certain characteristics [LN]. It is used in statements pertaining to age [BAGD].

c. ἀνήρ (LN 9.24, 10.53) (BAGD 1. p. 66): 'husband' [BAGD, LN (10.53)] 'man' [BAGD, LN (9.24)]. The clause ἑνὸς ἀνδρὸς γυνή 'of one husband a wife' is translated 'a wife of one man' [Herm], 'one husband's wife' [Lns, NTC], 'who had only one husband' [GW], 'she must have been married only once' [TEV; similarly AB; NRSV], 'having been the wife of one man' [KJV, NASB], 'she has been the wife of one husband' [HCSB; similarly BNTC, ECC; NET, REB], 'a one-man woman' [WBC], 'if she has been faithful to her husband' [LSA], 'she must have been faithful to her husband' [NCV; similarly NLT], 'she must have been faithful in marriage' [CEV]. This noun denotes an adult male of marriageable age [LN (9.24)], or a man who is married to a woman. [LN (10.53)].

QUESTION—What relationship is indicated by the use of the participle γεγονυῖα 'being'?

The verb is a conditional participle, meaning '*if* she is' [WBC; NASB, NRSV], 'unless she is' [BNTC; HCSB, NET, NIV, TEV].

QUESTION—What list would a widow would be put on if she were qualified?

1. This is a list of the widows who would receive regular aid from the church [BKC, ICC, NAC, NIBC, NICNT, NTIC, WBC; HCSB, NLT]. These were the truly needy widows who had no family to help them [NICNT]. Nothing is said of there being two groups of widows receiving help, with one group also being appointed to a ministry in the church. All of the qualifications are in the past tense and point to the already established good character of widows applying for church aid [ICC]. This does not imply that other needy widows who were not on the list would be refused help [NAC].

2. This is a list of widows who are both supported by the church and have duties given them by the church [Alf, BNTC, ECC, EGT, Lns, My, NIGTC, NTC, TC, WP]. The requirements for having lived a good life (5:9–10) and taking a pledge (5:12) seem to imply that widows who were

elderly and godly with no one else to care for them were enrolled to receive help from the church and also have a part in the Church's ministry as tasks arose [NIGTC]. The verb 'be enrolled' is a technical term for being put on a recognized list and this paragraph gives the qualifications of enrollment in the order of widows and hints of the duties involved [BNTC]. Such 'real' widows were publicly enrolled in the order of widows after they pledged their lives to Christ and to charitable service of others [ECC]. Probably such widows received aid from the church and were given special duties in the church [TNTC]. They probably counseled younger women, visited the sick, prayed, and fasted [NTC]. It is doubtful that there was any overseer order that would require its members to enter it at the advanced age of sixty, so perhaps their ministry consisted of prayer, intercession, and giving thanks [EGT]. Or, this was a special order of widows who were selected to be overseers and not just deaconesses [TC]. This does not imply that the church would not also help other widows who were younger than sixty or who did not meet all the requirements for being enrolled [Alf, NIGTC]. Poor widows would also be helped by the church without being placed in this special class of widows [My].

QUESTION—What is the significance of the age requirement of being at least sixty years old?

Sixty was the recognized age when one became an old man or old woman in that time [BNTC, ECC, WBC]. Upon reaching the old age of sixty, it was not likely that a widow would be able to provide for her needs [ICC]. After reaching sixty, it was not likely that a widow would be sought for a second marriage [Lns, NAC, NIBC]. The reason younger widows were not included is given in 5:11–16 [BKC, TH]. The advice for younger widows in 5:14 is to remarry [NIGTC]. This does not imply that a younger disabled widow would be refused help until she turned sixty [NAC].

QUESTION—What is meant by the phrase ἑνὸς ἀνδρὸς γυνή 'of one husband a wife'?

This is the counterpart of the requirement μιᾶς γυναικὸς ἄνδρα 'of one wife a husband' for an overseer (3:2) and deacons (3:12).

1. 'Husband' is used in an extended sense and means that a widow must not have any other sexual partners besides her legal husband, thus prohibiting adultery [Herm, ICC, Lns, My, NAC, NICNT, NIGTC, NTC, WBC; NLT]. This applies whether she was married only once or if she was married a second time [Herm].

2. This means that the widow is to have had only one husband in her lifetime [Alf, BNTC, ECC, EGT, NIBC, TC, TG, TH, TNTC, WP]. What is expressly forbidden by this phrase is contracting a second marriage under any circumstances, whether after the death or divorce of the first spouse [BNTC, EGT]. The meaning of this phrase must take into consideration the parallel phrase in 3:2: ἑνὸς ἀνδρὸς γυνή 'wife of one husband' [Alf, EGT, TC]. For ordinary Christians, remarriage after the death of a mate

was not forbidden, but it was forbidden to the bishop and the deacon, and even the widows who were put on the church's list, since they were to uphold the highest ideal [EGT, TC]. Evidence from literature and funerary inscriptions, both pagan and Jewish, indicate that remaining unmarried after the death of a spouse or after divorce was considered exemplary, while remarriage was taken as a sign of moral weakness and self-indulgence [BNTC].

3. This means that a widow must not have remarried after a divorce [NCBC].

5:10 **by good deeds being-attested,**[a]

LEXICON—a. pres. pass. participle of μαρτυρέω (LN 33.263) (BAGD 2.b. p. 493): 'to be well attested' [BAGD], 'to be well spoken well of, to be approved of' [BAGD, LN]. The clause ἐν ἔργοις καλοῖς μαρτυρουμένη 'by good deeds being attested' is translated 'attested in good works' [Lns], 'she must be well attested for her good works' [NRSV; similarly Herm], 'well attested for noble deeds' [NTC], 'being witnessed to by good deeds' [WBC], 'well reported of for good works' [KJV], 'and is well known for her good deeds' [NIV; similarly HCSB, NCV], 'and if it is well known that she has done good deeds' [LSA], 'having a reputation for good works/deeds' [AB; NASB, NET, TEV], 'having acquired a reputation for good works' [BNTC; similarly REB], 'she must also be well-known for doing all sorts of good things' [CEV], 'she must have public attestation of fine deeds' [ECC], 'people should tell about the good things she has done' [GW], 'she must be well respected by everyone because of the good she has done' [NLT]. Being in the passive voice, it means that she was well spoken of, she was well know for her good deeds [NICNT]. This widow is someone to whom Christians would give testimony in connection with her good works [Lns]. Probably these good deeds were done while her husband was still alive and prosperous [NCBC].

if she-raised-children,[a] **if she-showed-hospitality,**[b]

LEXICON—a. aorist act. indic. of τεκνοτροφέω (LN 35.51) (BAGD p. 809): 'to raise children' [Herm, LN, WBC; CEV, GW, NCV, NET], 'to rear children' [AB, ECC, LN, NTC], 'to bring up children' [BAGD, LN, Lns; HCSB, KJV, NASB, NIV, NLT, NRSV, TEV], 'to take care of children' [REB], 'to look after children' [BNTC]. The clause εἰ ἐτεκνοτρόφησεν 'if she raised children' is translated to indicate the implied quality of the rearing: 'and be a woman who reared her children well' [**LN**], 'who brought up her children well' [TEV; similarly NLT], 'for example, she has brought up children properly' [LSA]. This verb means to raise a child to maturity by providing for its physical needs [BAGD, LN, TH], psychological needs [LN], and spiritual needs [BAGD].

b. aorist act. indic. of ξενοδοχέω (LN 34.57) (BAGD p. 548): 'to show hospitality' [BAGD, LN, WBC; HCSB, NIV, NRSV, REB], 'to practice

hospitality' [BNTC, Herm; NET; similarly Lns], 'to be hospitable' [**LN**,
LSA; GW], 'to show hospitality to strangers' [AB; NASB], 'to welcome
strangers' [NCV], 'to welcome guests' [ECC], 'to receive a stranger as a
guest' [**LN**], 'to receive strangers in her home' [TEV], 'to be kind to
strangers' [NLT], 'to give food to strangers' [CEV], 'to lodge strangers'
[KJV]. This verb means to receive and show hospitality to someone who
is not regarded as a member of the extended family or a close friend [LN].

QUESTION—What relationship is indicated by the conditional marker εἰ 'if' in
the five 'if' clauses?

The 'if' clauses are connected grammatically to the verb 'be put on the list'
in 5:9 [NIGTC]: *let a widow be put on the list if these things are true about
her.* However, instead of making these clauses dependent on the verb, they
should be taken to explain what is meant by good deeds [EGT, My]. The
conditional 'if' implies either '*one should enquire whether* she has reared
children, etc.' or '*she can be placed on the list if* she has reared children,
etc.' [NTC]. It means 'if at any time' she has done this [Alf, TC]. The list
gives *some* of the good deeds covered by good works, not all of them
[NICNT, TG, TH]. It is a list of possible conditions in which she performed
good deeds, but it is not a check-list of particular requirements which must
all be met by every candidate [ICC, WBC]. The five 'if' clauses give
examples of the good deeds spoken of in the initial clause of this verse [AB,
Alf, BKC, BNTC, ECC, Lns, NAC, NTC, TH; HCSB, NCV, NET, NIV,
NLT, NRSV, TEV]. These five 'if' clauses are the indirect questions that
would be asked when examining her qualifications, and the fifth question
moves from a specific quality to a wider general question [Lns]. The final
'if' clause generically sums up all of the other good deeds that are not
specified by the first four clauses [NICNT, TH]. In the first four conditional
clauses the conjunction 'if' is translated 'such as', while in the last clause 'if'
is translated 'in short' [AB]. The first four 'if' clauses give examples of the
good deeds spoken of in the initial clause of this verse, while the final 'if'
clause is an amplification of the initial requirement [NIBC, NICNT, NTC;
REB].

QUESTION—Whose children did the widow raise?

1. They are her own children [ECC, EGT, Lns, NICNT, NTC, NTL, TG,
   TH, WBC; probably NCV, NLT, TEV which refer to 'her children']. The
   children are obviously her own [TH]. This question refers to the widow's
   younger days and concerns her character in practicing motherhood [Lns,
   NICNT]. This refers to the widow's offspring and any orphans she has
   adopted, and it assumes that she has outlived them [ECC]. This is not a
   requirement for childless widows [NCBC, WBC]. She must be
   experienced in doing this in order to counsel others about rearing their
   children [NTC].

2. They are probably the children of other people that she has raised [Alf,
   BNTC, Herm, ICC, NIGTC]. The following conditions refer to good
   deeds done for those outside the widow's family, so the children may well

be outside her family members also [NIGTC]. Since the widow spoken of here has no children or grandchildren to support her, this joins the other requirements for service to others and refers to other people's children, including orphans (although it doesn't exclude her own children) [ICC]. Considering this paragraph as a unity, it refers to orphans rather than the widow's own children [Herm]. Childless widows are not being excluded here, so it must refer to caring for orphans, which is something a childless woman could do [Alf, BNTC].

QUESTION—Who received hospitality?

This speaks of hospitality shown to traveling Christians [BNTC, ICC, NAC, NICNT, NIGTC, NTL], especially those who were traveling about in order to preach and teach [NIGTC]. In the widow's younger days, her husband would invite guests, and her part would concern cooking, seeing to the beds, and doing whatever housework was needed for the guests. This generous hospitality continued to be worthy of praise in her days of widowhood [Lns]. The aorist tense of the verb indicates things done in the past, since a 'real' widow would not have the means to provide for strangers' needs at the present time [TH]. Or, this talks about her present sharing of her starvation rations with any traveling prophet [ECC].

if she-washed (the) saint's[a] **feet, if she-helped**[b] **(the ones) being-afflicted,**[c]

LEXICON—a. ἅγιος (LN 11.27) (BAGD 2.a.β. p. 10): The plural substantive ἁγίων 'saints' [AB, Herm, Lns, WBC; HCSB, KJV, NASB, NET, NIV, NRSV] is also translated 'God's people' [LN, LSA; CEV, NCV, REB], 'believers' [GW], 'Christians' [BNTC, ECC; TEV]. The clause εἰ ἁγίων πόδας ἔνιψεν 'if she washed the saint's feet' is translated so as to broaden her activities: 'welcoming God's people into her home' [CEV], 'taking care of believers' needs' [GW], 'and served other believers humbly' [NLT], 'performed humble duties for other Christians' [TEV]. This pronominal adjective 'saints' denotes people who belong to God [LN]. This name was traditionally used in the church of Christians in general [ICC].

b. aorist act. indic. of ἐπαρκέω (LN 35.1) (BAGD p. 283): 'to help' [AB, BAGD, LN, LSA, WBC; all versions except KJV, NASB, REB], 'to come to the help of' [ECC], 'to aid' [BAGD], 'to come to the aid of' [Herm], 'to assist' [NASB], 'to support' [REB], 'to relieve' [BNTC; KJV]. This verb means to assist in supplying what may be needed [LN]. See this word in another domain at 5:16.

c. pres. pass. participle of θλίβω (LN 22.21) (BAGD 3. p. 362): 'to be afflicted' [BAGD, LSA], 'to be distressed' [BAGD], 'to be troubled, to be persecuted, to suffer hardship' [LN]. This substantive is translated 'the afflicted' [WBC; HCSB, KJV, NRSV], 'the suffering' [GW], 'the oppressed' [ECC, Herm], 'those in distress' [NASB, NET], 'those who are in trouble' [AB; NCV, NIV, NLT; similarly TEV], 'those in distress'

[BNTC; REB], 'people in need' [CEV]. This verb means to cause someone to suffer trouble or hardship [LN].

QUESTION—What is involved in the requirement of washing the saints' feet?

1. This is connected with the preceding requirement of showing hospitality [ECC, Herm, LSA, My, NAC, NTC, NTL, TC, TG, WBC, WP]. When guests entered a house, their feet would be dirty from walking in the dusty streets, so it was customary to have a servant take off the guests' sandals and wash their feet [TG]. This follows the requirement for showing hospitality to travelers, so washing the feet of the saints is probably a particular act of showing hospitality to traveling Christians [ECC, LSA], or the feet of others, such as guests, husbands, parents, and teachers, who had been walking in the dry and dusty roads [WBC]. However, 'feet' is probably a synecdoche where the part represents the whole with the result that this refers not only to washing a guest's feet, but to all of the hospitality shown to such travelers [LSA, NTC]. It is a symbol of Christian humility and hospitality [Herm].

2. The reference to washing feet is used figuratively to refer to being involved in the most humble tasks in the church [AB, Lns, NICNT, NIGTC, TH; CEV, GW, NLT, TEV]. Hospitality has already been covered, so this is used figuratively for giving any menial service to the Christians in the congregation who needed such assistance, whether they came to her house for help or she went to their homes [Lns]. This may be a synecdoche for the entire activity of service shown to the church [AB].

QUESTION—What kind of affliction is meant here?

This probably refers to ordinary human afflictions [Alf, ICC, NIGTC, TH], such as bereavement and destitution [ICC], poverty [NICNT], troubles [BKC, TH], or social pressure [NICNT]. It refers to people in need [NTL, TG, WBC]. It could include persecution, but it is used in a more comprehensive sense than being limited to that [ICC, Lns, NIGTC]. Many were oppressed and persecuted because they were Christians [NTC], but this probably does not refer to external hostility [NICNT, WBC]. She helped others in the way that she now needs help herself [AB].

if she-was-devoted-to[a] every good-work.

LEXICON—a. aorist act. indic. of ἐπακολουθέω (LN 25.79) (BAGD 2. p. 282): 'to devote oneself to' [BAGD, BNTC, LN; HCSB, NASB, NIV, NRSV, TEV], 'to be dedicated to' [AB] 'to give oneself to' [LN], 'to zealously do' [LSA], 'to exhibit' [NET], 'to earnestly pursue' [WBC], 'to diligently follow' [KJV], 'to follow after' [Lns]. This clause is translated 'and always making herself useful' [CEV], 'or always doing good things' [GW], 'and giving her life to do all kinds of good deeds' [NCV], 'by doing good at every opportunity' [REB], 'has she always been ready to do good?' [NLT], 'did she set out to do every excellent deed possible?' [ECC]. This verb means to give or commit oneself wholeheartedly to something [LN].

DISCOURSE UNIT: 5:11–16 [TNTC]. The topic is the younger widows.

5:11 **But younger widows refuse/avoid.**[a] **Because when they-are drawn-away-by-strong-sexual-desires**[b] **from-the Christ, they-want-to-marry**
LEXICON—a. pres. mid./pass. (deponent = act.) impera. of παραιτέομαι (LN
   34.35) (BAGD 2.a. p. 616): 'to refuse' [BAGD], 'to refuse to accept, to
   reject' [LN]. This imperative παραιτοῦ is translated 'refuse' [KJV],
   'refuse to enroll' [LSA, WBC; HCSB], 'refuse to put on the list' [NTC;
   NASB, NRSV], 'reject' [Herm], 'do not accept' [**LN**], 'do not accept on
   the list' [NET], 'do not admit' [BNTC], 'do not admit to the roll' [REB],
   'do not put on the/that list' [CEV, NCV; similarly NIV, NLT], 'do not
   include on the/your list' [GW, TEV], 'avoid' [AB], 'have nothing to do
   with' [ECC], 'decline to be bothered with' [Lns]. This verb means to
   refuse to accept someone into a particular association, and here it is
   talking about not accepting younger widows into the list of those to
   receive support from the church [LN]. Here it means to refuse to enroll
   widows who are younger than sixty years of age [BAGD]. It means 'don't
   enroll them but reject them' [ICC].
   b. aorist act. subj. of καταστρηνιάω (LN 25.30) (BAGD p. 419): 'to
   become wanton against, to feel sensuous impulses that alienate' [BAGD],
   'to have lust, to experience strong physical desires' [LN], 'to become
   sensual' [LSA]. The phrase ὅταν καταστρηνιάσωσιν τοῦ Χριστοῦ
   'when they are drawn away by strong sexual desires from Christ' is
   translated 'when they are drawn away from Christ by desire' [HCSB],
   'when sensuous impulses lead them from Christ' [Herm], 'when their
   sensual desires alienate them from Christ' [NRSV], 'their passions may
   lead them away from Christ' [NET], 'when they feel sensual desires in
   disregard of Christ' [NASB], 'when they grow wanton against Christ'
   [AB, WBC; similarly KJV], 'when desire makes them restive against
   Christ' [BNTC], 'whenever their natural desires become stronger than
   their devotion to Christ' [GW], 'when their sensual desires overcome their
   dedication to Christ' [NIV], 'their physical desires will overpower their
   devotion to Christ' [NLT], 'often when, contrary to their pledged devotion
   to Christ, they grow restless with desire' [NTC], 'after they give
   themselves to Christ, they are pulled away from him by their physical
   needs' [NCV], 'whenever they feel attractions that are incompatible with
   their commitment to Christ' [ECC], 'whenever they act high and mighty
   against Christ' [Lns], 'they may later have a strong desire (to get married).
   Then they will turn away from Christ' [CEV]. This verb means to
   experience strong physical desires, particularly of a sexual nature [LN].
QUESTION—What relationship is indicted by δέ 'but'?
   The previous topic in 5:9–10 about putting widows on the list is now
   contrasted with refusing enrollment to another type of widows [ICC,
   NIGTC, WBC]. The widows of sixty years of age and older are contrasted
   with widows younger than sixty [ICC, NICNT, TG, TH]. The general tone of

the verse seems to focus on a younger age group than sixty since 5:14 counsels them to remarry and bear children [ICC, NIGTC]. Instead of 'younger', the adjective can be rendered simply 'young' [EGT].

QUESTION—What is implied by the conjunction ὅταν 'when'?

This conjunction indicates the condition in which the following clause about wanting to marry depends [ICC, NIGTC], and it also implies that this is very likely to happen [NIGTC]. Some translations leave out a condition and simply state that it will happen [NCV, NLT], while others translate with 'may' to indicate that it is only a possibility [CEV, NET].

QUESTION—Does the command παραιτοῦ mean that Timothy is to *refuse* or to *avoid* the younger widows?

1. The command is to refuse to enroll younger widows [Alf, BNTC, ECC, EGT, ICC, LN, Lns, LSA, NAC, NCBC, NIBC, NICNT, NIGTC, NTIC, NTL, TC, TH, WBC; all versions]. This command is in contrast with the command χήρα καταλεγέσθω 'let a widow be put on the list' in 5:9 and means that Timothy is to refuse to enroll the younger widows [Alf, ECC, LSA, NICNT, NIGTC, TH, WBC]. This refers to the official list of supported widows, and the widows of an age when they can remarry are to be excluded from that list [NICNT]. The church can aid younger widows, but it must not enroll them in a formal and ongoing financial relationship [NAC, TC, TNTC, WBC]. It does not mean to avoid younger widows because of fear for scandal [Alf].

2. The command is to avoid younger widows [AB, My]. It means that these widows are to be avoided personally [My]. This would also include to avoid placing them on the list of supported widows [AB, My].

QUESTION—What is the meaning of the verb καταστρηνιάσωσιν 'they are drawn away by strong sexual desires'?

The verb's prefix κατά means 'against' [EGT, NICNT, NIGTC] and the stem στρηνιάω means 'to live in sensuality or luxury' [NICNT], 'to have a strong sexual desire' [NIGTC], 'to be dominated by sensual or sexual desire' [TG]. This is talking about their desires taking control of them so that they want to get married [TH]. It is natural that having a strong sexual desire will bring about a strong desire to marry [BNTC, ECC, NAC, NIGTC, NTC], and in 5:14 Paul even states that he wants them to marry again [NTC]. Or, although the verb does not mean they would be sexually promiscuous, the context suggests that this could be a part of the problem [WBC]. It is implied that they would live a life of sexual misbehavior [NICNT].

QUESTION—What is meant by the genitive phrase τοῦ Χριστοῦ 'from the Christ'?

The verb prefix κατά 'against' requires that its object τοῦ Χριστοῦ 'the Christ' be in the genitive case [ECC, NIGTC]. The prefix means 'contrary to Christ' with the meaning that this is contrary to their pledged devotion to the work of Christ that they have pledged to do (4:12) [NTC]. When Christ becomes the recipient of this opposition, the idea seems to be that the young widows will reject their dedication to Christ by adopting a lifestyle of sexual misbehavior, yet the idea of sexual immorality seems too strong when the result is that they want to marry [NICNT]. It means that they will have sexual impulses that become a temptation to lead them away from devotion to Christ. Since they want to marry, it does not imply that they will fall into sexual sin, but it appears that when a widow is enrolled on the church list for support, her desire for marriage is wrong [ICC]. Their desire for marriage will overcome their devotion to Christ [BKC, NIBC], and perhaps this means that this would result in marrying an unbeliever [NIBC]. Even the desire to remarry would cause the women who undertook the widow's office to be unfaithful to Christ, their heavenly bridegroom [Alf, EGT, TC]. The following verse explains what is meant by such widows turning against Christ [AB].

5:12 having judgment[a] because they-have-broken[b] the first pledge/faith.[c]

LEXICON—a. κρίμα (LN 56.30) (BAGD 4.b. p. 450): 'condemnation' [BAGD, LN]. The participial phrase ἔχουσαι κρίμα 'having judgment' is translated 'having a judgment resting on them' [Lns], 'and so incur judgment' [NET], 'and come under judgment' [WBC], 'thus they bring judgment on themselves' [NIV], 'they will be judged' [NCV], 'then they would be guilty' [NLT], 'therefore they would be guilty' [LSA], 'and so become guilty' [TEV; similarly CEV, REB], 'and so they incur condemnation' [NRSV], 'thus incurring condemnation' [NTC; NASB; similarly BNTC], 'they earn condemnation' [AB], 'and will therefore receive condemnation' [HCSB], 'they stand condemned' [ECC], 'they condemn themselves' [GW], 'and thus are under the verdict that' [Herm], 'having damnation' [KJV]. This noun denotes the result of being judged guilty and thus liable for punishment [LN].

b. aorist act. indic. of ἀθετέω (LN 76.24) (BAGD 1.a. p. 21): 'to break, to nullify, to set aside' [BAGD], 'to do away with, to invalidate, to make invalid' [LN]. The clause ὅτι τὴν πρώτην πίστιν ἠθέτησαν 'because they have broken the first pledge/faith' is translated 'because they have broken their first pledge' [NIV; similarly BNTC, ECC], 'for breaking their former pledge' [NET], 'for having violated their first pledge' [NRSV], 'because they have set aside their previous pledge' [NASB], 'because they have renounced their original pledge' [HCSB; similarly NTC], 'breaking their earlier pledge of faithfulness' [LN (33.289)], '(become guilty of) breaking their promise to him' [CEV], 'of breaking their previous pledge' [NLT], 'of breaking their earlier vow to him' [REB], 'of breaking their earlier promise to him' [TEV], 'for not doing what they first promised to do' [NCV], 'because they have not done what they promised to do for Christ' [LSA], 'they have put aside their first commitment' [AB], 'they have broken their first faith' [Herm], 'since they abandoned their former faith' [WBC], 'because they set aside the first faith' [Lns], 'by rejecting the Christian faith, the faith they first accepted' [GW], 'because they have cast off their first faith' [KJV]. This verb means

to completely invalidate something that has been in force [LN]. The verb
has a range on meanings: 'to reject, to set aside, to nullify, to ignore, to
refuse' [NICNT].

c. πίστις (LN **33.289**) (BAGD 1.b. p. 662): 'pledge' [BNTC, ECC, NTC;
HCSB, NASB, NET, NIV, NLT, NRSV], 'pledge to be faithful' [LN],
'promise' [LN; CEV], 'solemn promise' [LN; TEV], 'what is promised'
[LSA; NCV], 'vow' [REB], 'oath' [BAGD], 'commitment' [AB], 'faith'
[Herm, Lns, WBC; KJV], 'the Christian faith' [GW]. This noun denotes a
promise or pledge to be faithful and loyal [LN].

QUESTION—What relationship is indicated by the use of the participle
ἔχουσαι 'having'?

It indicates the result of the widows' desire to remarry [BNTC, Herm, LSA,
NICNT, NIGTC, WBC; CEV, HCSB, NASB, NET, NIV, NLT, NRSV,
REB, TEV].

QUESTION—What is meant by the widows ἔχουσαι κρίμα 'having
judgment'?

This could be God's judgment as in 3:6 or public criticism as in 3:7; 5:7–8,
14; 6:1, or both, and the choice is affected by whether the following noun
πίστιν means 'pledge' or 'faith' [NICNT].

1. They incur judgment in the sense of being censured by others [AB, ECC,
NIGTC, TNTC]. They will earn public disapproval [AB].

2. God is the one who judges and condemns them [Alf, ICC, NICNT, TG,
TH; probably Lns, NAC, NIBC, NTIC, WBC; HCSB, KJV which take
this to refer to the Christian faith].

3. Their own consciences condemn them [My].

QUESTION—What relationship is indicated by ὅτι 'because'?

This conjunction explains why they would be judged for wanting to remarry
[AB, ECC, Lns, LSA, NIGTC, NTC, WBC; HCSB, KJV, NASB, NCV,
NET, NIV, NRSV].

QUESTION—What is meant by τὴν πρώτην πίστιν 'the first pledge/faith'?

1. This refers to the pledge they made when being enrolled as widows [AB,
Alf, BKC, BNTC, ECC, Herm, LSA, My, NCBC, NIGTC, NTC, TC, TG,
TH, TNTC, WP; all versions except HCSB, KJV]: *they have broken their
first pledge.* When they were accepted as an enrolled widow, they pledged
to devote their lives to serving the Lord [My, NIGTC]. They vowed to be
devoted to Christ instead of to a husband [NCBC, TC]. They vowed to
remain single in order to serve in the church [BKC, BNTC, ECC, NTC,
TH, WP]. They committed themselves to pray for the Christian
community in exchange for financial support [AB].

2. This refers to the Christian faith they had first accepted when they became
Christians [ICC, Lns, NAC, NIBC, NICNT, NTL, WBC; HCSB, KJV]:
they have rejected their original faith. This refers to apostatizing from the
faith they previously held [ICC]. The more common meaning of πίστις
'faith in 5:8 is retained here [NICNT, WBC], and since remarriage is
spoken of approvingly in 5:14, this must be speaking of young widows

who behave in a promiscuous manner so that they even marry unbelievers and adopt their new husbands' religion [NICNT, NTL]. The word 'faith' refers to her commitment to serve only Christ, so this kind of remarriage indicates that she has turned away from him [NAC, NIBC, WBC] and disobeyed biblical commands [NAC]. This refers to leaving her initial faith and commitment to Christ to marry an unbeliever [ICC, Lns, WBC]. There are two types of marriage in this paragraph, and here it is marriage with unbelievers while in 5:14 it is marriage with believers [ICC, NICNT].

5:13 **And at-the-same-time**[a] **also they-learn**[b] **(to be) idle**[c] **going-around**[d] **the houses,**

LEXICON—a. ἅμα (LN 67.34) (BAGD 1.a. p. 42): 'at the same time' [BAGD, BNTC, ECC, Herm, LN, Lns, NTC, WBC; GW, HCSB, NASB], 'besides' [CEV, NIV], 'besides that' [NCV, NET, NRSV], 'moreover' [AB], 'and withal' [KJV], 'and if they are on the list' [NLT], not explicit [TEV]. This adverb refers to a point of time that is emphatically simultaneous with another point of time [LN].

    b. pres. act. indic. of μανθάνω (LN 27.12) (BAGD 4. p. 490): 'to learn' [AB, BAGD, ECC, Herm, LN, Lns, NTC, WBC; all versions except CEV, NIV], 'to be instructed, to be taught' [LN], 'to qualify as' [BNTC], 'to become' [LSA; CEV], 'to get into the habit of' [NIV]. This verb means to acquire information, either in an informal or formal context of instruction [LN]. Here this means to learn through experience or practice rather than though instruction [BAGD, NIGTC]. This verb is also connected with the two adjectives in the following clause [NIGTC]: *they learn to be idle and also learn to be gossipy and meddling.* Since 'they learn' is in the present tense, it seems to mean that their idling was in the process of developing [TH].

    c. ἀργός (LN 42.46) (BAGD 2. p. 104): 'idle' [BAGD, LN, Lns, LSA, NTC; HCSB, KJV, NASB, NIV, NRSV], 'lazy' [BAGD, ECC; CEV, NET, NLT]. This adjective is also translated as a noun: 'idlers' [AB, BNTC, WBC], 'idleness' [Herm]; as a verb phrase: 'to waste their time' [NCV]. The whole clause is translated 'they learn to go around from house to house since they have nothing else to do' [GW]. This noun denotes the state of not working [LN]. For the widows to be 'idle' means that they had no work to do since they had no children to care for or housework to do [ICC]. It refers to wasting their time [TH].

    d. pres. mid./pass. (deponent = act.) of περιέρχομαι (LN **15.23**) (BAGD p. 647): 'to travel about, to wander about' [LN]. The phrase περιερχόμεναι τὰς οἰκίας 'going around the houses' is translated 'wandering around to the houses' [Lns], 'going around from house to house' [**LN**; GW, NET, REB, TEV; similarly AB; HCSB, NCV], 'as they go around from house to house' [NASB], 'and going about from house to house' [NIV], 'circulating from house to house' [ECC], 'wandering about

from house to house' [KJV], 'gadding around/about from house to house'
[BNTC, NTC; NRSV], 'flitting about among houses' [WBC], 'when they
run from house to house' [Herm], 'they just go about from house to
house' [LSA], 'and get into the habit of going from house to house'
[CEV], 'and will spend their time (gossiping) from house to house'
[NLT]. This verb means to move about from place to place [LN].

QUESTION—What relationship is indicated by the phrase ἄμα δέ 'and at the
same time'?

This is another thing that could happen if younger widows are put on the list
[ICC, WP]. It introduces a parallel and concurrent development among other
young widows [NICNT]. It is a second reason for refusing to enroll young
widows [BKC, ICC, LSA, NIBC, NIGTC, NTC, TC, TH]. Not all young
widows would be like this, but since it was likely to happen the rule should
be followed [NTC].

QUESTION—What is meant by the phrase ἀργαὶ μανθάνουσιν 'idleness they
learn'?

The infinitive εἶναι 'to be' is to be supplied [AB, EGT, ICC, Lns, My,
NICNT, NIGTC, NTC, TNTC, WBC; HCSB, KJV, NASB, NET, NLT,
NRSV, REB]: *they learn to be idle.* Or, the verb 'they learn' connected with
a substantive is an idiomatic construction, and here it is sarcastic and means
'they qualify as idlers' [BNTC].

QUESTION—What relationship is indicated by the use of the participle
περιερχόμεναι 'going around'?

1. This participle describes in what sense they were idle [LSA, NICNT
   WBC; TEV]: *they learn to be idle, that is, they go around from house to
   house.* 'They waste their time in going around from house to house'
   [TEV]. The description of these young widows in Ephesus as being idle is
   further explained by the participle [WBC].
2. This participle indicates an attendant circumstance of learning to be idle
   [NIGTC, NTC, TC; NASB, NET]: *they learn to be idle as they go around
   from house to house.*
3. This participle gives an example of their being idle [TH]: *they learn to be
   idle, such as going around from house to house.*
4. This participle is a result of being idle [CEV]: *they learn to be idle and
   then get into the habit of going from house to house.*

QUESTION—What is meant by going around the houses?

The plural 'houses' should be translated as going 'from house to house'
[NICNT].

1. This refers to going from house to house in the course of their church
   duties of visitation [BNTC, Herm, NIGTC, NTC, TC]. Part of their work
   for the church would be going from house to house in order to give
   assistance and counsel [NTC].
2. This means that they wasted their time in gadding about from house to
   house [AB, BKC, ICC, NIBC, NICNT, NTL, WBC]. These widows did
   not have their former household responsibilities, so they visited in other

houses to chat and gossip [NICNT, NTL]. This is not misusing visitation duties, but using spare time to gad about [ICC]. Although they should be spending their time in prayer and good deeds, they were spending their time going from house to house [WBC].

and not only idle but also (become) gossipy/nonsense-talking[a] and meddling,[b] saying[c] the (things) they-ought not.

LEXICON—a. φλύαρος (LN **33.375**) (BAGD p. 862): 'gossipy' [BAGD, LN, NTC], 'foolish' [BAGD]. This plural adjective is also translated as a substantive: 'gossips' [AB, BNTC, ECC, Herm, WBC; HCSB, NASB, NET, NIV, NRSV, REB, TEV], 'tattlers' [KJV]; as a verb phrase: 'they gossip' [GW], 'they begin to gossip' [LSA; NCV], 'they will start gossiping' [CEV], 'they talk nonsense' [LN], '(they will spend their time) gossiping' [NLT]. This adjective is derived from the verb φλυαρέω 'to talk nonsense' and describes one who talks nonsense, and perhaps here it could be translated 'gossipy' since one who speaks nonsense about someone else is normally gossiping [LN].

b. περίεργος (LN **88.244**) (BAGD 1. p. 646): 'meddling' [LN], 'meddlesome' [NTC], 'nosy (gossips)' [ECC]. This plural adjective is also translated as a substantive: 'busybodies' [AB, BNTC, Herm, LN, Lns, WBC; CEV, HCSB, KJV, NET, NIV, NRSV, TEV]; as a verb phrase: 'they begin to meddle' [LSA], 'meddling in other people's business' [NLT], 'they get involved in other people's business' [GW], 'they busy themselves with other people's lives' [NCV]. This adjective describes one who meddles in someone else's business [LN].

c. pres. act. participle of λαλέω (LN 33.70) (BAGD 2.b. p. 463): 'to say, to talk' [LN], 'to speak' [BAGD, LN]. The phrase λαλοῦσαι τὰ μὴ δέοντα 'saying the things they ought not' is translated 'saying things they shouldn't say' [NTC; GW, HCSB, NCV, NRSV; similarly AB, BNTC; NIV], 'they say what they should not say' [LSA], 'saying what they have no right to say' [ECC], 'talking about/of things they should not' [Lns; NET, NLT, TEV], 'speaking things which they ought not' [KJV], 'speaking about things that should not be spoken' [WBC], 'then they say what is not proper' [Herm], 'talking about things not proper to mention' [NASB], 'talking about things that are none of their business' [CEV]. This verb means to speak or to talk [LN].

QUESTION—What is meant by οὐ μόνον δὲ ἀργαί 'and not only idle'?

1. This adds another reason that young widows should not be enrolled [LSA, WBC].

2. This introduces a worse aspect of what would happen to idlers [ICC, NIBC, NICNT, TG, TH]. This means 'and even more than idlers' [NIGTC]. Not only do they do nothing constructive as idlers, they also do destructive things as being gossips and busybodies [NIBC]. It is the result of being idle [WBC].

QUESTION—What is meant by φλύαρος 'gossipy/nonsense talking'?

1. It means to gossip about other people [AB, BNTC, ECC, Herm, LSA, NIGTC, WBC; all versions].

2. It means to talk nonsense [ICC, LN, NIBC, NICNT, WBC]. This adjective means talking too much and saying nothing worthwhile, and in this context the problem is that they would talk nonsense, not that they would gossip about people [ICC]. The following clause about saying things that they shouldn't suggests that in their conversation they were promoting false teaching, and so this adjective means that they were talking nonsense [ICC, NIBC, NICNT].

QUESTION—What is meant by περίεργος 'meddling'?

This refers to those who pay attention to things that do not concern them and involve themselves in the concerns of others [NICNT, NIGTC]. They are nosy busybodies [NICNT]. It involves offering unsolicited advice [TG].

QUESTION—What relationship is indicated here by the use of the participle λαλοῦσαι 'saying'?

This participle expands on what they would gossip about [ECC]. It indicates a specific instance of both gossiping and meddling [AB, LSA], describing in more detail the nature of the two activities [WBC]. It refers to talking nonsense, and if their meddling is primarily verbal, that is also included [TH]. This could refer to the false teaching they have heard from the heretical teachers [ICC, NICNT], although this might be inadvertent addition to other things they talk about [NICNT]. They speak in the manner of gossips and busybodies, that is, speaking not for the benefit of others, but to their harm [AB].

5:14 **Therefore I-want[a] younger (widows) to-marry, to-bear-children, to-manage-the-home,[b]**

LEXICON—a. pres. mid./pass. (deponent = act.) indic. of βούλομαι (LN 25.3) (BAGD 2.a.δ. p. 146): 'to want' [AB, BAGD, LN; GW, HCSB, NASB, NCV, NET], 'to desire' [LN, LSA], 'to prefer' [CEV, TEV], 'to will' [NTC; KJV, NRSV], 'to advise' [NLT], 'to counsel' [NIV], 'to intend' [Lns], 'to wish' [Herm, WBC], 'to be one's wish' [BNTC, ECC; REB]. This verb means to desire to have or experience something [LN]. This verb expresses a degree of authority [Herm, NICNT]. It is a polite way of giving an order [TG]. It is a definite command [My, NAC, NICNT]. See this verb at 2:8.

b. pres. act. infin. of οἰκοδεσποτέω (LN **46.2**) (BAGD p. 558): 'to manage a home' [**LN**, LSA, NTC; GW, NCV, NIV], 'to manage a house' [BNTC], 'to manage a household' [BAGD, Herm; HCSB, NET, NRSV, REB], 'to direct a household' [LN], 'to rule the house' [Lns], 'to rule a household' [WBC], 'to run a household' [AB], 'to run a home' [ECC], 'to guide the house' [KJV], 'to take care of a home' [NLT, TEV], 'to keep house' [NASB], 'to look after a family' [CEV]. This verb means to command a household and give leadership to it [LN]. There is no difficulty about a woman being in charge of what went on in her own home [ICC].

QUESTION—What relationship is indicated by γάρ 'therefore'?

This conjunction indicates the conclusion for 5:11–13 [Alf, ICC, LSA, My, NICNT, NIGTC, TC, WBC]. The dangers involved with enrolling younger widows cause Paul to give this recommendation [ICC].

to-give no occasion[a] to-the (one) opposing[b] for reproach.[c]

LEXICON—a. ἀφορμή (LN **22.46**) (BAGD p. 127): 'occasion' [BAGD, LN, Lns, NTC, WBC; KJV, NASB, NRSV, REB], 'opportunity' [AB, BAGD, Herm, LN; HCSB, NET, NIV], 'favorable circumstances' [LN], 'reason' [NCV], 'a good reason for' [**LN**], 'a chance' [GW, TEV], 'pretext' [ECC], 'a loophole' [BNTC]. The whole clause is translated 'Then the enemy won't have any reason to say insulting things about us' [CEV], 'Then the enemy will not be able to say anything against them' [NLT], 'and that they do nothing about which an enemy can slander them' [LSA]. This noun denotes a set of circumstances that is favorable for a particular activity [LN].

b. pres. mid./pass. (deponent = act.) participle of ἀντίκειμαι (LN 39.1) (BAGD p. 74): 'to oppose' [BAGD, LN], 'to be hostile toward, to show hostility' [LN]. The phrase τῷ ἀντικειμένῳ 'the one opposing' is translated 'the one who opposes' [AB], 'the opponent' [BAGD], 'the adversary' [BAGD, ECC, Herm, Lns, NTC; HCSB, KJV, NET, NRSV], 'the Adversary' [BNTC], 'the Accuser' [WBC], 'the enemy' [BAGD; CEV, GW, NASB, NIV, NLT, REB], 'an enemy' [LSA], 'our enemies' [TEV], 'no enemy (will have any reason)' [NCV]. This verb means to oppose someone [LN].

c. λοιδορία (LN 33.393), (BAGD p. 479): 'reproach' [BAGD; NASB], 'reviling' [AB, ECC, Lns], 'slander' [BNTC, Herm, NTC, WBC; NIV], 'abuse' [BAGD], 'scandal' [REB], 'insult' [LN]. This noun is translated as a verb: 'to slander' [LSA], 'to accuse' [HCSB], 'to speak reproachfully' [KJV], 'to speak evil of' [TEV], 'to criticize' [NCV], 'to say insulting things' [CEV], 'to revile' [NRSV], 'to vilify' [NET], 'to ridicule' [GW], 'to say anything against them' [NLT]. This noun denotes something said in a highly insulting manner [LN].

QUESTION—What relationship is indicated by the use of the infinitive διδόναι 'to give'?

1. The infinitive indicates the purpose of Paul's instructions in the preceding clause [Lns; NET, NRSV, TEV]: *I want them to do this in order that they not give occasion for reproach.* Some translate with 'then' to state the result Paul wants BNTC, [CEV, NLT, REB].

2. The infinitive indicates the reason for the instructions [TH; NCV]: *I want them to do this because then they will not give occasion for reproach.*

3. The infinitive indicates an addition to what he wants [ECC, Herm, LSA; GW, HCSB, KJV, NASB, NIV]: *and I want them to do nothing that an enemy can slander them about.*

QUESTION—Who is τῷ ἀντικειμένῳ 'the one opposing'?

1. The one who opposes is expressed as a collective singular for human adversaries [AB, Alf, EGT, TC, TG, TH, TNTC]. The enemies are the non-Christians who are enemies of the Christians community [TG]. It refers to any human adversary, whether he is a Jew or a Gentile [NTC]. This avoids the problem of determining how Satan could insult the members of the church, and being a collective noun, it is best to translate with the plural 'the enemies' [TH].

2. The one who opposes is Satan [AB, BNTC, Lns, NAC, NCBC, NIBC, NICNT, NTL]. The article with the noun indicates that this refers to Satan, and he opposes the church by using the wicked men to revile the church [Lns, NAC, NIBC, WBC]. The criticism of people outside the church would be used by Satan to attack the reputation of the church and thus hinder the promotion of the gospel [NICNT]. The reference to Satan in the next verse supports this interpretation [AB, Lns, WBC], as does the reference to the devil in 3:6 [BNTC, WBC].

QUESTION—Who will be reproached?

1. Since the widows are the culprits, they will be the ones reproached [LSA; GW, NCV, NLT]: *for reproaching them.*

2. Since the widows belong to the church, their actions would cause the whole church to receive a bad reputation [Alf, EGT, ICC, NAC, NICNT, TG, TH, WBC; CEV, HCSB, NET, NRSV, TEV]: *for reproaching us.* Paul is addressing the total Christian community, so the inclusive 'us' should be used [TH].

5:15 Because[a] already some have-turned-away[b] after[c] Satan.

LEXCON—a. γάρ (LN 89.23): 'because' [Herm, LN, LSA], 'for' [AB, ECC, LN, NTC, WBC; HCSB, KJV, NASB, NET, NLT, NRSV, REB, TEV], 'as it is' [BNTC], 'but' [NCV], not explicit [CEV, GW, NIV]. This conjunction indicates the cause or reason between events [LN].

b. aorist pass. indic. of ἐκτρέπομαι, ἐκτρέπω (LN 31.65) (BAGD p. 246): 'to turn away' [BAGD, LN], 'to go astray' [LN], 'to turn' [BAGD]. The phrase τινες ἐξετράπησαν ὀπίσω τοῦ Σατανᾶ 'some have turned away to follow Satan' [LN (23.178); CEV, GW, HCSB, NCV, NIV, NRSV; similarly Herm; TEV], is also translated 'some have wandered away to follow Satan' [NET], 'some have turned aside to follow Satan' [NASB], 'some women have turned aside after Satan' [AB; similarly KJV], 'some have strayed after Satan' [ICC], 'some have gone astray after Satan' [BNTC], 'some of them have gone astray and now follow Satan' [NLT], 'some of them have slipped off after Satan' [ECC], 'there have been some who have taken the wrong turning and gone over to Satan' [REB], 'some younger widows have stopped obeying Christ in order to obey Satan'

[LSA]. This verb is a figurative expression for turning away from the truth and believing something that is different [LN]. See this word at 1:6.

c. ὀπίσω (LN **36.35**) (BAGD 2.a.β. p. 575): 'after' [LN]. This preposition is also translated as a verb: '(have turned away) to follow' [**LN**]. This preposition marks someone who is followed as a leader [LN]. See the preceding lexical item for translations of this preposition.

QUESTION—What relationship is indicated by γάρ 'because'?

The conjunction indicates the reason why Paul has just given the preceding instructions [BNTC, ECC, My, NTC, TC, TNTC]. It gives the grounds for the implied statement: '*I need to say this because, etc.*' [LSA]. It explains that Paul is giving these instructions on the basis of experience, not theoretically [NTC]. It is used to reinforce the argument [NICNT].

QUESTION—What is the function of the forefronted adverb ἤδη 'already'?

The adverb 'already' refers to what has happened prior to the time that Paul was writing this letter to Timothy, and it does not have the added meaning that he was surprised that it had happened in such a sort time after the church was founded [WBC]. It indicates the urgency of Paul's concern over the situation [BKC, ICC, NAC, NIBC, NIGTC, WBC]. The urgency is expressed by an exclamation, 'Look what's already happened to some of the young widows!' [CEV].

QUESTION—What is meant by the verb ἐξετράπησαν 'have turned away'?

They have turned aside from the right path [Alf, NTC], that is, from the Christian path of life [My]. They were unfaithful to their pledge (5:12) [TC]. This refers to something worse that a second marriage [EGT]. They rejected their first faith as described in 5:11–12 and cast off Christ and his spiritual restraint [Lns]. They have committed apostasy by turning away from the apostolic faith [ICC, NICNT]. Or, it is not referring to a formal apostasy, but it suggests that they were living a worldly lifestyle [My, NAC].

QUESTION—What is meant by 'following after' Satan?

Instead of following Christ they have left him to follow Satan [ICC, NICNT]. This does not tell what is involved, but it is evident that it is sinful [NIGTC]. It refers to what is described in 5:11b [ICC]. It refers to a way of life involving sexual promiscuity and rejection of traditional values [NICNT]. They became godless [Lns], and immoral [TNTC]. They have become prostitutes [NCBC].

5:16 **If any believing[a] (woman) has[b] widows,**

TEXT—Instead of πιστή 'believing-woman' some versions and Church Fathers read πιστός 'believing-man' and some manuscripts read πιστὸς ἢ πιστή 'believing-man or believing-woman'. GNT reads πιστή believing-woman' with a B decision, indicating that the text is almost certain. 'Believing-man or believing-woman' is read by KJV.

LEXICON—a. πιστός (LN 31.36) (BAGD 2. p. 665): 'believing, trusting' [BAGD, LN]. This feminine nominative is translated 'a/any believing woman' [BNTC, NTC, WBC; HCSB, NET, NRSV], 'any woman believer' [Lns], 'a/any woman who is a believer' [ECC; GW, NCV, NIV, NLT], 'a woman who believes in Christ' [LSA], 'a Christian woman' [REB, TEV], 'a/any woman who is a follower' [CEV, NASB], 'a/any faithful woman' [AB, Herm]. This adjective describes the act of trusting [LN].

b. pres. act. indic. of ἔχω (LN 57.1) (BAGD I.2.b.β. p. 332): 'to have, to own, to possess' [LN]. The phrase ἔχει χήρας 'has widows' [BNTC, Herm, Lns, NTC, WBC; HCSB, NET; similarly KJV] is also translated 'has widows in her family' [LN (35.32); CEV, NCV, NET, NIV, REB, TEV], 'has widows in her household' [LSA], 'has relatives who are widows' [AB; GW, NLT], 'has relatives who are really widows' [NRSV], 'has dependent widows' [NASB], 'who welcomes widows into her home' [ECC]. This verb means to have or possess objects or property in the sense of having control over such objects [LN]. It means to have possession of persons to whom one has close relationships [BAGD].

QUESTION—Why are these instructions directed to women who are believers?

This is addressed to a woman because the woman of the household would have the main responsibility of caring for a widow [My, NIGTC]. The woman head of the household would be one to make the arrangements for caring for a needy widow [ICC, TH]. If a man were unmarried or a widower, it would not be suitable for him to undertake the care of a widow, and if he were married, the practical aspects of caring for a widow in the household would rest upon his wife [BNTC, WBC]. This woman believer is a young widow or single woman who remains unmarried and has the means to take care of another widow in her family [NIGTC, WBC]. However, it is not necessary that this Christian woman be a widow herself [ICC]. This refers to a Christian woman who is well-to-do or wealthy [ECC].

QUESTION—What is meant by a Christian woman 'having' widows?

The verb 'has' indicates a family relationship [My, NIGTC], and it is also used in this way in 5:4: 'if any widow has children or grandchildren' [NICNT]. The context shows that the needy widows are in the Christian woman's household [TH], and it could refer to widowed mothers, sisters, aunts, and sisters-in-law [NCBC, TG]. The plural noun 'widows' covers mother, grandmother, mother-in-law, and other relatives [WBC]. Since the case of caring for widows who are close relatives such as mothers or grandmothers has been dealt with in 5:4 [Alf, BNTC] this extends the list to more distant relatives [Alf]. This refers to widows who are servants, dependants, or friends of the well-to-do Christian woman [BNTC]. Or, 'having widows' implies that a well-to-do Christian woman has gathered needy widows into her home to support them [ECC].

let-her-support[a] them and not (let) the church be-burdened,[b] in-order-that it-may-support the (ones) (who are) really[c] widows.

LEXICON—a. imperf. act. indic. of ἐπαρκέω (LN **35.32**): 'to support' [BNTC, **LN**; REB], 'to provide for' [AB, Herm, LN], 'to care for' [WBC], 'to take care of' [LSA; NCV, NLT, TEV], 'to help' [CEV, GW, HCSB, NET, NIV; similarly ECC], 'to assist' [NTC; NASB, NRSV], 'to relieve' [Lns; KJV]. This verb means to provide continuous assistance and help by supplying the needs of someone [LN]. This might involve giving a needy widow a home, or work, or financial support [Lns]. See this word in another semantic domain at 5:10.

b. pres. pass. impera. of βαρέομαι, βαρέω (LN 22.18) (BAGD p. 133): 'to be burdened' [AB, BAGD, ECC, Herm, LN, Lns, LSA, NTC, WBC; GW, HCSB, NASB, NET, NIV, NRSV], 'to have the burden' [BNTC; CEV], 'to have to take care of' [NCV], 'to be charged' [KJV], '(must be relieved of) the burden' [REB]. This passive verb is also translated actively: 'put the burden on' [TEV], 'put the responsibility on' [NLT]. The verb means to experience difficulty because of burdensome and troublous obligations [LN]. Here, this refers to financial burdens [BAGD].

c. ὄντως (LN 70.2) (BAGD 2. p. 574): 'really' [BAGD, LN], 'certainly, truly' [LN]. The phrase ταῖς ὄντως χήραις 'the ones who are really widows' [NTC] is also translated 'those who are real widows' [AB; NRSV], 'those who are genuinely widows' [HCSB, NET], 'genuine widows' [BNTC, Lns], 'the true widows' [Herm, WBC], 'who are truly widows' [NCV], 'who are widows indeed' [KJV, NASB], 'the widows proper' [ECC], 'those who are widows in the full sense' [REB], 'the really destitute widows' [LSA], 'widows who are really/truly in need' [CEV, NET, NIV], 'the widows who are all alone' [TEV], 'widows who are truly alone' [NLT], 'widows who have no families' [GW]. See this word at 5:2, 5.

QUESTION—How would the church be burdened?
This refers to an economic burden [NICNT]. The church would be burdened financially or because it would entail additional work [NIGTC].

DISCOURSE UNIT: 5:17–6:2a [AB; CEV]. The topic is more community directives [AB], church leaders [CEV].

DISCOURSE UNIT: 5:17–25 [ECC, ICC, NAC, NCBC, NIBC, NICNT, NIGTC, WBC; HCSB, NASB]. The topic is elders [NASB], instructions about elders [ICC, NIBC], payment and discipline of elders [WBC], the proper handling of leaders [NAC], honoring the elders [HCSB], the order of presbyters [ECC], how to deal with presbyters (with an inset at 5:23 about advice on diet) [NCBC], proper recognition and discipline of elders [NICNT], compensation, discipline, and ordination of elders [NIGTC].

DISCOURSE UNIT: 5:17–21 [TH]. The topic is responsibilities toward elders.

DISCOURSE UNIT: 5:17–20 [Herm, NAC, TNTC]. The topic is elders [TNTC], presbyters [Herm], recognition and discipline of leaders [NAC].

DISCOURSE UNIT: 5:17–19 [NTL]. The topic is the rights of elders.

5:17 **(Let) the elders (who) have-led[a] well be-considered-worthy[b] of-double honor/pay,[c]**

LEXICON—a. perf. act. participle of προΐσταμα, προΐστημι (LN 36.1) (BAGD 1. p. 707): 'to lead, to guide' [LN], 'to direct' [BAGD, LN], 'to manage, to rule' [BAGD]. The phrase οἱ καλῶς προεστῶτες πρεσβύτεροι 'the elders who have led well' is translated 'the elders who lead the church well' [LSA; NCV], 'the elders who are good leaders' [HCSB], 'elders who give good service as leaders' [REB], 'elders who exercise leadership well' [BNTC], 'the elders who have been serving well' [WBC], 'the elders who do good work as leaders' [LN (65.18); TEV], 'elders who do their work well' [NLT], 'elders who provide effective leadership' [NET], 'the elders who direct the affairs of the church well' [NIV], 'church leaders who do their job well' [CEV], 'the elders that/who rule well' [NTC; KJV, NASB, NRSV], 'elders who govern well' [AB], 'the excellently presiding elders' [Lns], 'spiritual leaders who handle their duties well' [GW], 'the presbyters who have given outstanding direction' [ECC], 'the presbyters who govern well as presiding officers' [Herm]. This verb means to influence others so as to cause them to follow a recommended course of action [LN]. This verb is commonly used to refer to the activities of officials and administrators of the church [BAGD]. In respect to the church, this verb refers to guiding, administering, and caring for the members of the congregation, but 'ruling' is too strong a word for this setting [NAC, NICNT]. The perfect tense indicates that these elders had been serving well and are now doing so [NIGTC]. The perfect tense signifies a present activity here [Alf].

b. pres. pass. impera. of ἀξιόω (LN **65.18**) (BAGD 1.a. p. 78): 'to be considered worthy of' [**LN**], 'to be regarded as worthy of' [BAGD, LN], 'to be considered as meriting, to be regarded as being valuable for' [LN], 'to be deserving of' [BAGD]. See translations of this word in the following lexical item. This verb means to consider something of a comparable merit or worth [LN].

c. τιμή (LN **57.167**, 87.4) (BAGD 2.e. p. 818): 'honor, respect, status' [LN (87.4)], 'compensation, honorarium' [BAGD, LN (57.167)], 'pay' [LN (57.167)]. The phrase διπλῆς τιμῆς ἀξιούσθωσαν 'let them be considered worthy of double honor/pay' is translated 'let them be considered worthy of double honor' [WBC; NRSV; similarly NTC; KJV, NET], 'let them be counted worthy of twofold honor' [Lns], 'should receive double honor' [NCV], 'should be greatly honored by the church' [LSA], 'are to be considered worthy of double honor' [NASB], 'are worthy of double honor' [NIV], 'give double honor to' [GW], 'should be respected and paid well' [NLT], 'should be considered worthy of double compensation' [AB], 'should be deemed worthy of double remuneration' [BNTC], 'should be considered worthy of an ample honorarium' [HCSB], 'should be considered worthy of double pay' [**LN** (65.18); similarly TEV], 'should be reckoned worthy of a double stipend' [REB], 'should be considered worthy of receiving double compensation' [LN (57.167); similarly Herm], 'deserve to get double pay' [ECC], 'deserve to be paid twice as much' [CEV]. This noun denotes honor as an element in the assignment of status to a person [LN], or it denotes the compensation that is given for special service, and it implies that this is a way by which honor or respect may be shown [LN].

QUESTION—Who were the πρεσβύτεροι 'elders'?

This is the same word used at 5:2 for 'older man' in contrast with the younger men. Here it is used as a technical term for leaders of the congregation [LSA, My, NTC, NTL, TC, WP]. They were a recognized group of church leaders [NICNT, NIGTC, WBC]. The offices of πρεσβύτερος 'elder' and ἐπίσκοπος 'overseer' (in 3:2) are two designations for the same group of persons [BNTC, ECC, Lns, NAC, NIBC, NIGTC, NTC, NTL, TC, WBC, WP]. They were the older men in charge of the congregation [TG]. The term 'elder' pertains to one's age and dignity while 'overseer' pertains to his function [Lns, NTC]. Or, elders seem to be church leaders in a town, while overseers were leaders over a much wider area [TH].

QUESTION—What is meant by τιμῆς 'honor/pay'?

1. This refers to being honored by the church [Alf, LSA, My, NICNT, NTC; GW, KJV, NASB, NCV, NRSV]: *the elders should be highly honored by the church*. The elders were householders and did not need double pay, so this instruction urges the congregation to acknowledge the faithfulness of such elders [NIGTC]. This primarily concerns the attitude of respect that the church should have for the elders, but it does not exclude honoring them by paying them what they deserve [Alf, LSA, My, NICNT, NTC].

2. This refers specifically to being paid by the church [AB, BAGD, BKC, ECC, EGT, Herm, LN, NCBC, NTIC, TC, TG, TH, TNTC; CEV, HCSB, REB, TEV]: *the elders should receive double pay from the church*. Here the word τιμή has the concrete meaning of wages [AB, TG]. This speaks of doubling the payment given them, rather than the dubious idea of doubling the honor shown them [AB].

3. This refers to both being respected and being paid by the church [NAC, NIBC, NIGTC, NTL, TH, WBC; NET, NLT].

QUESTION—What is meant by διπλῆς 'double' honor or pay?

1. This refers to double honor [Lns, LSA, My, NTC; GW, KJV, NASB, NCV, NIV, NRSV].

1.1 'Double' merely means that they should receive *great* honor [Alf, Lns, LSA, NTC, TNTC]. Elders should receive honor and those who serve well should receive extra honor [Lns, NTC], but it is implied that when necessary, they should also be honored in a material way [NTC]. Double honor means honor in greater measure [Lns].

1.2 'Double' means that there are *two reasons* for honoring them: they should be honored for their office and also for their good work [My].

1.3 'Double' means that there are two kinds of honor; they are worthy to receive both respect and remuneration [NAC, NIBC, NIGTC, NTL, TH].

1.4 'Double' means that they are to be honored with receiving double-seized portions at the church meal [ICC]. An example of this kind of honoring someone at a meal is in Gen. 43:34 where Benjamin's portion was five times that of what his brothers received [ICC].

2. This refers to paying them double for their work [AB, BKC, BNTC, ECC, EGT, Herm, LN, TC, TG, TNTC, WBC; CEV, HCSB].

2.1 'Double' merely means that they should receive ample pay [EGT, TC, TNTC, WBC; HCSB]. This refers not to a set salary, but to an honorarium, so instead of saying that some sum was to be doubled, it means that they should receive a generous amount of money as an honorarium [WBC].

2.2 'Double' means that they are to receive twice as much pay [BKC, BNTC, ECC, Herm, LN, TG; CEV]. They are to be paid twice as much as those elders who have lesser duties [BNTC, ECC, Herm, TG]. There seems to be a few elders who devoted themselves to full time service, while there were others who only worked part time and thus had other jobs to support themselves [ECC].

especially/namely[a] the (ones) working-hard[b] in preaching[c] and teaching.

LEXICON—a. μάλιστα (LN 78.7) (BAGD 1. p. 489): 'especially' [AB, Alf, BAGD, BNTC, Herm, LN, Lns, LSA, NAC, NTC; all versions except GW, REB], 'particularly' [ECC], 'in particular' [REB], 'this is especially true for' [GW], 'above all' [LN], 'namely' [WBC]. This adverb denotes a very high point on a scale of extent [LN].

b. pres. act. participle of κοπιάω (LN 42.47) (BAGD 2. p. 443): 'to work hard, to toil, to labor' [LN]. The phrase οἱ κοπιῶντες ἐν λόγῳ καὶ διδασκαλίᾳ 'the ones working hard in preaching and teaching' is translated 'those who labor in preaching and teaching' [NTC], 'those who work hard in/at preaching and teaching' [HCSB, NASB, NET, NLT, REB, TEV; similarly CEV, NCV, NRSV], 'those who are laboring hard at preaching and teaching' [WBC], 'those whose work is preaching and teaching' [NIV], 'those occupied with preaching and teaching' [BNTC], 'those whose jobs are preaching and instructions' [ECC], 'those who labor in speech and in teaching' [AB], 'those who are engaged in speaking and teaching' [Herm] 'they who labor in the word and doctrine' [KJV], 'if they work hard at teaching the word of God' [GW], 'toiling in connection with Word and teaching' [Lns], 'those who preach and those who teach' [LSA]. This verb means to engage in hard work, and it implies that there are difficulties and trouble involved in doing so [LN]. This kind of work is described as being in the category of preaching and teaching [ICC, NICNT].

c. λόγος (LN 33.99) (BAGD 1.a.β. p. 477): 'preaching' [BAGD; HCSB, NASB, NET, NIV, NLT, NRSV, REB], 'speaking' [LN; NCV, NET], not explicit [GW]. This noun is also translated as an active verb: 'to preach' [LSA; CEV]. This noun denotes the act of speaking [LN]. The meaning depends on the context and in conjunction with διδασκαλία 'teaching' it means 'preaching' [BAGD].

QUESTION—What is meant by μάλιστα 'especially/namely'?

1. This means 'especially' or 'above all' [Alf, BKC, BNTC, ECC, EGT, Herm, Lns, LSA, NAC, NICNT, NTC, NTIC, NTL, TC, TG, TH, WP; all versions]. This verse refers to two groups of elders plus a subgroup of one group: (1) those elders who did not lead well, (2) those elders who did lead well in their various duties, and (3) especially those in the second group who worked hard as preachers and teachers [ECC, NICNT]. Or, the word τιμή 'honor' in itself does not mean honorarium or salary, so all elders who rule well deserve double honor, but in the case of those who have given themselves entirely to the work of preaching and teaching, honoring them might include giving them a good salary to enable them to continue in that work [NTC].

1.1 It implies that some elders preached and taught while other elders had other duties [Alf, BNTC, ECC, EGT, NAC, TG, TH, TNTC]. Some elders were involved with administration and pastoral care, but the primary work was preaching and teaching [TH]. Some elders did not preach and teach, but those who did especially deserved to be paid double the usual amount paid to elders [TG].

1.2 It implies that while all the elders preached and taught, some worked harder at this than others [Lns, NTC]. All of the elders were required to teach (3:2) but some of them showed special zeal for this work [Lns]. All of the elders ruled and to some extent taught, but in addition to ruling some labored in preaching to the congregation and teaching the youth [NTC].

2. This means 'namely' and identifies the ones who lead well as being those who work hard at preaching and teaching [ICC, NIGTC, WBC]. There are two groups of elders: (1) those elders who did not lead well, (2) those elders who did lead well in their preaching and teaching [ICC, NIGTC].

QUESTION—How are preaching and teaching distinguished from each other?

'Preaching' is used in the sense of exhortation and application, while the subject of these activities is the 'teaching' [NIGTC]. They preached by proclaiming the gospel, and they taught the doctrinal instructions of the gospel [WBC]. Preaching refers to proclaiming the message of the gospel to believers and especially to nonbelievers, while teaching was directed to the believers, explaining what Christians should believe and the implications this had for their lives [TH]. The two activities are not to be sharply distinguished from each other, and they may refer to two types of teaching [ICC]. Both activities deal with the gospel, so their distinction involves the audience: the gospel was preached to unbelievers, and it was taught to the

church [ICC, NICNT]. Elders in general had the responsibility of teaching,
but senior executive elders would also have the responsibility of preaching
[BNTC].

5:18 Because the Scripture[a] says, "You-shall- not -muzzle[b] an-ox treading-
out-the-grain"[c] and, "Worthy[d] (is) the workman of his wages."[e]

LEXICON—a. γραφή (LN 33.53) (BAGD 2.b.β. p. 166): 'Scripture' [BAGD,
LN], 'Scripture passage' [LN]. This singular noun is translated 'Scripture'
[BNTC, WBC; GW, REB], 'the Scripture' [AB, ECC, Herm, Lns, LSA,
NTC; all versions except CEV, GW, REB], 'the Scriptures' [CEV]. This
singular noun denotes a particular passage of the Old Testament [LN]. Or,
it designates Scripture as a whole [BAGD]. The noun can refer to either a
specific passage or to the whole of Scripture, and here it means 'the
Scripture says in this particular verse' [ICC, NICNT].

   b. fut. act. indic. of φιμόω (LN **44.6**) (BAGD 1. p. 861): 'to muzzle' [AB,
BAGD, BNTC, Herm, **LN**, Lns, LSA, NTC, WBC; all versions except
NCV, NLT], 'to tie shut' [BAGD], 'to tie shut the mouth' [ECC], 'to keep
from eating' [LN], 'to muzzle an ox to keep it from eating' [NLT], 'to
cover its mouth to keep it from eating' [NCV]. This verb means to put
something over or around the mouth of an animal in order to prevent it
from eating [LN]. This is a declarative future tense [LSA], and it functions
as in imperative in this context [ICC, LSA, NIGTC; CEV].

   c. pres. act. participle of ἀλοάω (LN **43.19**) (BAGD p. 41): 'to tread out the
grain' [**LN**], 'to thresh' [LN]. The participle ἀλοῶντα 'treading out the
grain' [WBC; similarly BNTC; KJV] is also translated 'that is threshing'
[AB], 'that is threshing grain' [ECC; HCSB], 'a threshing (ox)' [Lns,
NTC]. This participle is also translated with an indication of its temporal
relationship: 'when/while it is treading out the grain' [Herm, LN, LSA;
NET, NIV, NRSV, REB], 'as it treads out the grain' [NLT], 'while he is
threshing' [NASB], 'when it is threshing grain' [GW], 'when an ox is
working in the grain' [NCV], 'when you are using it to thresh grain'
[TEV], 'when you are using it to grind grain' [CEV]. The verb means to
separate the grain from the husks of plants, either by beating or by being
tread on by farm animals [LN].

   d. ἄξιος (LN 65.17) (BAGD 2.a. p. 78): 'worthy' [BAGD, LN]. The phrase
ἄξιος ὁ ἐργάτης 'worthy is the workman' is translated 'worthy is the
worker' [NTC, WBC], 'the worker/laborer is worthy of' [Herm; HCSB,
KJV, NASB; similarly Lns], 'workers are worth' [CEV], 'a/the
worker/workman/laborer deserves' [AB, BNTC; GW, NET, NIV, NRSV],
'the workman is deserving of' [ECC], 'one who works deserves' [LSA],
'the worker earns' [REB], 'a worker should be given' [NCV]. 'workers
should be given' [TEV]. This adjective describes something as having a
relatively high degree of comparable merit or worth [LN]. Here 'worthy'
has the sense of being entitled to wages [NIGTC].

e. μισθός (LN 57.173) (BAGD 1. p. 523): 'wages/wage' [BAGD, BNTC, ECC, Herm, LN, WBC; HCSB, NASB, NIV], 'pay' [AB, BAGD, LN, Lns, NTC; CEV, GW, NCV, NET, REB, TEV], 'reward' [KJV]. This noun is also translated as a verb phrase: 'to be paid' [NRSV], 'that he be paid' [LSA]. This noun denotes the payment offered someone for services or work that was done [BAGD, LN]. Although the noun can also mean 'reward', here it means 'wages' since it is given to the worker in return for his work, not as an undeserved gift [TH].

QUESTION—What relationship is indicated by the conjunction γάρ 'because'?

This conjunction indicates the grounds for saying that payment should be given to the elders [Alf, BKC, BNTC, ECC, ICC, Lns, My, NAC, NCBC, NIBC, NICNT, NIGTC, NTL, TH, WBC]. The preceding principle is true because it is a commandment given by God [NIGTC].

QUESTION—What is indicated by using the verb 'it says' in connection with Scripture rather than the more commonly used phrase 'it is written'?

Although the phrase 'it is written' is used more frequently in the NT, the expression 'Scripture says' is used in five other places in the NT [TH]. This verb personifies Scripture as though it could speak [TH]. Paul considered God to be directly speaking through Scripture [ECC, NIGTC]. The present tense λέγει 'says' indicates that the OT has a continuing authority for Paul [WBC].

QUESTION—Where does Scripture say, "You shall not muzzle an ox treading out grain" and how is it applied?

This is quoted from Deuteronomy 25:4 [all commentaries] in the slightly reorganized wording of the Septuagint [NICNT]. It is also quoted in 1 Corinthians 9:9 [TG, WBC], where Paul applies it in the same way [BNTC], by commenting "But was God concerned only about an ox? No, he wasn't! He was talking about us." [CEV]. The statement in Deuteronomy commands that a farmer must not prevent an ox from taking its share of the harvest [ICC]. This refers to the practice of driving oxen over a threshing floor so as to trample the grain with their hooves in order to separate the grain from the chaff [ICC, NICNT]. This action took place on a circular piece of level ground where sheaves of grain were untied and spread out. Sometimes the ox pulled a wooden sledge so as to more thoroughly loosen the grain from the sheaves. Sometimes a muzzle was placed over the mouth of the ox to prevent it from eating the grain as it walked around [NTC, TH]. The command in Deuteronomy about not muzzling an ox was given to allow the animal an occasional bite as it was working at the threshing floor, and Paul took this command as a principle that was broader than a mere statement about caring for animals [NAC]. It is quoted here to imply that just as an ox is entitled to eat while threshing, so an elder is entitled to provision for his needs while ministering [ICC]. Like an ox gets its food from the grain it is threshing, so elders should get material support for their labors from the very people they benefit [TH]. God has given to every worker, whether an ox, a workman, or a minister of the gospel, the right to partake of the fruits of his work [NTC]. Paul was using the common rabbinic principle of biblical interpretation of using an argument from the lesser to the greater: if animals are fed when they work, even more so should preachers and teachers be compensated for their work [NTL]. Since God showed concern for a laboring ox, then the congregation should show proper concern for their elders [NAC].

QUESTION—Where does Scripture say, "Worthy is the workman of his wages"?

The conjunction καί 'and' joins this quotation with the previous quotation from the OT, but here the actual text does not appear in the OT [ECC]. The conjunction 'and' indicates that Jesus' words in this quotation are of equal authority with the OT [Lns]. This quotation is in verbal agreement with Luke 10:7 [ICC, NIGTC, TH; NET], and in the parallel passage in Matthew 10:10 where the word 'food' is used instead of 'wages' [ICC, NIGTC]. This indicates that the sayings of Jesus had been given the status of Scripture [ICC, NAC, NIGTC, TNTC, WBC]. Since Luke had been with Paul during his imprisonment in Rome (Col. 4:14 and Philemon 24), it could be that Luke had finished writing his Gospel so that Paul could quote from it, or it is possible that Paul was quoting form a collection of Jesus' sayings that Luke used as a source for his Gospel [NTC]. Or, the reference to Scripture only refers to the preceding quotation, and Paul added by way of explanation and confirmation this quotation which may be a familiar proverb [Alf, EGT, My, TC]. Workmen usually work for wages, so they should get paid what is due them [TH]. This implies that διπλῆς τιμῆς 'double honor' in 5:17 refers to material support [BNTC, ECC], or at least includes it [NAC, NIBC, NICNT]. Or, 'double honor' refers only to honor and not material wages, so this is saying that diligent elders should be given honor just as an ox treading out grain is given the privilege of eating from that grain and as workers are given wages for their work [Lns].

5:19 Do not accept[a] an accusation[b] against (an) elder, unless[c] on[d] (the testimony of) two or three witnesses.[e]

LEXICON—a. pres. mid./pass. (deponent = act.) impera. of παραδέχομαι (LN **31.52**) (BAGD 1. p. 614): 'to accept' [BAGD, Herm, **LN**, WBC; HCSB, NET, NRSV], 'to receive' [BAGD, LN; KJV, NASB], 'to pay attention to' [LSA; GW], 'to listen to' [CEV, NCV, NLT, TEV], 'to entertain' [BNTC; NIV], 'to consider' [AB], 'to give a hearing' [ECC]. This verb means to come to believe something to be true and to respond accordingly, with some emphasis upon the source [LN]. The verb means to acknowledge an accusation as being correct [NIGTC].

   b. κατηγορία (LN **33.428**) (BAGD p. 423): 'accusation' [AB, BAGD, **LN**, WBC; GW, HCSB, KJV, NASB, NET, NIV, NLT, NRSV, TEV], 'charge' [BNTC, ECC, LN; CEV], 'complaint' [Herm], 'what a person accuses an elder of' [LSA]. This noun is also translated as a verb phrase: 'someone who accuses' [NCV]. This noun denotes the content of an accusation or a charge made against someone [LN], and in this verse it could refer either to the content of the accusation or to the event of accusing [LN, TH]. It has the sense of a legal accusation [AB].

c. ἐκτός εἰ μὴ (BAGD 1. p. 246): 'unless' [AB, BAGD, ECC, Herm, LSA; CEV, GW, HCSB, NET, NIV, NLT, REB, TEV], 'except' [BAGD, BNTC, WBC; NASB, NRSV], 'but' [KJV], 'without' [NCV].

d. ἐπί (LN 90.6) (BAGD I.1.b.β. p. 286): 'by, from' [LN]. The phrase ἐπὶ 'on (the testimony/evidence of)' [BNTC], is also translated 'on the basis of' [BAGD, Herm, WBC; NASB], 'on the evidence of' [BAGD; NRSV], 'it is supported by' [GW, HCSB], 'it is confirmed by' [NLT], 'it can be confirmed by' [NET], 'it is brought by' [NIV, TEV], 'before' [KJV], not explicit [NCV]. The phrase 'on the testimony of two or three witnesses' is translated 'the evidence comes from two or three witnesses' [ECC], 'at least two or three people bring the same charges' [CEV], 'two or three witnesses support it' [AB], 'there are two or three persons who testify as to what he did wrong' [LSA]. This preposition indicates an agent, and often implies that the agent is being used as an instrument [LN]. This has the meaning 'on the basis of' [NICNT].

e. μάρτυς (LN 33.270) (BAGD 1. p. 494): 'witness' [AB, BAGD, BNTC, ECC, Herm, LN, WBC; GW, HCSB, KJV, NASB, NCV, NET, NIV, NLT, NRSV, TEV], 'one who testifies' [LN], 'a person who brings a charge' [CEV], 'a person who testifies what the accused did wrong' [LSA]. This noun denotes a person who witnesses [LN]. Here it is someone who gives testimony in regard to legal matters [NICNT].

QUESTION—How is this verse connected with the previous matters?

One form of honor to be shown elders is to safeguard them from even having to answer a charge unless it is supported by at least two witnesses [Lns, NTC, NTL]. The preceding paragraph was about the elders who have led well, and now Paul naturally considers the elders who were serving unsatisfactorily [EGT, My]. This shifts to another administrative matter that Timothy had to handle at Ephesus when some unknown charges were brought against one or more of the elders [NICNT]. Apparently formal charges were being brought against some elders, saying that they were guilty of extravagance and insubordination [WBC]. The return to second-person singular imperatives imply that Timothy had regional authority to deal with problems of church discipline [ICC], and that he was to act with the authority given him by Paul [NICNT]. Since Timothy was supervising the various churches, every accusation against an elder would be brought to him, but accusations against ordinary members of the congregation would be referred to the elders of that congregation [Lns]. Timothy is now commanded to take the role of judge when an accusation is made against an elder, and this command is given in the form of when not to entertain an accusation [ECC].

QUESTION—What is the purpose of having two or three witnesses before acting on an accusation?

In the OT, two or three witnesses are required in a case where a person could be punished by death (Deut. 17:6), and in any case where a person might be punished if found guilty (Deut. 19:15) [NICNT]. This principle was deeply rooted in the teaching of the early church and is also mentioned in 1 Cor. 13:1 [BNTC, NICNT]. The phrase 'two or three witnesses' means 'two or *more*' witnesses [TG], the minimum number of witnesses being two people [TH]. It is implied that it was preferable to have three witnesses [Lns]. This was not giving elders any special treatment, it was just giving them as much protection as an ordinary Jew had under the law [NAC]. This requirement would protect elders from malicious or unsubstantiated accusations [WBC], or from frivolous or ill-natured complaints [BNTC]. Ill will or hatred might trump up a change against an elder, but without two or more witnesses, Timothy was not to take further steps about the matter [Lns].

QUESTION—What is meant by μάρτυς 'witness'?

This may include an eyewitness, but it is referring to someone who can testify against the elder at the trial [TH]. This matter would probably be addressed at a church meeting of the whole congregation [TG, TH]. Since there was no limitation of the number of witnesses, it is probable that this was public meeting [WBC].

DISCOURSE UNIT: 5:20–25 [NTL]. The topic is the pastoral care of sinners.

5:20 **The (ones) sinning[a] rebuke[b] in-front-of[c] all, in-order-that also the rest may-have fear.[d]**

LEXICON—a. pres. act. participle of ἁμαρτάνω (LN 88.289): 'to sin, to engage in wrongdoing' [LN]. The phrase τοὺς ἁμαρτάνοντας 'the ones sinning' is translated 'those who sin' [HCSB, NIV, NLT; similarly KJV], 'those who are sinning' [AB, ECC, Lns], 'those who do commit sins' [REB], 'those who do wrong' [BNTC, NTC], 'the elders who sin' [LSA], 'those leaders who sin' [GW], 'if any of them sin' [Herm], 'those who continue in sin' [NASB], 'those who continue sinning' [NCV], 'those who persist in sin' [NRSV], 'those who persist in sinning' [WBC], 'if any of the leaders should keep on sinning' [CEV], 'those guilty of sin' [NET], 'all those who commit sins' [TEV]. This verb means to disobey God's will and his law [LN, NICNT].

   b. pres. act. impera. of ἐλέγχω (LN 33.417) (BAGD 3. p. 249): 'to rebuke' [AB, LN, Lns, LSA; HCSB, KJV, NASB, NET, NIV, NRSV, REB, TEV], 'to reprimand' [GW, NLT], 'to reproach' [LN], 'to reprove' [BAGD, Lns], 'to correct' [BAGD; CEV], 'to convict' [Herm], 'to confront' [WBC], 'to refute' [ECC], 'to tell...that they are wrong' [NCV], 'to expose' [BNTC]. This verb means to state that someone has done wrong, and it implies that there is adequate proof of such wrongdoing [LN].

c. ἐνώπιον (LN 83.33) (BAGD 2.a. p. 270): 'in front of, before' [LN], 'in the sight of, in the presence of' [BAGD]. The phrase ἐνώπιον πάντων 'in front of all' is translated 'before all' [KJV, NET], 'before everyone' [WBC], 'in front of everyone' [GW], 'in the presence of all' [AB, Lns, NTC; NASB, NRSV], 'in public' [REB], 'before the whole church' [LSA], 'in front of the whole church' [NCV, NLT], 'in front of the whole group' [CEV], 'in the presence of all presbyters' [Herm], 'while all the presbyters look on' [ECC]. The preposition is also translated as an adjective: 'publicly (rebuke)' [BNTC; HCSB, NIV, TEV]. This preposition indicates a position in front of an object [LN]. It means 'in the presence of' [NIGTC].

d. φόβος (LN 25.251) (BAGD 2.a.α. p. 863): 'fear' [BAGD, LN]. The phrase καὶ οἱ λοιποὶ φόβον ἔχωσιν 'also the rest may have fear' is translated 'the others too may have fear' [Herm; similarly Lns], 'others also may fear' [KJV], 'the rest might be in fear' [WBC], 'the rest will also be afraid' [HCSB], 'the rest may/might be afraid' [AB, BNTC; similarly TEV], 'the rest also may stand in fear' [NRSV], 'also the others may be filled with fear' [NTC], 'to put fear into the others' [REB], 'the others will have a warning' [NCV], 'others may take warning' [NIV], 'as a warning to the rest' [NET], 'as a warning to everyone else' [CEV], 'this will serve as a strong warning to others' [NLT], 'the rest will be fearful of sinning' [NASB] 'to put fear of wrongdoing into the rest of them' [ECC], 'the other leaders will also be afraid' [GW], 'the rest of the elders will fear to sin' [LSA]. This noun denotes a state of severe distress caused from an intense concern for impending pain, danger, evil, etc. [LN].

QUESTION—Who are the antecedents of τοὺς ἁμαρτάνοντας 'the ones sinning'?

1. This refers to elders who sin [Alf, BKC, BNTC, ECC, Herm, ICC, Lns, LSA, My, NAC, NCBC, NIBC, NICNT, NIGTC, NTC, TC, TG, TNTC, WBC, WP; CEV, GW, NET]. Paul is still speaking about the problem of the Ephesian elders, and this is the third statement about elders in this section [WBC]. This refers to the class of elders in 5:19 who have been proven guilty by adequate testimony [BKC, BNTC, ICC, Lns, LSA, NIBC, NICNT, NIGTC, TC, WBC], and it is in contrast with 'the elders who lead well' in 5:17 [LSA]. Although the context applies this to the elders, this is a general principle that would apply to the rest of the congregation as well [ICC, NIGTC].

2. This refers to the pastoral care of the sinners within the church community [NTL].

QUESTION—What is the significance of the present tense of the participle ἁμαρτάνοντας 'sinning'?

Many think that this indicates that the sinning is continuing and persistent [Alf, ECC, EGT, ICC, NAC, NCBC, NIBC, NICNT, NTL, TH, WBC, WP; CEV, NASB, NCV, NRSV]. It could then be implied that the elders who had previously sinned but were not at the moment doing so should not be publicly rebuked [TH]. This describes an elder who continues to live a life of sin after being confronted as in 5:19 [WBC]. But it may not have such an inference and simply refer to those elders who have been shown to have been sinning [BNTC, NICNT]. Or, this present tense is iterative, referring to the various cases that might occur, not to one case of an elder who steadily kept on sinning [Lns]. The point is that they have committed sin [NIGTC].

QUESTION—What is meant by rebuking them?

It means to correct the person by showing him his sin and summoning him to repent [NIGTC]. The purpose of exposing a person's sin is to bring about correction [NET]. It is a remedial confrontation for the purpose of encouraging proper behavior [WBC]. This likely means to reprove, correct, and even punish the sinner [AB]. The context does not indicate the severity of the rebuke, but in the case of elders it may include the threat of removal from leadership and even excommunication [NICNT]. This reproof would not be referring to such sins as fornication, drunkenness, and the like, since for the more serious sins the elders would not be allowed to stay in office [Lns, NAC].

QUESTION—What is meant by rebuking those sinners in front of πάντων 'all'?

1. This refers to the rebuking them in front of the whole local congregation [Alf, BKC, BNTC, ICC, LSA, NAC, NIBC, NICNT, NIGTC, NTC, NTL, TG, TH, TNTC, WBC; CEV, HCSB, NCV, NIV, NLT, TEV]. This was to be done publicly [HCSB, NIV, REB, TEV].
2. This refers to rebuking them in front of all the rest of the elders [ECC, Herm, ICC, Lns, My, NCBC, NTC, TC; GW].

QUESTION—What relationship is indicated by the conjunction ἵνα 'in order that'?

This conjunction indicates the purpose for such a rebuke being made in front of all [AB, ICC, NICNT, NIGTC]. The addition of the adverb καί 'also' indicates that the purpose of the rebuke is not only in reference to the effect it has on the elder himself but also to the effect on the rest [NICNT]. It indicates that this disciplinary action was also made in public to bring about the fear of committing such sins in those who witnessed the rebuke [NIGTC].

QUESTION—Who are the people referred to as οἱ λοιποὶ 'the rest'?

1. This refers to all the rest of the elders [AB, BKC, BNTC, ECC, LSA, My, NCBC, NIBC, NTC, TC, TG, WBC; GW]: *so that the other elders will be afraid.*
2. This refers to everyone else in the church [Alf, ICC, NAC, NICNT, NIGTC, NTL, TNTC]: *so that everyone else in the congregation will be afraid of the consequences of sin.* Of course it includes the rest of the elders, but it must include the rest of the church since it was to be done publicly [ICC, NAC, TNTC].

QUESTION—What would they fear?

The elders would be afraid of the consequences of sinning [ECC, Lns, LSA; NASB]. They would be afraid to do the same thing the one sinning had done [TG]. Not only would they be afraid to sin, they would also be afraid of being publicly rebuked and disgraced [Alf, NIGTC, TH]. They would realize that if they sinned, they also would be held accountable by the church [WBC]. The fear would be produced by realizing the gravity of the sin that brought about the rebuke and discipline [NICNT]. They would fear God's discipline administered through the congregation [BKC].

DISCOURSE UNIT: 5:21–25 [Herm, NAC, TNTC]. The topic is Timothy's own behavior [TNTC], exhortation to Timothy [Herm], special directions to Timothy [NAC].

5:21 **I-charge**[a] **(you) in-the-presence-of**[b] **God and Christ Jesus and the chosen**[c] **angels,**

TEXT—Instead of Χριστοῦ Ἰησοῦ 'Christ Jesus' some manuscripts read Κυρίου Ἰησοῦ Χριστοῦ 'Lord Jesus Christ'. GNT does not mention this variant. 'Lord Jesus Christ' is read by KJV.

LEXICON—a. pres. mid./pass. (deponent = act.) indic. of διαμαρτύρομαι (LN 33.319, 33.425) (BAGD 1. p. 186): 'to charge' [AB, BAGD, NTC; KJV, NIV], 'to solemnly charge;' [WBC; HCSB, NASB, NET, REB], 'to command' [LSA; NCV], 'to solemnly command' [NLT], 'to order' [CEV], 'to insist' [LN (33.319)], 'to solemnly call upon' [GW, TEV], 'to adjure' [BAGD, BNTC, ECC, Herm], 'to earnestly testify' [Lns], 'to warn' [BAGD, LN (33.425); NRSV]. This verb means to emphatically state a desire [LN (33.319)], or to admonish or instruct someone from personal knowledge about some future happening or action [LN (33.425)]. The verb has a strong sense of charging, warning, and adjuring [ICC].

b. ἐνώπιον (LN 83.33) (BAGDS 2.b. p. 270): 'in the presence of' [BAGD, LSA; CEV, NASB, NLT, NRSV, TEV], 'before' [AB, Herm, LN, LSA, WBC; HCSB, KJV, NCV, NET, REB], 'in front of' [LN], 'in the sight of' [BAGD, BNTC, Lns, NTC; GW, NIV], 'as they look on' [ECC]. This preposition refers to a position in front of someone [LN]. See this word at 6:13.

c. ἐκλεκτός (LN 30.93) (BAGD 1.a. p. 242): 'chosen' [BAGD, Herm, LN, LSA; CEV, NASB, NCV, REB], 'elect' [AB, BNTC, ECC, Lns, NTC, WBC; HCSB, KJV, NET, NIV, NRSV], 'holy' [NLT, TEV], 'select' [BAGD]. This adjective describes something as having been chosen [LN].

QUESTION—What is the significance of giving this charge before God, Christ Jesus, and the chosen angels?

To show how solemn this charge is, Paul calls on the Father and the Son, along with the angels who are with them, to witness that he is giving this charge to Timothy [AB, BKC, EGT, My, NIGTC, TG, TH, WBC]. This emphasizes the seriousness of the charge [NICNT, WBC]. This charge functions as an oath formula [NTC, TH, WBC]. Or, this solemn preamble is not the equivalent of giving an oath, but Paul is impressing Timothy with the fact that they both were standing in the presence of God, and Christ, along with the angels who were spectators of what happens in the church [Lns]. This pictures God seated on his throne, with Jesus seated at God's right hand, and the angels surrounding the throne [TH]. Timothy is to realize that he is responsible to God and the Son, who will judge his actions [NIGTC]. Timothy is always in their presence and is accountable to them [WBC]. Timothy is to use his judicial functions as their representative, bearing in mind that he himself will be judged by them [BNTC]. God is pictured as acting as a judge surrounded by heavenly beings [ICC, My]. God, Jesus Christ, and the angels are named because the final judgment will be in their hands [AB, BNTC]. Paul was, in effect, putting Timothy under oath to obey this solemn charge that was given under the eye of God with his full approval. God will judge all men in the final judgment. At that time God, through Christ, will judge Timothy if he breaks this oath. The angels will accompany Christ at the judgment, and they will be the ones who gather the redeemed and the wicked before his judgment throne [NTC]. Or, instead of referring to the last judgment, it refers to the present state of things [My].

QUESTION—What is meant by τῶν ἐκλεκτῶν ἀγγέλων 'the chosen angels'?

1. It means that God had chosen the angels for some service [Alf, Herm, TNTC; CEV, NASB, NIV, REB]: *and their chosen angels*. The angels were chosen by God and Christ Jesus [CEV]. God or Christ has chosen these angels to be his heavenly servants [Alf, TH]. God chose them to do his special tasks [WBC], to be his agents to carry out his will [NIGTC], to serve him and to watch over the affairs of humans [TC, TNTC]. God also chose them to take part in the final judgment [NIGTC]. In this context, probably the angels were chosen to be God's instruments of judgment [ICC].

2. It means the elect angels [AB, BNTC, ECC, EGT, Lns, My, NAC, NIGTC, NTC, WBC, WP; HCSB, KJV, NIV, NRSV]. The designation 'elect' contrasts them with the fallen angels [BNTC, EGT, NAC, NIGTC, NTC, WP]. Or, the contrast is not in focus [My, WBC], since the single term 'angels' consistently refers to angels who did not fall and adding 'elect' would be superfluous [WBC]. God elected angels just as he elects men to be his own forever [Lns]. He has chosen them to be the objects of his love [My]. God decreed from all eternity to give these angels the grace of perseverance so they would not fall as did other angels [NTC].

3. It means the holy angels [TG; NLT, TEV]. This is a way of speaking about the angels as a group, without trying to specify some action or state for which they were chosen [TG].

that you-keep[a] these (things) without discrimination,[b] doing nothing according-to partiality.[c]

LEXICON—a. aorist act. subj. of φυλάσσω (LN 36.19) (BAGD 1.f. p. 868): 'to keep' [BAGD, ECC, LN, WBC; NIV, NRSV], 'to observe' [AB, BAGD,

BNTC, Herm, Lns, NTC; HCSB, KJV], 'to obey' [LN, LSA; NLT, TEV], 'to follow' [BAGD; CEV, GW], 'to maintain' [NASB, REB], 'to carry out' [NET], 'to do' [NCV]. This verb means to keep on obeying orders or commandments [LN]. The verb has the sense of keeping a law from being broken [ICC, WBC], and here it means 'to observe' or 'to follow' the previous instructions [ICC].

b. πρόκριμα (LN **30.79**) (BAGD p. 708): 'discrimination, prejudgment' [BAGD], 'partiality, prejudice' [LN]. The phrase χωρὶς προκρίματος 'without discrimination' is translated 'without showing any partiality' [**LN**; similarly NIV], 'doing nothing with partiality' [WBC], 'do nothing on the basis of partiality' [AB], 'without prejudice' [ECC, Herm, NTC; HCSB, NET, NRSV], 'without showing any prejudice' [TEV], 'without bias' [NASB], 'without prejudgment' [Lns; similarly WBC], 'without prejudging the issue' [BNTC; similarly REB], 'without prejudging an elder' [LSA], 'without favoritism' [AB], 'without preferring one before another' [KJV], 'without taking sides' [NLT], 'be impartial' [GW], 'be fair with everyone' [CEV]. The phrase 'without discrimination, doing nothing according to partiality' is translated 'without showing favor of any kind to anyone' [NCV]. This noun denotes a decision that is based upon an unjustified preference, and implies that that it was prejudged [LN].

c. πρόσκλισις (LN **88.241**) (BAGD p. 716): 'partiality, prejudice' [LN]. The clause μηδὲν ποιῶν κατὰ πρόσκλισιν 'doing nothing according to partiality' [Herm] is also translated 'doing nothing from partiality' [NTC], 'doing nothing on the basis of partiality' [NRSV], 'doing nothing in a spirit of partiality' [NASB; similarly KJV], 'without being partial' [LSA], 'but acting with strict impartiality' [REB], 'not doing anything out of partisanship' [ECC], 'doing nothing out of favoritism' [BNTC; HCSB], 'don't have any favorites' [CEV], 'without favoritism of any kind' [NET], 'without showing favoritism to anyone' [NLT], 'do nothing out of favoritism' [NIV], 'never play favorites' [GW], 'without showing any favor to anyone in anything you do' [TEV], '(I call upon you) not to show prejudice in anything you do' [**LN**]. See the preceding lexical item for this translation [NCV]. This noun denotes a decided and unjustified preference for something or someone [LN].

QUESTION—What relationship is indicated by the conjunction ἵνα 'that'?
It indicates the content of the charge [Lns, NIGTC, WBC].

QUESTION—What are ταῦτα 'these things' that Timothy is to keep?
These things are instructions [ICC, NTC, TH; CEV, NIV, NLT, NRSV, TEV], commands [LSA; NET], rules [BNTC; REB], requirements [NIGTC], directives [ECC], principles [NASB], matters [AB], what Paul has told Timothy [GW].

1. This refers backward. These 'things' are the instructions about church discipline given in 5:19–20 [AB, Alf, EGT, ICC, Lns, My, NICNT, NIGTC, TC, TG, WBC], and because of the seriousness of this charge to

Timothy, it probably does not go back as far as 5:17–18 [NIGTC]. These commands refer to the commands in 5:l7 primarily, but may also refer to 5:19–20 [LSA]. This refers to the instructions given in 5:17–20 [NAC, TH] about dealing with elders [NAC].

2. This refers forward. It refers to instructions about the readmission of those have sinned or who are heretics [Herm].

QUESTION—What is meant by keeping these commands 'without discrimination'?

When Timothy listens to charges against the elders and confronts those who refuse to repent, he is to do so without having a preconceived judgment about their guilt or innocence [NIGTC]. He is not to come with preformed opinions [ICC], or prejudgments [NAC, NICNT, TH]. He must carefully weigh the facts before making a judgment about an elder [NICNT].

QUESTION—What is meant by doing nothing 'according to partiality'?

Timothy should take no action of discipline as a result of his favoring one of the accused men [NIGTC]. His personal bias must not affect his judgment [WBC]. He must not lean toward either the accuser or the accused until all the important facts in the case are fully established [NTC]. He is not to be partial to one party or the other [ICC]. This word is almost synonymous with the preceding word 'discrimination' and means an unjustified preference for something or someone [TH]. This phrase rewords the preceding instruction in a negative form: 'that is, not doing anything out of partisanship' [ECC].

DISCOURSE UNIT: 5:22–25 [TH]. The topic is some other matters.

5:22 (Let) no-one lay-on[a] hands hastily[b] nor participate[c] in-sins of-others.

LEXICON—a. pres. act. impera. of ἐπιτίθημι (LN 85.51) (BAGD 1.a.α. p. 303): 'to lay (hands) on' [AB, BAGD, BNTC, Herm, LN, Lns, LSA, WBC; HCSB, KJV, NASB, NCV, NET, NIV], 'to impose (hands) on' [ECC], 'to put on' [BAGD, LN]. This verb is also translated as a noun phrase: 'the laying on of hands' [NIV, REB]; as a clause that makes explicit the purpose of laying on hands on a person: 'to place your hands on anyone to ordain him' [GW], 'to lay hands of ordination upon anyone' [NTC], 'to lay hands on people to dedicate them to the Lord's service' [TEV], 'to accept people into the service of the Lord by placing your hands on them' [CEV], 'to ordain anyone' [NRSV], 'about appointing a church leader' [NLT]. This verb means to place something on something [LN]. See also ἐπίθεσις 'to lay on' at 4:14 which is in the same lexical domain as this verb.

b. ταχέως (LN 67.110) (BAGD 1.b. p. 806): 'hastily' [AB, Lns, LSA, NTC; NET, NRSV], 'too hastily' [NASB], 'quickly' [WBC], 'suddenly' [KJV]. This is also translated as a verb phrase 'be hasty' [ECC, Herm; NIV], 'be over-hasty' [REB], 'be in a hurry' [BNTC; GW, NLT, TEV], 'be too quick' [CEV, HCSB], 'think carefully before' [NCV]. This adverb indicates a very short extent of time [LN]. Here the adverb is used in an unfavorable sense, such as 'too quickly', 'too easily', or 'hastily' [ICC, NIGTC].

  c. pres. act. impera. of κοινωνέω (LN **4.14**) (BAGD 1.b.β. p. 438): 'to participate, to share' [BAGD], 'to join in doing, to share in doing' [LN]. The phrase μηδὲ κοινώνει ἁμαρτίαις ἀλλοτρίαις 'nor participate in sins of others' is translated 'neither be a partaker in the sins of others' [NTC], 'do not join up with others in sinning' [**LN**], 'do not participate in the sins of others' [GW, NRSV], 'and do not share in the sins of others' [HCSB, NCV, NIV, NLT; similarly WBC], 'incur no responsibility for the sins of others' [ECC], 'do not associate yourself with other people's sins' [AB], 'don't sin because others do' [CEV], 'neither be partaker of other men's sins' [KJV], 'take no part in the sins of others' [TEV], 'and do not have any part in the sins of others' [Herm], 'do not join in another person's sins' [**LN**], 'and so identify with the sins of others' [NET], 'don't associate yourself with another man's sins' [BNTC], 'nor fellowship with other people's sins' [Lns], 'or you may find yourself implicated in other people's misdeeds' [REB], 'and thereby share responsibility for the sins of others' [NASB], 'because if you do, you will be responsible if you approve a person who sins' [LSA]. This verb means to join in some activity with others [LN]. It means to be equally responsible for the deeds of others [BAGD].

QUESTION—What is meant by the command, 'Let no one lay on hands quickly'?

  1. This refers to ordaining or installing someone as an elder [AB, Alf, BKC, BNTC, ICC, Lns, LSA, NIBC, NICNT, NIGTC, NTC, TC, TH, WBC; NET], a church leader [NLT], someone in a Christian office [NAC, TNTC], or one who is in the service of the Lord [CEV, TEV]. This act refers to ordaining someone [TG; GW], setting someone apart to be an elder [NIGTC], accepting someone into the service of the Lord [CEV], or dedicating someone to the Lord's service [TH]. This refers to commissioning an elder, whether he be a new elder or a repentant elder who had been caught in a sin [WBC]. Timothy, along with the other elders, would lay their hands on individuals to set them apart as elders [NIGTC]. This was a ritual signifying the bestowal of authority [AB]. 'Hastily' does not refer to the speed of the movement of the hands as they are laid on a person; it means that he is not to hastily approve of a person's appointment to some position, that is, he is to take time to make sure that a candidate for the office of elder is both qualified and suitable for the work [LSA]. Timothy must not fail to make extensive examinations of candidates in the selection of elders, deacons, and 'real' widows [NICNT]. This instruction is given to avoid the problem discussed in 5:19–20 about what to do when elders sin [TH]. This instruction is not for Timothy alone, he is to see to it that no one chooses an unfit candidate for the office [Lns].

2. This refers to the forgiveness and restoration of a church member who had been disciplined [EGT, Herm, NCBC, NTL]. Verse 6:20 is a transitional passage, so 6:22 is unconnected with the preceding passage about elders and now the concern is with the readmission of sinners and heretics [Herm]. This is connected with disciplinary rebuke of sin in 5:20, and hands were laid on reconciled sinners to signify their readmission to church communion [EGT].

3. This refers to both of the above, whatever the occasion might be [My].

QUESTION—What is indicated by the conjunction μηδέ 'nor'?

1. This conjunction closely links this clause with the preceding clause [ICC, My, NICNT, TH, WBC]. If the elder whom they appointed without ascertaining his qualifications and moral standing later acted immorally, in a real sense they would be participating in his sins [TH]. It gives the reason why he is not to lay hands on someone hastily [My, NICNT]. Timothy is not to hastily approve a person for the office of elder, because if he does, he will be held in some degree responsible if that person commits sin while in office [BNTC, LSA, WBC].

2. This conjunction gives a separate command [Lns]. This warning is not confined to a warning of the consequences of hastily ordaining an unfit elder who may sin in the future. It includes any elder who may properly be accused of sin (5:20), since Timothy would fellowship in the sins of that elder if he refused to consider the accusation against him and did not rebuke him [Lns].

QUESTION—What is meant by the clause μηδὲ κοινώνει ἁμαρτίαις ἀλλοτρίαις 'nor participate in the sins of others'?

1. It means to share in the responsibility for the sins committed by an unworthy elder [Alf, BKC, LSA, My, NAC, NICNT, NIGTC, NTC, NTL, TC, TNTC, WBC; NASB, NET, REB], or by an unrepentant sinner [EGT]. Following the command that he should not hastily lay hands on someone to appoint him to the office of an elder, this probably means that if Timothy should appoint an unworthy person to that office, then Timothy would share the responsibility for the sins committed by that unworthy elder [LSA, NICNT]. By placing someone who would behave sinfully in an office that required the person to be above reproach (3:2), Timothy and the other elders would seem to be condoning those sins and thus their hasty action of appointing him would make them become responsible for the sins of such an unqualified elder [NIGTC, WBC]. By showing a positive attitude toward a sinner, Timothy would appear to approve of the actions of that person, and thus shares in the responsibility and guilt of those sins [ICC]. The sins of the unqualified person could be those already committed before being ordained or those that will be committed while in office, but here the emphasis lies on the future sins since the person who appoints a man to office is responsible for what the person he appointed does while holding office [ICC].

2. It means to sin along with others [NIBC, TG, TH; CEV]. This means that he must not get involved in the sins of others, not go along with them in the sins they commit [TG]. It means to abstain from anything immoral and sinful, and to live in an honest, sincere, and acceptable manner [TH].

Keep yourself pure.[a]

LEXICON—a. ἁγνός (LN 88.28) (BAGD 1. p. 12): 'pure' [BAGD, LN], 'without defect' [LN]. The command σεαυτὸν ἁγνὸν τήρει 'keep yourself pure' [AB, Herm, NTC, WBC; KJV, NCV, NET, NIV, NLT, NRSV] is also translated 'keep yourself morally' [GW], 'keep yourself chaste' [ECC], 'keep yourself unstained' [BNTC], 'keep, thyself clean' [Lns], 'keep yourself free from sin' [NASB], 'keep yourself above reproach' [REB], 'stay close to God' [CEV], 'do not become guilty of this' [LSA]. This adjective describes someone who is without moral defect or blemish, and is therefore pure [LN].

QUESTION—What is meant by Timothy keeping himself ἁγνός 'pure'?

This is closely related to the preceding clause, so it means to be pure and free from fellowship with other men's sins [Alf, Lns]. Timothy would not be pure if he shared responsibility for the sins committed by an unworthy elder [LSA]. In this context, Timothy would keep himself pure when he commissioned new elders without any discrimination or partiality [WBC]. He must keep pure by not participating in another man's sins [My, TG], and be pure in all other respects as well [TC]. He must fully conform to God's moral law in the ordaining of elders and in all other matters [NTC]. Some do not connect this so closely to the previous clause. Here there is an abrupt personal charge to Timothy [TNTC]. 'Pure' is used in a moral sense [NIGTC; GW]. It means to be free from sin [NIGTC; NASB], to be guiltless and blameless [ICC], honorable and upright [EGT, TNTC]. It has the same sense as the word ἁγνεία 'purity' at 4:12 [TG]. This refers to being separate from immorality and being single-minded in purpose [NAC]. Timothy could not deal with another's sin if his own life was not pure [BKC]. In Ephesus, it would mean staying away from financial and sexual improprieties that some of the elders apparently were charged with [AB]. A Christian leader who must make judgments and punish others must himself be above reproach [BNTC].

5:23 No-longer[a] drink water, but use[b] a-little wine because-of the stomach[c] and your frequent illnesses.[d]

LEXICON—a. μηκέτι (LN 67.130) (BAGD 6.a p. 518): 'no longer' [BAGD, LN, LSA; KJV], 'not from now on' [BAGD]. The command 'no longer drink water' is translated 'no longer be a water drinker' [Lns], 'no longer drink only water' [NTC, WBC; NRSV; similarly AB, ECC], 'do not drink only water' [Herm; NLT, TEV], 'stop drinking only water' [CEV, GW, NCV, NIV, REB], 'stop drinking just water' [NET], 'don't go on drinking only water' [BNTC], 'no longer drink water exclusively' [NASB], 'don't continue drinking only water' [HCSB]. The word refers to an extension of time up to a certain point, but not beyond [LN].

b. pres. mid./pass. (deponent = act.) imperative of χράομαι (LN **42.23**) (BAGD 1.a. p. 884): 'to use' [AB, BAGD, **LN**, Lns, LSA, NTC, WBC; KJV, NASB, NET, NIV], 'to take' [BNTC, ECC, Herm; CEV, NRSV, REB, TEV], 'to make use of' [BAGD, LN], 'to drink' [GW, NCV, NLT]. This verb means to make use of something [LN].

c. στόμαχος (LN **8.66**) (BAGD p. 770): 'stomach' [BAGD, LN]. The phrase διὰ τὸν στόμαχον 'because of the/your stomach' [Herm, Lns; HCSB, NIV] is also translated 'on account of your stomach' [WBC], 'for your stomach' [GW], 'for the sake of your stomach' [**LN**, NTC; NASB, NLT, NRSV; similarly KJV], 'to help your stomach' [NCV], 'for your bad stomach' [ECC], 'to help your stomach trouble' [CEV], 'to help your digestion' [REB, TEV], 'for your digestion' [NET], 'for the sake of your digestion' [AB, BNTC]. In some languages it might be more meaningful to translate this 'for the sake of your digestion' or even more specifically, 'in order to help your digestion' [**LN**]. See the following lexical item for how this clause is combined with the following clause [LSA]. This noun denotes the upper part of the digestive tract, but it is used especially to refer to the stomach [LN].

d. ἀσθένεια (LN 23.143) (BAGD 1.a. p. 115): 'illness, disability' [LN], 'weakness' [BAGD, LN]. The clause καὶ τὰς πυκνάς σου ἀσθενείας 'and your frequent illnesses' [NTC, WBC; HCSB, NET, NIV, NRSV] is also translated 'and your frequent ailments' [NASB], 'and your frequent sicknesses' [NCV], 'and for your frequent weakness' [AB], 'and frequent attacks of weakness' [Lns], 'and your frequent ill health' [Herm], 'and thine often infirmities' [KJV], 'and your frequent bouts with illness' [ECC], 'and the other illnesses you always have' [CEV], 'because you are frequently sick' [GW], 'because you are sick so often' [NLT], 'since you are sick so often' [TEV], 'in view of your frequent ailments' [REB], 'in view of your frequent indispositions' [BNTC]. The two clauses διὰ τὸν στόμαχον καὶ τὰς πυκνάς σου ἀσθενείας 'because of the stomach and your frequent illnesses' are combined: 'in order to cure your stomach's frequent illnesses' [LSA]. This noun denotes the state of being ill and thus being incapacitated in some manner [LN].

QUESTION—How is this verse related to its context?

It seems to be a parenthetical digression from the theme that is resumed in the following verse [AB, BKC, BNTC, EGT, ICC, NCBC, WBC]. The verse is translated as a separate paragraph [CEV, GW, NASB, NCV, NIV, NRSV, REB, TEV], or as a parenthetical comment in the midst of a paragraph [WBC; NET, NLT]. The preceding command in 5:22 was for Timothy to keep himself pure, and that led to this personal instruction about drinking a little wine with water for the sake of his health [BNTC, ECC, ICC, NCBC, NIBC, NIGTC, TH, TNTC, WBC]. Although most commentaries take 5:23 to be parenthetical, one finds a closer connection with 5:24 in that by conserving his health, Timothy would be better able to deal with the cases that come up for his decisions about appointing elders [Alf]. The verb ὑδροποτέω 'to drink water' could be more accurately translated 'to be a water-drinker' [Lns, My], and it was used only of someone who made water his exclusive drink, thus one who abstained from wine [My, NICNT]. Perhaps Paul knew that Timothy was abstaining from wine in an attempt to keep himself pure [BKC, BNTC, EGT, NIBC, NICNT, NIGTC, TC], since drunkenness would be incompatible with spiritual purity and self-control [ICC]. Probably Timothy abstained from alcohol for religious reasons, and here the advice is that a moderate use of wine for health reasons was permissible [ICC]. Timothy's opponents in Ephesus were drunkards, and so Timothy had disassociated himself from them and their teaching by not drinking wine at all [WBC]. Or, because of Timothy's illnesses he was not able to efficiently perform the duties required by his office [Alf].

QUESTION—How absolute is the command not to drink water, and what is the reason for using a little wine?

1. Timothy was not told to stop drinking water altogether, but to stop drinking only water [AB, Alf, BKC, BNTC, ECC, EGT, ICC, LSA, My, NAC, NIBC, NIGTC, NTC, NTIC, NTL, TC, TG, TH, TNTC, WBC, WP; all versions except KJV]. He was to drink wine in addition to water [WBC]. Many translations give this understanding with 'no longer drink *only* water' [AB, BNTC, LSA, NTC, WBC; all versions except KJV, NASB, NET], 'no longer drink *just* water' [NET], 'no longer drink water *exclusively*' [NASB]. Here a little amount of wine was advised for medicinal purposes [BKC, NAC, NIBC, NICNT, NIGTC, NTC, NTIC, TG, TNTC, WBC, WP], not as a beverage or for social drinking [NTC, WBC]. Probably there was the danger of contaminated water that threatened Timothy's health [ICC]. Probably it was to help Timothy's digestion [LN, NAC, TG; NET, REB, TEV]. Or, there may have been some other medicinal reasons for using wine [ICC]. This was a standard prescription of his day [ECC, NICNT]. The alcohol content of the wine that was mixed with the water would act as a purifying agent, and this would act as a tonic or antidote to the effects of impure water [TH].

2. Paul was telling Timothy to quit drinking water, which was contaminated and would cause dysentery, and told him to substitute wine for it. Paul had no fear that Timothy would overindulge [Lns].

QUESTION—What relationship is indicated by καί 'and' in the phrase 'and your frequent illnesses'?

1. This conjunction indicates a coordinate clause [AB, BKC, ECC, Herm, Lns, NICNT, TC, TG, WBC, WP; CEV, HCSB, KJV, NASB, NCV, NET, NIV, NRSV]: *drink a little wine because of your stomach and because of your frequent illnesses.* The frequent illnesses were in addition to his stomach problems [WBC]. His stomach trouble was probably concerned with digestion, but the nature of his frequent illnesses is not known [TG].

2. This is a hendiadys in which the two nouns in the phrase 'stomach and illnesses' are not coordinate, but one defines or qualifies the other [LSA, TH]: *your frequent stomach illnesses.*

3. This conjunction functions to indicate the reason for the previous clause [BNTC, TH; GW, NLT, REB, TEV]: *drink a little wine because of your stomach, (and you need the wine) because of your frequent illnesses.*

5:24 The sins of-some men are obvious,[a] going-before[b] (them) to judgment, but they- also -follow-after[c] some.

LEXICON—a. πρόδηλος (LN **28.60**) (BAGD p. 704): 'obvious' [AB; GW, NET, NIV, NLT], 'very obvious' [**LN**], 'immediately obvious' [BNTC], 'so obvious' [REB], 'obvious enough' [ECC], 'evident' [BAGD, Herm, WBC; HCSB], 'clear, known to all' [BAGD], 'very clear, very easily known' [LN], 'clearly evident' [NTC], 'entirely evident' [Lns], 'quite evident' [NASB], 'conspicuous' [NRSV], 'easy to see' [NCV], 'plain to see' [TEV], 'open beforehand' [KJV]. The clause 'the sins of some men are obvious' is translated 'some people sin openly' [LSA], 'some people get caught in their sins right away' [CEV]. This adjective describes something as being easily seen and known by the public [LN]. It means clear, evident, known to everyone [ICC].

b. pres. act. participle of προάγω (LN 15.143) (BAGD 2.b. p. 702): 'to go before' [BAGD, Herm, WBC; HCSB, KJV, NASB, NET], 'to go ahead' [GW, TEV], 'to go in front of' [LN], 'to go on in advance' [Lns], 'to proceed ahead' [NTC], 'to precede (them)' [LN; NRSV, REB], 'to run ahead' [BNTC], 'to escort (them)' [ECC], 'to parade before' [AB]. The clause προάγουσαι εἰς κρίσιν 'going before them to judgment' is translated 'reaching the place of judgment ahead of them' [NIV], 'leading them to certain judgment' [NLT], 'are easy to see even before they are judged' [NCV], 'so that it is known what they have done before they are judged' [LSA], 'even before the time of judgment' [CEV]. This verb means to move in front of or ahead of someone [LN]. This pertains to a temporal relationship [BAGD].

c. pres. act. indic. of ἐπακολουθέω (LN 13.113) (BAGD 2. p. 282): 'to follow after' [BAGD], 'to happen' [LN]. The clause τισὶν καὶ ἐπακολουθοῦσιν 'they also follow after some' is translated 'some men they also follow after' [Lns; similarly KJV], 'the sins of others follow them' [HCSB; similarly Herm, Lns], 'the sins of others follow them there' [NRSV; similarly GW], 'for others, their sins follow after' [NASB], 'the sins of others trail behind them' [NIV; similarly AB, BNTC], 'they also follow after some' [WBC], 'and (there are) others whose offences have not yet caught up with them' [REB], 'others trail their sins behind them' [ECC], 'there are others whose sins will not be revealed until later' [NLT], 'but the sins of others are seen only later' [NCV, TEV], 'but for others, they show up later' [NET], 'but other people's sins don't show up until later' [CEV], 'some people sin secretly so that it is not known what they have done until after they are examined' [LSA]. This verb means to have come or to be present with respect to some temporal reference point [LN]. This is a figurative use of the verb to indicate a contrast with προάγω 'to go in front of' [BAGD].

QUESTION—How is this verse and the next related to what precedes?

The personal advice to Timothy in 5:23 is over, and now the text returns to talking about men in the third person in order to make two closing observations [ECC]. This verse and the next give the grounds for Paul's command not to lay hands on someone hastily to appoint him to office (5:22) [Alf, BKC, BNTC, ECC, EGT, ICC, LSA, NAC, NIBC, NIGTC, NTC, TC, WBC]: do not *hastily* appoint elders, *since,* although the sins of some can be seen right away, *the sins of others only come to light later; and also,* although the good deeds of some can be seen right away, *the good deeds of others only come to light later.* Before accepting or rejecting a candidate, time is needed to allow sins or good deeds to come to light [NIGTC].

QUESTION—What is the judgment that this refers to?

1. The judgment in view is conducted by Timothy or by church elders [AB, BKC, ECC, EGT, Lns, My, NAC, NIBC, NIGTC, NTC, TC, TH, WBC]. This judgment is the activity of the church, especially Timothy [TH]. This is the only kind of judgment that is meaningful in this context [NIGTC, WBC], since the sins must eventually become obvious so that Timothy can make decisions about which men to appoint as elders [WBC].

   1.1 This involves the examination of candidates for the office of elders [BKC, ECC, EGT, Lns, My, NAC, NIBC, NIGTC, NTC, TC]. It is directed to Timothy and perhaps several of the elders in regard to judging the fitness of men for the ministry [Lns].

   1.2 This involves the examination of accused sinners of the congregation by church leaders [AB, TH]. It especially concerns the judgment of accused elders, but could also include other church members who are accused of sin [TH].

2. The judgment in view is conducted by God at the final judgment [BNTC, Herm, ICC, NCBC, NICNT, TNTC]. Extreme care must be taken in selecting elders since although some people cannot conceal the fact that they are incurring God's wrath even while they are alive, there are some whose sins will not be apparent until they stand before God's judgment [BNTC].

QUESTION—What is meant by the sins of some men going ahead of them to judgment?

1. This pictures sins as if they were a herald who goes before the man to proclaim that he is a sinner and ineligible for the office of elder [Lns, TC, WBC]. Or, this gives a picture of sins arriving at the trial ahead of the sinner [AB, NICNT]. The picture is of a courtroom, and the sins of some march ahead of them into the courtroom to appear as witnesses against them [AB]. This is a metaphor of men's sins leading those men into court to be judged [LSA]. The picture is of sins dragging the men who

committed the sins to court where they will certainly be judged guilty
[ICC, LSA]. A bad report about the sins of some men comes to the
attention of the judge before the man himself appears before the judge
[Alf, EGT]. Some sins are so obvious that an early judgment can be made
about candidates [NIGTC]. Some translations avoid the use of verbs that
picture sin as a participant at the trial [LSA, NIGTC, TH; CEV, NCV,
NLT]. The sins are so obvious that the sinner's guilt is already evident
before judgment is conducted [TH].

QUESTION—In the clause τισὶν δὲ καὶ ἐπακολουθοῦσιν literally 'but some
also they follow after', what is the referent of the pronominal adjective τισίν
'some' and what is the subject of the verb ἐπακολουθοῦσιν 'follow after'?

This masculine pronoun τισίν 'some' refers to some other men who sin [Alf,
ECC, EGT, Lns, LSA, NICNT, NIGTC, WBC; KJV, NASB, NET, NLT,
REB], and the understood subject of the verb is αἱ ἁμαρτίαι 'their sins'
[AB, NIGTC, NTC, WBC]: *but for some (men), (their sins) follow after
(them)*. Many translate so as to parallel the statement of the first clause by
translating the same idea as though the pronoun 'some' refers to the sins of
other men [AB, BNTC; CEV, GW, HCSB, NCV, NIV, NRSV, TEV]: *but
some (sins) follow after (other men)*. The indefinite reference of the pronoun
τισίν could be translated 'some', but it is an idiom here for 'others'
[NICNT].

QUESTION—What is meant by the sins of other men following after them to
judgment?

1. Most think the judgment is conducted by Timothy (perhaps with other
   elders) to judge the qualifications of a person for a church office. This
   gives a picture of some of the sins following after the sinner so that they
   arrive during the trial conducted by Timothy [AB]. These sins trail along
   after the people so that the people are visible before their sins are [AB,
   NTIC]. This means that such sins will show up later [NAC]. The obvious
   sins make adverse judgments easy. It is the hidden sins that are the
   problem when choosing elders, yet those sins will march right into the
   meeting behind the candidates and disqualify them. There may be
   exceptional cases in which the sins do not become apparent, but Timothy
   will not be guilty of fellowshipping in such sins [Lns]. Their sins will be
   made manifest during the trial [My]. Or, their sins will not be known until
   after the examination [Alf]. This is a way of saying that it is necessary to
   know some men for a considerable time before their sins become apparent
   [NIGTC]. Only a thorough examination will uncover the sins that would
   indicate that the candidate is unfit for office [BKC, NTC].
2. Some think the judgment is conducted by God at the final judgment of all
   people. For those who think that the judge represents God, a lengthy
   examination by Timothy would do no good since the sins will not be
   known until the final judgment [ICC]. Then, it is possible that this is
   meant to comfort Timothy if he makes the mistake of appointing someone
   who later turns out to be a sinner [ICC, NCBC, NICNT].

5:25 Likewise[a] also the good deeds[b] (of some people) (are) obvious,

LEXICON—a. ὡσαύτως (LN 64.16) (BAGD p. 899): 'in the same way, in like manner' [LN]. The phrase ὡσαύτως καί 'likewise also' [Herm; KJV, NASB] is also translated 'likewise' [HCSB], 'in like manner also' [Lns], 'in a similar way' [LSA], 'similarly also' [ECC; NET], 'similarly' [NTC], 'in the same way also' [WBC], 'in the same way' [AB, BNTC; GW, NIV, NLT], 'it is the same with' [CEV], 'so also' [NCV, NRSV], 'so too' [REB]. This adverb indicates a similarity that approximates identity [LN].

   b. ἔργον (LN 42.11) (BAGD 1.c.b. p. 308): 'deed' [LN], 'act' [LN]. The clause τὰ ἔργα τὰ καλὰ πρόδηλα 'the good deeds are obvious' is translated 'good deeds are obvious' [AB; NIV], 'good deeds may be immediately obvious' [BNTC], 'fine deeds are obvious' [ECC], 'good works are obvious' [HCSB, NET], 'the good works are evident' [WBC], 'the excellent works are entirely evident' [Lns], 'the noble deeds are clearly evident' [NTC], 'deeds that are good are quite evident' [NASB], 'good works are evident' [Herm], 'good works are conspicuous' [NRSV], 'the good things people do are obvious' [GW], 'the good deeds of some people are obvious' [NLT], 'with good deeds; they may be obvious' [REB], 'the good works of some are manifest beforehand' [KJV], 'good deeds are easy to see' [NCV], '(It is the same with) good deeds, some are easily seen' [CEV], 'although some people do good deeds openly so that it is known what they have done' [LSA]. This noun denotes that which is done [LN].

QUESTION—What relationship is indicated by the phrase ὡσαύτως καί 'likewise also'?

   It means that what is true for sins, is also true for good deeds [BNTC, ICC, NICNT, NIGTC].

QUESTION—What is implicit in this clause?

   The parallel statement in 5:24 implies that these are the good deeds τινῶν ἀνθρώπων 'of some men' and also the verb εἰσιν 'are' is to be supplied with the adjective 'obvious' [NIGTC]: *the good deeds of some men are obvious.*

and the (things) being otherwise[a] are- not -able to-be-hidden.[b]

LEXICON—a. ἄλλως (LN **58.36**) (BAGD p. 41): 'different' [LN]. The phrase τὰ ἄλλως ἔχοντα 'the things being otherwise' is translated 'the ones that are otherwise' [Lns; similarly KJV, NASB], 'even those that are otherwise' [NTC], 'the ones that are not' [NET; similarly Herm, WBC], 'even those that are not' [NIV], 'even when they are not' [BNTC; NRSV; similarly REB], 'even those that are not so plain' [TEV], 'those that are not obvious' [ECC; GW, HCSB], 'but even those that are not easily seen' [NCV], 'those that are different' [**LN**], 'deeds that are not' [AB], 'the good deeds done in secret' [NLT], 'some people do good deeds secretly' [LSA], '(some are easily seen), but none of them (can be hidden)' [CEV].

This adverb indicates something that is different in kind or class from all other entities [LN].

   b. aorist pass. infin. of κρύπτω (LN 28.79) (BAGD 2.a. p. 454): 'to be hidden, to be kept secret, to be concealed' [BAGD, LN]. The clause κρυβῆναι οὐ δύνανται 'are not able to be hidden' [WBC] is also translated 'cannot be hidden' [NIV; similarly Lns; KJV], 'cannot remain hidden' [AB, NTC; GW, HCSB, NET, NRSV], 'cannot stay hidden' [NCV], 'cannot stay hidden always' [ECC], 'cannot be concealed' [BNTC; NASB], 'cannot be concealed for ever' [REB], 'cannot remain secret either' [LSA], '(none of them) can be hidden' [CEV], 'will some day come to light' [NLT]. This verb means to cause something not to be known [LN]. They are not able to be hidden from people's notice [TG].

QUESTION—What is meant by τὰ ἄλλως ἔχοντα 'the (things) being otherwise'?

   1. The contrast is between the good deeds that are obvious and the good deeds that are not immediately obvious [AB, Alf, BNTC, EGT, ICC, Lns, My, NAC, NIBC, NICNT, NIGTC, NTC, NTIC, TC, TH, WBC, WP]: *but the good deeds which are not immediately obvious cannot be kept concealed.*

   2. The contrast is between the good deeds of some people and the bad deeds of other people [AB]: *but the bad deeds of others cannot be hidden forever.*

QUESTION—When will the good deeds be brought to light?

   1. They will finally come to people's notice [BKC, Lns, NIBC, NIGTC, NTC, TG, TH]. Delay in appointing elders may make possible the discovery of their being worthy of the office [NIGTC]. An investigation will soon bring the good deeds to light, and then men who are really qualified will be appointed [Lns]. While 5:24 is a warning against approving a candidate too hastily, this verse is a warning against rejecting a candidate too hastily [My].

   2. They will come to light at the final judgment [BNTC, ICC, NCBC].

DISCOURSE UNIT—6:1–21 [NASB]. The topic is instructions to those who minister.

DISCOURSE UNIT—6:1–10 [NAC]. The topic is a warning to slaves and sinners.

DISCOURSE UNIT—6:1–2 [ECC, NCBC, NIGTC, NTL, TNTC]. The topic is slaves and masters [NTL], servants and masters [TNTC], instructions for slaves [NIGTC], advice for Christian slaves [NCBC], part 2 of the domestic code [ECC].

DISCOURSE UNIT—6:1–2a [Herm, ICC, LSA, NAC, NIBC, TH, WBC; HCSB]. The topic is slaves [Herm, WBC], instructions about slaves [ICC, NIBC], teaching regarding slaves [TH], the responsibility of Christian slaves [NAC], honoring masters [HCSB], slaves should honor their masters [LSA].

6:1 As-many-as are under a-yoke[a] (as) slaves let-them-consider[b] the(ir) own masters worthy[c] of all honor,

LEXICON—a. ζυγός (LN 6.8, **87.80**) (BAGD 1. p. 339): 'yoke' [BAGD, LN (6.8)]. The phrase ὅσοι εἰσὶν ὑπὸ ζυγὸν δοῦλοι 'as many as are under a yoke (as) slaves' is translated 'all who are slaves under a yoke' [NCV; similarly AB, Herm], 'as many as are under the yoke, namely slaves' [NTC], 'all who are under the yoke as slaves' [BNTC; HCSB, NASB; similarly Lns, WBC; NET], 'all who are under the yoke of slavery' [NIV, NRSV], 'as many servants as are under the yoke' [KJV], 'all who wear the yoke of slavery' [REB], 'those Christians who are bound in slavery' [ECC]. Many drop the idiom about a yoke: 'those who are slaves' [**LN** (87.80); TEV], 'all slaves' [LSA; NLT], 'all slaves who believe' [GW], 'if you are a slave' [CEV]. The noun 'yoke' denotes a wooden bar or frame that joins two draft animals by their heads or necks so that they can work together effectively as they pull a plow or a wagon [LN (6.8)]. In the NT this word is only used figuratively of any burden [BAGD].

b. pres. mid./pass. (deponent = act.) impera. of ἡγέομαι (LN 31.1) (BAGD 2. 343): 'to consider' [BAGD, LN, Lns, LSA, WBC; NIV, REB, TEV], 'to regard' [AB, ECC, LN, NTC; HCSB, NASB, NET, NRSV], 'to deem' [BNTC], 'to count' [Herm; KJV], not explicit [CEV, GW, NCV, NLT]. This verb means to hold a view or opinion about something [LN].

c. ἄξιος (LN 65.17) (BAGD 2.a. p. 78): 'worthy' [BAGD, LN]. The phrase πάσης τιμῆς ἀξίους 'worthy of all honor' [Lns, NTC, WBC; KJV, NASB, NRSV] is also translated 'worthy of full/all respect' [AB, Herm; NIV, REB, TEV], 'to be worthy of all respect' [HCSB], 'worthy of complete respect' [BNTC], 'as deserving of full respect' [NET], 'as deserving all esteem' [ECC], 'are worthy to be honored by them in every way' [LSA]. The phrase 'let them consider their own masters worthy of all honor' is translated 'must give complete respect to their own masters' [GW], 'should show full respect to their masters' [NCV, NLT], 'you should respect and honor your owner' [CEV]. This adjective pertains to having a relatively high degree of comparable merit or worth [LN].

QUESTION—Who are the slaves this is speaking about and what is meant by being under the yoke?

There were very many slaves at that time. Some became slaves by being captured in war and others became slaves by being sold into slavery because of economic reasons. The children of slaves were automatically slaves [TH]. Here the antecedent of 'as many as' is not expressed and this simply means 'all who' are slaves, and since this instruction is quite general, it refers to all Christian slaves [ICC]. The pronoun 'as many as' refers to those who belong to a particular group, here the group being slaves who are subject to the will of their masters and have to work for them whether they like it or not [NIGTC]. There are different views about the designation ὑπὸ ζυγὸν δοῦλοι 'under the yoke slaves'.

1. The idiom 'those under the yoke' and the following noun 'slaves' are two ways of saying the same thing [BNTC, LN, My]. The phrase εἰσὶν ὑπὸ ζυγὸν 'are under a yoke' is an idiom meaning to be in a state of slavery, and followed here by the word δοῦλοι 'slaves' the phrase simply emphasizes the status of being a slave [LN (87.80)]. Perhaps 'slaves' was added to indicate that a different metaphor was intended [AB]. Since in Titus 1:1 and 2 Tim. 2:24 'slave' is a title for Paul or Timothy, 'under the yoke as slaves' allows no mistake in understanding who these people were [ECC]. The grammar has 'slaves' as the predicate, so it says 'as many as are slaves under the yoke', the words 'under the yoke' being added for emphasis [Alf, WBC]. Some leave out the idiom and merely translate this as 'slaves' [LSA; CEV, GW, NLT, TEV]. Although 'under the yoke' signifies the galling and humiliating result of slavery, Paul is thinking about all slaves, and in view of the contrast to believing masters in 6:2, he was thinking particularly of slaves who had unbelieving masters [ICC, NAC].

2. Probably using the figure being under the yoke of slavery indicates an oppressive attitude on the part of a non-Christian master who regarded his slave as little more than his oxen [Lns, NCBC, NIGTC, TNTC].

QUESTION—In the phrase τοὺς ἰδίους δεσπότας 'the own master' what is implied by speaking of the slave's *own* master?

The addition of 'own' emphasizes the slaves' relationship to their masters [Alf]. Slaves were not required to be obedient to masters of other slaves [ICC]. However, the force of ἰδίους 'own' was so weakened by that time that probably it means no more than αὐτῶν 'of them' [EGT, NTC]. Some translations omit 'own' and say 'their masters' [BNTC, ECC, Herm; CEV, NCV, NIV, NLT, NRSV, REB, TEV]. In this context, the master is primarily a non-Christian master [Alf, ECC, EGT, ICC, Lns, My, NAC, NCBC, NIGTC, TG, TH, TNTC]. Or, this is talking about masters who are believers since that is where the problem lies [AB]. Or, this is talking about masters in general, including both Christians and non-Christians [BNTC, WBC].

QUESTION—What is meant by considering one's master to be worthy of honor and respect?

This concerns the slave's attitude [NIGTC, NTIC, TH]. The master is in authority over the sphere of the slave's work, so it is appropriate for the slave to recognize that his master's position is worthy of respect [NIGTC]. This refers to the respectful attitude that is due any master [TH]. In this context it refers to a slave's total obedience to his master [TG]. Paul is not giving his approval of slavery here, but he is concerned about the reputation of the gospel and God's reputation among the heathen [WBC].

in-order-that[a] the name of-God and the teaching[b] not be-blasphemed.[c]

LEXICON—a. ἵνα 'in order that' [Lns, LSA, NTC, WBC], 'so that' [HCSB, NASB; similarly BNTC, Herm; KJV, NIV, NLT, NRSV, REB], 'so' [AB;

NCV, TEV], 'thus' [ECC], 'in this way' [GW], 'for the purpose of, so that' [LN], 'this will keep people from (saying bad things about God)' [CEV], 'this will prevent' [NET]. This conjunction indicates the purpose for events and states [LN, NIBC]. It gives the motive or reason for treating the master with complete respect [BNTC, ECC].

b. διδασκαλία (LN 33.224) (BAGD 2. p. 191): 'teaching' [BAGD, LN]. The phrase 'the teaching' [AB, Herm, WBC] is also translated 'the instruction' [ECC], 'the doctrine' [Lns, NTC], 'our teaching' [CEV, NCV, NIV, TEV], 'our doctrine' [NASB], 'what we teach' [GW], 'that which we apostles teach' [LSA], 'the Christian teaching' [BNTC; NET, REB], 'his teaching' [HCSB, NLT], 'his doctrine' [KJV]. This noun denotes the instruction obtained in either a formal or informal setting [LN].

c. pres. pass. subj. of βλασφημέω (LN 33.400) (BAGD 2.b.β. p. 142): 'to be blasphemed' [AB, BAGD, Herm, LN, Lns, WBC; HCSB, KJV, NRSV], 'to be reviled' [LN, NTC], 'to be defamed' [ECC, LN], 'to be spoken against' [NASB], 'to be discredited' [NET], 'to be brought into disrepute' [REB], 'to be slandered' [NIV], 'to be exposed to scandal' [BNTC]. This passive verb is also translated actively: 'to speak against' [LSA; NCV], 'to speak evil of' [GW, TEV], 'to say bad things about' [CEV], 'to bring shame on' [NLT]. This verb means to speak against someone in such a way as to harm or injure that person's reputation [LN]. It means to defame or injure the reputation of someone [AB].

QUESTION—What is meant by the name of God?

The name of God refers to God's reputation in the world [AB, BKC, WBC; CEV]. It refers to God's nature and character [TH]. It refers to that by which God makes himself known [NIGTC]. It refers to God's revelation of himself in his gospel [Lns]. For the phrase 'the name of God', some translate just 'God' [LSA, TG; CEV, GW, NLT, TEV].

QUESTION—What is meant by ἡ διδασκαλία 'the teaching'?

'The teaching' is the teaching about God as Savior [AB, NIGTC]. Some translate this as 'our teachings' [CEV, GW, NASB, NCV, NIV, TEV]. The 'teachers' would include Paul and the apostles [LSA]. But perhaps the teachers are all Christian in general, that is, the Christian teaching [ICC, Lns, TG; NET, REB]. But others take the article ἡ 'the' to be equivalent to a possessive pronoun [Alf] and translate it 'his (God's) teachings' [HCSB, KJV, NLT]. The teaching refers to the gospel [NAC, NIBC, WBC], or the Christian faith [EGT, TNTC]. Or, it refers to the OT teachings about slaves as interpreted by Paul [ECC].

QUESTION—Why would the failure to consider one's master to be worthy of honor and respect cause God's name and the teaching to be blasphemed?

If a slave failed to obey his master, people would say that the Christian teaching developed wrong social attitudes [ICC], and that God and the gospel made slaves less respectful and poorer workers [NIGTC]. A master would say that Christian slaves were not as dependable as non-Christian slaves [WP]. The master would curse the slave's God, his religion, and the teaching the slave had accepted [Lns].

6:2 **And/but[a] the (ones) having believing[b] masters let-them- not -despise/be-disrespectful-to[c] (them) because[d] they are brothers,[e]**

LEXICON—a. δέ (LN 89.87, 89.93, 89.124) (BAGD 1., 2., 3. p. 171): This conjunction can mark a sequence of closely related events: 'and, and then' [LN (89.87)], or an additive relation that is not coordinate: 'and, and also, also, in addition, even' [LN (89.93)], or a contrast: 'but, on the other hand' [LN (89.124)]. It can emphasize a contrast: 'but', or mark a simple transition: 'now, then', or mark a resumption of an interrupted discourse: 'and also, but also' [BAGD]. Here it is translated 'and' [AB, Lns, NTC, WBC; HCSB, KJV], 'moreover' [ECC], 'but' [Herm; NET], not explicit [BNTC, LSA; all versions except HCSB, KJV, NET].

b. πιστός (LN 31.86) (BAGD 2. p. 665) 'believing' [BAGD], 'trusting' [BAGD, LN]. The phrase 'believing masters' [BNTC, NTC, WBC; HCSB, KJV, NET, NIV, NRSV] is also translated 'masters who are believers' [ECC, Herm; similarly NCV, NLT], 'whose masters also believe' [GW], 'believers as their masters' [AB, Lns; NASB], 'masters who believe in Christ' [LSA], 'Christian masters' [REB, TEV], 'owners who are followers' [CEV]. This adjective describes the act of trusting [LN]. See this word at 5:16.

c. pres. act. impera. of καταφρονέω (LN 88.192) (BAGD 1. p. 420): 'to despise' [AB, BAGD, LN, Lns, WBC; KJV, TEV], 'to scorn' [BAGD, LN], 'to disdain' [ECC], 'to look down on' [BAGD, LN, NTC], 'to think lightly of' [Herm], 'to be disrespectful' [LSA; HCSB, NASB, NLT, NRSV], 'to show less respect' [NCV, NET, NIV], 'to take liberties with' [BNTC; REB]. The negative command 'let them not be disrespectful' is translated positively: 'should respect' [GW], 'should show them respect' [CEV]. This verb means to feel contempt for someone he thinks is bad or without value [LN]. The basic meaning of the verb is to despise someone, but it can have the weakened sense of treating someone without the full consideration due that person's station [WBC]. See this word at 4:12.

d. ὅτι (LN 89.33): 'because' [AB, Herm, LN, Lns, LSA, NTC, WBC; HCSB, KJV, NASB, NCV, NET], 'just because' [REB], 'since, in view of the fact that' [LN], 'on the ground that' [NRSV], 'even though' [GW], 'for (they are believers too)' [TEV], 'after all' [ECC], not explicit [CEV, NLT]. This conjunction indicates the cause or reason for something, and it is based on an evident fact [LN].

e. ἀδελφός (LN 11.23) (BAGD 2. p. 16): 'brother' [AB, BAGD, ECC, Herm, LN, Lns, LSA, NTC, WBC; HCSB, KJV, NASB, NET, NIV, REB], 'fellow believer' [LN], 'believer' [GW, NCV, TEV], 'follower of Christ' [CEV], 'member of the church' [NRSV], not explicit [NLT]. This noun denotes a close associate in a group of persons having a well-defined membership, and in the NT the term refers to a fellow believer in Christ

[LN]. The term indicates a spiritual relationship Christians have with one another as members of the family of God [NIGTC].

QUESTION—What relationship is indicated by δέ 'but'?

1. This conjunction indicates a related topic to that of the preceding verse [BNTC, Lns, NIBC, NTC, WBC; HCSB, KJV]: *and.* Paul now considers a second case [BNTC]. The previous verse is about slaves in general or functions as a preface to this verse, so δέ means 'indeed, those slaves, etc.' [NIBC].

2. This conjunction indicates a contrast [Alf, ECC, ICC, My, NAC, NIGTC; NET]: *but.* The contrast is between Christian slaves who have pagan masters (6:1) and Christian slaves who have Christian masters (6:2) [ECC, ICC, My, NIGTC, NTL].

QUESTION—Does the verb καταφρονέω mean to despise their masters or does it have the weakened meaning of being disrespectful to them?

1. It means the slaves must not despise their Christian masters [AB, ECC, Lns, NIGTC, TG, TNTC, WBC; KJV, TEV]. The verb is the opposite of 'holding them in honor' and means to think contemptuously of them, or to show contempt toward them [AB]. This means 'despise' or 'look down on' them, the same kind of attitude spoken of in 4:12 [TG].

2. It means the slaves must not be disrespectful to their Christian masters [Alf, BNTC, LSA, My, NAC, NIBC, TH; HCSB, NASB, NCV, NET, NIV, NLT, NRSV, REB]. This does not mean that they despise their masters, but that they do not treat them with the full consideration due their station in society [BNTC]. This concerns not showing their masters the proper respect and obedience due them [ICC, TH].

QUESTION—What relationship is indicated by ὅτι 'because'?

It indicates the reason the slaves might despise their Christian masters or be disrespectful to them [AB, BNTC, ICC, Lns, My, NAC, NIGTC, NTC, NTIC, TG; GW, NRSV, REB; probably HCSB, NASB, NCV, NET, NIV which appear to relate the reason to why they are disrespectful]: *let them not despise/be disrespectful to them on the grounds that they are merely brothers.* This explains their contempt or disrespect, not Paul's prohibition [AB, My]. The Christian slaves may have disdained their masters because they thought that their masters had no right to be on a higher plane and have authority over them since both were equals in the church [ICC]. They might think that they didn't have to obey Christians in the same way they would have to obey non-Christian masters [TG]. Probably the slaves and the masters were members of the same congregation, and the slaves might start thinking that since slaves and masters were the same before God, they did not have to give their masters the extra obedience and respect that a slave was normally required to give a master [TH]. The slave might think that a master who keeps someone who is his equal in church as a slave is not a very good Christian [NTC]. Or, the slaves might have despised their Christian masters because their masters had relaxed their discipline over them since they regarded their slaves as Christian brothers [TNTC].

but[a] even-more[b] let-them-serve[c] (them),

LEXICON—a. ἀλλά (LN 89.125): 'but' [BNTC, Herm, LN, Lns, NTC, WBC; HCSB, KJV, NASB], 'instead' [LN; TEV], 'on the contrary' [**LN**], 'quite the contrary' [REB], 'instead' [ECC; NET, NIV], 'rather' [AB, LSA; NRSV], not explicit [CEV, GW, NCV]. This conjunction indicates an emphatic contrast [LN].

   b. μᾶλλον (LN 89.12) (BAGD 2.a. p. 489): 'even more, more, to a greater degree' [LN], 'all the more' [WBC; NASB, NET, NRSV], 'better' [AB, LSA; HCSB], 'even better' [ECC, LN (89.125); GW, NCV, NIV, TEV], 'all the better' [BNTC, NTC; REB], 'all the harder' [NLT], 'all the more eagerly' [Herm], 'the best you can' [CEV], 'the rather' [Lns], 'rather' [KJV]. This adverb indicates a degree which surpasses in some manner a point on a scale of extent [LN].

   c. pres. act. impera. of δουλεύω (LN 35.27) (BAGD 2.a. p. 205): 'to serve' [AB, LN, LSA, NTC, WBC; GW, HCSB, NASB, NCV, NET, NIV, NRSV, TEV], 'to do (them) service' [KJV], 'to do their work' [REB], 'to serve and help' [CEV], 'to work' [NLT], 'to slave (for them)' [Lns], 'to be slaves' [BNTC, ECC]. This verb means to serve, and normally service is to be done in a humble manner and in response to the demands or commands of others [LN]. The meanings 'serve' or 'obey' may here have the stronger literal sense of 'perform the duties of a slave' [NIGTC]. The verb means 'to be a slave' and 'to perform the duties of a slave by serving and obeying' [ICC].

QUESTION—What relationship is indicated by ἀλλά 'but'?

This conjunction indicates the alternative to the attitude expressed in the preceding clause [BNTC, ECC, Lns, NIGTC, NTC, TH, WBC, WP]. The very opposite attitude is called for [NTC]. Rather than being disrespectful to their masters, the fact that their masters are Christians should be an incentive to serve them even better than they did before [NIGTC, TH].

QUESTION—What is meant by μᾶλλον 'even more'?

   1. This adverb means to serve their masters to an even greater degree of service [AB, ECC, EGT, My, NIGTC, NTC, TG, TH, TNTC, WBC; GW, HCSB, NASB, NCV, NET, NIV, NRSV, TEV]: *but let the slaves serve their believing masters all the better.* They should be even better slaves [BNTC, TG], and serve their masters better that they did before [TG, TH]. The slaves should work even harder at their tasks [TH, WBC].

   2. This adverb means that they have all the more reason to serve their masters [BNTC, Herm, NAC, NIBC; NLT, NTL]: *but let the slaves serve their believing masters with all the more respect and devotion.* It does not mean to serve their Christian masters better than they would serve pagan masters [BNTC, NAC, NIBC]. It would make them more eager to serve [Herm]. They would serve a Christian master more enthusiastically [NAC].

3. This adverb means 'instead of something else' [ICC, Lns, WP; KJV]: *let them not be disrespectful, rather let them serve them (respectfully)*. Rather than despising their masters, let them serve them [ICC].

because the (ones) receiving/giving-the-benefit[a] of-the good-work[b] are believers and beloved.[c]

LEXICON—a. pres. mid. participle ἀντιλαμβάνομαι (LN **25.79**, or **65.48**) (BAGD 2., or 3. p. 74): 'to enjoy a benefit, to be benefited' (LN 65.48)], 'to enjoy, to benefit by' [BAGD (3.)]; or, 'to devote oneself to, to give oneself to' [LN (25.79)], 'to take part in, to devote oneself to, to practice' [BAGD (2.)]. The phase οἱ τῆς εὐεργεσίας ἀντιλαμβανόμενοι 'the ones receiving/giving the benefit of the good work' is translated 'those who are benefited by their good work' [**LN** (25.79)], 'those who benefit from/by their service' [HCSB, NET, NIV, NRSV], 'those who benefit from their work' [TEV], 'those benefiting from their act of kindness' [WBC], 'those who are receiving their benefaction' [AB], 'those who receive the benefit of their work' [GW], 'those who receive the benefit of their service' [REB], 'those who partake of the benefit' [NASB; similarly KJV], 'who reciprocate this kind service' [NTC], 'the recipients of their good service' [BNTC], 'so you should serve and help them' [CEV], 'their efforts are helping (other believers)' [NLT], 'they are helping' [NCV], ' those who are devoted to doing kind things' [**LN** (25.79)], 'who devote themselves to good works' [Herm], 'they have masters who practice kindness' [ECC], 'they too taking hold of the well-doing' [Lns]. This verb means to experience a benefit from someone [LN (65.48)], or it means to give or commit oneself wholeheartedly to something [LN (25.79)].

b. εὐεργεσία (LN 88.7) (BAGD 1. p. 319): 'service, the doing of good' [BAGD], 'good deed' [LN]. This noun denotes a deed that is good and beneficial to someone [LN]. It means 'the doing of good, a good deed, a benefit, or a service' [ICC, NIGTC]. See translations of this word in the preceding lexical item.

c. ἀγαπητός (LN 25.45) (BAGD 2. p. 6.c): 'beloved' [AB, BAGD, BNTC, ECC, LN, Lns, NTC, WBC; KJV, NRSV], 'dearly beloved' [HCSB], 'dearly loved' [NET], 'one who is loved' [LN], 'beloved by God' [Herm]. The substantive is also translated as verb phrase: 'their masters are loved by God' [LSA], 'he (Christ) loves them' [CEV], 'whom they love' [GW, TEV; similarly NCV], 'who are well loved' [NLT], 'dear to them' [NIV], 'are one with them in (faith and) love' [REB]. This verbal adjective denotes one who is loved [LN].

QUESTION—What relationship is indicated by ὅτι 'because'?

This indicates the grounds for commanding the slaves to serve their Christian masters even better [BNTC, ECC, NAC, NIBC, NIGTC, NTL, TG, TH].

QUESTION—Who receives the benefit of the good work in the phrase οἱ τῆς εὐεργεσίας ἀντιλαμβανόμενοι 'the ones receiving/giving the benefit of the good work'?

The verb ἀντιλαμβάνομαι can mean either 'to give' or 'to receive' the benefit [AB].

1. The masters, because they are believers and beloved, receive the benefit of their slaves' good work [AB, BKC, BNTC, EGT, ICC, LSA, NIBC, NIGTC, NTIC, NTL, TC, TG, TH, WBC; CEV, GW, HCSB, NASB, NCV, NET, NIV, NRSV, REB, TEV]: *slaves should work all the more since the master who receives the benefit of their work is a believer and beloved.* Here it means that the masters receive something that results in their benefit [TH]. The phrase 'believers and beloved' is the predicate of the sentence, and so 'the ones receiving the benefit' are the masters who have already been called 'believers' at the beginning of the verse [NIGTC, TC].

2. The masters, because they are believers and beloved, give the slave the benefit of their good deed [ECC, EGT, Herm, Lns, My, NTC]: *slaves should work all the more because their masters are believers and devote themselves to doing good deeds for their Christian slaves.* The masters devote themselves to the benefit of their Christian slaves because the masters were themselves Christian believers and beloved by God [ECC]. The master would do this in appreciation of the good service rendered by the Christian slave [NTC].

3. The masters, who share with the slaves in Christian service, are believers and beloved [Alf, NAC, NCBC]. It means, 'since the masters, who share with slaves in Christian service, are believers and beloved [NCBC]. Masters and slaves mutually interchange service in the Christian life [Alf]. The masters and the slaves share in their Christian service to God [NAC]

QUESTION—Who loves the 'beloved'?

1. God loves them [AB, ECC, Herm, LSA, My, NTC]. If the slaves have to be admonished to serve their masters, then the one who loves the masters must be God [Herm]. The close connection with 'believers' supports this interpretation [My]. Also their fellow-believes love them [NTC].

2. Christ loves them [CEV].

3. The masters are loved by both God and by fellow-believers [NTC].

4. The beloved are the masters who are loved by the slaves [BNTC, ICC, Lns, NIBC, NIGTC, TG, TH, WBC; GW, NCV, NIV, TEV]. The masters are believers, and therefore they are loved by the Christian slaves [ICC, WBC].

DISCOURSE UNIT—6:2b–21 [WBC; GW, REB]. The topic is final instructions [WBC; REB], guidelines for living a godly life [GW].

DISCOURSE UNIT—6:2b–21a [ICC]. The topic is the true and the false teachers contrasted.

DISCOURSE UNIT—6:2b–19 [NET]. The topic is a summary of Timothy's duties.

DISCOURSE UNIT—6:2b–10 [AB, ICC, NIBC, WBC; CEV, HCSB, NLT, NRSV, TEV]. The topic is teachers with false doctrines and motives [ICC], the final discussion of the opponents [WBC], the final indictment of the false teachers [NIBC], false teaching and true wealth [CEV, NLT, NRSV, TEV], false doctrine and human greed [HCSB], cravings for wealth [AB].

DISCOURSE UNIT—6:2b–5 [Herm, NAC, TH]. The topic is a further warning against false teachers [TH], the indictment of the false teachers [NAC], warning against false doctrine [Herm].

DISCOURSE UNIT—6:2b [LSA]. The theme is the command to teach these things and exhort people to do them.

These (things) teach[a] and encourage.[b]

LEXICON—a. pres. act. impera. of διδάσκω (LN 33.224) (BAGD 1., 2.f. p. 192): 'to teach' [AB, BAGD, BNTC, ECC, Herm, LN, Lns, LSA, NTC, WBC; all versions]. This verb means to provide instruction in a formal or informal setting [LN]. The present imperatives of the two verbs indicate the necessity of constant repetition, 'keep on teaching, keep on urging' [NTC].

b. pres. act. impera. of παρακαλέω (LN 25.150) (BAGD 2. p. 617): 'to encourage' [BAGD, ECC, LN; HCSB], 'to exhort' [BAGD; KJV, NET], 'to urge' [AB, Lns, NTC, WBC; NIV, NRSV], 'to preach' [BNTC, Herm; NASB, NCV, REB, TEV]. The clause 'these things…encourage' is translated 'encourage everyone to obey them' [NLT], 'encourage people to do these things' [GW], 'exhort people that they do them' [LSA], 'these are the things you must…tell the people to do' [CEV]. This verb means to cause someone to be encouraged or consoled [LN]. Following the command to teach these things, Timothy is told to appeal to his listeners to apply the teaching to their lives [NIGTC].

QUESTION—How is this clause related to its context, and what do 'these things' refer to?

1. This concludes the preceding section [Alf, BKC, ECC, EGT, Lns, LSA, My, NCBC, NIGTC, NTC, NTL, TC, TH; NASB, NCV, NIV]. 'These things' refer to 5:1–6:2 [ECC, TH], or to the instructions about slaves in 6:1–2 [Alf, Lns, NTC, TC; NASB]. Before turning to personal things Paul urges Timothy to teach and exhort the preceding truths [NIGTC]. The phrase 'these things' occurs at 4:6, 11, 15; 5:7, 21; 6:17, and they all seem to refer to what precedes rather than what follows [NIGTC, TH].

2. This begins a new section [AB, BNTC, Herm, ICC, NAC, NCBC, NIBC, NTIC, TNTC, WBC; CEV, GW, HCSB, NET, NLT, NRSV, REB, TEV]. This is a transitional sentence connected both backward and forward [ICC, WBC]. This new section begins with a transitional sentence in which 'these things' refer to the preceding material, and yet this positive

statement about teaching these things is closely connected with the following contrast with Paul's opponents who teach otherwise [ICC, WBC]. 'These things' refers to all the subjects and instructions given in the letter [BNTC], to 6:1–2 [NAC], to 5:3–6:2a [NIBC, WBC], or it may even go back to 2:1 [NIBC].

DISCOURSE UNIT—6:3–21 [TNTC]. The topic is miscellaneous injunctions.

DISCOURSE UNIT—6:3–21a [LSA]. The theme is live according to the Christian doctrine and complete what I have commanded you to do.

DISCOURSE UNIT—6:3–19 [ECC]. The topic is the commission in relation to problems.

DISCOURSE UNIT—6:3–10 [NIGTC, NTL; NCV, NIV]. The topic is false teaching [NTL], false teaching and true riches [NCV], love of money [NIV], final indictment of false teachers and warning against love of money [NIGTC].

DISCOURSE UNIT—6:3–5 [ECC, LSA, NCBC, NIGTC, TNTC]. The topic is more about false teachers [TNTC], a denunciation of false teachers [NCBC], a final indictment of false teachers [NIGTC], the heterodox [ECC], false teachers are conceited, know nothing, and argue about words [LSA].

6:3 **If anyone teaches-differently**[a]
LEXICON—a. pres. act. indic. of ἑτεροδιδασκαλέω (LN 33.235) (BAGD p. 314): 'to teach differently' [BNTC, LSA, NTC], 'to teach otherwise' [AB; KJV, NRSV, REB], 'to teach something different' [LN; CEV], 'to teach a different doctrine' [BAGD, LN, Lns, WBC; TEV], 'to teach other doctrine' [HCSB], 'to teach false doctrine' [GW, NIV], 'to have a different teaching' [NCV], 'to advocate a different doctrine' [NASB], 'to propound strange teachings' [ECC], 'to contradict (our) teaching' [NLT], 'to spread false teachings' [Herm; NET]. This verb means to teach something that is different from what should be taught [LN]. It refers to teaching a heretical doctrine [BAGD]. See this word at 1:3.
QUESTION—What relationship is indicated by the conjunction εἰ 'if'?
This indicates a condition that is regarded as being true [ICC, NIBC, NIGTC, WBC]. Paul is quite certain of the facts [NIBC]. The condition is given in 6:3, and the consequences are given in 6:4–5 [NIBC, NIGTC, WBC]. This pertains to any of the false teachers that were there [ICC].
QUESTION—What is meant about someone teaching 'differently'?
1. This refers to teaching anything different from the instructions and teaching *contained in this letter* [Alf, BNTC, ICC, TC, TH, WBC]. This is speaking of the instructions given in this letter, not doctrine in general [BNTC, TH]. The verb 'to teach differently' directly contrasts with the command in the preceding verse, 'these things teach' [ICC, WBC]. It concerns that which is different from Paul's teachings and what he instructs Timothy to teach [WBC]. The false teachers were advising a different conduct from that taught by Paul [Alf].

2. This refers to teaching a doctrine that is different from the doctrines of the Christian faith [BAGD, BKC, Lns, NIGTC, TG; probably LN; GW, HCSB, NASB, NIV, TEV which use the word 'doctrine']. This verb has already appeared in 1:3, so its occurrence now signals that Paul is referring to that same group of false teachers who teach a different doctrine from the apostolic teaching [BKC, NIGTC, TG]. This refers to heretical teaching [TG].

and does- not -agree-with[a] (the) being-sound[b] words, (namely) the (words) of our Lord, Jesus Christ

LEXICON—a. pres. mid./pass. (deponent = active) indic. of προσέρχομαι (LN **31.19**) (BAGD 2.b. p. 713): 'to agree with' [BAGD, **LN**, LSA; GW, HCSB, NASB, NCV, NET, NIV, TEV], 'to consent to' [KJV], 'to adhere to' [Herm, WBC], 'to come over to' [NTC], 'to come to' [Lns], 'to give his mind to' [BNTC], 'to attend to' [AB], 'to devote himself to' [REB], 'to have recourse to' [ECC]. The negative phrase 'does not agree with' is also translated 'to disagree with' [CEV], 'to contradict' [NLT]. This verb means to come to a position of holding the same opinion as someone else [LN]. It refers to occupying oneself to the teaching, and thus has the idea of agreeing with it [WBC]. When someone does 'not agree' with such words, it means that he considers the words to be false [TH].

b. pres. act. participle of ὑγιαίνω (LN 72.15) (BAGD 2. p. 832): 'to be sound, to be correct, to be accurate' [BAGD, LN]. The phrase ὑγιαίνουσιν λόγοις τοῖς τοῦ κυρίου ἡμῶν 'the being sound words, namely the words of our Lord' is translated 'sound words (that is, those of our Lord)' [NET], 'sound words, those of our Lord' [NASB], 'sound precepts—that is, those of our Lord' [REB], 'healthy words, those of our Lord' [Lns], 'wholesome words, even the words of the Lord' [KJV], 'the wholesome message, that of our Lord' [BNTC]. Some simplify the sentence structure by downplaying the plural article τοῖς 'the (words)' before the phrase 'of our Lord': 'the sound words of our Lord' [Herm, NTC; NRSV], 'the sound teaching of our Lord' [HCSB], 'the sound instruction of our Lord' [NIV], 'the healthy words of our Lord' [AB, WBC], 'the wholesome teachings of the Lord' [NLT], 'the wholesome sayings that come from our Lord' [ECC], 'the correct teaching of our Lord' [CEV], 'the true teaching of our Lord' [NCV], 'the true words of our Lord' [TEV], 'the accurate words of our Lord' [GW], 'the correct teaching which is about our Lord' [LSA]. This verb means to be correct in one's views [LN]. In the Pastoral Epistles the verb 'to be healthy' is used figuratively with reference to Christian teaching and describes the teaching as being correct because it is reasonable and appeals to sound intelligence [BAGD]. This is a medical term used to describe 'healthy' doctrine [BKC, NAC]. See this word at 1:10.

QUESTION—What relationship is indicated by καί 'and' at the beginning of this clause?

This describes what is meant by the preceding reference to teaching differently [BNTC, ECC, ICC, Lns, My, NIGTC]. The difference of the teaching involves not agreeing with the correct words of the Lord [NIGTC]. This is the basic cause of the false teacher's deviation [BNTC].

QUESTION—What is meant by the ὑγιαίνουσιν 'being sound' words of our Lord?

1. It retains the metaphor of the words being healthy and wholesome [AB, BKC, BNTC, Lns, NAC, NIBC, NTIC, TC, WBC; KJV, NLT]. The gospel is healthy in itself and also imparts spiritual well-being to the one who has faith in it [BNTC].
2. It simply means that the words are correct [LSA; CEV, GW, TEV]. It means correct in the sense that they are true, in contrast with what is false [NICNT].

QUESTION—What is meant by the genitive construction, 'the words of our Lord Jesus Christ'?

1. This is a subjective genitive and means the words that were spoken by our Lord [ECC, Lns, My]. The 'words' refers to the collected words of Jesus [ECC]. Jesus 'words' refers to those in a Gospel and the plural form refers to the many doctrines Jesus taught in it [Lns].
2. This is a subjective genitive and means the teachings coming from our Lord in the sense that they come directly from him or through his apostles and teachers [Alf, EGT, NAC, NIBC, NIGTC, TC]. Christ can be seen as the authority behind the teaching [NAC, NIGTC]. It refers to the gospel message [NAC]. This does not mean the actual words spoken by Jesus, but that Jesus is the *source* of sound doctrine, and his words furnish the standard [TC]. These are words agreeing with Jesus' teachings and expressing his will [Alf].
3. This is an objective genitive and means the words that are about our Lord [LSA; TNTC, WBC]. This defines the content of the words, which is the gospel message about Christ [WBC].

and (with) the according-to godliness[a] teaching,

LEXICON—a. εὐσέβεια (LN 53.1 53.5) (BAGD p. 326): 'godliness' [BAGD, LN (53.5)], 'piety' [BAGD, LN (53.1, 53.5)], 'religion' [BAGD, LN (53.1)]. The phrase τῇ κατ᾽ εὐσέβειαν διδασκαλίᾳ 'the according to godliness teaching' is translated 'the doctrine which is according to godliness' [KJV; similarly Lns], 'the teaching that is according to godliness' [WBC], 'the teaching that accords with godliness' [AB; NET], 'the teaching that is in accordance with godliness' [NRSV], 'the teaching which is in accordance with (right) religion' [Herm], 'the doctrine that harmonizes with godliness' [NTC], 'the doctrine conforming to godliness' [NASB], 'the teaching which accords with sound religion' [BNTC], 'the doctrine about how we should live a godly life' [LSA], 'godly teaching'

[CEV, GW, NIV], 'the teaching that promotes godliness' [HCSB], 'these teachings promote a godly life' [NLT], 'the godly instruction' [ECC], 'the teaching that shows the true way to serve God' [NCV], 'the teaching of our religion' [TEV], 'good religious teaching' [REB]. This noun denotes the appropriate beliefs and devout practice of obligations relating to supernatural persons and powers [LN (53.1)], or the behavior that reflects correct religious beliefs and attitudes [LN (53.5)]. See this noun at 2:2; 4:7; 6: 5, 11.

QUESTION—What relationship is indicated by καί 'and' at the beginning of this clause?

1. This adds to the preceding description of 'different teaching' [NIGTC, WBC]. Not only do the contents of the teaching disagree with the words of our Lord, but its results do not accord with godliness [NIGTC, WBC].
2. In addition to Paul's instructions and the Lord's message, this is a third body of teaching [TH].

QUESTION—What is meant by the teaching that is 'according to godliness'?

The preposition κατά 'according to' can mean that the teaching conforms to godliness or that the goal of the teaching is godliness [WBC]. It can mean either the teachings of the Christian faith or the teachings that result in morally upright living [TH]. The teaching is in accordance with godliness [AB, Alf, BNTC, Herm, NTC; NASB, NET, NRSV]. Or, it means that the teaching promotes godliness [ICC, NIGTC, WP; HCSB, NCV, NLT]. Or, the teaching is about godliness [LSA]. It is what our religion teaches [REB, TEV].

QUESTION—What is meant by 'godliness'?

1. Godliness refers to a life of reverence before God and obedience to him [My, NIGTC, NTL]. This is the kind of religious devotion that is accompanied by a corresponding way of life [NTL]. It is Christian piety [My].
2. Godliness refers to the Christian religion [BNTC, TG]. This refers to the orthodox faith that Paul and Timothy hold to [BNTC].

6:4 he-has-become-conceited/foolish,[a] having-understood[b] nothing,

LEXICON—a. perf. pass. indic. of τυφόομαι, τυφόω (LN 88.218) (BAGD 1. or 2. p. 831): 'to be conceited' [BAGD (1.), ECC, LSA; HCSB, NASB, NET, NIV, NRSV], 'to be a conceited person' [GW], 'to be extremely proud, to be very arrogant' [LN], 'to be proud' [KJV], 'to be full of pride' [NCV], 'to be proud of oneself' [CEV], 'to be pompous' [Herm], 'to be blinded with conceit' [NTC], 'to be arrogant' [NLT], 'to be puffed up' [BAGD (1.), Lns], 'to be swollen with pride' [TEV], 'to be a swollen-headed person' [BNTC], 'to be a pompous (ignoramus)' [REB], 'to be foolish' [BAGD (2.), WBC], 'to be stupid' [BAGD (2.)], 'to be deluded' [AB]. This verb is a figurative extension of τυφόομαι 'to be crazy, to be demented', and means to be insanely arrogant [LN]. The perfect tense 'has become foolish' emphasizes the established and permanent state of

their condition [WBC], it is a continuing condition [Lns]. Many translate
with the present tense [NTC, WBC; all versions]: he is conceited/foolish.
See this word at 3:6.

b. pres. mid./pass. (deponent = act.) participle of ἐπίσταμαι (LN **32.3**)
(BAGD 1. p 300): 'to understand' [AB, BAGD, Herm, **LN**, Lns, LSA,
WBC; GW, HCSB, NASB, NCV, NET, NIV, NRSV], 'to be aware of, to
really know' [LN], 'to know' [NTC; CEV, KJV, TEV]. The phrase
'having understood nothing' is translated 'lacks understanding' [NLT],
'possessing no real knowledge' [BNTC], 'is a (pompous) ignoramus'
[REB], 'become a (conceited) ignoramus' [ECC]. This verb means to
have or to gain insight, and it focuses upon the process [LN].

QUESTION—What is meant by τυφόομαι 'being conceited/foolish'?

This describes the kind of person who dares to teach something different
from that which Christ taught [TH]. It is the main characterization of the
person who does not agree with the sound words of our Lord Jesus Christ
[NIGTC]. This is developed by the two following participial phrases 'having
understood nothing' and 'having a morbid craving' [NIGTC, WBC]. Either
meaning of the verb is possible with what follows: a person who knows
nothing but craves to be involved in disputes may be either filled with a
baseless pride or he is simply foolish [ICC, WBC].

1. He is conceited [BKC, BNTC, ECC, Herm, Lns, NAC, NIBC, NIGTC,
NTC, TH, WP; all versions], proud [Alf, ICC, TNTC], and arrogant [TH].
This is undoubtedly the meaning of the word at 3:6 and it fits here also
[NIGTC]. He thinks he is wise and becomes puffed up with self-
importance [NIBC]. He thinks that by his own intellect he has obtained
the correct answer [NIGTC].

2. He is foolish [AB, WBC]. Since this is parallel with 'understand nothing',
the word 'foolish' appears to be the meaning here, although at 3:6 this
same word appears to mean 'to be conceited' when applied to the danger
of appointing a novice to the office of elder too quickly [WBC]. It means
to be deluded and stupid [AB].

QUESTION—What relationship is indicated by the use of the participial phrase
'having understood nothing'?

If the first description means 'conceited', then the participle is concessive: he
is conceited *even though* he understands nothing. But if the first description
means 'foolish', the participle intensifies the statement: he is foolish and
understands nothing [WBC]. Or, this is an attendant circumstance: he is
besotted with pride, being one who does not know [Alf].

QUESTION—What is meant by 'understanding nothing'?

He is ignorant [TH]. Despite his arrogance, he doesn't have real spiritual
knowledge [NAC]. His knowledge is limited to fables, and he doesn't know
the truth [My]. He knows nothing about the subject that he teaches [Lns]. He
claims to have superior knowledge about religious and theological subjects,
yet he has no real knowledge about them [BNTC]. This condition is
described in 1:7 where it speaks of the false teachers as 'not understanding

what things they say nor concerning what things they confidently speak'
[AB].

but having-a-morbid-craving[a] **for controversies/speculations**[b] **and disputes-over-words,**[c]

LEXICON—a. pres. act. participle of νοσέω (LN **25.10**) (BAGD p. 543): 'to
have a morbid desire, to desire in an unhealthy manner' [LN], 'to have a
morbid craving for something' [BAGD, ECC; NRSV], 'to have a morbid
interest' [NASB], 'to have a morbid enthusiasm' [REB], 'to be morbid
about something' [Lns], 'to be morbidly taken up with' [BNTC], 'to be
possessed with a morbid craving' [NTC], 'to have an unhealthy desire'
[**LN**; GW, NLT, TEV], 'to have an unhealthy interest' [NET, NIV], 'to
have a sickly craving' [WBC], 'to have a sick interest' [HCSB], 'to be
sick with a love for' [NCV], 'to be sick from' [AB], 'to be diseased with'
[Herm], 'to abnormally desire' [LSA], 'to dote about' [KJV]. This verb is
also translated as a description: 'their minds are sick and they like to...'
[CEV]. This verb means to have an unhealthy or morbid desire for
something [LN].
  b. ζήτησις (LN 27.34, 33.440) (BAGD 1. or 2. p. 339): 'controversy' [AB,
  BAGD (2.), NTC; NET, NIV, NRSV], 'disputes' [LN (33.440); HCSB],
  'arguing' [NCV], 'controversial questions' [NASB], 'speculations' [ECC,
  WBC], 'mere speculations' [REB], 'idle speculations' [BNTC], 'investigation' [BAGD (1.)], 'racking of the brain' [Herm], 'information' [LN
  (27.34)], 'questions' [KJV], 'questionings' [Lns]. This noun is also translated as a verb: 'to argue' [CEV, GW, TEV]; as a verb phrase: 'he disputes
  about unimportant questions' [LSA]. This noun denotes the expression of
  forceful differences of opinion [LN (33.440)], or it denotes an attempt to
  learn something by careful investigation or searching [LN (27.34)]. The
  noun may denote the investigation of religious and theological problem
  [BAGD (1.)], or controversy about questions [BAGD (2.)].
  c. λογομαχία (LN **33.454**) (BAGD p. 477): 'disputes about words' [BAGD,
  Herm; NASB, NRSV], 'fights about words' [WBC], 'battles about words'
  [Lns], 'word-battles' [BAGD, NTC], 'verbal disputers' [NET], 'quarrels
  about words' [**LN**; NIV], 'verbal quibbles' [BNTC], 'quibbling about
  terminology' [ECC], 'controversies' [AB], 'arguments over words'
  [HCSB], 'strifes of words' [KJV], 'quibbles' [REB]. The noun is also
  translated as a verb phrase: 'to argue about words' [LSA], 'to quarrel
  about words' [GW, TEV], 'to fight about words' [NCV]. The two nouns
  are combined: 'to argue over words' [CEV], 'to quibble over the meaning
  of words' [NLT]. This noun denotes an argument or quarrel about the
  meaning or use of words [LN].
QUESTION—What relationship is indicated by the use the participial phrase
  that begins with 'having a morbid craving'?
  This phrase is parallel with the preceding phrase 'having understood
nothing' and both modify 'he is conceited/foolish' [WBC].

QUESTION—What is a 'morbid craving' for controversies and disputes?

The verb literally means to be physically ill, but here it is applied to the mental state of unrest and instability [AB]. This uses the figure of having a sick or unhealthy craving for the following two attributes [NIGTC]. Calling the craving 'unhealthy' pictures it as an ailment of some kind [TH]. This word contrasts with the healthy (sound) words of the Lord (6:3) [NIBC, TNTC]. It carries on the metaphor in 6:3 in which they disagree with 'healthy' (sound) words and now have a 'sick' or 'unhealthy' craving for arguments about words [BNTC, WBC].

QUESTION—What is meant by ζητήσεις 'controversies/speculations'?

1. It means controversies [AB, BKC, ICC, LSA, NAC, NIBC, NIGTC, NTC, NTL, TH, TNTC; CEV, GW, HCSB, NCV, NET, NIV, NRSV, TEV]. This concerns discussions and debates [AB, ICC]. They forcefully express their differences of opinion without a real interest in seeking a solution [TH]. These are religious controversies about OT matters and interpretations [ECC]. Perhaps this is about theological problems [BKC].

2. It means speculations [Alf, BNTC, ECC, Herm, Lns, NIGTC, WBC; KJV, REB]. It concerns a sectarian preoccupation with pseudo-intellectual theorizing [BNTC]. It concerns controversial questions [NIGTC].

QUESTION—What is meant by λογομαχίας 'disputes over words'?

1. This word is literally 'word-battles' and means disputes about words [Alf, BNTC, EGT, ICC, NIBC, NIGTC, TH, WBC, WP]. This describes arguments and quarrels about the meaning and use of words [TH]. Apparently these disputes were over the law [NTC].

2. A war of words means dispute in which words are used as weapons [BKC, TC]. It describes a battle of words [BNTC]. This is equivalent to controversy [TC].

out of-which come[a] envy,[b] strife,[c] insults[d] evil suspicions,[e]

LEXICON—a. The phrase ἐξ ὧν γίνεται 'out of which come' [WBC; similarly Herm, Lns] is also translated 'out of which arise' [NASB], 'out of which proceed' [NTC], 'that result in' [NIV], 'this gives rise to' [NET; similarly BNTC; REB], 'from these come' [HCSB, NRSV; similarly AB], 'these in turn produce' [ECC], 'this produces' [GW], 'this stirs up arguments ending in' [NLT], 'they cause' [CEV], 'this brings' [NCV], 'this brings on' [TEV], 'whereof come' [KJV].

b. φθόνος (LN 88.160) (BAGD p. 857): 'envy' [AB, BAGD, LN, Lns, NTC, WBC; HCSB, KJV, NASB, NET, NIV, NRSV], 'jealousy' [BAGD, BNTC, ECC, Herm, LN; CEV, GW, NCV, NLT, REB, TEV]. The noun is also translated as a verb phrase: 'people envy one another' [LSA]. This noun denotes a state of ill will toward someone because of some real or presumed advantage experienced by that a person [LN].

c. ἔρις (LN 39.22) (BAGD p. 309): 'strife' [AB, BAGD, LN, Lns, WBC; KJV, NASB, NIV], 'discord' [BAGD, LN], 'contention' [BAGD], 'controversy' [ECC], 'disagreements' [CEV], 'dissension' [NET, NRSV], 'division' [NLT], 'quarreling' [BNTC, Herm; HCSB, REB], 'disputes' [TEV], 'wrangling' [NTC], 'fighting' [NCV], 'rivalry' [GW]. This noun denotes a conflict that results from rivalry and discord [LN].

d. βλασφημία (LN 33.400) (BAGD 1. p. 143): 'reviling' [LN, NTC], 'slander' [BAGD, BNTC, WBC; HCSB, NET, NLT, NRSV, REB], 'slandering' [Herm], 'defamation' [BAGD], 'speaking against others' [NCV], 'malicious talk' [NIV], 'unkind words' [CEV], 'abusive language' [NASB], 'railings' [KJV], 'reviling speech' [AB], 'insults' [TEV], 'cursing' [GW], 'vituperations' [ECC], 'blasphemies' [Lns]. The noun is also translated as a verb phrase: 'they slander one another' [LSA]. This noun denotes speaking against someone in such a way as to harm or injure his or her reputation [LN].

e. ὑπόνοια (LN **31.32**) (BAGD p. 846): 'suspicion' [BAGD, LN; GW], 'conjecture' [BAGD]. The phrase ὑπόνοιαι πονηρα 'evil suspicions' [AB, WBC; CEV, HCSB, NASB, NET, NIV, NLT, TEV] is also translated 'evil mistrust' [NCV], 'evil surmisings' [KJV]. 'base suspicions' [BNTC, NTC; NRSV, REB], 'false suspicions' [Herm], 'wicked suspicions' [Lns], 'vicious insinuations' [ECC]. The phrase 'out of which come...evil suspicions' is translated 'this causes...people to suspect evil', or 'to suspect falsely', or 'to be suspicious' [**LN**]. This noun denotes an opinion based on scant evidence, and this often results in accepting a false opinion to be true [LN].

QUESTION—What relationship is indicated by the phrase ἐξ ὧν γίνεται 'out of which comes'?

The phrase indicates the results coming from the preceding traits [AB, ECC, LSA, NAC, NIGTC, NTC, NTL, TH, WP]: *as a result people do the following*. This introduces the vices that develop out of ignorant controversies [ICC].

QUESTION—What is meant by φθόνος 'envy'?

It refers to an eager desire to have what another has, either their possessions or their abilities [TH]. This means holding a grudge against someone because of a desire to have what the other possesses [NIGTC]. It is jealousy [NTL]. They envied the success of others [NAC].

QUESTION—What is meant by ἔρις 'strife'?

An opponent in a debate becomes unwilling to admit defeat, so discord follows with one constantly contradicting the other [NTC]. This is the act of separating from one another or creating divisions that undermine the unity of the group [TH].

QUESTION—What is meant by βλασφημία 'insults'?

This means abusive speech [NIGTC]. It is abusive language directed toward others [TH]. It is a typical result of arguments and controversy [ICC]. It refers to slander among people, not blasphemy against God [Alf, ICC, TC]. It is slander and defamation directed toward an opponent in a debate [Alf, NTC]. The plural form indicates that these are frequent and that a number of people are involved [TH].

QUESTION—What is meant by ὑπόνοιαι πονηραί 'evil suspicions'?

A man suspects every action and word of his opponent [NTC]. They found fault with others and had misgivings about their integrity [NAC]. They suspected the honesty of others [EGT].

6:5 **wranglings**[a] **(between) men having-been-corrupted**[b] **(as to) their minds and having-been-deprived**[c] **of-the truth,**[d]

LEXICON—a. διαπαρατριβή (LN **33.452**) (BAGD p. 187): This plural form is translated 'wrangling' [NRSV], 'endless wrangles' [REB], 'constant wranglings' [AB], 'persistent wranglings' [BNTC], 'constant arguments' [TEV], 'constant arguing' [LN], 'continuous arguing' [LN], 'constant disagreement' [HCSB], 'constant bickering' [NET], 'incessant bickerings' [ECC], 'constant friction' [NASB, NIV], 'constant irritations' [WBC], 'perverse disputings' [KJV], 'quarrelsome disputes' [Herm], 'constant quarrels' [NCV], 'nasty quarrels' [CEV], 'conflict' [GW], 'mutual altercations' [NTC], 'irritations' [Lns], 'mutual or constant irritation' [BAGD]. This noun is also translated as a verb: 'they wrangle (with one another)' [LSA], 'these people always cause trouble' [NLT]. This noun denotes the state of engaging in continuous and repeated arguing [LN]. The verb prefix δια- adds the sense of continuance [Alf, EGT] and intensification [My]. The prefix is an emphatic indication of the persistency and obstinacy of the disputes [TC]. The plural form stresses the frequency and constancy of the arguments [TH]. They are a continual source of irritation as they interact with others [WBC].

b. perf. pass. participle of διαφθείρω (LN **88.266**) (BAGD 2. p. 190): 'to be depraved, to be perverted, to cause the moral ruin of' [LN], 'to be ruined' [BAGD, LN]. The phrase 'having been corrupted as to their minds' [Lns] is also translated 'corrupted in their minds' [NET], 'who have been corrupted in their mind' [WBC], 'who have a corrupted mind' [Herm], 'whose minds are corrupted' [BNTC; REB], 'with corrupted minds' [AB; similarly GW], 'their minds are corrupt' [NLT], 'of corrupt minds' [KJV, NIV], 'they have wicked minds' [CEV], 'who have evil minds' [NCV], 'with depraved minds' [LN], 'depraved in mind' [NTC], 'of depraved mind' [NASB], 'who are depraved in mind' [NRSV], 'whose minds are depraved' [HCSB], 'whose minds do not function' [TEV], 'whose minds are a shambles' [ECC], 'because they have corrupt attitudes' [LSA]. This verb means to be caused to become perverse or depraved [LN].

c. perf. pass. participle of ἀποστερέω (LN 57.47) (BAGD p. 99): 'to be deprived of' [BAGD, LN], 'to be caused to not possess something' [LN]. The clause 'having been deprived of the truth' is translated 'being deprived of the truth' [LN; similarly NET], 'who have been deprived of the truth' [Herm], 'deprived of the truth' [NTC; HCSB, NASB], 'destitute of the truth' [KJV], 'who have lost the truth' [NCV], 'who have lost their grip of the truth' [REB], 'who have lost their hold of the truth' [BNTC], 'who have been robbed of the truth' [ECC; NIV; similarly WBC], 'having been bereft of the truth' [Lns; similarly NRSV], 'who no longer have the truth' [TEV], 'they have missed out on the truth' [CEV], '(whose corrupt minds) have been robbed of the truth' [GW], 'defrauded from the truth' [AB], 'they have turned their backs on the truth' [NLT], 'because they are no longer taught the true doctrine' [LSA].

QUESTION—What relationship is indicated by the use of the participles 'having been corrupted' and 'having been deprived'?

1. The two participles indicate the reason they wrangle with one another [LSA, NICNT, NIGTC]: *wranglings between men because they have been corrupted...and deprived....* The present conditions are due to past actions or decisions they have made [NICNT]. When people lose hold on the truth they become corrupt in mind and start quarrels that bring about strife [ICC].

2. The participles describe these people [WBC]: *wranglings between men who have been corrupted...and deprived...*

QUESTION—What is meant by 'having been corrupted as to their minds'?

This refers to the moral and intellectual breakdown of their minds through which the truth of God's revelation is meant to be understood [NICNT]. Their depraved minds oppose the truth [NTC]. The word 'mind' refers to their inner disposition and their moral and intellectual capacity to make decisions [WBC]. Mind refers to more than reasoning powers, it refers to their whole mental and moral attitude or way of thinking [BNTC]. The passive participle implies that the devil is the one who has corrupted their minds [NIGTC].

QUESTION—What is meant by 'having been deprived of the truth'?

The word 'deprived' has the sense of a person being deprived of something to which he has a right, so to be deprived of the truth means that they no longer have the truth that was once theirs [EGT]. People are deprived of the truth when others spread false teaching that drives out the truth from their minds [ICC]. They have lost the ability to apprehend the truth of the Christian revelation [BNTC, NICNT], because of their teachings and disputing [NICNT]. The truth was once theirs, or could have been theirs, but now they are bereft of the truth and keep undermining the health of the church [Lns]. The 'truth' is the gospel [ICC, NICNT], the content of the absolute truth of Christianity [NIGTC]. The passive voice of this participle implies that the devil is the one who has deprived them of the truth [NIGTC]. They have been robbed of the truth by Satan [BKC]. Verse 4:1 implies that they have lost this by the influence of demons [My].

thinking godliness[a] to-be (a means of) gain.[b]

TEXT—Following εὐσέβειαν 'godliness' some manuscripts add ἀφίστασο ἀπὸ τῶν τοιούτων 'keep away from such ones'. 'Keep away from such-ones' is read by KJV.

LEXICON—a. εὐσέβεια (LN 53.1 53.5) (BAGD p. 326): 'godliness' [BAGD, LN (53.5)], 'piety' [BAGD, LN (53.1, 53.5)], 'godly faith' [BAGD], 'religion' [BAGD, LN (53.1)]. See translations of this word in the following lexical item b. This noun denotes the appropriate beliefs and devout practice of obligations relating to supernatural persons and powers [LN (53.1)], or the behavior that reflects correct religious beliefs and attitudes [LN (53.5)]. See this noun at 2:2; 4:7; 6: 3, 11.

b. πορισμός (LN 57.194) (BAGD p. 693): 'gain, profit, wealth' [LN], 'a means of gain' [BAGD]. The clause 'thinking godliness to be a means of gain' is translated 'supposing their godliness to be a means of gain' [Lns], 'thinking that godliness is a means of profit' [WBC], 'who suppose that godliness is a means of gain' [NASB], 'who think that godliness is a means to financial gain' [NIV; similarly AB], 'supposing that gain is godliness' [KJV], 'they think godliness is a means for gain' [ECC], 'they think that religion is a way to gain wealth' [LN], 'who imagine that godliness is a way to material gain' [HCSB], 'who imagine that the practice of godliness is gain' [NTC], 'imagining that godliness is a means of gain' [NRSV], 'they think that a godly life is a way to make a profit' [GW; similarly NET], 'who think that religion is a profit-making business' [Herm], 'they think that religion is a way to become rich' [TEV], 'they think that serving God is a way to get rich' [NCV], 'these people think religion is supposed to make you rich' [CEV], 'they think religion should yield dividends' [REB], 'who regard religion as a source of profit' [BNTC], 'they think that they should practice religion only in order that they may gain money' [LSA], 'to them, a show of godliness is just a way to become wealthy' [NLT]. This noun denotes a means of gaining a profit or wealth [LN]. Here the noun 'gain' refers to 'a means of gain' [ICC, NIGTC].

QUESTION—What relationship is indicated by the use of the participle 'thinking'?

This can mean either an expression of their corrupt nature or a further characteristic of these people [ICC]. The change to the present tense of this participle connects this to the preceding statement by describing one way in which they have been robbed of the truth [NICNT]. The participle indicates the result of being corrupted and deprived [LSA].

QUESTION—In what way do they think that godliness is gain?

The word 'gain' refers to financial gain or profit and the focus is on the means they use to obtain this wealth [TH]. The noun means 'source of gain', that gain being financial gain [AB]. They think that they can get rich by being religious [TG]. In order to become rich they made a show of their religion and also charged large fees for giving their religious instructions [NTC]. In this context, this means that they exacted fees for the religious instructions they gave to their followers [BNTC]. They had only the appearance of piety, but it was not actual piety [My]. They get an actor's salary and for them religion is a livelihood [ECC]. 'Their godliness' was not the true godliness of 6:3, but the kind of godliness these men conceived it to be [Lns].

DISCOURSE UNIT—6:6–10 [ECC, Herm, LSA, NAC, NCBC, TH, TNTC]. The topic is riches, part 1 [ECC], the greed of the false teachers [NAC], the perils of wealth [TNTC], a warning against avarice [Herm], warnings against rich Christians [TH], the need for moderation in lifestyle [NCBC], a person gains great benefit when he lives godly and is content, but ruins himself spiritually when he aspires to be rich [LSA].

DISCOURSE UNIT—6:6–8 [NIGTC]. The topic is that godliness with contentment is great gain.

6:6 But/and[a] a-great[a] gain is godliness with contentment/self-sufficiency.[c]

LEXICON—a. δέ (LN 89.87, 89.93, 89.124) (BAGD 1., 2., 3. p. 171): This conjunction can mark a sequence of closely related events: 'and, and then' [LN (89.87)], or an additive relation that is not coordinate: 'and, and also, also, in addition, even' [LN (89.93)], or a contrast: 'but, on the other hand' [LN (89.124)]. It can emphasize a contrast: 'but', or mark a simple transition: 'now, then', or mark a resumption of an interrupted discourse: 'and also, but also' [BAGD]. Here it is translated 'and' [NTC; CEV], 'and indeed' [Herm], 'now' [AB, Lns, WBC; NET], 'well' [TEV], 'of course' [NRSV], 'and of course' [REB], 'anyway' [Herm], 'yet' [NLT], 'however' [ECC], 'but' [HCSB, KJV, NASB, NIV], not explicit [BNTC; GW].

b. μέγας (LN **59.22**) (BAGD 2.a.β. p. 497): 'great' [BAGD, LN], 'much, big, extensive' [LN]. The phrase ἔστιν πορισμὸς μέγας ἡ εὐσέβεια 'a great gain is godliness' is translated 'godliness is great gain' [**LN**; HCSB, KJV, NIV], 'godliness is a great profit' [WBC], 'there is great gain in godliness' [NRSV], 'true godliness is itself great wealth' [NLT], 'godliness brings gain, great gain' [ECC], 'godliness brings great profit' [NET], 'godliness actually is a means of great gain' [NASB], 'godliness…actually is a great means of gain' [Lns], 'godliness is a great source of gain' [AB] 'a godly life brings huge profits' [GW], 'religion is indeed a great source of profit' [BNTC], 'religion does make us very rich' [TEV], 'religion does make your life rich' [CEV], 'religion is of great profit' [Herm], 'religion does yield high dividends' [REB], 'it is great gain, namely the practice of godliness (with…)' [NTC], 'a person gains great benefit when he lives godly' [LSA], 'serving God does make us very rich' [NCV]. This adjective means a large quantity involving extent [LN].

c. αὐτάρκεια (LN **25.83**) (BAGD 2. p. 122): 'contentment' [BAGD, LN], 'self-content, contentment with what one has' [LN]. The phrase μετὰ αὐταρκείας 'with contentment' [WBC; HCSB, KJV, NIV, NLT] is also translated 'combined with contentment' [NET, NRSV], 'together with contentment' [Lns], 'when accompanied by contentment' [NASB], '(when he lives godly) and is content' [LSA], 'if we are satisfied with what we have' [NCV], 'if it is accompanied by contentment with what one has' [**LN**], 'if we are satisfied with what we have' [TEV], 'to people who are content with what they have' [GW], 'for the man with a contented spirit' [BNTC], 'but only to those who are content with what they have' [REB], 'for someone contented with what he has' [ECC], 'with soul sufficiency' [NTC], 'when it is accompanied by self-sufficiency' [AB], 'if it is coupled with self-sufficiency' [Herm], 'by making you content with what you have' [CEV]. This noun denotes the state of being content with one's circumstances or lot in life [LN].

QUESTION—What relationship is indicated by δέ 'but/and'?

1. This conjunction indicates a contrast [Alf, ECC, My, NIBC, NIGTC, TC, TH; HCSB, KJV, NASB, NIV, NLT]: but, yet. This is in emphatic contrast with what the false teachers think [ECC, TC]. They are wrong in their thinking, but there is a sense in which such an idea is true [Alf, NIBC]. Paul takes up the word 'gain' in 6:5 and gives the true sense of it in the material side of life in contrast with the misunderstanding of the false teachers [NIGTC].

2. This conjunction indicates an additive relation that is not coordinate [AB, Herm, ICC, Lns, LSA, NAC, NICNT, NTC, WBC; CEV, NET, NRSV, REB, TEV]: and, now, well, of course. This enlarges his discussion by stating there is another kind of profit to be derived from Christian service [WBC]. It has the intensive idea of 'indeed' [Herm, NAC]. Paul is affirming that those who thought that godliness leads to gain were correct, because there is a spiritual profit in true godliness [NAC]. There is a paragraph break here since Paul will deal with different groups [Lns].

QUESTION—What is the great gain acquired by living a godly life?

1. The word 'gain' is used in a spiritual sense, not a material sense related to money [AB, Alf, BNTC, ECC, ICC, NAC, NIBC, NIGTC, NTC, TC, TG, TH, WBC]. The gain is peace with God, spiritual joy, assurance of salvation, and the conviction that all things work together for good [NTC]. It is lots of good things in one's heart, or a life full of good things [TH]. It is the happiness of being above the vexations, temptations, dangers, and disappointments encountered by the mercenary men described in 6:9–10 [Lns]. This gain is both in this world and in the next [ICC, NAC, TC]. The profit is the promise of life in the present life, and in the life to come [BNTC, NIGTC].

2. The gain is in being godly and contented [AB, Alf, BKC]. Instead of giving gain, godliness is itself the gain [BKC]. The gain is the life of godliness itself [AB]. The gain is not one's reward in heaven, but the possession of a godliness that is joined with contentment [Alf].

3. Contentment is the great gain we receive from godliness [WP; CEV]. Religion makes our lives rich by making us content with what we have [CEV].

QUESTION—What relationship is indicated by the prepositional phrase μετὰ αὐταρκείας 'with contentment'?

1. This phrase explains the kind of godliness Paul has in mind, it is godliness accompanied by contentment [AB, Alf, BKC, ECC, ICC, Lns, LSA, My, NAC, NIGTC, NTC, NTIC, NTL, TC, TG, TH, WBC; HCSB, KJV, NET,

NIV, NLT, NRSV]. The preposition is not causal or conditional, nor does it indicate that there are two kinds of godliness. Rather, it indicates that contentment always goes with true godliness [Lns]. It explains the nature of the godliness that produces great gain [ICC]. It is the godliness of a person who is content with what he has [TG]. Godliness is the source of contentment and the combination produces great gain [NIGTC].

2. This phrase indicates the condition that must be met in order to receive great gain from one's godliness [BNTC, Herm, NASB, NCV, NIBC, REB, TEV]: godliness brings great gain to a person *if that person is content with what he has*. This is an essential condition [BNTC]. There is great (metaphorical) profit in godliness, provided it is accompanied by contentment [NIBC].

QUESTION—What is meant here by the word αὐτάρκεια 'contentment/self-sufficiency'?

This word was commonly used to describe the Greek virtue of being self-sufficient so that one had enough resources in himself that he lacked nothing, or it can mean being content with one's state and condition in life [TH]. The Greek Stoics considered it a virtue to be self-sufficient and rely on one's own inner resources without outside help, but the word can also refer to the state of a person who has enough and is not longing for more [ICC].

1. This means being contented [BNTC, ECC, ICC, Lns, LSA, NAC, TC, TG, TH, WBC; all versions]. It is being content with one's state or condition in life [TH], to be satisfied with what one has [ICC, NTC]. It is to be satisfied with food and clothing (6:8) [ECC, WBC], and it goes beyond such material things to accept all situations that are encountered [ECC]. A contented person has no need for stored earthly goods, which can never satisfy his soul [NTC]. He must have a spirit that gratefully accepts what God gives him and is satisfied with that [BNTC]. Contentment is satisfaction with what one has, and this enables him to live above both want and plenty as in Philippians 4:13 [NIBC]. He is not self-sufficient, but is Christ-sufficient [ICC, NAC, NIBC]. It is resting serene and safe in God's care, since God provides what is needed [Lns].

2. This means being self-sufficient [AB, BKC, EGT, Herm, NTC, NTIC, TNTC]. Such a person is independent and indifferent to any circumstance [EGT, TNTC]. This refers to self-sufficiency, a detachment and freedom from any claims made by any sort of possession, and positively it is called contentment [AB]. This self-sufficiency is not in the unfavorable of sense of self-satisfaction or extreme self-confidence, but it has the favorable sense of 'soul-sufficiency' so that one has an inherent and adequate capacity for every activity, and it includes the element of contentment [NTC]. This sufficiency is described in Philippians 4:11–12, and the Greek moralists would have accepted all of that thought except when Paul added that he could do all things 'in Christ' who strengthened him [NICNT]. This self-sufficiency is due to a God-given sufficiency that does not depend on material circumstances [BKC].

6:7 Because we-brought[a] nothing into the world, because/that we-are- not -
able to-take-out[b] anything.

TEXT—Instead of ὅτι 'because/that' some manuscripts read δῆλον ὅτι '(it is)
certain that', some manuscripts read ἀληθὲς ὅτι '(it is) true that', and a few
version manuscripts and Church Fathers omit ὅτι 'because/that'. GNT reads
ὅτι 'that/because' with an A decision, indicating that the text is certain. '(It
is) certain that' is read by KJV.

LEXICON—a. aorist act. indic. of εἰσφέρω (LN 15.194) (BAGD 1. p. 233): 'to
bring into' [AB, BAGD, BNTC, ECC, Herm, LN, Lns, NTC, WBC; all
versions], 'to carry in' [BAGD, LN]. Implicit information is added: 'we
brought nothing when we were born' [LSA]. This verb means to carry or
to bring something into an area [LN]. This refers to bringing something
material with us when we are born [NIGTC].

b. aorist act. infin. of ἐκφέρω (LN 15.197) (BAGD 1. p. 246): 'to take out'
[AB, BNTC, ECC, Herm, LN, WBC; all versions except CEV, GW,
KJV], 'to carry out' [LN, NTC; KJV], 'to bring out' [BAGD, LN, Lns].
This is also translated with the positive counterpart: 'we can take nothing
out' [GW]. Some add implicit information: 'we won't take anything with
us when we leave' [CEV], 'we cannot take anything out of it when we
die' [LSA]. This verb means to carry something out of an area [LN]. It
refers to departing from the world at death [NIGTC].

QUESTION—What relationship is indicated by the first conjunction γάρ
'because'?

This conjunction indicates the grounds for making the statement in 6:6
[BKC, BNTC, ECC, LSA, My, NAC, NIBC, NIGTC, WBC]: there is a great
gain is godliness with contentment, *because we brought nothing into the
world, and we are not able to carry anything out of it when we leave it.* This
gives the reason why a person can have a contented attitude [BNTC]. It
amplifies and explains 6:6 [Herm, Lns]. It especially explains what a blessed
source of gain 'contentment' is [Lns].

QUESTION—What is indicated by the use of the first-person plural 'we' in the
verbs?

This gives a proverb-like quality to this verse [AB, ICC, NIGTC]. 'We'
includes all human beings [ECC, TG], people in general [TH].

QUESTION—What relationship is indicated by the conjunction ὅτι 'because/
that'?

1. The conjunction indicates reason [ICC, Lns]. There is no reason to bring
   anything into the world because we are not able to bring anything out
   [Lns]. There is an ellipsis and filled out it means '(and there was no point
   in bringing anything into the world) because we shall not be able to take
   anything out of it' [ICC].
2. It appears that the conjunction has a weakened sense and simply means
   'and' [BNTC, LSA, WBC; CEV, GW, HCSB, NIV, NLT, REB]: *and
   neither are we able to take out anything.*

3. The conjunction indicates result [BAGD (1.d.γ. p. 589), ECC; NASB, NCV, NET, NRSV]: *so we cannot take anything out.* This is a special use of the conjunction and has the consecutive meaning 'so that' [BAGD].

4. The conjunction means 'that' [NIGTC, NTC; KJV]. There is an ellipsis, and filled out it means 'just as it is evident that' [NTC], or 'it is clear that' [NIGTC; KJV].

5. The conjunction is resumptive [TC]: *(I say) that neither can we carry anything out.*

6. This difficult conjunction is best ignored [NCBC, TG, TH; TEV]. 'When people are born, they bring nothing into this world; when they die, they take nothing out of this world' [TH], 'when we were born, we had nothing; after we die, we will have nothing' [TG].

QUESTION—What is the point of this verse?

Acquiring things like the false teachers want to do has no ultimate or final benefit [NIGTC]. The results of greediness are only temporary [WBC]. In view of our brief stay on earth, material gain is irrelevant, and greed is irrational [NAC, NIBC]. The conclusion is that we need not seek more than we need while we are in the world [ICC].

6:8 **But having food**[a] **and clothing/coverings,**[b] **with these we-will-be-satisfied.**[c]

LEXICON—a. διατροφή (LN **5.1**) (BAGD p. 190): 'food' [AB, BAGD, BNTC, Herm, **LN**, LSA, WBC; all versions], 'nourishment' [Lns, NTC], 'subsistence' [BAGD], 'keep' [ECC]. This noun denotes any kind of food or nourishment [LN].

b. σκέπασμα (LN **6.163**) (BAGD p. 753): 'clothing' [BAGD, BNTC, Herm, **LN**, LSA, WBC; HCSB, NIV, NLT, NRSV, REB], 'clothes' [CEV, GW, NCV, TEV], 'apparel' [LN], 'raiment' [KJV], 'covering' [AB, BAGD, ECC; NASB], 'coverings' [Lns], 'shelter' [NTC; NET]. This noun denotes clothing as a covering [LN]. This denotes anything that serves as a shelter and protection, so besides clothing it could also refer to a house [BAGD].

c. fut. pass. indic. of ἀρκέω (LN 59.46) (BAGD 2. p. 107): 'to be satisfied' [BAGD], 'to be content' [BAGD, ECC, Herm, Lns], 'to regard (these) as sufficient' [NTC], 'to be adequate, to be enough' [LN]. The passive voice is also translated 'we will be satisfied' [LSA; NCV, NET], 'we will be content' [AB, BNTC, WBC; HCSB, NASB, NIV, NRSV], 'let us be content' [KJV, NLT], 'let us rest content' [REB], 'we should be satisfied' [CEV, GW], 'that should be enough for us' [TEV]. This verb means to be sufficient or adequate for a particular purpose, and it implies that it leads to satisfaction [LN].

QUESTION—What relationship is indicated by δέ 'but'?

1. This conjunction indicates a contrast [AB, Alf, EGT, My, NAC, NIGTC, NTC, NTIC; HCSB, NCV, NET, NIV, NRSV]: *but.* This contrasts the believer's attitude with the attitude of the greedy heretics [Alf, My, NAC].

We shall not strive after earthly riches, but be content with these [NTC]. It is a counterbalance to 6:7: we do not bring anything into the world and can take nothing out of it, but we do need some essential things while living in this world [EGT, NIGTC].

2. It indicates an addition [Lns; KJV]: *and/now*. This resumes the main thought of 6:6 [Lns].

3. This indicates a conclusion arising from 6:7 [ECC, TH; CEV, NLT, TEV]: *so then, if we have food and clothing, we should be satisfied.*

QUESTION—What relationship is indicated by the use of the participle ἔχοντες 'having'?

1. It indicates the condition for being satisfied [AB, BNTC, ECC, Herm, ICC, NTIC, TC; HCSB, NASB, NCV, NET, NIV, NLT, NRSV, REB, TEV]: *if we have food and clothing, then we will be satisfied with these* [BNTC, ICC; HCSB, NASB, NCV, NET, NIV, NRSV], or, *let us be satisfied with these* [NLT, REB, TEV].

2. It indicates the grounds for being satisfied [Alf, Lns, LSA, NIGTC]: *since we have food and clothing, we will be satisfied with these.* 'Having' indicates that food and clothing are already possessed [Alf, NIGTC].

QUESTION—What is meant by σκεπάσματα 'clothing/coverings'?

1. This means clothing [BAGD, BNTC, ECC, Herm, LN, LSA, My, NAC, NCBC, TC, WBC; HCSB, NIV, NLT, NRSV, REB].

2. This means coverings and includes both clothing and shelter [AB, Alf, Lns, NTC, TNTC]. This includes the house in which a person resides as well as the garment he wears [NTC].

3. This means shelter [NET].

QUESTION—What relationship is indicated by the use of the future tense 'we will be satisfied'?

1. It indicates a consequence [AB, Alf, ECC, Herm, Lns, My, NTC, NTIC, TC; NASB, NCV, NET, NIV, NRSV]: *if we have food and clothing, then we will be satisfied.*

2. It indicates a command or exhortation [BNTC, NIGTC, TG, WBC; CEV, GW, KJV, NLT, REB, TEV]: *let us be satisfied with these.* This is probably a Hebrew usage to indicate an imperative: 'let us be content' or 'we should be content' [BNTC, NIGTC].

DISCOURSE UNIT—6:9–10 [NIGTC]. The topic is the love of money being a root of all sorts of evil.

6:9 **But the (ones) desiring to-be-rich fall[a] into temptation[b] and a-trap[c]**

TEXT—Instead of παγίδα 'trap' some manuscripts read παγίδας 'traps', and some manuscripts read παγίδα τοῦ διαβόλου 'trap of the devil'. GNT reads παγίδα 'trap' with an A decision, indicating that the text is certain.

LEXICON—a. pres. act. indic. of ἐμπίπτω (LN 15.121, 90.71) (BAGD 2. p. 256): 'to fall' [AB, BAGD, BNTC, Herm, LN (15.121), Lns, NTC, WBC; CEV, HCSB, KJV, NASB, NIV, REB], 'to topple' [ECC], 'to stumble' [NET], 'to experience' [LN (90.71)]. This verb is translated differently for the two items with which it is connected: 'fall into temptation and caught in the trap' [TEV], 'bring temptation to themselves and are caught in a trap' [NCV], 'fall into temptation and are trapped by...desires' [NLT, NRSV; similarly GW]. This verb means to fall into a particular point or location [LN (15.121)], or to suddenly experience something that is difficult or bad [LN (90.71)]. The present tense indicates what usually happens to such people [NIGTC]. They keep falling [GW]. See this word at 3:6, where it is used in the same way [ICC].

b. πειρασμός (LN 88.308) (BAGD 2.b. p. 641): 'temptation' [AB, BAGD, BNTC, ECC, Herm, LN, Lns, NTC, WBC; all versions], 'an enticement to sin' [BAGD]. The clause 'they fall into temptation' is translated 'they are tempted' [LSA]. This noun denotes an attempt to cause someone to sin [LN].

c. παγίς (LN **21.4**) (BAGD 2. p. 602): 'trap' [AB, ECC, LN; CEV, HCSB, NCV, NET, NIV, TEV], 'snare' [BNTC, Herm, Lns, NTC, WBC; KJV, NASB, REB], 'danger' [**LN**]. The clause 'they fall into a trap' is translated 'they are trapped' [GW, NLT, NRSV], 'they are caught in a trap' [LSA]. This noun is a figurative extension of 'trap', (6.23) and it denotes that which brings, or is a means of, sudden danger [LN]. This figurative use of 'trap' or 'snare' denotes something that brings sudden and unexpected danger or death [BAGD].

QUESTION—What relationship is indicated by δέ 'but'?

This conjunction indicates contrast [Alf, BKC, ECC, Herm, ICC, Lns, My, NIBC, NIGTC, NTC, TC, TH, WBC; GW, HCSB, KJV, NASB, NET, NLT, NRSV, TEV]. This verse is in contrast with 6:8 [Alf], or with 6:6–8 [My, NIBC, NIGTC]. The contrast is between the attitude of the godly and the attitude of those who seek to be rich [ICC, Lns, TG]. This contrasts the satisfaction of those who have the necessities of life with the dissatisfaction of those who want more [WBC].

QUESTION—What relationship is indicated by the use of the participle βουλόμενοι 'desiring'?

It indicates the reason for what follows [LSA]: *because they desire to be rich, they fall into the following things.* This 'desire' is to be rich at any cost and to do it quickly [WP]. It does not indicate whether or not they succeed in becoming rich [Lns]. This does not condemn money, but the love of money [TC, NAC].

QUESTION—What are they tempted to do?

This is the kind of temptation that comes from pursuing riches [Alf, WBC]. They are tempted to acquire money in a wrong way [LSA, My].

QUESTION—What is meant by falling into a trap?

This may refer to a trap which takes someone unaware or a snare from which one cannot escape after being caught in it [ICC]. Falling into a trap is a result of failing to resist the temptation [Alf, WBC]. The temptations entangle them in the snare [Alf]. This is probably the snare of the devil as in 3:7 [NIBC, NIGTC, NTL, TG, TH, TNTC].

and/even many foolish[a] and harmful[b] desires[c]

LEXICON—a. ἀνόητος (LN 32.50) (BAGD 2. p. 70): 'foolish' [BAGD, Herm, LN, WBC; all versions except GW, NET, NRSV], 'stupid' [LN; GW], 'senseless' [AB, ECC, NTC; NET, NRSV], 'irrational' [BNTC], 'thoughtless' [Lns], 'without understanding' [LN]. This adjective describes an unwillingness to use one's mental faculties in order to understand [LN]. The desires are foolish because they cannot be logically explained [EGT]. They are foolish since they produce harm instead of gain [NAC]. They are foolish because wealth has nothing to do with godliness [NIBC].

   b. βλαβερός (LN **20.13**) (BAGD p. 142): 'harmful' [AB, BAGD, Herm, LN, WBC; all versions except KJV], 'hurtful' [Lns, NTC; KJV], 'injurious' [ECC], 'pernicious' [BNTC]. This adjective describes something that causes physical, moral, or spiritual harm [LN]. They are harmful because they hinder true happiness [EGT]. They plunge the greedy into ruin and destruction [NIBC].

   c. ἐπιθυμία (LN **25.20**) (BAGD 3. p. 293): 'desire' [BAGD, BNTC, Herm, LN; all versions except KJV, NCV], 'craving' [AB, NTC], 'passion' [WBC], 'lust' [LN, Lns; KJV]. The clause 'many foolish and harmful desires' is translated 'they want many foolish and harmful things' [NCV], 'they foolishly desire many things that cause them to get hurt' [LSA]. This noun denotes a strong desire to have something that belongs to another person, or to engage in an activity that is morally wrong [LN]. Used in a bad sense, it denotes a desire for something forbidden [BAGD].

QUESTION—What relationship is indicated by καί 'and/even'?

   1. This conjunction adds these desires as the third result of desiring to be rich [AB, Alf, BNTC, ECC, Herm, LSA, My, NTC, NTIC; GW, HCSB, KJV, NASB, NET, NIV, REB]: *and*.

   2. This conjunction specifies the nature of the trap [Lns, NIBC, TH; CEV, GW, NLT, NRSV, TEV]: a trap, *that is, many foolish and harmful desires*. When they fall into temptation, they are enmeshed in a snare which holds them with the cords of these desires [Lns].

QUESTION—What are these desires?

The desires are probably concerned with becoming rich [NIBC, TH]. The desire for riches is generally accompanied by the desire for honor, popularity, power, ease, and pleasing fleshly desires [NTC].

which plunge[a] people into ruin[b] and destruction.[c]

LEXICON—a. pres. act. indic. of βυθίζω (LN **90.95**) (BAGD 2. p. 148): 'to plunge' [AB, BAGD, NTC, WBC; HCSB, NASB, NET, NIV, NLT, NRSV, REB], 'to drown' [GW, KJV], 'to engulf' [ECC], 'to sink' [Herm, Lns], 'to submerge' [BNTC], 'to drag down' [CEV], 'to bring upon' [LN], 'to pull down to' [LN; TEV], 'to cause' [LN, LSA]. The whole clause is translated 'that ruin and destroy people' [NCV]. This verb is a figurative extension of the verb 'to cause to sink' (15.115), and means to cause someone to experience serious consequences [LN]. Figuratively, it refers to moral decline [AB].

b. ὄλεθρος (LN **20.33**) (BAGD p. 563): 'ruin' [AB, BAGD, BNTC, **LN**, NTC, WBC; HCSB, NASB, NET, NIV, NLT, NRSV, REB, TEV], 'destruction' [BAGD, Herm, LN, Lns; GW, KJV], 'death' [BAGD]. This noun is also translated as a verb phrase: 'that ruin…people' [NCV], 'they become ruined' [LSA]. The whole clause is translated 'they drag them down and destroy them' [CEV], 'the kind that engulf people in utterly ruinous destruction' [ECC]. This noun denotes a state of utter ruin or destruction [LN].

c. ἀπώλεια (LN 20.31) (BAGD 2. p. 103): 'destruction' [AB, BAGD, BNTC, LN, NTC, WBC; HCSB, NASB, NET, NIV, NLT, NRSV, REB], 'perdition' [Lns; KJV], 'ruin' [Herm; GW, TEV]. This noun is also translated as a verb phrase: 'that…destroy people' [NCV], 'they are destroyed' [LSA]. This verb means to destroy or to cause the destruction of persons, objects, or institutions [LN].

QUESTION—What does αἵτινες 'which' refer to?

'Which' refers to 'desires' [Alf, ECC, ICC, Lns, LSA, NTC, TH, WP; CEV, GW, NASB, NCV, NIV, NLT, NRSV, TEV]: *many foolish and harmful desires that plunge men into ruin and destruction.* The men drown in those lusts [WP]. If there is a progression (being tempted, then falling into a trap, and then having desires), this relative pronoun refers to the last item 'desires'. But it may refer to all three preceding nouns, in which case it takes its feminine gender from the second and third nouns [NIGTC].

QUESTION—What is meant by ὄλεθρος 'ruin'?

This is practically synonymous with the following word 'destruction', and the repetition may be intended to highlight the complete and total ruin of the one who pursues riches [ECC, ICC, NAC, TC, TH, WBC; CEV]. The combination 'ruin and destruction' means utter ruin [AB]. These terms describe the final judgment, so the two refer to spiritual judgment [ICC]. Or, the word 'ruin' refers to the destruction of what is material, and the following word 'destruction' refers to the destruction of what is spiritual [BNTC].

QUESTION—What is meant by ἀπώλεια 'destruction'?

This is the usual term for the eternal destruction of the wicked [WBC].

6:10 Because (a/the) root of all the evils[a] is the love-of-money,[b]

LEXICON—a. κακός (LN 88.106) (BAGD 1.c. p. 397): 'evil' [BAGD, LN], 'bad' [BAGD, LN]. The phrase ῥίζα πάντων τῶν κακῶν 'root of all the evils' [Lns] is also translated 'a root of all the evils' [NTC], 'a root of all kinds of evils' [WBC; HCSB, NIV, NRSV], 'a root for every kind of wickedness' [AB], 'a root of all sorts of evil' [NASB], 'the root of all kinds of evil' [GW, NLT], 'the root of all evil' [Herm; KJV, NET, REB], 'a source of all kinds of evil' [TEV], 'the source of all kinds of evil' [LN (25.107)], 'the root that lies under all evils' [ECC], 'evils of every kind are rooted in' [BNTC]. The clause 'the root of all evils is the love of money' is translated 'all kinds of evil things happen when people desire to have money' [LSA], 'the love of money causes all kinds of evil' [NCV], 'the love of money causes all kinds of trouble' [CEV]. This substantive denotes something that is bad, and it is implied that it is harmful and damaging [LN].

b. φιλαργυρία (LN 25.107) (BAGD p. 859): 'love of money' [AB, BAGD, BNTC, ECC, Herm, LN, Lns, NTC, WBC; all versions except NIV], 'love of wealth' [LN], 'avarice, miserliness' [BAGD]. This noun is also translated as a verb phrase: 'eager for money' [NIV], 'people desire to have money' [LSA]. This noun denotes the state of loving money or wealth [LN]. This noun is literally 'a love of silver', in which 'silver' is a metonymy for money [LSA, WBC].

QUESTION—What relationship is indicated by γάρ 'because'?

This conjunction indicates the grounds for the description of what happens to people desiring to be rich that is given in 6:9 [ECC, LSA, My, NAC, NIBC, NICNT, NTC, NTL, TH]. It explains why the desire for wealth is so destructive [ICC].

QUESTION—What is meant by the love of money being a ῥίζα 'root'?

The noun ῥίζα 'root' is often used as a symbol for the beginning from which something grows or develops [ICC]. It means the love of money is the *source* of all evils [NIGTC]. This anarthrous noun may mean '*a* root' or '*the* root' [ICC].

1. This speaks of 'a root' of all kinds of evil [AB, BNTC, NAC, NIGTC, NTC, NTIC, TG, TH, WBC, WP; HCSB, NASB, NIV, NRSV, TEV]. The article 'the' could have been included, but since it is absent, '*a* root' is intended [NIGTC]. Love of money is not the only source of evil [BNTC, NAC, TH]. It is a root, one among several roots, and this does not even imply that it is the most significant root, but it was a serious problem in the Ephesian church [WBC]. It does not mean that the love of money causes all sins [NAC]. This refers to all the evils that arise from the love of money [My].

2. This speaks of 'the root' of all *kinds* of evils [Alf; GW, NLT]. It does not mean the only root, but it is the root from which all kinds of evil may and do arise [Alf].

3. This speaks of 'the root' of all evils [ECC, EGT, ICC, Lns, NIBC, TNTC; KJV, NET, REB]. This meaning is supported by the forcefulness of the saying [EGT, ICC], but probably this is a hyperbolical statement since it does not necessarily mean that the love for money is literally the source of every evil there is [ICC]. It is a hyperbole since some evils are not related to love for money [NET]. This is a proverb and proverbs often overstate a point for effect [NIBC]. This is a proverbial expression, but there may be other sources of evil as well [ECC].

QUESTION—What is meant by the noun 'evils'?

It refers to things that are morally wrong [ICC, My, NICNT, TC], and can also include things that are injurious to self or to others [ICC, My]. It refers to troubles [CEV]. Examples are fraud, divorces, perjuries, robberies, poisonings, murders, and wars [NTC].

of-which some craving[a] **(money) wandered-away**[b] **from the faith**

LEXICON—a. pres. mid. participle of ὀρέγομαι, ὀρέγω (LN 25.15) (BAGD p. 579): 'to crave' [ECC; HCSB, NLT], 'to strive for, to desire' [BAGD], 'to long for' [LN, LSA; NASB], 'to be eager for' [NIV], 'to be eager to have it' [TEV], 'to set ones' heart on (getting rich)' [GW], 'to reach for' [WBC; NET], 'to reach out after' [NTC], 'to aspire to' [Lns], 'to pursue' [AB; REB], 'to make as an objective' [BNTC], 'to strive to attain' [LN], 'to be inflamed by desire' [Herm], 'to covet after' [KJV], 'to want to get' [NCV], 'to want so much' [CEV], '(in their) eagerness (to be rich)' [NRSV]. Some translations specify the object of their craving: 'it' [HCSB, NASB, NET], 'money' [LSA; CEV, NCV, NIV, NLT], 'getting rich' [GW]. This verb means to eagerly desire to accomplish some goal or purpose [LN].

    b. aorist pass. indic. of ἀποπλανάομαι, ἀποπλανάω (LN **31.11**) (BAGD p. 97): 'to wander away' [BAGD], 'to wander from the truth, to stray from the truth, to go astray from' [LN]. The phrase in its passive form ἀπεπλανήθησαν ἀπὸ τῆς πίστεως 'were led away from the faith' [WBC] is also translated 'have been led astray from the faith' [AB, BNTC], 'were made to wander away from the faith' [Lns]. This passive verb is also translated actively: 'they have wandered from the faith' [**LN**, NTC; NASB, NIV, REB; similarly HCSB, NLT], 'have wandered away from the faith' [NRSV, TEV; similarly GW], 'they have gone astray from the faith' [BAGD, Herm], 'have strayed from the faith' [NET], 'have strayed off from the faith' [ECC], 'have left the faith' [NCV], 'they have given up their faith' [CEV], 'they have erred from the faith' [KJV], 'they stopped believing the doctrine which all of us believe' [LSA]. This verb means to no longer believe what is true, but to have started to believe what is false [LN].

QUESTION—What relationship is indicated by the use of the pronominal adjective ἧς 'of which'?

This introduces a specific instance of the kind of evils that is meant [LSA, WBC].

    1. 'Which' refers to the love of money [Lns, WBC]. It refers back to the noun 'love of money' [WBC].

    2. 'Which' refers to money [Alf, EGT, Herm, ICC, LSA, My, NICNT, NTC, TH; CEV, GW, NCV, NIV, NLT]. Although grammatically it refers to the event noun 'love of money', it logically refers to the object of that love, 'money' [EGT, NICNT, NTC]. The love of money is itself a desire, and men cannot properly be said to crave a desire [Alf, Herm].

3. 'Which' refers to money-making [BNTC].

QUESTION—What is meant by the phrase ἀπεπλανήθησαν ἀπὸ τῆς πίστεως 'were led away from the faith'?

1. The passive indicates that something caused this [AB, BNTC, Lns, NTIC, TNTC, WBC]: *they were led away*. They were led away by their vice [AB], by their aspirations [Lns]. The passive form does not mean they were led away by another person since it says that they pierced themselves and knew what they were doing [WBC].

2. The passive is translated with an active meaning so that they are the actors [ECC, Herm, NIGTC, NTC, TH; GW, HCSB, KJV, NASB, NCV, NET, NIV, NLT, NRSV, REB, TEV]: *they wandered away*. They have wandered away in their inner attitude and their outer conduct [NTC].

QUESTION—What is meant by τῆς πίστεως 'the faith'?

'The faith' refers to the doctrine that is to be believed by Christians [ICC, WBC; GW]. It is the truth as confessed by the church [NTC]. It is the objective content of the Christian faith, which is a necessary part of becoming and living as a Christian, and here it speaks of people straying from their trust in God and Christ as the central desire and love of their life [NIGTC]. It is described in 6:3 as 'the sound words, namely the words of our Lord, Jesus Christ' [NTL].

QUESTION—What relationship is indicated by the use of the participle ὀρεγόμενοι 'craving'?

1. This participle indicates the reason why they wandered away from the faith [NICNT; NCV, TEV]: *because some craved money*, they wandered away from the faith.

2. This participle indicates the means by which they pierce themselves [WBC; HCSB, NASB]: *by craving money*, they wandered away from the faith.

and they-pierced[a] themselves (with) many pains.[b]

LEXICON—a. aorist act. indic. of περιπείρω (LN 90.73) (BAGD p. 649): 'to pierce through, to impale' [BAGD], 'to undergo, to experience' [LN]. The phrase ἑαυτοὺς περιέπειραν 'they pierced themselves with' [Herm, Lns, NTC, WBC; HCSB, KJV, NASB, NIV, NLT, NRSV] is also translated 'have skewered themselves' [ECC], 'have got themselves spiked with' [BNTC], 'they have pierced themselves to the heart with' [BAGD], 'have stabbed themselves with' [NET], 'spiked themselves on (many a painful thorn)' [REB], 'have tortured themselves with' [AB], 'have broken their hearts with' [TEV], 'they have caused themselves' [CEV, GW, NCV], 'they have caused themselves to experience (severe grief)' [LN; similarly LSA]. The verb means to experience something that is adverse and severe [LN].

b. ὀδύνη (LN 25.235) (BAGD p. 555): 'pain' [BAGD, Lns, WBC; CEV, HCSB, NET, NRSV], 'woe' [BAGD], 'grief' [GW, NASB, NIV], 'pangs' [BNTC, NTC], 'sorrow' [KJV, NCV, NLT, TEV], 'pain' [Herm; HCSB,

NET], 'agony' [AB], 'torture' [ECC], 'distress, anxiety' [LN], 'a painful (thorn)' [REB]. This noun is a figurative extension of ὀδύνη 'physical pain' and means a state of severe emotional anxiety and distress [LN]. Here it refers to the remorse of one's conscience [BAGD].

QUESTION—What is meant by the metaphor, 'they pierced themselves with many pains'?

The picture is of a man piercing himself with a spear [TC]. The figure of piercing oneself so as to suffer from the pains of this stabbing figuratively refers to the terrible mental distress and grief of the soul [NIGTC]. It means to experience what is severe and painful [TH]. The pains are concerned with the unfulfilled desires for wealth [ICC]. It can refer to the pangs of guilt, conscience, remorse, and actual pains caused by these sins [WBC], remorse and disillusionment [BNTC], unrest, boredom, dissatisfaction, gloom, and envy [TC]. It refers to the stings of conscience [My]. These are probably the griefs brought on by the sins themselves, whether or not one has any pangs of conscience about it [NIGTC].

DISCOURSE UNIT—6:11–21 The topic is the closing commission [AB], Paul's charge to Timothy [NIV], Paul's final instructions [NLT], personal instructions [TEV], instructions to Timothy and the wealthy [NAC], some things to remember [NCV], fighting a good fight for the faith [CEV].

DISCOURSE UNIT—6:11–19 [NRSV]. The topic is the good fight of faith.

DISCOURSE UNIT—6:11–16 The topic is encouragement to Timothy [WBC], a final exhortation to Timothy [NIBC, NIGTC, NTL], a charge to a man of God [TNTC], a charge to one newly ordained [NCBC], an ordination charge [ECC], proper conduct as a minister of Christ [TH], instructions on true teaching [ICC], a program for godliness [NAC], compete for the faith [HCSB], the battle of faith [Herm].

DISCOURSE UNIT—6:11–12 The theme is the charge to conduct yourself in a godly manner and make sure you obtain eternal life [LSA].

6:11 But you, O[a] man of-God, flee-from[b] these (things).

LEXICON—a. ὦ (LN 91.14): 'O' [LN]. This particle marks direct address and is functionally equivalent to the traditional vocative [LN]. The phrase σὺ ὦ ἄνθρωπε θεοῦ 'you, O man of God' [AB, ECC, Lns, NTC, WBC; KJV] is also translated 'you, man of God' [BNTC, Herm; GW, HCSB, NASB, NCV, NIV, REB, TEV], 'as for you, man of God' [NRSV], 'you, as a person dedicated to God' [NET], 'you who are a man who serves God' [LSA], 'you, Timothy, are a man of God (so...)' [NLT], 'you belong to God' [CEV].

b. pres. act. impera. of φεύγω (LN 13.161) (BAGD 3. p. 856): 'to flee from' [BAGD, Herm], 'to flee away from' [NTC], 'to flee' [AB, Lns, WBC; KJV, NASB, NIV], 'to escape' [LN], 'to run away' [NCV, NLT], 'to run from' [HCSB], 'to avoid' [BAGD, LN; GW, TEV], 'to keep away from'

[CEV, NET], 'to shun' [BNTC, ECC; NRSV, REB], 'to not do' [LSA]. This verb means to become safe from danger by avoiding or escaping it [LN]. The present tense indicates that Timothy is to constantly flee from those things and not be involved in them [Lns, TH].

QUESTION—What relationship is indicated by δέ 'but'?

1. It indicates a contrast [AB, Alf, BKC, BNTC, Herm, ICC, Lns, My, NAC, NIBC, NIGTC, WBC; all versions except CEV, HCSB]: *but you*. This conjunction indicates a contrast with the preceding section [WBC]. Paul turns from Timothy's opponents to Timothy himself [ICC]. The phrase 'you, O man of God' is emphatic and contrasts with 'some' (false teachers) in 6:10 [Alf, BKC, BNTC, LSA, My], and also 'anyone' (a greedy person) in 6:3 [BNTC, LSA, NAC]. Timothy is contrasted with the ones who wander from the faith [NIGTC]. It marks a contrast from the preceding vices that have been condemned to the virtues Timothy is to develop [Lns, NTC].

2. It indicates a new topic [HCSB; probably CEV which uses no conjunction]: *now*.

QUESTION—How are the nouns related in the genitive construction ἄνθρωπε θεοῦ 'man of God'?

The relationship probably focuses on serving God [Alf, LSA, NAC, TG], although representing God might also be included in the meaning [LSA]. It refers to Timothy's function as God's representative and also to Timothy's dedication to God's service [ICC]. He is a man who belongs to God [Lns, NTC, NTL, TH; CEV], and represents God [TH]. This refers to a man who is entrusted by God to deliver his message [TC]. This is an apt description of a pastor as a man who is in God's service, representing God and speaking in his name [BNTC].

QUESTION—What is the function of addressing Timothy as a man of God?

The following virtues are those that befit a man of God [BNTC, NTC; NET].

QUESTION—What things is he to flee from?

It refers to 'evil things' [CEV]. 'These things' at least refer to the previous section about a desire to be rich and the evils that accompany such a desire [BNTC, EGT, My, NIGTC, TC, TH, WBC]. This is shown in 6:17 where he continues the subject of riches [My]. It probably also refers to everything wrong with his opponents mentioned in 6:2–10 [WBC]. 'These things' are those described in 6:3–5 and 9–10 [LSA]. Besides the love of money, it refers to the false and disastrous courses that the false teachers encouraged [BNTC]. He is to flee from things such as wickedness, craving for money, error, envy, wrangling, and reviling [NTC].

But/and pursue[a] righteousness,[b] godliness,[c] faith, [d]

LEXICON—a. pres. act. impera. of διώκω (LN 68.66) (BAGD 4.b p. 201): 'to pursue' [AB, BAGD, ECC, Herm, Lns, WBC; GW, HCSB, NASB, NET, NIV, NLT, NRSV, REB], 'to run after' [NTC], 'to strive for/toward' [BAGD, LN; TEV], 'to seek after, to aspire to' [BAGD], 'to aim at'

[BNTC], 'to follow after' [KJV], 'to try one's best' [CEV], 'to determine to do' [LSA], 'to live (in the right way)' [NCV], 'to do with effort, to strive toward' [LN]. This is a figurative extension of the verb 'to pursue' and means to do something with intense effort along with a definite purpose or goal [LN].

b. δικαιοσύνη (LN 88.13) (BAGD 2.b. p. 196): 'righteousness' [AB, BAGD, LN, Lns, NTC, WBC; HCSB, KJV, NASB, NET, NIV, NLT, NRSV, TEV], 'uprightness' [BAGD, Herm], 'upright conduct' [ECC], 'integrity' [BNTC], 'justice' [REB], 'what God approves of' [GW]. This noun is also translated as a verb phrase: 'live in the right way' [NCV], 'doing what God requires' [LN], 'doing what is right' [LN, LSA], 'to please God' [CEV]. This noun denotes the act of doing what God requires [LN].

c. εὐσέβεια (LN 53.5) (BAGD p. 326): 'godliness' [AB, BAGD, ECC, LN, Lns, NTC, WBC; HCSB, KJV, NASB, NET, NIV, NRSV, TEV], 'piety' [BAGD, BNTC, Herm, LN; REB], 'a godly life' [GW, NLT]. The noun is also translated as a verb phrase: 'to serve God' [NCV], 'to be godly' [LSA], 'to be like God' [CEV]. This noun denotes behavior that reflects correct religious beliefs and attitudes [LN]. See this noun at 2:2; 4:7; 6: 3, 5.

d. πίστις (LN 31.85) (BAGD 2.d.γ. p. 663): 'faith' [AB, BAGD, BNTC, Herm, LN, Lns, My, NTC, WBC; GW, HCSB, KJV, NASB, NIV, NLT, NRSV, TEV], 'trust' [LN], 'faithfulness' [ECC; NET], 'integrity' [REB]. The noun is also translated as a verb phrase: 'have faith' [NCV], 'trust God' [LSA], 'be faithful' [CEV]. This noun denotes the act of believing to the extent of complete trust and reliance [LN]. See this word at 1:2, 4, 5, 14, 19; 3:13; 4:12.

QUESTION—What relationship is indicated by δέ 'but'?

1. It indicates a contrast [AB, Alf, BNTC, ECC, ICC, Lns, NAC, NIBC, NIGTC, TH, TNTC, WBC; HCSB, NCV, NET, NIV]: *but, instead*. This turns from the preceding negative command to this equally necessary positive command [ICC, NIGTC, TH]. It indicates a contrast between the activities of fleeing from the evil things and of pursuing the good virtues listed here [Alf, Lns, TNTC, WBC].

2. It is a continuative [NTC; KJV, NASB, NIV, REB]: *and*.

QUESTION—What is meant by δικαιοσύνη 'righteousness'?

It means upright conduct [ECC, Herm, NAC, NIBC]. This has the ethical sense of living in accordance with the demands laid on a person who has been justified [WBC]. It describes conduct that is in accord with God's will and is pleasing to him [NIGTC]. It is the conduct that God expects and requires of Christians [TH]. It is a state of living in harmony with God's law [EGT, NTC]. It is conforming to what is right, both in relation to God and to people [TNTC].

QUESTION—What is meant by εὐσέβεια 'godliness'?

This describes a life fully consecrated to God [WBC]. It is pious conduct [EGT, Lns, NTC], accompanied with reverence toward God [Lns]. It is the Christian way of life that is acceptable to God [TH]. It is a devout and correct religious attitude [BNTC].

QUESTION—What is meant by πίστις 'faith'?

1. Faith is used here in the sense of 'trust' in God [Alf, BNTC, NAC, NIBC, NIGTC, NTC, WBC; probably AB, Herm, Lns, My; GW, HCSB, KJV, NASB, NIV, NLT, NRSV, TEV which translate this as 'faith']. Faith is reliance on God and his promises [Lns, NTC].
2. It is the attribute of faithfulness [ECC; CEV, NET].

love,[a] endurance,[b] gentleness.[c]

LEXICON—a. ἀγάπη (LN 25.43) (BAGD I.1.a. p. 5): 'love' [AB, BAGD, Herm, LN, Lns, NTC, WBC; all versions except CEV, NCV], 'charity' [ECC]. The noun is also translated as a verb phrase: 'to have love' [NCV], 'to be loving' [CEV], 'to love people' [LSA]. This noun denotes love for someone based on sincere appreciation and high regard [LN]. See this word at 1:5, 14; 2:15; 4:12.

   b. ὑπομονή (LN 25.174) (BAGD 1. p. 846): 'endurance' [AB, BAGD, LN, NTC, WBC; GW, HCSB, NET, NIV, NRSV, TEV], 'patience' [BAGD, Herm, Lns; KJV], 'perseverance' [BAGD; NASB, NLT], 'fortitude' [BAGD; REB], 'steadfastness' [BAGD, BNTC, ECC]. The noun is also translated as a verb phrase: 'to have patience' [NCV], 'to endure difficult circumstances' [LSA], 'to be dependable' [CEV]. This noun denotes the capacity to continue to bear up under difficult circumstances [LN].

   c. πραϋπαθία, πραϋπάθεια (LN 88.59) (BAGD p. 698): 'gentleness' [BAGD, BNTC, ECC, Herm, LN, NTC, WBC; GW, HCSB, NASB, NET, NIV, NLT, NRSV, REB, TEV], 'meekness' [LN, Lns; KJV], 'mildness' [LN], 'a generous temper' [AB]. The noun is also translated as a verb phrase: 'to have gentleness' [NCV], 'to be gentle' [LSA; CEV]. This noun denotes gentleness of attitude and behavior and contrasts with harshness in dealing with others [LN].

QUESTION—What is meant by ἀγάπη 'love'?

Love concerns benevolence and goodwill toward others [NAC]. Here the object of love is probably people [LSA, NIGTC, TH]. It is love for God, believers, and everyone [Lns, NTC].

QUESTION—What is meant by ὑπομονή 'endurance'?

This noun probably has the comprehensive sense of patience, endurance, fortitude, steadfastness, perseverance, and expectation as listed in BAGD [NIGTC]. This quality endures evil and suffering [WBC]. It is the ability to persevere in the faith and not give up, and it is accompanied by a life full of hope [NTC, TH]. It endures with patience under privations and suffering without complaining [Lns].

QUESTION—What is meant by πραϋπαθία 'gentleness'?

It means being gentle with other people [TH], having patience with them [NTC]. This word has the sense of being considerate of others, and being willing to forego one's rights, the opposite of jealousy and selfish ambition [WBC]. This quality is needed as Timothy deals with cantankerous heretics and wavering Christians [NAC], and his opponents [ICC, NAC].

6:12 Struggle[a] the good struggle of-the faith,

LEXICON—a. pres. mid./pass. impera. of ἀγωνίζομαι (LN 39.29) (BAGD 2.b. p. 15): 'to struggle, to fight' [BAGD, LN]. The clause ἀγωνίζου τὸν καλὸν ἀγῶνα τῆς πίστεως 'struggle the good struggle of the faith' is translated 'fight the good fight of the faith' [WBC; NIV, NRSV], 'fight the noble fight of the faith' [NTC], 'fight a good fight for the faith' [CEV], 'fight the good fight for the faith' [HCSB], 'fight the good fight for the true faith' [NLT], 'fight the good fight for the Christian faith' [GW], 'compete well for the faith' [NET], 'be a contestant in the noble contest for the faith' [Lns], 'engage the noble athletic contest for the faith' [AB]. Instead of 'the faith' some have 'faith': 'fight the good fight of faith' [Herm; KJV, NASB, NCV], 'run the great race of faith' [REB], 'run your best in the race of faith' [TEV], 'contend in the fine contest, the contest in the arena of faith' [ECC], 'play your part in the noble contest of faith' [BNTC], 'earnestly engage in what is like a good contest, that is, live in accordance with what you believe' [LSA]. This verb means to engage in an intense struggle that involves physical or nonphysical force against strong opposition [LN]. It means to fight or struggle and can be used figuratively of any type of struggle or striving [BAGD]. The present imperative indicates that this is a continuing struggle [BNTC, EGT, Lns, NAC, NIBC, NIGTC, NTC, TC]. See this word at 4:10.

QUESTION—What is meant by 'struggle the good struggle'?

Whether it is an athletic or a military metaphor, the focus is on the struggle involved [LSA, NIGTC, TNTC], a desperate struggle to win [ICC].

1. This is an athletic metaphor [AB, BKC, BNTC, ECC, EGT, ICC, Lns, LSA, NAC, NCBC, NIBC, NTC, TC, TG, TNTC, WBC; CEV, GW, HCSB, KJV, NASB, NCV, NET, REB, TEV; probably NIGTC, TH]: *compete strenuously in the good athletic competition.* This command is a summary statement of the personal instructions to Timothy in the previous verse, so this metaphor concerns Timothy's personal life on earth, which has as its goal the eternal life of the age to come [LSA]. The following allusion to the prize or goal of eternal life indicates that this is an athletic metaphor [ICC]. It refers to striving for a prize in an athletic event [Lns]. The athletic contest is a foot race [TG; REB, TEV]. The competition could be a race, a boxing match, or a wrestling match [NAC; NET]. Since Paul does not make it clear that this is a race as he does in other racing metaphors, this probably compares the Christian life to any athletic contest except a race [NTC].

2. This is a military metaphor similar to the command στρατεύῃ...τὴν καλὴν στρατείαν 'war the good warfare' in 1:18 [Alf]: *fight the good fight*. This speaks of the Christian as being a soldier of Christ [Alf]. If so, this is a further instruction to Timothy to do his best to oppose and overcome the arguments of those opponents of the Christian faith LSA].

QUESTION—Why is the struggle called good?

It is good because it is done for God and for the gospel which was making its way into the world [NIGTC]. It is good in that it is of supreme worth and is required by God [ICC]. It is good in contrast with the evil pursuit of wealth [TH]. It is a contest that is noble [AB, BNTC, EGT, Lns, NTC], fine [ECC], and great [REB]. Literally 'compete in the good competition for the faith', it can be translated 'compete well for the faith' [NET].

QUESTION—What is meant by the genitive construction ἀγῶνα τῆς πίστεως 'struggle of the faith'?

1. This refers to Timothy's own faith [BNTC, ICC, LSA, NIBC, NIGTC, NTC, TC, WBC].
   1.1 The struggle is engaged in because of Timothy's faith, or through his faith [NIGTC, NTC]: *struggle the good struggle because of your faith*. The good struggle springs from and is inspired by Timothy's faith [NTC].
   1.2 The struggle is to maintain Timothy's own faith [BNTC, ECC, ICC, NIBC, TC, WBC]. This refers to daily perseverance in the struggle against the world and the flesh [WBC]. It is the warfare with evil that is experienced by every Christian [BNTC, TC]. Faith must be preserved to the end since it is the characteristic quality of the Christian life [ICC] His whole Christian life is a contest that requires discipline and purpose [NIBC]. It is a call to faithfulness [WBC].
2. This refers to the contents of the Christian faith [Alf, BKC, EGT, Lns, LSA, TG; GW, NLT; probably CEV, HCSB, NET, NIV, NRSV which translate this as 'the faith']. The struggle is identified as the race of the faith, the Christian religion [TG]. It does not mean to fight to maintain his own faith in his heart, but to defend the substance of the Christian faith, the gospel that is attacked by his opponents [Lns]. The struggle is to further the faith [BKC]. The struggle is that which one's profession of the faith entails [EGT]. He is to live in accordance with the Christian faith [LSA].
3. There are both subjective and objective elements of this faith [ECC, NAC]. Faith is the arena in which he struggles to remain true to the revelation God gave him [ECC].

take-hold[a] of-the eternal life to which you-were-called[b]

LEXICON—a. aorist mid. (deponent = act.) impera. of ἐπιλαμβάνομαι (LN **90.63**) (BAGD 2.b. p. 295): 'to take hold' [BAGD] 'to experience, to undergo' [LN]. The phrase ἐπιλαβοῦ τῆς αἰωνίου ζωῆς 'take hold of the eternal life' [AB; NASB, NIV, NRSV] is also translated 'take hold of eternal life' [Herm; HCSB, REB], 'take hold of everlasting life' [NTC; GW], 'lay hold on eternal life' [ECC], 'lay hold of the eternal life' [Lns], 'lay hold of that eternal life (you were called for)' [NET], 'seize hold of the eternal life' [WBC], 'hold tightly to the eternal life' [NLT], 'lay hold on eternal life' [KJV], 'grabbing hold of the life that continues forever' [NCV], 'make sure that you obtain eternal life' [LSA], 'claim eternal life' [CEV], 'and win eternal life for yourself' [TEV], 'possess yourself of eternal life' [BNTC], 'experience eternal life' [**LN**]. This verb means to experience some event or state [LN]. 'To take hold of' is used figuratively of taking hold of something in order to make it one's own [BAGD, NIGTC]. The aorist tense points to a single act [BNTC, ECC, EGT, TC, TNTC].

b. aorist pass. indic. of καλέω (LN 33.312) (BAGD 2. p. 399): 'to be called' [BAGD, LN]. The phrase εἰς ἣν ἐκλήθης 'to which you were called' [BNTC, NTC, WBC; GW, HCSB, NASB, NIV] is also translated 'into which thou wast called' [Lns], 'whereunto thou art also called' [KJV], 'to which you were called' [NRSV], 'to which God has called you' [NLT], 'to this you have been called' [Herm], '(that eternal life) you were called for' [NET], 'you were called to it' [AB], 'you were called into that life' [ECC], 'you were called to have that life' [NCV], 'for to this you were called' [REB], 'for it was to this life that God called you' [TEV], 'because you were called by God to obtain this life' [LSA], 'God offered it to you' [CEV]. This verb means to be urgently invited by someone to accept responsibilities for a particular task [LN]. When the verb is passive and the one who calls is unnamed, it is to be understood that God is the one who is calling [LSA, NIGTC; CEV, NLT, TEV].

QUESTION—How does this command relate to the preceding one?

1. This command extends the metaphor to focus on the prize awaiting the outcome of the contest [BNTC, NAC, NIBC, NIGTC, TC, TG, TH]. This pictures the victor receiving the champion's trophy of eternal life [TH]. Eternal life is the prize held out for perseverance in struggling for the faith [WBC]. The future eternal life is the final outcome of the ongoing struggle, so the command is to struggle the struggle of persevering in faith and at the end of the struggle lay hold of eternal life [NIGTC]. It is eternal life in heaven [TG]. Or, eternal life can be enjoyed in some measure in the present life [BNTC, NIBC]. Since Timothy was called to eternal life, perhaps it means that this life was in his grasp, but not completely held [NAC].

2. This is a second command and it is not part of the preceding metaphor [Alf, ECC, ICC, Lns, NTC, WBC]. This says to 'take hold' of eternal life, not to 'reach after it', so this refers to the blessings of eternal life both now and forever [ICC]. The image has been dropped and now the realities of the Christian life are in view [Alf]. This is to be Timothy's response to God's call [WBC]. The aorist tense shows that this is a decisive act of laying hold on eternal life in this world [ECC]. The aorist tense shows that

this speaks of the fact that by putting up a successful fight, Timothy is already getting a firm grip on eternal life to which he was called at his conversion [NTC]. Or, this does not continue the athletic metaphor since the victor in a Greek contest did not lay hold of the prize, but a wreath was placed on his head. Rather this clause interprets the preceding metaphor by taking us to the last supreme moment of the contest that lasts all life long when we may grasp eternal life in heaven [Lns].

QUESTION—What is the function and meaning of the phrase εἰς ἣν ἐκλήθης 'to which you were called'?

It is a reason why Timothy should take hold of eternal life [BNTC, WBC]. God called us by the gospel [Lns]. Eternal life is the goal to which God called Timothy at the time of his conversion [ICC, Lns]. This refers to God's inner and effective call to eternal life [NIGTC]. God promised Timothy this eternal life when he called him [TG].

and confessed[a] the good confession before many witnesses.[b]

LEXICON—a. aorist act. indic. of ὁμολογέω (LN 33.274) (BAGD 4. p. 568): 'to confess' [BAGD, LN], 'to profess' [LN], 'to declare publicly, to acknowledge' [BAGD]. The phrase καὶ ὡμολόγησας τὴν καλὴν ὁμολογίαν 'and confessed the good confession' [WBC] is also translated 'and didst confess the noble confession' [Lns], 'and hast professed a good profession' [KJV], 'and made the noble confession' [BNTC], 'and you have made the good confession' [NASB], 'and about which you made a good testimony' [GW], 'and for which you made the good confession' [NRSV], 'and made your good confession for' [NET], 'and for it you made that fine profession' [ECC], 'and you pronounced the noble profession' [AB], 'and have made a good confession' [HCSB], 'and because you professed...that you believe what is good to profess' [LSA], 'when you made your good confession' [NIV], 'when you confessed the good confession' [NCV], 'when you confessed your faith nobly' [REB], 'when you confessed the beautiful confession' [NTC], 'when you clearly told about your faith' [CEV], 'when you firmly professed your faith' [TEV], 'which you have confessed so well' [NLT], 'this you professed in the good confession of faith' [Herm]. This verb means to openly express one's allegiance to a proposition or person [LN].

b. μάρτυς (LN 33.270) (BAGD 2.b. p. 494): 'witness' [BAGD, LN], 'one who testifies' [LN]. The phrase ἐνώπιον πολλῶν μαρτύρων 'before many witnesses' [AB, Herm, WBC; HCSB, KJV, NCV, NLT, REB, TEV] is also translated 'in the presence of many witnesses' [BNTC, Lns, NTC; NASB, NET, NIV, NRSV], 'in the presence of many people' [LSA], 'in front of many witnesses' [GW], 'before the eyes of many witnesses' [ECC], 'while so many people listened' [CEV]. This noun denotes a person who witnesses [LN].

QUESTION—What is the function of this clause?

This is another reason why Timothy should take hold of eternal life [BNTC, LSA, WBC].

QUESTION—When did Timothy confess the good confession before many witnesses?

The article in '*the* good confession' indicates that Timothy's confession was well known [WBC]. It was when he publicly acknowledged Jesus as the resurrected Lord [NET].

1. This refers to Timothy's baptism when he confessed his faith in Jesus Christ [Alf, BKC, BNTC, EGT, ICC, Lns, LSA, NAC, NCBC, NIBC, NTC, TC, TG, TH, TNTC, WBC, WP]. The call to eternal life occurred at the same time of his conversion [WBC]. At his baptism he professed his faith publicly [BNTC, NTC]. The confession was to his belief in Jesus Christ [TH, WBC]. He confessed Jesus Christ as Lord [ICC, TG]. The many witnesses would be those present at his baptism [TH]. The witnesses were members of the congregation [BNTC, Lns], and perhaps even the chosen angels of 5:21 [Lns].

2. This refers to Timothy's ordination as a minister of the gospel (1:18; 4:14) [AB, NIGTC]. This occasion was probably intended because Timothy is being addressed as a leader here and the many witnesses would be the elders who laid their hands on him at the ordination service [NIGTC].

QUESTION—What is a good confession?

The confession is good in that it was a Christian confession approved by God [ICC]. The confession was ordained, accepted, and confirmed by God [NIGTC]. It was a confession that was noble [Lns], and beautiful [NTC]. It does not mean that it was good in regard to the way it was said, but refers to a definite confession of Christ [My].

DISCOURSE UNIT—6:13–16 [LSA]. The theme is obey what you have been commanded to do.

6:13 **I-command**[a] **you in-the-presence-of**[b] **God the (one) giving-life-to/preserving-alive**[c] **all (things)**

TEXT—Some manuscripts omit σοι 'you'. GNT includes σοι 'you' with a C decision, indicating that the committee had difficulty making the decision.

LEXICON—a. pres. act. indic. of παραγγέλλω (LN 33.327) (BAGD p. 613): 'to command' [AB, BAGD, Herm, LN, LSA; TEV], 'to give a command' [NCV], 'to order' [BAGD, LN, Lns], 'to charge' [BNTC, ECC, NTC; HCSB, NASB, NET, NIV, NLT, NRSV, REB], 'to give charge to' [KJV], 'to direct' [BAGD], 'to instruct' [BAGD], 'to insist that' [GW], 'to urge' [WBC], 'to ask to make a promise' [CEV]. This verb means to announce what must be done [LN (33.327)]. See this word at 1:3; 4:11; 5:7; 6:17.

b. ἐνώπιον (LN 83.33) (BAGD 2.b. p. 270): 'in the presence of' [BAGD, BNTC, Herm, LSA, NTC; CEV, HCSB, NASB, NRSV, REB], 'in front of' [LN], 'before' [AB, LN, WBC; NET, NLT, TEV], 'in the sight of' [BAGD, Lns; GW, KJV, NCV, NIV], 'before the eyes of' [ECC]. This preposition refers to a position in front of someone [LN]. See this word at 5:21.

c. pres. act. participle of ζῳογονέω (LN **23.92**, 23.89) (BAGD 1. p. 341): 'to give life to, to make live' [BAGD, **LN** (23.92)], 'to keep alive, to preserve alive' [LN (23.89)]. The phrase τοῦ ζῳογονοῦντος τὰ πάντα 'the one giving life to all things' is translated 'who gives life to all things' [AB, BNTC, **LN**, LSA, WBC; NASB, NET, NRSV, REB, TEV], 'who gives life to everything' [Herm; GW, NCV, NIV], 'who gives life to all' [CEV, HCSB, NLT], 'who quickeneth all things' [KJV], 'who endues all things with life' [NTC], 'the one generating life in everything' [Lns], 'who keeps all things alive' [ECC]. This verb means to cause something to live [LN (23.92)], or to cause something to continue to live [LN (23.89)].

QUESTION—How is this verse connected with the previous one?

To emphasize the importance of this new command, the words of the preceding command 'take hold of the eternal life to which you were called and confessed the good confession before many witnesses' are used in relation to God and Jesus Christ who are called upon to witness this serious command now given to Timothy [ICC].

QUESTION—What is meant by the participle ζῳογονοῦντος 'giving life to/preserving life'?

1. This means that God is the one who gives life to all things [AB, Alf, BNTC, Herm, ICC, LN (23.93), Lns, LSA, My, NCBC, NIGTC, NTC, NTIC, TG, TH, WBC, WP; all versions]. 'All things' refers to all humans and everything else that possess life [NIGTC]. The present tense of the participle, suggests God's omnipotence in continuously giving life to all things in the universe [ICC]. Or, this probably reflects a baptismal liturgy and refers to the new life given to a believer at conversion and symbolized in baptism [BNTC, WBC].

2. This means that God preserves the life of all things [ECC, EGT, NIBC, TC]. In the context of a call to steadfastness, 'to preserve and maintain life' seems more likely here [NIBC]. This assures Timothy that he is in the care of God, whose protective power is universal [EGT].

3. This means that God both gives life and maintains it [NAC]. God has given Timothy life through the gospel, and he has given him stamina for service and protection in the face of danger [NAC].

and (in-the-presence-of) Christ Jesus the (one) having-testified[a] before/in-the-time-of[b] Pontius Pilate the good confession,[c]

LEXICON—a. aorist act. participle of μαρτυρέω (LN 33.263) (BAGD 1.d. p. 493): 'to testify, to bear witness' [BAGD], 'to witness' [LN]. The phrase τοῦ μαρτυρήσαντος...τὴν καλὴν ὁμολογίαν 'the one having testified the good confession' is translated 'who testified the good confession' [NASB], 'who testified to the good confession' [Herm], 'who testified to the noble profession' [AB], 'who witnessed the good confession' [WBC], 'the one who witnessed the noble confession' [Lns], 'who bore witness to the same noble confession' [BNTC], 'who professed what was good to profess' [LSA], 'who in his testimony made the good confession' [NRSV]. 'who while testifying made the beautiful confession' [NTC], 'who witnessed a good confession' [KJV], 'who himself made that noble confession in his testimony' [REB], 'who publicly attested to the fine profession' [ECC], '(who) made the good confession' [NCV], 'who made the/his good confession' [NET, NIV], 'who gave a good testimony' [GW, HCSB, NLT], 'who firmly professed his faith' [TEV], 'who told about his faith' [CEV]. This verb means to provide information about a person or an event concerning which the speaker has direct knowledge [LN].

b. ἐπί (LN 83.35, 67.33) (BAGD I.1.a.δ. p. 286): 'before' [AB, BAGD, ECC, Herm, LN (83.35), Lns, NTC; all versions except CEV, GW], 'in front of' [GW], 'in the presence of' [LSA], 'openly (told)' [CEV], 'when, at the time of' [LN (67.33)], 'in the time of' [WBC], 'in (Pontius Pilate's) time' [BNTC]. This preposition refers to a position before someone with authority [LN (83.35)], or it refers to a point of time which is simultaneous to or overlaps with another point of time [LN (67.33)].

c. ὁμολογία (LN 33.274) (BAGD 2. p. 568): 'confession' [BAGD, LN]. See translations of this word in lexical item a. This noun denotes the open expression of one's allegiance to a proposition or person [LN].

QUESTION—Does the preposition ἐπί mean 'in the presence of' Pontius Pilate or 'in the time of' Pontius Pilate?

1. It means that Jesus testified in the presence of Pontius Pilate [AB, Alf, ECC, Herm, ICC, Lns, LSA, My, NAC, NIGTC, NTC, NTL, TG, TH, WP; all versions]: *the one having testified in the presence of Pontius Pilate.* Here the context suggests an appearance at a court [ICC].

2. It means that Jesus testified during the time of Pontius Pilate's rule [BNTC, NIBC, WBC]. This confession probably refers to what Jesus did and said during his ministry and at his death, not just when he appeared before Pilate [NIBC, WBC].

QUESTION—What was the good confession before Pontius Pilate?

The article 'the' in the phrase 'the good confession' indicates it was a well-known confession [WBC].

1. The confession refers to what Jesus said [AB, Alf, BNTC, ECC, ICC, Lns, My, NAC, NIGTC, TG, TH, WP; CEV, GW, HCSB]. Jesus testified in regard to himself when he stated who he was [Lns]. Jesus publicly affirmed that he was the king of the Jews [BNTC, ECC, ICC; NET]. It was a good confession in that he made this confession is spite of the risk involved [ICC, NIGTC]. The good confession was Jesus' whole testimony to the truth of his own person [Alf].

2. The confession refers to what Jesus did [NIBC, WBC]. Jesus persevered in his mission during his life and especially in his death [NIBC, WBC].

This is mentioned to inspire Timothy to remain true to his commitment to Jesus and to continue in his tasks [WBC].

6:14 to-keep[a] the commandment[b] spotless[c] irreproachable[d]

LEXICON—a. aorist act. infin. of τηρέω (LN 13.32, 13.37) (BAGD 2.b. p. 815): 'to keep' [AB, BNTC, ECC, Herm, LN (13.32, 13.37), NTC, WBC; HCSB, KJV, NASB, NIV, NRSV], 'to obey' [LN (13.37), LSA; GW, NET, NLT, REB, TEV], 'to do' [NCV] 'to promise to obey' [CEV], 'to keep unharmed, to preserve' [BAGD], 'to guard' [Lns], 'to cause to continue, to retain' [LN (13.32)]. This verb means to continue to obey orders or commandments [LN (13.37)], or to cause a state to continue as it was [LN (13.32)].

b. ἐντολή (LN 33.330) (BAGD 2.f. p. 269): 'commandment' [BAGD, LN], 'order' [LN]. The phrase τὴν ἐντολήν 'the commandment' [AB, Lns, WBC; HCSB, NASB, NRSV] is also translated 'this commandment' [Herm; KJV], 'this command' [GW, NET, NIV, NLT], 'what you were commanded' [NCV], 'what you have been commanded by me' [LSA], 'your orders' [REB, TEV], 'the commission' [NTC], 'your commission' [BNTC], 'the apostolic command' [ECC], 'all that you have been told' [CEV]. This noun denotes that which is authoritatively commanded [LN]. The whole Christian religion is spoken of as a new command or law [BAGD].

c. ἄσπιλος (LN 79.59) (BAGD 2. p. 117): 'spotless' [AB, BAGD, BNTC, Lns], 'without spot' [NTC; HCSB, KJV, NIV, NRSV], 'morally spotless, pure' [LN], 'without stain' [NASB], 'unblemished' [Herm, WBC], 'without blemish' [BAGD], 'beyond blemish' [ECC], 'without fault' [NET, REB], 'without wrong' [NCV], 'without failing in anything' [LSA]. This adjective is also translated as an adverb: '(obey) completely' [CEV]. The words 'spotless, irreproachable' are translated 'completely' [GW], 'without wavering' [NLT], '(keep them) faithfully' [TEV]. This adjective is a figurative extension of ἄσπιλος 'spotless, without stain', and describes someone as being without anything that might mar his moral character [LN].

d. ἀνεπίλημπτος (LN 33.415) (BAGD p. 65): 'irreproachable' [BAGD, Lns], 'without reproach' [NASB], 'free from reproach' [BNTC], 'above reproach' [LN, NTC, WBC], 'beyond reproach' [ECC], 'unrebukeable' [KJV], 'above criticism' [LN], 'blameless' [AB], 'without blame' [HCSB, NCV, NIV, NRSV], 'without failure' [NET], 'in a way no one can reproach you about' [LSA], 'undamaged' [Herm]. This adjective is also translated as an adverb: '(obey) fully' [CEV]. The two adjectives 'spotless irreproachable' are translated 'completely' [GW], 'without wavering' [NLT], '(keep them) faithfully' [TEV]. This adjective refers to what cannot be criticized [LN]. See this word at 3:2.

QUESTION—How is this connected to the preceding verse?

This resumes the thought of the initial verb in 6:13 (I command you, etc.) [WBC]. This is the actual command and it proves to be worthy of the emphasis given it in 6:13 [ICC]. Some translations rearrange the wording of 6:13 so that the initial verb 'I command' appears at the end of that verse, thus making a smooth connection with this verse [HCSB, NIV, NRSV, REB, TEV], or the verb is moved to 6:14 [GW].

QUESTION—What is τὴν ἐντολὴν 'the commandment'?

1. The commandment concerns all that Timothy has been commissioned to do with respect to his ministry and the government of the church [AB, BKC, Herm, ICC, NTC, TH, WBC; NET]. This refers to what Timothy has been told to do, and this would include all of the instructions in this letter [BKC, ICC, TH]. The commandment is more general than any detail in the immediate context, and in fact it includes the whole letter and concerns Timothy's commitment to Christ and his whole ministry [WBC]. This is the entire commission from Paul in this letter [AB].

2. The commandment is that which was given to Timothy when he confessed the good confession before many witnesses (6:12). If it refers to Timothy's baptism, it would concern his duties as a Christian, but if it refers to his ordination, it would refer to his duties as a minister [TG].

2.1 It refers to his baptism [BNTC, TC]. The commandment was the baptismal charge given to Timothy [TC]. Since it was probably given at his baptism, the commandment would refer to the whole law of Christ [BNTC]

2.2 It refers to his ordination [ECC, NTL]. The ministerial task was entrusted to Timothy when he was commissioned [NTL].

3. The commandment is the one given in 4:16 concerning persevering in his faith and ministry [NAC, NIBC].

4. The commandment is the gospel viewed as the rule of life, commanding people to repent, believe, etc. [Alf, BNTC, EGT, Herm, My, NIGTC]. Instead of referring to any special command in this letter, it refers to the rule of the gospel, which regulates our lives and thoughts [Alf]. The law of the gospel is the divine standard by which a Christian is to regulate his life [My]. This means the rule of faith and life that is commanded by the gospel, the very thing that Timothy had pledged himself to follow at his baptism, and now as a leader he was a trustee of this commandment [BNTC].

QUESTION—What is meant by the phrase τηρῆσαί σε τὴν ἐντολὴν ἄσπιλον ἀνεπίλημπτον 'to keep the commandment spotless irreproachable'?

1. It means '(I command you) to preserve the commandment in its spotless and irreproachable state' [AB, Alf, BKC, BNTC, ECC, EGT, ICC, Lns, NCBC, NTC, NTL, TC, WBC]. When 'keep' means to preserve or guard the commandment, this says that the purity of the commandment must be guarded and preserved so that no one can criticize it, and this interpretation goes well with the idea that the commandment refers to the

gospel (or the Christian doctrine) being understood as a new law that should be guarded and preserved [TH]. The adjectives modify the commandment, and Timothy keeps it that way by not becoming defiled in his doctrine or life [WBC]. The commandment is spotless and irreproachable in itself, so Timothy is told to preserve this condition by keeping it immune from the contaminations of the false teachers [BNTC]. It is to be kept the way Christ gave it to us [Lns]. By his godly life and faithful ministry Timothy was to preserve the command from stain or reproach [BKC]. Timothy's attitude and conduct must be such that the commandment remains without spot and above reproach [NTC]. Although the two adjectives are connected grammatically to the verb, they really apply to Timothy, and the commandment is kept pure by not spotting it with disobedience [ICC]. As Paul chose these adjectives to qualify the commandment, he had in mind that Timothy should keep himself spotless and irreproachable in order that the commandment would be maintained flawless as far as he was concerned [EGT].

2. It means '(I command you) to obey the commandment in a spotless and irreproachable way' [LSA, NAC, NIBC, NIGTC, TH, TNTC; CEV, GW, NCV, NET, NLT, REB, TEV]. When 'keep' means to obey the commandment, the two adjectives qualify the way in which the commandment must be obeyed, that is, in a such a perfect way that no one can criticize Timothy about the way he obeyed the commandment, and this interpretation goes well with the idea that that the commandment refers to the instructions Timothy received at his baptism or ordination [TH]. The two adjectives refer to Timothy's keeping of the commandment, and he does so by not transgressing it and by keeping its positive aspects [NIGTC]. Timothy can best stop the work of the false teachers as he himself remains steadfast in his faith and calling [NIBC].

3. It means '(I command you) to obey the spotless commandment in an irreproachable way' [My]. In the phrase τὴν ἐντολὴν ἄσπιλον ἀνεπίλημπτον 'the commandment spotless irreproachable', the first adjective is closely connected to the commandment ('spotless commandment'), and the second adjective 'irreproachable' indicates how Timothy was to keep the spotless commandment, so that this says Timothy was to keep this commandment, which in itself is spotless, in such a way that he would not expose it to any blame [My].

QUESTION—What is meant by ἄσπιλος 'spotless'?

This adjective was used in describing an animal that was appropriate for a sacrifice, one that was unblemished in any way [WBC]. The lamb that was offered as a sacrifice had to be free from any defect [TH]. In a moral sense, it means free from fault and could be described as keeping the commandment faithfully and completely [TG]. When applied to the commandment, it is not a personal quality, but means unblemished or uninjured [Herm].

QUESTION—What is meant by ἀνεπίλημπτος 'irreproachable'?

It means to be above criticism so that nothing can be said against either the commandment itself or the way in which it is kept [TH]. When applied to the commandment, it means undamaged [Herm].

untilᵃ the appearingᵇ of-the Lord of-us, Jesus Christ.

LEXICON—a. μέχρι (LN 67.119) (BAGD 1.b. p. 515): 'until' [AB, BAGD, BNTC, ECC, Herm, LN, Lns, LSA, NTC, WBC; all versions except NLT], 'to' [LN], 'from now until' [NLT]. This preposition indicates the continuous extent of time up to a point [LN].

b. ἐπιφάνεια (LN 24.21) (BAGD 1. p. 304): 'appearing' [LN, NTC, WBC; HCSB, KJV, NASB, NET, NIV], 'appearance' [AB, Herm, LN; REB], 'manifestation' [BNTC; NRSV], 'revelation' [ECC], 'epiphany' [Lns]. This noun is also translated as a verb phrase with the Lord as subject: 'appears' [LSA], 'comes' [GW], 'comes again' [NLT], 'returns' [CEV], 'the Day when (our Lord Jesus Christ) will appear' [TEV]. This noun denotes someone's appearance to someone or at some place [LN].

QUESTION—What is meant by keeping the command in this way μέχρι 'until' the appearing of the Lord?

The 'appearing' is the appearing of Jesus in glory at the end of the age [AB, ECC, Lns, NTC]. This clause is added since at the time of judgment the Lord will determine how well Timothy has obeyed this command [BNTC, Lns, TG]. The word 'until' covers the whole Christian era, and at the end of it Christ will return and Timothy, along with every Christian, will have to give an account of himself to Christ [NIGTC]. The Last Day might come at any time, so Paul speaks as one who does not know whether Timothy will live to see that day or will die before it comes [Lns]. This means keeping this commission until the day of Timothy's death, or if the time of the end of the age comes before his death, then until that time when the Lord appears [NTC]. Death may close our time on earth before the Lord's appearance, but we shall not render account of our stewardship until the Lord's appearance at the Last Day [EGT]. This does not imply that Paul thought Timothy would be alive through this whole era [EGT, NCBC, NIGTC, TC]. Or, Paul spoke as though Timothy was to maintain the commandment through the whole time span that would end with the coming of the Lord, so the appearing of the Lord was considered to be a possibility in Timothy's lifetime [ICC].

6:15 which he-will bring-aboutᵃ in-its own times,ᵇ

LEXICON—a. fut. act. indic. of δείκνυμι (LN 28.47) (BAGD 1.a. p. 172): 'to bring about' [HCSB, NASB, NIV, NRSV, REB, TEV], 'to make known' [BAGD, LN, WBC; GW], 'to show' [BAGD, Herm, LN, Lns; KJV], 'to reveal' [AB; NET], 'to display' [NTC], 'to make visible' [BNTC], 'to make that happen' [NCV; similarly LSA]. The phrase 'which he will bring about' is translated 'he will send Jesus Christ back again' [CEV], 'that revelation God will make' [ECC], 'for Christ will be revealed from heaven' [NLT]. This verb means to make known the character or significance of something [LN]. The verb means 'will be done' or 'will be made to happen' [TG].

    b. καιρός (LN 67.1) (BAGD 3. p. 395): 'time' [BAGD, LN], 'occasion' [LN]. The phrase καιροῖς ἰδίοις 'in its own times' is translated 'in its own time' [Herm], 'in his own time' [HCSB, NIV], 'in his own good time' [REB], 'at the appropriate time' [BNTC], 'at the proper time' [LSA, WBC; NASB], 'at the right time' [GW, NCV, NET, NRSV, TEV], 'at just the right time' [NLT], 'at the proper season' [AB], 'at its own season' [Lns], 'in due time' [NTC], 'in due season' [NTC], 'at the time that God has already decided' [CEV]. This noun denotes points of time consisting of occasions for particular events [LN]. See the phrase 'in its own times' at 2:6.

QUESTION—How is this verse connected with the preceding one?

Having mentioned the appearing of Jesus Christ in 6:14, this verse and the next assert the certainty of that appearance by saying that God is the one who brings it about, and then an exalted description of God is given [TH]. It suggests a reason why Timothy should keep the commandment spotless and irreproachable by implying that he will receive a reward for this when Jesus will appear [NTC].

QUESTION—What is the referent of ἔν 'which' and who will bring this about?

The pronominal adjective ἔν 'which' has as its antecedent 'the appearing' [BNTC, ECC, ICC, NIGTC, TG; CEV, NET], and God is the one who will bring this about in his own time [AB, BNTC, ECC, ICC, NAC, NIGTC, NTC, TG; CEV, GW, NCV, NIV, REB, TEV]. God controls and determines the moment when Jesus Christ will appear [NIGTC].

the blessed[a] and only ruler,[b] the king of the (ones) being-kings[c] and Lord of the (ones) being-lords.[d]

LEXICON—a. μακάριος (LN 25.119) (BAGD 2. p. 487): 'blessed' [AB, BAGD, BNTC, ECC, Herm, LN, Lns, LSA, NTC, WBC; all versions except CEV], 'fortunate, happy' [BAGD, LN], 'glorious' [CEV]. This adjective describes the state of being happy because of enjoying favorable circumstances [LN]. See this word at 1:11.

    b. δυνάστης (LN **37.62**) (BAGD 1.a. p. 208): 'Ruler' [AB, BAGD, Herm, **LN**, LSA; CEV, GW, NCV, NIV, TEV], 'Sovereign' [BAGD, BNTC, NTC, WBC; HCSB, NASB, NET, NRSV, REB], 'Potentate' [Lns; KJV], 'suzerain' [ECC], 'almighty God' [NLT]. This noun denotes someone who is in a position of authority to command others [LN].

    c. pres. act. participle of βασιλεύω (LN 37.69) (BAGD 1.a. p. 136): 'to rule, to be a king' BAGD, LN], 'to reign' [LN]. The phrase ὁ βασιλεὺς τῶν βασιλευόντων 'the king of the ones being kings' is translated 'the King of those reigning as kings' [Lns], 'the king of those who act as kings' [ECC], 'the King of kings' [AB, BNTC, Herm, NTC, WBC; all versions except NCV, NLT], 'the King of all kings' [NCV, NLT], 'who reigns over people who reign' [LSA]. This verb means to rule as a king, and it implies having complete authority [LN].

d. pres. act. participle of κυριεύω (LN 37.50) (BAGD 1. p. 458): 'to be lord, to rule' [BAGD, LN], 'to govern, to reign over' [LN]. The phrase κύριος τῶν κυριευόντων 'Lord of the ones being lords' is translated 'Lord of those ruling as lords' [Lns], 'lord of those who act as lords' [ECC], 'the Lord of lords' [AB, BNTC, Herm, NTC, WBC; all versions except NCV, NLT], 'the Lord of all lords' [NCV, NLT], 'who rules over people who rule' [LSA]. This verb means to rule or reign over [LN].

QUESTION—How is this clause connected to the preceding one in this verse?

Here Paul breaks into a doxology [AB, BKC, BNTC, Lns, My, NAC, NIBC, NTC, NTL, TNTC, WBC]. Some translations imply that a hymn is either being quoted or composed by using a poetic format for 6:15b–16 [ECC, NTC; HCSB], or 6:15–16 [CEV]. The time of Jesus' appearing will be at the time determined by God who has absolute power to do what he determines [EGT]. This implies that Timothy should persevere because God is so powerful [WBC].

QUESTION—What is meant by God being called μακάριος 'blessed'?

This is an attribute of God and means that all happiness is contained in God, and he is the one who bestows happiness on people [NIGTC]. God is blessed since he is to be pronounced fortunate in his exalted state by those who worship him [ICC].

QUESTION—What is meant by God being the only ruler?

God is the only absolute ruler, and this fact is supported by the statement that he possesses the highest power over all who possess power and has full control over all who exercise control [NIGTC]. All forces in the universe are subject to God [ICC].

6:16 the only (one) having immortality,[a] living[b] in-light unapproachable,[c]

LEXICON—a. ἀθανασία (LN 23.126) (BAGD p. 20.c): 'immortality' [AB, BAGD, BNTC, ECC, LN, Lns, NTC, WBC; HCSB, KJV, NASB, NET, NRSV, REB]. The phrase 'the only one having immortality' is translated 'who/he alone is immortal' [**LN**, NIV, TEV], 'the only immortal one' [Herm], 'who alone is intrinsically immortal' [LSA], 'he is the only one who always exists' [**LN**], 'only God lives forever' [CEV], 'he alone can never die' [NLT], 'he is the only one who never dies' [NCV, **LN**], 'he is the only one who cannot die' [GW]. This noun denotes the state of not being subject to death, of never dying [LN].

b. pres. act. participle of οἰκέω (LN **85.67**) (BAGD 2. p. 557): 'to live' [Herm, LN; CEV, NCV, NET, NIV, NLT, TEV], 'to dwell' [AB, BAGD, BNTC, LN, NTC, WBC; HCSB, KJV, NASB, NRSV, REB], 'to inhabit' [ECC, Lns]. This verb means to live or dwell in a place [LN].

c. ἀπρόσιτος (LN **15.80**) (BAGD p. 102): 'unapproachable' [AB, BAGD, BNTC, LN, NTC, WBC; HCSB, NASB, NET, NIV, NRSV], 'inapproachable' [Lns], 'cannot be approached' [LN], 'inaccessible'

[ECC; Herm]. The phrase φῶς οἰκῶν ἀπρόσιτον 'living in light unapproachable' is translated 'he lives in light that no one can approach' [**LN** (88.567), LSA]. 'he lives in light that no one can come near' [CEV, GW], 'dwelling in the light which no man can approach unto' [KJV], 'he lives in the light that no one can approach' [TEV], 'he lives in the light that cannot be approached by anyone' [**LN** (15.80)], 'he lives in light so bright no one can go near it' [NCV], 'he lives in light so brilliant that no human can approach him' [NLT]. This adjective describes something that is not capable of being approached [LN].

QUESTION—In what sense does God have immortality?

Immortality is not continuing to live after death, but freedom from death [ICC]. It is to live on forever without experiencing death [TH]. God is deathless and self-existing [NAC]. God's essential property is his endless existence [EGT]. 'Having immortality' indicates that God alone has life and only he can confer life to others [ICC]. Creatures derive their immortality from God and are dependent upon him for it [Lns, NTC, WBC], so this is saying that God is the only one who is intrinsically immortal [BNTC, Lns, LSA, TNTC, WBC].

QUESTION—What is the significance of God living in unapproachable light?

This light emphasizes God's transcendent majesty, and probably this thought is based on Exod. 24:17 where God's glory was visible as a fire on the top of the mountain [WBC]. The purpose for the light is to make people unable to see God's face [TH]. Light is regarded as the element of the divine, and the light is so bright that people cannot look at it, or it is so intense that it would burn them up if they approached it [ICC].

whom no-one of men saw[a] or is-able to-see.

LEXICON—a. aorist act. indic. of ὁράω (LN 24.1): 'to see' [LN]. The clause 'whom no one of men saw' is translated 'whom no one/person/man has seen' [Herm, WBC; NASB, NIV; similarly KJV], 'whom not a single man has seen' [Lns], 'whom no person has ever seen' [LSA; similarly NTC; NET, NRSV], 'whom no human being has seen' [BNTC], 'the one whom no human being ever saw' [ECC], 'no human eye has ever seen him' [NLT], 'no one has seen him' [GW], 'no one has ever seen him' [TEV; similarly REB], 'no one has ever seen God' [NCV], 'no human being has ever seen him' [AB; similarly CEV], 'whom none of mankind has seen' [HCSB].

QUESTION—What is the significance of men being unable to see God?

God's holiness separates him from his creation [WBC]. God is so holy that sinful mankind cannot see him and live [NICNT, TH]. God is infinitely holy, therefore no human being can see him and live (Exod. 33:20) [NAC].

to-whom (be) honor[a] and power[b] eternal,[c] amen.

LEXICON—a. τιμή (LN 87.4) (BAGD 2.b. p. 818): 'honor' [AB, BAGD, BNTC, Herm, LN, Lns, NTC, WBC; all versions except CEV, GW], 'respect' [BAGD, LN]. The phrase 'to whom be honor' is translated 'may he be honored' [LSA], 'God will be honored' [CEV], 'to whom belong honor (and might)' [ECC], 'honor (and power) belong to him' [GW]. This noun denotes the element of honor in the assignment of status to a person [LN]. This means that God is worthy of receiving esteem and reverence [NAC]. Honor consists of esteem, reverence, worship, and adoration [Lns]. See this word at 1:17.

b. κράτος (LN 76.6) (BAGD 4. p. 449): 'power' [AB, BAGD, BNTC, Herm, LN; CEV, GW, KJV, NET, NLT, TEV], 'might' [ECC, LN, WBC; HCSB, NIV], 'strength' [Lns, NTC], 'sovereignty' [BAGD], 'dominion' [NASB, NRSV, REB]. The phrase 'to whom be power' is translated 'may he rule' [LSA], 'may power belong to God' [NCV]. This noun denotes the power to rule or control [LN].

c. αἰώνιος (LN 67.96) (BAGD 3. p. 28): 'eternal' [BAGD, LN]. This adjective modifies both nouns: 'eternal' [AB], 'everlasting' [KJV]; or it modifies only 'power': 'eternal' [BNTC, ECC, Herm, NTC; HCSB, NASB, NET, NRSV, TEV]. This adjective is also translated as an adverb modifying the implied verb: '(be) forever' [LSA, WBC; GW, NCV, NIV, NLT, REB], '(will last) forever' [CEV]. This adjective pertains to an unlimited duration of time [LN].

QUESTION—What is meant by God's 'power'?

This emphasizes God's sovereignty [WBC]. Power implies God's rule, sovereignty, or dominion [NICNT, TH]. God is a potentate who is supreme over those who would be his rivals [BNTC]. 'Might' refers to God's power expressed in his sovereign acts [NAC].

DISCOURSE UNIT—6:17–19 [ECC, Herm, ICC, LSA, NAC, NCBC, NIBC, NIGTC, NTL, TH, TNTC, WBC; HCSB]. The topic is riches, part 2 [ECC], words to the rich [WBC; HCSB], a word for those already rich [NIBC], riches for the wealthy [Herm], an exhortation for the wealthy [NTL], advice to wealthy men [TNTC], what to teach to the rich [ICC], the theme of life-style resumed [NCBC], further instructions for rich Christians [NIGTC, TH], a promise for the prosperous [NAC], command the rich people to trust God and do good [LSA].

6:17 **Command[a] the rich in the present age[b] not to-be-conceited[c] or to-hope[d] on the uncertainty[e] of-riches**

LEXICON—a. pres. act. impera. of παραγγέλλω (LN 33.327) (BAGD p. 613): 'to command' [BAGD, Herm, LN, LSA; NCV, NET, NIV, NRSV, TEV], 'to order' [BAGD, LN], 'to give orders to' [Lns], 'to charge' [ECC, NTC; KJV], 'to give charge to' [KJV], 'to direct' [BAGD], 'to instruct' [BAGD, BNTC; HCSB, NASB, REB], 'to teach' [NLT], 'to urge' [WBC], 'to tell' [AB; GW], 'to warn' [CEV]. This verb means to announce what must be done [LN]. The word 'command' is too strong for a church setting, so here it means 'to urge' [WBC]. Here the verb has the sense of 'to warn' or 'to strongly urge' [TH]. See this word at 1:3; 4:11; 5:7; 6:13.

b. αἰών (LN 67.143) (BAGD 2.a. p. 27): 'age' [BAGD, ECC, LN, WBC; HCSB, NRSV], 'world' [AB, LSA; CEV, KJV, NASB, GW, NCV, NIV,

NLT], 'era' [LN], 'eon' [Lns]. The phrase 'in the present age' is translated 'in terms of this present age' [NTC], 'so far as the present world goes' [BNTC], 'in this world's goods' [NET, REB], 'in the things of this life' [TEV]. This noun denotes a unit of time as a particular stage or period of history [LN].

   c. pres. act. infin. of ὑψηλοφρονέω (LN **88.209**) (BAGD p. 850): 'to be conceited' [NASB], 'to be haughty' [BAGD, BNTC, LN, LSA, WBC; NET, NRSV], 'to be arrogant' [AB, LN; GW, HCSB, NIV], 'to be proud' [BAGD, Herm; CEV, NCV, NLT, REB, TEV], 'to be high-minded' [Lns, NTC; KJV], 'to be snobbish' [ECC]. This verb means to have an arrogant or haughty attitude [LN].

   d. perf. act. infin. of ἐλπίζω (LN 25.59) (BAGD 3. p. 252): 'to put one's hope in something' [AB, BAGD, Herm], 'to place one's confidence (in)' [GW], 'to fix/set/put/place one's hope (on)' [BNTC, ECC, Lns, NTC, WBC; HCSB, NASB, NET, NIV, NRSV, REB, TEV], 'to hope' [LN; NCV], 'to hope for' [LN], 'to trust in' [LSA; CEV, KJV, NLT]. This verb means to confidently look forward to something that is good and beneficial [LN]. See this word at 4:10.

   e. ἀδηλότης (LN 71.20) (BAGD p. 16): 'uncertainty' [AB, BAGD, Herm, LN, NTC, WBC; HCSB, NASB, NRSV]. This noun is also translated as an adjective modifying 'riches': 'uncertain' [Lns; GW, KJV, NCV, NET, NIV, REB, TEV], 'unreliable' [NLT], 'precarious' [ECC], 'unstable' [BNTC]. The phrase ἠλπικέναι ἐπὶ πλούτου ἀδηλότητι 'to hope on the uncertainty of riches' is translated 'to trust in wealth that is easily lost' [CEV], 'trust in their rich possessions because a person cannot be certain how long they will have them' [LSA]. This noun denotes the uncertainty of some event or state [LN].

QUESTION—Who are the rich?

   The rich are the wealthy members of the church [NIBC, NTC, TC, TH]. They are those who are actually rich, not those in 6:9 who desire to become rich [Lns, NAC, NTC, TNTC]. These people have become rich in a legitimate and irreproachable way [Lns].

QUESTION—What is meant by the qualification of being rich 'in the present age'?

   Material wealth is wealth only in regard to the present world [BNTC]. This gives the idea of being rich in earthly wealth [Lns]. This refers to the present transitory world as long as it lasts, and it may imply that although they are rich by the world's standards, they may be poor in respect to the next world [ICC]. The limiting factor of this present age or world prepares for the contrast of what happens for the future in 6:19 [BNTC, NIGTC]. It implies that the rich will have their wealth only in this age [NAC].

QUESTION—Why would the rich be in danger of being haughty?

   They might think that having greater wealth than others would indicate that they themselves were of greater value than the others [NIGTC]. Instead of realizing that all they possess is a gift from God, they might develop an attitude of superiority over the poor [WBC]. It is not so much being proud of themselves as being scornful of those who have not gained a high social position based on their possessions [ICC].

QUESTION—What is meant by 'to hope on the uncertainty of riches'?

The rich must not place their confidence in wealth since being of this age their riches are uncertain [WBC]. Wealth is only temporary [NAC, TH], and it cannot always be depended upon to provide for one's needs [TH]. Their riches cannot be depended on. and also earthly wealth is no basis for security in the world to come [ICC].

but (hope) on God the (one) giving[a] us all (things) richly[b] for enjoyment,[c]

TEXT—Instead of ἀλλ' ἐπὶ θεῷ 'but on God' some manuscripts read ἀλλ' ἐπὶ τῷ θεῷ 'but on the God', some manuscripts read ἀλλ' ἐπὶ θεῷ ζῶντι 'but on God living', some manuscripts read ἀλλ' ἐπὶ τῷ θεῷ τῷ ζῶντι 'but on the God the living', and one manuscript omits ἀλλ' ἐπὶ θεῷ 'but on God'. GNT reads ἀλλ' ἐπὶ θεῷ 'but on God' with an A decision, indicating that the text is certain. 'But on the God the living' is read by KJV.

LEXICON—a. pres. act. participle of παρέχω (LN 90.91) (BAGD 1.b. p. 626): 'to give' [LN; KJV, NCV, NLT, TEV], 'to grant' [BAGD, Herm, WBC], 'to provide' [BNTC, ECC, LSA, NTC; GW, HCSB, NET, NIV, NRSV, REB], 'to furnish' [Lns], 'to supply' [AB; NASB], 'to cause to experience' [LN], 'to bless' [CEV]. This verb means to cause someone to experience something [LN].

b. πλουσίως (LN **59.57**) (BAGD p. 673): 'richly' [AB, BAGD, BNTC, Herm, LN, Lns, NTC, WBC; all versions except CEV, TEV], 'abundantly' [BAGD, LSA], 'in abundance' [**LN**], 'generously' [TEV], 'in large amount' [LN], 'lavishly' [ECC]. This adverb is also translated as a noun: '(God, who is) rich' [CEV]. This adverb pertains to that which exists in a large amount and implies that it is valuable [LN]. The adverb πλουσίως 'richly' is probably a live metaphor in the context of πλουσίοις '(the) rich', πλούτου 'riches', and πλουτεῖν 'to be rich' (6:18) [LSA]. Many point out this play on the words concerning riches [AB, ECC, Herm, Lns, NIGTC, NTC, WBC].

c. ἀπόλαυσις (LN **25.115**) (BAGD p. 94): 'enjoyment' [AB, BAGD, LN], 'satisfaction' [ECC]. The phrase εἰς ἀπόλαυσιν 'for enjoyment' [Herm, Lns] is also translated 'for our enjoyment' [BNTC, NTC, WBC; NET, NIV, NLT, NRSV, TEV], 'to enjoy' [**LN**; GW, HCSB, KJV, NASB, NCV, REB], 'in order that we may enjoy it' [LSA], 'to enjoy life' [CEV]. This noun denotes enjoyment that is based upon the satisfaction of one's desires [LN]. It is enjoyable because God gives it. and it is his intention that we enjoy it [WBC].

QUESTION—Is there any significance in the statement that God gives all things richly to *us* instead of to *them*, the rich?

By saying 'to us', Paul indicates that he is stating a general truth that applies to all people whether they are rich or not [NIGTC, WBC].

QUESTION—What are the 'all things' that God richly gives us?
This means all the things that we receive from God [ICC, LSA], everything
we need [ICC]. It refers to all that we have, whether it is much or little [Lns].
It does not mean everything people could possible want, and 6:18 limits it to
human needs of food and clothing [WBC]. Yet 'richly' indicates that God
gives beyond our needs [ICC].

6:18 **to-do-good,**[a] **to-be-rich**[b] **in good deeds, to-be generous,**[c] **ready-to-share,**[d]

LEXICON—a. pres. act. infin. of ἀγαθοεργέω (LN **88.3**) (BAGD p. 2): 'to do
good' [BAGD, BNTC, ECC, Herm, **LN**, WBC; all versions except CEV,
NLT], 'to do what is good' [NTC], 'to do good deeds' [LSA; CEV], 'to
do good work' [AB], 'to perform good deeds/works' [LN], 'to be working
good' [Lns], 'to use their money to do good' [NLT]. This verb means to
engage in doing what is good [LN].

   b. pres. act. infin. of πλουτέω (LN **59.58**) (BAGD 2. p. 674): 'to be rich in
something' [BAGD, LN], 'to have a great deal of' [LN]. The phrase
πλουτεῖν ἐν ἔργοις καλοῖς 'to be rich in good deeds' [WBC; KJV,
NASB, NET, NIV], is also translated 'to be rich in good works' [Herm,
LN; HCSB, NLT, NRSV, TEV], 'to be rich in excellent works' [Lns], 'to
be rich in noble deeds' [NTC], 'to be rich in doing good deeds' [NCV],
'to be rich in well-doing' [REB], 'to be rich in deeds of kindness'
[BNTC], 'to be wealthy in noble deeds' [AB], 'to become wealthy in fine
deeds' [ECC], 'to do a lot of good things' [GW], 'to do many good deeds'
[LSA], 'to have an abundance of good works, to do many good works'
[**LN**]. The two commands 'to do good, to be rich in good deeds' is
translated 'instruct them to do as many good deeds as they can and to help
everyone' [CEV]. This verb means to have a large amount of something
that has value [LN].

   c. εὐμετάδοτος (LN **57.97**) (BAGD p. 323): 'generous' [BAGD, Herm,
WBC; CEV, GW, HCSB, NASB, NCV, NIV, NRSV, TEV], 'munificent'
[ECC], 'liberal' [**LN**]. This adjective is also translated as a phrase
'generous givers' [NET], 'generous in giving' [AB], 'generous in sharing'
[**LN**], 'generous to those in need' [NLT], 'eager to give to people' [LSA],
'ready to distribute' [KJV], 'to be quick to give' [NTC], 'to be ready to
give generously' [REB], 'to be open-handed' [BNTC], 'to be sharing
well' [Lns]. This adjective describes one who is generous in sharing [LN].

   d. κοινωνικός (LN **57.100**) (BAGD p. 439): 'ready to share' [Herm, **LN**,
NTC; NASB, NCV, NRSV], 'ready to share with others' [REB, TEV],
'willing to share' [HCSB, NIV], 'sharing' [WBC], 'liberal' [BAGD],
'generous' [BAGD, BNTC]. The adjective 'ready to share' is translated
'always being ready to share with others' [NLT], 'and to share' [GW],
'and share what they have' [CEV], 'sharing with others' [NET], 'sharing
all around' [ECC], 'and to be sharers of possessions' [AB], 'to generously
share what they have' [LSA], 'willing to communicate' [KJV],

'fellowshipping' [Lns]. This adjective describes one who is willing and ready to share [LN].

QUESTION—How is this verse related to the preceding verse?

The three infinitives depend on the verb παράγγελλε 'command' in 6:17 [AB, NIBC, NICNT, TH, WBC]. Many translations repeat the verb of 6:17 here [AB, ECC, NTC; all versions except KJV, NCV, REB]: *command them to do good, etc.* All four actions are the natural result of realizing that everything one has is really a gift from God [WBC]. This describes the practical outworking of the commands to the rich and of setting their hope on God [NICNT]. The thought of the generosity of God leads to what the rich should do [BNTC].

QUESTION—How are the three infinitives and the adjective related?

The first command is to do good, then the next is more specific by stating that this means to richly do good deeds, and then good deeds is explained as being generous in a sharing way [AB, WBC]. The first two infinitives are synonymous [TG, TH], but the second is intensified to bring out the importance of doing good deeds [TH].

QUESTION—What is meant by 'to do good'?

They are to use their wealth to do good [BNTC]. The good is what is beneficial to others [Lns]. The first two commands probably include more than giving monetary help since that need is emphasized in the next command [NAC]. Doing good consists of demonstrating one's love to others [ICC].

QUESTION—What is the function of the adjective κοινωνικούς 'ready to share' after the three infinitives?

The adjective 'sharing' joins with the preceding verb 'to be generous' to present the idea that the rich should be generous by sharing with the poor [NTL, WBC]. The two words are close in meaning [ICC, TH]. Being generous is sharing with others by gladly giving them a share of what one owns [NICNT]. The word εὐμετάδοτος 'generous' is an unusual term not found elsewhere in the NT, so 'ready to share' is added as an explanation of what Paul intended by that word [ECC, TC]. The rich person will always be ready to share what he has with others in the community of believers [NTC]. Or, the adjective means 'fellowshipping', being ready to fellowship and actually doing so [Lns].

6:19 **treasuring-up**[a] **for-themselves a-good foundation**[b] **for the coming (age),**[c]

LEXICON—a. pres. act. participle of ἀποθησαυρίζω (LN 65.11) (BAGD p. 91): 'to treasure up' [**LN**], 'to store up a treasure' [NTC; GW, NLT, TEV; similarly NASB], 'to lay up treasure' [NIV], 'to save a treasure' [NCV], 'to save up a treasure' [NET], 'to acquire a treasure' [REB], 'to store up' [AB, BAGD, BNTC, LSA; HCSB, NRSV], 'to lay' [CEV], 'to lay up' [BAGD, Herm, Lns, WBC], 'to lay up in store' [KJV], 'to keep safe' [LN], 'to make deposits in' [ECC]. This verb is derived from

θησαυρός 'treasure' and it means to keep something that is of great value
safe [LN].

b. θεμέλιον, θεμέλιος (LN **89.12**) (BAGD 2.c. p. 356): 'foundation' [LN,
WBC], 'basis' [**LN**], 'treasure, reserve' [BAGD]. The phrase 'a good
foundation' [BNTC, Herm, WBC; GW, HCSB, KJV, NASB, NLT] is also
translated 'a solid foundation' [CEV, TEV], 'a firm foundation' [NET,
NIV], 'a strong foundation' [NCV], 'a noble foundation' [AB], 'an
excellent foundation' [NTC], 'the treasure of a good foundation' [NRSV],
'an excellent stock' [Lns]. The phrase 'a good foundation for the coming
age' is translated 'which will be a good basis on which they may rely for
the future' [LSA], 'which will form a good foundation' [REB], 'an excellent fund' [ECC]. This noun is a figurative extension of θεμέλιονα
'foundation' [BAGD, LN], and it denotes the basis for some action or
event [LN]. It means about the same as 'treasure' or 'reserve' [BAGD].

c. pres. act. participle of μέλλω (LN **67.135**) (BAGD 2. p. 501): The
participial phrase τὸ μέλλον 'the coming' is translated 'the coming age'
[WBC; NIV], 'the age to come' [NTC; HCSB], 'the time to come' [KJV],
'the future' [AB, BAGD, BNTC, ECC, Herm, **LN**, Lns; CEV, NASB,
NCV, NET, NLT, NRSV, REB, TEV]. This phrase refers to an unlimited
extent of time beginning with the time of the discourse [LN]. The future is
the age that follows this age [NICNT].

QUESTION—What relationship is indicated by the use of the participle
ἀποθησαυρίζοντας 'treasuring up'?

This indicates the results of the actions described in the preceding verse [AB,
Alf, BNTC, NAC, NIBC, NTC, TH, WBC; GW, NLT, NRSV, REB, TEV].
It explains what rich believers will do by those actions [ICC]. Not only do
the rich benefit others by their good and generous actions, they also benefit
themselves [NIGTC].

QUESTION—What is meant by 'treasuring up' for themselves?

When they are generous (6:18), they are not losing their wealth; instead they
are laying it away in heaven [WBC]. The same paradox is expressed in Matt.
6:19–20 [WP]. This has the idea of storing up treasure in heaven [AB, BKC,
BNTC, TC]. The treasure in heaven consists of a good conscience (1:5), an
enthusiastic reception by those who have benefited from his generosity
(Luke 16:9), and in general, an entrance into all the joys and glories of
heaven [NTC]. The word 'themselves' is emphasized to make the point that
they will not only be helping others, but they will actually be piling up great
benefits for themselves [BNTC, NAC].

QUESTION—What is meant by 'a foundation'?

1. The idea of treasuring up a foundation is a mixing of metaphors [AB,
BKC, BNTC, EGT, ICC, My, NIBC, NTC, NTIC, NTL, TNTC, WBC;
GW, NCV, NET, NIV, REB, TEV]. This mixing is due to a condensation
of language here [EGT]. By laying away treasure in heaven, the rich
establish a firm foundation on which they can build for the future, that is,
for the real life [WBC]. The treasure is defined later as the real life

[BNTC, NIBC]. They store up a treasure that will serve as a good foundation for the future [NTC, NTL; GW, NCV, NET, NIV, REB, TEV]. 'They will lay up treasure for themselves as a firm foundation for the coming age' [NIV], they will 'acquire a treasure which will form a good foundation for the future' [REB], 'they will store up for themselves a treasure which will be a solid foundation for the future' [TEV]. By giving away their wealth, the rich will gather for themselves a treasure, and they will also lay a good foundation on which their future salvation is built [My]. Being conscious of having enjoyed the heavenly treasure will be a firm foundation for expecting everything good on the Day of Judgment [NTC].

2. There is one metaphor here. They store up treasure, that treasure being the foundation [ECC, Lns; NASB, NRSV; possibly Herm; HCSB, KJV which say that they store up a good foundation]: 'storing up for themselves the treasure of a good foundation for the future' [NASB, NRSV]. The word θεμέλιον can mean either 'a foundation' (a base for a building) or 'a fund' (money that is deposited), and here this is translated 'making their deposits in an excellent fund for the future' [ECC]. What is laid up is a capital sum invested and thus laid up for the future [Lns].

3. This is presented as a building metaphor [CEV]. 'They will lay a solid foundation' [CEV]

that[a] they-may-lay-hold[b] of-the real[c] life.

TEXT—Instead of ὄντως 'real' some manuscripts read αἰωνίου 'eternal' and one manuscript reads αἰωνίου ὄντως 'eternal real'. GNT reads ὄντως 'real' with an A decision, indicating that the text is certain. 'Eternal' is read by Herm; KJV.

LEXICON—a. ἵνα (LN 89.49, 89.59): 'that' [Herm; KJV], 'in order that' [Lns, WBC], 'in order to, for the purpose of' [LN (89.59)], 'so that' [AB, ECC, LN (89.59); HCSB, NASB, NLT, NRSV], 'so as a result, that' [LN (89.49)], 'so that' [BNTC, LN (89.49); CEV, NIV], 'in this way' [GW], 'and so' [NET], 'then' [NCV, REB, TEV]. This conjunction indicates the purpose for events [LN (89.59)], or the result, although in some cases it implies that there is an underlying or indirect purpose [LN (89.49)].

b. aorist mid. (deponent = active) subjunctive of πιλαμβάνομαι (LN 90.63): 'to lay hold of/on' [AB, ECC; KJV, NET], 'to seize hold' [LN, WBC], 'to take hold of' [Lns; GW, HCSB, NASB, NIV, NRSV], 'to grasp' [REB], 'to obtain' [Herm, LSA], 'to win' [TEV], 'to have' [NCV], 'to possess' [BNTC], 'to experience' [LN; NLT], 'to know' [CEV]. This verb means to experience some event or state [LN].

c. ὄντως (LN 70.2) (BAGD 2. p. 574): 'really, certainly [BAGD, LN], truly' [LN], 'in truth' [BAGD]. The phrase τῆς ὄντως ζωῆς 'the real life' is translated 'real life' [AB], 'what is truly life' [WBC], 'eternal life which is the real life' [LSA], 'life that is real' [HCSB], 'the life that is life indeed' [BNTC; REB], 'the life that is true life' [NCV, TEV], 'the life that really is life' [NRSV], 'the life that is truly life' [NIV], 'that which is life indeed' [NASB], 'what is truly life' [NET], 'the genuine life' [Lns], 'what life really is' [GW], 'true life' [NLT], 'what true life is like' [CEV], 'the life which deserves that name' [ECC]. This adjective describes something as having actual existence [LN]. See this word in 5:3 in regard to 'real' widows.

QUIESTION—What relationship is indicated by the conjunction ἵνα 'that'?

1. It indicates the purpose for obeying the commands in 6:17–18 [AB, Alf, BNTC, ECC, ICC, Lns, LSA, My, NAC, NIBC, WBC; GW, HCSB, NASB, NLT, NRSV]: *the rich should do this in order that they obtain the real life*. It is the purpose for which the treasuring up takes place [NIGTC], and defines the nature of that treasure [BNTC].

2. It indicates the result of obeying the command of 6:17–18 [ICC, WBC; CEV, GW, NCV, NET, NIV, REB, TEV]: *the rich should do this and so obtain the real life*. Because the real life is a gift of God, this does not imply that by obeying the command they will earn the real life. Rather, the real life is the result of living in this way [WBC]. These actions are the result of one's faith and not an attempt to earn God's favor [WBC]. This does not mean that people can get credit for their generous deeds and because of that win a reward in the next life. Rather, it indicates that the lack of expressing faith by good works shows a lack of faith itself, and conversely [ICC].

QUESTION—What is meant by τῆς ὄντως ζωῆς 'the real life'?

This refers to the real or true life, another designation for eternal life, the spiritual life God gives to the believer through Christ, a life that has a future dimension as well as a present one [NIGTC]. The real life is eternal life [AB, BNTC, LSA]. The true life is eternal life in the coming age, not the life of this age [NIBC, WBC]. Or, it is the eternal life mentioned 6:12, a life that begins in the present world, but is finally consummated and perfected in the future [TH].

DISCOURSE UNIT—6:20–21 [Herm, NAC, NIBC, NIGTC, NTL, TH, TNTC, WBC; HCSB, NET, NRSV]. The topic is the conclusion [NET], the epistolary closing [NTL], the final encouragement to Timothy [WBC], a final charge to Timothy [NIBC, NIGTC], a final admonition to Timothy [TNTC], concluding instructions to Timothy [TH], guard the heritage [HCSB], a concluding caution [NAC], warning against false "gnosis" [Herm], personal instructions and benediction [NRSV].

DISCOURSE UNIT—6:20–21a [ECC, ICC, LSA, NCBC]. The topic is a renewed warning against false teaching [NCBC], a final warning to Timothy, a closing summary [ECC], summing up earlier themes [ICC], guard the true doctrine which has been entrusted to you and avoid what is falsely called 'knowledge' [LSA].

6:20 O[a] Timothy, what-has-been-entrusted[b] (to you) guard[c]

LEXICON—a. ὦ (LN 91.14) (BAGD 1. p. 895): 'O' [AB, ECC, Herm, LN, Lns, NTC, WBC; KJV, NASB, NET], not explicit [BNTC; all versions except KJV, NASB, NET]. This particle functions to indicate direct address (as a traditional vocative) and it is often left untranslated [LN]. It expresses emotion at the beginning of a clause [BAGD, NIBC, NIGTC]. It adds solemnity and urgency to what Paul is saying to Timothy [NIGTC]. It indicates solemn earnestness [Lns, NTC].

   b. παραθήκη (LN 35.48) (BAGD p. 616): 'what has been entrusted' [BAGD, LN] The clause τὴν παραθήκην φύλαξον 'what has been entrusted to you guard' [NTC] is also translated 'guard what has been entrusted to you' [WBC; HCSB, NASB, NRSV], 'guard what has been entrusted to your care' [NIV], 'guard the deposit' [Lns], 'keep what has been deposited with you' [ECC], 'guard the deposit which has been entrusted to you' [Herm], 'guard what God has entrusted/trusted to you' [LSA; NCV, NLT], 'guard what God has placed in your care' [CEV], 'protect what has been entrusted to you' [NET], 'keep safe what has been entrusted to you' [REB], 'keep safe what has been entrusted to your care' [LN; TEV], 'keep safe the trust committed to you' [BNTC], 'keep that which is committed to thy trust' [KJV], 'guard the Good News which has been entrusted to you' [GW], 'protect the tradition' [AB]. This noun denotes something that has been entrusted to the care of someone [LN].

   c. aorist act. impera. of φυλάσσω (LN 37.120) (BAGD 1.c. p. 868): 'to guard' [BAGD, LN], 'to protect' [BAGD]. See translations of this verb in the preceding lexical item. This verb literally means to hold someone in close custody [LN].

QUESTION—What is meant by the noun παραθήκην 'that which has been entrusted' to Timothy, and what has been entrusted to him?

   Used as a legal technical term, the noun παραθήκη means 'a deposit, a property entrusted to another for safekeeping and to be returned when required', but when used figuratively, it refers to passing on teaching [ICC]. In this context it means 'to commit to one's charge' or 'to place in one's care' [TH]. There is a question of who deposited the deposit with Timothy: (1) the depositor is God who entrusted the deposit to Paul who then passes it on to Timothy, or (2) the depositor is Paul himself, as the author of the letter. However, neither of the alternatives is decisive [ICC].

   1. This refers to the Christian doctrine, the gospel [AB, Alf, BKC, BNTC, EGT, Herm, ICC, Lns, LSA, NAC, NIGTC, NTC, NTL, TC; GW]. It refers to the apostolic teaching of the gospel [ICC, NIGTC; GW]. This probably refers to Christian teachings since the rest of the verse is about teachings [LSA]. A cognate verb παράθου 'entrust' is used in 2 Tim. 2:2 where the teaching Timothy heard from Paul was to be entrusted to faithful men [LSA, NIGTC]. God is the one who entrusted this to Timothy [LSA]. To guard the doctrine, Timothy must not change it himself, and he must defend it from being changed or contradicted by

others [LSA, NTC]. From these two verses, it must mean to guard the truth of the gospel and pass it on to future believers, and also to avoid the profane foolish talk and contradictions of the heresy in Ephesus [WBC]. He is to guard the gospel against the attacks of the heretics [BKC, ICC]. This includes guarding the orders and teachings in this letter [NTC]. 'Guard' has the dual meanings of observing and protecting the traditions [AB]. He is to resist the false teachers and keep his life pure as he faithfully proclaims the truth [NAC]. The following clause describes what is involved in this guarding [Lns].

2. This refers to the commands Paul has given in this letter [NCBC, NIBC, WBC]. Coming at the end of the letter, this refers to at least this letter, and perhaps it includes the gospel and Timothy's ministry as a whole [WBC]. In this letter Timothy was given the task of resisting the false teachers, doing this by keeping his own life pure, and faithfully teaching the truth [NIBC].

3. This refers to the ministry entrusted to Timothy [My, TG]. It concerns Timothy's responsibilities that God entrusted to him as a pastor and as a teacher of the Christian faith [TG]. The main purpose of this letter is to instruct Timothy about his conduct in the ministry entrusted to him [My].

avoiding[a] the profane[b] foolish-talk[c] and contradictions[d] of-the wrongly-called[e] knowledge,

LEXICON—a. pres. mid. participle (imperative sense) of ἐκτρέπομαι (LN **13.155**): 'to avoid' [AB, **LN**, LSA, WBC; HCSB, KJV, NASB, NET, NLT, NRSV, TEV], 'to stay away from' [NCV], 'to keep one's distance from' [ECC], 'to steer clear of' [BNTC], 'to not become involved' [LN], 'to not pay attention to' [CEV], 'to turn away from' [Herm, Lns, NTC; GW, NIV], 'to turn a deaf ear to' [REB]. This verb means to avoid becoming involved in some type of activity [LN]. This participle has the force of an imperative so that Timothy must determine to guard (aorist tense) the truth, and then every day he must avoid (present tense) the foolish talk of the opponents [WBC].

b. βέβηλος (LN 88.115) (BAGD 1. p. 138): 'profane' [AB, BAGD, BNTC, ECC, Lns, NTC; KJV, NET, NRSV, TEV], 'worldly' [BAGD, LN; NASB], 'godless' [Herm, LN; CEV, NIV, NLT], 'unholy' [WBC], 'irreligious' [LSA; REB], 'irreverent' [HCSB], 'foolish' [NCV]. This adjective is also translated as a phrase: '(discussions and claims) that people use to oppose the Christian faith' [GW]. This adjective refers to being profane in the sense of being godless or worldly [LN]. See this word at 1:9; 4:7.

c. κενοφωνία (LN 33.376) (BAGD p. 428): 'foolish talk' [LN], 'stupid talk' [CEV], 'empty talk' [BAGD, LN], 'empty speech' [HCSB], 'empty chatter' [NTC; NASB, REB], 'chatter' [BAGD, BNTC, Herm, LSA, WBC; NET, NIV, NRSV], 'chattering' [AB], 'drivel' [ECC], 'babblings' [Lns], 'foolish discussions' [NLT], 'pointless discussions' [GW], 'useless talk' [NCV], 'vain babblings' [KJV]. This noun is also translated as an adjective: 'foolish (arguments)' [TEV]. This noun denotes talk that lacks significant content [LN].

d. ἀντίθεσις (LN **33.457**) (BAGD p. 74): 'contradictions' [AB, BAGD, Herm, **LN**, NTC, WBC; HCSB, NRSV, REB], 'opposition' [KJV], 'opposing arguments' [NASB], 'opposing ideas' [NIV], 'counter-affirmations' [BNTC], 'arguments' [NCV, TEV], 'objection' [BAGD], 'inconsistent teachings' [LSA], 'absurdities' [NET], '(with those who) oppose you' [NLT], 'dialectic' [ECC], 'antitheses' [Lns], not explicit [CEV, GW]. This noun denotes a statement that involves direct contradiction or is logically inconsistent [LN].

e. ψευδώνυμος (LN **33.130**) (BAGD p. 892): 'wrongly called' [**LN**], 'falsely called' [BAGD, LN], 'falsely named' [LN]. The clause τῆς ψευδωνύμου γνώσεως 'the falsely called knowledge' is translated 'what is wrongly called knowledge' [LN], 'what is falsely called knowledge' [BNTC, LSA; NASB, NCV, NIV, NRSV], 'what is falsely styled "knowledge"' [NTC], 'what is falsely named "knowledge"' [WBC], 'the "knowledge" that falsely bears that name' [HCSB], 'the claims of false knowledge' [GW], 'the false "knowledge"' [Herm], 'so-called "know-ledge"' [AB, ECC; NET, NLT], 'of "knowledge" so-called' [REB], 'the knowledge falsely so named' [Lns], 'science falsely so called' [KJV], '(that godless and stupid talk) that sounds smart but really isn't' [CEV]. This adjective describes something as being falsely or wrongly called by some term [LN].

QUESTION—What is meant by the command to 'avoid' these things?

Timothy must avoid being enticed by the heretical teachings, and it may also mean that Timothy is to keep those who accept those teachings out of the church since debate with the heretics would be a waste of time [ICC]. He must not pay attention to them or listen to them [NAC, TH], or waste time on them [NTC]. He is to guard the gospel by continually turning away from these things, not refuting them since there is nothing that needs to be refuted in the myths and fictional stories made up on the basis of the Mosaic genealogies [Lns].

QUESTION—What is meant by βέβηλος 'profane talk'?

The adjective modifies both foolish talk and contradictions and describes them as being profane and unholy, a common description of heresy [ICC, TC, WBC]. It means non-Christian talk [TG], words that show no reverence for God [TH].

QUESTION—What is meant by κενοφωνία 'foolish talk'?

It is roughly equivalent to meaningless discussions (1:6), old-womanish myths (4:7), and disputes over words (6:4) [WBC]. It lacks sense and therefore is futile [ICC]. This empty talk is described by the next two items [My].

QUESTION—What is meant by ἀντιθέσεις 'contradictions'?

1. It refers to teachings that are self-contradictory [WBC].

2. It refers to teachings that contradict and oppose the Christian doctrine [BKC, BNTC, TH]. Claiming superior knowledge, they developed their teachings in opposition to, and in contradiction with, the teachings of sound Christian teachers, and this amounted to a denial of the gospel [BNTC].

3. It refers to objections made by teachers of the false knowledge [EGT, NTL].

QUESTION—How is the word γνώσεως 'knowledge' used?

The false teachers claimed to teach the true knowledge, but Paul named it 'false knowledge' [NAC]. The false knowledge of the heretics was probably concerned with their 'endless fables and genealogies', their asceticism in regard to food and sex [BNTC, NAC, TNTC], and their denial of the resurrection [BNTC]. The use of the word 'knowledge' doesn't have a specific reference to Gnosticism, and it could be used in regard to having a knowledge of the Jewish Law [ICC], but probably it was a term used by the opponents themselves who called their instructions 'knowledge' [ICC, WBC]. It may be that some form of Gnosticism was present at the time [BNTC, TH]. The essential teachings of Gnosticism about spiritual hierarchies and of finding salvation by 'knowledge, or by escape from the world of matter are not mentioned in this letter [NIBC].

6:21 which some professing[a] missed-the-mark[b] concerning the faith.

LEXICON—a. pres. mid./pass. participle of ἐπαγγέλλομαι (LN 2.10), (BAGD 2. p. 281): 'to profess' [BAGD, LN], 'to assert' [LN], 'to claim, to lay claim to, to give oneself out as an expert in something' [BAGD]. The phrase 'which some professing' [KJV] is also translated 'which some have professed' [Herm; NASB, NIV], 'because some people who claim to have this knowledge' [LSA], 'which some, by professing' [Lns], 'some, who profess to have this at their disposal' [ECC], 'for by laying claim to it' [REB], 'for some have claimed to possess it' [TEV], 'some have professed it' [AB], 'by professing which' [WBC], 'by professing it' [NTC; HCSB, NET, NRSV], 'by believing this talk' [CEV], 'by saying they have that "knowledge"' [NCV], 'by following such foolishness' [NLT]. This verb means to emphatically announce something openly [LN]. The word means to acknowledge and to advocate something [TH].

b. aorist act. indic. of ἀστοχέω (LN 31.68) (BAGD p. 118): 'to miss the mark, to deviate, to depart' [BAGD], 'to abandon the truth, to lose one's way' [LN]. The phrase 'some...missed the mark concerning the faith' is translated 'some/they have missed the mark as regards the faith' [AB, Lns; NRSV], 'some have departed from the faith' [WBC], 'some...have wandered from the faith' [NIV], 'some people have deviated from the faith' [HCSB], 'some have strayed from the faith' [NET], 'some have strayed far from the faith' [REB], 'some people have wandered from the faith' [NLT], 'certain individuals have wandered away with respect to the faith' [NTC], 'some...have in fact deviated in their faith' [ECC], 'some...have fallen away from faith' [Herm], 'as a result they have lost the way of faith' [TEV], 'and thus gone astray from the faith' [NASB], 'some have missed the true faith' [NCV], 'they have abandoned the faith' [GW], 'have stopped believing the doctrine which all of us believe' [LSA], 'some people have even lost their faith' [CEV], 'have erred concerning the faith' [KJV]. This verb means to go astray as the result of departing from the truth [LN]. See this word at 1:6.

QUESTION—What is the referent of the pronoun ἥν 'which'?

It is the so-called knowledge with all its foolish talk and contradictions [Alf, ICC, NIGTC, NTC, WBC; all versions]. It is the teaching of Paul's opponents [ICC].

QUESTION—What is the function of this relative clause?

It indicates the grounds for telling Timothy to avoid the teachings of the so-called knowledge [LSA, NIGTC, NTC]: *because some people professing to accept such "knowledge" have missed the mark concerning the faith.* It is a warning that Timothy is to give to the churches since he himself is not in danger of losing his own faith [Lns].

QUESTION—What relationship is indicated by the use of the participle ἐπαγγελλόμενοι 'professing'?

It indicates the means by which some people have departed from the faith [Lns, NTC, WBC; CEV, HCSB], by professing this so-called knowledge, they have missed the mark.

QUESTION—What is meant by professing this so-called knowledge?

They have laid claim to this erroneous system [NIGTC]. It refers to their allegiance to a particular group or teaching [Herm]. It means to acknowledge this teaching to be theirs and then to advocate it [TH]. They proclaimed it and made propaganda for it [NTC]. They made it their business to teach this so-called knowledge [Lns].

QUESTION—What is meant by these people missing the mark concerning the faith?

1. It means that they have departed from the Christian faith [Lns, NTC, TG, TH, WBC; GW]. They have ceased being a member of the church and have stopped believing the true Christian doctrine [TH, WBC]. They have abandoned the faith [GW]. They have forsaken the truth, even though they might have remained in the church [NTC].

2. They have deviated from the faith [ICC; HCSB, NASB, NCV, NET, NIV]. They have missed the true faith [NCV]. It does not have to mean that they have reached the final stage of apostasy, so there may be the possibility of them returning to the truth [ICC].

DISCOURSE UNIT—6:21b [ECC, ICC, LSA, NCBC]. The topic is a final greeting [ICC, NCBC], a final prayer [ECC], may you be given grace by God [LSA].

6:21b **Grace[a] (be) with you (plural).**

TEXT—Instead of ἡ χάρις μεθ' ὑμῶν 'grace (be) with you (plural)' some
manuscripts read ἡ χάρις μετὰ σοῦ 'grace (be) with you (singular)', some
manuscripts read ἡ χάρις μεθ' ὑμῶν. ἀμήν 'grace (be) with you (singular).
Amen'. GNT reads of ἡ χάρις μεθ' ὑμῶν 'grace (be) with you (plural)' with
an A decision, indicating that the text is certain. 'Grace (be) with you
(singular). Amen' is read by KJV.

LEXICON—a. χάρις (LN 88.66) (BAGD 2.c. p. 877): 'grace' AB, [BAGD,
    BNTC, ECC, LN, Lns, NTC, WBC; HCSB, KJV, NASB, NCV, NET,
    NIV, NRSV, REB], 'God's grace' [NLT, TEV], 'kindness' [LN], 'favor,
    gracious help, good will' [BAGD], 'God's good will' [GW]. The clause
    'grace be with you' is translated 'may you be given grace by God' [LSA],
    'I pray that the Lord will be kind to all of you!' [CEV]. See this word at
    1:2, 14.

QUESTION—In this letter written to Timothy, why is the benediction given to
ὑμῶν 'you' plural?

It refers to Timothy and his fellow Christians in Ephesus [TG, TH].
Although the letter is addressed to Timothy, this shows that Paul intended
that the letter be read to the church as a whole [BNTC, ICC, My, NAC,
NCBC, NIBC, NIGTC, NTC, WBC]. It also indicates that all along Paul had
the congregation in view as he wrote the letter [NIGTC]. Some translate
μεθ' ὑμῶν 'with you' as 'with you all' [NET, NLT, REB, TEV], 'with all of
you' [GW, HCSB], 'to all of you' [CEV].